graphic JAVA™ 1.2

Mastering the JFC 3RD EDITION

VOLUME I

AWT

THE SUN MICROSYSTEMS PRESS
JAVA SERIES

▼ **_Core Java 1.1_** _Volume I: Fundamentals_
Cay S. Horstmann & Gary Cornell

▼ **_Core Java 1.1_** _Volume II: Advanced Features_
Cay S. Horstmann & Gary Cornell

▼ **_Graphic Java 1.2_** _Volume I: AWT_
David M. Geary

▼ **_Graphic Java 1.2_** _Volume II: Swing_
David M. Geary

▼ **_Graphic Java 1.2_** _Volume III: 2D API_
David M. Geary

▼ **_Inside Java WorkShop 2.0,_** _Second Edition_
Lynn Weaver

▼ **_Instant Java,_** _Second Edition_
John A. Pew

▼ **_Java by Example,_** _Second Edition_
Jerry R. Jackson & Alan L. McClellan

▼ **_Java Studio by Example_**
Lynn Weaver & Leslie Robertson

▼ **_Jumping JavaScript_**
Janice Winsor & Brian Freeman

▼ **_Just Java 1.1 and Beyond_**
Peter van der Linden

▼ **_Not Just Java_**
Peter van der Linden

graphic

JAVA 1.2™

Mastering the JFC 3RD EDITION

VOLUME I
AWT

DAVID M. GEARY

Sun Microsystems Press
A Prentice Hall Title

The publisher offers discounts on this book when ordered in bulk quantities.
For more information, contact: Corporate Sales Department, Phone: 800-382-3419;
Fax: 201-236-7141; E-mail: corpsales@prenhall.com; or write: Prentice Hall PTR,
Corp. Sales Dept., One Lake Street, Upper Saddle River, NJ 07458.

Editorial/production supervision: *Patti Guerrieri*
Cover design director: *Jerry Votta*
Cover designer: *Scott Weiss*
Cover illustration: *Karen Strelecki*
Manufacturing manager: *Alexis R. Heydt*
Marketing Manager: *Kaylie Smith*
Acquisitions editor: *Gregory G. Doench*
Sun Microsystems Press publisher: *Rachel Borden*

10 9 8 7 6 5 4

ISBN 0-13- 079666-2

Sun Microsystems Press
A Prentice Hall Title

For RoyBoy

Contents

Chapter 10
Components, Containers, and Layout Managers, 327

Part 4   AWT Components

Preface

The 1.2 JDK (Java Development Kit) offers vastly improved support over its predecessors for developing graphical user interfaces and graphical applets/applications in the form of the Java Foundation Classes.The Java Foundation Classes are represented by four APIs: AWT, Swing, Accessibility and the 2D API.

The Abstract Window Toolkit (AWT) is Java's original user interface toolkit that provides a basic set of components such as labels, buttons, scrollbars etc. The AWT also includes a great deal of infrastructure for graphical components such as a delegation event model, layout management, and support for data transfer and lightweight components.

Swing is a second user interface toolkit that is built on the AWT's infrastructure. Swing offers a much more extensive set of components than the AWT; Swing's 40 components outnumber the AWT by a 4:1 ratio. Some Swing components (labels, buttons, etc.) are designed to replace their AWT counterparts, whereas other Swing components provide extra capabilities not found in the AWT (trees and tables).

The Accessibility API allows developers to implement Java applets and applications that are accessible to users with disabilities. The Accessibility API can also be used to develop alternative interfaces for nomadic users, such as a hypothetical Java navigational system that tells drivers (instead of showing them with a map display) went to turn in an audible fashion.

The 2D API encompasses a number of major enhancements to the AWT's graphics model in terms of manipulating colors, shapes and images and text.

Why The AWT and Why This Book?

The 1.2 JDK comes with the Swing set of components which includes a complete set of lightweight replacements for the AWT's heavyweight components. As a result, a common misconception is that Swing is a replacement for the AWT, but that is not the case.

Swing is built on top of the AWT, and in fact, every Swing component is a bonafide AWT component. Because Swing components are in fact AWT components, it is imperative to have a good grasp of how AWT components behave and a what makes the AWT tick.

Graphic Java is meant, first and foremost, to help you *master* the AWT. Both fundamental and advanced concepts of the AWT are fully explored in the pages that lie ahead. Each AWT component is examined in detail, and AWT Tips are provided to illuminate some of the AWT's dark corners. No stone is left unturned.

What You'll Find Inside

After reading *Graphic Java*, you will have a thorough grasp of how the AWT is designed, and how to best take advantage of that design.

This volume of *Graphic Java* covers fundamental and advanced concepts of the AWT, but does not cover the other JFC APIs that are included in the AWT packages, namely the 2D API. For a discussion of the 2D API, see the third volume of *Graphic Java*.

The following is a sample of the coverage provided in the pages that lie ahead.

Peers

You will understand the peer architecture of the AWT, along with the pros and cons of the peer approach. For instance, you'll know which `Component` methods behave differently if invoked before a component's peer has been created, and what to do about it.

Clipboard and Data Transfer

You'll understand the data transfer model employed by the AWT, and how to utilize both local clipboards and the system clipboard. While the AWT only provides the ability to transfer strings to and from a clipboard, *Graphic Java* shows you how to put other data types on the clipboard, with examples of transferring both images and custom components.

Lightweight Components

In addition to being able to implement lightweight custom components, you'll also know how to drag them across a double buffered container, and even how to animate them on a playfield. You will understand how double buffering works, and why lightweight components should be displayed in a double buffered container. You will know the pitfalls of placing lightweight components in a container, and why lightweight containers must be manually fitted with a layout manager.

Layout Managers

You will have a complete grasp of layout managers, including the behemoth, GridBagLayout, and you will be able to implement custom layout managers with ease. You will understand how to force a container to layout its components, and why it is sometimes necessary to do so.

Internationalization and Serialization

You'll be able to internationalize a graphical user interface, and serialize both AWT components and their event listeners.

Scrolling

You will be able to scroll any number of components in a container by using a scrollpane. You'll also understand the limitations of the scrollpane class and why it is sometimes necessary to have a peerless scrolling framework. Of course, we'll discuss the implementation of such a scrolling framework from the Graphic Java Toolkit, which you are free to use for your own purposes.

Graphic Java Content

The delegation event model, lightweight components, clipboard and data transfer, desktop colors, mouseless operation, and printing are all thoroughly covered. You'll also find extensive coverage of scrolling, menus (including popup menus), image manipulation, graphics, fonts and fontmetrics, dialogs, text components, etc.

Audience

This book is written for object-oriented developers working in Java. There are numerous books explaining details of the Java language and how it works vis-a-vis Visual Basic, C, C++, etc. The details of the language are left to those books.

Internet Sources of Information

There are several online sources of information on Java. You can find online guides and tutorials on Sun's home page:

`http://java.sun.com/`

There is an active net newsgroup dedicated to Java:

`comp.lang.java`

There is also a mailing list where Java aficionados exchange ideas, questions, and solutions. For information about the mailing list, look on the World Wide Web at:

`http://java.sun.com/mail.html`

From these newsgroups and web sites, you'll be able to locate countless other resources, tutorials, Frequently-Asked-Questions (FAQs), and online magazines dedicated to Java.

For updates about this book and information about other books in the SunSoft Press Java Series, look on the web at:

`http://www.sun.com/books/books/Geary/Geary.html`

For some cool graphics, take a look at:

`http://www.pixelsight.com:80/PS/pixelsite/pixelsite.html`

Conventions Used in This Book

Table P-1 shows the coding conventions used in this book.

Table P-1 Coding Conventions

Convention	Example
Class names have initial capital letters.	`public class LineOfText`
Method names have initial lowercase and the rest of the words have an initial capital letter.	`public int getLength()`
Variable names have initial lowercase and the rest of the words have an initial capital letter.	`private int length` `private int bufferLength`
`static` variables begin with an underscore.	`protected static int _defaultSize = 2;`

Note that, for the most part, methods are referred to without their arguments; however, we include the arguments when the discussion warrants including them.

Table P-2 shows the typographic conventions used in this book.

Table P-2 Typographic Conventions

Typeface or Symbol	Description
![CD icon]	Indicates that the accompanying code, command, or file is available on the CD that accompanies this book.
`courier`	Indicates a command, file name, class name, method, argument, Java keyword, HTML tag, file content, or code excerpt.
`bold courier`	Indicates a sample command-line entry.
italics	Indicates definitions, emphasis, a book title, or a variable that you should replace with a valid value.

Acknowledgments

I'd like to thank the many folks that have had a hand in *Graphic Java*. From co-workers to publishers to reviewers, to those that have filed bug reports and errata, you have all made this book better in some fashion.

Rachel Borden and John Bortner of Sun Microsystems Press, along with Greg Doench and Patti Guerrieri from Prentice Hall, have all bent over backwards to go above and beyond the call time after time. Lisa Iarkowski, Gail Cocker-Bogusz and Mary Treacy have all had a hand in one facet of the book or another.

Mary Lou Nohr, the book's editor, has once again done a splendid job of pointing out things like omitting commas before conjunctions in sentences with compound predicates. Her keen eye is greatly appreciated.

Thanks to the reviewers, whose insights and perspectives add a great deal to the book: Jeff Dinkins, Rob Gordon, Shawn Bertini and Wally Wedel.

Our immense appreciation goes to Keith Ohlfs of Pixelsite for granting permission to use all the cool images. You can see more of Keith's handiwork at:

`http://www.pixelsight.com:80/PS/pixelsite/pixelsite.html`

Finally, I'd like to say a special thank you to Ashley Anna Geary, who is a bug finder extrordinaire—more software developers should have 9-year olds test their software. And to my wife Lesa, who endures the droning of my voice well into the night.

PART ONE

Introduction: The Java Foundation Classes, The AWT, Applets, and Applications

CHAPTER
1

Introduction

The Java Foundation Classes

The Java Foundation Classes—also known as the JFC—are a set of java packages encompassing the following Apis:

- Abstract Window Toolkit (1.1 and beyond)
- Swing Components
- Java 2D Api
- Accessibility Api

Some of the Apis listed above span multiple packages. The 2D Api has classes in both `java.awt` and `java.awt.image`, for instance. Although specific packages, such as `java.awt.geom`, support the 2D Api, a good deal of the foundation for the 2D Api resides in the `java.awt` package.

The core of the JFC is the AWT (1.1 and beyond), which is the subject matter of this book. The AWT provides the following infrastructure for JFC components:

- Delegation event model
- Lightweight components
- Clipboard and data transfer
- Printing and mouseless operation

The Abstract Window Toolkit

Developing Java™ applets and graphical applications requires working with the Abstract Window Toolkit to some degree. Commonly referred to as the *AWT*, the Abstract Window Toolkit is part of the freely distributed Java Development Kit (JDK).

The AWT provides basic user interface components, such as buttons, lists, menus, textfields, etc. AWT components are platform independent and are primarily used to build graphical user interfaces. In addition, the AWT also provides an event handling mechanism, support for clipboard and data transfer, and image manipulation.

With the advent of the 2D Api, the AWT also includes packages for advanced font manipulation, printing, geometry accessibility, and input methods. The AWT is composed of the Java packages listed in Table 1-1.

Table 1-1 AWT Packages

AWT Package	Description
`java.awt`	Basic component functionality
`java.awt.accessibility`	Assitive technologies
`java.awt.color`	Colors and color spaces
`java.awt.datatransfer`	Clipboard and data transfer support
`java.awt.dnd`	Drag and drop
`java.awt.event`	Event classes and listeners
`java.awt.font`	2D Api font package
`java.awt.geom`	2D Api geometry package
`java.awt.im`	Input methods
`java.awt.image`	Fundamental image manipulation classes
`java.awt.peer`	Peer interfaces for component peers
`java.awt.print`	2D Api support for printing
`java.awt.swing`	Swing components
`java.awt.test`	A single applet that tests a limited subset of AWT functionality

The current AWT is vastly improved over the original incarnation, which was designed for simple applets with simple user interfaces. With a redesigned event model, support for clipboard and data transfer, printing and mouseless operation, the AWT is now much more comparable to industrial-strength user interface frameworks such as Parc Place's VisualWorks™ or Borland's Object Windows Library™ (OWL).

Note that this volume of *Graphic Java* does not cover all of the `java.awt` packages. For instance, this volume does not discuss the `java.awt.font` or `java.awt.geom` packages, which are addressed in *Volume III: The 2D Api.*

Peers and Platform Independence

As the programming interface for applet and graphical application development, the AWT provides a generalized set of classes that can be used without concern for platform-specific windowing issues. This feature is made possible by a set of AWT classes known as *peers*. Peers are native GUI components that are manipulated by the AWT classes. The way peers work and their influence on program development is sometimes confusing, so we'll take a closer look at them here and in subsequent chapters in this book.

The AWT components delegate a great deal of functionality to their peers. For example, when you use the AWT to create an instance of the Menu class, the Java runtime system creates an instance of a menu peer. It is the menu peer that does the real work of displaying and managing the menu behavior. In the case of a menu, the Solaris™ JDK would create a Motif® menu peer; the Windows 95™ JDK would create a Windows 95 menu peer; the Macintosh® JDK would create a Macintosh menu peer, and so on. Figure 1-1 shows how peers fit into the process of displaying components in native windowing systems.

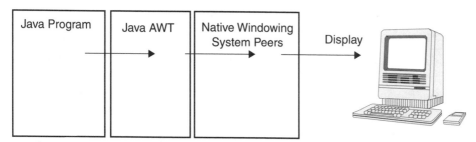

Figure 1-1 Peers at Work
A Java program creates and displays an AWT component, which creates and displays a native component (a peer).

The decision by the original AWT development team to use a peer approach enabled rapid development of a cross-platform window toolkit. Using peers obviates the need to reimplement the functionality encapsulated in native windowing components. Additionally, the use of peers enables applets and applications using the AWT to retain the look-and-feel of the native windowing system because peers are actually native components. The AWT classes are just wrappers around the peers and delegate functionality to them.

Although using the AWT rarely requires you to deal directly with peers, you will most likely be influenced by their presence. For instance, certain `java.awt.Component` methods will not work as expected until the component's peer has been created.

The peer approach resulted in the implementation of a GUI toolkit in record time; however, the peer design is fundamentally flawed and does not scale well. See "Components and Peers" on page 439 for more on the drawbacks of the peer approach.

Lightweight Components

The AWT's components are all heavyweight, meaning they have peers and are rendered in their own native (opaque) windows. As a result, they are expensive to use and are not amenable to being subclassed in order to modify default behaviors. Additionally, they must be rectangular and cannot have transparent backgrounds.

Peers yielded a high return on investment as far as quickly producing a UI toolkit. Because of reliance on native peers to do much of the actual gruntwork, AWT classes were implemented as veneers that were relatively easy to develop. The original AWT took a scant 6 weeks to develop; however, the quick time to market was offset by the underlying peer architecture, a limited event model, and a high number of bugs attributed to mismatches between peers and their AWT counterparts.

The 1.1 AWT introduced the notion of lightweight components. Lightweights directly extend either `java.awt.Component` or `java.awt.Container`. Lightweights do not have peers and are rendered in their heavyweight container's window instead of one of their own. As a result, lightweights do not incur the performance penalties associated with having their own opaque window and can have transparent backgrounds. The ability to have transparent backgrounds means that lightweights can appear to be nonrectangular, even though their bounding boxes are rectangular in nature.

The AWT and the Swing Components

The Swing components are (mostly) lightweight components that offer replacements for the heavyweight AWT components. Additionally, the Swing components include many other useful components, from separators and image buttons, to document editors and color choosers. The Swing components are covered in *Graphic Java Mastering the JFC Volume II: Swing Components*.

The AWT and the 2D Api

The original AWT provided a respectable, albeit incomplete, graphics package. For instance, the image package provided the infrastructure for image filtering but neglected to offer anything other than a one-pixel-sized square for the graphics pen.

The 2D Api consists of a set of classes for 2D graphics and images. The 2D Api encompasses the following packages:

```
java.awt.color
java.awt.font
java.awt.geom
java.awt.print
```

Additionally, the 2D Api extends other AWT packages. For instance, `java.awt.Composite` and `java.awt.Stroke`, are part of the 2D Api. The java.awt.image package also contains many of the 2D Api packages.

This volume of *Graphic Java* does not venture into the 2D Api; however, the basic graphics and imaging capabilities provided by the AWT are explored in detail. For an exploration of the 2D Api, see *Graphic Java Mastering the JFC Volume III: The 2D Api*.

Components—The Foundation of the AWT

The AWT is a world of components; approximately half of the classes in the AWT are extensions of the `java.awt.Component` class. The `Component` class and its supporting cast are the foundation upon which the AWT is built:

- `Component` – An abstract base class for components such as menus, buttons, labels, lists, and so on.

- `Container` – An abstract base class that extends `Component`. Classes derived from `Container`, most notably `Panel`, `Applet`, `Window`, `Dialog`, and `Frame`, can contain multiple components.

- `LayoutManager` – An interface that defines methods for positioning and sizing objects within a container. Java defines several default implementations of the `LayoutManager` interface.

- `Graphics` class – An abstract class that defines methods for performing graphical operations in a component. Every component has an associated `Graphics` object.

Figure 1-2 shows a class diagram of the relationships between components, containers, and layout managers.[1]

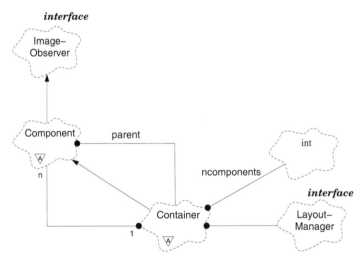

Figure 1-2 Components, Containers, and Layout Managers

Components, Containers, and Layout Managers

`Component` and `Container` form a simple, yet fundamental, relationship of the AWT: containers may contain components. All containers come equipped with a layout manager,[2] which positions and shapes (*lays out*) the container's

---

1. Graphic Java contains many class diagrams that show relationships between classes. "AWT Class Diagrams" on page 845 provides an introduction to class diagrams and a complete set of class diagrams for the AWT.
2. Except for the `java.awt.Container` class itself.

components. A layout manager's responsibilities are defined by the
`java.awt.LayoutManager` and `java.awt.LayoutManager2` interfaces.
Much of the action that takes place in the AWT occurs between components,
containers, and their layout managers.

Components

In Java parlance, user interface controls, such as panels, scrollbars, labels,
textfields, buttons, and so on are generically referred to as *components* because
they all extend `java.awt.Component`. Table 1-2 lists the AWT component
classes that are ultimately derived from `java.awt.Component`.

Table 1-2 AWT Components

Component	Superclass	Description
Button	Component	A textual button for triggering an action
Canvas	Component	A canvas for painting graphics
Checkbox	Component	A checkable boolean component
Choice	Component	Popdown menu of textual entries
Dialog	Window	A window that can be modal
FileDialog	Dialog	A platform-dependent dialog for selecting files
Frame	Window	Top-level window with titlebar and optional menubar
Label	Component	Component that displays a string
List	Component	A scrollable list of textual entries
Panel	Container	A generic container of components
Scrollbar	Component	An `adjustable` component for scrolling items
ScrollPane	Container	A scrollable container
TextArea	TextComponent	A multiline, scrollable textfield
TextComponent	Component	Base functionality for `TextArea` and `TextField`
TextField	TextComponent	A single-line component for entering text
Window	Container	A borderless window with no title

Figure 1-3 shows each of the standard Java AWT components with the exception
of classes that extend `java.awt.Window`.

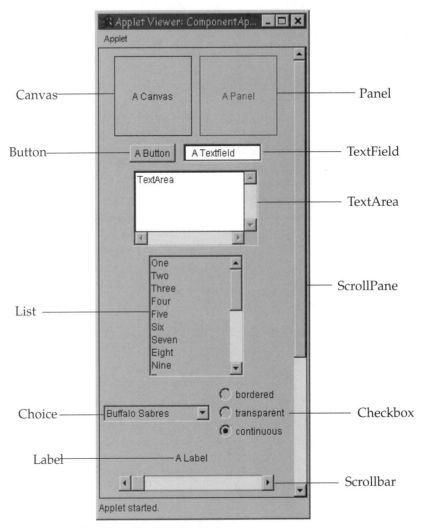

Figure 1-3 AWT Components
The AWT provides a basic set of user interface components.
Components that extend `java.awt.Window` are not shown.

Basic Component Functionality

The `java.awt.Component` class is an abstract class that provides a great deal of functionality for the classes that extend it. For example, a `Component` has the following affiliated with it:

- `Graphics` object
- Location
- Size
- Native peer
- Parent container
- Fonts and font dimensions (referred to as font metrics in the AWT)
- Foreground and background colors
- Locale
- Minimum, maximum, and preferred sizes

Containers

`java.awt.Container` class is also an abstract class that extends `Component`. A `Container` can contain multiple components. Using containers, you can group-related components and treat them as a unit. This technique simplifies an applet's design and is useful in arranging components on the display. Note that the `Applet` class is a subclass of `Panel`, which extends `Container`, so all applets inherit the ability to contain components.

Table 1-3 lists the AWT containers derived from the `java.awt.Container` class.

Table 1-3 `Container` Subclasses

Subclasses	Description
`Applet`	An extension of `Panel`. `Applet` is the superclass of all applets
`Dialog`	An extension of `Window` that can be modal or nonmodal
`FileDialog`	A `Dialog` for selecting a file
`Frame`	An extension of `Window`, `Frame` is the container for an application.. A `Frame` may have a menubar, but an `Applet` may not.
`Panel`	An extension of `Container`, `Panel` is a simple container
`ScrollPane`	Scrolls a component
`Window`	An extension of `Container`, windows have no menu or border. `Window` is rarely extended directly; it is the superclass of `Frame` and `Dialog`

Layout Managers

Containers merely keep track of the components they contain; they delegate the positioning and shaping of their components to a layout manager. The LayoutManager interface defines methods for laying out components and calculating the preferred and minimum sizes of their containers. The AWT provides five classes that implement either the LayoutManager or LayoutManager2 interfaces.

- BorderLayout – Lays out North/South/East/West/Center components
- CardLayout – Displays one panel at a time from a deck of panels
- FlowLayout – Specifies that components flow left to right, top to bottom
- GridBagLayout – Imposes constraints on each component in a grid
- GridLayout – Lays out components in a simple grid; components are stretched to fill the grid

We'll discuss layout managers extensively—both the standard AWT layout managers and how to implement custom layout managers. For now, the important point is to understand at a high level how they fit into the big picture of the AWT and applet/application development.

Summary

The AWT is a platform-independent window toolkit. It relies on *peers*, which are native windowing components that are delegated to by AWT classes. Although their presence influences the development of graphical applets and applications, you do not generally need to deal directly with peers.

There are four main classes in the Java Abstract Window Toolkit: the Component class, Container class, Graphics class, and the LayoutManager (and LayoutManager2) interfaces.

Containers contain components, and layout managers position and shape the components contained in a container. The Graphics class provides the means to display text and graphics within a component. These classes and the relationships between them form the foundation of the AWT.

CHAPTER 2

Applets and Applications

In this chapter, we will cover the basics of developing graphical Java applets and applications. We'll include some simple code that highlights the key methods used in any applet or application, and we'll discuss the relationship between an applet and the `java.awt` package. First, we'll take a look at applets, and then we'll go into some detail about applications, noting differences and implications of each as we proceed.

Java Applets

Applets are Java programs that execute within a Java-enabled web browser. Most of the graphical support required for an applet to execute is built in to the browser. The major implication for applet developers is that they don't need to worry about creating a frame for the applet to execute in.

Using the Appletviewer

Applets are launched by embedding the `applet` HTML tag in a web page and then viewing that page with a Java-enabled browser or the appletviewer that comes with the Java Development Kit (JDK).

For consistency and ease of illustration, all of the applets in this book are used in the following way:

```
appletviewer applet_name.html
```

In this syntax, *applet_name*.html is a minimal HTML file that can be used as an argument to the appletviewer. The HTML file looks like this:

```
<title>Applet Title</title>
<hr>
<applet code="applet_name.class" width=width height=height>
</applet>
<hr>
```

Each applet on the CD included with *Graphic Java* has a corresponding HTML file that can be used as an argument to appletviewer. Of course, these applets could also be displayed within a Java-enabled web browser, as long as the web page includes the appropriate HTML applet tag to call the applet. The appletviewer ignores all but the applet HTML tag, so it can be used on any HTML file with an applet tag.

The Browser Infrastructure

When applets are executed in a Java-enabled browser, the browser provides a great deal of the infrastructure necessary for an applet's execution. For example, when a web page containing an applet is visited, the browser calls the set of methods required to initialize and start the applet. When the web page containing an applet is no longer displayed, the browser calls methods to terminate the applet's execution.

One point that sometimes confuses developers new to Java is the absence of a main() statement in the applet code. In applets, main() is unnecessary because control for executing the applet is managed by the browser.

The java.awt.Applet Class

All applets extend java.applet.Applet, which extends java.awt.Panel, as illustrated in Figure 2-1. Since Panel is an AWT container, it has a default layout manager—a FlowLayout,[1] which lays out the applet's components.

---

1. See "The FlowLayout Layout Manager" on page 351.

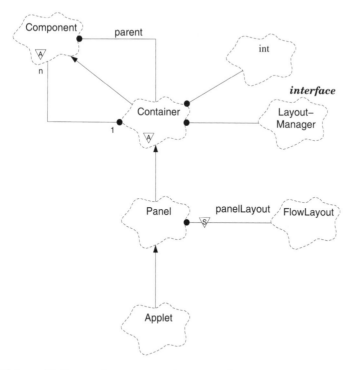

Figure 2-1 `Applet`, `Container`, and `LayoutManager` Class Diagram
An `Applet` is a container with a default layout manager, `FlowLayout`.

Key Applet Methods

The `Applet` class provides a basic set of methods that define the overall behavior of applets. An applet's execution is controlled by four methods: `init()`, `start()`, `stop()`, and `destroy()`. You don't typically call these methods directly—rather, they are invoked automatically either by the browser or the appletviewer. Note, however, that these methods are commonly overridden in classes that extend `Applet`. Table 2-1 summarizes their use.

Example 2-1 shows a simple applet and the use of the `init()`, `start()`, `stop()`, and `destroy()` methods; the first two are commonly overridden. `StarterApplet` overrides them simply to highlight when they are executed. The `start` method also adds a "Starter" label to the applet every time it is called. Additionally, note that `StarterApplet`, like all applets, extends the `java.applet.Applet` class.

Table 2-1 Commonly Used `applet.Applet` **Methods**

Key `Applet` Methods	Description
`init()`	When a document with an applet is opened, the `init` method is called to initialize the applet
`start()`	When a document with an applet is opened, the `start` method is called after the `init` method to start the applet
`stop()`	When a document with an applet is no longer displayed, the `stop` method is called. This method is always called before the `destroy` method is called
`destroy()`	After the `stop` method has been called, the `destroy` method is called to clean up any resources that are being held

Example 2-1 `Starter Applet`

```
import java.applet.Applet;
import java.awt.Label;

public class StarterApplet extends Applet {
    private Label label;

    public void init() {
        System.out.println("Applet::init()");
    }
    public void start() {
        System.out.println("Applet::start()");
        label = new Label("Starter");
        add(label);
    }
    public void stop() {
        System.out.println("Applet::stop()");
        remove(label);
    }
    public void destroy() {
        System.out.println("Applet::destroy()");
    }
}
```

The applet can be executed by invocation of appletviewer on the following HTML file:

```
<title>Starter Applet</title>
<hr>
<applet code="StarterApplet.class" width=300 height=100>
</applet>
<hr>
```

Figure 2-2 shows the applet window.

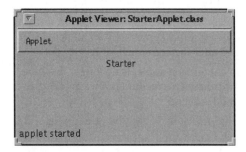

Figure 2-2 A Starter Applet

Running the applet results in the following output:

```
Applet.init()
Applet.start()
```

Exiting the applet results in the following output:

```
Applet.stop()
Applet.destroy()
```

java.awt.Component Display Methods

The java.awt.Component class implements methods to update its display: paint(), repaint(), and update(). Table 2-2 summarizes how they work.

Table 2-2 Commonly Used Component Methods

Component Display Methods	Description
paint()	Paints the component
repaint()	Schedules a call to the component's update method as soon as possible
update()	Is responsible for redrawing the component. The default version redraws the background and calls the paint method

java.awt.Component provides a number of overloaded repaint methods that specify either a delay before repainting or a subsection of the component to be repainted. "Rendering Components" on page 443 discusses the mechanics of painting and repainting AWT components in detail.

Java Applications

Applications are invoked from the command line and executed by the java interpreter. From the developer's point of view, there are primarily two differences between a Java applet and a Java application:

- An application must include a main method.
- If the application requires a window, it must extend the AWT Frame class.

A Frame is a window in which the application is displayed and, like all containers, comes with a layout manager for positioning and sizing its components. Additionally, a frame has insets that must be taken into account when objects are manually placed—see "Differences Between Applets and Applications" on page 110.

There is one other notable distinction between a Java application and a Java applet. An application does not have the same security restrictions that an applet does. Whereas untrusted applets cannot write or modify files, an application can perform file I/O. Applications are not constrained by the security restrictions that Java-enabled browsers enforce on applets.

Setting Up an Application

Unlike applets, applications must extend the Frame class in order to provide a window in which to run, as in Example 2-2.

Example 2-2 Starter Application

```
import java.awt.Event;
import java.awt.Frame;
import java.awt.event.*;
import java.awt.Label;

public class StarterApplication extends Frame {
    public static void main(String args[]) {
        StarterApplication app =
                new StarterApplication("Starter Application");

        app.setSize(300,100);
        app.show ();
        System.out.println("StarterApplication::main()");
```

```
    }
    public StarterApplication(String frameTitle) {
        super(frameTitle);
        add  (new Label("Starter", Label.CENTER), "Center");

        addWindowListener(new WindowAdapter() {
            public void windowClosing(WindowEvent event) {
                dispose();
                System.exit(0);
            }
        });
    }
}
```

This is a simple application, but it's worth noting exactly how it works since it is different from the "Starter Applet" on page 18 in several ways. The first thing to note is that the application does not import and extend `java.applet.Applet`. Instead, it imports and extends `java.awt.Frame`.

The next important distinction is that the application implements a `main` method. All Java applications require a `main` method, just like a C or C++ program; `main()` is the first method invoked in an application. The `main` method of the `StarterApplication` creates an instance of a `StarterApplication` (a `Frame`), which it resizes and shows. The constructor for the `StarterApplication` class initializes a `StarterApplication` instance.

Finally, a window listener is added to the frame, to dispose of the window and exit the application when the window is closed.[2]

Displaying Applications

Graphical applications, like all other Java applications, are executed directly by the `java` interpreter. For example, the compiled application in Example 2-2 is executed in the following manner:

```
java StarterApplication
```

2. See "Frames Don't Close by Default" on page 582.

The Java interpreter then runs the application, as shown in Figure 2-3.

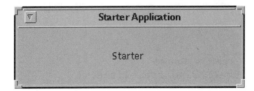

Figure 2-3 A Java Application
The `StarterApplication` implements a `WindowListener` that exits the application when the user activates the quit menu from the system menu.

Combining Applet and Application Code

There are a number of ways to write a Java program so that it can execute either from within a browser or as a standalone application. One way to do this is to center an `Applet` within a `Frame`, as in Example 2-3.

Example 2-3 Combining Applet and Application Code

```java
import java.applet.Applet;
import java.awt.Event;
import java.awt.Frame;
import java.awt.Label;
import java.awt.event.*;

public class StarterCombined extends Applet {
    private Label label;

    public static void main(String args[]) {
        StarterCombinedFrame app =
            new StarterCombinedFrame("Starter Application");

        app.setSize(300,100);
        app.show  ();
        System.out.println("StarterCombinedFrame::main()");
    }
    public void init() {
        System.out.println("Applet::init()");
    }
    public void start() {
        System.out.println("Applet::start()");
        label = new Label("Starter");
        add(label);
    }
    public void stop() {
        System.out.println("Applet::stop()");
```

```
            remove(label);
        }
        public void destroy() {
            System.out.println("Applet::destroy()");
        }
    }

    class StarterCombinedFrame extends Frame {
        public StarterCombinedFrame(String frameTitle) {
            super(frameTitle);

            StarterCombined applet = new StarterCombined();
            applet.start();
            add   (applet, "Center");

            addWindowListener(new WindowAdapter() {
                public void windowClosing(WindowEvent event) {
                    dispose();
                    System.exit(0);
                }
            });
        }
    }
}
```

The import statements import the essential classes needed for both an applet and an application. Putting the main method in the applet class enables the program to be executed with the same argument, whether it is going to run as an applet or as an application. For example, the following command would execute the code as an application:

---

java StarterCombined

Using the appletviewer on the following HTML file would execute the code as an applet:

```
<title>Starter Combined Test</title>
<hr>
<applet code="StarterCombined.class" width=300 height=100>
</applet>
<hr>
```

If the program is run as an applet, the main method is ignored; instead, the browser or appletviewer invokes the init() and start methods to start the applet.

`StarterCombinedFrame` provides a `Frame` for the application to run in. StarterCombinedFrame creates an instance of the applet, which is created and centered in the `Frame`.

Summary

Both applets and applications are executed by the Java interpreter. Applications must create their own frame, whereas applets run in the frame provided by the Java-enabled web browser or appletviewer. As a result, applications must handle window closing events, whereas an applet's execution is controlled by the browser or appletviewer. Applications are free to read and write files, but untrusted applets are not permitted to do so.

PART TWO

Graphics and Images

CHAPTER
3

Graphics

The AWT provides user interface components such as buttons, lists, menus, dialogs and so on, but it does not include anything analogous to purely graphical objects. For instance, the AWT does not provide Line or Circle classes.

The AWT does provide Rectangle, Polygon, and Point classes; however, those classes were added as afterthoughts to the original AWT. Since the design of the original AWT did not allow for purely graphical objects, Rectangle, Polygon, and Point wound up without any graphical capabilities. In other words, Rectangle, Polygon, and Point do not come equipped with a draw method. You can only set and get information about the geometric entity each represents.

Instead of providing purely graphical objects, the AWT employs a simpler—albeit less flexible and extensible—model. Every AWT component comes complete with its own java.awt.Graphics object, through which graphical operations can be performed in the associated component.

Graphics are also used to draw into various output devices, such as offscreen buffers and printers—see "Double Buffering" on page 789 and "Printing" on page 642.

java.awt.Graphics

java.awt.Graphics is an abstract class that defines a veritable kitchen sink of graphical operations. Its 47 public methods can be used for rendering images and text, drawing and filling shapes, clipping graphical operations, and much more.

Nearly all applets (and applications) that use the AWT manipulate a Graphics for at least one graphical service. For example, even simple Hello World applets are quick to use a Graphics to display their clever verbiage:

```
public class HelloWorld extends Applet {
    public void paint(Graphics g) {
        g.drawString("Hello Graphic Java World", 75, 100);
    }
}
```

In addition to performing graphical operations within a component, each Graphics also keeps track of the following graphical properties:

- The color used for drawing and filling shapes
- The font used for rendering text
- A clipping rectangle
- A graphical mode (XOR or Paint)
- A translation origin for rendering and clipping coordinates

To provide an overall picture of the role that the Graphics class plays in the AWT (and the JDK), two tables are provided below. Table 3-1 lists JDK methods that are passed a reference to a Graphics.

Table 3-1 JDK Methods That Are Passed a Graphics Reference [1]

Package	Class	Methods
java.awt	Canvas	paint(Graphics g)
	Component	paint(Graphics g)
	Component	paintAll(Graphics g)
	Component	print(Graphics g)
	Component	printAll(Graphics g)
	Component	update(Graphics g)
	Container	paint(Graphics g)
	Container	paintComponents(Graphics g)
	Container	print(Graphics g)
	Container	printComponents(Graphics g)

Table 3-1 JDK Methods That Are Passed a Graphics Reference (Continued)[1]

Package	Class	Methods
	ScrollPane	printComponents(Graphics g)
java.beans	Property-Editor	paintValue(Graphics g, Rectangle r)
	Property-EditorSupport	paintValue(Graphics g, Rectangle r)

1. java.awt.peer methods omitted

Nearly all of the methods that are passed a reference to a Graphics reside in the java.awt.package. Furthermore, notice that many of the methods are used to paint or print AWT components.

Table 3-2 lists methods that return a Graphics reference. The most commonly used method from Table 3-2 is Component.getGraphics(), which returns a reference to the Graphics associated with a java.awt.Component.

Table 3-2 JDK Methods That Return a Graphics Reference[1]

Package	Class	Methods
java.awt	Component	getGraphics()
	Image	getGraphics()
	PrintJob	getGraphics()
	Graphics	create()
	Graphics	create(int x, int y, int w, int h)

1. java.awt.peer methods omitted

Images and print jobs also provide a getGraphics method. Image.getGraphics() is often used for double buffering by rendering into an offscreen buffer—see "An Introduction to Double Buffering" on page 177.

Graphics.create() clones the Graphics on whose behalf create() was called. The version of create() that takes four arguments sets the origin and clipping rectangle for the newly created copy. The origin is specified by the x and y arguments. The clipping rectangle is the intersection of the Graphics' current clipping rectangle and the rectangle defined by the arguments passed to create().

Graphics Parameters

The Graphics class fulfills two major responsibilities:

- Set and get graphical parameters
- Perform graphical operations in an output device

The main focus of attention for the Graphics class is the second item, to which most of this chapter is devoted. This section takes a brief look at the graphical parameters that are maintained by the Graphics class:

- Color
- Font and font metrics
- Clipping rectangle
- Graphics mode

The Graphics class provides get and set methods for color, font, and clipping rectangle. Graphics mode is a write-only property, while font metrics is a read-only property.[1]

Each Graphics maintains a single color, representing the color that will be used for the next rendering operation:

- `void setColor(Color color)`
- `Color getColor()`

The font used to draw text may be specified and read by the following methods:

- `void setFont(Font f)`
- `Font getFont()`

Font metrics are represented by the `java.awt.FontMetrics` class, which provides information about a particular font, such as the height of the font, its ascent, leading, etc. The Graphics class provides two methods that return a reference to a FontMetrics:

- `FontMetrics getFontMetrics()`
- `FontMetrics getFontMetrics(Font f)`

1.   Font metrics are associated with a specific font, so font metrics can be changed by changing the Graphics' font.

The no-argument version of the method returns the font metrics associated with the Graphics' current font. The second method returns the font metrics associated with the specified font. Although there is no setter method, you can specify font metrics indirectly by setting a particular font. Fonts and font metrics are discussed in the "Colors and Fonts" chapter beginning on page 75.

Each Graphics also maintains a clipping rectangle. Graphical operations are clipped to the rectangle specified by a Graphics' clipping rectangle:

- void setClip(int x, int y, int w, int h)
- Rectangle getClipBounds()

- void setClip(Shape)
- Shape getClip()

- void clipRect(int x, int y, int w, int h)

The clipping rectangle can be specified either by four integers representing the bounding box of the rectangle or by a java.awt.Shape. The Shape interface is part of the Java2D Api, which is discussed at length in the third volume of *Graphic Java*. Shapes can be nonrectangular, so it is possible to define a nonrectangular clipping rectangle for an output device.

The last method listed above computes a new clipping rectangle that is the intersection of the previous clipping rectangle with the rectangle specified by the method's arguments. In early versions of the AWT, Graphics.clipRect() was the only way to modify a clipping rectangle.

Finally, graphics mode, which is discussed in detail in "Graphics Modes" on page 63, determines how text and shapes are drawn over existing graphics. Two methods are provided to set the mode:

- void setPaintMode()
- void setXORMode()

setPaintMode() sets the graphics mode to *paint*, meaning subsequent rendering operations will overwrite existing graphics. setXORMode() allows for drawing and erasing without disturbing the graphics underneath. Paint mode is the default graphics mode, whereas XOR mode comes in handy in a number of situations, such as rubberbanding or layering graphics in a drawing program, for example.

The Graphics Coordinate System

The graphics coordinate system is anchored in the upper left-hand corner of a component, with coordinates increasing down and to the right, as depicted in Figure 3-1.

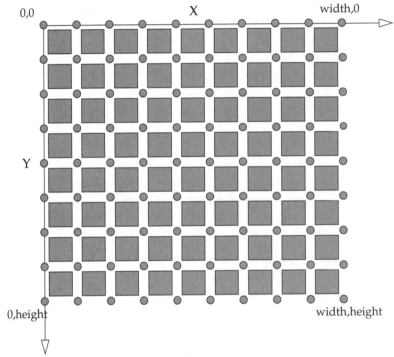

Figure 3-1 Graphics Coordinate System
Circles represent coordinates, and squares represent pixels.
Coordinates lie between pixels.

Coordinates lie between pixels of the output device. Operations that draw outlines of shapes, such as `Graphics.drawRect()`, traverse a coordinate path with a pen that hangs beneath and to the right of the path. The size of the pen is always one pixel wide and one pixel high.

Drawing Shapes

Example 3-1 lists an applet that invokes `Graphics.drawRect()` to draw a small rectangle in the upper left-hand corner of the applet.

Example 3-1 `RectTest Applet`

```
import java.applet.Applet;
import java.awt.*;

public class RectTest extends Applet {
    public void paint(Graphics g) {
        g.drawRect(2,2,4,4);
    }
}
```

Although the applet has a simple implementation, it illustrates an important point.

At first glance, it may appear that the arguments to `drawRect(2,2,4,4)` define the bounds of the rectangle to be drawn in pixel coordinates. In reality, as shown in Figure 3-2, the arguments specify a *coordinate path* that the graphics' pen will traverse when drawing the rectangle. The coordinate path starts at (2,2) and is 4 coordinates wide and 4 coordinates high:

$$(2,2) \longrightarrow (6,2) \longrightarrow (6,6) \longrightarrow (2,6) \longrightarrow (2,2)$$

The graphics pen traverses the path, hanging down and to the right of the path. As the pen traverses the path, it colors pixels that it comes in contact with. The color used by the pen is specified by invoking `Graphics.setColor(Color)`.

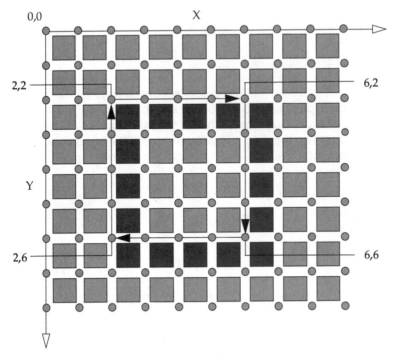

Figure 3-2 Drawing Shape Outlines
The 5-pixel square shown above is the result of
g.drawRect(2,2,4,4). Lines with filled arrows indicate the
coordinate path. The pen traverses the path, hanging down and
to the right, coloring pixels it comes in contact with.

Drawing a rectangle by invoking Graphics.drawRect() results in an extra
row of pixels on the right and bottom sides of the rectangle. This is because the
arguments passed to Graphics.drawRect() define the *coordinate path that the
pen will follow*, and *not the size of the rectangle itself*. Since the pen hangs beneath and
to the right of the coordinates along the path, the statement
g.drawRect(2,2,4,4) actually draws a rectangle whose width and height are
5 pixels—not 4 pixels as you might expect.

AWT TIP ...

Coordinates Lie Between Pixels

Graphics coordinates lie between pixels, not on them. Graphics methods that specify coordinates specify a path that the graphics' pen—always a pixel-sized square—will traverse. The pen paints pixels below and to the right of the coordinates on the path. As a result, Graphics methods that paint outlines of shapes draw an extra row of pixels on the right and bottom sides of the shape's outline. For example, the statement `g.drawRect(x,y,10,10)` paints a rectangle 11 pixels wide and 11 pixels high. The arguments to Graphics.drawRect() specifies the coordinate path—not the dimensions of the rectangle.

Drawing a Border Around a Component

When drawing a border around a component for the first time, newcomers to the AWT often override the component's `paint` method like so:[2]

```
public void paint(Graphics g) {
    Dimension size = getSize();
    g.drawRect(0, 0, size.width, size.height);
}
```

However, as we know, the rectangle will be one pixel wider and one pixel taller than the size of the component. As a result, the right and bottom edges of the border will be drawn outside of the component and therefore will not be visible.

The solution, of course, is to subtract one pixel from both the width and the height:

```
Dimension size = getSize();
g.drawRect(0, 0, size.width-1, size.height-1);
```

Filling Shapes

Example 3-2 lists another simple applet, which is identical to the one listed in Example 3-1 on page 33, except that the rectangle is filled.

---

2. `getSize()` is a Component method—see Table 11-2 on page 433.

Example 3-2 `FillTest Applet`

```
import java.applet.Applet;
import java.awt.*;

public class FillTest extends Applet {
    public void paint(Graphics g) {
        g.fillRect(2,2,4,4);
    }
}
```

The arguments passed to `fillRect()` specify the same coordinate path as the previous call to `drawRect()`. However, `Graphics` methods that fill shapes fill the *interior of the path*, and therefore the filled rectangle is 4 pixels wide and 4 pixels high, as depicted in Figure 3-3.

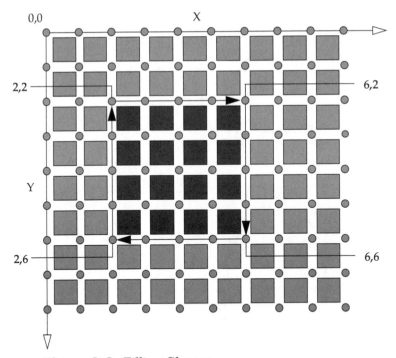

Figure 3-3 Filling Shapes
The filled rectangle shown above is a result of
`g.fillRect(2,2,4,4)`. `Graphics` methods that fill shapes fill
the interior of the path.

The fact that shape fills are smaller than shape outlines can be confusing. Additionally, the arguments passed to drawRect() and fillRect() define a coordinate path, but are often mistaken for representing the bounds of the rectangle in pixels. All Graphics methods that draw outlines and fills exhibit a discrepancy in size. The effect for arcs can be seen in Figure 3-10 on page 51, which draws an outline and fill of an arc.

Graphics References

There are two ways to obtain a reference to a component's Graphics: override one of the methods listed in Table 3-1 on page 28 that are passed a Graphics reference or invoke one of the methods listed in Table 3-2 on page 29, all of which return a Graphics reference.

It is worth mentioning that the Graphics reference returned from getGraphics() in Component, Image, and PrintJob does not, as the name might seem to imply, return a reference to a single Graphics reference. Instead, the methods return a copy of the original Graphics. As we'll see in the next section, this has some important consequences.

Graphics References Refer to Copies

It is important to emphasize that Graphics references refer to *copies* of the actual Graphics associated with a component. Consider the applet listed in Example 3-3—an applet that merely draws a line from its upper left-hand corner to the lower right-hand corner.

Example 3-3 CopyTest Applet

```
import java.applet.Applet;
import java.awt.*;

public class CopyTest extends Applet {
    public void paint(Graphics g) {
        setForeground(Color.yellow);
        g.drawLine(0,0,getSize().width-1, getSize().height-1);
    }
}
```

The applet sets its foreground color to yellow, then draws a line from the upper left-hand corner to the lower-right hand corner of the applet. However, this applet may not perform as you expect—the line will not be yellow the first time it is drawn.

The applet is shown in Figure 3-4.

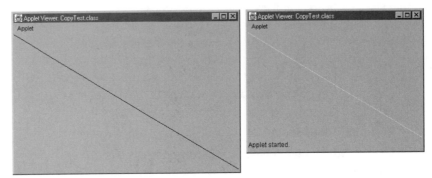

Figure 3-4 `Graphics` References Passed to `paint()` Refer to Copies

The picture on the left shows the applet in its initial state; the line is drawn in the default foreground color for the applet, which, for Windows 95, is black. The picture on the right shows the applet after it has been resized and, therefore, repainted. After the initial painting of the applet, subsequent calls to `paint()` result in a yellow line. Here's why:

The call to `Component.setForeground()` changes the current color of the component's `Graphics`—in this case, to yellow. `setForeground()` affects the applet's `Graphics`, but *not the copy* of the `Graphics` that was passed to `paint()`. Therefore, when `paint()` is invoked for the first time, the line will not be yellow; the `Graphics` passed to `paint()` is out of synch with the actual `Graphics` when the call to `drawLine()` is made.

Subsequent calls to `paint()` are passed new copies of the applet's `Graphics`, and by then the call to `setForeground()` has resulted in the current color of the applet's `Graphics` being set to yellow.

If the applet is modified as listed in Example 3-4, the line will initially be drawn in yellow.

Example 3-4 `CopyTest2` Applet

```
import java.applet.Applet;
import java.awt.*;

public class CopyTest2 extends Applet {
    public void paint(Graphics g) {
        setForeground(Color.yellow);

        // the next line would do just as well as the following
        // g.setColor(Color.yellow);
```

```
Graphics copy = getGraphics();
try {
    System.out.println("g=" + g.getColor() +
                        " copy=" + copy.getColor());

    copy.drawLine(0,0,
                    getSize().width-1, getSize().height-1);
}
finally {
    copy.dispose();
}
}
}
```

The Graphics passed to paint() is ignored. Instead, getGraphics() is called to obtain a new Graphics reference which is used to draw the line. Since the Graphics is obtained after the call to setForeground(), the current color of the Graphics, and therefore the color of the line, will be yellow.

The first time paint() is called, it prints the following output:[3]

g=java.awt.Color[r=0,g=0,b=0] copy=java.awt.Color[r=255,g=255,b=0]

Notice that the Graphics returned by Component.getGraphics() is disposed of before the method returns by invoking Graphics.dispose(), while the Graphics passed to paint() is not disposed of. See "Disposing of a Graphics" on page 40 for more on when it is sometimes necessary to dispose of a Graphics.

Lifetime of a Graphics Reference

In addition to referring to a copy of the real thing, references to Graphics that are passed to methods such as paint() and update() are only valid during the execution of the method they are passed to. Once the method returns, the reference is no longer valid.

Consider the foolish applet listed in Example 3-5, which tries to reuse the Graphics reference initially passed to paint(). The line will be drawn the first time paint() is invoked, but subsequent calls to paint() will result in the line being drawn into an invalid Graphics, and the line no longer shows up (the applet can be forced to repaint by resizing the window).

3. Under Windows 95.

Example 3-5 HoldRef Applet

```
import java.applet.Applet;
import java.awt.*;
import java.awt.event.*;

public class HoldRef extends Applet {
    private Graphics oldg;
    private boolean first = true;

    public void paint(Graphics g) {
        if(first) {
            oldg = g;
            first = false;
        }
        oldg.drawLine(0,0,getSize().width-1, getSize().height-1);
    }
}
```

Graphics references passed to methods have short life-spans because they are a finite resource that must be disposed of. Each Graphics represents a graphics context supplied by the native windowing system. Such graphics contexts are usually available in a finite quantity, and callers that pass references to a Graphics are careful to dispose of it when the call returns. For example, when a call to Component.paint() returns, the caller disposes of the Graphics that was passed to paint().

Although Java has garbage collection, there are a couple of places in the AWT where it is up to the developer to dispose of system resources, and disposing of Graphics is one of them.[4] There are two issues related to disposing of a Graphics: When it needs to be done and how it is done.

Disposing of a Graphics

Here's a simple rule for when you should dispose of a Graphics: If you obtain a reference to a Graphics by invoking one of the getGraphics methods listed in Table 3-2 on page 29 or by creating a Graphics via Graphics.create(), then you are responsible for disposing of it.

If you override a method that is passed a Graphics reference, such as Component.paint() or Component.update(), then you are off the hook—it is the caller's responsibility to dispose of the reference.

Disposing of a Graphics is accomplished by invoking Graphics.dispose(), as the code fragment below demonstrates.

---

4.   Windows and dialogs must also be disposed of. See "Windows, Frames, and Dialogs" on page 569.

```
public void someMethodInAComponent() { // code fragment
    Graphics g = getGraphics();

    if(g != null) {
        try {
            // do something with g - if an exception is thrown,
            // the finally block will be executed
        }
        finally {
            g.dispose() // crucial
        }
    }
}
```

Calling `dispose()` is crucial because neglecting to do so can cause the windowing system to run out of graphics contexts, which on most operating systems is not a pretty sight.

Also note that it is not merely paranoia that causes the check for g against `null`. `getGraphics()` can indeed return `null` if it is invoked before the component's peer has been created—see "`java.awt.Component` Methods That Depend Upon Peers" on page 440.

The call to `Graphics.dispose()` is placed in a `finally` block; manipulation of the `Graphics` is performed within a corresponding `try` block. This ensures that the call to `dispose()` will be made in the event that an exception is thrown from within the `try` block.

AWT TIP ...

Graphics References Passed to Methods Refer to Copies

Graphics represent native graphics contexts, which are typically a finite resource. Therefore, Graphics references returned by a method must be disposed of by calling `Graphics.dispose()`.

Graphics references passed to methods, such as `Component.paint()`, do not need to be manually disposed of by the method—the caller of the method is responsible for disposing of the Graphics when the calls return.

More on Drawing and Filling Shapes

The `Graphics` class provides methods for rendering the following:

- Lines
- PolyLines
- Rectangles

- Arcs
- Ovals
- Polygons
- Text
- Images

Rectangles, arcs, ovals, and polygons can also be filled. In this section, we will explore all but the last item listed above—for information on displaying and filtering images, the *Loading and Displaying Images* chapter on page 103 and the *Image Filtering* chapter on page 129.

Drawing Lines

Lines are drawn by use of Graphics.drawLine(int x, int y, int x2, int y2). The AWT is not capable of drawing lines of variable thickness; the graphics' pen, and therefore the lines it draws, are always one pixel thick. In addition, lines are always drawn solid—there is no provision for patterned lines such as dotted or dashed. However, the Java 2D Api provides extensive support for various linestyles and pen sizes.

The applet shown in Figure 3-5 draws lines at random locations. The lines are also fitted with random lengths, directions, and colors.

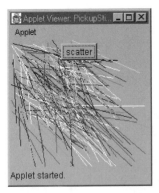

Figure 3-5 Drawing Lines
The applet draws lines at random locations, lengths, and colors.

The applet shown in Figure 3-5 is listed in Example 3-6. Activation of the "scatter" button causes the applet to repaint. `Math.random()` is used to randomize the line's parameters. `random()` returns a pseudorandom[5] number between 0.0 and 1.0. That number is multiplied by some factor of ten to give reasonable bounds to the line's location and size.

Example 3-6 `PickupSticks Applet`

```
import java.applet.Applet;
import java.awt.*;
import java.awt.event.*;

public class PickupSticks extends Applet {
    private static Color[] colors = {
        Color.white, Color.black, Color.blue, Color.red,
        Color.yellow, Color.orange, Color.cyan, Color.pink,
        Color.magenta, Color.green };

    public void init() {
        Button button = new Button("scatter");

        add(button);

        button.addActionListener(new ActionListener() {
            public void actionPerformed(ActionEvent event) {
                repaint();
            }
        });
    }
    public void paint(Graphics g) {
        for(int i=0; i < 500; ++i) {
            int x = (int)(Math.random()*100);
            int y = (int)(Math.random()*100);
            int deltax = (int)(Math.random()*100);
            int deltay = (int)(Math.random()*100);

            g.setColor(colors[(int)(Math.random()*10)]);
            g.drawLine(x,y,x + deltax, y + deltay);
        }
    }
}
```

The arguments to `Graphics.drawLine(int x, int y, int x2, int y2)` represent the endpoints of the line. Notice that the line, like all other shapes drawn by a `Graphics`, is drawn in the `Graphics`' current color. The applet listed above uses a random number between 1 and 10 to select an index into the `colors` array in order to randomize the color of the line.

---

5. Pseudorandom number generators have repeating sequences.

Drawing Polylines

A polyline is a series of connected line segments, which are drawn by
`drawPolyline(int[] xPoints, int[] yPoints, int numPoints)`.
The method is passed two arrays, one specifying the x coordinates of each point,
and the other representing the y coordinates. Additionally, the method takes an
integer value signifying the number of points to be drawn.[6] The figure drawn by
`drawPolyline()` is not closed if the first and last points differ.

The applet shown in Figure 3-6 randomly generates polylines. The applet
contains a repaint button, which causes the applet to repaint when activated. The
number of points and their locations, in addition to the color of the polyline,
varies in a pseudorandom fashion.

The applet shown in Figure 3-6 is listed in Example 3-7.

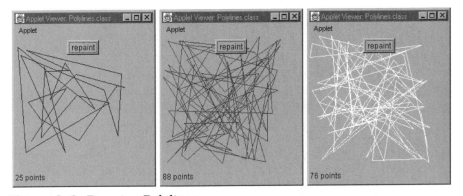

Figure 3-6 Drawing Polylines
The applet generates randomly colored polylines with randomly
located points.

Example 3-7 Polylines Applet

```
import java.applet.Applet;
import java.awt.*;
import java.awt.event.*;

public class Polylines extends Applet {
    private static Color[] colors = {
        Color.white, Color.black, Color.blue, Color.red,
        Color.yellow, Color.orange, Color.cyan, Color.pink,
        Color.magenta, Color.green };
```

6. The number of points equals the number of line segments - 1.

```
public void init() {
    Button button = new Button("repaint");
    add(button);
    button.addActionListener(new ActionListener() {
        public void actionPerformed(ActionEvent event) {
            Polylines.this.repaint();
        }
    });
}
public void paint(Graphics g) {
    int arraySize = ((int)(Math.random()*100));
    int[] xPoints = new int[arraySize];
    int[] yPoints = new int[arraySize];

    for(int i=0; i < xPoints.length; ++i) {
        xPoints[i] = ((int)(Math.random()*200));
        yPoints[i] = ((int)(Math.random()*200));
    }
    g.setColor(colors[(int)(Math.random()*10)]);
    g.drawPolyline(xPoints, yPoints, xPoints.length);

    showStatus(arraySize + " points");
}
}
```

Drawing Rectangles

In contrast to lines, the Graphics class provides a wealth of support for rectangles; three types of rectangles are supported:

- solid
- rounded
- 3D

The Graphics methods for painting and filling rectangles are listed below:

- void clearRect(int x, int y, int w, int h)
- void drawRect(int x, int y, int w, int h)
- void drawRoundRect(int x, int y, int w, int h, int arcWidth, in arcHeight)
- void draw3DRect(int x, int y, int w, int h, boolean raise)
- void fillRoundRect(int x, int y, int w, int h, int arcWidth, int arcHeight)
- void fillRect(int x, int y, int w, int h)
- void fill3DRect(int x, int y, int w, int h, boolean raise)

It is important to remember that the x, y, w, and h arguments passed to each of the functions listed above define a coordinate path—which is not necessarily the size of the rectangle. See "Drawing Shapes" on page 33.

The methods for drawing and filling 3D rectangles take an argument in addition to x, y, w, and h. The boolean argument specifies whether the 3D effect is raised or inset; true equates to raised, and false equates to inset.

The methods for drawing and filling round rectangles take two additional arguments: arcWidth and arcHeight, both integer values. arcWidth specifies the arc's horizontal diameter in pixels, and arcHeight specifies the vertical diameter of the arc. Figure 3-7 illustrates the horizontal and vertical diameters of the arcs.

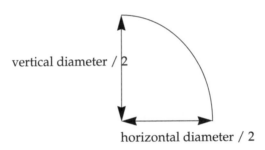

vertical diameter / 2

horizontal diameter / 2

Figure 3-7 Rounded Rectangles
The vertical and horizontal diameters of the arc for rounded corners is specified in Graphics methods that draw rounded rectangles. The size of the vertical diameter may differ from the size of the horizontal diameter.

The applet shown in Figure 3-8 paints rectangles with random parameters for color, size, and location. All three types of rectangles supported by the Graphics class are drawn.

 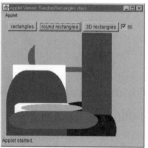 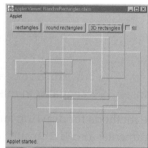

Figure 3-8 Drawing Rectangles
The applet generates rectangles, round rectangles, and 3D rectangles at random locations, sizes, and colors.

The applet comes equipped with three buttons and a checkbox. Each button represents the type of rectangle to be drawn; activating a button results in a repaint using the type of rectangle the button represents.

A checkbox is also included for specifying whether or not the rectangles are filled.

The applet is rather lengthy, but a good percentage of it is concerned with constructing the buttons and checkbox and their corresponding event handling. Our concern, namely, drawing rectangles, is encapsulated in the applet's paint method.

```
public class RandomRectangles extends Applet {
    ...
    private boolean fill = false, raise = false,
                round = false, threeD = false;
    ...
    public void paint(Graphics g) {
        for(int i=0; i < numRects; i++) {
            Point lhc = randomPoint(); // left hand corner
            Dimension size = randomDimension();

            g.setColor(colors[(int)(Math.random()*10)]);

            if(round) {
                if(fill)
                    g.fillRoundRect(
                        lhc.x,lhc.y,size.width,size.height,
                        (int)(Math.random()*250),
                        (int)(Math.random()*250));
                else
                    g.drawRoundRect(
                        lhc.x,lhc.y,size.width,size.height,
```

```
                    (int)(Math.random()*250),
                    (int)(Math.random()*250));
        }
        else if(threeD) {
            g.setColor(Color.lightGray);
            if(fill)
                g.fill3DRect(
                    lhc.x,lhc.y,size.width,size.height,raise);
            else
                g.draw3DRect(
                    lhc.x,lhc.y,size.width,size.height,raise);
        }
        else {
            if(fill)
                g.fillRect(lhc.x,lhc.y,size.width,size.height);
            else
                g.drawRect(lhc.x,lhc.y,size.width,size.height);
        }
        raise = raise ? false : true;
    }
}
...
}
```

`Boolean` class members keep track of which button was last activated and whether or not the fill option is currently checked.

All of the rectangles drawn by the applet are drawn with a one-pixel-square pen, because that is the only size the AWT provides.

When 3D rectangles are drawn, the `Graphics'` color is set to light gray before drawing the rectangle, because `draw3DRect()` and `fill3DRect()` draw rectangles that only look three-dimensional if they are drawn in light gray.

The applet is listed in its entirety in Example 3-8.

 Example 3-8 RandomRectangles Applet

```
import java.applet.Applet;
import java.awt.*;
import java.awt.event.*;

public class RandomRectangles extends Applet {
    private static Color[] colors = {
        Color.white, Color.black, Color.blue, Color.red,
        Color.yellow, Color.orange, Color.cyan, Color.pink,
        Color.magenta, Color.green };

    private int numRects = 10;
    private boolean fill = false, raise = false,
                    round = false, threeD = false;
```

```
public void init() {
    Button rectsButton = new Button("rectangles");
    Button roundButton = new Button("round rectangles");
    Button threeDButton = new Button("3D rectangles");
    Checkbox fillCheckbox = new Checkbox("fill");

    add(rectsButton);
    add(roundButton);
    add(threeDButton);
    add(fillCheckbox);

    rectsButton.addActionListener(new ActionListener() {
        public void actionPerformed(ActionEvent event) {
            round = false;
            threeD = false;
            repaint();
        }
    });
    roundButton.addActionListener(new ActionListener() {
        public void actionPerformed(ActionEvent event) {
            round = true;
            threeD = false;
            repaint();
        }
    });
    threeDButton.addActionListener(new ActionListener() {
        public void actionPerformed(ActionEvent event) {
            threeD = true;
            round = false;
            repaint();
        }
    });
    fillCheckbox.addItemListener(new ItemListener() {
        public void itemStateChanged(ItemEvent event) {
            fill = ((Checkbox)(event.getSource())).getState();
        }
    });
}
public void paint(Graphics g) {
    for(int i=0; i < numRects; i++) {
        Point lhc = randomPoint(); // left hand corner
        Dimension size = randomDimension();

        g.setColor(colors[(int)(Math.random()*10)]);

        if(round) {
            if(fill)
                g.fillRoundRect(
                    lhc.x,lhc.y,size.width,size.height,
                    (int)(Math.random()*250),
                    (int)(Math.random()*250));
            else
```

```
            g.drawRoundRect(
                lhc.x,lhc.y,size.width,size.height,
                (int)(Math.random()*250),
                (int)(Math.random()*250));
        }
        else if(threeD) {
            g.setColor(Color.lightGray);

            if(fill)
                g.fill3DRect(
                    lhc.x,lhc.y,size.width,size.height,raise);
            else
                g.draw3DRect(
                    lhc.x,lhc.y,size.width,size.height,raise);
        }
        else {
            if(fill)
                g.fillRect(lhc.x,lhc.y,size.width,size.height);
            else
                g.drawRect(lhc.x,lhc.y,size.width,size.height);
        }
        raise = raise ? false : true;
    }
}
private Dimension randomDimension() {
    return new Dimension((int)(Math.random()*250),
                        (int)(Math.random()*250));
}
private Point randomPoint() {
    return new Point((int)(Math.random()*250),
                    (int)(Math.random()*250));
}
}
```

Drawing Arcs

`java.awt.Graphics` provides the following methods for drawing and filling arcs:

- `void drawArc(int x, int y, int w, int h, int startAngle, int endAngle)`
- `void fillArc(int x, int y, int w, int h, int startAngle, int endAngle)`

Both methods are passed the same list of arguments. The first four arguments specify a coordinate path for a bounding box into which the arc will be drawn (or filled). The last two arguments specify the start and end angles of the arc in degrees. For example, the applet shown in Figure 3-9 draws an arc with a start angle of 0 degrees and an end angle of 270 degrees whose width and height are specified as 151 and 101 pixels, respectively. The applet is listed in Example 3-9.

(10,10)

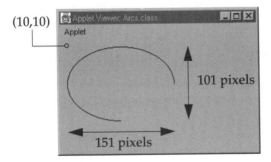

Figure 3-9 Drawing Arcs
Arcs are drawn by specifying a bounding rectangle and start/end angles.

Example 3-9 DrawArc Applet

```
import java.applet.Applet;
import java.awt.*;

public class DrawArc extends Applet {
    public void paint(Graphics g) {
        g.setColor(Color.black);
        g.drawArc(10,10,150,100,0,270);
    }
}
```

Graphics.fillArc() fills the interior of the coordinate path specified by the arguments it is passed. The applet listed in Example 3-9 on page 51 is modified to fill the arc in addition to drawing it, as shown in Figure 3-10.

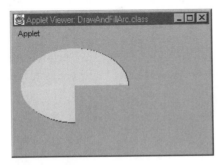

Figure 3-10 Drawing and Filling Arcs

Notice that the black outline of the arc is visible on the right and bottom sides of the arc, even though the calls to `drawArc()` and `fillArc()` specify the same coordinate path. As noted previously, `Graphics` methods that draw shape outlines draw an extra row of pixels on the left and bottom sides of the shape.

Arcs are the only unclosed shape that can be filled. Filled arcs are closed by drawing lines that emanate from the center of the arc to its endpoints. The applet shown Figure 3-10 is listed in Example 3-10.

Example 3-10 DrawAndFillArc Applet

```
import java.applet.Applet;
import java.awt.*;

public class DrawAndFillArc extends Applet {
    public void paint(Graphics g) {
        g.setColor(Color.black);
        g.drawArc(10,10,150,100,0,270);
        g.setColor(Color.yellow);
        g.fillArc(10,10,150,100,0,270);
    }
}
```

Drawing Ovals

The `Graphics` class provides methods for drawing and filling elliptical shapes:

- void drawOval(int x, int y, int w, int h)
- void fillOval(int x, int y, int w, int h)

The arguments passed to both methods specify a coordinate path for a bounding rectangle for the ellipse. If the width and height of the coordinate path are equal, then a circle is drawn. The oval is centered at the center of the bounding box and just fits inside it.

As with other `Graphics` methods that draw shapes, `drawOval()` draws an ellipse that fits into a rectangle that is w+1 pixels wide and h+1 pixels high.

Drawing Polygons

Polygons may be drawn and filled by the following Graphics methods:

- void drawPolygon(int[] xPoints, int[] yPoints, int
                   numPoints)
- void drawPolygon(Polygon polygon)
- void drawPolygon(int[] xPoints, int[] yPoints, int
                   numPoints)
- void drawPolygon(Polygon polygon)

A polygon may be drawn or filled by specifying either a Polygon object or arrays of x and y values specifying the points of the polygon. Polygons are automatically closed if the first and last points are not the same.

It is interesting to note that although the AWT provides nongraphical Polygon and Rectangle classes, no drawRect(Rectangle) method is provided by the Graphics class, although there is a drawPolygon(Polygon).

Drawing Text

The Graphics class provides three methods for rendering text:

- void drawString(String s, int x, int y)
- void drawChars(char[], int offset, int length, int x,
                 int y)
- void drawBytes(byte[], int offset, int length, int x,
                 int y)

The text may be specified as a string, an array of characters, or an array of bytes, depending upon which method is invoked.

All three methods for rendering text are passed an x,y location at which to draw the text. The location corresponds to the baseline of the text, and not the upper left-hand corner of the text, as is the case for rectangles, as depicted in Figure 3-11.

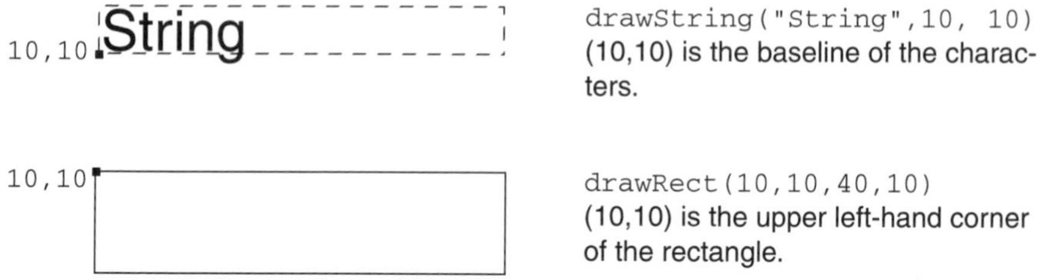

10,10 **String**

`drawString("String",10, 10)`
(10,10) is the baseline of the characters.

10,10

`drawRect(10,10,40,10)`
(10,10) is the upper left-hand corner
of the rectangle.

Figure 3-11 Drawing Strings with the `drawString()` Method
The `drawString` method uses the text baseline as the point of
origin. The `drawRect` method uses the upper left-hand corner as
the point of origin.

The offset and length arguments passed to `drawChars()` and `drawBytes()`
specifies an offset into the array at which to start drawing, and the number of
characters to draw, respectively.

The `Graphics` class does not provide the capability to rotate text.

AWT TIP ...

Locations for Strings and Shapes Differ

The location specified for drawing a string specifies the baseline of the text,
whereas the location specified for drawing a shape refers to the upper left-hand
corner of the shape's boundary. If a string and rectangle are drawn with the
same location specified for each, the string will appear above the rectangle.

Translating a Coordinate System's Origin

Unless specified otherwise, the origin of a `Graphics'` coordinate system
coincides with the upper left-hand corner of its associated component, image or
print job, as illustrated in "The Graphics Coordinate System" on page 32.

`Graphics.translate()` can be used to translate the origin to a new location.
The `translate` method is passed two `integer` values representing a point in
the original coordinate system that will become the origin of the translated
coordinate system.

Translating a coordinate system's origin is done for numerous reasons; one reason is to scroll the contents of a container without scrollbars, as our next applet illustrates.

The applet shown in Figure 3-12 displays an image that can be scrolled by dragging the mouse within the applet.

The scrolling is accomplished by translating the origin of the Graphics' coordinate system whenever a mouse drag event is detected and subsequently repainting the image.

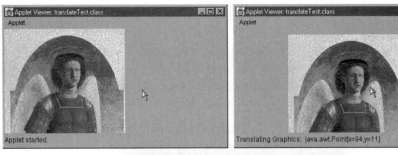

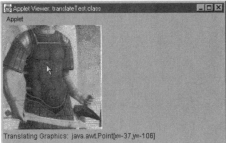

Figure 3-12 Translating a Coordinate System's Origin
Dragging the mouse changes the origin of the coordinate system, so that the image is scrolled.

The top left picture in Figure 3-12 shows the applet in its initial state. The top right picture shows the applet after the origin has been translated and the image has been redrawn. The bottom picture illustrates that the origin may be translated to negative x and y values.

The applet's `init` method loads the image, and its `paint` method draws the image at (0,0).

```
public void init() {
    image = getImage(getCodeBase(), "saint.gif");
    try {
        MediaTracker mt = new MediaTracker(this);
        mt.addImage(image, 0);
        mt.waitForID(0);
    }
    catch(InterruptedException e) {
        e.printStackTrace();
    }
}
public void paint(Graphics g) {
    g.drawImage(image, 0, 0, this);
}
```

`init()` employs an instance of `MediaTracker` to ensure that the image is fully loaded before it is displayed, but loading images is not the focus of our discussion here. For more on loading images and the use of `MediaTracker`—the *Loading and Displaying Images* chapter on page 103.

The applet defines inner-class versions of mouse and mouse motion listeners. When the mouse is pressed in the applet, the location of the mouse press is saved.

```
public class TranslateTest extends Applet {
    Image image;
    Point pressed = new Point(), lastTranslate = new Point();
    ...
    public void init() {
        ...
        addMouseListener(new MouseAdapter() {
            public void mousePressed(MouseEvent e) {
                Point loc = e.getPoint();
                // adjust mouse press location for
                // translation ...
                pressed.x = loc.x - lastTranslate.x;
                pressed.y = loc.y - lastTranslate.y;
            }
        });
        ...
    }
    ...
}
```

Again, the focus of our discussion here concerns translating the origin of a coordinate system and not event handling or inner classes—the *The Delegation Event Model (AWT 1.1 and Beyond)* chapter on page 237 for more on event handling and inner classes. The gist of the event handling code is that when a mouse press occurs in the applet, `mousePressed()` listed above, is invoked.

The location of the mouse press is adjusted for the last translation point. The lastTranslate point is initially (0,0),[7] so the first time the mouse is pressed, the pressed location is the same as the mouse press coordinates. lastTranslate is updated every time the coordinate system is translated as the result of a mouse dragged event.

It is important to realize that the mouse press location is adjusted for the last translation because the translations apply only to the *copy* of the component's Graphics obtained from the call to getGraphics(). The actual Graphics associated with the applet is *never* translated; only the copies of the actual Graphics get translated.

The call to Graphics.translate() takes place in mouseDragged():

```
public class TranslateTest extends Applet {
    ...
    public void init() {
        ...
        addMouseMotionListener(new MouseMotionAdapter() {
            public void mouseDragged(MouseEvent e) {
                Point loc = e.getPoint();
                Point translate = new Point(loc.x - pressed.x,
                                            loc.y - pressed.y);
                Graphics g = getGraphics();

                try {
                    g.clearRect(0,0,
                                getSize().width,getSize().height);
                    g.translate(translate.x, translate.y);
                    showStatus("Translating Graphics:  " +
                                translate);

                    g.drawImage(image, 0, 0, TranslateTest.this);
                }
                finally {
                    g.dispose();
                }
                lastTranslate = translate;
            }
        });
    }
    ...
}
```

As the mouse is dragged, a translate point is calculated by subtracting the coordinates of the original mouse press event from the coordinates of the mouse dragged event, as shown in Figure 3-13.

---

7.   The Point no-argument constructor sets the point's location to (0,0).

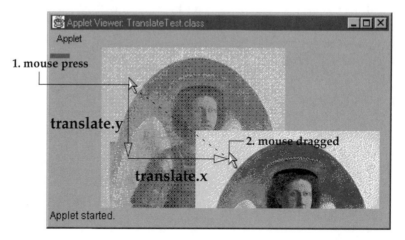

Figure 3-13 Translation Coordinates
An image is dragged from an initial location (shown partially dissolved) to a new location by translating the origin of the coordinate system. The translation coordinates are calculated by subtracting the mouse press location from the mouse dragged location.

The copy of the `Graphics` obtained from `getGraphics()` has its origin translated to the calculated value.

There are a couple of points regarding the previous example worth reiterating concerning `Graphics`.

The first point is that a call is made to `Graphics.drawImage()` to redraw the image after the translation. Since the applet's `paint` method also draws the image at (0,0), it might be tempting to simply call `repaint()` after translating the origin and let `paint()` take care of rendering the image. However, remember that the `Graphics` object obtained in `mouseDragged()`, like the `Graphics` passed to `paint()`, is a copy of the actual graphics context associated with the component. Invoking `g.translate(translate.x, translate.y)` translates the origin of the copy of the `Graphics` returned from `getGraphics()` but not of the copy that would be passed to `paint()`.[8]

---

8.   Which is also the reason we must track the last translation point, as previously noted.

Second, notice that a call is made to dispose of the `Graphics` obtained from the call to `Component.getGraphics()`. It is not necessary to dispose of the `Graphics` passed to `paint()`—see "Disposing of a Graphics" on page 40.

Finally, if you run the applet from the CD in the back of the book, you will notice that the image flickers as it is being dragged. The flickering is due to the erasing and rendering of the image, which is done in the onscreen graphics. The applet could easily be double buffered to eliminate the flicker. "An Introduction to Double Buffering" on page 177 discusses a simple implementation of double buffering.

The `TranslateTest` applet is listed in its entirety in Example 3-11.

Example 3-11 `TranslateTest` Applet

```
import java.applet.Applet;
import java.awt.*;
import java.awt.event.*;

public class TranslateTest extends Applet {
    Image image;
    Point pressed = new Point(), lastTranslate = new Point();

    public void init() {
        image = getImage(getCodeBase(), "saint.gif");
        try {
            MediaTracker mt = new MediaTracker(this);
            mt.addImage(image, 0);
            mt.waitForID(0);
        }
        catch(InterruptedException e) {
            e.printStackTrace();
        }
        addMouseListener(new MouseAdapter() {
            public void mousePressed(MouseEvent e) {
                Point loc = e.getPoint();

                // adjust mouse press location for
                // translation ...
                pressed.x = loc.x - lastTranslate.x;
                pressed.y = loc.y - lastTranslate.y;
            }
        });
        addMouseMotionListener(new MouseMotionAdapter() {
            public void mouseDragged(MouseEvent e) {
                Point loc = e.getPoint();
                Point translate = new Point(loc.x - pressed.x,
                                            loc.y - pressed.y);
                Graphics g = getGraphics();
```

```
        try {
           g.clearRect(0,0,
                      getSize().width,getSize().height);
           g.translate(translate.x, translate.y);
           showStatus("Translating Graphics:  " +
                      translate);

           g.drawImage(image, 0, 0, TranslateTest.this);
        }
        finally {
           g.dispose();
        }
        lastTranslate = translate;
      }
   });
  }
  public void paint(Graphics g) {
     g.drawImage(image, 0, 0, this);
  }
}
```

Clipping

Every Graphics has an associated clipping rectangle. Clipping rectangles are so named because they clip rendering to the rectangle they represent. In addition, with the advent of the Java 2D Api, clipping can be set to an arbitrary shape instead of being restricted to a rectangle.

The methods below, which are repeated from "Graphics Parameters" on page 30, are provided by java.awt.Graphics for setting and getting the clipping region:

- void setClip(int x, int y, int w, int h)
- void setClip(Shape)

- Rectangle getClipBounds()
- Shape getClip()

- void clipRect(int x, int y, int w, int h)

The first two methods set the clipping region. The first method sets the clipping region to a rectangle, and the second sets it to an arbitrary shape.

The next two methods return the clipping region—the first returns a rectangle, and the second returns a shape.

The last method sets the clipping rectangle to the intersection of the current clipping rectangle and the rectangle specified by the arguments to the method.

Figure 3-14 shows the applet shown in Figure 3-8 on page 47 and listed in Example 3-8 on page 48. The applet's `paint` method has been modified to display the clipping rectangle of the `Graphics` it is passed in the applet's status bar. Since that is the only modification to the applet, we won't bother to list it here.

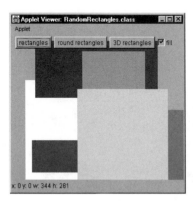
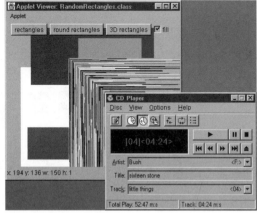

Figure 3-14 Clipping Graphics
As the smaller window is dragged over the applet, repainting is clipped to the damaged region of the applet's window.

When the applet is initially displayed, as depicted by the left-hand picture in Figure 3-14, the clipping rectangle is equal to the size of the applet itself (note the applet's status bar). This case restricts rendering to the extent of the applet. Any graphical operations that are performed outside the bounds of the applet are not rendered, which explains why you can inadvertently draw outside the bounds of a component without any dire consequences.

If another window is dragged across the applet, as depicted in the right-hand picture, the applet is repainted. Since the applet paints a fresh set of random rectangles every time it is repainted and since repainting is clipped to the damaged area of the applet, the result is a series of repainted regions of the applet. It is important to realize that the entire applet is actually redrawn every time the smaller window is dragged; however, the drawing is clipped to the damaged area of the applet's window.

The clipping rectangle in the right-hand picture in Figure 3-14 has a width of 150 pixels but a height of only 1 pixel. The one-pixel height indicates that the smaller window was last dragged vertically—if the window had been dragged horizontally, the width would have been one pixel. If the window is dragged diagonally, the clipping rectangle would be equal to the area underneath the window being dragged.

Clipping is especially important when implementing double buffering and animations, as we shall see in "Double Buffering" on page 789 and "Sprite Animation" on page 813. When dragging or animating components over the surface of a component, it is much more efficient to restore only damaged areas of the component, rather than repainting the entire component and relying upon clipping to restrict rendering to damaged areas.

AWT TIP ...

Component.paint() Is Often Passed a Clipped Graphics

Unbeknown to AWT newcomers, paint methods are often passed a Graphics whose clipping rectangle is smaller than the size of the component. As a result, most overridden paint methods do not bother to check the clipping rectangle of the Graphics they are passed. When `paint()` paints the contents of the component, the rendering operations are clipped to the current clipping region; however, all rendering operations are still performed. In some instances, such as double buffering or animation, much better performance can be achieved by refreshing only the clipped region instead of painting the entire component and relying upon clipping to clip the rendering operations.

Graphics Modes

`java.awt.Graphics` provides two graphics modes: paint and XOR. Paint mode is the default; graphical operations performed in paint mode simply overwrite existing graphics. XOR mode, on the other hand, allows graphical operations to be performed over existing graphics without disturbing the affected areas. Until now, all of the rendering in this chapter has been done in paint mode, so we will concentrate on XOR mode in this section.

The documentation for `Graphics.setXORMode(Color)` describes XOR mode as follows:

When drawing operations are performed, pixels which are the current color are changed to the specified color, and vice versa.

Pixels that are of colors other than those two colors are changed in an unpredictable but reversible manner; <u>if the same figure is drawn twice, then all pixels are restored to their original values</u>.

The bottom line is the underlined portion of the last sentence: If a rendering operation is performed in XOR mode twice in succession, the underlying graphics is unaffected.

Perhaps the most common use of XOR mode is for rubberbanding shapes over existing graphics. Rubberbanding is commonly used in drawing programs and also for selecting multiple objects.

Figure 3-15 shows an applet that employs XOR mode to rubberband a rectangle over an image.

The applet shown in Figure 3-15 loads the image in its `init` method and paints the image in `paint()`. All of the action, as far as XOR mode is concerned, takes place in an event handler that reacts to mouse dragged events:

Figure 3-15 XOR Mode

XOR mode is used to rubberband a rectangle over the image.
When the rubberbanding is complete, the Graphics is clipped to
the rubberband rectangle, and the image is redrawn.

```
addMouseMotionListener(new MouseMotionAdapter() {
    public void mouseDragged(MouseEvent e) {
        Point loc = e.getPoint();
        Graphics g = getGraphics();

        try {
            g.setXORMode(getBackground());

            if(firstRect) {
                firstRect = false;
            }
            else {
                g.drawRect(pressed.x, pressed.y,
                        Math.abs(pressed.x - last.x),
                        Math.abs(pressed.y - last.y));
            }
            g.drawRect(pressed.x, pressed.y,
                        Math.abs(loc.x - pressed.x),
                        Math.abs(loc.y - pressed.y));
            last = e.getPoint();
        }
        finally {
            g.dispose();
        }
    }
});
```

Whenever the mouse is dragged, the graphics mode for the applet is set to XOR mode. Passing the background color to setXORMode() means that subsequent graphical operations result in pixels that are the current Graphics color being rendered in the background color, and vice versa. All other colors are changed unpredictably; however, if a graphical operation is performed twice in XOR mode, the underlying pixels will be left in their original color.

If mouseDragged() is being called for the first time immediately after a mouse pressed, firstRect is true, and therefore there is no previous rectangle to erase. Subsequent drags result in the last rectangle being redrawn, which effectively erases the previous rectangle, leaving the underlying graphics intact. Then, a new rectangle is drawn at the current drag location.

For good measure, after the rubberbanding operation is complete, the applet's background is cleared, the Graphics is clipped to the rubberband rectangle, and the image is redrawn:

```
public void mouseReleased(MouseEvent e) {
    if(pressed != null) {
        Point  released = e.getPoint();
        Rectangle clip = new Rectangle();
        Graphics g = getGraphics();
        Dimension size = getSize();

        try {
            clip.x = pressed.x;
            clip.y = pressed.y;
            clip.width  = Math.abs(released.x - pressed.x);
            clip.height = Math.abs(released.y - pressed.y);

            g.clearRect(0,0,size.width,size.height);
            g.setClip(clip);
            g.drawImage(image, 0, 0, xortest.this);
        }
        finally {
            g.dispose();
        }
    }
}
```

Of course, both mouse handler methods in Example 3-12 are careful to dispose of the Graphics obtained by calls to Component.getGraphics(). In addition, mouseReleased() paints the image itself instead of invoking paint() after setting the clipping rectangle because only the copy of the Graphics obtained via getGraphics() is affected by the call to setClip().

The algorithm used for drawing the rubberband rectangle is faulty. If the rectangle is dragged above or to the left of the mouse press point, it will not be properly rendered. We will see how to correct this shortcoming in "Rubberbanding" on page 765.

The applet is listed in its entirety in Example 3-12.

Example 3-12 xortest Applet

```java
import java.applet.Applet;
import java.awt.*;
import java.awt.event.*;

public class xortest extends Applet {
    Pointpressed, last;
    Image image;
    boolean firstRect;

    public void init() {
        image = getImage(getCodeBase(), "saint.gif");
        try {
            MediaTracker mt = new MediaTracker(this);
            mt.addImage(image, 0);
            mt.waitForID(0);
        }
        catch(InterruptedException e) {
            e.printStackTrace();
        }
        addMouseListener(new MouseAdapter() {
            public void mousePressed(MouseEvent e) {
                firstRect = true;
                pressed   = e.getPoint();
            }
            public void mouseReleased(MouseEvent e) {
                if(pressed != null) {
                    Point  released = e.getPoint();
                    Rectangle clip = new Rectangle();
                    Graphics g = getGraphics();
                    Dimension size = getSize();

                    try {
                        clip.x = pressed.x;
                        clip.y = pressed.y;
                        clip.width  =
                            Math.abs(released.x - pressed.x);
                        clip.height =
                            Math.abs(released.y - pressed.y);

                        g.clearRect(0,0,size.width,size.height);
                        g.setClip(clip);
                        g.drawImage(image, 0, 0, xortest.this);
                    }
```

```
                    finally {
                        g.dispose();
                    }
                }
            }
            public void mouseClicked(MouseEvent e) {
                repaint();
            }
        });
        addMouseMotionListener(new MouseMotionAdapter() {
            public void mouseDragged(MouseEvent e) {
                Point loc = e.getPoint();
                Graphics g = getGraphics();

                try {
                    g.setXORMode(getBackground());

                    if(firstRect) {
                        firstRect = false;
                    }
                    else {
                        g.drawRect(pressed.x, pressed.y,
                                Math.abs(pressed.x - last.x),
                                Math.abs(pressed.y - last.y));
                    }
                    g.drawRect(pressed.x, pressed.y,
                            Math.abs(loc.x - pressed.x),
                            Math.abs(loc.y - pressed.y));
                    last = e.getPoint();
                }
                finally {
                    g.dispose();
                }
            }
        });
    }
    public void paint(Graphics g) {
        g.drawImage(image, 0, 0, this);
    }
}
```

Creating a Graphics

When implementing a method that is passed a Graphics reference, it is best to
ensure that the method results in no net change to the Graphics. In other words,
when the method returns, the Graphics should be in the same state that it was in
before the method was invoked.

There are exceptions to this rule, of course. For instance, we can have a high degree of certainty that callers of paint (Graphics) will merely dispose of the Graphics when the call to paint () returns. Therefore, it is acceptable to modify the Graphics passed to paint () with wanton disregard to maintaining its state.

However, in other situations it is not so clear as to whether the Graphics must retain its initial state. In such cases, it is best to take the safe route and ensure that the Graphics is unchanged. This can be done in two ways.

First, all of the initial attributes of the Graphics can be stored locally and reset before the method returns:

```
// code fragment
public void notSureIfGraphicsShouldChangeState(Graphics g) {
    Color oldColor = g.getColor();
    Font oldFont = g.getFont();

    // modify g's color and font and perform graphical operations

    g.setColor(oldColor); // restore old color
    g.setfont(oldFont); // restore old font
}
```

When modifications are made to only one or two properties, restoring the properties is simply a minor inconvenience. However, if a number of properties are to be modified and then restored, it's more convenient to create a copy of the Graphics and use it instead of the Graphics passed to the method:

```
public void notSureIfGraphicsShouldChangeState(Graphics g) {
    Graphics copy = g.create();
    try {
        // use copy for rendering
    }
    finally {
        g.dispose(); // crucial
    }
}
```

As discussed previously in "Disposing of a Graphics" on page 40, it is imperative that Graphics obtained by calls to Graphics.create() are disposed of, as we've done in the pseudocode above.

Another motivation for creating a Graphics results from the need to hold onto a Graphics reference passed to a method after the method returns. Typically, this is done in lieu of repeatedly modifying properties of a Graphics reference in an associated paint method—it is more efficient to hold onto a copy of a Graphics with the appropriate properties modified.

Recall our ill-fated applet in Example 3-5 on page 40 that held on to a `Graphics` reference. Since the `Graphics` passed to `paint()` is disposed of by the caller, the `Graphics` reference is valid only for the duration of the call to `paint()`. However, we can create a copy of the `Graphics` that will not be disposed of after the call to `paint()`, as shown in Example 3-13.

Example 3-13 `HoldRef2` Applet

```java
import java.applet.Applet;
import java.awt.*;
import java.awt.event.*;

public class HoldRef2 extends Applet {
    private Graphics copy;
    private boolean first = true;

    public void paint(Graphics g) {
        if(first) {
            // note: copy is never disposed of
            copy = g.create();

            copy.setColor(Color.red);
            copy.setFont(new Font("Times Roman", Font.BOLD, 14));
            first = false;
        }
        copy.drawString("Red Text", 10, 10);
    }
}
```

The `Graphics` created in Example 3-13 modifies its color and font and is subsequently used to draw a string in the upper left-hand corner of the applet. Of course, we are committing a mortal sin by not disposing of the copy of the `Graphics`. In real life, one would probably make the `copy` reference a class member and dispose of it in another method at the appropriate moment in time.

The `Graphics` class provides two methods for creating a `Graphics`:

- `Graphics create()`
- `Graphics create(int x, int y, int w, int h)`

The first method, as we have seen, creates an exact duplicate of the `Graphics` on whose behalf the method is invoked.

The second method also creates a duplicate; however, the arguments specify a translation `(x,y)` and a new clipping rectangle `(x,y,w,h)`. The origin of the `Graphics` returned from `create(int,int,int,int)` is translated to the `(x,y)` coordinates, whereas the clipping rectangle winds up being the intersection of the original clipping rectangle with the specified rectangle.

The applet shown in Figure 3-16 displays an image twice—once using the Graphics passed to paint(), and a second time using a Graphics copy that has had its origin translated and clipping rectangle modified by the call to create().

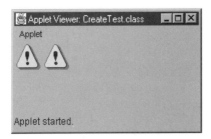

Figure 3-16 Creating a Graphics
The applet draws the same image twice—once with the original Graphics, and once with a copy whose origin has been translated.

The applet is listed in its entirety in Example 3-14.

Example 3-14 CreateTest Applet

```java
import java.applet.Applet;
import java.awt.*;

public class CreateTest extends Applet {
    private Image image;

    public void init() {
        MediaTracker mt = new MediaTracker(this);
        image = getImage(getCodeBase(), "image.gif");

        try {
            mt.addImage(image, 0);
            mt.waitForID(0);
        }
        catch(Exception e) {
            e.printStackTrace();
        }
    }
    public void paint(Graphics g) {
```

```
Graphics copy = g.create(image.getWidth(this),0,100,100);

try {
    System.out.println("g:   " + g.getClip().toString());
    System.out.println("copy: " +
                        copy.getClip().toString());

    g.drawImage(image, 0, 0, this);
    copy.drawImage(image, 0, 0, this);
}
finally {
    copy.dispose();
}
}
}
```

An image is loaded—see "Loading and Displaying Images" on page 103—and the applet's paint method creates a copy of the Graphics it is passed. The copy has its origin translated to (imw,0), where imw represents the width of the image.

The copy also has its clipping rectangle set to the intersection of the original Graphics' clipping rectangle and the rectangle specified by (image.getWidth(this),0,100,100). Since the original Graphics' clipping rectangle covers the area occupied by the applet, the intersection of the two rectangles winds up being (image.getWidth(this),0,100,100).

The tip-off that the copy's Graphics has been translated comes from the fact that both calls to drawImage() draw the image at (0,0).

Summary

Unlike some object-oriented graphical toolkits, the AWT does not provide classes for specific shapes, such as Line and Circle classes. Instead, each AWT component comes with a Graphics object that is used to perform graphical operations in the component. In addition to components, other output devices, such as printers and offscreen images, also have associated Graphics for performing graphical operations.

java.awt.Graphics provides a wealth of methods for drawing and filling shapes, drawing text, and setting graphical parameters such as the color and font used for the next rendering operation. However, in some respects Graphics are quite limited—for instance, the pen used for drawing is restricted in size to a one-pixel square. The Java 2D Api remedies many of the shortcomings of the Graphics class; however, the 2D Api is not strictly a part of the AWT and is beyond the scope of this book (see *Graphic Java Mastering the JFC Volume III: The 2D Api* for an in-depth look at the 2D Api).

The coordinate system for graphical operations is anchored in the upper left-hand corner of the device, with x and y coordinates increasing down and to the right, respectively. Coordinates lie in between pixels instead of on them, and Graphics methods that draw outlines of shapes are passed arguments that define the shape in terms of coordinates instead of pixels. The graphics pen hangs down and to the right of the coordinate path, and therefore outlines of shapes result in an extra row of pixels on the right and bottom sides of the shapes. Shape fills, on the other hand, fill the interior of the shape, and therefore the fill is the same size as the coordinate path. This discrepancy in size between shape outlines and fills is often a stumbling block to newcomers to the AWT.

Each Graphics corresponds to a graphics context from the underlying native windowing system. As a result, Graphics represent a finite resource that must be manually disposed of. If a Graphics is obtained by invoking a method that returns a reference to a Graphics, Graphics.dispose() must be called for the Graphics to free system resources. On the other hand, methods that are passed a Graphics reference are generally absolved from having to dispose of the Graphics. In general, it is up to the caller of such methods to dispose of the Graphics.

The Graphics class also comes with a number of handy features such as: translating the origin of the coordinate system, clipping graphical operations to a specified shape, and the ability to create a copy of an existing Graphics.

CHAPTER
4

Colors and Fonts

This chapter introduces the use of colors and fonts.

Colors are interpreted by color models, so our discussion of colors starts by looking at the two types of color models the AWT offers: index color models and direct color models. After discussing the use of color models, we'll take a look at the `java.awt.Color` class. Colors and color models are most pertinent to image manipulation; therefore, the discussion in this chapter serves as a basis for the "Image Filtering" chapter beginning on page 129.

The font discussion centers around the `Font` and `FontMetrics` classes and the AWT's font model, which is similar to that used in the X Window System.

Although this chapter is geared toward colors and fonts in the 1.2 release of the JDK, we have omitted color and font facilities provided by the 2D Api. The 2D Api is beyond the scope of this book and is covered in *Graphic Java Volume III: The 2D Api*.

Color Models

Color models translate pixel values into their red, green, blue, and alpha constituents, as presented in Table 4-1, which lists the methods from the abstract `java.awt.image.ColorModel` class (minus the 2D Api methods introduced in the 1.2 JDK).

Table 4-1 `java.awt.image.ColorModel` **Methods (2D Api Methods Omitted)**

Method	Implementation or Intent
`static ColorModel getRGBdefault()`	Returns the default RGB color model
`abstract int getAlpha(int)`	Returns the color's alpha component
`abstract int getBlue(int)`	Returns the color's blue component
`abstract int getGreen(int)`	Returns the color's green component
`abstract int getRed(int)`	Returns the color's red component
`int getRGB(int)`	Returns the color of the pixel in RGB format
`int getPixelSize()`	Returns the size of pixels in bits

The `java.awt.image` package supports two types of color models: index color models and direct color models. Index color models interpret colors as an index into an array of colors. Direct color models directly interpret the bits of a color value.

Index Color Model

When an index color model extracts the red, green, blue, or alpha components of a color, it interprets the color as an index into an array of colors, commonly referred to as a colormap. The colors in the colormap are specified when the index color model is instantiated.

Figure 4-1 shows an applet that creates an image using an instance of `IndexColorModel`. The color model is constructed with the red, green, and blue components of each color in the colormap. An array of colors is used to create an image with the aid of an instance of `MemoryImageSource`.

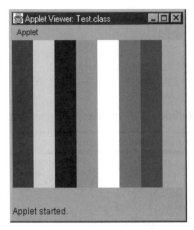

Figure 4-1 An `IndexColorModel` is Used to Paint Stripes

The applet instantiates the array of `Colors` and employs `Color.getRed()`, `Color.getBlue()`, and `Color.getGreen()` to extract the individual color components into separate arrays.

```
Color[] colors = {
        Color.red, Color.yellow, Color.blue, Color.cyan,
        Color.white, Color.green, Color.magenta,
        Color.orange};

byte[] reds = {
        (byte)colors[0].getRed(),(byte)colors[1].getRed(),
        (byte)colors[2].getRed(),(byte)colors[3].getRed(),
        (byte)colors[4].getRed(),(byte)colors[5].getRed(),
        (byte)colors[6].getRed(),(byte)colors[7].getRed() };

byte[] greens = {
        (byte)colors[0].getGreen(),(byte)colors[1].getGreen(),
        (byte)colors[2].getGreen(),(byte)colors[3].getGreen(),
        (byte)colors[4].getGreen(),(byte)colors[5].getGreen(),
        (byte)colors[6].getGreen(),(byte)colors[7].getGreen()
        };
```

```
byte[] blues = {
        (byte)colors[0].getBlue(),(byte)colors[1].getBlue(),
        (byte)colors[2].getBlue(),(byte)colors[3].getBlue(),
        (byte)colors[4].getBlue(),(byte)colors[5].getBlue(),
        (byte)colors[6].getBlue(),(byte)colors[7].getBlue()};
```

The `IndexColorModel` is constructed with the number of bits per pixel, the size of the arrays containing red, green, and blue components for each color in the colormap, and the arrays themselves. Since no alpha components are specified, all the colors in the colormap will be fully opaque.

```
IndexColorModel icm = new IndexColorModel(
                    8, // bits per pixel
                    8, // size of arrays that follow
                    reds,  // red components
                    greens, // green components
                    blues);// blue components
```

`IndexColorModel` provides other constructors that are passed either an array of alpha values for each color or a transparent pixel index into the colormap.

The values in the `imageBits` array represent indices into the colormap specified when the `IndexColorModel` was constructed, namely, the `colors` array. For instance, the value 1 is interpreted as the color yellow, whereas the value 3 is interpreted as cyan.

```
int[] imageBits = new int[] {
            0,0,0,1,1,1,2,2,2,3,3,3,4,4,4,5,5,5,6,6,6,7,7,7,
            0,0,0,1,1,1,2,2,2,3,3,3,4,4,4,5,5,5,6,6,6,7,7,7,
            0,0,0,1,1,1,2,2,2,3,3,3,4,4,4,5,5,5,6,6,6,7,7,7,
            0,0,0,1,1,1,2,2,2,3,3,3,4,4,4,5,5,5,6,6,6,7,7,7,
            0,0,0,1,1,1,2,2,2,3,3,3,4,4,4,5,5,5,6,6,6,7,7,7,
            0,0,0,1,1,1,2,2,2,3,3,3,4,4,4,5,5,5,6,6,6,7,7,7,
            0,0,0,1,1,1,2,2,2,3,3,3,4,4,4,5,5,5,6,6,6,7,7,7,
            0,0,0,1,1,1,2,2,2,3,3,3,4,4,4,5,5,5,6,6,6,7,7,7,
            0,0,0,1,1,1,2,2,2,3,3,3,4,4,4,5,5,5,6,6,6,7,7,7,
            0,0,0,1,1,1,2,2,2,3,3,3,4,4,4,5,5,5,6,6,6,7,7,7};
```

An instance of `MemoryImageSource` is used to create an image from the `imageBits` array. See "Memory Image Source" on page 193 for more on constructing images from arrays of bits.

```
MemoryImageSource mis = new MemoryImageSource(
                    24,10,  // width, height of image
                    icm,// ColorModel
                    imageBits, // bits of image
                    0,      // offset
                    24);// scansize
image = createImage(mis);
```

The applet displays the image in its `paint` method. The entire applet is listed in Example 4-1.

Example 4-1 An Applet That Demonstrates the Use of an
IndexColorModel

```java
import java.applet.Applet;
import java.awt.*;
import java.awt.image.*;
import java.awt.event.*;

public class Test extends Applet {
    Color[] colors = {
            Color.red, Color.yellow, Color.blue, Color.cyan,
            Color.white, Color.green, Color.magenta,
            Color.orange};

    byte[] reds = {
            (byte)colors[0].getRed(),(byte)colors[1].getRed(),
            (byte)colors[2].getRed(),(byte)colors[3].getRed(),
            (byte)colors[4].getRed(),(byte)colors[5].getRed(),
            (byte)colors[6].getRed(),(byte)colors[7].getRed() };

    byte[] greens = {
            (byte)colors[0].getGreen(),(byte)colors[1].getGreen(),
            (byte)colors[2].getGreen(),(byte)colors[3].getGreen(),
            (byte)colors[4].getGreen(),(byte)colors[5].getGreen(),
            (byte)colors[6].getGreen(),(byte)colors[7].getGreen()
            };

    byte[] blues = {
            (byte)colors[0].getBlue(),(byte)colors[1].getBlue(),
            (byte)colors[2].getBlue(),(byte)colors[3].getBlue(),
            (byte)colors[4].getBlue(),(byte)colors[5].getBlue(),
            (byte)colors[6].getBlue(),(byte)colors[7].getBlue()};

    IndexColorModel icm = new IndexColorModel(
                        8, // bits per pixel
                        8, // size of arrays that follow
                        reds,  // red components
                        greens, // green components
                        blues);// blue components
    Image image;

    public void init() {
        int[] imageBits = new int[] {
                0,0,0,1,1,1,2,2,2,3,3,3,4,4,4,5,5,5,6,6,6,7,7,7,
                0,0,0,1,1,1,2,2,2,3,3,3,4,4,4,5,5,5,6,6,6,7,7,7,
                0,0,0,1,1,1,2,2,2,3,3,3,4,4,4,5,5,5,6,6,6,7,7,7,
                0,0,0,1,1,1,2,2,2,3,3,3,4,4,4,5,5,5,6,6,6,7,7,7,
                0,0,0,1,1,1,2,2,2,3,3,3,4,4,4,5,5,5,6,6,6,7,7,7,
                0,0,0,1,1,1,2,2,2,3,3,3,4,4,4,5,5,5,6,6,6,7,7,7,
                0,0,0,1,1,1,2,2,2,3,3,3,4,4,4,5,5,5,6,6,6,7,7,7,
                0,0,0,1,1,1,2,2,2,3,3,3,4,4,4,5,5,5,6,6,6,7,7,7,
                0,0,0,1,1,1,2,2,2,3,3,3,4,4,4,5,5,5,6,6,6,7,7,7,
```

```
                0,0,0,1,1,1,2,2,2,3,3,3,4,4,4,5,5,5,6,6,6,7,7,7};

        MemoryImageSource mis = new MemoryImageSource(
                        24,10,  // width, height of image
                        icm,// ColorModel
                        imageBits, // bits of image
                        0,      // offset
                        24);// scansize
        image = createImage(mis);
    }
    public void paint(Graphics g) {
        g.drawImage(image,0,0,240,200,this);
    }
}
```

If a different constructor is used in the applet listed in Example 4-1, a transparent
pixel can be specified. For example, the following will create an index color model
with a transparent pixel at index 3:

```
IndexColorModel icm = new IndexColorModel(
                8, // bits per pixel
                8, // size of arrays that follow
                reds,  // red components
                greens, // green components
                blues,// blue components
                3);  // transparent pixel index
```

When the image generated from `imageBits` is drawn, the color value stored in
the colormap at index 3 will be interpreted as the transparent pixel, and the applet
will look like the one in Figure 4-2.

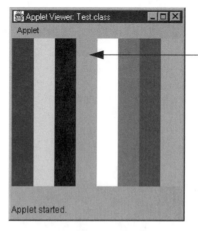

The transparent pixel is specified as the
third index in the colormap.

Figure 4-2 Transparent Pixels in Index Color Models

Direct Color Model

Direct color models directly interpret the bits of color values. The `java.awt.image` package provides a default RGB color model, which is accessible via the `static ColorModel.getRGBdefault()`. The default RGB color model allocates 8 bits per pixel for red, green, blue, and alpha color components, as depicted in Figure 4-3.

bits 24-31   bits 16-23   bits 8-15   bits 0-7

0001111 00000000 00000000 11111111

alpha   red   green   blue

Figure 4-3 Colors in the Default RGB Color Model
Colors interpreted by the default RGB color model have 8 bits each for r, g, b, and alpha values. The color above is a semitransparent blue.

The blue component is stored in bits 0–7, green in bits 8–15, red in 16–23, and alpha in 24–31. Since each component is stored in 8 bits, values can range from 0 to 255. The higher the number, the more intensity the color component has. For instance, an alpha value of 0 is completely transparent, while a value of 255 is fully opaque.

Figure 4-4 shows an applet that specifies colors by using the default RGB color model.

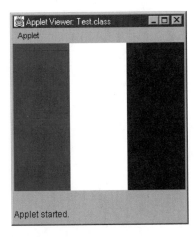

Figure 4-4 Colors Specified with the Default RGB Color Model

Example 4-2 lists the applet shown above.

Example 4-2 Using the Default RGB Color Model

```java
import java.applet.Applet;
import java.awt.*;
import java.awt.image.*;
import java.awt.event.*;

public class Test extends Applet {
    ColorModel defaultRGB = ColorModel.getRGBdefault();
    Image image;

    public void init() {
        int rp = 0xff << 24 | 0xff << 16;
        int bp = 0xff << 24 | 0xff;
        int wp = 0xff << 24 | 0xff << 16 | 0xff << 8 | 0xff;

        int[] imageBits = new int[] {
                rp,rp,rp,wp,wp,wp,bp,bp,bp,
                rp,rp,rp,wp,wp,wp,bp,bp,bp,
                rp,rp,rp,wp,wp,wp,bp,bp,bp,
                rp,rp,rp,wp,wp,wp,bp,bp,bp,
                rp,rp,rp,wp,wp,wp,bp,bp,bp,
                rp,rp,rp,wp,wp,wp,bp,bp,bp,
                rp,rp,rp,wp,wp,wp,bp,bp,bp,
                rp,rp,rp,wp,wp,wp,bp,bp,bp,
                rp,rp,rp,wp,wp,wp,bp,bp,bp,
                rp,rp,rp,wp,wp,wp,bp,bp,bp };

        MemoryImageSource mis = new MemoryImageSource(
                        9,10,  // width, height of image
                        defaultRGB,// ColorModel
                        imageBits, // bits of image
                        0,     // offset
                        9); // scansize
        image = createImage(mis);
    }
    public void paint(Graphics g) {
        g.drawImage(image,0,0,240,200,this);
    }
}
```

The red, blue, and white pixels are specified by turning on the appropriate bits in separate integers.

```java
int rp = 0xff << 24 | 0xff << 16
int bp = 0xff << 24 | 0xff
int wp = 0xff << 24 | 0xff << 16 | 0xff << 8 | 0xff;
```

`Oxff << 24` shifts two bytes 24 places to the left, which causes each color to be fully opaque. `Oxff << 16` shifts two bytes 16 places to the left, tripping all of the red bits, `Oxff << 8` fills in the green bits, and `Oxff` fills in blue bits. The values are used directly in the `imageBits` array in order to draw the strips of red, white, and blue.

If the wp integer is modified so that its alpha value is zero, it will be transparent. Figure 4-5 shows the applet listed in Example 4-2 with the white color's alpha value set to zero.

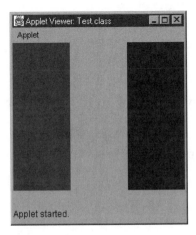

Figure 4-5 A Transparent Color Specified with the Default RGB Color Model.

The transparency is set like this:

```
...
public void init() {
    int rp = 0xff << 24 | 0xff << 16;
    int bp = 0xff << 24 | 0xff;
    int tp = 0x00 << 24 | 0xff << 16 | 0xff << 8 | 0xff;

    int[] imageBits = new int[] {
            rp,rp,rp,tp,tp,tp,bp,bp,bp,
            rp,rp,rp,tp,tp,tp,bp,bp,bp,
            rp,rp,rp,tp,tp,tp,bp,bp,bp,
            rp,rp,rp,tp,tp,tp,bp,bp,bp,
            rp,rp,rp,tp,tp,tp,bp,bp,bp,
            rp,rp,rp,tp,tp,tp,bp,bp,bp,
```

```
    rp,rp,rp,tp,tp,tp,bp,bp,bp,
    rp,rp,rp,tp,tp,tp,bp,bp,bp,
    rp,rp,rp,tp,tp,tp,bp,bp,bp,
    rp,rp,rp,tp,tp,tp,bp,bp,bp };
. . .
```

The transparent pixel—tp—has the value 0x00 shifted into the alpha bits of the integer. Therefore, the alpha value for tp is zero, and the color is completely transparent.

The java.awt.Color Class

The java.awt.Color class offers three services:

1.   static convenience methods

2.   instance methods

3.   color constants

The static convenience methods mostly involve constructing a Color from a String. Instance methods provide access to the color's rgb makeup, return darker or brighter shades of a color, perform an equality test, etc. The color constants are final static Colors that are used to represent commonly used colors and are listed below.

```
Color.black
Color.blue
Color.cyan
Color.darkGray
Color.gray
Color.green
Color.lightGray
Color.magenta
Color.orange
Color.pink
Color.red
Color.white
Color.yellow
```

Most use of the Color class involves accessing the constants listed above. Colors can be constructed, if need be, by one of seven constructors:

```
Color(float r, float g, float b)

Color(float r, float g, float b, float alpha)

Color(int r, int g, int b)

Color(int r, int g, int b, int alpha)

Color(int rgb)

Color(int rgb, boolean hasAlpha)

Color(ColorSpace, float[] components, float alpha)
```

The first four constructors are passed separate values for the red, green, and blue components of the color. The float versions expect values between 0.0 and 1.0, whereas the integer versions expect values between 0 and 255. Both versions allow the alpha value of the color to be specified.

A color may also be constructed with a single integer representing the color in the default RGB format. The last constructor is passed a ColorSpace. The ColorSpace class is part of the 2D Api and is covered in *Graphic Java Volume III: The 2D Api*.

Table 4-2 lists the static convenience methods. Methods are provided to convert from RGB to HSB, and vice versa, obtain colors from the system properties, and decode strings into a color.

Table 4-2 java.awt.image.Color **Static Convenience Methods**

Method	Implementation
int HSBtoRGB(float,float,float)	Returns RGB representation of HSB
float[] RGBtoHSB(int,int,int,float[])	ReturnS HSB representation of RGB
Color decode(String) throws NumberFormatException	Converts string representing decimal, hex or octal number to a color
Color getColor(String)	Returns a color from system properties, or color equal to decoded String value

Table 4-2 `java.awt.image.Color` **Static Convenience Methods (Continued)**

Method	Implementation
`Color getColor(String, int)`	Returns a color from system properties, or color equal to decoded String value
`Color getColor(String, Color)`	Returns a color from system properties, or color equal to decoded String value
`Color getHSBColor(float,float,float)`	Creates a color based on HSB

`decode()` uses `Integer.decode()` to turn the `String` into an `Integer` value. The integer value is then interpreted as a color value in the default RGB color model, the rgb values are extracted, and a new `Color` is instantiated and returned. `Integer.decode()` can decode integer, hex, or octal numbers.

Each `getColor` method uses `Integer.getInteger()` to see if the string passed in represents a name in the system properties. If so, the integer is parsed for rgb values, which are used to construct a `Color`. The additional `int` and `Color` arguments passed to the overloaded `getColor` methods are used as defaults in case the system property with the given name is not found.

Table 4-3 lists the instance methods provided by the `Color` class. Given a specific color, brighter or darker representations of a color may be obtained, as well as the rgb components of the color. The `equals` method returns `true` if the `Object` it is passed a `Color` whose rgb components are equal to the color on whose behalf the method is invoked.

Table 4-3 `java.awt.image.Color` **Instance Methods**

Static Method	Implementation
`Color brighter()`	Returns a brighter color
`Color darker()`	Returns a darker color
`boolean equals(Object)`	Returns `true` if `Object` is a color with same rgb components, `false` otherwise
`int getAlpha()`	Returns the alpha component
`int getBlue()`	Returns the blue component
`int getGreen()`	Returns the green component
`int getRGB()`	Returns the rgb representation, with the alpha value specified as `0xff`
`int getRGBA()`	Returns the rgb representation, including the alpha component

Table 4-3 `java.awt.image.Color` Instance Methods (Continued)

Static Method	Implementation
`int getRed()`	Returns the red component
`int getTransparency()`	Returns the transparency mode of the color
`float[] getColorComponents(` `float[])`	Returns an array of color components in the color's color space
`float[] getColorComponents(` `ColorSpace, float[])`	Returns an array of color components in the specified color space
`float[] getRGBComponents(` `float[])`	Returns an array of color components in the default RGB color model
`float[] getRGBColorComponents(` `ColorSpace, float[])`	Returns an array of color components in the default RGB color model, excluding alpha components
`int hashCode()`	Computes hash code
`String toString()`	String represents rgb components

Colors and color models are most interesting in relation to image manipulation. The previous sections on colors and color models will serve as a foundation for the "Image Filtering" chapter beginning on page 129.

System Colors

System colors represent colors used for native GUI controls. The colors are available as `public static` members of the `java.awt.SystemColors` class and are listed in Table 4-4.

Table 4-4 AWT SystemColor Instances and Default Values

Instance Name	Represents	Default Value
`activeCaption`	Active caption background	Color(0,0,128)
`activeCaptionBorder`	Active caption border	lightGray
`activeCaptionText`	Active caption text	white
`control`	Control background	lightGray
`controlDkShadow`	Control dark shadow	black
`controlHighlight`	Control highlight	white
`controlLtHighlight`	Control light highlight	Color(224,224,224)
`controlShadow`	Control shadow	gray
`controlText`	Control text	black
`desktop`	Desktop background	Color(0,92,92)

Table 4-4 AWT SystemColor Instances and Default Values (Continued)

Instance Name	Represents	Default Value
inactiveCaption	Inactive caption background	gray
inactiveCaptionBorder	Inactive caption border	lightGray
inactiveCaptionText	Inactive caption text	lightGray
info	Info background	Color(224,224,0)
infoText	Info text	black
menu	Menu background	lightGray
menuText	Menu text	black
scrollbar	Scrollbar background	Color(224,224,224)
text	Text background	lightGray
textHighlight	Text highlight	Color(0,0,128)
textHighlightText	Text highlight text	white
textInactiveText	Inactive text	gray
textText	Text	black
window	Window background	white
windowBorder	Window border	black
windowText	Window text	black

System colors fall into two general categories: those with which you must concern yourself and those that are automatically handled by the AWT. For instance, the AWT will ensure that windows it creates have a border color of SystemColor.windowBorder. Developers, on the other hand, should ensure that any custom components they create have a background color of SystemColor.control. Note that the default values in Table 4-4 are used in case there is no appropriate value for a particular platform.

All that's required to use a system color is to access the appropriate static instance of SystemColor. For instance, in a custom component's paint method, you could paint the background of the component and draw some text in the following manner:

```
public void paint(Graphics g) {
    Dimension size = getSize();

    g.setColor(SystemColor.control);
    g.clearRect(0,0,size.width-1,size.height-1);
    g.setColor(SystemColor.controlText);
    g.drawString("CustomComponent", x, y);
}
```

AWT TIP ...

Custom Components Should Use System Colors Whenever Applicable

While standard AWT components use system colors automatically, developers are responsible for ensuring that any custom components they create use system colors where appropriate. Custom components developed under previous versions of the AWT that hardcoded colors should be refactored to use system colors instead.

Fonts and FontMetrics

The AWT includes two classes that support font manipulation: `Font` and `FontMetrics`.

The `Font` class provides a basic set of fonts and font styles. Because Java is platform independent, fonts such as Helvetica, Times Roman, and so on are always mapped to an available font on the native platform.

The `FontMetrics` class allows access to the metrics associated with a particular font, including the font's height, leading, ascent and descent, the width of a specified string, etc.

Fonts

With the advent of the Java 2D Api, the `Font` class has been extended a great deal. In addition, the 2D Api provides a `java.awt.font` package containing advanced support for fonts, glyphs, and ligatures. Our discussion here will focus on the aspects of the `Font` class that are unrelated to the Java 2D Api. For an in-depth discussion of font support provided by the 2D Api, see *Graphic Java Volume III: The 2D Api*.

A font is a collection of glyphs, which are shapes that represent a particular character. A font is instantiated by specification of its logical font name, style, and point size.

The logical font name is mapped to a native font for the underlying windowing system. The logical font names supported in the 1.2 JDK are listed below:

```
Dialog

SansSerif

Serif

Monospaced

Helvetica
```

```
TimesRoman
Courier
DialogInput
ZapfDingbats
```

The font styles specified when constructing a font are defined by the following constants:

```
Font.BOLD
Font.ITALIC
Font.PLAIN
```

Each constant represents a bit in a style `integer` that the `Font` class maintains. As a result, the `BOLD` and `ITALIC` constants can be combined. `Font.PLAIN` has a zero value, so combining it with `BOLD` or `ITALIC` will result in `BOLD` or `ITALIC`, respectively.

Font point sizes are specified with an integer value. One point corresponds to roughly 1/72 of an inch. The AWT tries to accommodate all point sizes, but it is not guaranteed that the point size requested can be mapped onto the system font. To determine the exact size of a font, a `FontMetrics` object must be used.

The applet shown in Figure 4-6 allows the selection of a logical font name, in addition to a style and point size. An example of the selected font is shown in the panel below the lists. The same applet (under a different name) is discussed in Example 13-5 on page 509 in order to illustrate usage of the `java.awt.List` class, so we won't bother to list it again here; instead, we'll highlight the code for font creation.

The lists are populated by invoking `Toolkit.getFontList()` to obtain a list of the supported logical font names. The styles list is populated with the different font styles available. The point sizes list is populated with some random point sizes.

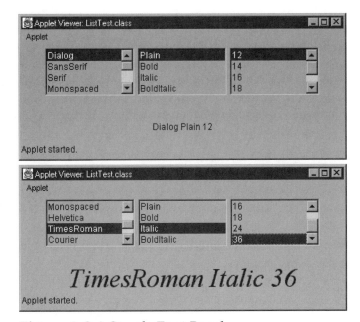

Figure 4-6 A Simple Font Panel

```
private void populateFonts() {
    String fontNames[] = getToolkit().getFontList();

    for(int i=0; i < fontNames.length; ++i)
        familyList.add(fontNames[i]);
}
private void populateStyles() {
    styleList.add("Plain");
    styleList.add("Bold");
    styleList.add("Italic");
        styleList.add("BoldItalic");
    }
    private void populateSizes() {
        String sizes[] = {"12", "14", "16", "18", "24", "36"};

        for(int i=0; i < sizes.length; ++i)
            sizeList.add(sizes[i]);
    }
```

All of the lists in the applet share a single `ItemListener` that updates the label text.

```
public class Listener implements ItemListener {
    public void itemStateChanged(ItemEvent event) {
        listTest.updateLabel(getSelectedFont());
    }
}
```

The selected font is instantiated by the `getSelectedFont` method.

```
public Font getSelectedFont() {
    return new Font(familyList.getSelectedItem(),
                styleList.getSelectedIndex(),
                Integer.parseInt(
                    sizeList.getSelectedItem())));
}
```

The label is updated by setting its text and font.

```
public void updateLabel(Font font) {
    label.setText(fullNameOfFont(font));
    label.setFont(font);
}
```

The full name of the font is obtained by invoking `Font.getFamily()` which returns the platform-dependent family name of the font. The style is obtained by invoking `Font.getStyle()`.

```
private String fullNameOfFont(Font font) {
    String family = font.getFamily();
    String style  = new String();

    switch(font.getStyle()) {
        case Font.PLAIN:  style = " Plain ";  break;
        case Font.BOLD:   style = " Bold ";   break;
        case Font.ITALIC: style = " Italic "; break;

        case Font.BOLD + Font.ITALIC:
            style = " Bold Italic ";
            break;
    }
    return family + style + Integer.toString(font.getSize());
}
```

FontMetrics

The `FontMetrics` class provides metrics about an associated font. Before discussing the `FontMetrics` class in detail, we must first introduce the AWT font model.

The AWT font model is similar to the one used in the X Window System™. Figure 4-7 shows how font height, ascent, descent, and leading are calculated in the AWT.

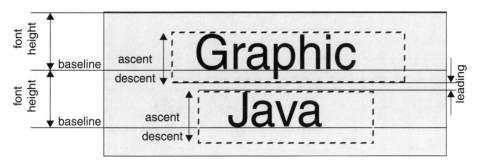

Figure 4-7 The AWT Font Model

The font ascent is measured from the baseline to the top of the characters, and the descent is measured from the baseline to the bottom of the characters. The leading is the distance from the descent of one line to the ascent of the next line of text. The font height is the sum of the ascent, descent, and leading.

The `FontMetrics` class has no public constructors. In order to obtain a reference to a `FontMetrics`, invoke one of the following methods:

```
FontMetrics Component.getFontMetrics(Font)

FontMetrics Graphics.getFontMetrics()

FontMetrics Graphics.getFontMetrics(Font)

FontMetrics Toolkit.getFontMetrics(Font)

FontMetrics AbstractAccessible.getFontMetrics(Font)

FontMetrics AbstractAccessible.getFontMetrics(Font)

FontMetrics ComponentPeer.getFontMetrics(Font)
```

The most commonly used method for obtaining the font metrics associated with an AWT component is the second one listed above. This method involves first obtaining a reference to the component's `Graphics`, and then invoking `Graphics.getFontMetrics()`, like so:

```
public void paint(Graphics g) {// code fragment
    FontMetrics fm = g.getFontMetrics();
    ...
}
```

Note that a number of JDK methods return the font metrics associated with a specified font.

The `FontMetrics` class provides the `public` methods listed in Table 4-5.

Table 4-5 `java.awt.FontMetrics` **Public Methods**

Method	Implementation
`int bytesWidth(byte[],int,int)`	Returns the pixel width of the array of bytes
`int charWidth(char)`	Returns the width of the character specified
`int charWidth(int)`	Returns the width of the character specified
`int charsWidth(char[],int,int)`	Returns the pixel width of the array of chars
`int getAscent()`	Returns the font ascent in pixels
`int getDescent()`	Returns the font descent in pixels
`int getFont()`	Returns the associated font
`int getHeight()`	Returns the font height in pixels
`int getLeading()`	Returns the font leading in pixels
`int getMaxAdvance()`	Returns the maximum advance in pixels
`int getMaxAscent()`	Returns the maximum ascent in pixels
`int getMaxDescent()`	Returns the maximum descent in pixels
`int[] getWidths()`	Returns the pixel widths of the first 256 characters in the associated font
`int stringWidth(String)`	Returns the pixel width of the specified string
`String toString()`	Returns a string representation of the font metrics

`FontMetrics` methods return information about the ascent, descent, leading, and height of the font with which the font metrics is associated. Additionally, methods are provided for obtaining the pixel width of an array of characters or bytes.

Although the descent represents the distance from the baseline to the bottom of the descender, it is not necessarily the *maximum* descent; some characters in the font may extend below the descent. As a result, in addition to reporting a font's descent, the `FontMetrics` class also provides a method for returning the maximum descent for its associated font. The same is true for the ascent; the `FontMetrics` class includes a method that returns the maximum ascent of its font.

The advance width is the pixel distance between the left edge of a given character to the left edge of the next character. Although the advance width is typically the same as the width of the character, such is not always the case; oblique and italic fonts often have characters whose top-right corner extends slightly beyond the advance width. The `FontMetrics` class provides a method for obtaining the maximum advance width for a font.

Figure 4-8 shows an applet that uses an instance of `FontMetrics` to illustrate the ascent, descent, and leading of a font. The applet is similar to the one shown in Figure 4-6 on page 91, except that it displays the font metrics for the selected font in addition to highlighting the ascent, descent, and leading of the font.

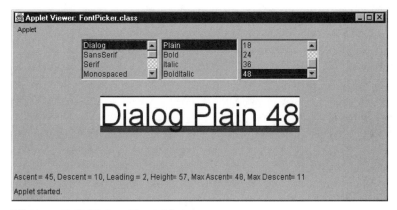

Figure 4-8 Using Font Metrics

Font metrics information is displayed with a label that is displayed at the bottom of the applet. Whenever the font is changed by a selection in one of the lists, the applet's `updateMetricsInfo` method is invoked.

```
public void updateMetricsInfo(Font font) {
    FontMetrics fm = getFontMetrics(font);
    metricLabel.setText(
        "Ascent = " + fm.getAscent() + ", " +
        "Descent = " + fm.getDescent() + ", " +
        "Leading = " + fm.getLeading() + ", " +
        "Height= " + fm.getHeight() + ", " +
        "Max Ascent= " + fm.getMaxAscent() + ", " +
        "Max Descent= " + fm.getMaxDescent());
}
```

The ascent, descent, and leading are all highlighted with filled rectangles in white, red, and black, respectively. In addition, a black line is drawn along the baseline of the font. All of this is implemented in `MetricPanel.paint()`.

```java
public void paint(Graphics g) {
    Dimension size = getSize();
    FontMetrics fm = g.getFontMetrics();
    Point  bl     = new Point();  // bl = baseline
    int    sw     = fm.stringWidth(text),
           ascent = fm.getAscent(),
           descent = fm.getDescent(),
           leading= fm.getLeading();

    bl.x = size.width/2 - sw/2;
    bl.y = size.height/2;

    // draw leading rectangle
    g.setColor(Color.black);
    g.fillRect(bl.x, bl.y - ascent - leading, sw, leading);

    // draw ascent rectangle
    g.setColor(Color.white);
    g.fillRect(bl.x, bl.y - ascent, sw, ascent);

    // draw descent rectangle
    g.setColor(Color.red);
    g.fillRect(bl.x, bl.y, sw, descent);

    g.setColor(getForeground());
    g.drawLine(bl.x, bl.y, bl.x + sw, bl.y);
    g.drawString(text, bl.x, bl.y);
}
```

The size of the component, the width of the string displayed, and the ascent, descent, and leading are all used to place the string and calculate the bounds of the rectangles. The baseline of the font is placed in the center of the component, and the highlighting rectangles are all calculated from the baseline.

The y coordinate of the upper left-hand corner of the leading rectangle is obtained by subtracting the ascent and leading from the baseline—recall from "The Graphics Coordinate System" on page 32 that y coordinates increase from top to bottom.

The highlighting rectangle for the ascent and descent are calculated in a similar fashion; both are based on the baseline of the font. The widths of each rectangle is equal to the width of the string displayed, and the heights are set to the ascent, descent, or leading values obtained from the `FontMetrics` methods.

The applet is listed in its entirety in Example 4-3.

Example 4-3 Using Font Metrics

```
import java.applet.Applet;
import java.awt.*;
import java.awt.event.*;

public class FontPicker extends Applet {
    private FontPanel fontPanel = new FontPanel(this);
    private MetricPanel metricPanel = new MetricPanel();
    private LabelmetricLabel = new Label();

    public void init() {
        setLayout(new BorderLayout());
        add(fontPanel, "North");
        add(metricPanel, "Center");
        add(metricLabel, "South");
    }
    public void start() {
        Font font = fontPanel.getSelectedFont();
        updateMetricPanel(font);
        updateMetricsInfo(font);
    }
    public void update(Font font) {
        updateMetricPanel(font);
        updateMetricsInfo(font);
    }
    public void updateMetricPanel(Font font) {
        metricPanel.setText(fullNameOfFont(font));
        metricPanel.setFont(font);
        metricPanel.repaint();
    }
    public void updateMetricsInfo(Font font) {
        FontMetrics fm = getFontMetrics(font);
        metricLabel.setText(
            "Ascent = " + fm.getAscent() + ", " +
            "Descent = " + fm.getDescent() + ", " +
            "Leading = " + fm.getLeading() + ", " +
            "Height= " + fm.getHeight() + ", " +
            "Max Ascent= " + fm.getMaxAscent() + ", " +
            "Max Descent= " + fm.getMaxDescent());
    }
    private String fullNameOfFont(Font font) {
        String family = font.getFamily();
        String style  = new String();

        switch(font.getStyle()) {
            case Font.PLAIN:  style = " Plain ";  break;
            case Font.BOLD:   style = " Bold ";   break;
            case Font.ITALIC: style = " Italic "; break;

            case Font.BOLD + Font.ITALIC:
                style = " Bold Italic ";
```

```
                    break;
            }
            return family + style + Integer.toString(font.getSize());
        }
}
class MetricPanel extends Panel {
    private String text;

    public void setText(String text) {
        this.text = text;
    }
    public void paint(Graphics g) {
        Dimension size = getSize();
        FontMetrics fm = g.getFontMetrics();
        Point  bl    = new Point();  // bl = baseline
        int    sw    = fm.stringWidth(text),
                ascent = fm.getAscent(),
                descent = fm.getDescent(),
                leading= fm.getLeading();

        bl.x = size.width/2 - sw/2;
        bl.y = size.height/2;

        // draw leading rectangle
        g.setColor(Color.black);
        g.fillRect(bl.x, bl.y - ascent - leading, sw, leading);

        // draw ascent rectangle
        g.setColor(Color.white);
        g.fillRect(bl.x, bl.y - ascent, sw, ascent);

        // draw descent rectangle
        g.setColor(Color.red);
        g.fillRect(bl.x, bl.y, sw, descent);

        g.setColor(getForeground());
        g.drawLine(bl.x, bl.y, bl.x + sw, bl.y);
        g.drawString(text, bl.x, bl.y);
    }
}
class FontPanel extends Panel {
    private FontPicker listTest;
    private List familyList = new List(),
                 styleList  = new List(),
                 sizeList   = new List();

    public FontPanel(FontPicker applet) {
        Listener listener = new Listener();
```

```
        listTest = applet;

        populateFonts();
        populateStyles();
        populateSizes();

        add(familyList);
        add(styleList);
        add(sizeList);

        familyList.addItemListener(listener);
        styleList.addItemListener (listener);
        sizeList.addItemListener  (listener);

        familyList.select(0);
        styleList.select(0);
        sizeList.select(0);
    }
    public class Listener implements ItemListener {
        public void itemStateChanged(ItemEvent event) {
            listTest.update(getSelectedFont());
        }
    }
    public Font getSelectedFont() {
        return new Font(familyList.getSelectedItem(),
                        styleList.getSelectedIndex(),
                    Integer.parseInt(
                        sizeList.getSelectedItem()));
    }
    private void populateFonts() {
        String fontNames[] = getToolkit().getFontList();

        for(int i=0; i < fontNames.length; ++i)
            familyList.add(fontNames[i]);
    }
    private void populateStyles() {
        styleList.add("Plain");
        styleList.add("Bold");
        styleList.add("Italic");
        styleList.add("BoldItalic");
    }
    private void populateSizes() {
        String sizes[] = {"12", "14", "16", "18",
                        "24", "36", "48"};

        for(int i=0; i < sizes.length; ++i)
            sizeList.add(sizes[i]);
    }
}
```

Summary

The AWT provides two color models: index color models and direct color models. Index color models interpret pixel values as indices into a colormap, whereas direct color models directly interpret the bits in a pixel value.

Colors are represented by the `java.awt.Color` class, which provides a set of constants for commonly used colors, in addition to convenience methods for obtaining darker and lighter shades of a color, comparing two colors for equality, etc.

Fonts are represented by the `java.awt.Font` class, which allows the construction of fonts by specifying a logical font name, style, and point size. Logical font names are always mapped onto native fonts so, for instance, a *SanSerif* logical name will map to different fonts on different platforms. The AWT also provides a `FontMetrics` class, which returns information about its associated font, such as the ascent, descent, and leading in pixel values.

The discussion of colors and color models in this chapter is most pertinent to image manipulation and serves as the basis for the "Image Filtering" chapter beginning on page 129.

CHAPTER

5

Loading and Displaying Images

The AWT provides support for loading and displaying GIF and JPEG images in addition to support for animating multframe images such as animated GIFs. Images are loaded and displayed in an asynchronous manner—as a result there are a number of techniques for loading and displaying images, which we will thoroughly explore in this chapter.

To make the most of this chapter, you will want to run the applets and applications discussed. Some paint images a line at time, some paint all at once, some have an annoying flicker, and some are nice and smooth—all characteristics which are not conducive to static screen snapshots.

The Image Class and the Image Package

The AWT provides a `java.awt.Image` class. References to `java.awt.Image` are passed to methods of other AWT objects for displaying and manipulating images. For instance, images can be displayed in a component by invocation of `Graphics.drawImage(java.awt.Image, int, int, ImageObserver)`.

`java.awt.Image` is an abstract class that defines methods which provide access to information about an image. The infrastructure for creating and manipulating images resides in the `java.awt.image` *package*, not to be confused with the `java.awt.Image` *class*.

Nearly all of the classes in the `java.awt.image` package are concerned with either producing images or consuming them. Image producers are responsible for producing the bits of an image and image consumers are the recipients of the bits.

The `ImageProducer` and `ImageConsumer` interfaces are implemented twice in the `java.awt.image` package: pixel grabbers and image filters are consumers, whereas filtered and memory image sources are producers.

The `java.awt.Image` class provides a reference to an image, but it is actually the `java.awt.image` package that undertakes all of the grunt work associated with producing images.

Table 5-1 lists the methods that are defined by the `java.awt.Image` class.

Table 5-1 `java.awt.Image` **Methods**

Return Value	Method
`int`	`getWidth(ImageObserver observer)`
`int`	`getHeight(ImageObserver observer)`
`ImageProducer`	`getSource()`
`Graphics`	`getGraphics()`
`Object`	`getProperty(String name, ImageObserver observer)`
`Image`	`getScaledInstance(int width, int height, int hints)`
`void`	`flush()`

An image can return its width and height, although as we will see shortly, the values returned are valid only after the image is completely loaded; the `ImageObserver` argument passed to `getWidth()` and `getHeight()`.

Every image is capable of returning a reference to its image producer via `Image.getSource()`. Obtaining a reference to the image producer associated with an image is required in order to filter an image—see "ImageConsumer Properties" on page 142.

Images, like AWT components, have a `Graphics` associated with them. Typically, `Image.getGraphics()` is invoked for images that are used for offscreen buffering.

Images can have a set of properties associated with them, which are defined by the format of the image. Properties are typically reserved for advanced image manipulation techniques. One property—"comment"—is reserved for describing the image, its source, or its author.

A scaled instance of an image can be obtained by invocation of
`Image.getScaledInstance()`. Additionally, the `Graphics` class provides a
set of overloaded `drawImage` methods that can draw a scaled representation of
an image—see "`Graphics.drawImage` Methods" on page 186.

Finally, `Image.flush()` flushes all of the resources being used by the image,
including cached pixel data and system resources. Flushing an image is essential
when an image needs to be completely reconstructed.

Image Producers and Image Observers

Image producers produce the bits associated with an image for delivery to an
image consumer.[1] Image production is an asynchronous activity, so the AWT also
provides image observers for monitoring the production of images by an image
producer. The `java.awt.image` package defines interfaces for image producers,
consumers, and observers.

Asynchronous Image Production

Much of the image manipulation that takes place in the AWT happens
asynchronously. For example, when the call to `drawImage()` returns in the code
fragment below, the image may not be showing at all. If none of the image was
loaded at the time of the call, `drawImage()` would have nothing to draw and
would simply start production of the bits associated with the image and return.

```
// Component extension's overridden paint() - code fragment

public void paint(Graphics g) {
    g.drawImage(image, 0, 0, this);
}
```

It may appear as though `drawImage()` is negligent in performing its duties, but
that's not the case—it just doesn't want to hold you up while the image is loading.
This begs the question, of course, as to how the image ever gets drawn, and the
answer to that question lies in the fourth argument passed to
`Graphics.drawImage()`.

Image observers can monitor the progress of an image producer as it is loading an
image. AWT components are image observers, and when they detect that an
image is fully loaded, they repaint themselves. Therefore, the call to
`drawImage()` above registers `this` component as being an observer. When the
image is fully loaded, the component is redrawn, `paint()` is called, and
`drawImage()` is invoked again to draw all the bits of the image.

---

1. See "Image Filtering" on page 129 for more details about image consumers.

Understanding that image-related tasks happen asynchronously and understanding the relationship between `ImageProducer` and `ImageObserver` are paramount to understanding image manipulation in the AWT.

ImageProducer

The bits associated with an image are not stored in a `java.awt.Image`. Instead, each image maintains an association with an `ImageProducer`, which is responsible for producing the bits of an image and for passing them along to an `ImageConsumer`. The `ImageProducer` interface is discussed in more detail in "The ImageProducer Interface" on page 129. For now, it will suffice to know that an image producer produces the bits of an image.

ImageObserver

The `ImageObserver` interface defines a collection of constants and one method, `ImageObserver.imageUpdate()`, which is defined as:

```
public boolean imageUpdate(Image img, int flags,
                           int x, int y, int width, int height);
```

The `flags` argument informs the image observer as to the status of image production. Table 5-2 lists the `ImageObserver` constants. The constants represent bits in the flags variable passed to `ImageObserver.imageUpdate()`.

Table 5-2 `ImageObserver` Constants

Constant	Indicates
ABORT	Image loading was aborted
ALLBITS	All bits have been loaded into the image
ERROR	An error occurred during loading
FRAMEBITS	Another complete frame of a multiframe image is available. Used for animated GIFs
HEIGHT	The height of the image is available
PROPERTIES	The image's properties are available
SOMEBITS	More bits are available for a scaled variation of the image
WIDTH	The width of the image is available

Implementors of `ImageObserver` are ubiquitous in the AWT because `java.awt.Component` implements `ImageObserver`. Every component, therefore, is an `ImageObserver` that can choose to be updated on the progress of a given `ImageProducer` when undertaking an asynchronous operation.

AWT TIP ...

All Components Are Image Observers

A number of asynchronous methods related to image manipulation in the AWT require an ImageObserver argument. For instance, obtaining the width of an image is accomplished by invoking Image.getWidth(ImageObserver). As a result, newcomers to the AWT often wonder where to get a reference to an ImageObserver to pass to asynchronous methods such as getWidth(). The answer is that every component in the AWT is an ImageObserver because java.awt.Component implements the ImageObserver interface. Therefore, any component can be passed to a method that takes an ImageObserver argument.

Loading and Displaying Images

Let's begin by taking a look at a very simple applet, shown in Figure 5-1 and listed in Example 5-1, that obtains a JPEG image and displays it.

Figure 5-1 A Simple Applet That Displays an Image

The applet prints the `codebase`—the URL defining the location of the applet—and the image's width and height, solely for the sake of illustration.

Example 5-1 A Simple Applet That Displays an Image

```
import java.net.URL;
import java.applet.Applet;
import java.awt.Graphics;
import java.awt.Image;

public class ImageTestAppletSimple extends Applet {
    private Image im;

    public void init() {
        URL codebase = getCodeBase();
        System.out.println(codebase);

        im = getImage(codebase, "saint.jpg");

        System.out.print  ("Image width=" + im.getWidth(this));
        System.out.println(" height=" + im.getHeight(this));
    }
    public void paint(Graphics g) {
        g.drawImage(im,0,0,this);
    }
}
```

`Applet.getImage()` returns a reference to an `Image`. To illustrate the asynchronous behavior of loading an image, the width and height of the image are printed immediately after `getImage()` returns. If you run the applet, you'll see the following output:

```
Image width=-1 height=-1
```

At first glance, it may seem that this is an extremely small image. In reality, the rather odd-looking values for width and height indicate that although `getImage()` has returned a reference to an `Image`, the bits that define the image are not yet loaded. In fact, the bits of an image associated with a `java.awt.Image` are not produced until they are needed. `Image.getWidth()` and `Image.getHeight()` return -1 until the image is fully loaded.

Asynchronous Image Loading and Drawing

When the applet in Example 5-1 is run, you can see the image being loaded chunks of bits at time, from top to bottom. Here's why:

The third argument to `Graphics.drawImage()` specifies the image observer. In our case, the image observer is `this`, meaning the applet itself. Since `java.applet.Applet` extends `java.awt.Component`, and `Component` implements `ImageObserver`, all applets qualify as bona fide image observers.

The first time `drawImage()` is invoked, none of the image has been loaded. As a result, since there are no bits of the image to draw, `drawImage()` just registers the image observer (in this case, the applet) with the image producer associated with the image. When the call returns, nothing has been drawn.

After the call to `drawImage()` returns, the image observer has its `imageUpdate()` invoked whenever a new portion of the image has been loaded. Since our applet does not override `imageUpdate()`, the inherited `Component.imageUpdate()` is invoked by the image producer whenever fresh bits of the image are loaded.

`Component.imageUpdate()`, when invoked with a batch of freshly loaded image bits, invokes `repaint()`, which results in a call to `paint()`. The applet's `paint()`, of course, invokes `drawImage()`, which draws as much of the image as is available at the moment.

This cycle of method invocations persists until the image is fully loaded: the image producer loads a portion of the image and invokes the image observer's `imageUpdate()`. When the image observer is an AWT component, `Component.imageUpdate()` invokes `repaint()`, which clears the background of the component and invokes `paint()`. In our case, the applet's `paint()` invokes `drawImage()`, which draws whatever bits of the image are available at the moment. The image producer loads the next chunk of the image and invokes the image observer's `imageUpdate()`, and the cycle repeats. When the image is fully loaded, the image producer ceases to invoke the observer's `imageUpdate()`, breaking the cycle.

As noted previously, the width and height of an image are reported as -1 until the image is completely loaded. In addition, `Graphics.drawImage()` returns a `boolean` value indicating whether the image is completely loaded; if the image is completely loaded, the method returns `true`—if not, it returns `false`. We can use the return value from `drawImage()` to verify the sequence of calls discussed above. Example 5-2 is a modified listing of Example 5-1 and prints the return value of the call to `drawImage()` every time it is invoked.

Example 5-2 Verifying Asynchronous Loading and Drawing

```java
import java.applet.Applet;
import java.awt.Graphics;
import java.awt.Image;

public class ImageTestAppletSimple2 extends Applet {
    private Image im;

    public void init() {
        im = getImage(getCodeBase(), "saint.gif");
    }
    public void paint(Graphics g) {
        System.out.println("drawing image ...");
        System.out.println(g.drawImage(im,0,0,this));
    }
}
```

When the applet is first invoked, output is as follows:

```
drawing image ...
false
drawing image ...
false
drawing image ...
false
drawing image ...
true
```

As you can see, `paint()` is invoked a total of four times[2] as a result of calls to `Component.imageUpdate()`. Each time, the bits of the image that have been loaded are drawn. After `drawImage()` returns `true`, indicating the image is completely loaded, the cycle of `load–>imageUpdate()–>repaint()–>load` is broken.

Differences Between Applets and Applications

Applets provide built-in support for obtaining images, namely, the `Applet.getImage` method. A Java application, however, does not extend `Applet`, so applications that incorporate images are implemented differently than their applet counterparts. Figure 5-2 shows an application that displays an image. The application is listed in Example 5-3.

---

2. On our system—your mileage may vary.

Figure 5-2 An Application That Displays an Image

Example 5-3 ImageTestApplication

```
import java.awt.*;
import java.awt.event.*;

public class ImageTestApplication extends Frame {
    Insets insets;
    Image  im;

    static public void main(String args[]) {
        ImageTestApplication app = new ImageTestApplication();
        app.show();
    }
    public ImageTestApplication() {
        super("Image Test");
        im = Toolkit.getDefaultToolkit().getImage("cougar.jpg");

        addWindowListener(new WindowAdapter() {
            public void windowClosing(WindowEvent event) {
                dispose();
                System.exit(0);
            }
        });
```

```
    }
    public void addNotify() {
        super.addNotify();// peer is created here
        insets = getInsets();
        setBounds(100, 100, 217 + insets.left, 321 + insets.top);
    }
    public void paint(Graphics g) {
        g.drawImage(im, insets.left, insets.top, this);
    }
}
```

The application obtains a reference to an Image in the ImageTestApplication constructor. Instead of calling Applet.getImage(), the application invokes getImage() from the Toolkit class.

First, the static getDefaultToolkit() from the Toolkit class is invoked, which returns the default toolkit for the platform the application is running on. Then, the toolkit's getImage method is invoked, which returns a reference to a java.awt.Image. It should be noted that Toolkit.getImage() is overloaded to take either a URL or a String as an argument.

Another difference between applets and applications is that the insets of the frame in which an application is displayed must be taken into account. If the image had been drawn at (0,0), as was the case for the applet in Example 5-1 on page 108, the top of the image would have been drawn underneath the frame's titlebar. The upper left-hand corner of an applet resides below the menubar of the applet, whereas the upper left-hand corner of an application resides at the top of its frame.

Notice that addNotify() is overridden to obtain a reference to the frame's insets in order to set the bounds of the frame. getInsets() returns an inset of (0,0,0,0) until the frame's peer is created—see "java.awt.Component Methods That Depend Upon Peers" on page 440. Peers are created by addNotify(), and therefore the call to getInsets() is made after the frame's peer has been created. See "Components and Peers" on page 439 for more information about peers and overriding addNotify().

Finally, notice that the size of the image has been hardcoded into the application, which is definitely not recommended practice:

```
    setBounds(100, 100, 217 + insets.left, 321 + insets.top);
```

As discussed previously, Image.getWidth() and Image.getHeight() return -1 until the image is fully loaded. A better approach would entail waiting for the image to load, and subsequently invoking the image's getWidth() and getHeight() to obtain the width and height of the image programmatically.

AWT TIP

Loading Images in Applications Vs. Applets

Applets provide two overloaded methods for loading an image:

```
Applet.getImage(URL url)
Applet.getImage(URL url, String string)
```

Since applications are not extension of the applet class—applications most often extend java.awt.Frame—they must use an alternative method of loading images. The following java.awt.Toolkit methods are commonly used by applications to load images:

```
Toolkit.getImage(URL url)
Toolkit.getImage(String string)
```

In addition, both applets and applications can load images as resources, which is typically the preferred method of image loading—see "Loading Images as Resources" on page 125.

Waiting for an Image to Load

Both the applet and application presented so far load and display their images in chunks, from the top of the image to the bottom, due to the asynchronous nature of image loading. A more aesthetically pleasing approach is to wait for the image to load completely before displaying it. There are a number of ways to accomplish this approach; one way is to implement imageUpdate(), which keeps us informed as to the progress of the loading of the image in question.

The applet in Example 5-4 is almost exactly like the one in Example 5-1 on page 108, except that it implements ImageObserver.imageUpdate().

Example 5-4 An Applet that Waits for An Image to Fully Load

```
import java.applet.Applet;
import java.awt.Graphics;
import java.awt.Image;

public class ImageTestAppletWithUpdate extends Applet {
    private Image im;

    public void init() {
        im = getImage(getCodeBase(), "saint.gif");

        System.out.print  ("Image width=" + im.getWidth(this));
        System.out.println(" height=" + im.getHeight(this));
    }
```

```
public void paint(Graphics g) {
  g.drawImage(im,0,0,this);
}
public boolean imageUpdate(Image image, int flags,
                   int x, int y, int w, int h)
{
    System.out.println("imageUpdate():  x=" + x + ", y=" +
                   y + "  w=" + w + ",h=" + h);

    if((flags & ALLBITS) == 0)
       return true;// need more updates
    else {
       repaint();
       return true;// image is fully loaded
    }
  }
}
```

The implementation of imageUpdate() prints the location, width, and height of each row of bits as they are passed in. If you run the applet, you'll see printed output something like this:

```
Image width=-1 height=-1
imageUpdate():   x=0, y=0  w=217,h=321
imageUpdate():   x=0, y=0  w=217,h=1
imageUpdate():   x=0, y=1  w=217,h=1
imageUpdate():   x=0, y=2  w=217,h=1
imageUpdate():   x=0, y=3  w=217,h=1
imageUpdate():   x=0, y=4  w=217,h=1
...
```

Note that the applet's implementation of imageUpdate() uses the ImageObserver constant ALLBITS to determine when all the bits of the image have been completely loaded. Once the flags ANDed with ALLBITS are non-zero, we know that all the bits for the image have been fully loaded.

Until the image is fully loaded, imageUpdate() returns true, signifying that further updates are required. Once the image is fully loaded, imageUpdate() returns false, indicating that no further updates are required, and repaint() is invoked to draw the image in one fell swoop.

The ImageObserver interface defines several constants besides ALLBITS, as shown in Table 5-2 on page 106.

Although the applet above displays its image all at once, it takes some time for the image to load (especially with statistics being printed from imageUpdate()). Naturally, the larger the image is, the longer it will take to load.

If you have a web page, for instance, with a number of large images, the delay incurred by waiting for each image to load may be burdensome. In such a case, you may wish to paint each scanline of the image as it becomes available. Painting a scanline at a time does not reduce the time required to load the image, but it does provide feedback that the image is being loaded. The next applet does exactly that.

Painting Images a Scanline at a Time

Example 5-5 lists an applet that is a variation of the previous applet. Instead of calling `repaint()` after all the bits have been loaded into the image, the applet calls `repaint()` every time `imageUpdate()` is called.

Example 5-5 Image Loading With Dynamic Updates

```
import java.applet.Applet;
import java.awt.Graphics;
import java.awt.Image;

public class ImageTestAppletWithDynamicUpdate extends Applet {
    private Image im;

    public void init() {
        im = getImage(getCodeBase(), "saint.gif");

        System.out.print  ("Image width=" + im.getWidth(this));
        System.out.println(" height=" + im.getHeight(this));
    }
    public void paint(Graphics g) {
      g.drawImage(im,0,0,this);
    }
    public boolean imageUpdate(Image image, int flags,
                        int x, int y, int w, int h)
    {
        System.out.println("imageUpdate():  x=" + x + ", y=" +
                        y + "  w=" + w + ",h=" + h);
        repaint();

        if((flags & ALLBITS) == 0)
            return true;// need more updates
        else
            return false;// image is fully loaded
    }
}
```

The applet, as advertised, paints each scanline as it becomes available. However, a horrible penalty has been incurred for keeping users informed as to the progress of our image loading: the image flickers as it is being drawn. Our next applet employs a simple mechanism to smoothly display each scanline without flickering.

Eliminating the Flicker

The culprit of the flicker is the applet's `update` method. Recall from the *Applets and Applications* chapter that a call to a component's `repaint` method results in the component's `update` method being called as soon as possible. Therefore, when `repaint()` is invoked in Example 5-5, a call to `update()` is scheduled. The default implementation of `Component.update()` erases the entire background of the component and invokes the component's `paint` method. Therefore, every time a scanline is available, `repaint()` is invoked, resulting in a call to `update()`, which erases the background and then invokes `paint()`. All of this erasing and repainting results in the flicker we seek to eliminate.

The simple solution, illustrated by Example 5-6, is to override `update()` to call `paint()` directly. This technique eliminates the erasure of the applet's background and results in the image being displayed in a smooth fashion.

Example 5-6 `Image Loading Without Flickering`

```
import java.applet.Applet;
import java.awt.Graphics;
import java.awt.Image;

public class ImageTestAppletWithSmoothDynamicUpdate extends
Applet {
    private Image im;

    public void init() {
        im = getImage(getCodeBase(), "saint.gif");

        System.out.print  ("Image width=" + im.getWidth(this));
        System.out.println(" height=" + im.getHeight(this));
    }
    public void paint(Graphics g) {
      g.drawImage(im,0,0,this);
    }
    public boolean imageUpdate(Image image, int flags,
                          int x, int y, int w, int h)
    {
        System.out.println("imageUpdate():  x=" + x + ", y=" +
                            y + "  w=" + w + ",h=" + h);
        repaint();

        if((flags & ALLBITS) == 0)
```

```
            return true;// need more updates
        else
            return false;// image is fully loaded
    }
    public void update(Graphics g) {
        paint(g);
    }
}
```

Overriding update() to invoke paint() directly is a common technique that is typically employed when a component needs to be continuously updated.

Of course, it still takes awhile for the image to paint, mostly because we are still doggedly printing out statistics for each scanline. You may wish to modify the applet so that it does not print out statistics each time a scanline is available; you will notice a considerable increase in speed by doing so.

AWT TIP

update() Clears the Background Before Invoking paint()

Component.update(), which is invoked whenever repaint() is called, first clears the background of the component and then calls paint(). While this is a desirable default behavior, it can cause flickering when a component is continuously updated. To eliminate the flicker, override update() to call paint() directly.

MediaTracker

The java.awt.MediaTracker class provides a more convenient way than we've illustrated thus far to manage the asynchronous loading of an image. Essentially, an instance of MediaTracker can *track* the loading of an image. The applet in Example 5-7 employs an instance of MediaTracker to fully load the image before it is drawn.

Example 5-7 Image Loading With the MediaTracker Class

```
import java.net.URL;
import java.applet.Applet;
import java.awt.Graphics;
import java.awt.Image;
import java.awt.MediaTracker;

public class ImageTestAppletWithMediaTracker extends Applet {
    private Image im;

    public void init() {
        MediaTracker tracker = new MediaTracker(this);
```

```
            im = getImage(getCodeBase(), "saint.gif");

            tracker.addImage(im, 0);
            try { tracker.waitForID(0); }
            catch(InterruptedException e) { e.printStackTrace(); }

            System.out.print  ("Image width=" + im.getWidth(this));
            System.out.println(" height=" + im.getHeight(this));
        }
     public void paint(Graphics g) {
        g.drawImage(im,0,0,this);
     }
   }
```

Using `MediaTracker` is a three-step process:

1. Create an instance of `MediaTracker`.

2. Use `MediaTracker.addImage()` to specify the image to be tracked.

3. Create a `try/catch` block. The `try` block waits for the image associated with ID to fully load. The `MediaTracker waitForID` method may throw an `InterruptedException`, so it's necessary to implement a `catch` block. In our case, we catch the exception and print a stack trace.

If you wish to wait for images to load entirely before displaying them, employing an instance of `MediaTracker` is probably the way to go. Using `MediaTracker` means that you need not override `imageUpdate()` and go through the trouble of ANDing the correct constant with the `flags` variable passed in to determine when the image is fully loaded.

However, using `MediaTracker` requires you to implement the three steps outlined above. The steps involved in using `MediaTracker` are best implemented once and for all in a utility method such as the one listed below:

```
public static void waitForImage(Component component,
                                    Image image) {
   MediaTracker tracker = new MediaTracker(component);
   try {
       tracker.addImage(image, 0);
       tracker.waitForID(0);
   }
   catch(InterruptedException e) { e.printStackTrace(); }
}
```

This code reduces waiting for an image to one simple statement—no overriding methods, fooling around with ANDing bits, or implementing `try/catch` blocks.

Animated GIFS

The AWT contains built-in support for animated GIFs; simply create a
`java.awt.Image` with an animated GIF in the manner described above, and it
will animate on its own. Figure 5-3 shows the frames of an animated GIF
displayed by the application listed in Example 5-8.

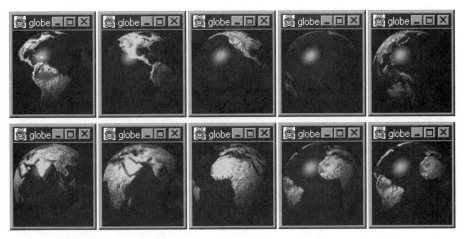

Figure 5-3 An Animated GIF
The globe animated GIF contains 10 frames, which are displayed from left
to right and top to bottom.

Example 5-8 An Application That Displays an Animated GIF

```
import java.awt.*;
import java.awt.event.*;

public class Globe extends Frame {
    Image globe;
    Toolkit tk = Toolkit.getDefaultToolkit();

    public static void main(String args[]) {
        Frame f = new Globe();
        f.show();
    }
```

```
public Globe() {
    super("globe");
    globe = tk.getImage("globe.gif");

    try {
        MediaTracker mt = new MediaTracker(this);
        mt.addImage(globe,0);
        mt.waitForID(0);
    }
    catch(Exception e) { e.printStackTrace(); }

    addWindowListener(new WindowAdapter() {
        public void windowClosing(WindowEvent event) {
            dispose();
            System.exit(0);
        }
    });
}
public void addNotify() {
    super.addNotify(); // this instantiates the peer

    Insets    insets = getInsets();
    Dimension scrnsz = tk.getScreenSize();
    Dimension globesz = new Dimension(globe.getWidth(this),
                                globe.getHeight(this));

    setBounds((scrnsz.width/2) - (globesz.width/2),
              (scrnsz.height/2) - (globesz.height/2),
              globesz.width + insets.left + insets.right,
              globesz.height + insets.top + insets.bottom);
}
public void paint(Graphics g) {
    Insets insets = getInsets();
    g.drawImage(globe,insets.left,insets.top,this);
}
public void update(Graphics g) {
    paint(g);
}
}
```

The application listed above employs the default toolkit to obtain a reference to the image. MediaTracker is subsequently called upon to ensure that the image is fully loaded before it is displayed. The fact that Example 5-8 is an application has no significance; an applet could just as easily display and animate the image.

As an added bonus, the application is centered on the desktop: thus the call to Toolkit.getScreenSize() and the subsequent calculations performed in the call to set the frame's bounds.

Controlling the Rate of Animation

If you run the application listed in Example 5-8, you'll notice that the earth's rotation is significantly faster than the real thing. In fact, the earth is spinning at such a dizzying rate that it can be hard to clearly see the continents as they whiz by. As a result, it might be beneficial to slow the rate at which the image is animated.

To control the rate of animation ourselves, we must take animating the image into our own hands. Not only will this intervention allow the rate of animation to be controlled, but it also affords us the opportunity to shed some light on the manner in which animated GIFs are animated behind the scenes.

Recall from "ImageObserver Constants" on page 106 that one of the constants refers to multiframe images—the FRAMEBITS constants. The FRAMEBITS flag is set whenever the next image in a multiframe image is available for display.

In order to manually animate the image, imageUpdate() is overridden. When the FRAMEBITS bit is set in the flags variable, we know that the next frame in the animation is ready to go, and we simply invoke repaint(). The revised application is listed in Example 5-9.

Example 5-9 Controlling the Rate of Animation for an Animated GIF

```java
import java.awt.*;
import java.awt.event.*;

public class Globe extends Frame {
    Image globe;
    Toolkit tk = Toolkit.getDefaultToolkit();

    public static void main(String args[]) {
        Frame f = new Globe();
        f.show();
    }
    public Globe() {
        super("globe");
        globe = tk.getImage("globe.gif");

        try {
            MediaTracker mt = new MediaTracker(this);
            mt.addImage(globe,0);
            mt.waitForID(0);
        }
        catch(Exception e) { e.printStackTrace(); }

        addWindowListener(new WindowAdapter() {
            public void windowClosing(WindowEvent event) {
                dispose();
```

```
                    System.exit(0);
            }
        });
    }
    public void addNotify() {
        super.addNotify(); // this instantiates the peer

        Insets    insets = getInsets();
        Dimension scrnsz = tk.getScreenSize();
        Dimension globesz = new Dimension(globe.getWidth(this),
                                    globe.getHeight(this));

        setBounds((scrnsz.width/2) - (globesz.width/2),
                (scrnsz.height/2) - (globesz.height/2),
                globesz.width + insets.left + insets.right,
                globesz.height + insets.top + insets.bottom);
    }
    public boolean imageUpdate(Image image, int flags,
                        int x, int y, int w, int h) {
        if((flags & FRAMEBITS) != 0) {
            try {
                Thread.currentThread().sleep(500);
            }
            catch(Exception e) {
                e.printStackTrace();
            }
            repaint();
        }
        return true;
    }
    public void paint(Graphics g) {
        Insets insets = getInsets();
        g.drawImage(globe,insets.left,insets.top,this);
    }
    public void update(Graphics g) {
        paint(g);
    }
}
```

To slow the rate of animation, the current thread is put to sleep for 500 milliseconds whenever the next frame in the image is ready to be displayed. This process incurs a half-second delay between frames, which slows the animation significantly.

Also, note that update() has once again been overridden to invoke paint() directly. Without the overridden update(), the background would be cleared every time a new frame is available, resulting a perceptible flicker.

AWT Components as Image Observers

As alluded to earlier, when an AWT component is specified as an image observer, `java.awt.Component.imageUpdate()` is invoked by the image's image producer—provided, of course, that the method has not been overridden in a subclass. None of the components provided by the AWT override `imageUpdate()`; all exhibit the behavior of `Component.imageUpdate()`, which is listed in Example 5-10.

Example 5-10 `java.awt.Component.imageUpdate()`

```
public boolean imageUpdate(Image img, int flags,
                int x, int y, int w, int h) {
    int rate = -1;

    if ((flags & (FRAMEBITS|ALLBITS)) != 0) {
        rate = 0;
    }
    else if ((flags & SOMEBITS) != 0) {
        if (isInc) {
            try {
                rate = incRate;

                if (rate < 0)
                    rate = 0;
            }
            catch (Exception e) {
                rate = 100;
            }
        }
    }
    if (rate >= 0) {
        repaint(rate, 0, 0, width, height);
    }
    return (flags & (ALLBITS|ABORT)) == 0;
}
```

If the `flags` integer has bits set that correspond to either FRAMEBITS or ALLBITS, then the repaint rate is set to zero and an overloaded version of `repaint()` is invoked. The rate specifies the maximum time in milliseconds before repainting. Therefore, in plain English, if all bits of the image are loaded or the next frame in a multiframe image is available, the component is repainted immediately.

If some, but not all, of the bits are loaded, then a repaint rate is determined (more on that in a moment) and the component is repainted within the allotted number of milliseconds, as long as the `isInc` variable is `true`, which indicates that the image should be painted incrementally.

`Component.imageUpdate()` returns `true` if all the bits of the image haven't been loaded and loading has not been aborted. Recall that a `true` return value indicates that more updates are required, meaning the image producer will continue to invoke `imageUpdate()`. Otherwise, the method returns `false`, indicating that no more updates are required. If the image has multiple frames, the method always returns `true`, resulting in continuous updating for multi-frame images.

The `Component` class keeps track of two variables: a boolean `isInc` and an integer `incRate`.

The `isInc` boolean variable depends upon the value of the system property `awt.image.incrementalDraw`; if the property is `false`, then no repainting is performed until the image is completely loaded. Otherwise, the image is repainted every time more bits of the image are loaded.

The `incRate` variable is set to the system property `awt.image.redrawrate`. If the property is not set, the `incRate` defaults to 100 milliseconds.

AWT TIP ...

Use System Properties to Control Image Redrawing in AWT Components

Two system properties affect redraw characteristics of images contained in AWT components:

```
awt.image.incrementalDraw
awt.image.redrawrate
```

If awt.image.ncrementalDraw is false, images will not be drawn incrementally as their bits are produced; instead, the image will be fully loaded before it is displayed.

awt.image.redrawrate determines the rate, in milliseconds, that a component incrementally draws images as the image bits become available. If unspecified, the redraw rate defaults to 100 milliseconds.

Creating Images

AWT components, in addition to being image observers, are also capable of creating images. `java.awt.Component` comes with two methods for creating images:

- `createImage(ImageProducer)`
- `createImage(int width, int height)`

The first version of `createImage()` creates an image, given an `ImageProducer` from which the bits of the image are obtained; we will find a use for this method in "Loading Images as Resources" on page 125.

The second version creates an image suitable for an offscreen buffer, as we shall discover in "Double Buffering" on page 789.

Additionally, the `java.awt.Toolkit` class is also capable of creating images and provides the following methods:

- `createImage(ImageProducer)`
- `createImage(byte[] bits)`
- `createImage(byte[] bits, int offset, int length)`

Like AWT components, the `Toolkit` class is capable of creating an image given an `ImageProducer`. In addition, the `Toolkit` class provides two methods for creating an image from a `byte` array. As we shall see in "Memory Image Source" on page 193, creating an image from an array of bits is a straightforward process.

Loading Images as Resources

Until now, we've loaded images by hardcoded URLs or file names. The Java Development Kit provides another method of loading resources that is independent of the actual path or URL of the resource.

`java.lang.Class` provides two methods for loading resources:

- `URL getResource(String)`
- `InputStream getResourceAsStream(String)`

Both methods delegate to the applet's class loader in order to load the resource. It should be noted that resources are not limited to images, for instance, audio clips can be accessed as resources.

The benefit to loading an image as a resource stems from the fact that the image does not have to reside in a well-known location. For instance, consider the manner in which an image was loaded in Example 5-1 on page 108:

```
URL codebase = getCodeBase();
Image im = getImage(codebase, "saint.gif");
```

The `codebase` URL returned from `Applet.getCodeBase()` corresponds to the directory from which the applet was launched. The string passed to `Applet.getImage()` specifies a file relative to the codebase. If the image had resided in an `images` directory off the applet's codebase, for example, it would be accessed like so:

```
Image im = getImage(codebase, "images/saint.gif");
```

Loading an image as a resource does not specify a hardcoded location. Instead, the string passed to Class.getResource() specifies a file that is *searched for* by the class loader associated with the class. The exact algorithm used for locating a resource depends upon the class loader used, but typically, the resource will be found if it resides anywhere in the user's CLASSPATH. Additionally, class loaders will typically search jar and zip files found in the CLASSPATH. If a jar or zip file is found that contains the resource, the resource will be extracted from the file.

Example 5-11 lists an applet that loads an image as a resource.

Example 5-11 Loading an Image as a Resource

```java
import java.applet.Applet;
import java.net.URL;
import java.awt.*;
import java.awt.image.ImageProducer;
import java.awt.event.*;

public class Test extends Applet {
    Image im;

    public void start() {
        URL url = getClass().getResource("globe.gif");
        try {
            im = createImage((ImageProducer)url.getContent());
            if(im == null)
                System.out.println("null image");
        }
        catch(Exception e) {
            e.printStackTrace();
        }
    }
    public void paint(Graphics g) {
        Insets insets = getInsets();
        g.drawImage(im, insets.left, insets.top, this);
    }
    public void update(Graphics g) {
        paint(g);
    }
}
```

Once the URL is returned from the call to Class.getResource(), URL.getContent() is invoked to get the contents of the resource associated with the URL. For images, the content is an image producer that is prodded into coughing up its image by invoking createImage().

AWT TIP ...

Load Images as Resources

Instead of loading an image by specifying a hardcoded URL or file name, in general, it is advisable to load images as resources. Resources are searched for in a manner defined by a class loader's algorithm, allowing resources to reside in a number of different locations, including zip and jar files. When loaded as a resource, the URL associated with the image returns an ImageProducer when its getContent method is invoked. Once the ImageProducer is in hand, Component.createImage(ImageProducer) can be invoked to return a reference to the image itself.

Loading images as resources provides a more general mechanism for loading images that does not depend on the image being in a known location. Additionally, custom class loaders can be developed that expand the search algorithm to search for resources over a network, for instance.

Summary

This chapter has discussed techniques for obtaining and displaying images. We've introduced image producers and image observers, and we've explored how they interact with each other when an image producer is loading an image. We've seen how to smoothly paint images a scanline at a time and how to display a multi-frame image without flicker.

Additionally, we've seen how the AWT animates multiframe images such as animated GIF and how to manually animate such images. We've also taken a look at how AWT components handle the loading of an image and how to load images as resources.

In the next chapter, we will delve into image filtering.

CHAPTER

6

Image
Filtering

The AWT provides extensive support for image filtering. A handful of image filters are provided in the `java.awt.image` package, but more importantly, a complete infrastructure is also provided for implementing custom image filters.

This chapter explores image filtering in detail. We will discuss the image filters provided by the `java.awt.image` package and how to use them. We will also discuss implementing custom filters, including those that filter one pixel (or color) at a time, and more sophisticated filters that do more than modify individual pixels.

Some of the examples in this chapter are applets, others are applications. The decision to implement examples as either applets or applications is entirely random; all of the examples will work equally as well as applets or applications. Also, all of the examples in this chapter load images as resources, as we advised in the AWT Tip "Load Images as Resources" on page 127.

The ImageProducer Interface

As discussed previously—see "ImageProducer" on page 106—image producers produce the bits of an image and pass them along to an image consumer. Every `java.awt.Image` has an associated image producer that reconstructs the image and produces the bits that constitute the image whenever necessary.

The methods defined by the `java.awt.image.ImageProducer` interface are listed in Table 6-1.

Table 6-1 `java.awt.image.ImageProducer` **Methods**

Method	Intent
void addConsumer(ImageConsumer)	Registers an image consumer with the producer
boolean isConsumer(ImageConsumer)	Returns `true` if the image consumer has been registered with the producer, `false` otherwise
void removeConsumer(ImageConsumer)	Removes an image consumer from the list of consumers associated with the producer
void requestTopDownLeftRightResend(ImageConsumer)	Requests a resend of the image data in a top-down, left-right (TDLR) order. Image producers are free to ignore the request if the data cannot be delivered in this manner.
void startProduction(ImageConsumer)	Registers the image consumer with the producer and immediately begins production of the image bits for delivery

Image producers maintain a list of image consumers that are passed image data by the producer. The `ImageProducer` interface provides methods for adding and removing image consumers from the list and for determining if an image consumer is currently registered with a producer.

`ImageProducer.startProduction()` registers the image consumer it is passed and causes the image producer to immediately begin reconstructing the image. The reconstructed image bits are passed along to all of the consumers currently registered with the producer.

`ImageProducer.requestTopDownLeftRightResend()` is typically invoked to enable the consumer (which is passed to the method) to receive image bits in a top-down, left-right order (TDLR—the same order in which you are reading this page). Some image consumers can implement more precise algorithms for filtering images if the data is received in a TDLR order. However, sometimes image producers are not able to send the data in a TDLR order and are, therefore, free to ignore the request. If the request can be filled, then the producer will invoke the following `ImageConsumer` methods:

```
setHints()
setPixels() (perhaps repeatedly)
imageComplete()
```

Two classes in the `java.awt.image` package implement the `ImageProducer` interface:

- `FilteredImageSource`
- `MemoryImageSource`

The ImageConsumer Interface

Image consumers receive image data from an image producer. The methods defined by the `ImageConsumer` interface are listed in Table 6-2.

Table 6-2 The `java.awt.image.ImageConsumer` **Interface**

Method	Intent
void imageComplete(int)	Signifies that the producer is finished delivering image data
void setColorModel(ColorModel)	Indicates the color model used for the majority of the calls to `setPixels()`
void setDimensions(int,int)	Specifies the width and height of the image
void setHints(int)	Indicates the order in which pixels will be delivered
void setProperties(Hashtable)	Sets properties associated with the filtered image
void setPixels(int,int,int,int, ColorModel, byte[], int, int)	Delivers pixels in a `byte` array
void setPixels(int,int,int,int, ColorModel, int[], int, int)	Delivers pixels in an `int` array

`imageComplete()` is passed an `integer` constant indicating the state of the image; Table 6-3 lists valid values for the `integer` value.

Table 6-3 Constants Passed to `ImageConsumer.imageComplete()`

Constant	Meaning
STATICIMAGEDONE	All of the image bits have been delivered.
SINGLEFRAMEDONE	A single frame of a multi-frame image has been delivered.
IMAGEERROR	An error occurred during loading or delivery.
IMAGEABORTED	Loading or delivery was deliberately aborted.

`setColorModel()` is passed a `ColorModel` that will be used for the *majority* of the pixels delivered. It is possible that an image producer may use more than one `ColorModel` during image delivery.

`setDimensions()` specifies the width and height of the image that is to be delivered. `setHints()` is passed an `integer` flag whose bits indicate the manner in which pixels will be delivered. The flag's bits are represented by one of the constants listed in Table 6-4.

Table 6-4 Constants Passed to `ImageConsumer.setHints()`

Constant	Meaning
RANDOMPIXELORDER	Pixels will be delivered in random order.
TOPDOWNLEFTRIGHT	Pixels will be delivered in top-down, left-right order.
COMPLETESCANLINES	Pixels will be delivered in complete scan lines.
SINGLEPASS	Each pixel is delivered exactly once.
SINGLEFRAME	The image contains a single static image.

The `integer` flag passed to `setHints()` may have more than one bit set, represented by the constants listed above. For instance, production of a single frame image could result in a flags argument with the following bits set: `TOPDOWNLEFTRIGHT|COMPLETESCANLINES|SINGLEPASS|SINGLEFRAME`.

`setProperties()` can be overridden to set properties related to the filtered image in a `java.util.Hashtable`. For instance, the `ImageFilter` class implements `setProperties()`, which adds a "filters" key to the hashtable with a value equal to the string returned from the filter's `toString()` method. If the filter's properties hashtable already contains a "filters" key, then the string representation of the filter (returned from `toString()`) is tacked onto the end of the value associated with the "filters" key. As a result, if an image is run through multiple filters, (see "Combining Image Filters" on page 140) the "filters" key in the last filter's properties hashtable has a value equal to the string representations of all the filters the image has been run through.

`setPixels()` is invoked to actually deliver the bits of the image and is overloaded to pass either arrays of `bytes` or arrays of `integers`, depending upon the manner in which images are stored natively. We will discuss each argument passed to `setPixels()` when we cover implementing image filters in "Extending ImageFilter" on page 151.

Two classes in the `java.awt.image` package implement the `ImageConsumer` interface:

- `ImageFilter`
- `PixelGrabber`

How Image Producers and Image Consumers Interact

Somehow, one or more image consumers are registered with a single image producer. Typically, this happens behind the scenes—unless you are filtering images or grabbing pixels, you rarely deal with image consumers directly.

At some point in time, the image producer invokes the image consumer's setDimensions(). Optionally, producers may invoke setHints() and setColorModel() to further inform consumers as to the properties of the image it is about to deliver.

Once production of the image starts, producers invoke one of the consumer's overloaded setPixels(). setPixels() may be called once, therefore delivering the entire image in one shot, or it may be called multiple times with regions of the image delivered in each call.

After the image has been delivered, producers invoke the consumer's imageComplete(). The flag passed to imageComplete() indicates whether the image bits were successfully delivered, whether delivery was aborted, or whether an error occurred during loading, as outlined above.

AWT Image Filters

We will discuss implementing image filters in detail in this chapter, but first we must illustrate how to use them. This will afford us the opportunity to explore the image filters provided by the java.awt.image package. It also gives us a chance to examine the interactions between a specific image producer and a specific image consumer—FilteredImageSource and ImageFilter respectively.

The java.awt.image package provides a handful of image filters:

- AreaAveragingScaleFilter
- CropImageFilter
- ReplicateScaleFilter
- RGBImageFilter

The CropImageFilter crops a rectangular region of an image. Both AreaAveragingScaleFilter and ReplicateScaleFilter scale an image by using different scaling algorithms. The RGBImageFilter is an abstract filter that delivers individual pixels to its extensions in the RGB color model.

The `java.awt.image` package also provides another image filter—
`BufferedImageFilter`, which is not part of the core AWT. Instead,
`BufferedImageFilter` is part of the Java 2D Api. The 2D Api is covered at
length in *Graphic Java Volume III: The 2D Api.*

Figure 6-1 shows the relationships between the image filtering classes in the AWT.

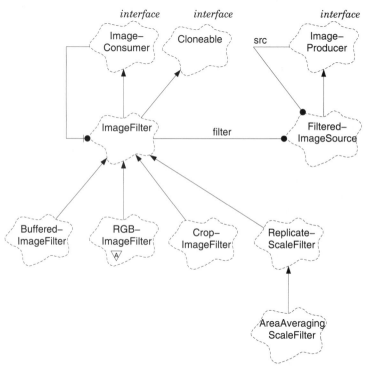

Figure 6-1 AWT Image Filters
The `java.awt.image` package offers a handful of image filters in
addition to providing the infrastructure for implementing custom
filters.

CropImageFilter

`CropImageFilter` crops a specific rectangle of an image. The cropped rectangle is specified in the filter's constructor. Figure 6-2 shows an applet that employs a `CropImageFilter` to crop an image.

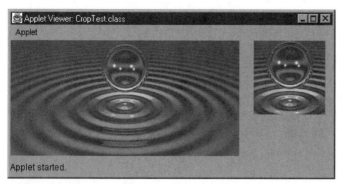

Figure 6-2 `CropImageFilter` in Action
The original image is on the left, and a cropped region of the image is displayed on the right.

The applet loads the original image as a resource, as outlined in "Loading Images as Resources" on page 125.

```
public void init() {
    MediaTracker mt  = new MediaTracker(this);
    URL url = getClass().getResource("pic.jpg");

    try {
        im = createImage((ImageProducer)url.getContent());
        mt.addImage(im, 0);
        mt.waitForID(0);
    }
    catch(Exception e) { e.printStackTrace(); }
    ...
```

An instance of `MediaTracker` is employed to fully load the image, although it is not a necessity to do so. The advantage to ensuring that the image is fully loaded is that the image will be drawn in one fell swoop, as outlined in "Waiting for an Image to Load" on page 113.

Next, the image is filtered. First, an instance of `CropImageFilter` is instantiated, and the cropped rectangle is specified as 110,5,100,100. Note that negative values for either the width or height will result in the filter using the original width and height of the image.

```
...
ImageFilter filter = new CropImageFilter(110,5,100,100);

FilteredImageSource fis =
       new FilteredImageSource(im.getSource(), filter);

cropped = createImage(fis);
```

Next, a `FilteredImageSource` is constructed and passed the image producer associated with the original image and the filter itself. Notice that a reference to the image producer associated with the original image is obtained by invoking `Image.getSource()`—see "`java.awt.Image` Methods" on page 104.

Finally, `Component.createImage()` is invoked and passed the `FilteredImageSource`. Since `FilteredImageSource` implements the `ImageProducer` interface, it is a valid argument to `createImage()`.

The applet shown in Figure 6-2 is listed in its entirety in Example 6-1.

Example 6-1 `CropTest` Applet

```
import java.net.URL;
import java.applet.Applet;
import java.awt.*;
import java.awt.image.*;

public class CropTest extends Applet {
    private Image im;
    private Image cropped;

    public void init() {
        MediaTracker mt  = new MediaTracker(this);
        URL url = getClass().getResource("pic.jpg");

        try {
            im = createImage((ImageProducer)url.getContent());
            mt.addImage(im, 0);
            mt.waitForID(0);
```

```
        }
        catch(Exception e) { e.printStackTrace(); }

        ImageFilter filter = new CropImageFilter(110,5,100,100);

        FilteredImageSource fis =
            new FilteredImageSource(im.getSource(), filter);

        cropped = createImage(fis);
    }
    public void paint(Graphics g) {
        g.drawImage(im,0,0,this);
        g.drawImage(cropped,im.getWidth(this)+20,0,this);
    }
}
```

Using Image Filters in General

The applet listed in Example 6-1 illustrates the manner in which all image filters are used to filter an image. Given an image and an instance of an image filter:

1. Instantiate the image filter.

2. Instantiate a `FilteredImageSource`, passing it the image producer associated with the original image and the filter.

3. Invoke `createImage()`, passing it the `FilteredImageSource`.

The `FilteredImageSource` class extends `ImageProducer` and keeps track of the original image and the filter used to filter it. When the filtered image source is asked to produce the image, it forwards the request to the original image's image producer, specifying the filter as the image consumer. Thus, the original image's image producer passes the bits of the image through the image filter, and the result is a filtered image.

ReplicateScaleFilter and AreaAveragingScaleFilter

The `ReplicateScaleFilter` scales images by using a simple algorithm that replicates rows or columns of image data for scaling up, and removing rows or columns of data for scaling down.

Figure 6-3 shows an applet that uses a `ReplicateScaleFilter` to scale an image.

Figure 6-3 ReplicateScaleFilter
The original image, on the left, is scaled using
ReplicateScaleFilter.

The applet shown in Figure 6-3 is listed in Example 6-2.

Example 6-2 ReplicateScaleTest Applet

```java
import java.net.URL;
import java.applet.Applet;
import java.awt.*;
import java.awt.image.*;

public class ReplicateScaleTest extends Applet {
    private Image im;
    private Image big, small;
    private int imw, imh;

    public void init() {
        MediaTracker mt  = new MediaTracker(this);
        URL url = getClass().getResource("pic.jpg");

        try {
            im = createImage((ImageProducer)url.getContent());
            mt.addImage(im, 0);
            mt.waitForID(0);
```

```
        }
        catch(Exception e) { e.printStackTrace(); }

        imw = im.getWidth(this);
        imh = im.getHeight(this);

        ImageFilter bigFilter =
            new ReplicateScaleFilter(imw*2, imh*2);

        ImageFilter smallFilter =
            new ReplicateScaleFilter(imw/2, imh/2);

        FilteredImageSource bigSource =
            new FilteredImageSource(im.getSource(), bigFilter);

        FilteredImageSource smallSource =
            new FilteredImageSource(im.getSource(), smallFilter);

        big = createImage(bigSource);
        small = createImage(smallSource);
    }
    public void paint(Graphics g) {
        g.drawImage(im,0,0,this);
        g.drawImage(small,imw,0,this);
        g.drawImage(big,imw,imh/2,this);
    }
}
```

The applet creates two instances of `ReplicateScaleFilter`: one that scales the image up and another that scales it down. The constructor for the `ReplicateScaleFilter` class is passed arguments representing the width and height of the scaled image. Two instances of `FilteredImageSource` are created and are used to create the scaled versions of the original image.

`AreaAveragingScaleFilter` is an extension of `ReplicateScaleFilter` that uses a more sophisticated algorithm for scaling images. An `AreaAveragingScaleFilter` is used in exactly the same manner as the `ReplicateScaleFilter`, but produces scaled images whose quality is better than images scaled using `ReplicateScaleFilter`.

However, the better image quality comes at a price— `AreaAveragingScaleFilter` is slower than `ReplicateScaleFilter`. Additionally, `AreaAveragingScaleFilter` can only be used with an image producer that can deliver pixels in a top-down, left-right order. If the producer cannot deliver pixels in a TDLR order, then the `AreaAveragingScaleFilter` falls back on the algorithm implemented by its superclass, `ReplicateScaleFilter`.

Combining Image Filters

Image filters can easily be combined to create a wide array of effects. For example, the applet shown in Figure 6-4 combines a `CropImageFilter` and a `ReplicateScaleFilter` to produce an image that is both cropped and scaled.

Figure 6-4 Combining Image Filters
The original image, on the left, is passed through two filters, resulting in the cropped and scaled image on the right.

First, a `FilteredImageSource` is instantiated with the image producer of the original image and a `CropImageFilter`.

```
FilteredImageSource fis =
        new FilteredImageSource(orig.getSource(),
                new CropImageFilter(25,200,155,125));
```

The resulting `FilteredImageSource` is passed to `createImage()`. Then, the image producer from the cropped image is passed to the constructor of a second `FilteredImageSource`, along with an instance of `ReplicateScaleFilter`.

```
fis = new FilteredImageSource(
        createImage(fis).getSource(),
        new ReplicateScaleFilter(310,250));
```

The final image is produced by passing the second `FilteredImageSource` to `component.CreateImage()`.

```
croppedAndScaled = createImage(fis);
```

141

In this manner, an image may be passed through multiple filters. Example 6-3 lists the applet shown in Figure 6-4.

Example 6-3 An Application That Passes an Image Through Two Filters

```java
import java.awt.*;
import java.awt.event.*;
import java.awt.image.*;
import java.net.URL;
import java.util.Hashtable;

public class Test extends Frame {
    Image orig, croppedAndScaled;

    public Test() {
        super("Combining Filters");

        URL url = getClass().getResource("tiger.gif");

        try {
            orig = createImage((ImageProducer)url.getContent());

            MediaTracker mt = new MediaTracker(this);
            mt.addImage(orig, 0);
            mt.waitForID(0);
        }
        catch(Exception e) {
            e.printStackTrace();
        }
        FilteredImageSource fis =
            new FilteredImageSource(orig.getSource(),
                    new CropImageFilter(25,200,155,125));

        fis = new FilteredImageSource(
                createImage(fis).getSource(),
                new ReplicateScaleFilter(310,250));

        fis = new FilteredImageSource(
                createImage(fis).getSource(),
                new PropertiesReportingFilter());

        croppedAndScaled = createImage(fis);
    }
    public void update(Graphics g) {
        paint(g);
    }
    public void paint(Graphics g) {
        Insets  i = getInsets();
        int ow = orig.getWidth(this);  // ow = Original Width

        g.drawImage(orig, i.left, i.top, this);
```

```
            g.drawImage(croppedAndScaled,
                    i.left + ow, i.top + 50, this);
        }
    public static void main(String args[]) {
        final Frame f = new Test();
        f.setBounds(100,100,650,380);
        f.setVisible(true);

        f.addWindowListener(new WindowAdapter() {
            public void windowClosing(WindowEvent e) {
                f.dispose();
                System.exit(0);
            }
        });
    }
}
class PropertiesReportingFilter extends ImageFilter {
    public void setProperties(Hashtable ht) {
        super.setProperties(ht);
        System.out.println(ht);
    }
}
```

ImageConsumer Properties

In "The ImageConsumer Interface" on page 131, we briefly discussed
ImageConsumer.setProperties(), which can be used to set properties
associated with an image consumer. setProperties() is a somewhat odd
method because there is no corresponding getProperties(). Properties are
used mainly as a debugging technique and are typically viewed in a debugger. If
you wish to view the properties associated with an image filter without the aid of
a debugger, you must implement a filter that overrides setProperties() and
prints out the properties.

For example, we can modify the applet listed in Example 6-3 so that the properties
associated with the ReplicateScaleFilter are printed out. First, an extension
of java.awt.image.ImageFilter is implemented that does nothing but
override setProperties().

```
class PropertiesReportingFilter extends ImageFilter {
    public void setProperties(Hashtable ht) {
        super.setProperties(ht);
        System.out.println(ht);
    }
}
```

The overridden setProperties() invokes super.setProperties() and
then prints the hashtable it is passed.

The PropertiesReportingFilter is then added to the chain of image filters.

```
FilteredImageSource fis =
    new FilteredImageSource(orig.getSource(),
                    new CropImageFilter(25,200,155,125));

fis = new FilteredImageSource(
            createImage(fis).getSource(),
            new ReplicateScaleFilter(310,250));

fis = new FilteredImageSource(
            createImage(fis).getSource(),
            new PropertiesReportingFilter());

croppedAndScaled = createImage(fis);
```

As a result, you will see the following output when the modified applet is run.

```
> java Test
{filters=java.awt.image.CropImageFil-
ter@1cce36java.awt.image.ReplicateScaleFilte
r@1cce32, croprect=java.awt.Rectan-
gle[x=25,y=200,width=155,height=125], rescale=
310x250}
```

Since we've listed the modifications to Example 6-3 on page 141, we won't bother to list the entire applet again. Also, only the modified version exists on the CD.

`ImageConsumer.setProperties()` is rarely used in practice, except as a debugging technique. The lack of `ImageConsumer.getProperties()` makes `setProperties()` awkward to use and adds little value to the image filtering process. It can also be rather puzzling to try and figure out how and why the method is used, which is why we've taken some time to discuss it here.

Implementing Custom Image Filters

The AWT provides two ways to implement custom image filters. One way is to extend the `ImageFilter` class. The `ImageFilter` class is a "null" filter that passes on the bits of an image, untouched, to another image consumer. As you might suspect, an image filter that makes no modifications to the original image is, in and of itself, of little use. The `ImageFilter` class is designed to be subclassed to implement filters that actually modify the original image. As we shall soon discover, extending the `ImageFilter` class can sometimes be a daunting task.

The second way to implement an image filter is to extend the `RGBImageFilter` class. `RGBImageFilter` extends `ImageFilter` and is much easier to subclass than its superclass. So, we will first discuss image filters that extend `RGBImageFilter` and then return to filters that extend the `ImageFilter` class.

Extending RGBImageFilter

RGBImageFilter is an abstract class that defines one abstract method:

```
int filterRGB(int x, int y, int rgb)
```

filterRGB() is passed the location of a pixel and an integer representation of the pixel in the default RGB color model. The method is expected to examine the RGB representation of the pixel and return either the same RGB representation or a modified color for the pixel in question. The following discussion assumes that you have a basic understanding of the RGB color model—see "Colors and Fonts" on page 75.

Many image filters are only concerned with modifying the colors of the pixels that constitute an image and are therefore suitable candidates for extensions of the RGBImageFilter class.

Furthermore, a certain percentage of image filters derived from RGBImageFilter are concerned only with the colors used in an image and are not interested in the position of each pixel in the image. For instance, a bleach filter that uniformly brightens every pixel in an image is not interested in the coordinates of the pixels. As a result, the RGBImageFilter class allows for a further simplification.

The RGBImageFilter class contains a protected boolean member— canFilterIndexColorModel. If an extension of RGBImageFilter sets the variable to true, then the filter will not be passed every *pixel* in the image. Instead, extensions will be passed RGB representations of every *color* in the image. This approach can result in a substantial boost in performance, especially for large images.

In this section, we will discuss two image filters derived from RGBImageFilter: a dissolve filter and a dissolve edge filter.

The dissolve filter alters the alpha value of *each color* in the image, so that the filtered image exhibits a certain degree of transparency.

The dissolve edge filter alters the transparency of pixels around the edge of the image, so that only the edges of the image exhibit a certain degree of transparency.

The dissolve filter can filter the index color model, meaning that it filters by the colors of the image, and not by individual pixels. The dissolve edge filter, on the other hand, is concerned with the location of each pixel in the image, and therefore filters by pixel instead of by color.

Additionally, we have included three other filters on the CD that are not discussed in the book: a black and white filter, a bleach filter, and a negative filter. The black and white filter drains the color out of an image, the bleach filter uniformly brightens an image, and the negative filter produces an effect similar to a negative of a photograph.

DissolveFilter

Figure 6-5 shows a dissolve filter in action.

Figure 6-5 Dissolve Filter Applet
The dissolve filter uniformly modifies the alpha values of each color in an image.

The image on the left is the original image, and the image on the right has been run through the dissolve filter and is partially dissolved. The applet shown in Figure 6-5 is listed below in Example 6-4.

Example 6-4 DissolveFilterTest Applet

```
import java.applet.Applet;
import java.awt.*;
import java.awt.image.*;
import java.net.URL;

public class DissolveFilterTest extends Applet {
    private Image   im, alpha;
    private int     alphaValue;
```

```
public void init() {
    loadImage();
    filterImage();
}
public void paint(Graphics g) {
    int imw = im.getWidth(this);

    g.drawImage(im,0,0,this);
    g.drawImage(alpha,imw,0,this);
}
private void loadImage() {
    try {
        URL url = getClass().getResource("tiger.gif");
        im = createImage((ImageProducer)url.getContent());
    }
    catch(Exception e) {
        e.printStackTrace();
    }

    MediaTracker mt = new MediaTracker(this);
    mt.addImage(im, 0);
    try {
        mt.waitForID(0);
    }
    catch(Exception e) {
        e.printStackTrace();
    }
}
private void filterImage() {
    alpha = createImage(new FilteredImageSource(
            im.getSource(), new DissolveFilter(50)));
}
}
```

The applet loads the original image as a resource and then creates the filtered version of the image by passing a filtered image source to createImage(). The filtered image source is constructed with the image producer associated with the original image, and an instance of DissolveFilter.

The DissolveFilter constructor is passed an alpha value for each color in the filtered image. Recall from "Direct Color Model" on page 81 that alpha values range from 0 to 255; a value of 0 results in a completely transparent image, whereas a value of 255 results in a completely opaque image.

The applet's paint() method draws both the original and filtered images, side by side.

The implementation of `DissolveFilter` is listed in Example 6-5.

Example 6-5 `DissolveFilter` Class Listing

```java
import java.awt.image.*;

public class DissolveFilter extends RGBImageFilter {
    private int alpha;

    public DissolveFilter() {
        this(0);
    }
    public DissolveFilter(int alpha) {
        canFilterIndexColorModel = true;

        if(alpha < 0 || alpha > 255)
            throw new IllegalArgumentException("bad alpha");

        this.alpha = alpha;
    }
    public int filterRGB(int x, int y, int rgb) {
        DirectColorModel cm =
            (DirectColorModel)ColorModel.getRGBdefault();

        int alpha = cm.getAlpha(rgb);
        int red   = cm.getRed  (rgb);
        int green = cm.getGreen(rgb);
        int blue  = cm.getBlue (rgb);

        alpha = alpha == 0 ? 0 : this.alpha;

        return alpha << 24 | red << 16 | green << 8 | blue;
    }
}
```

The `DissolveFilter` implementation is quite simple, thanks to the implementation of its superclass, `RGBImageFilter`, which delivers each color in the image to `DissolveFilter.filterRGB()`.

As noted previously, the `DissolveFilter` constructor is passed an alpha value for each color in the filtered image. Additionally, the constructor sets `canFilterIndexColorModel` to `true`, to filter by color instead of by pixel.

`filterRGB()` extracts the red, green, blue, and alpha components of each color it is passed by employing the default RGB color model. If the color is already transparent, its alpha value is untouched; otherwise, the alpha value passed to the constructor is used for the new color. The new color is then reconstructed and returned from the method.

AWT TIP

Filter by Color Index for Better Performance

Some image filters that extend java.awt.image.RGBImageFilter are not interested in the coordinates of individual pixels but instead modify only the colors contained in an image. Such filters should set the protected canFilterIndexColorModel variable from the RGBImageFilter class to true. Doing so will result in each *color* in the image being delivered to filterRGB() instead of to each *pixel* in the image. Filtering by color instead of by pixel can greatly increase performance, especially for large images.

DissolveEdgeFilter

The next image filter we will discuss also extends `RGBImageFilter` and dissolves an image. However, the `DissolveEdgeFilter` modifies only the alpha values of pixels around the edge of an image. Such an image filter might be employed to do a transition between images as part of a more sophisticated animation. Regardless, the intent here is to present an extension of `RGBImageFilter` that does not filter by color but instead must take the coordinates of each pixel into account when filtering an image.

Figure 6-6 shows an applet that exercises an instance of `DissolveEdgeFilter`.

Figure 6-6 DissolveEdge Filter
The `DissolveEdgeFilter` dissolves an area around the edges of an image.

The original image is filtered such that an inset around the edge of the image is partially dissolved. The applet is listed in Example 6-6.

Example 6-6 `DissolveEdgeFilterTest` Applet

```java
import java.applet.Applet;
import java.awt.*;
import java.awt.event.*;
import java.net.URL;
import java.awt.image.*;

public class DissolveEdgeFilterTest extends Applet {
    private Image    im, alpha;
    private int      alphaValue;

    public void init() {
        loadImage();
        filterImage();
    }
    public void paint(Graphics g) {
        int imw = im.getWidth(this);

        g.drawImage(im,0,0,this);
        g.drawImage(alpha,imw+10,0,this);
    }
    private void loadImage() {
        try {
            URL url = getClass().getResource("gjMedium.gif");
            im = createImage((ImageProducer)url.getContent());
        }
        catch(Exception e) {
            e.printStackTrace();
        }

        MediaTracker mt = new MediaTracker(this);
        mt.addImage(im, 0);
        try {
            mt.waitForID(0);
        }
        catch(Exception e) {
            e.printStackTrace();
        }
    }
    private void filterImage() {
        Insets insets = new Insets(15,15,15,15);
        alpha = createImage(new FilteredImageSource(
                im.getSource(),
                new DissolveEdgeFilter(175, insets)));
    }
}
```

The original image is loaded and filtered in exactly the same manner as the previous applet listed in Example 6-4 on page 145—the image is loaded as a resource, and a filtered image source is employed to filter the image. The original image and the filtered version are displayed side by side.

The `DissolveEdgeFilter` is listed in Example 6-7.

Example 6-7 DissolveEdgeFilter Class Listing

```java
import java.awt.*;
import java.awt.image.*;

public class DissolveEdgeFilter extends RGBImageFilter {
    private Insets insets;
    private int alpha;
    private int width, height;

    public DissolveEdgeFilter(int alpha, Insets insets) {
        this.insets = insets;

        if(alpha < 0 && alpha > 255)
            throw new IllegalArgumentException("bad alpha");

        this.alpha = alpha;
    }
    public void setDimensions(int width, int height) {
        this.width = width;
        this.height = height;
        super.setDimensions(width,height);
    }
    public int filterRGB(int x, int y, int rgb) {
        int modifiedRGB = rgb;

        if(x < insets.left || x > width - insets.right ||
            y < insets.top || y > height - insets.bottom)
                modifiedRGB = modifyAlpha(rgb);

        return modifiedRGB;
    }
    private int modifyAlpha(int rgb) {
        DirectColorModel cm =
            (DirectColorModel)ColorModel.getRGBdefault();

        int alpha = cm.getAlpha(rgb);
        int red   = cm.getRed  (rgb);
        int green = cm.getGreen(rgb);
        int blue  = cm.getBlue (rgb);

        alpha = alpha == 0 ? 0 : this.alpha;

        return alpha << 24 | red << 16 | green << 8 | blue;
    }
}
```

The filter is constructed with an alpha value for pixels around the edge of the image. The edge of the image is specified by an `Insets`, which is also passed to the constructor.

`filterRGB()` tests the coordinates of the pixels it is passed to see whether they lie within the insets. If so, the alpha value of the pixel is modified in the same manner as the `DissolveFilter` listed in Example 6-5 on page 147.

`DissolveEdgeFilter` must be aware of the width and height of the filtered image to determine if pixels lie in the insets surrounding the edge of the image. The width and height of the image are obtained by overriding `setDimensions()`, which invokes `super.setDimensions()` to ensure that the dimensions are passed on to the ultimate image consumer.

Extending ImageFilter

If an image filter modifies the color value of individual pixels within an image, it is straightforward enough to extend `RGBImageFilter`, as illustrated in the preceding sections. Filters that extend `RGBImageFilter` are shielded from the complexities of fulfilling the `ImageConsumer` interface by their superclass and merely have to deal with one pixel—or color—at a time.

However, more complex image filters, such as those that produce an image whose size differs from that of the original image, cannot be content to modify an image pixel by pixel. As a result, some image filters cannot extend `RGBImageFilter` but must instead extend the `ImageFilter` class directly.

Extending `ImageFilter` is considerably more complicated than extending `RGBImageFilter`. Implementing extensions of `ImageFilter` requires a knowledge of the role that the `ImageFilter` class plays and the manner in which pixels of the original image are delivered to the filter. That topic will occupy our discussion for the next two sections.

The ImageFilter Class

`java.awt.image.ImageFilter` is a concrete class implemented as a "null" filter. Extensions of `ImageFilter` are instantiated and passed as the second argument to the constructor of a `FilteredImageSource`, as we have done with extensions of `RGBImageFilter` in the preceding pages.

If you go to the trouble of instantiating an instance of `ImageFilter` and use it to filter an image, you will find that the bits of the "filtered" image pass through the filter untouched—thus earning `ImageFilter` the moniker "null filter." For the `ImageFilter` class to have a meaningful purpose, it must be extended to actually filter the bits associated with the original image. So far, so good—it is our intention (and presumably yours) to extend `ImageFilter` to implement meaningful filters. Now that we understand the purpose of the `ImageFilter` class, let's take a closer look at how it is implemented and used.

`ImageFilter` extends the `ImageConsumer` interface, which makes perfect sense because an image filter is passed the bits of an image for filtering. However, somehow the bits of the filtered image must be produced by the filter, which leads us to conclude that the `ImageFilter` class must also be somewhat of an image producer in addition to being an image consumer. However, `ImageFilter` does not implement the `ImageProducer` interface. How, then, does an image filter produce the filtered bits of an image? To answer that question, we must take a closer look at how image filters are used.

As we have seen previously, an extension of `ImageFilter` is passed as the second argument to the `FilteredImageSource` constructor. The resulting `FilteredImageSource`, which implements the `ImageProducer` interface, is passed to either `Component.createImage()` or `Toolkit.createImage()`, which somehow magically produces a filtered version of the original image, like so:

```
// code fragment. im is the original image, and filtered is the
// filtered image.

FilteredImageSource fis =
          new FilteredImageSource(im.getSource(), filter);

filtered = createImage(fis);
```

Since `FilteredImageSource` implements the `ImageProducer` interface, at some point in time it is told to produce the filtered bits of the image by a call to its `startProduction(ImageConsumer)` method.

`FilteredImageSource.startProduction(ImageConsumer)` invokes `ImageFilter.getFilterInstance(ImageConsumer)`, which assigns the image consumer to a `protected` member of `ImageFilter`. Nearly every method of the `ImageFilter` class delegates to the consumer. For example, here are the implementations of some of the `ImageFilter` methods:

```
// implementation of ImageFilter methods follow. The consumer
// member is passed to ImageFilter.getFilterInstance()

public void setDimensions(int width, int height) {
   consumer.setDimensions(width, height);
}
public void setHints(int hints) {
   consumer.setHints(hints);
}
```

```
public void setColorModel(ColorModel model) {
    consumer.setColorModel(model);
}
public void setPixels(int x, int y, int w, int h,
            ColorModel model, int pixels[], int off,
            int scansize) {
    consumer.setPixels(x, y, w, h, model, pixels, off, scansize);
}
public void imageComplete(int status) {
    consumer.imageComplete(status);
}
```

The rather lengthy discourse above illustrates that the `ImageFilter` class fulfills its role as an image producer, not by implementing the `ImageProducer` interface, but by delegating all of the methods it implements from the `ImageConsumer` interface to some other image consumer. For example, when the image filter is passed the pixels associated with the image, in the `setPixels()` method, it turns around and passes the same pixels on to the consumer.

Why is this important enough to warrant a couple of pages of discussion? First of all, it solves the mystery of how a filter, which produces filtered bits of an image, does so without implementing the `ImageProducer` interface. Second, when you extend the `ImageFilter` class, you must ensure that the consumer is delegated to by each method you override. This delegation can be accomplished in one of two ways—for overridden methods from the `ImageConsumer` interface named XXX that are passed arguments YYY:

1. invoke `super.XXX(YYY)` OR

2. invoke `consumer.XXX(YYY)`

Either approach listed above will ensure that the image consumer associated with your image filter is passed all of the information it needs to construct the filtered image. The second option is viable because `consumer` is a `protected` member of the `ImageFilter` class and is therefore available to extensions of the `ImageFilter` class.

At this point, you may wonder where the mysterious `ImageConsumer` passed to `FilteredImageSource.startProduction()` comes from in the first place. The answer is that it comes from deep in the guts of the AWT and is something that you never have to concern yourself with, except to ensure that it is delegated to in the manner prescribed above in your `ImageFilter` extensions.

How Image Bits Are Delivered to an Image Filter

The other hurdle that we must clear before we dive into implementing extensions of the `ImageFilter` class, is understanding how the bits of the original image are delivered to an image filter.

The `ImageConsumer` interface defines methods that specify characteristics of the image, such as the width and height of the image—`setDimensions()`—and hints about the order in which pixels will be delivered—`setHints()` (see Table 6-2 on page 131). In addition, `ImageConsumer` defines an overloaded pair of methods that actually deliver the pixels of the original image:

```
void setPixels(int x, int y, int w, int h, ColorModel model,
               int[] pixels, int offset, int scansize)

void setPixels(int x, int y, int w, int h, ColorModel model,
               int[] pixels, int offset, int scansize)
```

Depending upon how pixels are stored natively, one (and only one) of the `setPixels()` methods will be invoked. However, both of the `setPixels()` variants should be overridden in every image filter you develop, to ensure that your filter will work across platforms. This requirement is not as bad as it seems; the two `setPixels()` methods are invariably near mirror images of each other, except for minor details that arise from pixels being delivered in different formats (either `bytes` or `integers`).

Depending upon the format of the image and whether or not the source image has been fully loaded, `setPixels()` may be called once, with all the data in the source image, or it may be called repeatedly, with portions of the image passed each time around.

The first four arguments (`x`, `y`, `w`, `h`) passed to `setPixels()` define the rectangle of the image for which source image data is being supplied.

The `ColorModel` specifies the color model that must be used to translate pixels into color values.

The `pixels` array—in the form of `bytes` or `integers`—represents the array that is iterated over to extract pixel values.

The `offset` represents the offset into the array of the first pixel, and `scansize` represents an important variable in the stepping equation for extracting pixels.

On the surface, it all seems very straightforward. However, the arguments to `setPixels()` are frequently misinterpreted. The uninitiated often make the following assumptions:

1. w and h represent the width and height of the `pixels` array.

2. `scansize` is always equal to, or larger than, the width of the `pixels` array.

Both of the assumptions are misguided; `scansize` can sometimes be zero, for instance, when a GIF decoder needs to clear a portion of an image. Another scenario has the h value equal to the height of the source data, but the pixels array contains only one row of data. This scenario occurs when an interlaced GIF delivers the same row of data for each row in the source image.

Fortunately, it is not necessary to understand the rationale behind all possible combinations of arguments to `setPixels()`. All you have to do is implement the following stepping equation in your overridden `setPixels()` in order to extract pixel information.

```
for(int row=0; row < h; row++) {
    for(int col=0; col < w; col++) {
        int nextIndex = offset + row*scansize + col;
    }
}
```

In other words, the best approach is to view w, h, `offset`, and `scansize` as variables in a stepping equation used to extract pixel information. So, for a pixel in an image whose coordinates are (x, y), the equation for extracting the pixel from the `pixels` array is (`offset` + y*`scansize` + x).

The ColorModel Used to Deliver Pixels

One final word of advice concerning the color model used to decipher pixels delivered in `setPixels()`. Notice from Table 6-2 on page 131 that the `ImageConsumer` interface defines a `setColorModel(ColorModel)` method.

The color model specified by `setColorModel()` should not be used to extract color values from pixels passed to `setPixels()`. The reason is that `setColorModel()` specifies the color model that will *most likely be used for the majority* of the pixels delivered via calls to `setPixels()`. It is entirely possible that an image producer may use different color models to deliver different portions of the image to `setPixels()`. When decoding color values from pixels passed to `setPixels()`, you must use the color model passed to the `setPixels()` method.

Extending java.awt.image.ImageFilter

Extending java.awt.image.ImageFilter can sometimes be a difficult task. However, if you keep in mind a few guidelines, the difficulty is reduced considerably.

First, remember that setColorModel() specifies the color model that will be used for the majority of pixels delivered to setPixels(). Always use the color model that is passed to setPixels() for extracting color information from individual pixels.

Second, always regard the offset and scansize arguments passed to setPixels() as variables in a stepping equation for extracting pixels. Overridden setPixels() should use the following formula to access pixel(x,y): offset + y*scansize + x.

Third, always remember to pass on information, such as image dimensions and hints, to the consumer associated with your image filter. If you forget to do so, the consumer will not have adequate information to construct the filtered image.

A Dissolve Filter That Extends ImageFilter

Our first foray into filters that extend ImageFilter directly is the implementation of another dissolve filter. The filter has the same effect as the dissolve filter that extends RGBImageFilter—see "DissolveFilter" on page 145. Implementing the same type of filter will illustrate the differences involved in extending RGBImageFilter versus extending ImageFilter.

Since the filter has the same effect as the dissolve filter discussed previously, we won't bother to show or list the applet that exercises the filter. The two dissolve filters are used in an identical manner.

Like its counterpart that is extended from RGBImageFilter, the filter is instantiated with an alpha value for the pixels of the image. The no-argument constructor defaults the alpha value to 100.

```
class DissolveFilter extends ImageFilter {
    ColorModel defaultRGB = ColorModel.getRGBdefault();
    int pixelRow[], alpha;

    public DissolveFilter() {
        this(100);
    }
    public DissolveFilter(int alpha) {
        if(alpha < 0 || alpha > 255)
            throw new IllegalArgumentException(
                    "bad alpha argument");

        this.alpha = alpha;
    }
    ...
```

The default RGB color model is used to modify the transparency of each pixel and is obtained by invoking `ColorModel.getRGBdefault()`. See "Direct Color Model" on page 81 for more information on the default RGB color model. Regardless of the color model passed to the filter, the default RGB color model is passed on to the filter's `consumer` in `setColorModel()`. Recall that the color model passed to `setColorModel()` is the color model that will be used for the majority of the pixels delivered to the consumer. In our case, the default RGB color model is used for all the pixels in the image.

```
public void setColorModel(ColorModel model) {
    consumer.setColorModel(defaultRGB);
}
```

`setDimensions()` is overridden in order to allocate a buffer for storing each row of the image as it is delivered to `setPixels()`. The width and height are passed on to the `consumer`.

```
public void setDimensions(int width, int height) {
    pixelRow = new int[width];
    consumer.setDimensions(width, height);
}
```

As is the case with nearly every filter that extends `ImageFilter` directly, the two `setPixels()` methods are almost mirror images of each other. Hence, we will limit our discussion to the version that is passed a `byte` array (both versions are listed in Example 6-8 on page 159).

```
public void setPixels(int x, int y, int w, int h,
                      ColorModel cm, byte pixels[],
                      int offset, int scansize) {
    int pixel, index, originalAlpha;

    for(int row=0; row < h; row++) {
        for(int col=0; col < w; col++) {
            index = offset + row*scansize + col;
            pixel = cm.getRGB(pixels[index] & 0xff);

            originalAlpha = defaultRGB.getAlpha(pixel);

            pixel = originalAlpha == 0 ? 0 : alpha << 24 |
                    defaultRGB.getRed(pixel) << 16 |
                    defaultRGB.getGreen(pixel) << 8 |
                    defaultRGB.getBlue(pixel);

            pixelRow[col] = pixel;
        }
        consumer.setPixels(x,y+row,w,1,
                           defaultRGB,pixelRow,0,w);
    }
}
```

The stepping equation specified in "How Image Bits Are Delivered to an Image Filter" on page 154 is used to step through the pixels delivered to setPixels(). The integer representing the RGB pixel value is translated from the byte in the pixels array by means of the color model passed into the method. Recall that the color model passed into setPixels() must be used to translate the value from the array.

The red, green, and blue components of each pixel are extracted by the default RGB color model, and the alpha value is set appropriately. The image data is passed on to the filter's consumer one row at a time, using the buffer allocated in setDimensions() and the default RGB color model.

setProperties() is overridden as follows:

```
public void setProperties(Hashtable props) {
    String key = "dissolve";
    String val = Integer.toString(alpha);
    Object o = props.get(key);

    if (o != null && o instanceof String)
        val = ((String) o) + ", " + val;

    props.put(key, val);

    consumer.setProperties(props);
}
```

If the hashtable already has a "dissolve" key, then the alpha value for the filter is added to the values associated with the key, separated by a comma. Thus, if an image is run through successive dissolve filters, the alpha values of each filter will be recorded. If the hashtable does not have a "dissolve" key, then one is created with the alpha value. For more information on setProperties() and how it is used, see "ImageConsumer Properties" on page 142.

Notice that the filter does not override the setHints() method. The filter delivers pixels to the consumer in the same order they are received. Therefore, we are content to rely upon the inherited implementation of setHints(), which simply forwards the hints specified by the image producer.

Finally, the filter does not override imageComplete() because it has no business to attend to when the image has been completely delivered.

Some image filters buffer the entire image in setPixels(). Subsequently, in an overridden imageComplete(), modifications are made to the image as a whole, and a new array of pixel values is then passed on to the consumer in one shot. In general, with all other things being equal, it is better to avoid buffering the image, simply because of memory requirements for large images.

The dissolve filter is listed in its entirety in Example 6-8.

Example 6-8 Dissolve Filter That Extends
java.awt.image.ImageFilter

```
import java.awt.*;
import java.awt.image.*;
import java.util.Hashtable;

class DissolveFilter extends ImageFilter {
    ColorModel defaultRGB = ColorModel.getRGBdefault();
    int pixelRow[], alpha;

    public DissolveFilter() {
        this(100);
    }
    public DissolveFilter(int alpha) {
        if(alpha < 0 || alpha > 255)
            throw new IllegalArgumentException(
                    "bad alpha argument");

        this.alpha = alpha;
    }
    public void setDimensions(int width, int height) {
        pixelRow = new int[width];
        consumer.setDimensions(width, height);
    }
    public void setColorModel(ColorModel model) {
        consumer.setColorModel(defaultRGB);
    }
    public void setProperties(Hashtable props) {
        String key = "dissolve";
        String val = Integer.toString(alpha);
        Object o = props.get(key);

        if (o != null && o instanceof String)
            val = ((String) o) + ", " + val;

        props.put(key, val);
        consumer.setProperties(props);
    }
    public void setPixels(int x, int y, int w, int h,
                    ColorModel cm, int pixels[],
                    int offset, int scansize) {
        int pixel, index, originalAlpha;

        for(int row=0; row < h; row++) {
            for(int col=0; col < w; col++) {
                index = offset + row*scansize + col;
                pixel = cm.getRGB(pixels[index]);
                originalAlpha = defaultRGB.getAlpha(pixel);
```

```
                      pixel = originalAlpha == 0 ? 0 : alpha << 24 |
                              defaultRGB.getRed(pixel) << 16 |
                              defaultRGB.getGreen(pixel) << 8 |
                              defaultRGB.getBlue(pixel);

                      pixelRow[col] = pixel;
                   }
                   consumer.setPixels(x,y+row,w,1,
                                 defaultRGB,pixelRow,0,w);
            }
      }
      public void setPixels(int x, int y, int w, int h,
                          ColorModel cm, byte pixels[],
                          int offset, int scansize) {
         int pixel, index, originalAlpha;

         for(int row=0; row < h; row++) {
            for(int col=0; col < w; col++) {
               index = offset + row*scansize + col;
               pixel = cm.getRGB(pixels[index] & 0xff);

               originalAlpha = defaultRGB.getAlpha(pixel);

               pixel = originalAlpha == 0 ? 0 : alpha << 24 |
                       defaultRGB.getRed(pixel) << 16 |
                       defaultRGB.getGreen(pixel) << 8 |
                       defaultRGB.getBlue(pixel);

               pixelRow[col] = pixel;
            }
            consumer.setPixels(x,y+row,w,1,
                          defaultRGB,pixelRow,0,w);
         }
      }
   }
```

Wave Filter

The next filter we discuss also extends `ImageFilter` directly and runs the pixels
in the original image through a sine wave. An applet that exercises the wave filter
is shown in Figure 6-7.

The application shown in Figure 6-7 is listed in Example 6-9.

Figure 6-7 Wave Filter
The wave filter applies a sine wave to the pixels contained in the
original image.

Example 6-9 Application That Exercises the Wave Filter

```
import java.net.URL;
import java.awt.*;
import java.awt.event.*;
import java.awt.image.*;

public class Test extends Frame {
    Image original, wavey;

    public Test() {
        super("Wave Filter");
        URL url = getClass().getResource("tiger.gif");
        try {
            original =
                createImage((ImageProducer)url.getContent());

            MediaTracker mt = new MediaTracker(this);
            mt.addImage(original, 0);
            mt.waitForID(0);
        }
```

```
        catch(Exception e) {
            e.printStackTrace();
        }
        FilteredImageSource fis = new FilteredImageSource(
                                original.getSource(),
                                new WaveFilter());
        wavey = createImage(fis);
    }
    public static void main(String args[]) {
        final Frame f = new Test();
        f.setBounds(200,50,730,380);
        f.setVisible(true);

        f.addWindowListener(new WindowAdapter() {
            public void windowClosing(WindowEvent e) {
                f.dispose();
                System.exit(0);
            }
        });
    }
    public void paint(Graphics g) {
        Insets i = getInsets();
        int iw = original.getWidth(this);

        g.drawImage(original, i.left, i.top, this);
        g.drawImage(wavey, i.left + iw + 20, i.top, this);
    }
}
```

The applet loads the original image, then runs it through an instance of WaveFilter. The original image is drawn in the upper left-hand corner of the application, with the filtered image drawn on the right.

The wave filter differs from the previous dissolve filter in that the filtered image is a different size than the original image—it is the same width, but taller. As a result, unlike the dissolve filter, the wave filter cannot be implemented as an extension of RGBImageFilter. The wave filter stores the pixels of the original image at modified locations and then passes the entire filtered image to the consumer in imageComplete().

The wave filter keeps track of the amplitude and frequency of the wave, which can be specified with a constructor. Also supplied is a no-argument constructor that defaults the amplitude and frequency to 10 pixels. setDimensions() is overridden to allocate an integer array for storing pixels and to allocate and initialize a sinearray that contains values used to translate pixels of the original image.

```
class WaveFilter extends ImageFilter {
    ColorModel defaultRGB = ColorModel.getRGBdefault();
    int amplitude, frequency, width, height;
    int sineArray[], intPixels[];

    public WaveFilter() {
        this(10,10);
    }
    public WaveFilter(int amplitude, int frequency) {
        this.amplitude = amplitude;
        this.frequency = frequency;
    }
    public void setDimensions(int width, int height) {
        int x;
        this.width = width;
        this.height = height+(amplitude*2);

        intPixels= new int[width * this.height];
        sineArray = new int[width];

        for(x=0; x < width; ++x) {
            sineArray[x] =
                ((int)(amplitude*Math.sin(((double)(x)) /
                ((double)frequency)))));
        }
        consumer.setDimensions(width, this.height);
    }
    ...
}
```

`setProperties()` is overridden to record the amplitude and frequency of the wave.

```
public void setProperties(Hashtable props) {
    String akey = "wave amplitude", fkey = "wave frequency";
    String aval = Integer.toString(amplitude),
            fval = Integer.toString(frequency);

    Object o = props.get(akey);

    if (o != null && o instanceof String)
        aval = ((String) o) + ", " + aval;

    o = props.get(fkey);

    if (o != null && o instanceof String)
        fval = ((String) o) + ", " + fval;

    props.put(akey, aval);
    props.put(fkey, fval);

    //System.out.println(props);
    consumer.setProperties(props);
}
```

The print statement that is commented out prints out the contents of the properties hashtable. If the statement is uncommented, the output for the test applet listed above looks like this:

```
{wave frequency=10, wave amplitude=10}
```

The wave filter employs the default color model for converting pixels to an RGB representation and therefore specifies the default RGB color model in setColorModel().

```
public void setColorModel(ColorModel model) {
    consumer.setColorModel(defaultRGB);
}
```

setHints() is overridden to indicate that the pixels will be delivered in a TDLR order in complete scan lines. Notice that setHints() also ensures that the RANDOMPIXELORDER bit is not set in the integer value passed on to the consumer.

```
public void setHints(int hints) {
    hints |= TOPDOWNLEFTRIGHT | COMPLETESCANLINES;
    hints &= ~RANDOMPIXELORDER;
    consumer.setHints(hints);
}
```

Once again, the setPixels() methods are near mirror images of one another. The bytes version is listed below.

```
public void setPixels(int x, int y, int w, int h,
                      ColorModel cm, byte pixels[],
                      int offset, int scansize) {
    int index, destY, destIndex = 0;

    for(int row=0; row < h; row++) {
        for(int col=0; col < w; col++) {
            destY     = y + row + amplitude + sineArray[col];
            destIndex = (destY*w) + x + col;
            index     = offset + row*scansize + col;

            intPixels[destIndex] =
                        cm.getRGB(pixels[index] & 0x0ff);
        }
    }
}
```

setPixels() uses the standard stepping equation to step through the pixels it is passed, which we've emphasized in bold type. For each pixel, a new y value is calculated, in addition to the index into the intPixels array. The pixel value itself is untouched—only its location is modified.

`imageComplete()` is overridden to deliver the filtered pixels.

```
public void imageComplete(int status) {
    if(status == IMAGEERROR || status == IMAGEABORTED) {
        consumer.imageComplete(status);
        return;
    }
    consumer.setPixels(0,0,width,height,
                            defaultRGB,intPixels,0,width);
    consumer.imageComplete(status);
}
```

If the status indicates that an error occurred or the process was intentionally aborted, the bad news is simply passed on to the consumer. If no errors were encountered, the entire `intPixels` array is delivered to the `consumer` by invoking its `setPixels()`. After the filtered bits are delivered to the `consumer`, `imageComplete()` is invoked, and the `status` is passed on.

The `WaveFilter` is listed in its entirety in Example 6-10.

Example 6-10 WaveFilter Class Listing

```
import java.awt.*;
import java.awt.image.*;
import java.util.Hashtable;

class WaveFilter extends ImageFilter {
    ColorModel defaultRGB = ColorModel.getRGBdefault();
    int amplitude, frequency, width, height;
    int sineArray[], intPixels[];

    public WaveFilter() {
        this(10,10);
    }
    public WaveFilter(int amplitude, int frequency) {
        this.amplitude = amplitude;
        this.frequency = frequency;
    }
    public void setDimensions(int width, int height) {
        int x;
        this.width = width;
        this.height = height+(amplitude*2);
        intPixels= new int[width * this.height];

        sineArray = new int[width];
        for(x=0; x < width; ++x) {
            sineArray[x] =
                ((int)(amplitude*Math.sin(((double)(x)) /
                ((double)frequency))));
        }
        consumer.setDimensions(width, this.height);
    }
```

```
public void setProperties(Hashtable props) {
    String akey = "wave amplitude", fkey = "wave frequency";
    String aval = Integer.toString(amplitude),
           fval = Integer.toString(frequency);
    Object o = props.get(akey);

    if (o != null && o instanceof String)
        aval = ((String) o) + ", " + aval;

    o = props.get(fkey);

    if (o != null && o instanceof String)
        fval = ((String) o) + ", " + fval;

    props.put(akey, aval);
    props.put(fkey, fval);

    //System.out.println(props);
    consumer.setProperties(props);
}
public void setColorModel(ColorModel model) {
    consumer.setColorModel(defaultRGB);
}
public void setHints(int hints) {
    hints |= TOPDOWNLEFTRIGHT | COMPLETESCANLINES;
    hints &= ~RANDOMPIXELORDER;

    consumer.setHints(hints);
}
public void setPixels(int x, int y, int w, int h,
                      ColorModel cm, int pixels[],
                      int offset, int scansize) {
    int index, destY, destIndex = 0;

    for(int row=0; row < h; row++) {
        for(int col=0; col < w; col++) {
            destY     = y + row + amplitude + sineArray[col];
            destIndex = (destY*w) + x + col;
            index = offset + row*scansize + col;

            intPixels[destIndex] =
                cm.getRGB(pixels[index]);
        }
    }
}
public void setPixels(int x, int y, int w, int h,
                      ColorModel cm, byte pixels[],
                      int offset, int scansize) {
    int index, destY, destIndex = 0;
```

```
        for(int row=0; row < h; row++) {
            for(int col=0; col < w; col++) {
                destY     = y + row + amplitude + sineArray[col];
                destIndex = (destY*w) + x + col;
                index  = offset + row*scansize + col;

                intPixels[destIndex] =
                    cm.getRGB(pixels[index] & 0x0ff);
            }
        }
    }
    public void imageComplete(int status) {
        if(status == IMAGEERROR || status == IMAGEABORTED) {
            consumer.imageComplete(status);
            return;
        }
        consumer.setPixels(0,0,width,height,
                            defaultRGB,intPixels,0,width);
        consumer.imageComplete(status);
    }
}
```

Implementing the ImageConsumer Interface

As was previously mentioned in "The ImageProducer Interface" on page 129, image producers can have more than one image consumer added to them. Each image consumer registered with an image producer is passed the pixels of the image associated with the producer whenever the bits of the image are reconstructed. In this section, we will explore two subjects: implementing the ImageConsumer interface directly and registering an image consumer with an image producer.

An Image Dissolver

A dissolve filter, such as those implemented in "DissolveFilter" on page 145 and "A Dissolve Filter That Extends ImageFilter" on page 156, becomes much more interesting when used to animate an image by fading it in and out. This section presents a dissolver—an implementation of the ImageConsumer interface that uses a dissolve filter to create multiple images of varying transparency, for the purpose of fading an image in and out.

Figure 6-8 shows the dissolver in use.

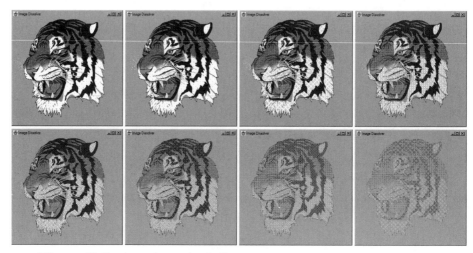

Figure 6-8 `Dissolver` in Action
`Dissolver` is an extension of `ImageConsumer` that uses a dissolve filter to fade an image in and out.

The application shown in Figure 6-8 animates the image with a thread that continuously fades the image in and out. Of course, static images in a book cannot effectively portray the animation, so you may wish to run the application from the CD in the back of the book.

Before examining the implementation of the `Dissolver` class, let's take a look at how it's used. The application shown in Figure 6-8 starts off by loading the image.

```java
public class Test extends Frame implements Runnable {
    Image  tiger;
    boolean showing = false;
    Dissolver dissolver = null;
    int       x,y;

    public Test() {
        super("Image Dissolver");

        MediaTracker mt  = new MediaTracker(this);
        URL url = getClass().getResource("tiger.gif");

        try {
            tiger = createImage((ImageProducer)url.getContent());
            mt.addImage(tiger, 0);
            mt.waitForID(0);
        }
        catch(Exception e) { e.printStackTrace(); }
    }
    ...
```

The frame's addNotify() is overridden because the insets of the frame, which are needed to place the image, are not available until after the frame's peer has been instantiated. See "Components and Peers" on page 439 for more on overriding addNotify().

```
public void addNotify() {
    super.addNotify();

    Insets i = getInsets();
    dissolver = new Dissolver(this, x=i.left, y=i.top);

    synchronized(dissolver) {
        ImageProducer ip = tiger.getSource();
        ip.startProduction(dissolver);

        try {
            dissolver.wait(); // wait for dissolved images ...
        }
        catch(Exception e) { // wait() was interrupted
            e.printStackTrace();
        }
    }
    try {
        Thread thread = new Thread(this);
        thread.start();
    }
    catch(Exception e) { // thread was interrupted
        e.printStackTrace();
    }
}
```

The dissolver is instantiated, passed a reference to the Frame, and passed a location at the top of the frame. The Dissolver class draws its images in the component specified in its constructor, at the location it is passed.

The dissolver will be registered with the image producer associated with the original image, which is obtained by invoking the image's getSource(). The dissolver is passed to the image producer's startProduction(), which registers the dissolver as an interested consumer and immediately begins production of the image.

Once the image is produced and handed off to the dissolver, the dissolver begins creating a number of images, each with a different degree of transparency. Since the creation of the images takes some time, addNotify() waits on the dissolver to finish creating its images. The dissolver, as we shall see shortly, invokes notifyAll() when it is done creating the images, and this method kicks us out of the wait(). Finally, a thread that repeatedly fades the image in and out is created and started.

The thread is straightforward. The application implements the `Runnable` interface and implements `run()`, like so:

```
public void run() {
    while(true) {
        if(isShowing()) {
            if(showing) dissolver.fadeOut();
            else        dissolver.fadeIn();

            showing = showing ? false : true;

            try {
                Thread.currentThread().sleep(1000);
            }
            catch(Exception e) { e.printStackTrace(); }
        }
    }
}
```

If the frame is showing—determined by a call to `Component.isShowing()`—the dissolver is told to fade the image either in or out, depending upon whether the image itself is currently showing. Subsequently, the application sleeps for one full second before starting the cycle again.

The application is listed in its entirety in Example 6-11.

Example 6-11 `Dissolver Test Application`

```
import java.net.URL;
import java.awt.*;
import java.awt.event.*;
import java.awt.image.*;

public class Test extends Frame implements Runnable {
    Image tiger;
    boolean showing = false;
    Dissolver dissolver = null;
    int       x,y;

    public Test() {
        super("Image Dissolver");

        MediaTracker mt  = new MediaTracker(this);
        URL     url = getClass().getResource("tiger.gif");

        try {
            tiger = createImage((ImageProducer)url.getContent());
            mt.addImage(tiger, 0);
            mt.waitForID(0);
        }
        catch(Exception e) { e.printStackTrace(); }
    }
```

```
public void addNotify() {
    super.addNotify();

    Insets i = getInsets();
    dissolver = new Dissolver(this, x=i.left, y=i.top);

    synchronized(dissolver) {
        ImageProducer ip = tiger.getSource();
        ip.startProduction(dissolver);
        try {
            dissolver.wait(); // wait for dissolved images ...
        }
        catch(Exception e) { // wait() was interrupted
            e.printStackTrace();
        }
    }
    try {
        Thread thread = new Thread(this);
        thread.start();
    }
    catch(Exception e) { // thread was interrupted
        e.printStackTrace();
    }
}
public void run() {
    while(true) {
        if(isShowing()) {
            if(showing) dissolver.fadeOut();
            else        dissolver.fadeIn();
            showing = showing ? false : true;

            try {
                Thread.currentThread().sleep(1000);
            }
            catch(Exception e) { e.printStackTrace(); }
        }
    }
}
public static void main(String args[]) {
    final Test f = new Test();
    f.setBounds(100,100,375,375);
    f.setVisible(true);

    f.addWindowListener(new WindowAdapter() {
        public void windowClosing(WindowEvent e) {
            f.dispose();
            System.exit(0);
        }
    });
}
}
```

Implementation of the Dissolver Class

The Dissolver class implements the ImageConsumer interface directly. It also keeps track of the component into which it will paint its images, and the location at which the images will be drawn.

Two constructors are provided, one that allows specification of the number of images used in the fade and another that specifies a pause interval, in milliseconds, between frames. The default for the number of images is 10, and the default pause is 50 milliseconds.

```java
class Dissolver implements ImageConsumer {
    Image   images[];
    Image   image;
    ColorModel defaultRGB = ColorModel.getRGBdefault();
    Component component;
    Graphicsg;
    int     intPixels[], x, y, width, height, pauseInterval;
    int     numImages;

    public Dissolver(Component c, int x, int y) {
        this(c,x,y,10,50);
    }
    public Dissolver(Component c, int x, int y,
                        int numImages, int pauseInterval) {
        this.component = c;
        this.numImages = numImages;
        this.pauseInterval = pauseInterval;
        this.x = x;
        this.y = y;
        images = new Image[numImages];
    }
```

Since the Dissolver class implements the ImageConsumer interface directly, it must implement every method defined by the interface, even though it is not really interested in doing so. As a result, some of the methods are implemented as no-ops.

```java
    public void setColorModel(ColorModel model) {
        // don't care - we use our own in imageComplete(),
        // and the one passed into setPixels()
    }
    public void setHints(int hints) {
        // don't care
    }
    public void setProperties(java.util.Hashtable props) {
        // don't care
    }
```

The `Dissolver` class is not interested in the color model used by the image producer, hints about the image, or in setting properties. It is, however, interested in the dimensions of the image, which it records for further reference. `setDimensions()` also allocates an `integer` buffer for storing the bits of the original image.

```
public void setDimensions(int width, int height) {
    this.width = width;
    this.height = height;
    intPixels = new int[width * height];
}
```

`Dissolver.setPixels()` is rather unspectacular; it merely stores the pixels of the image in the `intPixels` array in RGB format.

```
public void setPixels(int x, int y, int w, int h,
                      ColorModel model, byte[] pixels,
                      int offset, int scansize) {
    for(int r=0; r < h; ++r) {
        for(int c=0; c < w; ++c) {
            int index = offset + r*scansize + c;
            intPixels[index] =
                model.getRGB(pixels[index] & 0xff);
        }
    }
}
```

`Dissolver.imageComplete()` is more interesting.

```
public synchronized void imageComplete(int status) {
    if(status == IMAGEERROR || status == IMAGEABORTED) {
        return;
    }
    MemoryImageSource mis = new MemoryImageSource(
                            width, height, defaultRGB,
                            intPixels, 0, width);
    image = component.createImage(mis);
    makeDissolvedImages();  // this takes some time, so ...
    notifyAll();// notify all threads waiting on us
}
```

If an error has occurred or production has been aborted, then `Dissolver` is finished for the time being. Otherwise, the original image is created from the stored array of pixels by putting an instance of `MemoryImageSource` to work—see "Memory Image Source" on page 193. Once the original image is in hand, the array of images of varying transparency is created. Since creation of the images can be time consuming, `notifyAll()` is invoked when `makeDissolvedImages()` returns to notify threads that are waiting on instances of `Dissolver`, such as our application, that the dissolver is ready to go.

The `Dissolver` class implements two methods, one for fading the image in and another for fading it out.

```
public void fadeOut() {
    g = component.getGraphics();
    if(g != null) {
        try {
            for(int i=numImages-1; i >= 0; --i) {
                g.clearRect(x, y, width, height);
                g.drawImage(images[i], x, y, component);
                pause();
            }
        }
        finally {
            g.dispose();
        }
    }
}
public void fadeIn() {
    g = component.getGraphics();
    if(g != null) {
        try {
            for(int i=0; i < numImages; ++i) {
                g.clearRect(x, y, width, height);
                g.drawImage(images[i], x, y, component);
                pause();
            }
        }
            g.drawImage(image, x, y, component);
        }
        finally {
            g.dispose();
        }
    }
}
private void pause() {
    try { Thread.currentThread().sleep(pauseInterval); }
    catch(InterruptedException e) { }
}
```

Both methods obtain a reference to the component's `Graphics`, and both cycle through the array of partially dissolved images. In addition, both are careful to dispose of the component's `Graphics` in a `finally` block, as advised in "Disposing of a Graphics" on page 40.

The `Dissolver` class is listed in its entirety in Example 6-12.

Example 6-12 Dissolver Class Listing

```
import java.awt.*;
import java.awt.image.*;

class Dissolver implements ImageConsumer {
    Image   images[];
    Image   image;
    ColorModel defaultRGB = ColorModel.getRGBdefault();
    Component component;
    Graphics g;
    int     intPixels[], x, y, width, height, pauseInterval;
    int        numImages;

    public Dissolver(Component c, int x, int y) {
        this(c,x,y,10,50);
    }
    public Dissolver(Component c, int x, int y,
                     int numImages, int pauseInterval) {
        this.component = c;
        this.numImages = numImages;
        this.pauseInterval = pauseInterval;
        this.x = x;
        this.y = y;

        images = new Image[numImages];
    }
    public void setColorModel(ColorModel model) {
        // don't care - we use our own in imageComplete(),
        // and the one passed into setPixels()
    }
    public void setHints(int hints) {
        // don't care
    }
    public void setProperties(java.util.Hashtable props) {
        // don't care
    }
    public void setDimensions(int width, int height) {
        this.width = width;
        this.height = height;
        intPixels = new int[width * height];
    }
    public void setPixels(int x, int y, int w, int h,
                     ColorModel model, int[] pixels,
                     int offset, int scansize) {
        for(int r=0; r < h; ++r) {
            for(int c=0; c < w; ++c) {
                int index = offset + r*scansize + c;
                intPixels[index] =
                    model.getRGB(pixels[index] & 0xff);
            }
        }
    }
```

```
        }
        public void setPixels(int x, int y, int w, int h,
                            ColorModel model, byte[] pixels,
                            int offset, int scansize) {
            for(int r=0; r < h; ++r) {
                for(int c=0; c < w; ++c) {
                    int index = offset + r*scansize + c;
                    intPixels[index] =
                        model.getRGB(pixels[index] & 0xff);
                }
            }
        }
        public synchronized void imageComplete(int status) {
            if(status == IMAGEERROR || status == IMAGEABORTED) {
                return;
            }
            MemoryImageSource mis = new MemoryImageSource(
                            width, height, defaultRGB,
                            intPixels, 0, width);
            image = component.createImage(mis);

            makeDissolvedImages();  // this takes some time, so ...
            notifyAll();// notify all threads waiting on us
        }
        private void makeDissolvedImages() {
            MediaTracker mt = new MediaTracker(component);
            DissolveFilter filter;

            for(int i=0; i < images.length; ++i) {
                filter = new DissolveFilter((255/(numImages-1))*i);

                FilteredImageSource fis = new FilteredImageSource(
                                image.getSource(),
                                filter);
                images[i] = component.createImage(fis);
                mt.addImage(images[i], i);
            }
            mt.addImage(image, numImages);
            try { mt.waitForAll(); }
            catch(Exception e) { e.printStackTrace(); }
        }
        public void fadeOut() {
            g = component.getGraphics();

            if(g != null) {
                try {
                    for(int i=numImages-1; i >= 0; --i) {
                        g.clearRect(x, y, width, height);
                        g.drawImage(images[i], x, y, component);
                        pause();
                    }
                }
```

```
        finally {
            g.dispose();
        }
    }
}
public void fadeIn() {
    g = component.getGraphics();

    if(g != null) {
        try {
          for(int i=0; i < numImages; ++i) {
              g.clearRect(x, y, width, height);
              g.drawImage(images[i], x, y, component);
              pause();
          }
            g.drawImage(image, x, y, component);
        }
        finally {
            g.dispose();
        }
    }
}
private void pause() {
    try { Thread.currentThread().sleep(pauseInterval); }
    catch(InterruptedException e) { }
    }
}
```

An Introduction to Double Buffering

If you run the application listed in "Dissolver Test Application" on page 170, you will notice that the application flickers between frames. This flickering is due to the fact that the Dissolver class must clear the previous image every time it draws a partially dissolved image. Clearing the background of the component before drawing the next frame results in flickering, which can be eliminated by a technique known as double buffering.

In "Double Buffering" on page 789, we will examine double buffering in detail by discussing a set of classes that can be used for dragging and animating lightweight components. This section will serve as a foundation for that chapter.

Double buffering is a simple concept. Instead of drawing (and erasing) directly into the component, all of the erasing and drawing is done in an offscreen buffer. When the next frame has been rendered in the offscreen buffer, the contents of the offscreen buffer is *blitted*[1] to the component.

---

1. Blit is a term derived from the phrase "bit block transfer." A block transfer is sometimes referred to as a BLT; blit is short for a bit BLT.

Double buffering the `Dissolver` class is straightforward; all of the changes occur in `fadeIn()` and `fadeOut()` in addition to a few extra convenience methods. Since `fadeIn()` and `fadeOut()` are identical except for the order in which they draw the partially dissolved images, we will list only `fadeOut()` and the convenience methods below.

First, we have a couple of convenience methods for clearing the offscreen buffer and painting the image into the offscreen buffer and then blitting (copying) it to the screen. `offg` is the `Graphics` associated with the offscreen buffer, and `g` is the `Graphics` associated with the component.

```
private void clearOffscreen() {
    offg.setColor(component.getBackground());
    offg.fillRect(0, 0, width, height);
}
private void blitImage(Image im) {
    // paint image in offscreen graphics
    offg.drawImage (im, 0, 0, component);

    // blit the image onscreen
    g.drawImage(offscreen, x, y, component);
}
```

`fadeOut()` creates the offscreen buffer if it has not yet been instantiated; the buffer is created by a call to `Component.createImage()`. The overloaded `createImage()` invoked here is not the same as the one that we have been using throughout this chapter. Instead of an image producer being passed, the width and the height of the image are passed to `createImage()`. This variant of `createImage()` produces an uninitialized image, suitable for use as an offscreen buffer.

```
// double buffered version

public void fadeOut() {
    if(offscreen == null)
        offscreen = component.createImage(width,height);

    offg = offscreen.getGraphics();
    g = component.getGraphics();

    if(offg != null && g != null) {
        try {
            for(int i=numImages-1; i >= 0; --i) {
                clearOffscreen();
                blitImage(images[i]);
                pause();
```

```
            }
        }
        finally {
            offg.dispose();
            g.dispose();
        }
    }
}
```

After creation of the offscreen buffer if necessary, references are obtained to the offscreen `Graphics` and the component's `Graphics`.

For each image, the offscreen buffer is cleared—`clearOffscreen()`—and the image is drawn first in the offscreen buffer and then blitted to the component's `Graphics`—`blitImage()`. The component's graphics is never cleared—only the offscreen buffer is—which eliminates the flicker occasioned by drawing directly into the component itself.

`fadeOut()` is also careful to dispose of both the offscreen buffer's `Graphics`, and the component's `Graphics` in a `finally` block—see "Disposing of a Graphics" on page 40 for the rationale behind disposing of a `Graphics`.

The double buffered version of the `Dissolver` class is listed in Example 6-13.

Example 6-13 Double Buffered Dissolver Class Listing

```
import java.awt.*;
import java.awt.image.*;

class Dissolver implements ImageConsumer {
    Image   images[];
    Image   image, offscreen;
    ColorModel defaultRGB = ColorModel.getRGBdefault();
    Component component;
    Graphicsg, offg;
    int     intPixels[], x, y, width, height, pauseInterval;
    int         numImages;

    public Dissolver(Component c, int x, int y) {
        this(c,x,y,10,50);
    }
    public Dissolver(Component c, int x, int y,
                    int numImages, int pauseInterval) {
        this.component = c;
        this.numImages = numImages;
        this.pauseInterval = pauseInterval;
        this.x = x;
        this.y = y;
```

```
        images = new Image[numImages];
    }
    public void setColorModel(ColorModel model) {
        // don't care - we use our own in imageComplete(),
        // and the one passed into setPixels()
    }
    public void setHints(int hints) {
        // don't care
    }
    public void setProperties(java.util.Hashtable props) {
        // don't care
    }
    public void setDimensions(int width, int height) {
        this.width = width;
        this.height = height;
        intPixels = new int[width * height];
    }
    public void setPixels(int x, int y, int w, int h,
                          ColorModel model, int[] pixels,
                          int offset, int scansize) {
        for(int r=0; r < h; ++r) {
            for(int c=0; c < w; ++c) {
                int index = offset + r*scansize + c;
                intPixels[index] =
                    model.getRGB(pixels[index] & 0xff);
            }
        }
    }
    public void setPixels(int x, int y, int w, int h,
                          ColorModel model, byte[] pixels,
                          int offset, int scansize) {
        for(int r=0; r < h; ++r) {
            for(int c=0; c < w; ++c) {
                int index = offset + r*scansize + c;
                intPixels[index] =
                    model.getRGB(pixels[index] & 0xff);
            }
        }
    }
    public synchronized void imageComplete(int status) {
        if(status == IMAGEERROR || status == IMAGEABORTED) {
            return;
        }
        MemoryImageSource mis = new MemoryImageSource(
                             width, height, defaultRGB,
                             intPixels, 0, width);
        image = component.createImage(mis);

        makeDissolvedImages();  // this takes some time, so ...
        notifyAll();// notify all threads waiting on us
    }
    private void makeDissolvedImages() {
```

```
        MediaTracker mt = new MediaTracker(component);
        DissolveFilter filter;

        for(int i=0; i < images.length; ++i) {
            filter = new DissolveFilter((255/(numImages-1))*i);

            FilteredImageSource fis = new FilteredImageSource(
                                        image.getSource(),
                                        filter);
            images[i] = component.createImage(fis);
            mt.addImage(images[i], i);
        }
        mt.addImage(image, numImages);
        try { mt.waitForAll(); }
        catch(Exception e) { e.printStackTrace(); }
    }
    public void fadeOut() {
        if(offscreen == null)
            offscreen = component.createImage(width,height);

        offg = offscreen.getGraphics();
        g = component.getGraphics();

        if(offg != null && g != null) {
          try {
            for(int i=numImages-1; i >= 0; --i) {
                clearOffscreen();
                blitImage(images[i]);
                pause();
            }
          }
          finally {
             offg.dispose();
             g.dispose();
          }
        }
    }
    public void fadeIn() {
        if(offscreen == null)
            offscreen = component.createImage(width,height);

        offg = offscreen.getGraphics();
        g = component.getGraphics();

        if(offg != null && g != null) {
          try {
            for(int i=0; i < numImages; ++i) {
                clearOffscreen();
                blitImage(images[i]);
                pause();
            }
            blitImage(image);
```

```
            }
            finally {
                offg.dispose();
                g.dispose();
            }
        }
    }
    private void blitImage(Image im) {
        offg.drawImage (im, 0, 0, component);
        g.drawImage(offscreen, x, y, component);
    }
    private void clearOffscreen() {
        offg.setColor(component.getBackground());
        offg.fillRect(0, 0, width, height);
    }
    private void pause() {
        try { Thread.currentThread().sleep(pauseInterval); }
        catch(InterruptedException e) { }
    }
}
```

Summary

This chapter has explored the AWT's support for image filtering. You should have a good understanding of the `ImageProducer` and `ImageConsumer` interfaces and of how producers and consumers interact. You should also be familiar with the filters the `java.awt.image` package provides and know how to use and combine image filters.

Custom image filters are implemented typically by extending either `java.awt.image.ImageFilter` or `java.awt.image.RGBImageFilter`. At first glance, implementing `ImageFilter` directly can be very confusing, and we hope our discussion on the matter will make it easy for you to write your own filters.

We have one more chapter to go concerning image manipulation. In the next chapter, we'll focus on manipulating images without writing image filters.

CHAPTER

7

Image
Manipulation
Without
Filtering

Image filters usually get top billing when it comes to image manipulation, but there is a great deal that can be done without them. The AWT provides facilities for scaling and flipping images, grabbing pixels from the screen, constructing an image from an array of bits, and even performing animations, all without an image filter in sight. In a testament to the flexibility provided by the AWT's image package, everything that was done with filters in the "Image Filtering" chapter beginning on page 129 can be implemented in another fashion without implementing an image filter.

Scaling and Flipping Images

`java.awt.Graphics` provides several overloaded versions of `drawImage()`, which are listed in Table 7-1.

All of the methods are passed an image to draw and an image observer. If a method is passed a color, the color replaces any transparent bits in the image—the effect is as if the background of the image had been painted with the current background color and the image subsequently drawn over the background.

The `integer` values represent either a point in the image (source) or component (destination), or the width and height of the source and destination regions.

Figure 7-1 shows an application that exercises each of the methods listed in Table 7-1.

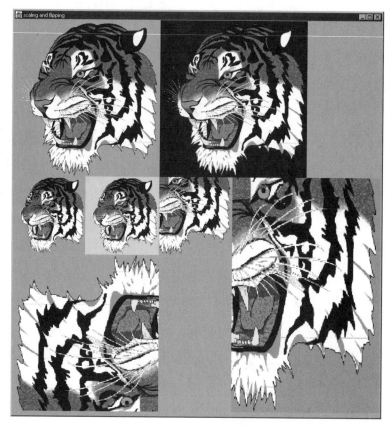

Figure 7-1 Scaling and Flipping Images
Overloaded `Graphics.drawImage` methods are used to scale and flip a
image.

Table 7-1 `Graphics.drawImage` **Methods**

Method
drawImage(Image,int,int,ImageObserver)
drawImage(Image,int,int,Color,ImageObserver)
drawImage(Image,int,int,int,int,ImageObserver)
drawImage(Image,int,int,int,int,Color,ImageObserver)
drawImage(Image,int,int,int,int,int,int,int,int,ImageObserver)
drawImage(Image,int,int,int,int,int,int,int,int,Color, ImageObserver)

The first row of images are drawn using the simplest versions of `drawImage()`:

```
public void paint(Graphics g) {
    Insets insets = getInsets();
    int il = insets.left, it = insets.top;
    int imw = im.getWidth(this), imh = im.getHeight(this);

    // top row
    g.drawImage(im, il, it, this);
    g.drawImage(im, il+imw, it, Color.blue, this);
    ...
```

The first image is drawn at the top of the application, adjusted for the application's insets. The second image is drawn to the right of the first image, with blue specified as the color used to replace the transparent bits of the image.

The second and third rows are drawn like so:

```
    ... // second row
    g.drawImage(im, il, it+imh, imw/2, imh/2, this);

    g.drawImage(im, il+imw/2, it+imh, imw/2, imh/2,
            Color.yellow, this);

    g.drawImage(im, il+imw, it+imh,
            il+imw+imw/2, it+imh+imh/2,
            100, 100, imw, imh, this);

    g.drawImage(im, il+imw+imw/2, it+imh,
            il+2*imw+imw/2, it+2*imh+imh/2,
            100, 100, imw, imh, Color.cyan, this);
    // third row
    g.drawImage(im, il, it+imh+imh/2,
            il+imw, it+imh+imh/2+imh,
            imw, imh, 100, 100, this);
```

The first image in the second row is drawn with a version of `drawImage()` that takes four integer arguments. The image is drawn at the location specified by the first two integer arguments and is scaled to the width and height specified by the second pair of integer arguments.

The second image is also drawn with a version of `drawImage()` that takes four integer arguments; however, yellow is specified as the color to be substituted for the image's transparent bits.

The last three images are drawn with a version of `drawImage()` that takes eight integer arguments. The first two integers specify the first destination corner, and the second pair of integers specifies the second destination corner. The third and fourth pairs of integers specify corners of the region of the image that is to be drawn. The region of the image that is drawn is scaled to the destination rectangle.

If the first corner of the image is above and to the left of the second corner, then the region's orientation is unchanged. However, if the first corner of the image is below and to the right of the second corner, the image is flipped, as is the case for the last image.

The application is listed in its entirety in Example 7-1.

Example 7-1 An Application That Scales and Flips an Image

```java
import java.awt.*;
import java.awt.event.*;

public class Test extends Frame {
    Image im = Toolkit.getDefaultToolkit().getImage("tiger.gif");

    public Test() {
        super("scaling and flipping");
        MediaTracker mt = new MediaTracker(this);

        mt.addImage(im, 0);
        try {
            mt.waitForID(0);
        }
        catch(InterruptedException e) {
            e.printStackTrace();
        }
    }
    public void paint(Graphics g) {
        Insets insets = getInsets();
        int il = insets.left, it = insets.top;
        int imw = im.getWidth(this), imh = im.getHeight(this);

        // top row
        g.drawImage(im, il, it, this);
        g.drawImage(im, il+imw, it, Color.blue, this);

        // second row
        g.drawImage(im, il, it+imh, imw/2, imh/2, this);

        g.drawImage(im, il+imw/2, it+imh, imw/2, imh/2,
                Color.yellow, this);

        g.drawImage(im, il+imw, it+imh,
                il+imw+imw/2, it+imh+imh/2,
                100, 100, imw, imh, this);

        g.drawImage(im, il+imw+imw/2, it+imh,
```

```
                    il+2*imw+imw/2,  it+2*imh+imh/2,
                    100, 100, imw, imh, Color.cyan, this);

        // third row
        g.drawImage(im, il, it+imh+imh/2,
                        il+imw, it+imh+imh/2+imh,
                        imw, imh, 100, 100, this);
    }
    public static void main(String args[]) {
        final Frame f = new Test();
        f.setBounds(100,100,800,850);
        f.setVisible(true);

        f.addWindowListener(new WindowAdapter() {
            public void windowClosing(WindowEvent e) {
                f.dispose();
                System.exit(0);
            }
        });
    }
}
```

Note that the resulting scaled and (possibly) flipped images are not cached—they are created on the fly, every time the call to `drawImage()` is made.

`java.awt.Image` provides a method that returns a scaled representation of itself, in the event that caching the image is desirable. The method takes three `integer` arguments: `Image.getScaledInstance(int, int, int)`. The first two `integers` specify the width and height of the image, and the third `integer` specifies the type of algorithm to be used for scaling the image. The different algorithms are listed in Table 7-2.

Table 7-2 Constants for Image Scaling Algorithms

Method	Implementation
SCALE_DEFAULT	Uses default image scaling algorithm
SCALE_FAST	Prefers speed over smoothness of scaled image
SCALE_SMOOTH	Prefers smoothness of scaled image to speed
SCALE_REPLICATE	Uses the algorithm employed by the ReplicateScaleFilter
SCALE_AVERAGING	Uses the algorithm employed by the AreaAveragingScaleFilter

The `ReplicateScaleFilter` and `AreaAveragingScaleFilter` are discussed in "Image Filtering" on page 129.

Grabbing Pixels

As we've seen, the AWT provides extensive support for filtering images. However, sometimes it is convenient to be able access the pixel data of an image without having to bother with implementing an image filter in order to access this data. That is precisely the role of the `PixelGrabber` class. `PixelGrabber` is an implementation of the `ImageConsumer` interface that grabs a rectangular region of pixels within a given image.

`PixelGrabber` provides three constructors that take the following arguments:

```
(Image im, int x, int y, int w, int h, boolean forceRGB)
(Image im, int x, int y, int w, int h, int[] buffer,
          int offset, int scansize)
(ImageProducer ip, int x, int y, int w, int h, int[] buffer,
          int offset, int scansize)
```

All of the constructors take either an `Image` or an `ImageProducer` from which pixels are extracted. Additionally, all take four `integers` representing the rectangle of bits to grab (x,y,w,h).

The first constructor allows the width and height arguments to be specified as negative numbers, in which case the width and height default to the dimensions of the image. This feature can be useful when grabbing pixels from an image that is not fully loaded. If the image is not fully loaded when the `PixelGrabber` is instantiated, the width and height of the image are unknown; in fact, `Image.getWidth()` and `Image.getHeight()` will return -1 until the image is loaded—see "Loading and Displaying Images" on page 107.

The first constructor is passed a `boolean` argument that specifies whether to force the pixels to be delivered in RGB format. A `true` value forces the pixels to be delivered in RGB format. A `false` value causes pixels to be delivered in whatever color model the image producer delivers pixels in. If the image producer delivers pixels using more than one color model, then the image producer uses the RGB color model. The other constructors deliver pixels in the RGB color model, regardless of the color model used by the original image producer.

The last two constructors are passed `integer` buffers in which to store the bits. If the first constructor is used, `PixelGrabber` will instantiate a buffer on its own.

The last two constructors also take an offset into the array where the first pixel will be stored, and take a scansize, which is the distance from one row of pixels to the next in the array. The offset and scansize are typically specified as zero and the width of the image, respectively, except when the array passed in is larger than the number of pixels grabbed.

It should be noted that the PixelGrabber class originally came equipped with only the last two constructors listed above; the first constructor was added in the 1.1 version of the AWT. Adding the constructor enabled PixelGrabber to deliver pixels in the format of the color model used by the image producer and allows PixelGrabber to be used without the need to allocate a buffer for the pixels.

Table 7-3 lists the PixelGrabber public methods.

Table 7-3 java.awt.image.PixelGrabber **Public Methods**[1]

Method	Implementation
boolean grabPixels(long) throws InterruptedException	Begins production of the image. Waits for all pixels to be delivered or until timeout.
void startGrabbing()	Starts fetching pixels
void abortGrabbing()	Aborts fetching pixels
ColorModel getColorModel()	Returns the color model used for pixels
int getWidth()	Returns the width of the pixel buffer
int getHeight()	Returns the height of the pixel buffer
Object getPixels()	Returns the array of pixels as either an array of bytes or an array of integers
int getStatus()	Returns the status of the pixel buffer

1. excluding methods implemented from the ImageConsumer interface

The applet shown in Figure 7-2 illustrates the use of PixelGrabber.

The applet uses an instance of PixelGrabber to grab all of the pixels in the image. Pixel values are extracted from the buffer of pixels returned by PixelGrabber as the mouse moves over the image. The RGB values for the pixel the mouse is currently over are displayed in the applet's status bar.

The applet is listed in Example 7-2.

red=108 green=144 blue=255 alpha=0

Figure 7-2 PixelGrabber in Action

Example 7-2 An Applet that Uses PixelGrabber

```
import java.applet.Applet;
import java.awt.*;
import java.awt.event.*;
import java.awt.image.*;
import java.net.URL;

public class Test extends Applet {
    private ColorModel defaultRGB = ColorModel.getRGBdefault();
    private Image image;
    private intimw, imh, pixels[];

    public void init() {
        MediaTracker mt = new MediaTracker(this);

        URL url = getClass().getResource("tiger.gif");

        try {
            image = createImage((ImageProducer)url.getContent());
            mt.addImage(image, 0);
            mt.waitForID(0);
        }
        catch(Exception e) {
            e.printStackTrace();
        }
        imw = image.getWidth(this);
```

```
    imh = image.getWidth(this);
    pixels = new int[imw*imh];

    try {
        PixelGrabber pg =
            new PixelGrabber(image, 0, 0, imw, imh,
                                pixels, 0, imw);
        pg.grabPixels();
    }
    catch(InterruptedException e) {
        e.printStackTrace();
    }

    addMouseMotionListener(new MouseMotionAdapter() {
        public void mouseMoved(MouseEvent e) {
            int mx = e.getX(), my = e.getY();

            if(mx > 0 && mx < imw && my > 0 && my < imh) {
                int pixel = ((int[])pixels)[my*imw + mx];

                int red = defaultRGB.getRed(pixel),
                    green = defaultRGB.getGreen(pixel),
                    blue = defaultRGB.getBlue(pixel),
                    alpha = defaultRGB.getAlpha(pixel);

                showStatus("red=" + red + " green=" + green +
                        " blue=" + blue + " alpha=" + alpha);
            }
        }
    });
}
public void paint(Graphics g) {
    Insets insets = getInsets();
    g.drawImage(image, insets.left, insets.top, this);
}
}
```

Memory Image Source

In addition to supporting grabbing pixels from an existing image, the AWT image package provides a mechanism for converting an array of pixels into an image. `java.awt.image.MemoryImageSource` implements the `ImageProducer` interface and can produce the bits of an image from an array of pixels.

Like `PixelGrabber`, the `MemoryImageSource` class is provided as a convenience that allows construction of an image without the need for custom image filters.

`MemoryImageSource` provides no less than six constructors that take the following arguments:

```
(int w, int w, ColorModel cm, byte[] pixels,
        int offset, int scansize)
(int w, int w, ColorModel cm, byte[] pixels,
        int offset, int scansize, Hashtable properties)
(int w, int w, ColorModel cm, int[] pixels,
        int offset, int scansize)
(int w, int w, ColorModel cm, int[] pixels,
        int offset, int scansize, Hashtable properties)
(int w, int w, int[] pixels,int offset, int scansize)
(int w, int w, int[] pixels,
        int offset, int scansize, Hashtable properties)
```

The first two arguments of each constructor specify the width and height of the image. All of the constructors are passed an array of either `bytes` or `integers` used to produce the image, in addition to the offset and scansize passed after the array.

If a constructor is not passed a color model, the pixels in the array are assumed to be stored in RGB format. The constructors also provide variants that allow a hashtable of image properties to be specified—see "ImageConsumer Properties" on page 142 for more on image consumer properties.

Table 7-4 lists the `MemoryImageSource` public methods.

Table 7-4 `java.awt.image.MemoryImageSource` **Public Methods**[1]

Method	Implementation
`setAnimated(boolean)`	Changes image to multiframe or static
`setFullBufferUpdates(boolean)`	Specifies whether to send the full buffer of pixels when animating
`newPixels()`	Flushes the image and produces a new image
`newPixels(byte[],ColorModel, int,int)`	Reproduces the image by using the `byte` array passed in
`newPixels(int,int,int,int)`	Sends the rectangular region specified to registered image consumers
`newPixels(int,int,int,int, boolean)`	Sends the rectangular region specified to registered image consumers
`newPixels(int[],ColorModel, int,int)`	Reproduces the image by using the `int` array passed in

1. excluding methods implemented from the `ImageProducer` interface

The methods listed in Table 7-4 are all concerned with the animation capabilities provided by MemoryImageSource, which we will discuss in "MemoryImageSource and Animations" on page 196.

Notice that although PixelGrabber has a method for grabbing pixels—grabPixels()—MemoryImageSource provides no analogous method for producing the image because MemoryImageSource implements the ImageProducer interface. To produce the image, an instance of MemoryImageSource is simply passed to either Component or Toolkit createImage(ImageProducer).

Cropping Images with MemoryImageSource

The applet shown in Figure 7-3 uses instances of PixelGrabber and MemoryImageSource to crop an image without the aid of an image filter.

Figure 7-3 Using MemoryImageSource to Crop an Image.

The applet uses an instance of PixelGrabber to grab the cropped rectangle of the image and subsequently turns the grabbed pixels into an image by using an instance of MemoryImageSource. The applet is listed in Example 7-3.

Example 7-3 An Applet That Crops an Image with MemoryImageSource

```java
import java.net.URL;
import java.applet.Applet;
import java.awt.*;
import java.awt.image.*;

public class CropTestWithPG extends Applet {
    private Image im;
    private Image cropped;
    private int w = 75, h = 200;

    public void init() {
        MediaTracker mt  = new MediaTracker(this);
        URL     url = getClass().getResource("pic.jpg");

        try {
            im = createImage((ImageProducer)url.getContent());
            mt.addImage(im, 0);
            mt.waitForID(0);
        }
        catch(Exception e) { e.printStackTrace(); }

        int[] pixels = new int[w*h];
        PixelGrabber pg = new PixelGrabber(im, 90, 5, w, h,
                                    pixels, 0, w);
        try {
            pg.grabPixels();
        }
        catch(InterruptedException e) {
            e.printStackTrace();
        }
        ImageProducer ip = new MemoryImageSource(w,h,pixels,0,w);
        cropped = createImage(ip);
    }
    public void paint(Graphics g) {
        g.drawImage(im,0,0,this);
        g.drawImage(cropped,im.getWidth(this)+20,0,this);
    }
}
```

MemoryImageSource and Animations

For efficiency, methods, such as Graphics.drawImage(), that display images
do not reconstruct the image every time it is drawn. For instance, in Example 7-3
on page 196, the cropped image is produced exactly once; subsequent calls to
drawImage() in the applet's paint() draw the image from a cached
representation. If a change is made to the array of pixels used to construct the
cropped image, that change is not reflected the next time the image was drawn.

The `Image` class provides a `flush` method that flushes the resources associated with the image it represents, including the bits of the image—see Table 5-1 on page 104. As a result, if we wished to animate the cropped image in Example 7-3, we could modify the buffer, flush the image, and redraw. However, doing so would reconstruct the entire image, which is not very efficient when animating a small portion of a large image.

For the 1.1 version of the AWT, `MemoryImageSource` was equipped with the capability to animate the image it represents. The methods used to animate an image are listed in Table 7-4 on page 194.

`setAnimated()` specifies whether the image produced by the `MemoryImageSource` is a multiframe image or a static image. If `setAnimated()` is passed `true`, the image is animated and `MemoryImageSource` will pass `ImageConsumer.SINGLEFRAMEDONE` as the argument to its consumer's `imageComplete` method when the next frame of the image is loaded. On the other hand, if `setAnimated()` is passed `false`, then the image is static and the `MemoryImageSource` will pass `ImageConsumer.STATICIMAGEDONE` to its consumers when the image is fully loaded. See "Constants Passed to `ImageConsumer.imageComplete()`" on page 131 for the possible values passed to `ImageConsumer.imageComplete()`.

`setAnimated()` must be called before any images are created with the `MemoryImageSource`. As a general rule, it's best to invoke `setAnimated()` immediately after the `MemoryImageSource` is constructed.

The `newPixels` method, provided in five variations, signifies that some part of the buffer containing the bits of the image has changed, and the image should be reconstructed. The five variants of `newPixels()` allow different regions of the image to be specified for reconstruction and also enable a new color model or new pixel buffers to be specified. All of the `newPixels` methods do nothing unless `setAnimated(true)` has been called previously.

`setFullBufferUpdates()` is also passed a `boolean` argument, indicating whether or not the entire image should be reconstructed whenever a call is made to `newPixels()`. If `setFullBufferUpdates()` is passed `true`, then the entire image is reconstructed whenever `newPixels()` is invoked; if it is passed `false`, then only the region of the image specified to the call to `newPixels()` will be reconstructed.

Figure 7-4 shows an applet that uses an instance of `MemoryImageSource` to animate an image. The applet implements a thread that continuously animates the image by "boxing" the image in and out, the effect of which is shown in Figure 7-4. If you want to see the full effect of the applet, you'll want to run it from the CD.

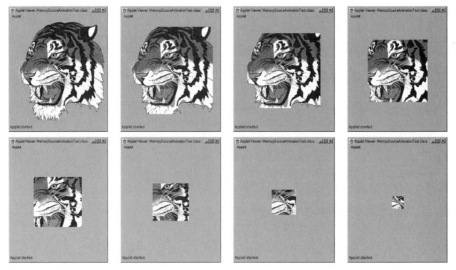

Figure 7-4 Using `MemoryImageSource` to Animate an Image

The applet is rather lengthy—it contains an inner class that extends `Thread` for animating the image and double buffers the image for smooth animation—so we'll highlight the code that uses the `MemoryImageSource` to animate the image before listing the entire applet. First, a general overview.

The applet tirelessly copies the next animation frame into an `integer` array that is simply named `pixels`. The array is associated with an instance of `MemoryImageSource`; the memory image source has been told, by invocation of `setAnimated(true)`, that the array represents an animated image. After copying the next animation frame, the applet invokes `newPixels()` for the memory image source and thus reconstructs the image from the array.

The applet keeps another `integer` array—`allPixels`—that contains the image in its entirety, thanks to an instance of `PixelGrabber`. Bits are copied from the `allPixels` array to the `pixels` array to build the next frame of the animation.

The applet's `init` method loads the image and uses an instance of
`MediaTracker` to wait for the image to fully load, so that the applet has
immediate access to the width and height of the image.

```
public class MemorySourceAnimationTest extends Applet {
    Image im, animatedImage, offscreen;
    MemoryImageSource mis;
    PixelGrabber pg;
    int imw, imh, allPixels[], pixels[];

    public void init() {
        MediaTracker mt  = new MediaTracker(this);
        URL url = getClass().getResource("tiger.gif");
        try {
            im = createImage((ImageProducer)url.getContent());
            mt.addImage(im, 0);
            mt.waitForID(0);
        }
        catch(Exception e) { e.printStackTrace(); }
        imw = im.getWidth(this);
        imh = im.getHeight(this);
        ...
```

After the image is fully loaded, the `pixels` and `allPixels` buffers are
allocated—`allPixels` contains all the pixels of the image at all times, and the
`pixels` array is passed to the `MemoryImageSource` constructor and thus used
for animating the image. Additionally, an offscreen buffer is instantiated for
double buffering.

```
        ...
        allPixels = new int[imw*imh];
        pixels    = new int[imw*imh];
        offscreen = createImage(imw, imh);
        ...
```

Then, the `MemoryImageSource` is instantiated. Notice that the array passed to
the constructor is an empty array; all of the values in the array are zero. As a
result, the image that is initially produced by the call to `createImage()` is also
empty.

After instantiation of the `MemoryImageSource`, a call is made to
`setAnimated()`, signifying that the image will be animated and not static.

```
        ...
        mis = new MemoryImageSource(imw,imh,pixels,0,imw);
        mis.setAnimated(true);
        animatedImage = createImage(mis);
        ...
```

Next, an instance of `PixelGrabber` fills the `allPixels` array with the pixels of the image. Finally, the `init` method winds up by creating an instance of `Animator`. `Animator` extends `Thread`, and its constructor is passed the number of intermediate images for boxing in and out. After the `Animator` is constructed, the thread is started, invoking the `Animator`'s run method.

```
    . . .
    try {
        pg = new PixelGrabber(im, 0, 0, imw, imh,
                             allPixels, 0, imw);
        pg.grabPixels();
    }
    catch(InterruptedException e) {
        e.printStackTrace();
    }
    Animator animator = new Animator(50);
    animator.start();
} // end of init method
```

The applet's `paint` method clears the offscreen buffer and draws the image produced by the `MemoryImageSource` into the offscreen buffer. Then, the offscreen buffer is blitted to the component's `Graphics`. Notice that it is only necessary to dispose of the offscreen `Graphics`, and not the `Graphics` passed to the `paint` method—see "Disposing of a Graphics" on page 40.

```
public void paint(Graphics g) {
    Graphics offg = null;
    Dimension size = getSize();

    try {
        offg = offscreen.getGraphics();
        offg.clearRect(0,0,size.width,size.height);
        offg.drawImage(animatedImage,0,0,this);
        g.drawImage(offscreen,0,0,this);
    }
    finally {
        offg.dispose();
    }
}
```

The `Animator` class instantiates another buffer, which is empty, for clearing out the image. The `run` method continuously invokes either `boxIn()` or `boxOut()`, depending upon the current state of the image, and pauses for a full second between calls.

```
class Animator extends Thread {
    private int numBoxes, curx, cury, curw, curh;
    private boolean showing = false;
    private Graphics g;
    private int[] emptyBuffer = new int[imw*imh];
```

```
        public Animator(int numBoxes) {
            this.numBoxes = numBoxes;
        }
        public void run() {
            while(true) {
                if(isShowing()) {
                    if(showing) boxIn();
                    else        boxOut();

                    showing = showing ? false : true;
                    pause(1000);
                }
            }
        }
    ...
```

boxOut() loops through the number of boxes specified in the Animator constructor, copying successively larger rectangles of pixels, starting at the center of the image, from the allPixels buffer to the pixels buffer. Recall that the pixels buffer was passed to the MemoryImageSource constructor, so when the call to newPixels() is made, it is the pixels buffer that is consulted for reconstructing the image.

boxOut() specifies that full buffer updates are not necessary. Since the current rectangle of pixels contains the previous rectangle, only the current rectangle needs to be updated.

The variant of newPixels() that is invoked in the while loop takes arguments specifying a rectangle of pixels to update. Only that portion of the image is reconstructed as a result of specifying that full buffer updates are not necessary.

After the largest rectangle has been updated, the entire image is copied to the pixels buffer, and newPixels() is invoked. The no-argument version of newPixels() updates the entire image, whether or not full buffer updates have been requested.

```
    private void boxOut() {
        mis.setFullBufferUpdates(false);

        curw = imw/numBoxes;
        curh = imh/numBoxes;

        while(curw < imw && curh < imh) {
            curx = imw/2 - curw/2;
            cury = imh/2 - curh/2;

            // copy each row of current rectangle from allPixels
            // to pixels buffer
```

```
        for(int i=0; i < curh; ++i) {
           System.arraycopy(allPixels,
                               (cury+i)*imw + curx, pixels,
                               (cury+i)*imw + curx, curw);
        }
        mis.newPixels(curx,cury,curw,curh);

        curw += imw/numBoxes;
        curh += imh/numBoxes;

        pause(50);
     }
     System.arraycopy(allPixels, 0, pixels, 0, imw*imh);
     mis.newPixels();
  }
```

boxIn() is the inverse of boxOut()—it copies successively smaller boxes, starting with the entire image, into the pixels array, and invokes newPixels() every time a new rectangle has been copied.

boxIn() invokes the no-argument version of newPixels() in a while loop, which reconstructs the entire image, no matter whether or not full buffer updates have been specified.

```
     private void boxIn() {
        curw = imw;
        curh = imh;

        while(curw > 0 && curh > 0) {
           curx = imw/2 - curw/2;
           cury = imh/2 - curh/2;

           // clear out all of the pixels in the pixels array
           System.arraycopy(emptyBuffer,0,pixels,0,imw*imh);

           // copy each row of current rectangle from allPixels
           // to pixels buffer
           for(int i=0; i < curh; ++i) {
              System.arraycopy(allPixels,
                                  (cury+i)*imw + curx, pixels,
                                  (cury+i)*imw + curx, curw);
           mis.newPixels();

           curw -= imw/numBoxes;
           curh -= imh/numBoxes;

           pause(50);
        }
        System.arraycopy(emptyBuffer,0,pixels,0,imw*imh);
        mis.newPixels(curx,cury,curw,curh);
     }
```

Every time through the loop, the `pixels` array is cleared out by copying the `emptyBuffer` into the `pixels` buffer. After the smallest box has been copied to the `pixels` buffer, it is erased by copying the `emptyBuffer` into the `pixels` buffer.

Before listing the entire applet, one concept should be reiterated. Notice that at no time is `repaint` ever invoked for the applet, yet, after each call to `newPixels()`, `repaint` gets called to redraw the reconstructed image.

Recall from "ImageObserver" on page 106 that all AWT components are image observers. Since `Applet` extends `java.awt.Panel`, it is therefore an image observer, which is verified by the fact that it is specified as the last argument to the call to `drawImage()` in the applet's `paint` method.

Furthermore, recall that when an image is reconstructed, a call is made to the `imageUpdate` method of any associated image observers.

Therefore, when the image is reproduced as a result of the call to `MemoryImageSource.newPixels()`, the applet's `imageUpdate()` is invoked. Finally, recall from "AWT Components as Image Observers" on page 123 that `java.awt.Component.imageUpdate()` immediately repaints the component whenever a new frame of a multiframe image is produced. Thus, the calls to `newPixels()` result in a call to the applet's `imageUpdate()`, which immediately repaints the applet.

The applet is listed in its entirety in Example 7-4.

Example 7-4 `MemorySourceAnimationTest` Applet

```
import java.net.URL;
import java.applet.Applet;
import java.awt.*;
import java.awt.image.*;

public class MemorySourceAnimationTest extends Applet {
    Image im, animatedImage, offscreen;
    MemoryImageSource mis;
    PixelGrabber pg;
    int imw, imh, allPixels[], pixels[];

    public void init() {
        MediaTracker mt  = new MediaTracker(this);
        URL     url = getClass().getResource("tiger.gif");

        try {
            im = createImage((ImageProducer)url.getContent());
            mt.addImage(im, 0);
            mt.waitForID(0);
```

```
        }
        catch(Exception e) { e.printStackTrace(); }

        imw = im.getWidth(this);
        imh = im.getHeight(this);

        allPixels = new int[imw*imh];
        pixels = new int[imw*imh];

        offscreen = createImage(imw, imh);

        mis = new MemoryImageSource(imw,imh,pixels,0,imw);
        mis.setAnimated(true);
        animatedImage = createImage(mis);

        try {
            pg = new PixelGrabber(im, 0, 0, imw, imh,
                                  allPixels, 0, imw);
            pg.grabPixels();
        }
        catch(InterruptedException e) {
            e.printStackTrace();
        }
        Animator animator = new Animator(25);
        animator.start();
    }
    public void update(Graphics g) {
        paint(g);
    }
    public void paint(Graphics g) {
        Graphics offg = null;
        Dimension size = getSize();
        try {
            offg = offscreen.getGraphics();
            offg.clearRect(0,0,size.width,size.height);
            offg.drawImage(animatedImage,0,0,this);
            g.drawImage(offscreen,0,0,this);
        }
        finally {
            offg.dispose();
        }
    }
    class Animator extends Thread {
        private int numBoxes, curx, cury, curw, curh;
        private boolean showing = false;
        private Graphics g;
        private int[] emptyBuffer = new int[imw*imh];

        public Animator(int numBoxes) {
            this.numBoxes = numBoxes;
        }
        public void run() {
            while(true) {
```

```
          if(isShowing()) {
              if(showing) boxIn();
              else    boxOut();

              showing = showing ? false : true;
              pause(1000);
          }
      }
}
private void boxIn() {
    curw = imw;
    curh = imh;

    while(curw > 0 && curh > 0) {
        curx = imw/2 - curw/2;
        cury = imh/2 - curh/2;

        System.arraycopy(emptyBuffer,0,pixels,0,imw*imh);

        for(int i=0; i < curh; ++i) {
            System.arraycopy(allPixels,
                        (cury+i)*imw + curx, pixels,
                        (cury+i)*imw + curx, curw);
        }
        mis.newPixels();

        curw -= imw/numBoxes;
        curh -= imh/numBoxes;

        pause(50);
    }
    System.arraycopy(emptyBuffer,0,pixels,0,imw*imh);
    mis.newPixels();
}
private void boxOut() {
    mis.setFullBufferUpdates(false);

    curw = imw/numBoxes;
    curh = imh/numBoxes;

    while(curw < imw && curh < imh) {
        curx = imw/2 - curw/2;
        cury = imh/2 - curh/2;

        for(int i=0; i < curh; ++i) {
            System.arraycopy(allPixels,
                        (cury+i)*imw + curx, pixels,
                        (cury+i)*imw + curx, curw);
        }
        mis.newPixels(curx,cury,curw,curh);

        curw += imw/numBoxes;
        curh += imh/numBoxes;
```

```
            pause(50);
        }
        System.arraycopy(allPixels, 0, pixels, 0, imw*imh);
        mis.newPixels();
    }
    private void pause(int milliseconds) {
        try {
            Thread.currentThread().sleep(milliseconds);
        }
        catch(InterruptedException e) {
            e.printStackTrace();
        }
    }
}
```

Summary

The AWT image package provides a number of different ways to manipulate images in addition to implementing filters. Images can be scaled on the fly by use of the Graphics class, or a scaled representation of an image can be obtained by invocation of Image.getScaledInstance().

Pixels can be grabbed from an image, and grabbed pixels can be turned into an image. You can then implement image filters that never involve the image filtering classes at all—simply grab all the pixels you need, modify them, and use MemoryImageSource to convert them into another image.

Even animations can be implemented rather painlessly with the animation capabilities of the MemoryImageSource class.

Support for image manipulation is extensive enough that there is often more than one way to modify an image with the same result. For example, in the previous chapter—"CropImageFilter" on page 135—a CropImageFilter is used to crop an image. The same thing is done in this chapter—"Memory Image Source" on page 193—by using the PixelGrabber and MemoryImageSource classes.

The java.awt.image package is arguably the most difficult aspect of the AWT at which to become truly proficient. Hopefully, the chapters on image loading, filtering, and manipulation will help to clearly enumerate the aspects of the package and how to best use its facilities.

Finally, *Graphic Java* contains more material on image manipulation that builds on this chapter and the previous two. The concepts presented in those chapters are used as the basis for exploring an in-depth double buffering framework, discussed in "Double Buffering" on page 789. Sprite animation is discussed in detail in "Sprite Animation" on page 813.

PART THREE

Events and Layout Management

CHAPTER

8

Inheritance-Based Event Handling (AWT 1.02 and Before)

This chapter covers the original AWT event model. With the advent of the 1.1 version of the JDK, the AWT has introduced a much-improved event model. We've left this chapter in Graphic Java, solely because the AWT still supports the old model. However, at some point in a future release of the AWT, the old model may cease to be supported. So, unless you are explicitly looking for information concerning the old model, we suggest that you skip this chapter and turn to the next, which discusses the new event model at length. We have also added a section at the end of this chapter that discusses the shortcomings of the original model and how they are rectified by the new model. This chapter will be removed in a subsequent version of Graphic Java.

Modern graphical user interfaces are typically event driven, meaning they spend much of their time idling, waiting for an event to occur; when an event occurs, an event handler responds to the event. Applets and applications developed with the AWT are no different, so in this chapter, we introduce event handling in AWT components and offer advice on a variety of points, including when to override event handling methods and when to handle an event or pass it on. We also introduce several applets to illustrate event handling techniques, such as sensing double clicks, managing action events, and generating and delivering events to custom components.

The Original AWT Event Model

As is the case with nearly all object-oriented user interface toolkits, the AWT is event driven. Actually, since the AWT uses a peer approach, the underlying event subsystem is native to the platform on which an applet or application is running. So, for instance, if an applet is executed under Motif, it uses the X Window event handling system. Our focus, however, is not on the underlying native event system but on the AWT layer through which we respond to events.

It should be noted that this chapter pertains to the original, inheritance-based event model, for AWT 1.0 and AWT 1.02. The current version[1] of the AWT has a new event model that is delegation based instead of inheritance based and is much improved over the original model. We suggest that you use the new event model instead of the original model. The AWT is backward compatible with the original event model, and therefore we have left this chapter, which was in the first edition of *Graphic Java*, intact.

The delegation event model is discussed in the next chapter. If you must use the old, inheritance-based model, then this chapter is for you; if you can use the delegation event model, then you should skip to the next chapter.

Overriding Event Handling Methods

Essentially, event handling using the original AWT event model is a fairly simple proposition: when an event occurs inside a component, a method of that component is invoked. If you want the component to respond to an event, you simply override the appropriate method. For instance, a component's void setSize(int w, int h) method is invoked when the component is resized. If you wanted to take some action when a resize event occurs, you would override setSize() and take care of business. There are a number of component methods which, like setSize(), are called in response to some event. Table 8-1 shows a partial list of such methods.

It is common to override the first group of methods in Table 8-1 when developing custom components. The methods in the second group in the table represent more obscure events, such as when a component needs to be laid out—see "Components, Containers, and Layout Managers" on page 327. It is rarely necessary to override the methods associated with these events. Of course, by overriding any of the methods in Table 8-1, you are rewriting what

1. From version 1.1 and later.

Table 8-1 Event-Driven Methods Used in Components

Method	Event
Component Methods Frequently Overridden	
`void setSize(int w,int h)`	Component has been resized.
`void setBounds(int x,int y,int w,int h)`	Component resized and/or moved.
`void paint(Graphics g)`	Component needs to be painted.
`void update(Graphics g)`	By default erase, then repaint.
`void addNotify()`	Peer created.
Component Methods Infrequently Overridden	
`void setLocation(int x, int y)`	Component moved to x,y location.
`void layout()`	Component needs to be laid out.
`void validate()`	If invalid, lay out.

the component does by default. As a result, you will often see event handler methods that call the superclass version before adding embellishments:

```
public addNotify() {    // Default version creates the peer
    super.addNotify();  // Peer created by this call
}
```

Propagated Events

The events discussed above occur in a component and are handled (or ignored) by the component in which the event occurred. Such events are of concern only to the component in which they occurred.

A second group of events is referred to as *propagated* events; whenever a propagated event occurs in a component, the component's `handleEvent(Event)` method is invoked. The component's `handleEvent` method may choose to propagate the event to its container or handle the event entirely on its own.

Note the distinction between propagated events and the events listed in Table 8-1. Propagated events are always handled by a component's `handleEvent` method, which is passed a `java.awt.Event`. Propagated events may be propagated to the component's container; if so, the container's `handleEvent` method is invoked and the `java.awt.Event` is passed along.

Since propagated events involve a java.awt.Event, they are generically referred to as AWT events. The rest of this chapter will only be concerned with such events.

Event Type Constants

Every java.awt.Event has an id field whose value indicates the type of event that has occurred. Typically, the first thing a component's handleEvent method does is to check the event's id field to determine the type of event. For instance, a handleEvent method concerned with mouse events might look something like this:

```
public boolean handleEvent(Event event) {
    if(event.id == Event.MOUSE_DOWN) {
        // react to mouse down
        return true; // event fully handled, do not propagate
    }
    else if(event.id == Event.MOUSE_UP) {
        // react to mouse up
        return true; // event fully handled, do not propagate
    }
    // let superclass handle event and decide to propagate
    return super.handleEvent(event);
}
```

Notice that this example returns true if the event is a mouse up or mouse down event, signifying that we have fully handled the event and therefore do not wish to propagate the event to the component's container. If the event is not a mouse up or mouse down, we give the superclass a chance to handle the event. If we were to return false, the event would be propagated directly to the component's container and the superclass would never have a chance to handle the event. Therefore, it is always a good idea to have overridden handleEvent methods return super.handleEvent(event) if they have not fully handled the event, instead of propagating the event directly to the component's container.

Table 8-2 shows the complete list of java.awt.Event type constants.

AWT TIP ...

Avoid Returning false From a handleEvent Method

Returning false from a handleEvent method propagates the event to the component's container without giving the component's superclass a chance to process the event. Therefore, it is a good idea to avoid returning false from a handleEvent method. Instead, if a class has not fully handled a particular event, it should always give its superclass a chance to process the event and let the superclass decide whether to propagate the event to the component's container. Even if you know that your superclass is not interested in a particular type of event, there are no guarantees that the superclass will not be modified in the future to process an event that you are not interested in.

Table 8-2 `java.awt.Event` Constants

Event Constants
Window Event Constants
WINDOW_DESTROY
WINDOW_EXPOSE
WINDOW_ICONIFY
WINDOW_DEICONIFY
WINDOW_MOVED
Keyboard Event Constants
KEY_PRESS
KEY_RELEASE
KEY_ACTION
KEY_ACTION_RELEASE
Mouse Event Constants
MOUSE_DOWN, MOUSE_UP
MOUSE_MOVE
MOUSE_ENTER, MOUSE_EXIT
MOUSE_DRAG
Scrollbar Event Constants
SCROLL_LINE_UP, SCROLL_LINE_DOWN
SCROLL_PAGE_UP, SCROLL_PAGE_DOWN
SCROLL_ABSOLUTE
List Event Constants

Table 8-2 `java.awt.Event` **Constants (Continued)**

Event Constants
`LIST_SELECT, LIST_DESELECT`

Action Event Constants
`ACTION_EVENT`
`LOAD_FILE`
`SAVE_FILE`
`GOT_FOCUS, LOST_FOCUS`

Propagated Event Handler Methods

Checking against the `id` field of an event to decipher the type of event in overridden `handleEvent` methods is rather ugly and requires keeping track of all the event constants listed in Table 8-2, which is not very object oriented.[2] As a result, `java.awt.Component` implements a `handleEvent` method that deciphers the type of event and invokes one of a number of convenience methods. Table 8-3 lists all of the convenience methods that are invoked by `java.awt.Component.handleEvent()`.

Table 8-3 Propagated Event Handler Convenience Methods

Method	Event
`boolean action (Event, Object)`	An action event
`boolean mouseUp (Event,int,int)`	Mouse up
`boolean mouseDown (Event,int,int)`	Mouse down
`boolean mouseDrag (Event,int,int)`	Mouse drag
`boolean mouseMove (Event,int,int)`	Mouse move
`boolean mouseEnter (Event,int,int)`	Mouse entered component
`boolean mouseExit (Event,int,int)`	Mouse exited component
`boolean keyUp (Event,int)`	Key up
`boolean keyDown (Event,int)`	Key down
`boolean gotFocus (Event,Object)`	Component has focus
`boolean lostFocus (Event,Object)`	Component lost focus

When handling propagated events, you can choose to do one of the following:

2. See Meyer, Bertrand. *Object Oriented Software Construction,* section 10.2.2. Prentice Hall, 1988.

- Override `handleEvent()` and check against the `id` field of the event to determine the type of event
- Override one of the convenience methods listed in Table 8-3

Let's take a look at the implementation of `Component.handleEvent(Event)` to see exactly how the convenience methods are invoked:

```
// java.awt.Component.handleEvent()
public boolean handleEvent(Event evt) {
    switch (evt.id) {
        case Event.MOUSE_ENTER:
            return mouseEnter(evt, evt.x, evt.y);

        case Event.MOUSE_EXIT:
            return mouseExit(evt, evt.x, evt.y);

        case Event.MOUSE_MOVE:
            return mouseMove(evt, evt.x, evt.y);

        case Event.MOUSE_DOWN:
            return mouseDown(evt, evt.x, evt.y);

        case Event.MOUSE_DRAG:
            return mouseDrag(evt, evt.x, evt.y);

        case Event.MOUSE_UP:
            return mouseUp(evt, evt.x, evt.y);

        case Event.KEY_PRESS:
        case Event.KEY_ACTION:
            return keyDown(evt, evt.key);

        case Event.KEY_RELEASE:
        case Event.KEY_ACTION_RELEASE:
            return keyUp(evt, evt.key);

        case Event.ACTION_EVENT:
            return action(evt, evt.arg);
        case Event.GOT_FOCUS:
            return gotFocus(evt, evt.arg);
        case Event.LOST_FOCUS:
            return lostFocus(evt, evt.arg);
    }
    return false;
}
```

`java.awt.Component.handleEvent(Event)` simply deciphers the type of event and then invokes a convenience method. All of the convenience methods are implemented in the `Component` class as *no-ops*; they exist solely for you to override them and give them some teeth.

Propagated Events Propagate Outward

Applets often have a fairly complex nested layout in which various extensions of `Panel` are nested within one another and positioned according to the container's layout manager. Indeed, this is the core of AWT development—an art that we explore throughout this book.

Events are propagated from the component in which the event occurred to the outermost container. However, any component along the chain of containers can halt the propagation of the event if its `handleEvent` method completely handles the event and returns `true`.

Overriding Propagated Event Handlers

As we discussed previously, methods that handle a propagated event return a `boolean` value, which indicates whether the event was handled or not. A `true` return value indicates that the event has been handled and should not be propagated to the component's container. A `false` return value signals that the event has not been handled completely and should be forwarded to the component's container. Table 8-4 summarizes the choices a component has when confronted with a propagated event.

Table 8-4 Component Choices When Handling Propagated Events

A Component Can Do This With a Propagated Event...	Then `handleEvent()`...
Propagate event to its container.	Returns `false`.
Not propagate event to its container.	Returns `true`.
Let superclass handle and decide to propagate.	Returns `super.handleEvent(event)`.

Whether you override `handleEvent()` or override one of the convenience methods listed in Table 8-3 on page 214, you must decide the manner in which you will return from the propagated event handler. In either case, if you have completely handled the event, then you can just return `true`, signifying the event is completely handled and should not be propagated. If you have not completely handled the event, then there are two guidelines to follow, as listed in Table 8-5.

Table 8-5 Event Handling Guidelines

If You Have Not Completely Handled the Event and You Have...	Then...
Overridden `handleEvent()`.	Call `super.handleEvent(event)` and let the superclass determine whether or not to propagate the event.
Overridden one of the convenience methods in Table 8-3.	Return the superclass implementation of the convenience method.

Let's look at the rationale for these guidelines. First, as we've already mentioned, it's preferable when using `handleEvent()` to leave the decision to propagate the event to the superclass's `handleEvent()`. It is just good practice to give the superclass a chance to handle the event. Additionally, when overriding a convenience method, it is also a good idea to give the superclass a crack at the event and let it determine whether to propagate the event.

One thing you don't want to do is to return `super.handleEvent(event)` from one of the convenience methods. If you were to override `mouseDown()`, for example, and return `super.handleEvent()`, you might wind up in an infinite loop. If none of your superclasses override `handleEvent()`, you will invoke `Component.handleEvent()`, which detects the mouse down event and invokes `mouseDown()`, putting you right back where you started. As a rule of thumb, when overriding the convenience methods, it is best to propagate the event directly to the container.

To highlight AWT event handling in action, we will provide a series of small applets in the rest of this chapter that illustrate various features and nuances of the AWT event model.

Event Modifier Constants

In addition to an `id` field, each `java.awt.Event` also contains a `modifier` field that provides additional information about the event. For example, you might want to know which key or which mouse button triggered an event. The `Event` class defines a handful of constants that provide such information. Table 8-6 lists the `modifier` constants. We'll show how to use these later in this chapter, but it's useful to have them handy for reference.

Table 8-6 Event Modifiers

Event Modifier Constant	Type	Meaning
ALT_MASK	Keyboard	ALT key is down.
ALT_MASK	Mouse Button	Button 2 is pressed.
CTRL_MASK	Keyboard	CONTROL key is down.
DOWN	Function Key	DOWN key is pressed.
END	Function Key	END key is pressed.
F1 - F12	Function Key	FUNCTION key 1 – 12 is pressed.
HOME	Function Key	HOME key is pressed.
LEFT	Function Key	LEFT key is pressed.
META_MASK	Keyboard	META key is down.
META_MASK	Mouse Button	Button 3 is pressed.
PGDOWN	Function Key	PAGE DOWN key is pressed.
PGUP	Function Key	PAGE UP key is pressed.
RIGHT	Function Key	RIGHT key is pressed.
SHIFT_MASK	Keyboard	SHIFT key or caps lock is down.
UP	Function Key	UP key is pressed.

Mouse Button Events

To illustrate handling mouse button events, we'll describe a MouseSensorApplet. The MouseSensorApplet uses a BorderLayout layout manager and places an instance of a MouseSensorCanvas in the center of the applet. Remember that an applet is an extension of Container, so components can be added to an applet. (Since most of the applets in this chapter simply place a blank canvas inside an applet, we won't show pictures of them unless there's something to illustrate.) The MouseSensorCanvas class overrides the mouseDown(), mouseUp(), and mouseDrag() convenience methods from java.awt.Component. It also implements a whichMouseButton method to print the mouse button that initiated the event. Example 8-1 shows the implementation for MouseSensorApplet.

Example 8-1 MouseSensorApplet Class Listing

```
import java.applet.Applet;
import java.awt.*;

public class MouseSensorApplet extends Applet {
    public void init() {
        setLayout(new BorderLayout());
        add(new MouseSensorCanvas(), "Center");
    }
```

```
    }

    class MouseSensorCanvas extends Canvas {
        public boolean mouseDown(Event event, int x, int y) {
            System.out.println(whichMouseButton(event) + ":  Down");
            return true;
        }
        public boolean mouseUp(Event event, int x, int y) {
            System.out.println(whichMouseButton(event) + ":  Up");
            return true;
        }
        public boolean mouseDrag(Event event, int x, int y) {
            System.out.println(whichMouseButton(event) + ":  Drag");
            return true;
        }
        private String whichMouseButton(Event event) {
            String s = new String("Mouse Button 1");

            if((event.modifiers & Event.META_MASK) != 0)
                s = "Mouse Button 2";
            else if((event.modifiers & Event.ALT_MASK) != 0)
                s = "Mouse Button 3";

            return s;
        }
    }
```

Notice that each of our convenience methods (`mouseUp()`, `mouseDown()` and `mouseDrag()`) prints information about the event, with the help of `whichMouseButton()`. These methods return `true`, indicating that the event is fully handled and should not be propagated to the container, which in this case is the applet.

The `whichMouseButton` method does the work of distinguishing between the different mouse buttons:

```
    private String whichMouseButton(Event event) {
        String s = new String("Mouse Button 1");

        if((event.modifiers & Event.META_MASK) != 0)
            s = "Mouse Button 2";
        else if((event.modifiers & Event.ALT_MASK) != 0)
            s = "Mouse Button 3";

        return s;
    }
```

To detect mouse button 2 and 3, this method simply uses a bitwise AND to combine the `modifiers` field of the event with the AWT `Event` class constants, `ALT_MASK` and `META_MASK`.

Note that we could have overridden `handleEvent()` and checked the `id` field of the event in order to sense mouse button events, but we have chosen to override convenience methods instead.

NOTE: In the JDK 1.0.2 release, there is a bug in the Windows 95 version of the AWT in which a mouse up with button 1 is detected as a mouse up with button 2.[3]

Of Mice and Buttons

Different platforms typically use different types of mice. Macintosh systems normally use a one-button mouse, PCs a two- or three-button mouse, and SPARC® systems a three-button mouse. Java deals with these differences by assuming that all mice have one button. For example, the AWT distinguishes only one mouse up event. Correspondingly, there is only one method (`mouseUp()`) to account for this. There's no `mouseUp1()`, `mouseUp2()`, `mouseUp3()` to account for the different mouse buttons that might initiate an event. This is also the case for mouse events such as a mouse down or mouse drag.

As we've seen in the `whichMouseButton` method above, the mechanism employed to determine which mouse button triggered an event is to look at the event's `modifier` field. If the `modifier` bit in `Event.META_MASK` is non-zero, then we know that mouse button 2 initiated the event, while an `ALT_MASK` represents mouse button 3. Therefore, on a system with a one-button mouse, mouse button 2 can be simulated by holding down the Meta key when clicking the mouse, and mouse button 3 can be simulated by holding down the Alt key.

There is no way to distinguish between a mouse button other than button #1 being pressed vs. pressing mouse button #1 and the suitable key. In other words, you cannot tell whether a one-button mouse has been pressed with the Meta key held down vs. button #2 on a two-button mouse with no modifier keys.

Monitoring Mouse Events

In the next applet, we'll illustrate monitoring mouse events such as the mouse moving, entering, and exiting an applet. This particular applet—called `EventMonitorApplet`—also monitors mouse up and down events and prints information about each event. `EventMonitorApplet` extends the `Applet` class (as do all applets). It includes an `EventPrinter` class that checks to see if an

---

3.   Note to all those left-handers out there: We generically refer to mouse buttons 1, 2, and 3 rather than left, middle, and right. Mouse button 1 represents the primary mouse button.

event is a mouse event, and if so, its `print` method prints which mouse event occurred. The `EventMonitorApplet` includes an instance of `EventPrinter` that is both `public` and `static`. It is `public` because both `EventMonitor` and `EventPrinter` classes use it. It is `static` because only one `EventPrinter` is required. Note that this applet is set up just like the `MouseSensorApplet`. It creates an applet, sets its layout to `BorderLayout`, and then positions an instance of a class that extends `Canvas` in the center of the applet. Example 8-2 shows the `EventMonitorApplet` in its entirety.

Example 8-2 EventMonitorApplet Class Listing

```java
import java.applet.Applet;
import java.awt.*;

public class EventMonitorApplet extends Applet {
    public static EventPrinter printer = new EventPrinter();

    public void init() {
        setLayout(new BorderLayout());
        add(new EventMonitor(), "Center");
    }
    public boolean handleEvent(Event event) {
        System.out.print("APPLET:   ");
        printer.print(event);
        System.out.println();
        return true;
    }
}

class EventMonitor extends Canvas {
    public boolean handleEvent(Event event) {
        System.out.print("CANVAS:   ");
        EventMonitorApplet.printer.print(event);
        System.out.println();
        return true;
    }
}

class EventPrinter {
    public void print(Event event) {
        String s = null;

        if(event.id == Event.MOUSE_DOWN)      s = "Mouse Down";
        else if(event.id == Event.MOUSE_UP)   s = "Mouse Up";
        else if(event.id == Event.MOUSE_DRAG) s = "Mouse Drag";
        else if(event.id == Event.MOUSE_MOVE) s = "Mouse Move";
        else if(event.id == Event.MOUSE_EXIT) s = "Mouse Exit";
        else if(event.id == Event.MOUSE_ENTER) s = "Mouse Enter";

        if(s != null)
```

```
        System.out.print(s);
    else
        System.out.print(event.id);
    }
}
```

The `EventMonitor` class, which extends `Canvas`, expands to fill the entire applet. The fact that the `EventMonitor` canvas expands to consume the entire applet area is the by-product of adding it centered in a `BorderLayout`. We'll talk more about `BorderLayout` and layout managers in general in—the *Components, Containers, and Layout Managers* chapter on page 327.

`EventMonitorApplet` and `EventMonitor` both override the `handleEvent` method, causing two things to occur when a mouse action takes place:

- Calls `System.out.print` to print `APPLET:` or `CANVAS:`, respectively
- Calls the `print` method in the `EventPrinter` class to print the mouse event that occurred (e.g., `MOUSE_UP`, `MOUSE_DOWN`)

So, when dragging the mouse over the applet, you'll see output similar to this:

```
APPLET:   Mouse Enter
CANVAS:   Mouse Enter
CANVAS:   Mouse Move
CANVAS:   Mouse Move
CANVAS:   Mouse Move
CANVAS:   Mouse Down
CANVAS:   Mouse Up
CANVAS:   Mouse Move
CANVAS:   Mouse Move
CANVAS:   Mouse Exit
APPLET:   Mouse Exit
```

The `EventMonitorApplet` illustrates that events are propagated from the component in which the event occurred to outermost container. Our containment strategy here is easy to expose: We have a `Canvas` (`EventMonitor`) contained inside an `Applet` (`EventMonitorApplet`). Both of them have overridden `boolean handleEvent(Event)`, ready to deal with whatever events come their way.

Of course, the return value of the `EventMonitor` `handleEvent` method determines whether `EventMonitorApplet` sees events that were generated in `EventMonitor`. In the previous output, the only events that `EventMonitorApplet` sees are mouse enter and mouse exit events; all the rest are effectively gobbled up by `EventMonitor`. (Note that a bug under Windows 95 results in some events being propagated up to the `EventMonitorApplet`, even though they are never explicitly propagated.)

If, for instance, the `EventMonitor` `handleEvent` method returned `false`, then events would be passed to the container's (`EventMonitorApplet`) `handleEvent` method. The applet output would change to look something like this:

```
APPLET:   Mouse Enter
CANVAS:   Mouse Enter
APPLET:   Mouse Enter
CANVAS:   Mouse Move
APPLET:   Mouse Move
CANVAS:   Mouse Down
APPLET:   Mouse Down
CANVAS:   Mouse Up
APPLET:   Mouse Up
CANVAS:   Mouse Down
APPLET:   Mouse Down
CANVAS:   Mouse Up
APPLET:   Mouse Up
CANVAS:   Mouse Move
APPLET:   Mouse Move
CANVAS:   Mouse Exit
APPLET:   Mouse Exit
APPLET:   Mouse Exit
```

Sensing Double Clicking

Sensing that the mouse has been *double-clicked* requires use of the `Event` `clickCount` field. To illustrate this, we've written the `DoubleClickApplet` program, which is set up like the previous event applets in this chapter. Example 8-3 shows the `DoubleClickApplet` code.

Example 8-3 `DoubleClickApplet` Class Listing

```java
import java.applet.Applet;
import java.awt.*;

public class DoubleClickApplet extends Applet {
    public void init() {
        setLayout(new BorderLayout());
        add(new DoubleClickCanvas(), "Center");
    }
}

class DoubleClickCanvas extends Canvas {
    public boolean mouseDown(Event event, int x, int y) {
        if(event.clickCount == 2)
            System.out.println("Double click");
        return true;
    }
}
```

The overridden `mouseDown` method simply checks to see if the `Event` `clickCount` field equals 2. If so, `mouseDown()` informs us that a double click has occurred. Regardless of whether a double click has occurred or not, `mouseDown()` returns `true` because our simple-minded applet is not prepared to deal with a propagated event.

There's an interesting aside here. Note that the location of the cursor seems to have no bearing upon whether or not `clickCount` is advanced. If you click the mouse at one location and then hastily move to another location and click again, it will register as a double click. This may lead one to the AWT source in search of an algorithm for advancing the `clickCount`; we do have the AWT source, after all. It may be hard to believe at first, but `clickCount` is not set anywhere other than at construction time, when it is set to zero; who, then, is responsible for advancing `clickCount`? The answer lies in the component's peer—the unseen laborer that implements much of the functionality of the AWT. Unless we have the source for the peers, which we do not, then we have no way of ever knowing the exact criterion for advancing `clickCount`.

Action Events

Action events are generated by the following classes:

- `Button`
- `Checkbox`
- `Choice`
- `List`
- `MenuItem`
- `TextField`

All of the components listed above are capable of generating action events, as you can see from Figure 7-5. Note that action events under the original event model do not necessarily equate to an `ActionEvent` under the delegation event model— see "Semantic Events" on page 269.[4]

`ActionTest` creates one of each of these AWT components. The unique characteristic of these AWT components is that *only* `Button`, `Checkbox`, `TextField`, `Choice`, `MenuItem`, **and** `List` components generate events that are routed through the `Component` `action` method. (In contrast, an event from any

---

4.   Specifically, checkboxes and choices generate item events instead of action events.

Figure 7-5 Action Events
Action events are events generated by selecting choice items,
checkboxes, buttons, or menu items, by entering a carriage
return in a textfield, or by double-clicking an item in a list.

other component will never result in a call to the Component action method.)
Now, let's look at ActionTest in Example 8-4 and then discuss the
ActionTest.action method.

Example 8-4 ActionTest Class Listing

```java
import java.awt.*;

class ActionTest extends Frame {
    Button    button = new Button("Cancel");
    Checkbox  checkbox = new Checkbox(
                            "Something to check about");
    TextField textfield = new TextField(25);
    Choice    choice = new Choice();
    List       list = new List();
    MenuItem  quitItem = new MenuItem("quit");

    static public void main(String args[]) {
        Frame frame = new ActionTest();
        frame.reshape(100,100,200,200);
        frame.show();
    }
    public ActionTest() {
        super("Action Test");

        MenuBar menubar  = new MenuBar();
        Menu    fileMenu = new Menu("File");

        fileMenu.add("menu item");
        fileMenu.add(quitItem);
        menubar.add(fileMenu);
```

```
        setMenuBar(menubar);

        choice.addItem("One");
        choice.addItem("Two");
        choice.addItem("Three");
        choice.addItem("Four");

        list.addItem("item One");
        list.addItem("item Two");
        list.addItem("item Three");
        list.addItem("item Four");
        list.addItem("item Five");
        list.addItem("item Six");

        setLayout(new GridLayout(0,1));
        add(button);
        add(checkbox);
        add(list);
        add(textfield);
        add(choice);
    }
    public boolean action(Event event, Object what) {
        if(event.target == quitItem) {
            System.exit(0);
        }
        System.out.print(event.target.getClass().getName());
        System.out.println(" " + what.getClass().getName() +
                            "= " + what);
        return true;
    }
}
```

The `action` method is passed an `event` and an object we have named `what`. This second argument differs according to the type of component that triggered the event. For example, if `event` is from an instance of `Button`, then `what` will be a `String` containing the label of the button. Table 8-7 shows how the value of the second argument is set, based on the component that generates the `event`.

For example, output from the ActionTest application[5] looks like this:

```
java.awt.TextField java.lang.String= text
java.awt.Choice java.lang.String= Three
java.awt.Checkbox java.lang.Boolean= true
java.awt.Button java.lang.String= Cancel
java.awt.MenuItem java.lang.String= menu item
java.awt.List java.lang.String= item One
```

5. ActionTest is an application because it has a menubar, which cannot be added to an applet.

Table 8-7 Value of the what Argument in the action Method

If the event Is From an Instance of...	Then the Second Argument is a...
Button	String with the text of label of the button.
Checkbox	Boolean value, which is true if the checkbox is checked and false if it is unchecked.
Choice	String that represents the text displayed in the choice.
List	String representing the item that was double-clicked.
MenuItem	String representing the menu item selected.
TextField	String representing the text in the text field.

A TextField generates an action event *only* after a carriage return. (The 1.0.2 version of the AWT provides no mechanism for being notified when a character other than a carriage return is typed into a text field.) Action events for Button, CheckBox, Choice, or MenuItem are generated when each is selected with the mouse. Finally, an action event is generated by double-clicking an item in a List.

Identifying Components by Label — Just Say No

It is standard AWT practice to check against the labels of certain components (in particular, buttons) to determine the component with which an event is associated. For instance, the following applet displays three buttons and uses the labels of the buttons to determine which one triggered an action event:

```java
import java.applet.Applet;
import java.awt.*;

public class ButtonActionApplet extends Applet {
    public void init() {
        Button buttonOne   = new Button("Button One");
        Button buttonTwo   = new Button("Button Two");
        Button buttonThree = new Button("Button Three");

        add(buttonOne);
        add(buttonTwo);
        add(buttonThree);
    }
    public boolean action(Event event, Object what) {
        if(what.equals("Button One"))
```

```
            System.out.println("Button One");
        if(what.equals("Button Two"))
            System.out.println("Button Two");
        if(what.equals("Button Three"))
            System.out.println("Button Three");

        return true;
    }
}
```

While this applet produces the desired effect, namely, it prints the identity of the button activated, it is fraught with difficulties. First of all, the labels of the buttons may very well change over time, causing modification of the action method each and every time a button has its label changed. This is not a consideration for a toy applet like the one above; however, in the real world it may be unacceptable for a complex applet or application to keep button labels in synch with event handling methods. Furthermore, identifying components by their labels has serious implications for internationalization.

A much better approach is to identify components by reference, instead of their labels, as depicted by the revised applet below:

```
import java.applet.Applet;
import java.awt.*;

public class ButtonActionByRefApplet extends Applet {
    private Button buttonOne   = new Button("Button One");
    private Button buttonTwo   = new Button("Button Two");
    private Button buttonThree = new Button("Button Three");

    public void init() {
        add(buttonOne);
        add(buttonTwo);
        add(buttonThree);
    }
    public boolean action(Event event, Object what) {
        if(event.target == buttonOne)
            System.out.println(buttonOne.getLabel());
        if(event.target == buttonTwo)
            System.out.println(buttonTwo.getLabel());
        if(event.target == buttonThree)
            System.out.println(buttonThree.getLabel());

        return true;
    }
}
```

Notice that we have moved the declarations for the buttons from being local to `init()` to private members of the class. Second, in the `action` method, we check the target of the event against the button references to identify which button triggered the action event.

This approach ensures that the applet continues to function properly even if we change the labels of the buttons. Note also that we get the label from the buttons themselves to print out the buttons' identity, instead of hardcoding the button labels in the `action` method.

AWT TIP

Identify Components by Reference, Not by Their Labels

It is standard AWT practice to identify components by their labels when handling certain events. This has some serious implications for maintaining applets and applications, since the methods that identify components must be kept in synch with the component's labels. A better approach is to identify components by reference.

Shortcomings of the Inheritance-Based Event Model

The original event model discussed in this chapter was appropriate for small applets with simple event handling needs, but the model did not scale well for a number of reasons, a few of which we will take the time to briefly explore. The new event model, covered in the next chapter, is delegation-based as opposed to the old model, which was inheritance-based. The inheritance-based model required a component to be extended in order to handle events. Example 8-5 is a simple example of the original event handling mechanism in action; `MouseCanvas` extends `Canvas` and overrides `handleEvent()` to process mouse down events, and `mouseUp()` to process mouse up events.

Example 8-5 `CanvasEventExample`—An Example of Inheritance-Based Event Model

```
import java.applet.Applet;
import java.awt.*;

public class CanvasEventExample extends Applet {
    public void init() {
        MouseCanvas canvas = new MouseCanvas();
        setLayout(new BorderLayout());
        add(canvas, "Center");
    }
}
```

```
class MouseCanvas extends Canvas {
    public boolean handleEvent(Event event) {
        if(event.id == Event.MOUSE_DOWN) {
            System.out.println("Mouse Down!");
            return true;  // event fully handled, don't propagate
        }
        return false; // event not fully handled, propagate
    }
    public boolean mouseUp(Event event, int x, int y) {
        System.out.println("Mouse Up!");
        return true;
    }
}
```

Propagation of Events

The original event model required you to determine whether or not an event was propagated to its container, by way of returning a `boolean` value from overridden event handling methods. `handleEvent()` and the related convenience methods (such as `mouseDown()`, `mouseUp()`, etc.) return a `boolean` value indicating whether or not the event will be propagated to the component's container. A `true` return value indicates that the event was fully handled by the component and therefore the event is not propagated, whereas `false` means that the event was not fully handled and should be propagated.

Propagation seems like a reasonable design; however, the interaction between propagation and the component hierarchy often resulted in subtle bugs. For instance, our applet in Example 8-5 never has its `mouseUp` method invoked because we have overridden `handleEvent()`. `Component.handleEvent()` dispatches events to convenience methods (like `mouseUp()`), and since we've overridden `Component.handleEvent()`, that dispatching is no longer invoked. The fix is to have `handleEvent()` return `super.handleEvent(event)`, so that the dispatching can take place, as we've done in Example 8-6.

Example 8-6 `CanvasEventExample` Revisited

```
import java.applet.Applet;
import java.awt.*;

public class CanvasEventExample extends Applet {
    public void init() {
        MouseCanvas canvas = new MouseCanvas();
        setLayout(new BorderLayout());
        add(canvas, "Center");
    }
}

class MouseCanvas extends Canvas {
```

```
    public boolean handleEvent(Event event) {
        if(event.id == Event.MOUSE_DOWN) {
            System.out.println("Mouse Down!");
            return true;  // event fully handled, don't propagate
        }
        return super.handleEvent(event);
    }
    public boolean mouseUp(Event event, int x, int y) {
        System.out.println("Mouse Up!");
        return true;
    }
}
```

As an aside, this is a classic case of inheritance breaking encapsulation. Classes that are unrelated by way of inheritance use each other only by accessing each other's *interface* (public methods). However, classes that are an extension of a (base) class must know a good deal[6] about the *implementation* of the base class they are extending. In this case, extensions of java.awt.Component must know that Component.handleEvent() dispatches events to convenience methods, in order to determine how to return from overridden handleEvent methods.

Returning false instead of super.handleEvent(event) is a common error among those new to the AWT. In fact, we felt compelled enough to write an AWT Tip on page 213 warning against the evils of depriving your superclass a crack at handling events.

OO TIP

Prefer Composition Over Inheritance

Instead of extending a class in order to reuse its functionality, it is sometimes preferable to delegate to an enclosed instance of the would-be base class; a technique known as composition. Composition results in less surface area than inheritance because inheritance requires extensions to be intimately familiar with the implementation of their superclass. Composition, on the other hand, requires that the delegator manipulate the delegate via the delegate's public interface (public methods) only, resulting in fewer dependencies and looser coupling between the classes in question.

---

6. How much one class needs to know about another class is referred to as *surface area*.

Inheritance Required

Requiring event handling to be implemented via inheritance can result in a plethora of extensions for functionally identical components that require different event handling algorithms. One can perhaps rightly argue that "plethora" is an exaggeration; however, it is a misplaced use of inheritance that requires you to extend a class in order to change a feature (attributes and/or methods) that varies between individual objects of the same type at runtime—`java.awt.Container` is guilty of this, by requiring you to extend it in order to change its insets. `Component`, by the same token, requires you to override `handleEvent()` (or one of the convenience methods) to handle events. The problem is greatly compounded when the feature is a candidate for frequent change, as is certainly true for event handling.

Embedding Event Handling in Component Classes

With inheritance-based event handling, event handling code becomes hardwired to a single component extension. It is interesting to note that the original designers of the AWT employed the strategy pattern for layout managers, thus decoupling containers from layout management, but neglected to take the same approach for event handling. Now, however, with the advent of the delegation-based event model, both layout management and event handling are accomplished by delegating to an object that encapsulates an appropriate algorithm for laying out components and handling events, respectively.

The Responsibility for Routing Events

With inheritance-based delegation, the onus for directing events lies squarely on the shoulders of the component that generates the event. Furthermore, the component in question has little choice as to where to route the event: events could be routed either to the superclass or to the container in which the component resides. With the delegation-based event model, it is the responsibility of event *listener*s to declare themselves interested in certain events associated with a particular component; the events are automatically sent to the listener via the AWT machinery.

The responsibility for routing events should be the purview of objects that are *listeners* of events, rather than objects that *generate* events; if a listener is interested in a button's activation, for instance, the listener should be responsible for registering interest in a particular button's action event—it should not be the responsibility of the button to arrange for events to be routed to the listener.

If the responsibility for routing events is left to the component that generates the event, then the component has to know who is interested in its events at the time the component is developed, which is quite restrictive.

When the responsibility for routing events is shifted from the component to the listener,[7] the component knows nothing about who is listening to its events, and therefore the component never needs to be extended for the purpose of routing events to listeners. When the component is responsible for routing events, it also becomes tightly coupled with the classes to whom it routes events. When the listener is responsible for registering interest in events, the component is decoupled from the objects that listen to its events. Such decoupling translates into much more modular code in which it is natural to separate out the user interface classes from the underlying object model.

handleEvent() Switch Statement

Another major drawback with the inheritance-based model was the fact that switch statements within overridden `handleEvent` methods work fine for simple applets but become a maintenance nightmare in complex surroundings. Switch statements that switch off an object's type (implied or concrete), are nearly always the result of a faulty object-oriented design. Instead of a switch statement, polymorphism should be employed in order to let the compiler (instead of the developer) decide what functionality to invoke given the type of object.[8] Typically, when a switch statement that switches off object types exists in object-oriented code, it should be refactored so that the constants signifying object types are turned into a hierarchy of classes. The switch statements are then rewritten to simply invoke a method on an object whose type is typically at (or near) the top of the hierarchy of classes. This is exactly what has happened for the 1.1 event model. Instead of integer constants that signify event types in the `Event` class, the delegation-based event model provides a hierarchy of event classes, such as: `AWTEvent, ActionEvent, ComponentEvent, KeyEvent, MouseEvent,` and so forth.

7. Strictly speaking, the responsibility for routing events is still shouldered by `java.awt.Component`. However, the responsibility for arranging for the event to be routed is the listener's.
8. See Cox, Brad. *Object Oriented Programming An Evolutionary Approach,* chapter 4. Addison-Wesley, 1984.

Summary

All applets involving the AWT are event driven. The applets display their components and patiently wait for some event to occur. There's a special group of event handling methods, generically referred to as propagated event handlers because they either handle an event or propagate it up to the container in which the component is displayed. A propagated event handler returns `true` to indicate the event has been completely handled and should not be propagated up to its container; it returns `false` to indicate that the event is to be propagated up to the container. Propagated events always work their way from the innermost component to the outermost container. We've seen that overridden `handleEvent` methods should never return `false` and directly propagate events to their containers but should instead return `super.handleEvent(event)` to give their superclass a crack at the event and decide whether to propagate the event. Additionally, we have seen that overridden convenience methods, such as `mouseDown()`, should not return `super.handleEvent()` because doing so may very well result in an infinite loop.

The AWT `Button`, `Checkbox`, `TextField`, and `Choice` components are unique in that they generate events that are routed through a `Component action` method. This method takes an `Event` argument and an `Object` argument. The latter is set according to the type of `Component` that generated the event.

While it is standard AWT practice to check against the label of certain components to identify the component with which an event is associated, we have advised you to check against object references rather than labels.

Finally, this chapter has covered the original, inheritance-based event model. The current version of the AWT has a new event model that is delegation based and vastly improved over the original. If possible, you should use the new event model, which is discussed at length in the next chapter.

CHAPTER
9

The Delegation Event Model (AWT 1.1 and Beyond)

The 1.1 version of the AWT introduced a new delegation-based event model that is vastly improved over the original, inheritance-based model. The delegation event model supports the inheritance-based (original) event model; however, the inheritance-based model will be phased out in a future release.

This chapter discusses the delegation event model. In "Shortcomings of the Inheritance-Based Event Model" on page 229, we discussed some of the drawbacks of the original event model, all of which are addressed by the new model. Applets (and applications) that use the original event model will still continue to work under the new model; however, the old API will be eliminated in a future release. For now, compiler warnings are issued if you are still using the old API, and mixing the two event models in a single component is not supported. We suggest that you migrate your old event handling code to the new model as soon as possible and that you use the new event model for any new development. Guidelines for doing so may be found in Event Handling Design on page 319.

The Delegation Event Model

The delegation event model derives its name from the fact that event handling is delegated from an event source to one or more event listeners.

The premise behind the delegation event model is simple: *components* fire *events*, which can be listened for and acted upon by *listeners*. Listeners are registered with a component by invoking one of a number of addXYZListener(*XYZ*Listener) methods. After a listener is added to a component, appropriate methods in the listener's interface will be called when the corresponding type of event is fired by the component.

Components, Events and Listeners

The applet shown in Figure 9-1 and listed in Example 9-1 illustrates the fundamental concepts of the delegation event model.

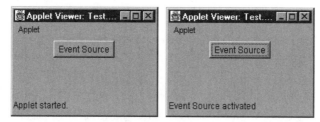

Figure 9-1 A Simple Illustration of the Delegation Event Model
The picture on the left shows the applet in its initial state. The picture on the right was taken after the button was activated. Note the applet's status bar.

The applet instantiates a ButtonListener and adds it to the button. ButtonListener implements the ActionListener interface and updates the applet's status bar when the button is activated.

Example 9-1 Listening for Action Events

```
import java.applet.Applet;
import java.awt.*;
import java.awt.event.*;

public class Test extends Applet {
    public void init() {
        Button eventSource = new Button("Event Source");
        eventSource.addActionListener(new ButtonListener(this));
        add(eventSource);
    }
}
class ButtonListener implements ActionListener {
    private Applet applet;

    public ButtonListener(Applet applet) {
        this.applet = applet;
    }
    public void actionPerformed(ActionEvent event) {
        Button source = (Button)event.getSource();
        applet.showStatus(source.getLabel() + " activated");
    }
}
```

java.awt.Button provides registration methods for ActionListeners—
addActionListener() and removeActionListener(). When a button is
activated, an ActionEvent is instantiated and fired to all ActionListeners
registered with the button at the time the event occurred. The Button class fires
action events by invoking actionPerformed() for every registered
ActionListener(). The actionPerformed method is passed a reference to
the ActionEvent instantiated by the button at the time the event occurred.

Figure 9-2 shows the sequence of events for firing an event from an event source
to a set of listeners. First, the listener must be added to the source as a specific
type of listener. Subsequent events of the specified type will cause the source to
invoke an *eventHandler* method defined in the listener's interface that takes a
single EventType argument.

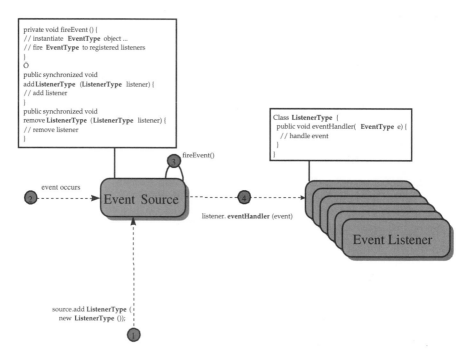

```
private void fireEvent () {
// instantiate  EventType  object ...
// fire  EventType  to registered listeners
}
Ö
public synchronized void
add ListenerType  (ListenerType  listener) {
// add listener
}
public synchronized void
remove ListenerType  (ListenerType  listener) {
// remove listener
}
```

```
Class ListenerType  {
    public void eventHandler(  EventType  e) {
      // handle event
    }
}
```

fireEvent()

event occurs

Event Source

Event Listener

listener. eventHandler (event)

source.add ListenerType (
new ListenerType ());

Figure 9-2 Firing an Event to a Set of Listeners
Event sources invoke a method defined by a listener interface,
passing an **EventType**.

Event sources implement listener registration methods such as
`Button.addActionListener(ActionListener)` and
`Button.removeActionListener(ActionListener)`, whereby event
listeners of a specified type may register and unregister interest in events fired by
the source. When an event occurs, the event source instantiates an appropriate
event, which is passed to the set of listeners that are registered with the source at
the time the event occurred.

Event listeners are responsible for implementing event handling methods. Event
handling methods are passed references to events, which are typically immutable,
and contain information about the event and a reference to the event source.

Event listeners are obligated to handle events in a timely manner. Calls made to event listeners are made on the source's thread, so the next listener can't get started until the current listener is done processing the event. One popular technique for event listeners that have long or indefinite event handling tasks is to use an adapter that queues events for delivery on another thread.

AWT TIP

The JDK Event Model

The JDK event model revolves around three types of objects:

- *Event Sources* fire events.
- *Event Listeners* handle events.
- *Events* represent an event at the time it occurred.

Event listeners register with an event source by invoking void Event-Source.addListenerType(ListenerType listener). Event sources fire events by instantiating an EventType, which is passed to void Listener-Type.eventHandler(EventType event).

Filtering Events

Under the inheritance-based event model, all events were sent to every component whether the component was interested in the event or not. The delegation event model filters events; events are only delivered to a component if:

- A listener interested in the event type is added to the component, OR
- Component.enableEvents(long mask) is invoked, where mask represents the events to be delivered.

Regardless of which approach is taken, events associated with either the mask or the type of listener will be fired by the component and either passed along to listeners or made available for overridden event handling methods.

The Big Picture

All of the action, as far as events and listeners are concerned, starts in the java.util package. java.util comes with a class and an interface— EventObject and EventListener, respectively, which form the foundation of the delegation event model. EventObject is a simple class that does nothing more than keep track of its event source, and EventListener is a *tagging*[1] interface, which all listeners extend. `EventListener` and `EventObject` anchor hierarchies of listeners and events, respectively. Figure 9-3 shows the event listeners, all of which extend the `java.util.EventListener` interface.

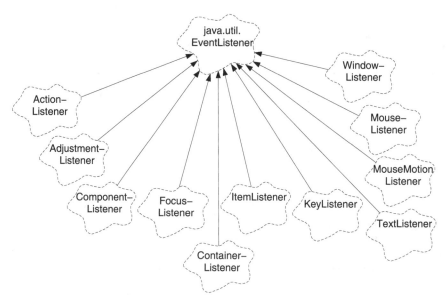

Figure 9-3 Event Listener Interfaces
All of the event listener interfaces shown above reside in the `java.awt.event` package, except for `java.util.EventListener`.

Figure 9-4 shows the hierarchy of AWT event classes.

`java.util.EventObject` maintains a reference to the source of the event,[2] and the `AWTEvent` class keeps track of the ID of the event and whether or not the event is consumed.[3] For the most part, the current version of the AWT has done away with `public` variables—access to the source and ID of an event are provided through public accessor methods on the appropriate class—see "AWT Event Classes (all classes are from the `java.awt.event` package)" on page 254.

1. A tagging interface does not define any methods.
2. Note that the event source is of type `Object`, and not `Component`.
3. Consumed events are not passed along to peers. See "Consuming Input Events" on page 267.

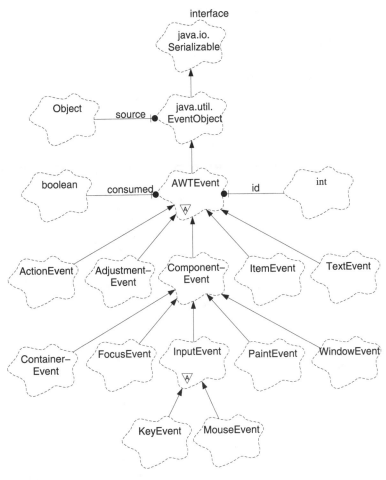

Figure 9-4 AWT Event Class Hierarchy

Events

Table 9-1 lists the public methods for `java.util.EventObject` and its extensions, excluding irrelevant methods such as `toString()`.

The delegation event model provides classes for events instead of representing events by integer constants, thereby eliminating the switch statement that resided in many overridden `handleEvent` methods under the original event model.

However, implementing a class for every possible event would result in an overwhelming number of event classes, so some event classes encompass a number of related events. For instance, WindowEvent represents events for activating, deactivating, closing, opening, iconifying, and deiconifying windows. As a result, some of the event classes define integer constants for encoding the particular type of event that they represent.[4] The constants, along with other constants defined by the event classes, are also listed in Table 9-1.

Table 9-1 JDK Event Classes: Public Methods and Constants

Class	Public Methods	Constants
java.util.Event Object	Object getSource()	
AWTEvent	int getId()	COMPONENT_EVENT_MASK, FOCUS_EVENT_MASK KEY_EVENT_MASK, MOUSE_EVENT_MASK MOUSE_MOTION_EVENT_MASK WINDOW_EVENT_MASK, ACTION_EVENT_MASK ADJUSTMENT_EVENT_MASK, ITEM_EVENT_MASK
ActionEvent	String getActionCommand() int getModifiers()	SHIFT_MASK, CTRL_MASK, META_MASK, ALT_MASK ACTION_FIRST, ACTION_LAST, ACTION_PERFORMED
AdjustmentEvent	Adjustable getAdjustable() int getValue() int getAdjustmentType()	ADJUSTMENT_FIRST, ADJUSTMENT_LAST ADJUSTMENT_VALUE_CHANGED UNIT_INCREMENT, UNIT_DECREMENT BLOCK_INCREMENT, BLOCK_DECREMENT, TRACK
ComponentEvent	Component getComponent()	COMPONENT_FIRST, COMPONENT_LAST COMPONENT_MOVED, COMPONENT_RESIZED COMPONENT_SHOWN, COMPONENT_HIDDEN
ContainerEvent	Container getContainer() Component getChild()	CONTAINER_FIRST CONTAINER_LAST CONTAINER_ADDED CONTAINER_REMOVED
FocusEvent	boolean isTemporary()	FOCUS_FIRST, FOCUS_LAST FOCUS_GAINED, FOCUS_LOST

4. Note that use of these constants can result in switch statements, but the switch statements will be simple and self-contained.

Table 9-1 JDK Event Classes: Public Methods and Constants (Continued)

Class	Public Methods	Constants
InputEvent	boolean isShiftDown() boolean isControlDown() boolean isMetaDown() boolean isAltDown() long getWhen() int getModifiers() void consume() boolean isConsumed()	SHIFT_MASK, CTRL_MASK, META_MASK, ALT_MASK BUTTON1_MASK, BUTTON2_MASK, BUTTON3_MASK
ItemEvent	ItemSelectable getItemSelectable() Object getItem() int getStateChange()	ITEM_FIRST, ITEM_LAST, ITEM_STATE_CHANGED, SELECTED, DESELECTED
KeyEvent	char getKeyChar() int getKeyCode() boolean isActionKey() void setKeyChar(char) void setKeyCode(int) void setModifiers(int) static String getKeyModifiersText(int) static String getKeyText(int)	KEY_FIRST, KEY_LAST KEY_TYPED, KEY_PRESSED, KEY_RELEASED KEY_ACTION_FIRST, KEY_ACTION_LAST HOME, END, PGUP, PGDN, UP, DOWN F1, F2, F3, F4, F5, F6, F7, F8, F9, F10, F11, F12, PRINT_SCREEN, SCROLL_LOCK, CAPS_LOCK, NUM_LOCK, PAUSE, INSERT, ENTER, BACK_SPACE, TAB, ESCAPE, DELETE
MouseEvent	int getClickCount() Point getPoint() int getX() int getY() void translatePoint(int x, int y) boolean isPopupTrigger()	MOUSE_FIRST, MOUSE_LAST MOUSE_CLICKED, MOUSE_PRESSED, MOUSE_RELEASED, MOUSE_MOVED, MOUSE_ENTERED, MOUSE_EXITED, MOUSE_DRAGGED

Table 9-1 JDK Event Classes: Public Methods and Constants (Continued)

Class	Public Methods	Constants
PaintEvent	Rectangle getUpdateRect() void setUpdateRect(Rectangle)	PAINT_FIRST, PAINT_LAST, PAINT, UPDATE
TextEvent	N/A	TEXT_FIRST TEXT_LAST TEXT_VALUE_CHANGED
WindowEvent	Window getWindow()	WINDOW_FIRST, WINDOW_LAST, WINDOW_ACTIVATED, WINDOW_DEACTIVATED, WINDOW_OPENED, WINDOW_CLOSING, WINDOW_CLOSED, WINDOW_ICONIFIED, WINDOW_DEICONIFIED

Components As Event Sources

Many AWT components are fitted with addXYZListener(XYZListener) methods to allow certain types of listeners to register interest in events. For instance, as you can see from Table 9-2, java.awt.Button comes with an addActionListener(ActionListener) method.

In order to handle a particular event for a given component, simply create a listener and pass it to the component's appropriate addXYZListener method, and the events in question will automatically be routed to the listener, meaning one of the methods in Table 9-2 will be invoked. Realize that all of the java.awt.Component extensions (Button, Choice, etc.) inherit the addXYZListener methods implemented in the Component class. Therefore, buttons, for instance, can support component, focus, key, mouse, and mouse motion listeners in addition to action listeners.

Note that more than one listener of a particular type can be registered with a single component. For instance, a button may have a number of action listeners, all of which listen for action events fired by the button. In such a case, the order in which events are delivered to the registered listeners is undefined. In practice, this is usually not a problem, but there are situations where the order of notification is important. You might think that the order of notification corresponds to the order in which the listeners are added to the component, but that is not necessarily the case. As a matter of fact, we will run across such a situation in "A Rubberband Panel" on page 776.

Table 9-2 AWT Component Listener Registration Methods

AWT Class/Interface	Listener Registration Methods
Button	void addActionListener(ActionListener)
Checkbox	void addItemListener(ItemListener)
CheckboxMenuItem	void addItemListener(ItemListener)
Choice	void addItemListener(ItemListener)
Component	void addComponentListener(ComponentListener) void addFocusListener(FocusListener) void addInputMethodListener(InputMethodListener) void addKeyListener(KeyListener) void addMouseListener(MouseListener) void addMouseMotionListener(MouseMotionListener)
Container	addContainerListener(ContainerListener)
List	void addActionListener(ActionListener) void addItemListener(ItemListener)
MenuItem	void addActionListener(ActionListener)
Scrollbar	void addAdjustmentListener(AdjustmentListener)
TextArea	void addTextListener(TextListener)
TextComponent	void addTextListener(TextListener)
TextField	void addTextListener(TextListener) void addActionListener(ActionListener)
Window	void addWindowListener(WindowListener)

AWT TIP ...

Notification Order for Multiple Listeners Is Undefined

If multiple listeners of a particular type are registered with a single component, the order in which the listeners are notified of events is undefined. Although it might seem that the order of notification should correspond to the order in which the listeners are added to the component, that is not necessarily the case. At any rate, you should not rely upon the observed order of notification for multiple listeners because it may vary from one platform to another.

Multicast Event Sources

All of the event sources listed in Table 9-2 on page 247 are multicast event sources. A multicast event source may have more than one event listener of a given type registered at any point in time. Multicast event sources should implement event listener registration methods that adhere to the following JavaBeans™ design pattern:

```
void addListenerType(ListenerType listener)

void removeListenerType(ListenerType listener)
```

addListenerType methods add the specified listener to the set of listeners of type ListenerType maintained by the event source. removeListenerType methods remove the specified listener from the set of listeners. Both methods should be synchronized in order to avoid race conditions. The order of event delivery to registered listeners is defined by the implementation.

Unicast Event Sources

Whenever possible, event sources should be multicast. There are situations, however, where it may be necessary to disallow multiple listeners for a given listener type. For instance, an image button may have a single listener that controls the manner in which the button reacts to mouse events.

Unicast event sources maintain a single event listener for a given type of event. Listener registration methods for a unicast event source are defined by the following JavaBeans design pattern:

```
void addListenerType(ListenerType listener)
    throws java.util.TooManyListenersException

void removeListenerType(ListenerType listener)
```

If the addListenerType method is invoked on a unicast event source that already has a listener of ListenerType registered, the registered listener should remain unchanged and the event source should throw a TooManyListenersException. For the listener associated with a unicast event source to be changed, the removeListenerType method must be invoked before the addListenerType method is called.

Unicast event sources may also be multicast event sources. For example, the image button mentioned above may have a single listener for reacting to mouse events but may also want to allow multiple listeners that react to action events.

Event Source Interfaces

The `java.awt` package contains two event source interfaces: `Adjustable` and `ItemSelectable`.[5] Adjustables have values that can be set between specified minimum and maximum amounts. They also fire `AdjustmentEvents` whenever their value changes.

An `ItemSelectable` has items, of which zero or more are selectable.

Listeners

The `java.awt.event` package defines eleven interfaces for different types of listeners. Each listener interface defines methods that will be invoked when a specific event occurs. For instance, as you can see from Table 9-3, `java.awt.event.ActionListener` defines a lone method: `actionPerformed()`, which is invoked when an *action* event is fired from a component with which the listener has registered interest.

Table 9-3 also lists the corresponding event constant and convenience methods from the inheritance-based event model to aid you in converting your code to the delegation event model. For example, handling an event under the old event model by checking the `id` field of the event for `ACTION_EVENT` or overriding `action()` gets replaced by an `ActionListener` that has its `actionPerformed` method invoked when an action event is fired.[6]

Table 9-3 java.awt.event Listener Interfaces and Methods

Interface	Methods	Corresponding Event/Method from 1.02
`ActionListener`	`void actionPerformed(ActionEvent)`	`ACTION_EVENT/action()`
`AdjustmentListener`	`void adjustmentValueChanged(AdjustmentEvent)`	N/A

`ComponentListener`	`void componentHidden(ComponentEvent)`
	`void componentMoved(ComponentEvent)`
	`void componentResized(ComponentEvent)`
	`void componentShown(ComponentEvent)`
		N/A
		COMPONENT_MOVED
		N/A
		N/A

`ContainerListener`	`void componentAdded(ContainerEvent)`
	
	`void componentRemoved(ContainerEvent)`
		N/A
		
		N/A

---

5. Event source interfaces are defined in the `java.awt` package, but listener interfaces are defined in `java.awt.event`.

Table 9-3 java.awt.event Listener Interfaces and Methods (Continued)

Interface	Methods	Corresponding Event/Method from 1.02
`FocusListener`	`void focusGained(FocusEvent)` `void focusLost(FocusEvent)`	`GOT_FOCUS/gotFocus()` `LOST_FOCUS/lostFocus()`

`InputMethodListener`	`void caretPositionChanged(`
	`InputMethodEvent)`
	
	`void inputMethodTextChanged(`
	`InputMethodEvent)`	

`ItemListener`	`void itemStateChanged(ItemEvent)`	`LIST_SELECT,` `LIST_DESELECT`

`KeyListener`	`void keyTyped(KeyEvent)`
	`void keyPressed(KeyEvent)`
	`void keyReleased(KeyEvent)`
		`N/A`
		`KEY_PRESS/keyDown()`
		`KEY_RELEASE/keyUp()`

`MouseListener`	`void mouseClicked(MouseEvent)`
	`void mouseEntered(MouseEvent)`
	`void mouseExited(MouseEvent)`
	`void mousePressed(MouseEvent)`
	`void mouseReleased(MouseEvent)`
		`MOUSE_UP/mouseUp()`
		`MOUSE_DOWN/mouseDown()`
		`MOUSE_UP/mouseUp()`
		`MOUSE_ENTER/mouseEnter()`
		`MOUSE_EXIT/mouseExit()`

`MouseMotion-Listener`	`void mouseDragged(MouseEvent)` `void mouseMoved(MouseEvent)`	`MOUSE_DRAG/mouseDrag()` `MOUSE_MOVE/mouseMove()`
`TextListener`	`void textValueChanged(TextEvent)`	`N/A`

`WindowListener`	`void windowActivated(WindowEvent)`
	`void windowDeactivated(WindowEvent)`
	`void windowClosed(WindowEvent)`
	`void windowOpened(WindowEvent)`
	`void windowClosing(WindowEvent)`
	`void windowIconified(WindowEvent)`
	`void windowDeiconified(WindowEvent)`
		`N/A`
		`N/A`
		`N/A`
		`WINDOW_DESTROY`
		`WINDOW_EXPOSE`
		`WINDOW_ICONIFY`
		`WINDOW_DEICONIFY`

JavaBeans Design Pattern for Event Handling Methods

All of the methods defined by the listener interfaces in Table 9-3 conform to the JavaBeans design pattern for event handling methods:

> void **eventHandler**(**EventType** evt)

The name of the method should reflect the type of event being handled. For instance, the event handling method for the `ActionListener` interface is `actionPerformed()`, indicating that an action of some type has been

6. There are actually a number of different approaches to take when converting event handling code from the old model to the new. See "Event Handling Design" on page 319.

performed. Event handling methods should be passed an event ultimately derived from `java.util.EventObject`. Event handling methods may also throw checked exceptions, in which case the method signature will include a `throws` clause.

Under exceptional circumstances, such as forwarding event notifications to external environments with different conventions, an alternate design pattern for event handling methods may be used:

```
void eventHandler(arbitrary-parameter-list)
```

Methods adhering to the alternate design pattern may take an arbitrary number of arguments of any Java type. Notice that the alternate design pattern specifies only that the method return `void`; the name of the method and the types and number of arguments could be anything. This alternate design pattern makes it difficult for humans and JavaBeans builder tools to identify such methods. As a result, the alternate design pattern should be used only when absolutely necessary.

AWT Adapters

Some of the interfaces listed in Table 9-3 on page 249 require implementing a fair number of methods. Listeners, a good percentage of the time, are only interested in implementing a small subset of the methods defined by listener interfaces. For instance, it is common to implement `WindowListener.windowClosing()` to handle the closing of the window, without any interest in the other six events defined by the `WindowListener` interface.

To free developers from having to implement every method defined in a listener interface, the AWT provides a number of adapter classes that provide no-op implementations of the methods defined in the appropriate interface. For example, `java.awt.event.MouseAdapter` implements all of the methods defined in `java.awt.event.MouseListener` as no-ops. Instead of implementing the `MouseListener` interface, it's preferable to extend the `MouseAdapter` class.

Example 9-2 lists an applet equipped with a single button. The button has a `ButtonMouseListener` added to it. `ButtonMouseListener` is only interested in mouse enter and exit events; it implements no-op versions of the other methods defined by `java.awt.event.MouseListener`.

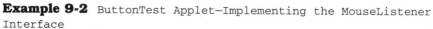

Example 9-2 `ButtonTest Applet—Implementing the MouseListener`
`Interface`

```
import java.awt.*;
import java.awt.event.*;
import java.applet.Applet;

public class ButtonTest extends Applet {
    public void init() {
        Button button = new Button("Press Me");
        button.addMouseListener(new ButtonMouseListener());
        add(button);
    }
}
class ButtonMouseListener implements MouseListener {
    public void mouseEntered(MouseEvent event) {
        System.out.println("Mouse Entered Button");
    }
    public void mouseExited(MouseEvent event) {
        System.out.println("Mouse Exited Button");
    }
    public void mousePressed (MouseEvent event) { }
    public void mouseClicked (MouseEvent event) { }
    public void mouseReleased(MouseEvent event) { }
}
```

Notice that `MouseListener` defines methods for a mouse click and a mouse
release. The `mouseClicked` method is invoked when the mouse button is
released immediately following a mouse press. The `mouseReleased` method is
invoked when the mouse button is released following a mouse drag.

As you might well imagine, it could become rather tedious to have to implement
all the methods associated with one or more listener interfaces if you are only
interested in giving meaningful purpose to a small percentage of the methods.

For instance, you might have a selectable object that you'd like to be selected with
a mouse press; if so, you'd want to implement `MouseListener` and override
`mousePressed()`. Since an interface is being implemented, however, the other
four `MouseListener` methods must be implemented, typically as no-ops, in
order for the class to be concrete (nonabstract).

Using adapter classes means that instead of implementing an interface and
having to code a handful of no-op methods, we can extend a class full of no-ops

and selectively override the methods that we're interested in. Example 9-3 isfunctionally identical to Example 9-2, except that `ButtonMouseListener` extends the `MouseAdapter` class instead of implementing the `MouseListener` interface.

Example 9-3 Extending MouseAdapter Instead of Implementing MouseListener

```java
import java.awt.*;
import java.awt.event.*;
import java.applet.Applet;

public class ButtonTest2 extends Applet {
    public void init() {
        Button    button = new Button("Press Me");
        button.addMouseListener(new ButtonMouseListener());
        add(button);
    }
}
class ButtonMouseListener extends MouseAdapter {
    public void mouseEntered(MouseEvent event) {
        System.out.println("Mouse Entered Button");
    }
    public void mouseExited(MouseEvent event) {
        System.out.println("Mouse Exited Button");
    }
}
```

Table 9-4 lists the adapter classes provided by the AWT, along with the listener interfaces they implement. Notice that there are no adapter classes for `ActionListener`, `AdjustmentListener`, `ItemListener`, and `TextListener` because those interfaces define only one method.

Table 9-4 AWT Adapter Classes

Adapter Class	Implements This Interface ...
ComponentAdapter	ComponentListener
ContainerAdapter	ContainerListener
FocusAdapter	FocusListener
KeyAdapter	KeyListener
MouseAdapter	MouseListener
MouseMotionAdapter	MouseMotionListener
WindowAdapter	WindowListener

Component Events

As evidenced by Figure 9-4 on page 243, there are two types of AWT events: component events, which extend `ComponentEvent`, and semantic events, which extend `AWTEvent`. Table 9-5 lists the classes representing the two types of events.

Table 9-5 AWT Event Classes (all classes are from the `java.awt.event` package)

Semantic Events	Component Events
ActionEvent	ComponentEvent
AdjustmentEvent	ContainerEvent
ItemEvent	FocusEvent
TextEvent	InputEvent
	KeyEvent
	MouseEvent
	MouseMotionEvent
	WindowEvent

Component events are fired when something specific happens to a component, for example: the mouse enters/exits the component or is pressed within it; the component gains or loses keyboard focus; the component is a window that is closing, etc. Component events are classified as either input events or noninput events; mouse and key events are input events. Input events are distinguished from noninput events because input events can be consumed. Consumed events are not passed to the component's peer.

Semantic events are not as specific as component events and are not necessarily triggered by an atomic action such as a mouse press. The exact definition of a semantic event depends upon the class that fires the event; for instance, lists fire action events when their items are double-clicked, whereas textfields fire action events when `enter` is typed in the field.

Component and Container Events

Whenever a component is shown, hidden, resized or moved, it fires a `ComponentEvent` to all registered `ComponentListeners`. In addition to firing component events, components that are containers also fire events when a component is added to or removed from the container.

Component events for showing or hiding a component are fired only when `Component.setVisible()` (or the deprecated `show()`/`hide()`) is invoked for a component. For instance, if an applet's window is temporarily hidden behind another window, the components contained in the applet will not fire `ComponentEvents` when the applet is hidden and shown.

The `ComponentListener` and `ContainerListener` interfaces are summarized in Table 9-3 on page 249, and the `ComponentEvent` and `ContainerEvent` classes are summarized in Table 9-1 on page 244.

The applet shown in Figure 9-1 has a `ContainerListener` that prints out container events as they occur. Likewise, the button in the applet has a `ComponentListener` that prints out component events. The two `Choice` components either show/hide the button or add/remove the button from its container (the applet).

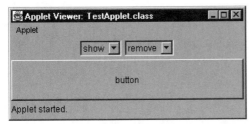

Figure 9-5 Component and Container Events
The applet has a `ContainerListener` added to it, and the button has a `ComponentListener`. Both listeners print events as they occur.

The applet is listed in Example 9-4.

Example 9-4 Handling Component and Container Events

```java
import java.applet.Applet;
import java.awt.*;
import java.awt.event.*;

public class TestApplet extends Applet {
    public void init() {
        final Button button = new Button("button");
        Choice visible = new Choice(), addRemove = new Choice();
        Panel  controls = new Panel();

        visible.add("show");
        visible.add("hide");

        addRemove.add("remove");
        addRemove.add("add");

        controls.add(visible);
        controls.add(addRemove);

        setLayout(new BorderLayout());
        add(button, "Center");
        add(controls, "North");

        button.addComponentListener(new ButtonListener());
        addContainerListener(new AppletListener());

        visible.addItemListener(new ItemListener() {
            public void itemStateChanged(ItemEvent e) {
                String s =
                    ((Choice)e.getSource()).getSelectedItem();

                if(s.equals("hide")) button.setVisible(false);
                else                 button.setVisible(true);
            }
        });
        addRemove.addItemListener(new ItemListener() {
            public void itemStateChanged(ItemEvent e) {
                String s =
                    ((Choice)e.getSource()).getSelectedItem();

                if(s.equals("add"))
                    add(button, "Center");
                else
                    remove(button);
            }
        });
    }
}
class ButtonListener implements ComponentListener {
    public void componentResized(ComponentEvent event) {
        Component c = (Component)event.getSource();
        System.out.println("button resized:  " +  c.getSize());
```

```
    }
    public void componentShown(ComponentEvent event) {
        System.out.println("button shown");
    }
    public void componentHidden(ComponentEvent event) {
        System.out.println("button hidden");
    }
    public void componentMoved(ComponentEvent event) {
        Component c = (Component)event.getSource();
        System.out.println("button moved:   " + c.getLocation());
    }
}
class AppletListener implements ContainerListener {
    public void componentAdded(ContainerEvent e) {
        Component c = e.getChild();
        System.out.println("container:  button added");
    }
    public void componentRemoved(ContainerEvent e) {
        Component c = e.getChild();
        System.out.println("container:  button removed");
    }
}
```

When the applet starts, the button is laid out by the applet's layout manager. As a result, the initial output of the applet looks like so:

```
button resized:  java.awt.Dimension[width=325,height=69]
button moved:   java.awt.Point[x=0,y=31]
```

Subsequently, when the button is shown or hidden, the `ButtonListener` is notified. If the button is added to or removed from the applet, the `AppletListener` is notified of the addition or removal.

Focus Events

At any given time, there is a maximum of one component with keyboard focus per windowing system. When a component has focus, keyboard events are delivered to the component in question.

Components with keyboard focus typically have a prominent appearance that distinguishes them from other components. For instance, buttons that have keyboard focus under Windows draw a dashed rectangle around the inside edge of their border (Windows buttons are interested in receiving focus because they can be activated with the spacebar or accelerators).

AWT components gain focus in one of the following ways:

1. Interact with the component
2. Invoke `Component.focusRequested()`
3. Type TAB and SHIFT-TAB to move the keyboard focus

Focus events are qualified as either FOCUS_LOST or FOCUS_GAINED events. FOCUS_LOST events are further qualified as either temporary or permanent.

Permanent focus events are fired when keyboard focus is deliberately given to a component within a given applet or application. The component that originally had focus fires a FOCUS_LOST event, followed by a FOCUS_GAINED event being fired by the component that gains the focus, in that order.

Temporary FOCUS_LOST events are fired when a component temporarily loses focus. For instance, if a component in an applet has focus and another window is activated, the component will temporarily lose focus, but focus will be restored when the applet/application window is subsequently activated.

Focus events are represented by `java.awt.event.FocusEvent`. A `FocusListener` is registered with the component in question; when a focus change occurs, the listener is notified and is passed an instance of `FocusEvent`.

Figure 9-6 shows an applet with two buttons, both of which have an instance of `ButtonFocusListener` added to them. `ButtonFocusListener` prints information about each focus event it receives.

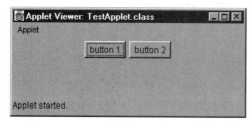

Figure 9-6 Handling Focus Events
Both buttons have a `FocusListener` added to them. The listener prints information about focus events fired by the buttons.

The applet is listed in Example 9-5.

Example 9-5 Handling Focus Events

```java
import java.applet.Applet;
import java.awt.*;
import java.awt.event.*;

public class TestApplet extends Applet {
    public void init() {
        Button button = new Button("button 1"),
               button2 = new Button("button 2");

        ButtonFocusListener listener = new ButtonFocusListener();

        button.addFocusListener(listener);
        button2.addFocusListener(listener);

        add(button);
        add(button2);
    }
}
class ButtonFocusListener implements FocusListener {
    public void focusGained(FocusEvent event) {
        report(event);
    }
    public void focusLost(FocusEvent event) {
        report(event);
    }
    private void report(FocusEvent event) {
        Button b = (Button)event.getComponent();

        if(event.getID() == FocusEvent.FOCUS_GAINED)
            System.out.print(b.getLabel() + " gained focus");
        else if(event.getID() == FocusEvent.FOCUS_LOST)
            System.out.print(b.getLabel() + " lost focus");

        if(event.isTemporary())
            System.out.println(": temporary");
        else
            System.out.println();
    }
}
```

When focus is shifted from button 1 to button 2, the applet's output looks like this:

```
button 1 lost focus
button 2 gained focus
```

Subsequently, if another window is activated, button 2 temporarily loses focus:

```
button 2 lost focus: temporary
```

When the applet window is reactivated, button 2 regains focus:

```
button 2 gained focus
```

Key Events

Key events are fired when a key is pressed or released in a component that has keyboard focus. There are three types of key events, all of which are encapsulated in the `java.awt.event.KeyEvent` class. Each type of event is represented by a constant and a corresponding method in the `KeyListener` interface, as listed in Table 9-6.

Table 9-6 Key Events

Event ID	KeyListener **Method**	Fired When ...
KEY_PRESSED	keyPressed(KeyEvent)	key is pressed
KEY_RELEASED	keyReleased(KeyEvent)	key is released
KEY_TYPED	keyTyped(KeyEvent)	key character is pressed

Figure 9-3 shows an applet that listens for key events fired from a textfield. The `KeyListener` associated with the textfield prints information about each key event that is fired.

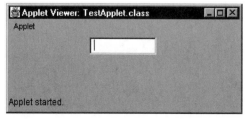

Figure 9-7 Handling Key Events
The textfield has a `KeyListener` that prints information about key events.

The applet shown in Figure 9-7 is listed in Example 9-6.

Example 9-6 Handling Key Events

```
import java.applet.Applet;
import java.awt.*;
import java.awt.event.*;

public class TestApplet extends Applet {
    private TextField tf = new TextField(10);

    public void init() {
        tf.addKeyListener(new TextfieldListener());
        add(tf);
    }
}
class TextfieldListener implements KeyListener {
    public void keyPressed(KeyEvent e) {
        System.out.println("KEY_PRESSED:  ");
        report(e);
    }
    public void keyReleased(KeyEvent e) {
        System.out.println("KEY_RELEASED:  ");
        report(e);
    }
    public void keyTyped(KeyEvent e) {
        System.out.println("KEY_TYPED:  ");
        report(e);
    }
    private void report(KeyEvent e) {
        int keyCode = e.getKeyCode();
        char keyChar = e.getKeyChar();
        String mods = e.getKeyModifiersText(keyCode);
        String txt = e.getKeyText(keyCode);

        if(keyCode != KeyEvent.KEY_UNDEFINED)
            System.out.println("Code:  " + keyCode);

        if(keyCode != KeyEvent.CHAR_UNDEFINED)
            System.out.println("Char:  " + keyChar);

        System.out.println("Modifiers:  " + mods);
        System.out.println("Text:  " + txt);

        if(e.isActionKey())
            System.out.println("ACTION");

        System.out.println();
    }
}
```

KEY_PRESSED and KEY_RELEASED events are fired when any key is pressed or released in a component that has focus. Each key on the keyboard is represented by a key code; `KeyEvent.getKeyCode()`[7] can be used to find out which key was pressed or released. Additionally, `KeyEvent.getKeyText()` returns a string representation of the key. For example, if the F1 key is pressed and subsequently released while the textfield in the applet listed in Example 9-6 has focus, the output is as follows:

```
KEY_PRESSED:
Code:   112
Modifiers:
Text:   F1
ACTION

KEY_RELEASED:
Code:   112
Modifiers:
Text:   F1
ACTION
```

The F1 key has a keycode of 112, and `KeyEvent.getKeyText()` returns the string "F1" when the F1 key is pressed or released.

KEY_TYPED events are fired when a key representing a valid unicode character is pressed. For example, if the 'g' key is pressed when the textfield in the applet listed in Example 9-6 has focus, the output is as follows:

```
KEY_PRESSED:
Code:   71
Char:   g
Modifiers:  Meta+Ctrl+Shift
Text:   G

KEY_TYPED:
Code:   0
Char:   g
Modifiers:
Text:   Unknown keyCode: 0x0

KEY_RELEASED:
Code:   71
Char:   g
Modifiers:  Meta+Ctrl+Shift
Text:   G
```

---

7.   `java.awt.event.KeyEvent` methods are listed in Table 9-3 on page 249.

Key events, like mouse events, are input events and therefore may be consumed—see "Consuming Input Events" on page 267. Additionally, KeyEvent is the only event class that is not immutable;[8] KeyEvent provides methods for setting the key code, character, and modifiers.

Under the (old) inheritance-based delegation model, key presses other than unicode characters were labeled action events. The KeyEvent class provides a corresponding isAction method to determine if the key pressed represents a valid unicode character.

Mouse and Mouse Motion Events

The delegation event model—unlike the inheritance event model—distinguishes between mouse events and mouse motion events by providing two listeners: MouseListener and MouseMotionListener. Both mouse and mouse motion events are represented by the same event class: MouseEvent.

Mouse moved and mouse dragged events are mouse motion events, whereas all other mouse events (enter/exit, pressed/released, and clicked) are simply mouse events. A mouse clicked event is fired when a mouse pressed is immediately followed by a mouse released event (without mouse drags in between).

Mouse events, like key events, are input events and therefore may be consumed—see "Consuming Input Events" on page 267.

The applet listed in Example 9-7 adds a mouse listener and mouse motion listener to the applet itself. The listeners print events as they occur.

Example 9-7 Handling Mouse Events

```
import java.applet.Applet;
import java.awt.*;
import java.awt.event.*;

public class TestApplet extends Applet {
    public void init() {
        addMouseListener(new TestMouseListener());
        addMouseMotionListener(new TestMouseMotionListener());
    }
}
class MouseReporter {
    public void report(MouseEvent e) {
        int clickCount = e.getClickCount();
        int mods       = e.getModifiers();
        Point p        = e.getPoint();
        boolean isPopupTrigger = e.isPopupTrigger();
```

8. PaintEvent provides a method for setting the update rectangle.

```
              String s          = "mouse ";

              if((mods & InputEvent.BUTTON3_MASK) != 0)
                  s += "button 3";
              else if((mods & InputEvent.BUTTON2_MASK) != 0)
                  s += "button 2";
              else if((mods & InputEvent.BUTTON1_MASK) != 0)
                  s += "button 1";
              else
                  s += "cursor";

              switch(e.getID()) {
                  case MouseEvent.MOUSE_PRESSED:
                      s += " pressed";
                      break;
                  case MouseEvent.MOUSE_RELEASED:
                      s += " released";
                      break;
                  case MouseEvent.MOUSE_CLICKED:
                      s += " clicked";
                      break;
                  case MouseEvent.MOUSE_MOVED:
                      s += " moved";
                      break;
                  case MouseEvent.MOUSE_ENTERED:
                      s += " entered";
                      break;
                  case MouseEvent.MOUSE_EXITED:
                      s += " exited";
                      break;
                  case MouseEvent.MOUSE_DRAGGED:
                      s += " dragged";
                      break;
              }
              System.out.println(s + " at:   " + p);
              System.out.println(" click count:   " + clickCount);
              System.out.println(" is popup trigger:   " +
                                  isPopupTrigger);
              System.out.println();
          }
  }
  class TestMouseListener implements MouseListener {
      private MouseReporter reporter = new MouseReporter();

      public void mouseClicked(MouseEvent e) {
          reporter.report(e);
      }
      public void mouseEntered(MouseEvent e) {
          reporter.report(e);
      }
      public void mouseExited(MouseEvent e) {
          reporter.report(e);
```

```
        }
        public void mousePressed(MouseEvent e) {
            reporter.report(e);
        }
        public void mouseReleased(MouseEvent e) {
            reporter.report(e);
        }
    }
    class TestMouseMotionListener implements MouseMotionListener {
        private MouseReporter reporter = new MouseReporter();

        public void mouseDragged(MouseEvent e) {
            reporter.report(e);
        }
        public void mouseMoved(MouseEvent e) {
            reporter.report(e);
        }
    }
```

The MouseEvent class provides methods that can be used to determine the
position of the mouse at the time of the event (getPoint(), getX(), and
getY()). Additionally, MouseEvent.getClickCount() is used to determine if
the mouse was double clicked. If the value returned from getClickCount() is
2, then the mouse event represents a double click.

Information pertaining to which mouse button was pressed/released or clicked is
stored in the modifiers field of the event, which is accessible via
InputEvent.getModifiers(). Since the AWT must be able to deal with mice
with differing numbers of buttons, mouse buttons are simulated with modifier
keys, as listed in Table 9-7.

Table 9-7 Modifier Keys for Simulating Multiple-Button Mice

Modifier	Button Simulated
NONE	Button 1
ALT	Button 2
META	Button 3

An unfortunate side effect of using modifiers to simulate multiple buttons is that
it is not possible to distinguish between a button 1 + modifier click from a button
other than button 1. For instance, it is not possible to distinguish between a button
1 + ALT versus button 2.

Window Events

Window events are fired only by instances of java.awt.Window (and its
extensions) and signify that the window has been activated/deactivated,
iconified/deiconified, opened/closed, or is in the process of closing.

Example 9-8 lists an applet that listens for events in an instance of
`java.awt.Frame`.

Example 9-8 Handling Window Events

```java
import java.awt.*;
import java.awt.event.*;

public class Test extends Frame {
    public Test() {
        super("WindowListener test");
    }
    public static void main(String args[]) {
        final Frame f = new Test();
        f.setBounds(100,100,250,150);
        f.setVisible(true);
        f.addWindowListener(new TestWindowListener());
    }
}
class TestWindowListener implements WindowListener {
    public void windowActivated(WindowEvent e) {
        System.out.println("window activated");
    }
    public void windowClosed(WindowEvent e) {
        System.out.println("window closed");
        System.exit(0);
    }
    public void windowClosing(WindowEvent e) {
        System.out.println("window closing ...");
        Window w = e.getWindow();
        w.dispose();
    }
    public void windowDeactivated(WindowEvent e) {
        System.out.println("window deactivated");
    }
    public void windowDeiconified(WindowEvent e) {
        System.out.println("window deiconified");
    }
    public void windowOpened(WindowEvent e) {
        System.out.println("window opened");
    }
}
```

The application listed in Example 9-8 invokes `Window.dispose()` to close the
window when a window closing event is detected. See "java.awt.Frame" on
page 579 for more on reacting to window closing events.

Focus and Key Events for Canvases and Panels

Although all components are capable of firing focus and key events, a component
must have keyboard focus in order to do so. Canvases and panels, by default, are
not typically[9] interested in obtaining keyboard focus and therefore will not fire

key or focus events. To handle key and/or focus events for a canvas or panel, you must invoke `requestFocus()` on the canvas or panel in question. Once the canvas or panel has keyboard focus, it will fire key and focus events.

Consuming Input Events

There are times when it would be convenient to block an event from making its way to a component's peer. For instance, GUI builders often have a build mode and a test mode. In build mode, it may be desirable to suppress the usual reaction to button clicks or keystrokes and instead bring up a property sheet, while the component should be fully functional in test mode.

The delegation event model allows the consumption of input events (meaning key and mouse events); once consumed, an event is not passed to its native peer. The `InputEvent` class provides a `consume` method, which causes the event in question to be consumed.

Figure 9-8 shows an applet containing a lone button. The button has a mouse listener added to it that consumes mouse pressed events; as a result, the button is not activated when clicked. Additionally, the applet has a key listener attached to it that consumes 'a' key presses.

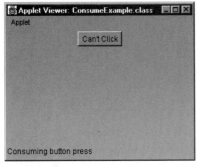

Figure 9-8 Consuming Input Events
The applet consumes 'a' key presses, and the button consumes mouse pressed events.

The applet is listed in Example 9-9.

---

9. Whether a component is interested in gaining focus is platform dependent.

Example 9-9 Consuming Input Events

```java
import java.applet.Applet;
import java.awt.*;
import java.awt.event.*;

public class ConsumeExample extends Applet {
    public void init() {
        Button button = new Button("Can't Click This");
        button.addMouseListener(new ConsumeButtonListener(this));

        addKeyListener(new ConsumeKeyListener(this));
        requestFocus();

        add(button);
    }
}
class ConsumeButtonListener extends MouseAdapter {
    private Applet applet;

    public ConsumeButtonListener(Applet applet) {
        this.applet = applet;
    }
    public void mousePressed(MouseEvent event) {
        applet.showStatus("Consuming button press");
        event.consume();
    }
}
class ConsumeKeyListener extends KeyAdapter {
    private Applet applet;

    public ConsumeKeyListener(Applet applet) {
        this.applet = applet;
    }
    public void keyPressed(KeyEvent event) {
        char key = event.getKeyChar();

        if(key == 'a') {
            applet.showStatus("Consuming 'a' key");
            event.consume();
        }
    }
}
```

Unlike listeners of most events, listeners of input events are notified of the event before it is passed on to the component's peer. If the event is consumed via `InputEvent.consume()`, the method is not passed on to the component's peer but is still passed on to all registered listeners (of the appropriate type, of course). For a button, for instance, this means that consumed mouse pressed events suppress the usual reaction to mouse presses, but the mouse pressed event is still sent to all of the button's registered mouse listeners.

Paint Events

Paint events are the odd man out as far as AWT events are concerned because they are not handled via the listener model. Paint events are handled internally and wind up resulting in calls to a component's `update` or `paint` methods. To handle paint events, a component's paint method is typically overridden in order to (re)paint the component. See "Rendering Components" on page 443 for more on painting and repainting components.

Semantic Events

The majority of AWT events are component events, such as mouse down, key pressed, etc. The AWT also provides *semantic* events, which are higher-level events, such as an action event. Semantic events do not equate to any single component event but describe an event that may consist of a number of component events. Semantic events, in contrast to component events, are always consumed—semantic events are not passed to a component's peer.

For instance, if you wheel the mouse (mouse moved) into a `java.awt.Button` (mouse entered), press the mouse button (mouse pressed), and release it inside of the button (mouse clicked), the button will fire an action event.

Semantic events are handled in exactly the same manner as component inputs; there are four semantic events in `java.awt.event`: `ActionEvent`, `AdjustmentEvent`, `ItemEvent`, and `TextEvent` as described in Table 9-8.

Table 9-8 Semantic Events

Semantic Events ...	are fired by ...	when ...
`ActionEvent`	Button	the button is activated
	List	the item is double-clicked
	MenuItem	the item is selected
	TextField	enter is typed in the field
`AdjustmentEvent`	Scrollbar	the thumb is moved
`ItemEvent`	Checkbox	the checkbox is toggled
	CheckboxMenuItem	the menu item is selected
	Choice	an item is selected
	List	an item is selected
`TextEvent`	TextComponent	the text changes

An `AdjustmentEvent` is fired only by components that can be adjusted—in the current release of the AWT, that would be all classes that implement the `Adjustable` interface, namely, `java.awt.Scrollbar`.[10]

Item events are fired by components that have items: `Checkbox`, `CheckboxMenuItem`, `Choice`, and `List`.

Text events are fired by components that have editable text, which means anything that extends `TextComponent`, namely, `TextField` and `TextArea`.

Which components fire action events is not so intuitive—`Button`, `List`, `MenuItem`, and `TextField` all fire action events. Note that `List` and `TextField` fire two different kinds of semantic events: a `List` fires item events when an item in the list is selected, and an action event when an item in the list is double-clicked. A `TextField` fires action events when enter is typed in the field and fires text events whenever its text is modified.

AWT TIP ...

Have Custom Components Fire Semantic Events When Appropriate

Custom components should fire semantic events when appropriate. The exact definitions of semantic events are intentionally left vague—an action event, for example, means different things depending upon the type of component that fires the event. For instance, image buttons should fire action events in a manner similar to the action events fired by a java.awt.Button, while custom components with selectable items should fire item events. Components that are adjustable should fire adjustment events, and components with editable text should fire text events.

Action Events

Figure 9-9 shows an application that handles action events for all of the components that fire them (see Table 9-8 on page 269). Two listeners are implemented: `ActionWindowListener`, which listens for the closing of the window, and `DebugActionListener`, which simply prints out information about action events as they are fired. Instances of `DebugActionListener` are added to each component, and they add an instance of `ActionWindowListener` is added to the frame itself. From there on out, the AWT machinery takes care of business for us.

10. Actually, a java.awt package private class, ScrollPaneAdjustable also implements Adjustable.

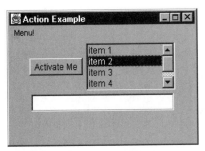

Figure 9-9 Action Events
Action events are generated by double-clicking list items,
activating buttons, and entering a carriage return in a textfield or
selecting a menu item.

The application is listed in Example 9-10.

Example 9-10 ActionExample2 Application

```java
import java.awt.*;
import java.awt.event.*;

public class ActionExample2 extends Frame {
    private Button    button    = new Button("Activate Me");
    private List      list      = new List();
    private TextField textfield = new TextField(25);
    private MenuItem  menuItem  = new MenuItem("Menu menuItem");

    static public void main(String args[]) {
        ActionExample2 f = new ActionExample2();
        f.setBounds(200,200,200,200);
        f.show();
    }
    public ActionExample2() {
        super("Action Example");
        MenuBar mbar = new MenuBar();
        Menu    menu = new Menu("Menu!");
        menu.add(menuItem);
        mbar.add(menu);
        setMenuBar(mbar);

        list.add("item 1");
        list.add("item 2");
        list.add("item 3");
        list.add("item 4");
        list.add("item 5");
```

```
        setLayout(new FlowLayout());
        add(button);
        add(list);
        add(textfield);

        button.addActionListener    (new DebugActionListener());
        list.addActionListener      (new DebugActionListener());
        textfield.addActionListener(new DebugActionListener());
        menuItem.addActionListener (new DebugActionListener());

        addWindowListener(new ActionWindowListener());
    }
}
class ActionWindowListener extends WindowAdapter {
    public void windowClosing(WindowEvent event) {
        Window window = (Window)event.getSource();
        window.dispose();
        System.exit(0);
    }
}
class DebugActionListener implements ActionListener {
    public void actionPerformed(ActionEvent event) {
        System.out.println("action event in:  " +
                        event.getActionCommand());
    }
}
```

The DebugActionListener in Example 9-10 identifies the component that fired the action event by invoking ActionEvent.getActionCommand(). The getActionCommand method returns a string; for buttons and menu items, the string is the label of the button or menu item. For lists, the string returned is the item that was double-clicked, whereas for textfields, the string contains the text that resided in the textfield when the event was fired.

Adjustment Events

Adjustment events are fired by classes that implement the Adjustable interface. Adjustables, as you can surmise from Table 9-9, are objects that maintain an integer value that can be adjusted between settable minimum and maximum values. Adjustables can have their values adjusted by incrementing or decrementing their unit and block increments or by having their value set directly. The exact meaning of unit and block depends on the object that implements the Adjustable interface, but typically a block is defined to be a certain number of units. For example, a text editor would probably define a unit to be a single line of text, and a block would correspond to a page.

The current version of the AWT contains only one public class that implements the `Adjustable` interface—`java.awt.Scrollbar`. Scrollbars can be incremented or decremented by their unit value by activation of the scrollbar arrows. They can also be incremented or decremented by their block value if clicked anywhere in the scrollbar outside of the arrows or the slider (thumb) of the scrollbar. The visible value of a scrollbar corresponds to the width of the slider of the scrollbar and is settable. (See "Applets and Applications" on page 15.)

Table 9-9 `Adjustable` **Interface**

Method	Intent
`void setMinimum(int)`	Sets minimum value
`void setMaximum(int)`	Sets maximum value
`void setUnitIncrement(int)`	Sets the unit increment—typically the smallest meaningful increment
`void setBlockIncrement(int)`	Sets the block increment—typically defined as a number of units
`void setVisibleAmount(int)`	Sets the length of proportional indicator
`void setValue(int)`	Sets the current value of adjustable
`int getOrientation()`	Returns either Adjustable.HORIZONTAL or Adjustable.VERTICAL
`int getMinimum()`	Returns the minimum value the adjustable can take on
`int getMaximum()`	Returns the maximum value the adjustable can take on
`int getUnitIncrement()`	Returns the unit increment
`int getBlockIncrement()`	Returns the block increment
`int getValue()`	Returns the current value
`int getVisibleAmount()`	Returns length of proportional indicator
`void addAdjustmentListener( AdjustmentListener)`	Adds an adjustment listener to adjustable
`void removeAdjustmentListener( AdjustmentListener)`	Removes an adjustment listener to adjustable

`java.awt.ScrollPane` contains two adjustables,[11] to which you can obtain a reference by invoking `ScrollPane.getHAdjustable()` and `ScrollPane.getVAdjustable()`.

Note that while a scrollpane's adjustables are actually scrollbars, the methods used to access the scrollbars return references to an `Adjustable`, not a `Scrollbar`. The reason for this is twofold. First, `Scrollbar` adds only one public method to the `Adjustable` interface:[12] `setOrientation()`. If `ScrollPane` were to return a reference to a `Scrollbar` instead of an `Adjustable`, the orientation of its scrollbars could be modified, which would be highly undesirable. Also, by returning a reference to an `Adjustable` instead of a `Scrollbar`, `ScrollPane` hides the implementation of its adjustables, which leaves it free to implement its adjustable components using something other than a scrollbar in the future or on different platforms.

The applet pictured in Figure 9-10 contains a scrollbar and a scrollpane and monitors the firing of adjustment events. The applet is listed in Example 9-11. Whenever the slider of a scrollbar is moved, adjustment events are fired, which we listen for and print out in the `adjustmentValueChanged` method for our `DebugAdjustmentListener`.

OO TIP

Hide Implementations of Enclosed Objects by Returning References to Interfaces

It is often the case that objects contain other objects—for instance, a ScrollPane contains two scrollbars for scrolling the contents of the scrollpane. Furthermore, it is sometimes desirable to provide accessors to contained objects. In such a case, it is generally preferable to return a reference to an interface that the enclosed objects implement instead of a reference to the actual class of the enclosed object. Doing so hides the actual implementation of the enclosed objects, which affords the enclosing object the freedom to change the actual class of the enclosed objects (as long as the class implements the interface returned).

---

11. Which may or may not be visible depending upon what is being scrolled and the scrollbar display policy of the scrollpane.
12. Excluding constructors.

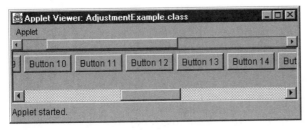

Figure 9-10 Adjustment Events
Adjustment events are fired by the `java.awt.Scrollbar`
component, the only adjustable component in the AWT. The
bottom scrollbar is part of a scrollpane that scrolls 25 cleverly
labeled Buttons. The top scrollbar is a loner.

Example 9-11 `AdjustmentExample` Applet

```java
import java.awt.*;
import java.awt.event.*;
import java.applet.Applet;

public class AdjustmentExample extends Applet {
    private ScrollPane scroller = new ScrollPane();
    private Scrollbar sbar = new Scrollbar(Scrollbar.HORIZONTAL);

    public void init() {
        setLayout(new BorderLayout());
        sbar.setValues(0,   // value
                       50,  // visible
                       0,   // minimum
                       100  // maximum
                       );
        sbar.setUnitIncrement (10);
        sbar.setBlockIncrement(20);
        add(sbar, "North");

        scroller.add(new ScrollMe(), 0);
        add(scroller, "Center");

        sbar.addAdjustmentListener(
                new DebugAdjustmentListener());

        scroller.getHAdjustable().addAdjustmentListener(
                new DebugAdjustmentListener());
        scroller.getVAdjustable().addAdjustmentListener(
                new DebugAdjustmentListener());
    }
}
```

```
class ScrollMe extends Panel {
    public ScrollMe() {
        for(int i=0; i < 25; ++i)
            add(new Button("Button " + i));
    }
}
class DebugAdjustmentListener implements AdjustmentListener {
    public void adjustmentValueChanged(AdjustmentEvent event) {
        Object obj = event.getSource();
        System.out.println(obj.toString());
    }
}
```

Item Events

Our next semantic event application deals with item events. An `ItemEvent` is fired any time you select or deselect an item in an item selectable component—see "Item Selectables: Checkboxes, Choices, and Lists" on page 493. As you can see from Table 9-8 on page 269, item events are fired by the AWT components that contain items: `Checkbox`, `CheckboxMenuItem`, `Choice`, and `List`. Figure 9-11 shows our `ItemExample` applet in action; Example 9-12 shows the source for our applet.

Figure 9-11 Item Events
ItemEvents are fired by components that contain items:
`Checkbox`, `CheckboxMenuItem`, `Choice`, and `List`.

Example 9-12 ItemExample Applet

```java
import java.awt.*;
import java.awt.event.*;
import java.applet.Applet;

public class ItemExample extends Frame {
    private Checkbox  cbox      = new Checkbox("Check Me");
    private Choice    choice    = new Choice();
    private List      list      = new List();
    private CheckboxMenuItem  menuItem =
                    new CheckboxMenuItem("Menu menuItem");

    static public void main(String args[]) {
        ItemExample f = new ItemExample();
        f.setBounds(200,200,200,200);
        f.show();
    }
    public ItemExample() {
        super("Item Example");
        MenuBar mbar = new MenuBar();
        Menu    menu = new Menu("Menu!");
        menu.add(menuItem);
        mbar.add(menu);
        setMenuBar(mbar);

        list.add("list 1");
        list.add("list 2");
        list.add("list 3");
        list.add("list 4");
        list.add("list 5");

        choice.add("choice 1");
        choice.add("choice 2");
        choice.add("choice 3");
        choice.add("choice 4");
        choice.add("choice 5");

        setLayout(new FlowLayout());
        add(cbox);
        add(list);
        add(choice);

        cbox.addItemListener   (new DebugItemListener());
        list.addItemListener   (new DebugItemListener());
        choice.addItemListener (new DebugItemListener());
        menuItem.addItemListener(new DebugItemListener());

        addWindowListener(new ItemWindowListener());
    }
}
```

```
class ItemWindowListener extends WindowAdapter {
    public void windowClosing(WindowEvent event) {
        Window window = (Window)event.getSource();
        window.dispose();
        System.exit(0);
    }
}

class DebugItemListener implements ItemListener {
    public void itemStateChanged(ItemEvent event) {
        Object obj = event.getSource();
        System.out.println(obj.toString());
    }
}
```

Text Events

Our final semantic event applet deals with text events. A TextEvent is fired by components that have editable text—TextField and TextArea, both of which extend TextComponent. A TextEvent is fired any time a text component's editable text is modified. You can see our applet in action in Figure 9-12—the corresponding source for the applet is listed in Example 9-13.

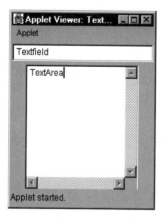

Figure 9-12 Text Events
A TextEvent is fired by components that contain editable text: TextField and TextArea (extensions of TextComponent).

Example 9-13 `TextExample Applet`

```
import java.awt.*;
import java.awt.event.*;
import java.applet.Applet;

public class TextExample extends Applet {
    private TextField textField = new TextField(25);
    private TextArea  textArea  = new TextArea(10, 20);

    public void init() {
        add(textField);
        add(textArea);

        textField.addTextListener(new DebugTextListener());
        textArea.addTextListener(new DebugTextListener());
    }
}
class DebugTextListener implements TextListener {
    public void textValueChanged(TextEvent event) {
        Object obj = event.getSource();
        System.out.println(obj.toString());
    }
}
```

Event Adapters

Event adapters are objects that are interposed between event sources and event listeners. Adapters implement an event listener interface and decouple one or more event sources from one or more event listeners.

Figure 9-13 illustrates the relationships between an event source, adapter, and listener. The adapter class stands in as a listener for a particular event by implementing an appropriate listener interface. When the adapter receives an event, it forwards it to the listener. The adapter may choose to act upon the event either before the event is forwarded to the listener or afterwards. Some adapters may queue events for pending delivery, for instance, whereas others may filter events that are passed on to the listener.

The relationship between adapters and listeners may vary. For instance, Figure 9-13 depicts a delegation relationship between the event adapter and the event listener. The adapter maintains a reference to the listener and invokes listener methods when it receives an event—the adapter *delegates to* the listener. On the other hand, AWT adapters—"AWT Adapters" on page 251—are related to their listeners through inheritance; the adapter *is the superclass of* the listener.

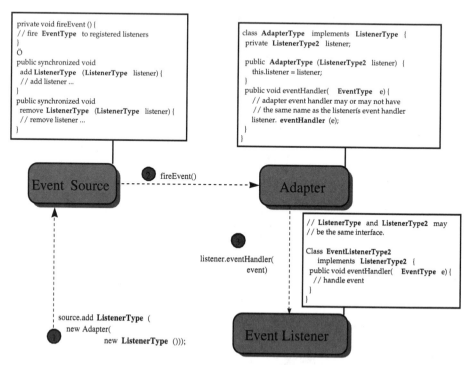

Figure 9-13 Event Adapters
Adapters are interposed between an event source and a listener.
Adapters perform services such as filtering, queuing, or routing
events.

AWT TIP ...

AWT Adapters Are Their Listener's Superclass

AWT event adapters are related to their listeners through inheritance, unlike the
relationship depicted in Figure 9-13.

Listeners extend AWT adapter classes, and therefore the adapter is the superclass of the listener. Instead of manually forwarding events from the adapter to
the listener, the listener overrides the AWT adapter's no-op methods.

Handling Events from Multiple Sources Without Adapters

It is not uncommon for a single event listener to register with more than one event source for a single type of event. Since a listener can implement a given listener interface only once, the listener must determine the source of the event and take appropriate action. For example, the YesNoDialog class listed in Example 9-14 implements the ActionListener interface and registers itself as an ActionListener with the two buttons it contains.

Example 9-14 YesNoDialog Without Adapters

```
import java.awt.*;
import java.awt.event.*;

class YesNoDialog extends Dialog implements ActionListener {
    private Button  yesButton  = new Button("Yes");
    private Button  noButton   = new Button("No");
    private boolean answer;

    public YesNoDialog(String title, String message,
                       boolean isModal) {
        super(new Frame(), title, isModal);

        Panel  buttonPanel = new Panel();
        Panel  labelPanel  = new Panel();

        buttonPanel.add(yesButton);
        buttonPanel.add(noButton);

        labelPanel.add(new Label(message));

        add(labelPanel, "Center");
        add(buttonPanel, "South");

        yesButton.addActionListener(this);
        noButton.addActionListener(this);

        pack();
    }
    public boolean getAnswer() {
        return answer;
    }
    public void actionPerformed(ActionEvent event) {
        Button button = (Button)event.getSource();

        if(button == yesButton)
            yesButtonActivated(event);
        else if(button == noButton)
            noButtonActivated(event);
    }
    public void yesButtonActivated(ActionEvent event) {
        answer = true;
        dispose();
```

```
        }
    public void noButtonActivated(ActionEvent event) {
        answer = false;
        dispose();
    }
}
```

The dialog implements the `ActionListener` interface and registers itself as an `ActionListener` for both of the dialog's buttons:

```
class YesNoDialog extends Dialog implements ActionListener {
    ...
    public YesNoDialog(String title,
                        String message, boolean isModal) {
        ...
        yesButton.addActionListener(this);
        noButton.addActionListener(this);
    }
    ...
}
```

The dialog's `actionPerformed` method obtains a reference to the event source by invoking `java.util.EventObject.getSource()` and then invokes the appropriate method, depending upon whether the event source is the `yesButton` or the `noButton`.

```
    ...
    public void actionPerformed(ActionEvent event) {
        Button button = (Button)event.getSource();

        if(button == yesButton)
            yesButtonActivated(event);
        else if(button == noButton)
            noButtonActivated(event);
    }
    public void yesButtonActivated(ActionEvent event) {
        answer = true;
        dispose();
    }
    public void noButtonActivated(ActionEvent event) {
        answer = false;
        dispose();
    }
    ...
```

For a simple class such as the dialog listed above, routing events through the `actionPerformed` method is nothing more than a minor inconvenience. However, for more complex listeners, code that routes event handling can become a significant maintenance burden. In addition, implementing a method by switching off an event type is unnatural from an object-oriented perspective. Object-oriented languages provide polymorphism to eliminate switching off object types. Adapters can provide a similar effect for events.

Figure 9-14 shows a simple applet that displays a `YesNoDialog`. The code for the applet follows the figure.

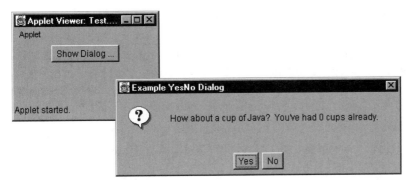

Figure 9-14 `YesNoDialog`

The test applet for the `YesNoDialog` shown above is listed in Example 9-15.

Example 9-15 An Applet That Uses a YesNoDialog

```java
import java.applet.Applet;
import java.awt.*;
import java.awt.event.*;

public class Test extends Applet {
    YesNoDialog dialog = new YesNoDialog("Yes/No Dialog",
                                         "Do you use adapters?",
                                true);  // true means modal

    Button launchButton = new Button("Show Dialog ...");

    public void init() {
        add(launchButton);

        launchButton.addActionListener(new ActionListener() {
            public void actionPerformed(ActionEvent event) {
                Point loc = launchButton.getLocationOnScreen();
                dialog.setLocation(loc.x + 10, loc.y + 10);
```

```
                    dialog.show();

                    if(dialog.getAnswer())
                        showStatus("Yes");
                    else
                        showStatus("No");
                }
            });
        }
    }
```

Type-Safe Demultiplexing Adapters

Without an adapter, the listener is responsible for invoking an appropriate method based on the identity of the event source; for instance, the YesNoDialog in Example 9-14 on page 281 decides whether to invoke yesButtonAcivated or noButtonActivated. Demultiplexing adapters assume that responsibility, resulting in a decoupling between event sources and event listeners.

YesAdapter and NoAdpater, listed below, decouple the event listener—the dialog—from the event sources, that is, the yes and no buttons.

```java
class YesAdapter implements ActionListener {
    YesNoDialog target;

    public YesAdapter(YesNoDialog dialog) {
        target = dialog;
    }
    public void actionPerformed(ActionEvent event) {
        target.yesButtonActivated(event);
    }
}
class NoAdapter implements ActionListener {
    YesNoDialog target;

    public NoAdapter(YesNoDialog dialog) {
        target = dialog;
    }
    public void actionPerformed(ActionEvent event) {
        target.noButtonActivated(event);
    }
}
```

Both adapter classes implement the ActionListener interface and are constructed with a reference to the YesNoDialog. The actionPerformed methods for each adapter class map the event to the appropriate method in the YesNoDialog class, thus decoupling the dialog from the buttons.

YesNoDialog creates instances of YesAdapter and NoAdapter, as listed in Example 9-16.

Example 9-16 YesNoDialog with Type-Safe Adapters

```java
import java.awt.*;
import java.awt.event.*;

class YesNoDialog extends Dialog {
    private Button yesButton   = new Button("Yes");
    private Button noButton     = new Button("No");
    private boolean answer;

    public YesNoDialog(String title, String message,
                        boolean isModal) {
        super(new Frame(), title, isModal);

        Panel  buttonPanel = new Panel();
        Panel  labelPanel  = new Panel();

        buttonPanel.add(yesButton);
        buttonPanel.add(noButton);

        labelPanel.add(new Label(message));

        add(labelPanel, "Center");
        add(buttonPanel, "South");

        yesButton.addActionListener(new YesAdapter(this));
        noButton.addActionListener(new NoAdapter(this));

        pack();
    }
    public boolean getAnswer() {
        return answer;
    }
    public void yesButtonActivated(ActionEvent event) {
        answer = true;
        dispose();
    }
    public void noButtonActivated(ActionEvent event) {
        answer = false;
        dispose();
    }
}
```

The instances of YesAdapter and NoAdapter are specified as listeners for the yes and no buttons. When one of the buttons is activated, an action event is fired to one of the adapters, which is mapped onto the appropriate YesNoDialog method. Use of adapters eliminates the event routing code from the previous version of YesNoDialog.

Notice that `YesAdapter` and `NoAdapter` are type-safe. The compiler attempts to validate that `yesButtonActivated` and `noButtonActivated` are valid methods for the `YesNoDialog` class. It is noteworthy because our next discussion concerns generic adapters that are not type-safe.

Generic Demultiplexing Adapters

Adapters, by design, require one adapter class per listener *method* invoked, which can result in a high number of adapter classes in practice. For instance, in the previous example `YesNoDialog` employed two types of adapters for two methods that handled the yes/no buttons.

Generic adapters, on the other hand, require one adapter class per listener *class*, which can result in a considerable reduction in the number of adapter classes. Such a reduction is not without penalty; generic adapters are not type-safe. Generic adapters employ the Java reflection API to invoke a method on an object at *runtime*. A single generic adapter can be used to invoke any method on any listener, anytime, anywhere.[13]

The drawback to generic adapters is that using them requires circumventing compile-time checking—type checking is handled entirely at runtime—which is no small transgression in a strongly typed language such as Java.

All other things being equal, it is better to check code at compile time than to defer checking until runtime. However, all other things are not equal in this case. Ultimately the developer is left to choose between a potentially high number of type-safe adapters or a relatively low number of type-unsafe generic adapters.

`YesNoDialog` is modified below to use two `GenericActionAdapters`.

```
// code fragment

class YesNoDialog extends Dialog {
    ...
    public void YesNoDialog(String title, String message) {
        ...
        yesButton.addActionListener(
            new GenericActionAdapter(this,
                                     "yesButtonActivated"));
        noButton.addActionListener(
            new GenericActionAdapter(this,
                                     "noButtonActivated"));
    ...
}
```

13. This was not possible prior to the 1.1 JDK.

The GenericActionAdapter constructor takes two arguments: an Object that is assumed to be the listener and a String representing the *name of the method* to be invoked on the listener. GenericActionAdapter uses Java reflection to invoke the named method on the specified listener. In other words, given a reference to a listener and the name of one of the listener's methods, the method is invoked on behalf of the listener. Here's how:

1. The listener's class is obtained via a call to Object.getClass().

2. The Class instance is used to obtain a reference to a Method representing the listener's method. Method Class.getMethod(String, Class[]) is passed the name of the method and an array of Class instances representing the types of the arguments to the method.

3. Once the method is in hand, it is invoked by calling its invoke method.

The Method reference is obtained in the GenericActionAdapter constructor:

```
public class GenericActionAdapter
                       implements ActionListener {
    . . .
    public Class[]  classTypes = { ActionEvent.class };
    . . .

    public GenericActionAdapter(Object listener,
                               String methodName) {
        . . .
        method = listener.getClass().getMethod(methodName,
                                             classTypes);
        . . .
    }
    . . .
}
```

Both event handling methods in the YesNoDialog take a single event of type ActionEvent; thus, the classTypes array passed to Class.getMethod(). Once the Method is in hand, all that's left is to invoke it on the listener.

```
public void actionPerformed(ActionEvent event) {
    args[0] = event;
    try {
        method.invoke(listener, args);
    }
    . . .
}
```

Generic adapters should be careful to handle all possible types of exceptions that can be thrown when the reflection API is used. Table 9-10 lists the types of exceptions that can be thrown from java.lang.reflect.Method.invoke.

Table 9-10 Exceptions Thrown from `java.lang.reflect.Method.invoke()`

Exception thrown	means ...
`IllegalAccess`	Underlying method is inaccessible.
`IllegalArgumentException`	Either the arguments to the method were invalid or unwrapping conversion failed.
`InvocationTargetException`	The underlying method threw an exception.
`NullPointerException`	The specified object is `null`.

In addition to the exceptions that may be thrown by `Method.invoke`, `GenericActionAdapter` must also check that a reference to the method can be had from the name of the method and the type of the listener. That verification requires catching a `NoSuchMethodException` and a `SecurityException`.

```
public GenericActionAdapter(Object listener,
                             String methodName) {
   this.listener   = listener;
   this.methodName = methodName;

   try {
      method =
      listener.getClass().getMethod(methodName, classTypes);
   }
   catch(NoSuchMethodException e) {
      System.out.println("method " +
                          methodName + " not found");
   }
   catch(SecurityException e) {
      System.out.println("search for method" + methodName +
                          " resulted in a security exception");
   }
```

The `GenericActionAdapter` class is listed in its entirety in Example 9-17.

Example 9-17 `GenericActionAdapter` Class Listing

```
import java.lang.reflect.*;
import java.awt.*;
import java.awt.event.*;

public class GenericActionAdapter implements ActionListener {
   public Object    listener;
   public String    methodName;
   public Method    method;
   public Object[]  args = new Object[1];
   public Class[]   classTypes = { ActionEvent.class };

   public GenericActionAdapter(Object listener,
                                String methodName) {
```

```
        this.listener   = listener;
        this.methodName = methodName;
        try {
            method =
            listener.getClass().getMethod(methodName, classTypes);
        }
        catch(NoSuchMethodException e) {
            System.out.println(
                "method " + methodName + " not found");
        }
        catch(SecurityException e) {
            System.out.println(
                "search for method" + methodName +
                " resulted in a security exception");
        }
    }
    public void actionPerformed(ActionEvent event) {
        args[0] = event;

        try {
            method.invoke(listener, args);
        }
        catch(NullPointerException e) {
            System.out.println("null object, or null method");
        }
        catch(IllegalAccessException e) {
            System.out.println("method " + methodName +
                                " cannot be legally accessed");
        }
        catch(IllegalArgumentException e) {
            System.out.println("bad arguments for method " +
                                methodName);
        }
        catch(InvocationTargetException e) {
            System.out.println("exception thrown from method" +
                                methodName);
        }
    }
}
```

A final observation about GenericActionAdapter: other than declarations, almost all of the code is in the business of handling exceptions. Using the Java reflection mechanisms to circumvent type-safety can be painful because type checking that is normally handled by the compiler at compile time must be manually coded by the developer and handled at runtime. It's not the way you'd want to spend much of your time coding and is motivation for working with Java's type system instead of against it.

Prefer Type Safety

The issue is not whether compile-time checking is preferable to runtime checking. Some object-oriented languages, such as Smalltalk, do not place much stock in compile time checking, whereas other languages, such as C++ and Java do. The issue is: Is circumventing type-safety worth the cost *in Java*? Most of the time, the answer is no. Java is a strongly typed language; as a result, circumventing the type system results in a great deal of manual error checking in addition to cutting across the grain of Java's type system.

Inner Classes

The 1.1 version of the JDK introduced a handy new construct: inner classes. Our intent here is not to provide an in-depth discussion of inner classes—if you are so inclined, you can find such a discussion from the Java home page (http://java.sun.com). Instead, we will show how inner classes can be used for handling events.

Inner classes are pertinent to event handling because they can be used to simplify the relationship between event sources and listeners. In Java, a class can be a top-level class or an inner class. Top-level classes are members of a package and were the only type of classes in the 1.0 JDK. Inner classes are classes that can be defined within a block or as part of a new expression.

ThreeDButton

To start off, we'll implement a simple custom component—ThreeDButton, shown in Figure 9-15; our exciting applet is listed in Example 9-18. Note, of course, that our ThreeDButton has no event handling associated with it and, therefore, is always drawn raised. As we go along, we'll add event handling behavior to illustrate various concepts.

Example 9-18 ThreeDButtonTest Applet

```
import java.applet.Applet;
import java.awt.*;
import java.awt.event.*;

public class ThreeDButtonTest extends Applet {
    public void init() {
        add(new ThreeDButton());
    }
}
```

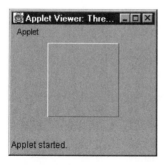

Figure 9-15 ThreeDButton—A Simple Custom Component With No Event Handling.

```
class ThreeDButton extends Canvas {
    static public  int BORDER_INSET = 0, BORDER_RAISED = 1;
            private int state = BORDER_RAISED;

    public void paint(Graphics g) {
        paintBorderRaised();
    }
    public Dimension getPreferredSize() {
        return new Dimension(100,100);
    }
    public int getState() {
        return state;
    }
    public void paintBorderRaised() {
        Graphics g = getGraphics();

        try {
          g.setColor(Color.lightGray);
          g.draw3DRect(0,0,
                    getSize().width-1,getSize().height-1, true);
            state = BORDER_RAISED;
        }
        finally {
            g.dispose();
        }
    }
    public void paintBorderInset() {
        Graphics g = getGraphics();

        try {
          g.setColor(Color.lightGray);
          g.draw3DRect(0,0,
                    getSize().width-1,getSize().height-1, false);
            state = BORDER_INSET;
```

```
        }
        finally {
            g.dispose();
        }
    }
}
```

Encapsulating Event Handling in a Separate Listener Class

Example 9-19 introduces a new class, ThreeDButtonListener, that handles mouse and mouse motion events for a ThreeDButton, similar to the manner in which such events are handled for java.awt.Button.

 Example 9-19 ThreeDButtonListener Class Listing

```
class ThreeDButtonListener extends    MouseAdapter
                             implements MouseMotionListener {
    public void mousePressed(MouseEvent event) {
        ThreeDButton button = (ThreeDButton)event.getSource();
        button.paintBorderInset();
    }
    public void mouseClicked(MouseEvent event) {
        ThreeDButton button = (ThreeDButton)event.getSource();
        button.paintBorderRaised();
    }
    public void mouseReleased(MouseEvent event) {
        ThreeDButton button = (ThreeDButton)event.getSource();
        button.paintBorderRaised();
    }
    public void mouseDragged(MouseEvent event) {
        ThreeDButton button = (ThreeDButton)event.getSource();

        if(button.contains(event.getX(), event.getY())) {
            if(button.getState() == ThreeDButton.BORDER_RAISED)
                button.paintBorderInset();
        }
        else {
            if(button.getState() == ThreeDButton.BORDER_INSET)
                button.paintBorderRaised();
        }
    }
    public void mouseMoved(MouseEvent event) {
    }
}
```

There are three things to notice about our event handling class:

First, every method (except mouseMoved()) in ThreeDButtonListener must, by invoking java.util.EventObject.getSource(), obtain a reference to the ThreeDButton that fired the event because each method manipulates the button in some fashion. An alternative implementation would be to have ThreeDButtonListener maintain a reference to the ThreeDButton with which it is associated, as we've done in Example 9-20. Regardless of which approach we take, since ThreeDButtonListener is a top-level class, we must somehow associate the listener to the button on whose behalf it is handling events.

Example 9-20 ThreeDButton Associated with ThreeDButtonListener

```
class ThreeDButtonListener extends    MouseAdapter
                             implements MouseMotionListener {
    private ThreeDButton button;
    public ThreeDButtonListener(ThreeDButton button) {
        this.button = button;
    }
    public void mousePressed (MouseEvent event) {
        button.paintBorderInset();
    }
    public void mouseClicked (MouseEvent event) {
        button.paintBorderRaised();
    }
    public void mouseReleased(MouseEvent event) {
        button.paintBorderRaised();
    }
    public void mouseDragged(MouseEvent event) {
        if(button.contains(event.getX(), event.getY())) {
            if(button.getState() == ThreeDButton.BORDER_RAISED)
                button.paintBorderInset();
        }
        else {
            if(button.getState() == ThreeDButton.BORDER_INSET)
                button.paintBorderRaised();
        }
    }
    public void mouseMoved(MouseEvent event) {
    }
}
```

Second, notice the curious (but bug-free) implementation of ThreeDButtonListener.mouseMoved(). The reason for the no-op implementation is due to the fact that ThreeDButtonListener implements the MouseMotionListener interface and therefore must implement every method defined in the interface in order to be a concrete (nonabstract) class. This, by the way, is the lesser of two evils: Had ThreeDButtonListener extended MouseMotionAdapter and implemented MouseListener, we would have had two no-op methods to implement: mouseEntered() and mouseExited().

Listening to Yourself

Third, ThreeDButtonListener really has no implementation other than manipulating the ThreeDButton with which it is associated. Perhaps such code would be better off placed in the ThreeDButton class itself, as we've done in

Example 9-21. Now, however, we have three no-op methods because
ThreeDButton already extends Canvas, and, therefore, we must implement
both the MouseListener and MouseMotionListener interfaces instead of
extending an adapter class.

Example 9-21 ThreeDButton Listening to Itself

```
class ThreeDButton extends      Canvas
                implements MouseListener, MouseMotionListener {
    static public  int BORDER_INSET = 0, BORDER_RAISED = 1;
    int state = BORDER_RAISED;
    ...
    public void mousePressed (MouseEvent event) {
        paintBorderInset();
    }
    public void mouseClicked (MouseEvent event) {
        paintBorderRaised();
    }
    public void mouseReleased(MouseEvent event) {
        paintBorderRaised();
    }
    public void mouseDragged(MouseEvent event) {
        if(contains(event.getX(), event.getY())) {
            if(state == ThreeDButton.BORDER_RAISED)
                paintBorderInset();
        }
        else {
            if(state == ThreeDButton.BORDER_INSET)
                paintBorderRaised();
        }
    }
    public void mouseEntered(MouseEvent event) { }
    public void mouseExited (MouseEvent event) { }
    public void mouseMoved  (MouseEvent event) { }
}
```

Although it might make sense to have ThreeDButton handle its own events
instead of giving that responsibility to another object (something discussed later
in this chapter), we're stuck either implementing no-op methods or associating a
separate listener class with the component that fires events.

Named Inner Classes

Enter inner classes. Example 9-22 shows an implementation of ThreeDButton
that defines two inner classes: ThreeDButtonMouseListener and
ThreeDButtonMouseMotionListener. Since inner classes have direct access
to the variables and methods defined in their enclosing class, there is no need to
maintain an association between the listener classes and the button. Also, since
the event handling is encapsulated in separate classes, each class can extend an

adapter class instead of implementing a listener and having to implement no-op methods to satisfy the requirement that concrete classes must implement all methods of the interfaces they implement.

Example 9-22 `ThreeDButton with Inner Classes for Event Handling`

```
class ThreeDButton extends Canvas {
    static public  int BORDER_INSET = 0, BORDER_RAISED = 1;
    int state = BORDER_RAISED;

    public ThreeDButton() {
        addMouseListener      (new ThreeDButtonMouseListener());
        addMouseMotionListener(
            new ThreeDButtonMouseMotionListener());
    }
    class ThreeDButtonMouseListener extends MouseAdapter {
        public void mousePressed (MouseEvent event) {
            paintBorderInset();
        }
        public void mouseClicked (MouseEvent event) {
            paintBorderRaised();
        }
        public void mouseReleased(MouseEvent event) {
            paintBorderRaised();
        }
    }
    class ThreeDButtonMouseMotionListener
                extends MouseMotionAdapter {
        public void mouseDragged(MouseEvent event) {
            if(contains(event.getX(), event.getY())) {
                if(state == ThreeDButton.BORDER_RAISED)
                    paintBorderInset();
            }
            else {
                if(state == ThreeDButton.BORDER_INSET)
                    paintBorderRaised();
            }
        }
    }
    ...
}
```

Anonymous Inner Classes

Notice that with our inner class implementation, `ThreeDButtonMouseListener` and `ThreeDButtonMouseMotionListener` are very unwieldy names for our event handling classes and really add no value, except to fulfill the requirement of a class name. Inner classes provide some syntactic sugar for eliminating such names: anonymous classes.

Example 9-23 is a rewrite of Example 9-22; it uses anonymous (as opposed to named) inner classes for handling mouse events. Anonymous inner classes are defined by inserting a class body after a new expression—the anonymous inner class is constructed on the fly and either implements or extends the interface or class, respectively, named in the new expression.

Example 9-23 ThreeDButton with Anonymous Inner Classes for Event Handling

```
class ThreeDButton extends Canvas {
    static public  int BORDER_INSET = 0, BORDER_RAISED = 1;
    int state = BORDER_RAISED;

    public ThreeDButton() {
        addMouseListener(new MouseAdapter() {
            public void mousePressed (MouseEvent event) {
                paintBorderInset();
            }
            public void mouseClicked (MouseEvent event) {
                paintBorderRaised();
            }
            public void mouseReleased(MouseEvent event) {
                paintBorderRaised();
            }
        });
        addMouseMotionListener(new MouseMotionAdapter() {
            public void mouseDragged(MouseEvent event) {
                if(contains(event.getX(), event.getY())) {
                    if(state == ThreeDButton.BORDER_RAISED)
                        paintBorderInset();
                }
                else {
                    if(state == ThreeDButton.BORDER_INSET)
                        paintBorderRaised();
                }
            }
        });
    }
    ...
}
```

Modifying Default Event Handling Behavior

At this point, the astute reader may observe that we've fused the event handling for ThreeDButton to the component class, and therefore ThreeDButton must be subclassed in order to modify its event handling algorithm, which was one of the major drawbacks of the old event model. Example 9-24 remedies this situation by allowing a ThreeDButton to be constructed with alternative listeners. Note that we've made the nondefault constructor public, but obviously you are free to change the scope of the constructor to suite your needs.[14]

14. In this case, it may actually make sense to allow only subclasses to change the default listeners.

Example 9-24 ThreeDButton with Interchangeable Default Event Handling

```
class ThreeDButton extends Canvas {
    static public  int BORDER_INSET = 0, BORDER_RAISED = 1;
    int state = BORDER_RAISED;

    public ThreeDButton() {
        this(new MouseAdapter() {
            public void mousePressed (MouseEvent event) {
                paintBorderInset();
            }
            public void mouseClicked (MouseEvent event) {
                paintBorderRaised();
            }
            public void mouseReleased(MouseEvent event) {
                paintBorderRaised();
            }
        },
        new MouseMotionAdapter() {
            public void mouseDragged(MouseEvent event) {
                if(contains(event.getX(), event.getY())) {
                    if(state == ThreeDButton.BORDER_RAISED)
                        paintBorderInset();
                }
                else {
                    if(state == ThreeDButton.BORDER_INSET)
                        paintBorderRaised();
                }
            }
        });
    }
    public ThreeDButton(MouseListener ml,
                        MouseMotionListener mml){
        addMouseListener      (ml);
        addMouseMotionListener(mml);
    }
    ...
}
```

Now we've placed the default implementation for handling events in the component that fires the events without having to implement any no-op methods or associate a separate listener with our component—all through the magic of inner classes. Additionally, the default event handling may be overridden by clients of the class. Again, this is not always a recommended approach, but in this case it is a good design.

The last observation that we'll make concerning inner classes is that they provide a mechanism similar to callbacks (function pointers) in C, or blocks in Smalltalk. The difference is that Java uses objects to provide such a mechanism, whereas C uses pointers to functions and Smalltalk uses untyped blocks.

Firing AWT Events from Custom Components

A good percentage of AWT components fire some sort of semantic event. Likewise, many custom components perform one or more actions that could be construed as semantic events. Equipping a custom component to fire semantic events is a fairly common and, thankfully, straightforward task that can be enumerated as follows:

1. Have the component implement a listener interface, if appropriate.

2. Add an appropriate listener member to the class.

3. Implement add*XXX*Listener() and remove*XXX*Listener().

4. Implement process*XXX*Event().

Example 9-25 lists the ThreeDButton class modified to fire action events under the same circumstances that java.awt.Button does.

Example 9-25 ThreeDButton That Fires Action Events

```
import java.applet.Applet;
import java.awt.*;
import java.awt.event.*;

public class ThreeDButtonTest extends Applet
                                    implements ActionListener {
public void init() {
     ThreeDButton button = new ThreeDButton();
     button.addActionListener(this);
     add(button);
}
   public void actionPerformed(ActionEvent event) {
      System.out.println(event.getActionCommand());
   }
}
class ThreeDButton extends Canvas {
   ...
   private ActionListener actionListener = null;
   ...

   public void addActionListener(ActionListener l) {
      actionListener =
          AWTEventMulticaster.add(actionListener, l);
   }
   public void removeActionListener(ActionListener l) {
      actionListener =
          AWTEventMulticaster.remove(actionListener, l);
   }
   public void processActionEvent() {
      if(actionListener != null) {
         actionListener.actionPerformed(
```

```
                new ActionEvent(this, ActionEvent.ACTION_PERFORMED,
                                "3DButton Action"));
        }
    }
}
```

An `ActionListener` reference is added to `ThreeDButton`, and `addActionListener()` and `removeActionListener()` are implemented to delegate to the `AWTEventMulticaster`. The `AWTEventMulticaster` implements an efficient event dispatching mechanism; we could have kept track of a vector (for instance) of action listeners that we manage ourselves, but the `AWTEventMulticaster` takes care of that headache for us in a manner that is more efficient than a vector implementation. Whenever a listener is added or removed via the `AWTEventMulticaster`, the multicaster returns a reference to a listener that is the first listener in the chain of listeners (of the appropriate type) that are currently registered with the component in question.

We have also implemented `processActionEvent()`, which invokes `actionPerformed()` on our action listener. Invoking `actionPerformed()` on the lone `actionListener` results in `actionPerformed()` being invoked for every action listener currently registered with our button.

`ThreeDButton.processActionEvent()` constructs an `ActionEvent`, signifying that the button is the source of the event, the type of action event is `ACTION_PERFORMED`, and the action command (a `String` representing the action) is "3DButton Action".

`ThreeDButtonTest` implements `ActionListener` and registers itself as an action listener with our button. In addition, it implements `actionPerformed()` and prints out the action command of the button that was the source of the event. It is important to realize that `ThreeDButtonTest` registers itself as an action listener and reacts to action events in exactly the same manner as it would for any AWT component that fires action events.

AWTEventMulticaster Limitations

If you were paying close attention to the above discussion, perhaps you found it somewhat curious that we can invoke `actionPerformed()` on the single `ActionListener` returned by the `AWTEventMulticaster` methods `add()` and `remove()`, and somehow have `actionPerformed()` invoked for every action listener currently registered with our component. This process works because the listener returned by the `AWTEventMulticaster` `add` and `remove` methods is actually an instance of `AWTEventMulticaster`!

`AWTEventMulticaster` implements every listener interface defined in the AWT and overrides all of the associated methods to turn around and invoke the same method for all currently registered listeners. So, for instance, when we invoke `AWTEventMulticaster.add()`, in Example 9-25, the `ActionListener` returned is actually an instance of `AWTEventMulticaster`. When we subsequently invoke `actionPerformed()` on the listener, `AWTEventMulticaster.actionPerformed()` is called; this method runs through the list of currently registered action listeners and invokes `actionPerformed()` for each one.

As a result of all this object-oriented tomfoolery, `AWTEventMulticaster` is only useful for the set of events defined by the AWT—if you wish to fire custom events, you must resort to maintaining a list of listeners yourself and ensure that the listeners are notified when your custom events are fired. This, of course, is a segue into our next section.

Firing Custom Events from Custom Components

Firing standard AWT events from custom components is relatively straightforward, as we've seen above. However, implementing custom events and firing them from a custom component is a little trickier. We'll outline the steps involved and then, for the sake of illustration, develop a custom component that fires custom events.

A Not-So-Contrived Scenario

Let's say that you've been tasked with developing a tree control similar to what you'd find in the Windows 95 Explorer application. For those of you unfamiliar with the Explorer, take a look at Figure 9-16. (A future version of the AWT will provide such a component.)

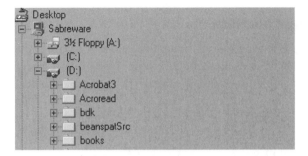

Figure 9-16 The Windows 95 Explorer Tree Control.

Being the good object-oriented developer that you are, you decide to encapsulate the functionality of the plus-minus buttons associated with each node in its own custom component. Furthermore, the plus-minus custom component will fire events whenever it is expanded or contracted, which will serve as notification to any registered listeners that the node has been either expanded or contracted.

If you take a look at the AWT events and listeners, you will find that no event/listener pairs correspond to expansion and contraction.[15] Therefore, a custom event class will need to be implemented in addition to the custom component. So, we have three tasks to accomplish:

- Implement a plus-minus custom component.

- Implement an event representing Expand/Contract events.

- Have the plus-minus component fire events implemented in the previous step when appropriate.

We should note that an alternative approach would be for the plus-minus component to simply fire item events. The `ItemEvent` class defines two constants, `ItemEvent.SELECTED` and `ItemEvent.DESELECTED`, that are used to signify the type of state change for the component in question. We could have used values for the state change other than the selection/deselection values to signify expansion/contraction. However, our intent here is to illustrate firing custom events, so we've chosen the alternative route of implementing a custom event class.

Steps Involved

Of course, the steps outlined above are specific to our plus-minus custom component and a bit too high level, so let's take a look at what's involved in general for developing a custom component that fires custom events:

1. Develop a custom event class.
2. Develop a listener interface.
    - `void XXXChanged(XXXEvent)`
3. Develop an interface for registering listeners.
    - public void addXXXListener(XXXListener).
    - public void removeXXXListener(XXXListener).

---

15. A 1.1 beta version of the AWT specified `ItemEvents` as encompassing expand/contract in addition to select/deselect, but it was thought that expand/contract was not general enough for `ItemEvent` and the feature was pulled.

- public void processXXXEvent(XXXEvent). // fire event to listeners

4. Develop a custom component that fires custom events.

   - Implements interface for registering listeners developed in previous step.

Of course, carrying out the steps listed above is easier said than done, so we will implement the plus-minus custom component in order to illustrate how it's done. Note that each step listed above is actually fairly straightforward to implement, but getting your arms wrapped around the task as a whole can take some practice.

Develop a Custom Event Class

In "Item Events" on page 276, we took a look at the ItemEvent class and noted that having a Checkbox fire an item event seemed to be somewhat of a stretch because a Checkbox has but one item (itself). The AWT provides one event/listener pair for components that have selectable items, whether they have one item or more than one item. We'll take the same approach with our expandable event and have it encompass components that have one expandable item, or components that may potentially have more than one expandable item.

Following the naming convention established by the AWT events, we'll name our custom event class ItemExpandEvent. ItemExpandEvent public methods are listed in Table 9-11.

Table 9-11 ItemExpandEvent **Public Methods**

Method	Description
ItemExpandable getItemExpandable()	Returns source of the event, which must be an ItemExpandable
Object getItem()	Returns the item that was expanded or contracted
int getExpandState()	Returns ItemExpandState.EXPANDED or ItemExpandState.CONTRACTED

The implementation of ItemExpandEvent is shown in Example 9-26.

Example 9-26 `ItemExpandEvent` Custom Event

```
import java.awt.AWTEvent;

public class ItemExpandEvent extends AWTEvent {
    public static final int EXPANDED   = 1;
    public static final int CONTRACTED = 2;

    Object item;
    int expandState;

    public ItemExpandEvent(ItemExpandable source, Object item,
                           int expandState) {
        super(source, -1);
        this.item = item;
        this.expandState = expandState;
    }
    public ItemExpandable getItemExpandable() {
        return (ItemExpandable)source;
    }
    public Object getItem() {
        return item;
    }
    public int getExpandState() {
        return expandState;
    }
    public String paramString() {
        String s = null;
        switch(expandState) {
          case EXPANDED:   s += "EXPANDED"; break;
          case CONTRACTED: s += "CONTRACTED"; break;
          default:         s += "unknown expand state";
        }
        return super.paramString() + "[expanded=" + s + "]";
    }
}
```

`ItemExpandEvent` extends `AWTEvent` and as a result inherits the ability to keep track of the source of the event. The source of the event must be an implementation of the `ItemExpandable` interface, as you can see from the `getItemExandable()` implementation.

`ItemExpandEvent` keeps track of the individual item (within the `ItemExpandable`) that was expanded or contracted and also provides access to the source of the event (the `ItemExpandable`).

It is interesting to note that not only will our plus-minus component implement `ItemExpandable`, but in all likelihood the tree control in which it resides would also implement `ItemExpandable`. The difference between the plus-minus component and the tree control is that the plus-minus component has but one expandable item (itself), whereas the tree control has potentially many expandable items (plus-minus or other ItemExpandable extensions).

ItemExpandEvent provides an accessor method, getExpandState() that returns either ItemExpandEvent.EXPANDED or ItemExpandEvent.CONTRACTED. Note that the expand state must be specified (along with the ItemExpandable and specific object being expanded or contracted) at construction time.

Finally, note that ItemExpandEvent provides a paramString method that will print out fascinating information whenever toString() is invoked on the event.

Develop a Listener Interface

The next thing that we need is an interface for listening to components that fire events of type ItemExpandEvent. The ItemExpandListener implementation is shown in Example 9-27.

Example 9-27 ItemExpandListener Interface

```
import java.util.EventListener;

public interface ItemExpandListener extends EventListener {
    void itemExpandStateChanged(ItemExpandEvent e);
}
```

As is typically the case, our listener interface is very simple. As is also typically the case, the listener interface extends the java.util.EventListener interface. Whenever the expansion state of an item in an ItemExpandable changes, the itemExpandStateChanged method of its listeners is invoked.

Define an Interface for Registering Listeners

Our plus-minus custom component will implement the ItemExpandable interface, which allows item expand listeners to register interest in item expand events and to obtain a reference to an array of all currently expanded items. The ItemExpandable interface is shown in Example 9-28.

Example 9-28 ItemExpandable Interface

```
public interface ItemExpandable {
    public Object[] getExpandedItems    ();
    public void     addExpandListener   (ItemExpandListener l);
    public void     removeExpandListener(ItemExpandListener l);
}
```

In addition to enabling listeners to register and unregister, the
`ItemExpandListener` interface also provides for returning an array of objects
that are currently expanded. When our plus-minus component is expanded, it
will return an array with itself as the lone item in the array; when our plus-minus
component is contracted, it will return `null` from `getExpandedItems()`. Other
components that implement the `ItemExpandable` interface may contain many
expandable objects and therefore may potentially return an array with any
number of objects from the `getExpandedItems` method.

Develop a Custom Component That Fires Custom Events

Our final step involves developing the custom component(s) that fire the custom
events. In our case, that would be our plus-minus component, which we'll name
`PlusMinus`. The `PlusMinus` class extends `Component`[16] and implements the
`ItemExpandable` interface defined above:

```
public class PlusMinus extends     Component
                       implements ItemExpandable {
    protected boolean  expanded      = false;
    private    Object[] expandedItems = new Object[1];
    private    Vector   listeners     = new Vector();
    ...
    public Object[] getExpandedItems() {
        if(expanded) {
            expandedItems[0] = this;
            return expandedItems;
        }
        else
            return null;
    }
    public void addExpandListener(ItemExpandListener l) {
        listeners.addElement(l);
    }
    public void removeExpandListener(ItemExpandListener l) {
        listeners.removeElement(l);
    }
...
```

If expanded, the `getExpandedItems` method sets the first element of the array
to the current instance of `PlusMinus`; otherwise, it returns `null` to signify that it
is not expanded. Of course, callers of `getExpandedItems()` must live with the
inconvenience of having to dig the instance of `PlusMinus` out of the first slot in
the array, which is the price they pay for the generality of the `ItemExpandable`
interface.

---

16. It's a lightweight component! See "Lightweight Components" on page 651.

Notice that we're not using the `AWTEventMulticaster` to broadcast events to listeners as we did when we fired AWT events from custom components in "Firing AWT Events from Custom Components" on page 298. As discussed in "AWTEventMulticaster Limitations" on page 299, the `AWTEventMulticaster` can only be used for the standard events that come with the AWT, and our event is a custom event. As a result, we've taken the easy way out and have kept track of a vector of listeners. Finally, we have `PlusMinus.processExpandEvent()`, which broadcasts expand events to registered listeners:

```
protected synchronized void processExpandEvent(
                                 ItemExpandEvent event) {
    Enumeration e = listeners.elements();

    while(e.hasMoreElements()) {
        ItemExpandListener l = (ItemExpandListener)
                                       e.nextElement();
        l.itemExpandStateChanged(event);
    }
}
```

`processExpandEvent()` simply cycles through the currently registered listeners and invokes `itemExpandStateChanged()` for each.

The `PlusMinus` constructor invokes `addMouseListener()` with an inner class version of `MouseAdapter` to handle mouse pressed events. Whenever a mouse pressed event occurs, the expansion state of the instance of `PlusMinus` is toggled and the component is repainted.

```
public PlusMinus() {
    addMouseListener(new MouseAdapter() {
        public void mousePressed(MouseEvent event) {
            if(expanded) contract();
            else         expand  ();
            repaint();
        }
    });
}
```

Example 9-29 shows the implementation of the `PlusMinus` class in its entirety.

Example 9-29 `PlusMinus` Class Listing

```
import java.util.*;
import java.awt.*;
import java.awt.event.*;

public class PlusMinus extends Component
                  implements ItemExpandable {
    protected boolean  expanded      = false;
    private    Object[] expandedItems = new Object[1];
```

```java
private   Vector   listeners     = new Vector();

public PlusMinus() {
    addMouseListener(new MouseAdapter() {
        public void mousePressed(MouseEvent event) {
            if(expanded) contract();
            else          expand  ();

            repaint();
        }
    });
}
public void paint(Graphics g) {
    drawBorder(g);
    drawPlusOrMinus(g);
}
public void expand() {
    ItemExpandEvent event =
        new ItemExpandEvent(this,  // we are event source
                            this,   // we are item
                    ItemExpandEvent.EXPANDED);
    expanded = true;
    processExpandEvent(event);
}
public void contract() {
    ItemExpandEvent event =
        new ItemExpandEvent(this,  // we are event source
                            this,   // we are item
                    ItemExpandEvent.CONTRACTED);
    expanded = false;
    processExpandEvent(event);
}
public Dimension getPreferredSize() {
    return new Dimension(11,11);
}
public Object[] getExpandedItems() {
    if(expanded) {
        expandedItems[0] = this;
        return expandedItems;
    }
    else
        return null;
}
public void addExpandListener(ItemExpandListener l) {
    listeners.addElement(l);
}
public void removeExpandListener(ItemExpandListener l) {
    listeners.removeElement(l);
}
protected synchronized void processExpandEvent(
                            ItemExpandEvent event) {
    Enumeration e = listeners.elements();
```

```
        while(e.hasMoreElements()) {
            ItemExpandListener l = (ItemExpandListener)
                                    e.nextElement();
            l.itemExpandStateChanged(event);
        }
    }
    private void drawBorder(Graphics g) {
        Dimension size = getSize();
        g.setColor(Color.darkGray.brighter());
        g.drawRect(0,0,size.width-1,size.height-1);
    }
    private void drawPlusOrMinus(Graphics g) {
        Dimension size = getSize();

        if(expanded) drawMinusSign(g, size, Color.black);
        else         drawPlusSign (g, size, Color.black);
    }
    private void drawMinusSign(Graphics g, Dimension size,
                                Color color) {
        g.setColor(color);
        g.drawLine(2,size.height/2,size.width-3,size.height/2);
    }
    private void drawPlusSign(Graphics g, Dimension size,
                                Color color) {
        g.setColor(color);
        g.drawLine(size.width/2,2,size.width/2,size.height-3);
        g.drawLine(2,size.height/2,size.width-3,size.height/2);
    }
}
```

Finally, we need an applet with which to test our custom component. This turns out to be trivial—the applet is shown in action in Figure 9-17. Our applet implements the `ItemExpandListener` interface, creates an instance of `PlusMinus`, and registers itself as being interested in expand events. The applet is listed in Example 9-30.

Example 9-30 `PlusMinusTest` Applet

```
import java.applet.Applet;
import java.awt.*;

public class PlusMinusTest extends    Applet
                            implements ItemExpandListener {
    public void init() {
        PlusMinus pm = new PlusMinus();
        pm.addExpandListener(this);
        add(pm);
    }
```

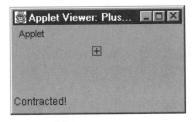 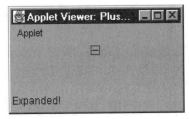

Figure 9-17 `PlusMinusTest` Applet
The picture on the left shows the `PlusMinus` custom component
contracted; on the right, it's expanded.

```
public void itemExpandStateChanged(ItemExpandEvent event) {
    ItemExpandable ie = event.getItemExpandable();
    Object[]       items = ie.getExpandedItems();

    if(items != null) showStatus("Expanded!");
    else              showStatus("Contracted!");
}
}
```

Whenever the plus minus component is expanded or contracted, it fires an
`ItemExpandEvent`, which the applet is listening for.

Dispatching Events and the AWT Event Queue

There are times when it is desirable to create an event and pass it to a specific
component for handling. For instance, some applications may wish to record a
sequence of events and play them back at a later time. Essentially, there are two
ways to send an event to a component: invoke `Component.dispatchEvent()`
or use an event queue.

`Component.dispatchEvent(AWTEvent)` processes the event it is passed in the
exact same manner as events that are initiated by user gestures. Figure 9-18 shows
an applet that contains two buttons; when the button on the right is activated,
mouse pressed and mouse released events are delivered to the button on the left.
The mouse events cause the left-hand button to activate and fire an action event.

Example 9-31 lists the applet.

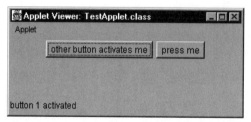

Figure 9-18 Dispatching Events Directly to a Component
When the button on the right is activated, mouse pressed and released
events are dispatched to the button on the left, causing it to fire an
action event.

Example 9-31 Dispatching Events Directly to a Component

```
import java.applet.Applet;
import java.awt.*;
import java.awt.event.*;

public class TestApplet extends Applet {
    public void init() {
        final Button
                button1 = new Button("other button activates me"),
                button2 = new Button("press me");

        add(button1);
        add(button2);

        button1.addActionListener(new ActionListener() {
            public void actionPerformed(ActionEvent e) {
                showStatus("button 1 activated");
            }
        });

        button2.addActionListener(new ActionListener() {
            public void actionPerformed(ActionEvent e) {
                MouseEvent press = new MouseEvent(
                                button1,
                                MouseEvent.MOUSE_PRESSED,
                                System.currentTimeMillis(),
                                0, 5, 5, 1, false);

                MouseEvent release = new MouseEvent(
                                button1,
                                MouseEvent.MOUSE_RELEASED,
                                System.currentTimeMillis(),
                                0, 5, 5, 1, false);
```

```
                button1.dispatchEvent(press);

                try {
                    Thread.currentThread().sleep(50);
                }
                catch(InterruptedException ex) {
                    ex.printStackTrace();
                }

                button1.dispatchEvent(release);
            }
        });
    }
}
```

The listener for the right-hand button creates two mouse events and sends them in succession—with a short delay between events[17]—to the button on the left. The button on the left has an `ActionListener` that updates the applet's status bar when the button has been activated.

Regardless of whether the button on the left is activated by clicking in the button itself or activating the right-hand button, the result is the same: the left-hand button reacts to the mouse events (in a platform-dependent manner) and fires an action event.

Instead of dispatching events directly to a component, it is sometimes preferable to post events to a queue and have the queue deliver events to the component in question. The AWT includes an event queue class—`java.awt.EventQueue`—that provides the methods listed in Table 9-12.

Table 9-12 `java.awt.EventQueue` **Public Methods**

Method	Description
`void postEvent(` `AWTEvent theEvent)`	Posts an `AWTEvent` to a queue
`AWTEvent getNextEvent()` `throws InterruptedException`	Returns the next event in a queue. This method removes the event from a queue.
`AWTEvent peekEvent()`	Returns the next event in a queue. This method does not remove the event from a queue.
`AWTEvent peekEvent(int id)`	Returns the next event in the queue of the specified type. This method does not remove the event from the queue.

17. A delay is incurred so that the button's reaction to the mouse events can be seen.

At any time, there exists only one system event queue, which can be accessed by invoking `Toolkit.getSystemEventQueue()`.[18] Additionally, events may be posted to a local event queue. Example 9-32 lists another version of the applet listed in Example 9-31 on page 310.

Example 9-32 `Dispatching Events to a Component Through an Event Queue`

```
import java.applet.Applet;
import java.awt.*;
import java.awt.event.*;

public class TestApplet extends Applet {
    public void init() {
        final Button
                button1 = new Button("other button activates me"),
                button2 = new Button("press me");

        final EventQueue queue = new EventQueue();

        add(button1);
        add(button2);

        button1.addActionListener(new ActionListener() {
            public void actionPerformed(ActionEvent e) {
                showStatus("button 1 activated");
            }
        });

        button2.addActionListener(new ActionListener() {
            public void actionPerformed(ActionEvent e) {
                MouseEvent press = new MouseEvent(
                                button1,
                                MouseEvent.MOUSE_PRESSED,
                                System.currentTimeMillis(),
                                0, 5, 5, 1, false);

                MouseEvent release = new MouseEvent(
                                button1,
                                MouseEvent.MOUSE_RELEASED,
                                System.currentTimeMillis(),
                                0, 5, 5, 1, false);

                queue.postEvent(press);

                try {
                    Thread.currentThread().sleep(50);
                }
                catch(InterruptedException ex) {
```

18. Subject to security restrictions.

```
                ex.printStackTrace();
            }

            queue.postEvent(release);
        }
    });
    }
}
```

Instead of dispatching the event directly to the left-hand button, an event queue is instantiated, and the mouse events are posted to the queue. Whenever an event queue is instantiated, an event dispatch thread is created and events are delivered on the dispatch thread. On the other hand, events that are dispatched directly to a component are not delivered on a separate thread.

Active Events

Prior to the 1.2 AWT, events posted to an event queue had to have either a Component or a MenuComponent specified as the source of the event in order for the event to be dispatched. When an event is dispatched by an event queue, either Component.dispatchEvent() or MenuComponent.dispatchEvent() is invoked for the source of the event, depending upon the type of the event source.

The 1.2 AWT introduces a new type of event—an active event. Active events are represented by the java.awt.ActiveEvent interface, which defines a lone method: void dispatch(). Active events are dispatched by invoking the *event's* dispatch method, instead of invoking a method provided by the event source. As a result, active events allow noncomponents to arrange for a certain behavior to occur on a different thread by posting the event to an event queue.

The applet shown in Figure 9-19 contains a button that posts an active event to an event queue. When the button is activated, an ActiveEvent is instantiated along with an EventQueue, and the event is posted to the queue.

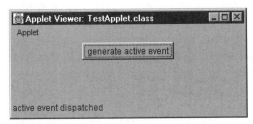

Figure 9-19 Active Events
Activating the button contained in the applet causes an ActiveEvent to be fired.

The applet is listed in Example 9-33.

Example 9-33 Using ActiveEvents

```java
import java.applet.Applet;
import java.awt.*;
import java.awt.event.*;

public class TestApplet extends Applet {
    public void init() {
        final Button
                button1 = new Button("generate active event");

        add(button1);

        button1.addActionListener(new ActionListener() {
            public void actionPerformed(ActionEvent e) {
                AnActiveEvent ae = new AnActiveEvent();
                EventQueue queue = new EventQueue();

                queue.postEvent(ae);
            }
        });
    }
}
class AnActiveEvent extends AWTEvent implements ActiveEvent {
    public AnActiveEvent() {
        super(new Object(), AWTEvent.RESERVED_ID_MAX + 1);
    }
    public void dispatch() {
        System.out.println("active event dispatched");
    }
}
```

Event queues expect events posted to them to be AWTEvents, so AnActiveEvent extends AWTEvent and implements the ActiveEvent interface.

Notice that the source of the event is specified as simply a new object; the source does not have to be a component or menu component. When the event queue sees that the event is an instance of ActiveEvent, it simply invokes the event's dispatch method instead of calling a method on the event source. The result is that each activation of the button results in an active event being posted to an event queue. In turn, the event queue processes the event by invoking ActiveEvent.dispatch, which is overridden in AnActiveEvent to simply print out a string.

Inheritance-Based Mechanism

Under certain circumstances, an inheritance-based event handling mechanism *may* be preferable to delegation. For instance, if a class provides some fundamental functionality that is tied to a particular event, an inheritance-based approach might possibly be preferred. The JDK documentation for the event model stresses that the inheritance-based mechanism is to be used sparingly, if at all.

The JDK delegation event model provides an inheritance-based alternative to using delegation for event handling. The inheritance-based mechanism is based upon the original JDK event model and suffers from its shortcomings; as a result, we reiterate the documentation warning: *the inheritance-based mechanism should be used sparingly, if at all.*

Using the inheritance-based mechanism involves overriding one of the following `java.awt.Component` methods:

```
void processEvent(AWTEvent event)

void processComponentEvent(ComponentEvent event)

void processFocusEvent(FocusEvent event)

void processKeyEvent(KeyEvent event)

void processMouseEvent(MouseEvent event)

void processMouseMotionEvent(MouseEvent event)
```

For every occurrence of an AWT event, `Component.processEvent()` is invoked. `processEvent()` determines the type of event that occurred and then invokes an appropriate `Component.process...Event` method. The `process...Event` method then fires the event to a set of listeners of the appropriate listener type.

For instance, when the mouse enters an AWT component, `Component.processEvent` is invoked. `processEvent()` is passed an `AWTEvent`, which is used to determine the type of the event. `processEvent()` invokes `Component.processMouseEvent()`, passing along the `AWTEvent`, which is cast to a `MouseEvent`. Finally, `processMouseEvent` invokes the `mouseEntered` method for every `MouseListener` that is registered with the component.

AWT TIP

Use Inheritance-Based Event Handling Sparingly

The documentation that comes with the AWT recommends that you use the inheritance-based mechanism sparingly. As we'll see later on in this chapter, the inheritance-based mechanism can be simulated by listening to yourself, in which case you get nearly all of the benefits associated with the inheritance-based mechanism, while avoiding all of its drawbacks.

Example 9-34 lists the implementation of a button that draws a 3D rectangle around the border of the button when the mouse enters and draws a flat border when the mouse exits, using the inheritance-based feature of the new event model. Under the original event model, we may have chosen to override `mouseEnter()` and `mouseExit()` in order to get the job done. With the new event model, we override `processMouseEvent()`, which must determine the actual type of mouse event and act accordingly.

Just as with the old (inheritance-based) event model, you can choose between overriding a kitchen-sink method, whereby all events are funneled through (`processEvent()`—the equivalent of `handleEvent()`), or you can override one of a number of convenience methods. Example 9-34 overrides `processMouseEvent()`, and Example 9-35 overrides `processEvent()`.

Note that you must call `enableEvents(long mask)` and specify the type(s) of event(s) that you'd like to be fired from the component (or alternatively add an appropriate event listener to the component), or your overridden methods will never be invoked. This is the one major difference between the inheritance-based event model and the delegation-based model. Figure 9-20 shows our highlight button test applet in action.

Example 9-34 Inheritance-Based Event Handling: Overriding processMouseEvent()

```
import java.applet.Applet;
import java.awt.*;
import java.awt.event.*;

public class HighlightButtonTest extends Applet {
    public void init() {
        HighlightButton leftButton  = new HighlightButton();
        HighlightButton rightButton = new HighlightButton();

        add(leftButton);
        add(rightButton);
```

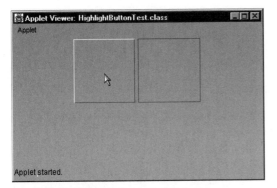

Figure 9-20 Using the Inheritance-Based Event Mechanism Uses inheritance-based event handling to draw a 3D border around a rectangle when the mouse enters (the mouse is in the rectangle on the left). Inheritance-based event handling is supported in the delegation-based event model.

```
        }
}

class HighlightButton extends Canvas {
    public HighlightButton() {
        // enableEvents() is a protected method, so we can
        // only call it in extensions of Component.  If we
        // added a MouseListener, it would undam the flow of
        // mouse events from the component
          enableEvents(AWTEvent.MOUSE_EVENT_MASK);
    }
    public void paint(Graphics g) {
        paintBorder();
    }
    public Dimension getPreferredSize() {
        return new Dimension(100,100);
    }
    public void paintBorder() {
        Graphics g = getGraphics();
        g.setColor(Color.gray);
        g.drawRect(0,0,getSize().width-1,getSize().height-1);
    }
    public void highlight() {
        Graphics g = getGraphics();
        g.setColor(Color.lightGray);
        g.draw3DRect(0,0,getSize().width,getSize().height, true);
    }
    public void unhighlight() {
        paintBorder();
    }
```

```
public void processMouseEvent(MouseEvent event) {
    if(event.getID() == MouseEvent.MOUSE_ENTERED) {
        HighlightButton canvas =
                (HighlightButton)event.getSource();
        canvas.highlight();
    }
    else if(event.getID() == MouseEvent.MOUSE_EXITED) {
        HighlightButton canvas =
                (HighlightButton)event.getSource();
        canvas.unhighlight();
    }
}
}
```

AWT TIP ...

Not All Events Are Delivered to Components

A common mistake when using the inheritance-based mechanism under the delegation event model is neglecting to call enableEvents(long). Under the inheritance-based event model, all events were delivered to a component, whether the component was interested in the event or not. The delegation event model is much more selective, delivering events only to components that indicate interest in the particular type of event by calling enableEvent(long) or adding a listener to the component. Therefore, if you must use the inheritance-based mechanism, don't forget to call enableEvents() for events you are interested in.

Example 9-35 illustrates overriding processEvent() instead of a convenience method. Note that we are careful to call super.processEvent() after we are finished processing the events we are interested in because, just like handleEvent() from the old event model, processEvent() dispatches events to convenience methods. If we had, for instance, also overridden processKeyEvent() in Example 9-35 and neglected to invoke super.processEvent(), our overridden processKeyEvent() would never be invoked.

Example 9-35 Inheritance-Based Event Handling: Overriding processEvent()

```
import java.applet.Applet;
import java.awt.*;
import java.awt.event.*;

public class HighlightButtonTest2 extends Applet {
    public void init() {
        HighlightButton leftButton  = new HighlightButton();
        HighlightButton rightButton = new HighlightButton();
```

```
        add(leftButton);
        add(rightButton);
    }
}

class HighlightButton2 extends Canvas {
    public HighlightButton2() {
        enableEvents(AWTEvent.MOUSE_EVENT_MASK);
    }
    public void paint(Graphics g) {
        paintBorder();
    }
    public Dimension getPreferredSize() {
        return new Dimension(100,100);
    }
    public void paintBorder() {
        Graphics g = getGraphics();
        g.setColor(Color.gray);
        g.drawRect(0,0,getSize().width-1,getSize().height-1);
    }
    public void highlight() {
        Graphics g = getGraphics();
        g.setColor(Color.lightGray);
        g.draw3DRect(0,0,getSize().width,getSize().height, true);
    }
    public void unhighlight() {
        paintBorder();
    }
    public void processEvent(AWTEvent event) {
        if(event.getID() == MouseEvent.MOUSE_ENTERED) {
            HighlightButton canvas =
                (HighlightButton)event.getSource();
            canvas.highlight();
        }
        else if(event.getID() == MouseEvent.MOUSE_EXITED) {
            HighlightButton canvas =
                (HighlightButton)event.getSource();
            canvas.unhighlight();
        }
        super.processEvent(event);   // must do
    }
}
```

Event Handling Design

Although the new event model is much improved over the old model, you may find yourself pining for the simplicity of the old model where you essentially had only one choice for handling events, namely, extending a component and

embedding event handling code in the extension.[19] The new model, coupled with inner classes, allows for much more flexibility than the old event model. For instance, when handling events with the delegation-based event model you can:

- Use the old event model
- Use the inheritance-based mechanism provided with the new model
- Have components listen to themselves
- Encapsulate the event handling code in a separate listener class

In addition to the approaches outlined above, you can also employ inner classes when handling events. In spite of all the choices you face when implementing event handling, deciding which approach to use is actually easier than it appears. As we shall soon discover, in nearly every case, the best approaches are the last two—the first two approaches are rarely (if ever) recommended. Let's take a look at each option and then discuss whether or not to use inner classes.

Using the Inheritance-Based Event Model

This option is viable because the new event model supports the old model. However, at some future time, the old model will cease to be supported, so it's a good idea to bite the bullet and revamp your event handling code sooner than later. Employing the old event model winds up being double work because you will eventually have to change it. Therefore, using the old event model is not recommended.

In nearly every case, listening to yourself or delegating to a separate event handling class is preferable to using the inheritance-based mechanism because the inheritance-based mechanism in the new event model suffers from the same deficiencies as the old event model. See "Shortcomings of the Inheritance-Based Event Model" on page 229 for a discussion of the old event model's deficiencies.

Listening to Yourself

You know the age-old question: "Are you crazy if you talk to yourself?" and the age-old reply: "Only if you answer." Perhaps you would be considered merely eccentric if you only listen to yourself. When handling events for a component, having the component register itself as a listener is a valid, and often recommended, approach.

---

19. Actually, you could manually delegate event handling to another object, but it's a lot of work and is quite error-prone.

When basic event handling for a component is not likely to change regardless of the manner in which the component is extended, it makes perfect sense to embed the event handling in the component by having the component listen to itself. Components listen to themselves by implementing a particular listener interface (or extending an adapter class) and then adding themselves as a listener:

```
public class SomeComponent extends Canvas
                                implements MouseAdapter{
    public SomeComponent() {
        addMouseListener(this); // listens to its own mouse events
    }
    public void mousePressed(MouseEvent event) {
        // React to mouse pressed
    }
    public void mouseEntered(MouseEvent event) { }
    public void mouseExited (MouseEvent event) { }
    public void mouseClicked(MouseEvent event) { }
    public void mouseReleased(MouseEvent event) { }
}
```

Of course, there are drawbacks to listening to yourself. First, you are almost certain to have to implement no-op event handling methods because you cannot extend an adapter class (components already extend either `Component` or an extension of `Component`). However, as we've seen in "ThreeDButton with Inner Classes for Event Handling" on page 295, we can employ inner classes to eliminate this drawback. In fact, our `SomeComponent` class can be rewritten as:

```
public class SomeComponent extends Canvas
    public SomeComponent() {
        addMouseListener(new MouseAdapter() {
            public void mousePressed(MouseEvent event) {
                // React to mouse pressed
            }
        });
    }
    . . .
```

Another drawback to listening to yourself is that it involves hardcoding event handling in the component that fires the events. However, as we saw in "ThreeDButton with Interchangeable Default Event Handling" on page 297, this drawback is easily obviated by providing a mechanism to replace the default listener(s). Also, you can decide whether you'd like to make the overriding mechanism available to all classes or whether you'd like to restrict such meddling to an extension of the component, by making the appropriate methods either public or protected, respectively.

There are a number of strategies to employ if you'd like to be able to swap default listeners at runtime. In "ThreeDButton with Interchangeable Default Event Handling" on page 297, we provided a constructor that took a listener argument for specifying an alternate listener. However, that approach allows the listener to be set at construction time only. For a more flexible approach, you can provide setters and getters for the suspect listener:

```
public class IHaveADefaultEventHandlerThatIsReplaceable
                    extends Component {
    private MouseListener listener;

    public IHaveADefaultEventHandlerThatIsReplaceable() {
        addMouseListener(listener = new MouseAdapter() {
            public void mousePressed(MouseEvent event) {
                // default event handling for mouse pressed
            }
        });
    }
    public void setMouseListener(MouseListener newListener) {
        if(listener != null)
            remove(listener);

        addMouseListener(listener = newListener);
    }
    ...
}
```

Notice that although a default mouse listener is added to the component in its constructor, it can be swapped out at any time by invocation of setMouseListener().

In short, basic event handling that is not likely to change (or will rarely change) is a good candidate for listening to yourself. Whether you also provide a mechanism for changing the default event handling behavior depends on just how stable you believe the event handling for the component in question happens to be.

Encapsulating Event Handling in a Separate Class

Encapsulating event handling in a separate class is preferable when you have default event handling for a basic component but you are fairly certain that the event handling will be modified, either at runtime or by extensions of the component. Of course, you're probably thinking that that's exactly what we just illustrated in the last section, by employing the "listen to yourself pattern." However, encapsulating the event handling in a separate class is a more flexible approach because, unlike listening to yourself, it provides a top-level base (event handling) class that others may extend to suit their needs.

The drawback to this approach is that you must implement a separate class, and you must somehow associate the event handling class with the component that fires the appropriate events. However, for event handling that is a likely candidate for change, this drawback is a small price to pay.

In general, then, it is a good idea to encapsulate event handling in a separate class when you can envision the event handling in question being modified for your component, especially when the default event handling is a candidate for subclassing.

Employing Inner Classes

Typically, the decision to use inner classes is most pertinent when you are listening to yourself, as we've seen with our ThreeDButton event handling discussion. Realize that inner classes are basically syntactic sugar. Syntactic sugar, in spite of the derogatory connotations usually associated with the term, can often be an exceedingly good thing.

We recommend that you use inner classes as long as their use does not require you to adopt an approach that is unsatisfactory for the given circumstance. For instance, if you are quite certain that some particular event handling functionality is likely to change for a given component, then using inner classes to fuse the event handling into the component class, without providing a mechanism for modifying the event handling in question, would be a pretty bonehead design decision.

Named Inner Classes vs. Anonymous Inner Classes

Of course, if you are going to use inner classes, then the next thing to consider is whether or not you want to give the class a name. The solution is quite straightforward: if you have components that will share the listener, then give the class a name. If the class has a name, then you can instantiate one listener for multiple components, as the following pseudocode illustrates:

```
Choice c1, c2, c3;
MyComponentListener listener = new MyComponentListener();
...
c1.add(listener);
c2.add(listener);
c3.add(listener);
...

class MyComponentListener extends ItemListener {
    // handle item state changes for all three choices
}
```

On the other hand, if the event handling is very specific to a particular component, an anonymous inner class is more convenient:

```
Button addButton = new Button("Add ...");

addButton.addActionListener(new ActionListener() {
   public void actionPerformed(ActionEvent event) {
      // Implementation specific to the add button only
   }
});
```

Propagating Events to Containers

We'll conclude our discussion of the new event model by making some observations about propagating events to a component's container. Note that automatic propagation is flat out not possible with the new event model. While some may argue that such a mechanism is indispensable, we'll go out on a limb here by voting for its exclusion in future versions of the AWT. For one thing, as we discuss in "Shortcomings of the Inheritance-Based Event Model" on page 229, mixing automatic propagation with the component hierarchy can result in subtle bugs, at least as it was implemented in the old model. For another thing, we believe that the best approach is to have objects interested in events fired by a particular component to explicitly register interest in those events. Surely, there are cases where one could argue that automatic propagation is a must-have, but such situations, in our humble opinion, are few and far between. Finally, relying on automatic propagation of events, instead of explicitly expressing interest in a set of events for a given component, often obfuscates code to such a degree that the inconvenience of explicitly registering interest is well worth it.

Summary

This chapter has covered the delegation-based event model that supersedes the inheritance-based model that came with the original AWT. Although the original event model was sufficient for applets (and applications) with simple event handling needs, it did not scale well for a number of reasons (see "Shortcomings of the Inheritance-Based Event Model" on page 229). The new event model addresses nearly all of the drawbacks of the original event model while maintaining compatibility, at least for the time being, with the old model.

We've explored many of the aspects of the new event model in this chapter: events, components, and listeners, along with semantic events, consuming events, firing standard and custom events from custom components, etc.

While the new event model is greatly improved over the original model, the developer is now faced with a number of choices with regard to implementing event handling. We've provided some guidelines for different approaches in "Event Handling Design" on page 319; these guidelines will help you move from the old event model to the new.

CHAPTER 10

Components, Containers, and Layout Managers

Perhaps the most fundamental relationship in the entire AWT is the relationship between components, containers, and layout managers. Understanding how the three relate to one another is paramount to developing nontrivial applets and applications using the AWT. As a result, a good deal of effort will be spent in this chapter to illustrate not only the relationships between components, containers, and layout managers, but also the standard AWT layout managers and the implementation of custom layout managers.

The Big Three of the AWT

To really get your teeth into the AWT, you're going to have to deal with components, containers, and layout managers in a fairly sophisticated fashion. This means you're going to have to be sensitive to the nuances of their relationship to one another. Primarily, you need to know where one stops working for you and where another starts.

A component contained in a container is quite likely to be subjected to a life of stretching, squashing, and being moved about. Although you might suspect the component's container of dishing out such punishment, containers are spatially challenged; they delegate the laying out—sizing and positioning—of their components to a layout manager. A container's layout manager is the sole force behind positioning and shaping the components contained in its associated container.

Figure 10-1 shows a class diagram for `java.awt.Container`.

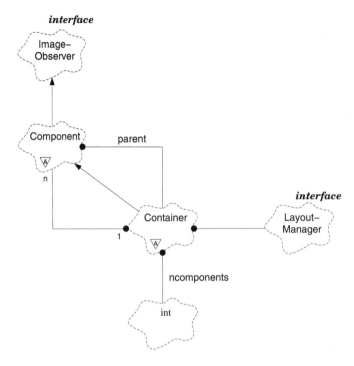

Figure 10-1 `Container` Class Diagram
Every container maintains a reference to a layout manager that
positions and shapes the components contained in the container.

Containers are simply components that can contain other components. The AWT
provides a handful of classes that extend `Container`, as illustrated in
Figure 10-2.

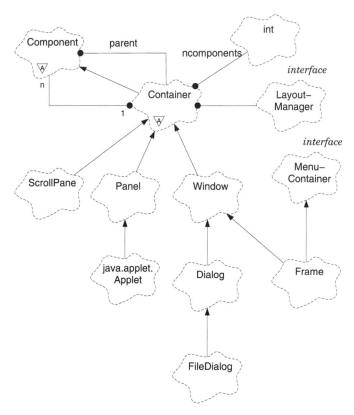

Figure 10-2 Container Extensions Class Diagram
The AWT provides a number of Container extensions. All
containers maintain a reference to a layout manager.

Every container has access to a LayoutManager that is responsible for
positioning and shaping the components contained in the container. When an
event occurs that causes a container to lay out its components (such as resizing a
window), the container's layout manager is called upon to lay out the
components that reside in the container.

Layout Management and the Strategy Pattern

Essentially then, containers farm out the job of laying out their components to a layout manager. Different layout managers implement different algorithms for laying out components, and containers are free to choose the layout algorithm of their choice by employing the appropriate layout manager. This technique of defining a family of algorithms and encapsulating each one in a class is known as the *strategy pattern*.[1] The delegation event model provided by the AWT is also an example of the strategy pattern—components delegate their event handling to a listener—see "The Delegation Event Model (AWT 1.1 and Beyond)" on page 237.

LayoutManagers

LayoutManager is an interface that defines the following methods:

```
void        addLayoutComponent    (String name, Component comp)
void        removeLayoutComponent (String name, Component comp)
Dimension   preferredLayoutSize   (Container parent)
Dimension   minimumLayoutSize     (Container parent)
void        LayoutContainer        (Container parent)
```

Layout managers are responsible for:

- Calculating the preferred and minimum sizes for a container
- Laying out the components contained in a container

It's important to note that while each container has exactly one layout manager, a single layout manager may wind up working for more than one container. Therefore, when a layout manager has to perform some work for a container, it must be passed a reference to the container requesting its services. In fact, if you look at Panel.java, you will see that instances of java.awt.Panel, by default, share a single and presumably overworked FlowLayout:

```
public class Panel extends Container {
    final static LayoutManager panelLayout = new FlowLayout();
    ...
    public Panel() {
        this(panelLayout);
    }
    public Panel(LayoutManager layout) {
        this.name = base + nameCounter++;
        setLayout(layout);
    }
...
}
```

---

1. See Gamma, Helm, Johnson, Vlissides. *Design Patterns*, p. 315. Addison-Wesley, 1994.

Since `panelLayout` is a static member, there is only one `panelLayout` for all instances of `Panel`. When a `Panel` equipped with its default layout manager is laid out, a reference to the `Panel` is passed to the `layoutContainer(Container)` method of the `static panelLayout` instance, which obliges by laying out the components in yet another `Panel`.

Two Types of Layout Managers

All layout managers lay out components for one or more containers. Some layout managers attach constraints to components that determine how the components are to be laid out. For instance, `BorderLayout` attaches compass points to its components in order to determine where the component is to be placed within the border. The constraints are specified as strings—"North", "South", "East", "West", and "Center". Other layout managers do not attach constraints to individual components—for instance, `FlowLayout` simply lays out components from left to right and top to bottom—as they fit within their container.

The AWT provides an interface for layout managers that associate constraints with their components: `LayoutManager2`, which extends the `LayoutManager` interface and adds the following methods:

```
void        addLayoutComponent (Component c, Object constraints)
Dimension   maximumLayoutSize  (Container)
float       getLayoutAlignmentX(Container parent)
float       getLayoutAlignmentY(Container parent)
void        invalidateLayout   (Container parent)
```

`addLayoutComponent()` allows a component to be added to a layout manager with constraints attached. The type of object that composes a constraint is up to the implementor of the `LayoutManager2` interface. For instance, the constraint for a `GridBagLayout` must be a `GridBagConstraints` reference, whereas a `BorderLayout` requires the constraint to be a `String`.

`maximumLayoutSize()` returns the maximum size for a container, given the current constraints of the component.

The `getLayoutAlignment...` methods are used by some layout managers to position components along the x and y axes.

`invalidateLayout()` signifies that the layout manager should discard any information it has cached concerning constraints.

Table 10-1 lists the layout manager interfaces implemented by the standard AWT layout managers. For layout managers that implement the `LayoutManager2` interface, the constraints are also listed.

Table 10-1 Interfaces Implemented by Standard AWT Layout Managers

Layout Manager	Implements	Component Constraints
BorderLayout	LayoutManager2	String specifying compass point
CardLayout	LayoutManager2	String specifying name
FlowLayout	LayoutManager	NONE
GridBagLayout	LayoutManager2	GridBagConstraints specifying grid constraints
GridLayout	LayoutManager	NONE

Layout Managers and Container Insets

Every container has a set of *insets* associated with it. Insets specify the container's top, bottom, left, and right inside margins, defined in pixels, as illustrated in Figure 10-3.

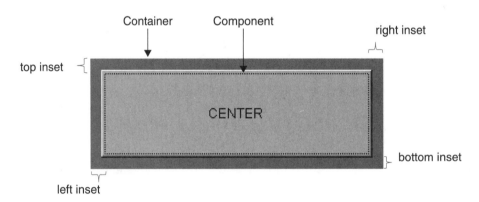

Figure 10-3 Container Insets
Layout managers are careful not to lay out components inside a container's insets; however, graphics can still be drawn in the insets region.

A container's insets values are important because layout managers are careful not to place components anywhere inside a container's insets,[2] although containers themselves can override `paint()` and paint into their insets area if they desire, which is how the border was painted in the container shown in Figure 10-3.

`java.awt.Container` defines the following `getInsets`[3] method that provides access to a container's insets:

```
Insets Container.getInsets()
```

The `Container` class does not define a separate method for setting its insets. If you want to set a container's insets, you must extend a class derived from `Container` and overwrite the `getInsets()` method, like so:

```
public Insets getInsets() {
    return new Insets(10,10,10,10);
}
```

Notice that `Container.getInsets()` is a little off-kilter with the rest of the AWT; most parameters of AWT classes have both a get and a set method, meaning you can query and/or change the parameter at runtime without having to extend a class to change a parameter. A container's insets cannot be set at runtime; a container must override `getInsets()` in order to change its insets. This requirement relegates setting a container's insets to a per-class basis instead of a per-object basis.

Frame Insets Are Unique

The insets for a Frame, by default, include the height of the title and menubars, if the frame is so equipped. This knowledge comes in handy if you accidentally draw into a frame underneath its menubar. While layout managers will not place components inside a container's insets, there is nothing to stop you from performing graphical operations inside a container's insets.

Peers and Insets

You might be curious to know what the default insets are for each extension of `java.awt.Container`.[4] Let's track this down by looking at `Insets Container.getInsets()`:

2. We speak only for the standard AWT layout managers. It is up to implementors of custom layout managers to respect the insets of a container.
3. `getInsets()` replaces the deprecated `insets()` for the 1.1 release of the AWT.
4. See "Components and Peers" on page 439 for a more in-depth look at peers.

```
// from java.awt.Container:

public Insets getInsets() {
   return insets();
}
```

`getInsets()` returns the insets calculated by the deprecated `insets()` method:

```
public Insets insets() {
    if (this.peer != null && this.peer instanceof ContainerPeer) {
        ContainerPeer peer = (ContainerPeer)this.peer;
        return peer.insets();
    }
    return new Insets(0, 0, 0, 0);
}
```

If a container does not override `getInsets()`, then its peer supplies the value. If the container does not yet have a peer, an `Insets` with zero for all four margins is returned. Now, if we look at `ContainerPeer.java` to find out the value that a container's peer returns for insets, we see this:

```
public interface ContainerPeer extends ComponentPeer {
    Insets getInsets();
}
```

Now we've hit a dead end, as is always the case when trying to track down peer behavior, because all peers are defined in terms of interfaces.

The reason we cannot find out a default value for insets is because there isn't one. Each container's peer is given leeway to return whatever insets make sense for the platform on which the peer resides, and therefore there is no cross-platform default for the insets of a `Container`. The peer approach—using native peer components—retains look-and-feel across platforms, and this is one of the trade-offs with which we must deal as a consequence—see "Components and Peers" on page 439 for more on the drawbacks of the peer architecture.

Layout Managers and Component Preferred Sizes

Components implement two methods that affect their interactions with layout managers:

```
// Component methods
public    Dimension getPreferredSize();
public    Dimension getMinimumSize();
```

As their names suggest, `getPreferredSize()` returns the preferred size of the component, and `getMinimumSize()` returns the minimum size a component can tolerate.

Layout managers are tasked with calculating the preferred and minimum sizes for a container by implementing the following methods from the `LayoutManager` interface:

```
// LayoutManager methods

Dimension preferredLayoutSize(Container)
Dimension minimumLayoutSize  (Container)
```

The methods typically cycle through all of the container's components and calculate preferred and minimum sizes for the container by taking into account each component's preferred and minimum sizes.

Layout managers lay out components in the `layoutContainer()` method:

```
void layoutContainer(Container)
```

While some layout managers completely ignore the preferred size of the components they lay out, others are infinitely receptive to each and every component's plea to be shaped according to their preferred size. Still other layout managers will pay attention to only half of a component's preferred size. `BorderLayout`, for instance, will respect a north component's preferred height, but stretches the component to fill its container horizontally, thereby ignoring the component's preferred width. Table 10-2 shows a list of the standard AWT layout managers and their attitudes toward a component's preferred and minimum sizes.

Table 10-2 Layout Managers and Preferred Sizes

Layout Manager	Respects Component's Preferred Size Like This...
BorderLayout	North and south components: Respects height, ignores width. East and west components: Respects width, ignores height. Center component: Ignores both preferred width and height.
FlowLayout	Respects preferred width and height if component has not been explicitly sized.
CardLayout	Ignores preferred width and height.
GridLayout	Ignores preferred width and height.
GridBagLayout	Varies depending on `GridBagConstraints` for the component. (See *GridBagLayout and GridBagConstraints* on page 357.)

Painting a Container's Components

Containers do not have to explicitly paint the heavyweight components they contain; a container's components are painted (or drawn, if you will) automatically. Custom components that extend `Container` need to override their `paint(Graphics)` method only if they need to perform graphical operations above and beyond painting the components they contain or if they contain lightweight components.[5]

TenPixelBorder

It's about time that we presented some code that illustrates the concepts we've discussed up to this point. We'll start with the `TenPixelBorder` class, which illustrates many of the topics we have covered so far. `TenPixelBorder` is a simple class, so we'll show you the code in Example 10-1 and then highlight the essentials of how it works.

Example 10-1 `TenPixelBorder` Class Listing

```
import java.awt.*;

public class TenPixelBorder extends Panel {
    public TenPixelBorder(Component borderMe) {
        setLayout(new BorderLayout());
        add(borderMe, "Center");
    }
    public void paint(Graphics g) {
        Dimension mySize   = getSize();
        Insets     myInsets = getInsets();

        g.setColor(Color.gray);

        // Top Inset area
        g.fillRect(0,
                   0,
                   mySize.width,
                   myInsets.top);

        // Left Inset area
        g.fillRect(0,
                   0,
                   myInsets.left,
                   mySize.height);

        // Right Inset area
        g.fillRect(mySize.width - myInsets.right,
                   0,
                   myInsets.right,
                   mySize.height);

        // Bottom Inset area
        g.fillRect(0,
```

---

5. Lightweights are explicitly drawn in `Container.paint()`. See "Remember to Invoke super.paint() When Overriding Container.paint()" on page 657.

```
                mySize.height - myInsets.bottom,
                mySize.width,
                mySize.height);
    }
    public Insets getInsets() {
        return new Insets(10,10,10,10);
    }
}
```

TenPixelBorder extends Panel, thereby inheriting the ability to contain components. An instance of TenPixelBorder must be constructed with a Component—borderMe—which it adds to itself. Notice that TenPixelBorder sets its layout manager to an instance of BorderLayout and adds borderMe as the center component. The result is that borderMe is reshaped to fill the entire space taken up by TenPixelBorder, minus the space taken up by the insets specified by the overridden TenPixelBorder.getInsets() method.[6]

Finally, TenPixelBorder overrides paint() and fills the insets area with a gray color. Remember that the components contained by TenPixelBorder, namely, borderMe, will be painted automatically, so the overridden TenPixelBorder.paint(Graphics) is only concerned with painting the border. Additionally, while the BorderLayout layout manager will ensure that borderMe does not encroach upon the area specified by TenPixelBorder.getInsets(), TenPixelBorder, like any container, is free to draw into its insets area. Figure 10-4 shows a simple applet that exercises an instance of TenPixelBorder.

Example 10-2 lists the TenPixelBorderTestApplet.

Example 10-2 TenPixelBorderTestApplet Class Listing

```
import java.applet.Applet;
import java.awt.*;

public class TenPixelBorderTestApplet extends Applet {
    public void init() {
        Button     button = new Button("CENTER");
        TenPixelBorder border = new TenPixelBorder(button);

        setLayout(new BorderLayout());
        add(border, "Center");
    }
}
```

6. Center components fill the available space that is not occupied by the north, south, east, and west components laid out by a BorderLayout. Since borderMe is the only component within TenPixelBorder, it fills the entire area of the panel minus insets.

Figure 10-4 `TenPixelBorderTestApplet` in Action
Components do not encroach on a container's insets; however,
components can still draw into their insets region. The panel in
the applet shown above has insets of 10 pixels all around.

The `TenPixelBorderTestApplet` passes a `button` to the `TenPixelBorder`
constructor. The border is then added to the applet as the center component. Since
the applet itself does not define any insets, the instance of `TenPixelBorder`
takes up all the available space in the applet.

Forcing a Container to Lay Out Its Components

It is not uncommon for situations to arise where it is necessary to force a container
to lay out its components. Since the recipe for programmatically forcing a layout
is not readily apparent, we'll take some time to explore the issue here.

Figure 10-5 shows an applet that contains a panel with a textfield and two buttons
for adjusting the textfield's font size—the applet itself is listed in Example 10-3.

Example 10-3 `ValidateApplet Class Listing`

```
import java.applet.Applet;
import java.awt.*;
import java.awt.event.*;

public class ValidateApplet extends Applet {
    private GrayPanel grayPanel = new GrayPanel();
    public void init() {
        add(grayPanel);
    }
```

Figure 10-5 `ValidateApplet`
The buttons adjust the size of the textfield's font. After the font size is adjusted, the applet needs to be laid out in order for the textfield and its container to resize to accommodate the new font size.

```
}
class GrayPanel extends Panel implements ActionListener {
    private TextField  field    = new TextField("TextField");
    private Button     lgButton = new Button   ("larger font");
    private Button     smButton = new Button   ("smaller font");

    public GrayPanel() {
        lgButton.addActionListener(this);
        smButton.addActionListener(this);

        add(field);
        add(lgButton);
        add(smButton);
        setBackground(Color.gray);
    }
    public void actionPerformed(ActionEvent event) {
        Button button  = (Button)event.getSource();
        Font   curFont = field.getFont();
        int    newSize = curFont.getSize();

        if(button == lgButton) newSize += 3;
        if(button == smButton) newSize -= 3;

        field.setFont(new Font(curFont.getFamily(),
                            curFont.getStyle(), newSize));
    }
    public void paint(Graphics g) {
        g.setColor(Color.black);
        g.drawRect(0,0,getSize().width-1,getSize().height-1);
    }
}
```

The applet contains an instance of `GrayPanel`—a panel with a gray background containing the textfield and buttons.

Changing the font size results in an immediate update in the textfield's font, but the textfield and its container do not grow or shrink to accommodate the text displayed in the textfield. In order for the textfield and its container to resize to accommodate the textfield's new font size, the applet needs to lay out its components. In other words, when the textfield's font is modified, we'd like to force a layout of the applet.

All components at any given time are either *valid* or *invalid*. Invalid components need to be laid out, whereas valid components do not. Calling `validate()` on a container that is invalid (and whose peer has been created) results in a call to the container's `layout` method. So our job is relatively easy—after setting the size of the field's font, we invalidate the field, and then invoke `validate()` on the parent container of the `GrayPanel`, which happens to be the applet.

```java
public void actionPerformed(ActionEvent event) {
    Button button  = (Button)event.getSource();
    Font    curFont = field.getFont();
    int     newSize = curFont.getSize();

    if(button == lgButton) newSize += 3;
    if(button == smButton) newSize -= 3;

    field.setFont(new Font(curFont.getFamily(),
                        curFont.getStyle(), newSize));
    field.invalidate();
    getParent().validate();
}
```

The revised applet is shown in Figure 10-6.

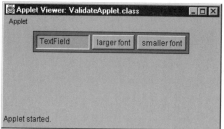 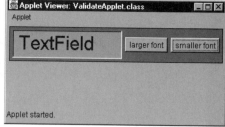

Figure 10-6 Forcing a Layout
After the textfield's font is modified, the textfield is invalidated and the applet is subsequently validated, resulting in a layout of the applet's components.

Realize that the applet itself is never explicitly invalidated. Recall that invoking `validate()` on a component will only result in a call to `layout()` if the component itself is invalid (and the component has a peer). How then, did the applet get invalidated?

Invalidating a component invalidates not only the component itself but also the container in which it resides. Containers behave in a similar fashion: if the container's layout manager is an instance of `LayoutManager2`, `invalidateLayout()` is invoked for the layout manager, and then `Container.invalidate()` invokes `super.invalidate()`. Therefore, a call to `invalidate()`, by default,[7] walks up the container hierarchy and invalidates all of the containers in the component's container hierarchy. As a result, the call to `field.invalidate()` above invalidated not only the textfield, but the `GrayPanel` and the applet itself. Subsequently invoking `validate()` on the applet forces the applet to be laid out.

Invalidation of a component occurs naturally as a side effect to a number of `java.awt.Component` and `java.awt.Container` methods, as you can see from Table 10-3.

`Component.setFont()` does not invalidate the component, and therefore the textfield in the `ValidateApplet` is not invalidated when its font is set. As a result, we must take matters into our own hands and invalidate the textfield by calling `invalidate()` ourselves. If we had also invoked one of the methods listed in Table 10-3 in addition to setting the font, then the call to `invalidate()` would not have been required.

In addition, windows are invalidated when they are resized, and frames are invalidated when their menubar is set. Scrollbars are invalidated when their orientation is changed, text areas are invalidated when the number of rows or columns changes, and textfields are invalidated when the number of columns in the field changes.

Forcing a Window to Resize

Another fairly common task is to force a window or dialog to resize when the components it contains change size.

---

7. We say *by default* because an extension of container could override its `invalidate()` method to behave differently—not a good idea, but possible nonetheless.

Table 10-3 Component and Container **Methods That Invalidate Components**

Method
void Component.addNotify()
void Component.show() (invalidates parent container)
void Component.hide() (invalidates parent container)
void Component.reshape(int x,int y,int width,int height)
void Component.setSize(int width,int height)
void Component.setBounds(int x,int y,int width,int height)
void Component.setLayout(LayoutManager)
void Container.add(Component)
void Container.remove(Component)
void Container.removeAll()
void Component.setLayout(LayoutManager)

Example 10-4 introduces a new class to our ValidateApplet (which is now ValidateApplet2): ValidateDialog, which contains an instance of GrayPanel. The applet itself has been modified so that it simply contains a button that launches the ValidateDialog.

Example 10-4 ValidateApplet2 Class Listing

```
import java.applet.Applet;
import java.awt.*;
import java.awt.event.*;

public class ValidateApplet2 extends Applet
                        implements ActionListener {
    Button launchButton = new Button("launch dialog ...");
    ValidateDialog validateDialog;

    public void init() {
        add(launchButton);
        launchButton.addActionListener(this);
    }
    public void actionPerformed(ActionEvent event) {
        if(validateDialog == null) {
            validateDialog =
                new ValidateDialog(new Frame(),
                            "Validate Dialog",
                            true);
        }
        validateDialog.show();
    }
}
class GrayPanel extends Panel implements ActionListener {
```

```java
    private TextField  field    = new TextField("TextField");
    private Button     lgButton = new Button  ("larger font");
    private Button     smButton = new Button  ("smaller font");

    public GrayPanel() {
        lgButton.addActionListener(this);
        smButton.addActionListener(this);

        add(field);
        add(lgButton);
        add(smButton);

        setBackground(Color.gray);
    }
    public void paint(Graphics g) {
        g.setColor(Color.black);
        g.drawRect(0,0,getSize().width-1,getSize().height-1);
    }
    public void actionPerformed(ActionEvent event) {
        Button button  = (Button)event.getSource();
        Font   curFont = field.getFont();
        int    newSize = curFont.getSize();

        if(button == lgButton) newSize += 3;
        if(button == smButton) newSize -= 3;

        field.setFont(new Font(curFont.getFamily(),
                               curFont.getStyle(),
                            newSize));
        field.invalidate();
        getParent().validate();
    }
}

class ValidateDialog extends Dialog {
    public ValidateDialog(Frame frame,
                          String title,
                          boolean modal) {
        super(frame, title, true);
        add("Center", new GrayPanel());
        pack();

        addWindowListener(new WindowAdapter() {
            public void windowClosing(WindowEvent event) {
                dispose();
            }
        });
    }
    public void validate() {
        setSize(getPreferredSize().width,
                getPreferredSize().height);
        super.validate();
    }
}
```

GrayPanel calls validate() on its container, which is now a
ValidateDialog. The dialog's validate() method is overridden, so that the
dialog is resized to its preferred size. After setting the dialog's size,
super.validate() is invoked in order to layout the dialog's components.
Figure 10-7 shows the dialog before and after the font size of the textfield has been
changed.

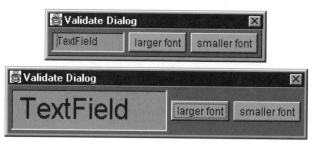

Figure 10-7 Forcing a Window to Resize
The dialog resizes when the font in its textfield is modified.

AWT TIP

Forcing a Container to Lay Out Its Components
Invoking Container.validate() forces the container to lay out its components.
However, the layout will only occur if the container is invalid. Containers are
invalidated implicitly by the methods listed in "Component and Container
Methods That Invalidate Components" on page 342. If none of the methods
listed in Table 10-3 has been invoked for any of the container's components,
then invalidate() must be called before invoking validate().

Standard AWT Layout Managers

The AWT comes with five standard layout managers, as shown in Table 10-4.

The designers of the AWT hit a home run with the implementation of layout
management and event handling by employing the strategy pattern for each.[8]
Containers are not responsible for laying out their own components; they
delegate that responsibility to a layout manager. By encapsulating the algorithm
for laying out components in a separate class, the layout functionality is available
for others to use (and extend), while containers may be fitted with different layout

8. See "Layout Management and the Strategy Pattern" on page 330.

Table 10-4 The AWT's Default Layout Manager Classes

Layout Manager	Description
BorderLayout	Lays out components around the sides and in the center of the container in north, east, west, south, and center positions. Gaps between components can be specified. BorderLayout is the default layout manager for Window, Dialog, and Frame containers.
CardLayout	Displays one component at a time from a *deck* of components. Components can be swapped in and out.
FlowLayout	Displays components left to right, top to bottom. FlowLayout is the default layout manager for panels and applets.
GridBagLayout	Arranges components in a grid, using an elaborate set of grid constraints.
GridLayout	Lays out components in a grid, with each component stretched to fill its grid cell. Horizontal and vertical gaps between components can be specified.

managers at runtime. The same benefits apply for the delegation-based event model. The AWT designers also did a decent job of providing a set of default layout managers, which are sufficient to handle probably 90 percent of all your layout needs.

The five layout managers in Table 10-4 provide a range of capabilities, from BorderLayout, a simple layout manager that is useful in an infinite variety of layouts, to the behemoth GridBagLayout, a very complex layout manager that can lay out nearly anything you can imagine.

Extensions of the Container class each have a default layout manager. BorderLayout is by far the AWT's most frequently used layout manager. As Table 10-5 shows, BorderLayout is the default layout manager for most of the AWT containers. Note that java.awt.Container itself has a null layout manager.

Table 10-5 Container Default Layout Managers

Container Class	Default Layout Manager
Container	null
Panel	FlowLayout
Window	BorderLayout
Dialog	BorderLayout
Frame	BorderLayout

Which Layout Manager to Use?

Programmers new to the AWT may be confused about which of the AWT's standard layout managers to employ in a given situation. In fact, that's largely the result of practice, trial, and error. However, Table 10-6 presents some high-level guidelines that you might find useful.

Table 10-6 Layout Manager Decision Table

Layout Manager	Use When...	An Example Is...
BorderLayout	A container divides its components into regions: north and south, or east and west. A single component needs to fill the entire area of the container it resides in.	TenPixelBorder
CardLayout	You want to control the visibility of sets of components under different circumstances.	A set of panels that presents itself as a stack of tabbed folders
FlowLayout	A container's components fill the container from left to right, top to bottom.	A container that places components one immediately following another
GridLayout	A container divides its components into a grid.	A calendar or spreadsheet
GridBagLayout	A container has complicated layout needs.	Input forms, such as a container that has components for name, address, zip code, etc.

The BorderLayout Layout Manager

Once you've worked on a few nested layouts, you'll come to appreciate the neat ability of BorderLayout to lay out components into geographical regions. Nearly every nested layout has a BorderLayout lurking somewhere inside.

BorderLayout, like CardLayout and GridBagLayout, implements the LayoutManager2 interface, meaning it attaches constraints to the components it lays out. The constraints are strings, which are passed to the container's add(Container, Object) method. The string specifies the location of the component—either "North", "South", "East", "West" or "Center".

Figure 10-8 shows an applet that uses an instance of BorderLayout.

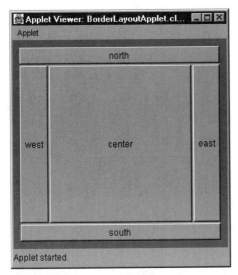

Figure 10-8 BorderLayoutApplet in Action
BorderLayout lays out at most five components as depicted
above.

Example 10-5 lists the implementation of the BorderLayoutApplet class,
which adds five buttons, one for each of the compass points and center.

Example 10-5 BorderLayoutApplet

```
import java.applet.Applet;
import java.awt.*;

public class BorderLayoutApplet extends Applet {
    private Button north, south, east, west, center;

    public void init() {
        Panel          buttonPanel = new Panel();
        TenPixelBorder border = new TenPixelBorder(buttonPanel);

        north  = new Button("north");
        east   = new Button("east");
        west   = new Button("west");
        center = new Button("center");
        south  = new Button("south");

        buttonPanel.setLayout(new BorderLayout(2,2));
        buttonPanel.add(north, "North");
        buttonPanel.add(south, "South");
```

```
            buttonPanel.add(east,  "East");
            buttonPanel.add(west,  "West");
            buttonPanel.add(center,"Center");

            setLayout(new BorderLayout());
            add(border,  "Center");
        }
    }
```

`BorderLayout` stretches the north and south components horizontally so that the components span the entire width of the container in which they reside, while sizing them vertically according to their preferred height. The east and west components are stretched vertically so that they span the entire height of the container in which they reside minus the combined heights of the north and south components; they are sized horizontally according to their preferred width. The center component gets whatever space is left over, regardless of its preferred size.

Notice that we've specified horizontal and vertical gaps between components of 2 pixels; the gaps specify the spacing between components. `BorderLayout` also provides set and get methods for specifying and obtaining the horizontal and vertical gaps.

The CardLayout Layout Manager

`CardLayout` keeps track of a deck, if you will, of components. From this deck, it can display or *deal* any one container at a time. Although it is nowhere near as versatile as the other AWT layout managers, it is nonetheless quite useful for components such as tabbed panels. `CardLayout` implements the `LayoutManager2` interface; component constraints are strings representing a name for the component.

Figure 10-9 shows an applet that uses a `CardLayout` to display four components in succession.

Table 10-7 lists the methods implemented by `CardLayout` (in addition to those defined in `LayoutManager` and `LayoutManager2`) that allow clients to control which component is currently displayed. Notice that the `show` method takes a string specifying the name of the component to be displayed. The `show` method is the rationale behind `CardLayout` implementing `LayoutManager2`, thus requiring constraints to be placed upon the components it lays out; the constraints are names of the components.

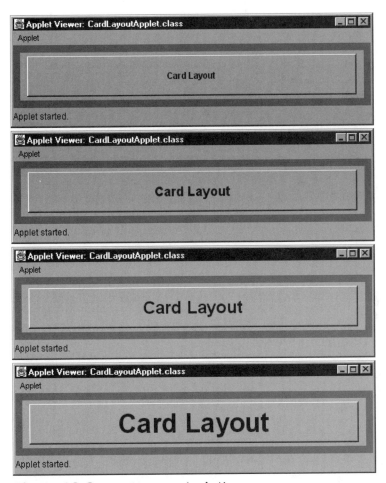

Figure 10-9 CardLayout in Action
The applet above employs a CardLayoutApplet to cycle through
four panels. Each panel displays a different image.

Example 10-6 lists the CardLayoutApplet code. Notice as you look through the
code that CardLayout is unique among layout managers in that it has methods
you can call directly to control which component is displayed. The overridden
mouseUp(), invokes one of those methods: CardLayout.next(Component).

Table 10-7 CardLayout **Stacking Methods**

Method	Description
void first(Container)	Displays the first component added to the container
void last(Container)	Displays the last component added to the container
void next(Container)	Displays the component added to the container after the currently displayed component. If the current component is the last, then the first component is displayed.
void previous(Container)	Displays the component added to the container before the currently displayed component. If the current component is the first, then the last component is displayed.
void show(Container, String)	Shows the component whose name matches the string passed in. If no components match the name, the method does nothing.

Example 10-6 CardLayoutApplet Class Listing

```
import java.applet.Applet;
import java.awt.*;
import java.awt.event.*;

public class CardLayoutApplet extends Applet {
    private Button tiny, small, med, lrg;
    private Panel cardPanel   = new Panel(),
                 tinyPanel    = new Panel(),
                 smallPanel   = new Panel(),
                 MediumPanel  = new Panel(),
                 LargePanel   = new Panel();

    private CardLayout card = new CardLayout(10,5);

    public void init() {
        TenPixelBorder border  = new TenPixelBorder(cardPanel);
        ButtonListener buttonListener = new ButtonListener();

        cardPanel.setLayout(card);

        // Panels share a FlowLayout by default ...
        tinyPanel.setLayout   (new BorderLayout());
        smallPanel.setLayout  (new BorderLayout());
        MediumPanel.setLayout (new BorderLayout());
        LargePanel.setLayout  (new BorderLayout());
```

```
    tiny  = new Button("Card Layout");
    small = new Button("Card Layout");
    med   = new Button("Card Layout");
    lrg   = new Button("Card Layout");

    tiny.setFont(new Font("Helvetica", Font.BOLD, 12));
    small.setFont(new Font("Helvetica", Font.BOLD, 18));
    med.setFont(new Font("Helvetica", Font.BOLD, 24));
    lrg.setFont(new Font("Helvetica", Font.BOLD, 36));

    tiny.addActionListener(buttonListener);
    small.addActionListener(buttonListener);
    med.addActionListener(buttonListener);
    lrg.addActionListener(buttonListener);

    tinyPanel.add  (tiny,  "Center");
    smallPanel.add (small, "Center");
    MediumPanel.add(med,   "Center");
    LargePanel.add (lrg,   "Center");

    cardPanel.add("tiny",  tinyPanel);
    cardPanel.add("small", smallPanel);
    cardPanel.add("med",   MediumPanel);
    cardPanel.add("lrg",   LargePanel);

    setLayout(new BorderLayout());
    add(border, "Center");
  }
  class ButtonListener implements ActionListener {
     public void actionPerformed(ActionEvent event) {
        card.next(cardPanel);
     }
  }
}
```

The CardLayout is instantiated with a horizontal gap of 10 pixels and a vertical gap of 5 pixels. Notice that the gaps have a different meaning than they did for BorderLayout. Since CardLayout only displays one component at a time, the gaps specify a margin around the components instead of *between* components, as is the case for BorderLayout.

The FlowLayout Layout Manager

FlowLayout simply shoves in components, left to right, top to bottom. Like BorderLayout, it is a basic layout that is handy in a variety of layout situations. Unlike BorderLayout, FlowLayout does not implement the LayoutManager2 interface and does not require constraints to be placed upon components it lays out.

Figure 10-10 shows how `FlowLayout` positions components when a window has been resized.

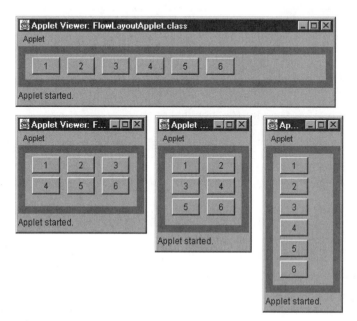

Figure 10-10 FlowLayout in Action
FlowLayout lays out components from left to right, top to bottom.

Example 10-7 lists the `FlowLayoutApplet` code.

Example 10-7 `FlowLayoutApplet Class Listing`

```
import java.awt.*;
import java.awt.event.*;
import java.applet.Applet;

public class FlowLayoutApplet extends Applet {
    public void init() {
        Button one = new Button("  1  "),
                two = new Button("  2  "),
                three = new Button("  3  "),
                four = new Button("  4  "),
                five = new Button("  5  "),
                six = new Button("  6  ");

        Panel      panel  = new Panel();
        TenPixelBorder border = new TenPixelBorder(panel);

        panel.setLayout(new FlowLayout(FlowLayout.LEFT, 10, 5));
        panel.add(one);
        panel.add(five);
        panel.add(two);
        panel.add(three);
        panel.add(four);
        panel.add(five);
        panel.add(six);

        setLayout(new BorderLayout());
        add(border, "Center");
    }
}
```

`FlowLayout` aligns the components it lays out, as shown in Figure 10-11. When an instance of `FlowLayout` is constructed, the alignment—LEFT, CENTER or RIGHT—can be specified, in addition to horizontal and vertical gaps.

The horizontal and vertical gaps specify not only the spacing between components but also the spacing between the edges of the component and the sides of the container. This specification is in contrast to `BorderLayout`, whose horizontal and vertical gaps specify only the space between components.

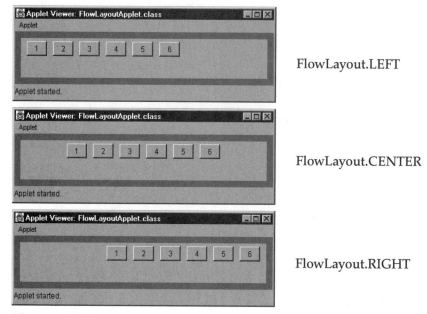

Figure 10-11 FlowLayout Alignment

FlowLayout is handy when you have a fixed-size component and you wish to lay out components in either a row or a column. FlowLayout is also the only AWT layout manager that sizes components according to their preferred widths and heights. See "Layout Managers and Component Preferred Sizes" on page 334.

The GridLayout Layout Manager

GridLayout, as you might guess, lays out components in a grid; clients can set the gap between components and the number of rows and columns either at construction time or after the GridLayout is constructed. GridLayout is obviously useful when you want to lay out components, such as spreadsheets or calendars, in applets. Figure 10-12 shows output from an applet with ImageButton components positioned by GridLayout.

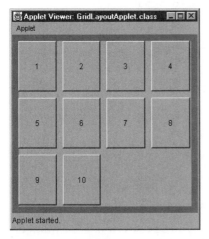

Figure 10-12 GridLayout in Action
GridLayout lays out components in a grid, where every grid cell
contains one component. The grid cells are all the same size.

Example 10-8 shows the GridLayoutApplet code. Notice that the applet
explicitly sets the number of rows and columns in the call to the GridLayout
constructor. The applet also sets the horizontal and vertical gaps between the
components to ten pixels.

Example 10-8 GridLayoutApplet Class Listing

```
import java.applet.Applet;
import java.awt.*;

public class GridLayoutApplet extends Applet {
    private Button one, two, three, four, five, six,
                        seven, eight, nine, ten;

    public void init() {
        Panel            buttonPanel = new Panel();
        TenPixelBorder border = new TenPixelBorder(buttonPanel);

        one   = new Button("  1  ");
        two   = new Button("  2  ");
        three = new Button("  3  ");
        four  = new Button("  4  ");
        five  = new Button("  5  ");
        six   = new Button("  6  ");
        seven = new Button("  7  ");
        eight = new Button("  8  ");
        nine  = new Button("  9  ");
        ten   = new Button("  10  ");
```

```
          buttonPanel.setLayout(new GridLayout(3,0,10,10));
          buttonPanel.add(one);
          buttonPanel.add(two);
          buttonPanel.add(three);
          buttonPanel.add(four);
          buttonPanel.add(five);
          buttonPanel.add(six);
          buttonPanel.add(seven);
          buttonPanel.add(eight);
          buttonPanel.add(nine);
          buttonPanel.add(ten);

          setLayout(new BorderLayout());
          add(border, "Center");
      }
  }
```

The applet constructs an instance of `GridLayout` by specifying the number of rows (3) and columns (0). If either the number of rows or columns is specified as zero, the value is computed. For instance, in the example above with 10 buttons, 3 rows will result in 4 columns. The horizontal and vertical gaps between components may also be specified.

Components laid out by a `GridLayout` completely fill the grid cell they occupy. Additionally, you cannot control any constraints concerning grid cell properties for a component. For instance, you cannot specify how many grid cells a component occupies because each component always occupies exactly one grid cell. `GridBagLayout`, on the other hand, allows constraints to be attached to each component that specify how much of the grid cell the component occupies and how many grid cells the component spans, in addition to a number of other constraints.

The GridBagLayout Layout Manager

Like `GridLayout`, `GridBagLayout` positions components in a grid. Unlike `GridLayout`, in which you explicitly specify the number of rows and columns in the grid, `GridBagLayout` determines the number of rows and columns from constraints placed upon the components it lays out. Also, unlike `GridLayout`, `GridBagLayout` allows components to span more than one grid cell— components may also overlap, as we shall soon discover.

`GridBagLayout` is capable of handling nearly any layout situation; however, it is one of the most complex and difficult classes in the AWT to use. Developers are often put off by its complexity, but it's an extremely useful layout manager. For that reason, we will apply a three-pronged approach to covering `GridBagLayout`.

First, we'll discuss the GridBagConstraints that are associated with components laid out by GridBagLayout, which is typically the most confusing aspect of the most maligned of layout managers.

Second, we've provided an applet on the CD that allows you to modify the GridBagConstraints associated with a grid of image buttons; we believe you will find the applet indispensable in furthering your understanding of how GridBagLayout works.

Third, we've included a section that covers laying out user input forms, which is a common task for GridBagLayout.

GridBagLayout and GridBagConstraints

GridBagLayout extends the LayoutManager2 interface and therefore attaches constraints to every component it lays out—see "Two Types of Layout Managers" on page 331. The constraints associated with a component are specified by an instance of GridBagConstraints. When components are added to a container equipped with a GridBagLayout, an instance of GridBagConstraints may be passed to the container's add(Component, Object) method. Alternatively, GridBagLayout provides a setConstraints method for setting the constraints apart from adding components to their container. Both techniques for specifying the constraints for a component are outlined below:

```
// In a method of a hypothetical java.awt.Container extension
...
GridBagLayout gbl = new GridBagLayout();
GridBagConstraints gbc = new GridBagConstraints();
...
setLayout(gbl);
...
// set variables contained in gbc, for example:
// gbc.anchor = GridBagConstraints.NORTH;
...
// specify constraints when adding component to container
add(anotherComponent, gbc);
...
// modify variables contained in gbc, for example:
// gbc.anchor = GridBagConstraints.WEST;
...
// specify constraints separately
gbl.setConstraints(component, gbc);
add(component);
...
```

As you can see from the pseudocode above, instances of GridBagLayout and GridBagConstraints are instantiated, and the container's layout manager is set to the instance of GridBagLayout. Constraints for each component are specified by setting variables in the GridBagConstraints instance, and subsequently either invoking GridBagLayout.setConstraints() or passing the constraints to the container's add method. The constraints are copied when they are set, so the same instance of GridBagConstraints can be used for multiple components.

GridBagLayout is unique among AWT layout managers because it is the only layout manager to attach constraints which are something other than a string to its component. BorderLayout and CardLayout, for instance, both of which also attach constraints to components,[9] use strings to specify component positions and component names, respectively.

The GridBagConstraints class provides a variety of instance variables and constants that control parameters associated with a component. Components laid out by a GridBagLayout can span multiple grid cells and can fill their grid cells wholly or partially. The grid cells themselves can consume a certain percentage of extra space over and above the preferred size of the component they contain.

Table 10-8 lists the variables and constants provided by the GridBagConstraints class.

Table 10-8 GridBagConstraints **Instance Variables and Valid Values**

Instance Variable	Default Value	Valid Values	Specifies
anchor	CENTER	CENTER EAST NORTH NORTHEAST NORTHWEST SOUTH SOUTHEAST SOUTHWEST WEST	Where to anchor a component within its grid cells
fill	NONE	BOTH HORIZONTAL VERTICAL NONE	The manner in which the component fills the grid cells it occupies

---

9.   See "Interfaces Implemented by Standard AWT Layout Managers" on page 332.

Table 10-8 `GridBagConstraints` **Instance Variables and Valid Values (Continued)**

Instance Variable	Default Value	Valid Values	Specifies
gridx gridy	RELATIVE	RELATIVE or integer values representing an x,y position in the grid.	The position of the component's upper left-hand grid cell
gridwidth gridheight	1 1	RELATIVE REMAINDER or integer values representing the width and height in grid cells.	The number of grid cells in both horizontal and vertical directions allotted for the component. Whether or not a component fills its grid cells depends upon the `fill` attribute.
ipadx ipady	0 0	Integer values representing number of pixels.	*Internal* padding that increases the component's preferred size. Negative values are allowed, which decreases the component's preferred size.
insets	(0,0,0,0)	An `Insets` object.	*External* padding between the edges of the component and the edges of its grid cells. Negative values, which cause the component to extend outside of its grid cells, are allowed.
weightx weighty	0.0 0.0	`Double` values representing weighting given to a component's grid cells relative to other components in the same row or column.	How extra space is consumed by the component's grid cells. Whether or not a component fills its grid cells depends upon the `fill` attribute. Values must be positive.

The mechanics of fitting a container with an instance of `GridBagLayout` and setting constraints for the components in the container is straightforward, as we've already discovered. The difficulty associated with using `GridBagLayout` comes from understanding exactly what each of the constraints listed in Table 10-8 means and how the constraints interact.

Grid Cells and Display Area

Since a component may be allotted more than one grid cell in both the horizontal and vertical directions—by specifying `gridwidth` and `gridheight` constraints—we'll refer to the area occupied by a component's grid cells as its *display area*.

For example, Figure 10-13 shows an input form laid out by `GridBagLayout` that winds up being four grid cells wide and seven grid cells high. The panel containing the buttons has a display area four grid cells wide in order to span the width of the form.

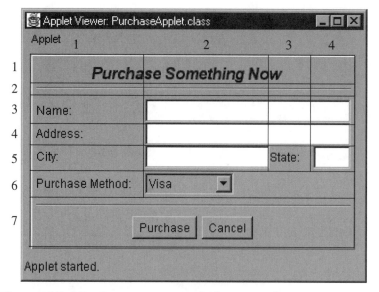

Figure 10-13 Components and Their Display Areas
The panel contains 7 rows and 4 columns.

Display Area vs. Component

One of the biggest obstacles to becoming proficient at using `GridBagLayout` is understanding the distinction between a component's display area and the component itself.

Some of the constraints associated with a component apply to the component's display area, other constraints apply to the component itself, and yet other constraints apply to both.

Table 10-9 lists the `GridBagConstraints` variables, what each specifies, and whether the constraint applies to the component, the component's display area, or both. The "Specifies" column in Table 10-9 summarizes the column of the same name in Table 10-8 on page 358.

Table 10-9 `GridBagConstraints` and Components

Constraint	Applies to	Specifies
anchor	Component	Position of component in display area
fill	Component	Region of display area component fills
gridx, gridy	Both	Upper left-hand corner of display area
gridwidth, gridheight	Display area, but may also affect component depending upon fill constraint	Width and height of display area in grid cells
weightx, weighty	Display area, but may also affect component size depending upon fill constraint	Percentage of extra space allotted. Extra space represents the space available in the display area above and beyond the component's preferred size.
insets	Both	External padding
ipadx, ipady	Both	Internal padding

The `anchor` constraint specifies the anchor position of a component within its display area. The `fill` constraint specifies the manner in which a component expands to fill its display area. The `anchor` and `fill` constraints have no effect on the component's display area; no matter how you specify the two constraints, the size of component's display area is unaffected.

The `gridx` and `gridy` constraints specify the upper left-hand grid cell for the component's display area. Since components reside somewhere in their display areas, making a change to the component's grid cell results in a change of location for both the display area and its associated component.

`gridwidth` and `gridheight` specify, in grid cells, the size of the component's display area. `weightx` and `weighty` specify how much *extra space over and above the component's preferred size* is occupied by the component's display area. Both the size and weight constraints apply only to the component's display area; however, the size of the component itself may also be affected depending upon the `fill` constraint associated with the component.

The `insets` constraint defines *external* padding between the edges of the component and the edges of component's display area. Setting the insets to a non-zero value can affect both the size of the component and the size of the component's display area.

The *internal* padding (specified by the `ipadx` and `ipady`) modifies the component's preferred size and may also modify the size of the component's display area, when the display area is equal to the preferred size of the component.

Components and Their Display Areas

Components laid out by a GridBagLayout are displayed in a grid of cells, collectively referred to as their display area. Some grid bag constraints placed upon components apply to the component itself, while others apply to the component's display area. Understanding this distinction is key to mastering the use of GridBagLayout.

Now, let's take a more in-depth look at each of the constraints used by `GridBagLayout` to lay out its components.

GridBagConstraints.anchor

The `GridBagConstraints.anchor` constraint specifies where a component is anchored in its display area.

It's important to note that setting the `anchor` constraint may seemingly have no effect if the component's `fill` constraint is set to anything other than `GridBagConstraints.NONE`, because the component will expand to fill a portion of its display area.

Although it is probably evident from the constants themselves, Table 10-10 lists the positions associated with the `GridBagConstraints.anchor` constraint.

Figure 10-14 shows a button laid out by a `GridBagLayout` at various anchor points within its display area.

Table 10-10 GridBagConstraints **Anchor Points**

Anchor Point	Results in the Component Being Positioned at ...
NORTHWEST	Upper left-hand corner of the display area
NORTH	Top of the display area—centered horizontally
NORTHEAST	Upper right-hand corner of the display area
EAST	Right side of the display area—centered vertically
CENTER	Center, both horizontal and vertical, of the display area
WEST	Left side of the display area—centered vertically
SOUTHWEST	Lower left-hand corner of the display area
SOUTH	Bottom of the display—centered horizontally
SOUTHEAST	Lower right-hand corner of the display area

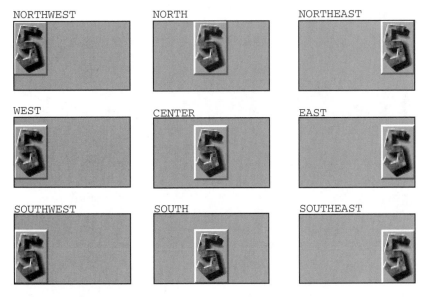

Figure 10-14 GridBagConstraints **Anchors**
The anchor constraint determines the position at which a component is anchored in its display area.

Realize that the anchor constraint does not necessarily equate to a compass point in a *single* grid cell because the anchor position is relative to the component's display area, not its (upper left) grid cell.

In Figure 10-15, button #2 has a display area that is 2 grid cells wide, 2 grid cells high, and an anchor constraint of CENTER. As a result, the button is centered in its display area, which causes it to overlap buttons #5 and #6.

Although the anchor constraint is relative to a component's display area, it does not affect the display area itself—only the placement of the component within the display area is affected.

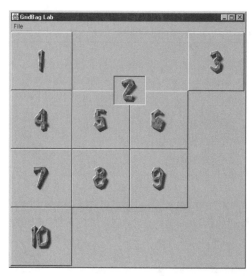

Figure 10-15 Anchor Constraint Is Relative to Display Area Image button #2 has a display area 2 grid cells wide and 2 grid cells high and is anchored in the center of its display area.

GridBagConstraints.fill

The `fill` constraint specifies how much of a component's display area is filled by the component.

Table 10-11 lists valid constants for the `GridBagConstraints.fill` constraint, along with the meaning associated with each constant. Setting the `fill` constraint to `GridBagConstraints.NONE` will cause a component to be sized according to its preferred width and height.

Table 10-11 `GridBagConstraints` Fill Constants

When `fill` Constant is ...	The Component ...
NONE	Is sized according to its preferred size
HORIZONTAL	Fills its display area horizontally—height is preferred height
VERTICAL	Fills its display area vertically—width is preferred width
BOTH	Fills its display area both horizontally and vertically

Figure 10-16 shows ten buttons, all of which have their `fill` constraint set to `GridBagConstraints.BOTH`, except for buttons #1, #7 and #10.

Button #1 has a display area 1 grid cell wide, 2 grid cells high, a `fill` constraint of VERTICAL, and an anchor constraint of CENTER. The button's width is sized to its preferred width.

Button #7 has a display area 3 grid cells wide, 1 grid cell high, a `fill` constraint of HORIZONTAL, and an anchor of CENTER. The button's height is its preferred height.

Button #10 has a display area 2 grid cells wide and 1 grid cell high, a `fill` constraint of NONE, and an anchor of CENTER.

Figure 10-16 GridBagConstraints Fill
The GridBagConstraints.fill constraint determines how much of its display area a component fills.

GridBagConstraints.gridx and GridBagConstraints.gridy

The gridx and gridy constraints specify the upper left-hand grid cell of a component's display area. Grid locations are zero-based, and therefore a grid cell in the upper left-hand corner of a container always has a (gridx,gridy) of (0,0).

In addition to specifying a numerical grid position, both gridx and gridy may be assigned GridBagConstraints.RELATIVE. A RELATIVE setting for gridx means that the component will be placed to the right of the last component added to the container. A RELATIVE setting for gridy means that the component will be placed in the row below the last component added to the container.

Table 10-12 enumerates the difference between specifying numerical values for gridx and gridy versus specifying GridBagConstraints.REMAINDER.

Table 10-12 GridBagConstraints gridx and gridy

gridx/gridy Values	Description
Integer	Specifies the position of a component's upper left-hand grid cell in its display area
RELATIVE	gridx: component is placed to the right of the last component added to container.
	gridy: component is placed in the row below the last component added to the container.

The applet shown in Figure 10-17 contains ten buttons laid out by an instance of GridBagLayout. button #1, of course, has a grid position of (0,0), while the grid position for button #10, for instance, is (0,3).

Figure 10-17 GridBagConstraints gridx and gridy
Grid locations are zero-based—image button #1 has a (gridx,gridy) of (0,0); image button #8, for instance, is at position (1,2).

When the buttons in Figure 10-17 were added to their container, they were added in numerical order, starting with button #1 and ending with button #10. As a result, the gridx constraint for buttons 2, 3, 5, 6, 8 and 9 could have been specified as GridBagConstraints.RELATIVE, which would place them to the right of buttons 1, 2, 4, 5, 7, and 8, respectively. Likewise, the gridy constraint for buttons 4, 7, and 10 could have been specified as GridBagConstraints.RELATIVE, placing them in rows 1, 2, and 3, respectively.

GridBagLayout is capable of anchoring more than one component in the same grid cell. If two components share the same grid cell, the component displayed on top is controlled by the component's zorder (see "Components and Zorder" on page 445).

Figure 10-18 shows the same applet displayed in Figure 10-17, with the constraints modified for button #2, such that its grid position is (0,0), and therefore is anchored in the same grid cell as button #1.

Figure 10-18 Two Components Anchored in the Same Grid Cell Buttons #1 and #2 are both anchored in the (0,0) grid cell. When two components share a grid cell, zorder determines which component is on top.

Since zorder determines which overlapping component is displayed on top and since button #1 was added to the container before button #2,[10] button #1 is always displayed on top of button #2. In order for button #2 to be visible, some constraints for button #1 had to be modified, namely,

`fill: GridBagConstraints.NONE`, and
`anchor: GridBagConstraints.NORTHWEST`.

GridBagConstraints.gridwidth and GridBagConstraints.gridheight

The `gridwidth` and `gridheight` constraints determine the size of a component's *display area*, not necessarily the size of the component itself.

In addition to integer values for `gridwidth` and `gridheight`, you can also specify the values `GridBagConstraints.RELATIVE` and `GridBagConstraints.REMAINDER`. `RELATIVE` means that the component will be the next to last component in its row (for `gridwidth`) or the next to last component in its column (for `gridheight`). A value of `REMAINDER` results in the component being the last component in its row (`gridwidth`) or column (`gridheight`). Specifying `REMAINDER` will cause the component's display area to expand into span as many grid cells as required in order to be the last component in its respective row or column.

Table 10-13 summarizes valid values that may be specified for `gridwidth` and `gridheight`.

Table 10-13 GridBagConstraints gridwidth **and** gridheight

gridwidth/gridheight Values	Description
Integer	The size of the component's display area in grid cells
RELATIVE	gridwidth: component is the next to last in its row.
	gridheight: component is the next to last in its column.
REMAINDER	gridwidth: component is the last in its row.
	gridheight: component is the last in its column.

Figure 10-19 shows two of the buttons that have had their `gridwidth` and `gridheight` values modified from the default values of 1, as follows: button #2 has a `gridwidth` of 2 and a `gridheight` of 1; button #9 has a `gridwidth` and a `gridheight` of `GridBagConstraints.REMAINDER`, which causes its display

---

10. The order in which components are added to their container determines zorder.

area to expand in order to become the last component in its respective row and column. Note that button #9 expands to fill its entire display area because its `fill` constraint has been set to `GridBagConstraints.BOTH`.

Figure 10-19 `GridBagConstraints` `gridwidth` and `gridheight`
The values assigned to `gridwidth` and `gridheight` determine the size of a component's display area in the horizontal and vertical directions, respectively. Image button #2 has a `gridwidth` of 2 and a `gridheight` of 1, and image button #9 has a `gridwidth` and a `gridheight` of `GridBagConstraints.REMAINDER`.

One of the subtleties of using `GridBagLayout` is the fact that a component's constraints interact to produce a desired (or undesired) effect. For instance, if the `fill` constraint for button #9 in Figure 10-19 is set to NONE, the button itself will not expand out to the edges of the container; however, its display area will.

GridBagConstraints.weightx and GridBagConstraints.weighty

If a container is larger than the combined preferred sizes of its components, then a component's weightx and weighty constraints determine how much of the extra space a component's *display area* consumes. The weightx and weighty constraints apply strictly to the component's display area, and not to the component itself, although components can be coaxed into filling their display areas in a number of different ways, by setting the fill constraint.

GridBagConstraints.weightx and GridBagConstraints.weighty are the only constraints that are specified as double values. Additionally, both weightx and weighty must be positive. Typically, weightx and weighty are specified as a number between 0.0 and 1.0, although numbers greater than 1.0 may be specified. The weighting of each component in a given row or column is relative to the weights of the other components that reside in the same row or column, so you can stick with numbers between 0.0 and 1.0 or use larger numbers if desired.

Up until now, the weights of every button in the GridBagLab application shown in the preceding figures have been (1.0, 1.0), and therefore each button's display area received an equal share of the extra space available in the container. If we modify the weight constraints to (0.0, 0.0) for each button, then none of the buttons are allotted any extra space, as you can see from Figure 10-20

The buttons in Figure 10-20 have also had their fill constraint set to NONE and their anchor constraint set to CENTER—in the previous figures they were set to BOTH and NORTHWEST, respectively.

Setting all of the component's weights to (0.0, 0.0) causes the components to be clumped together in the middle of the container— GridBagLayout puts all of the extra space between the outside of the grid of components and the inside of the container when none of the components have a weighting greater than 0.0.

To shed some light on exactly how weighting works, let's change the weightx to 1.0 for button #1 and leave all the other constraints as they were. You can see the results of our tinkering in Figure 10-21.

Since button #1 has a weightx of 1.0 and the other buttons in its row have a weightx of 0.0, the display area for button #1 takes up 100 percent of the extra space in the horizontal direction. Note that the button itself does not take up the extra space, although it would if its fill constraint were set to either BOTH or HORIZONTAL.

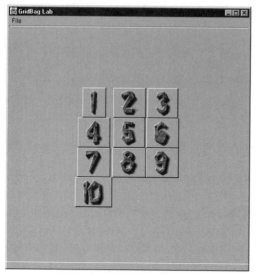

Figure 10-20 GridBagLayout Weight Constraints
weightx and weighty constraints determine how much extra
space a component's display area takes up. The buttons
displayed above all have weights of (0.0,0.0), and therefore none
of them get any extra space.

Another point of interest is the fact that all of the buttons in the same column as
button #1 have also had their display areas expanded to take up the extra space in
their respective rows, even though their weightx constraint is still set to 0.0. This
expansion is a necessity if a grid is to be maintained.

This automatic expansion leads us to an interesting conclusion: weighting is
applied on a column/row basis and not per component. For instance, in Figure
10-21 the weightx value for each *column* is 1.0, 0.0, and 0.0. Therefore, the left-
hand column is given all of the extra space in the horizontal direction.

AWT TIP

Weighting Is Applied on a Row/Column Basis

GridBagLayout maintains a *grid* of components. Each row and column is given
a weighting, which is determined from the weights of the row or column's components. The weighting of a row or column is equal to the weighting of the component with the highest weighting in the row or column.

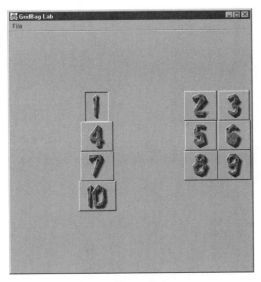

Figure 10-21 Weight Constraints Are Applied Per Row or Column
Button #1 has a weight of (1.0, 0.0). All of the other buttons have
weights of (0.0, 0.0).

A component's weighting affects not only how much extra space the component's
display area is given but also potentially affects the display areas of components
residing in the same row *and* the same column. Setting button #1's `weightx`
constraint in Figure 10-21 caused the display areas of the components in the same
column (#4, #7 and #10) to grow in the horizontal direction. If the buttons in the
same row (#2 and #3) had non-zero `weightx` constraints, their display areas may
also have been affected by modifying button #1's `weightx` constraint. All of this
is due to the fact that horizontal weighting is relative to components in the same
row, and vertical weighting is relative to components in the same column.

The `weightx` and `weighty` constraints are unique by virtue of the fact that their
values may affect not only the size of their own display area but also the size of
other components' display areas.

If we set the `weightx` constraint for both button #1 and button #2 to 0.5, then the
respective columns will each take up half of the extra space in the horizontal
direction, as you can see from Figure 10-22.

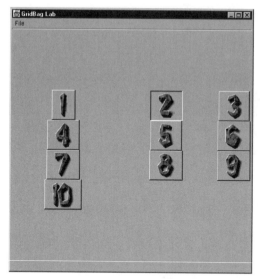

Figure 10-22 Weighting Determines Extra Space Allotted. Button #1 and button #2 both have a `weightx` of 0.5. All other buttons have weights of (0,0).

If you have a sharp eye (or a ruler handy), you may take exception to our claim that columns 1 and 2 each get half of the extra space. However, realize that this does not mean that columns 1 and 2 have the exact same width—in fact, they do not.

Columns 1 and 2 are not the same width because button #1 and button #2 do not have the same preferred widths. Let's suppose that the container is 100 pixels wide, and the preferred widths of buttons 1, 2, and 3 are 5, 10, and 7 pixels, respectively. When `GridBagLayout` sees that buttons #1 and #2 are evenly dividing the extra space in their row, it first calculates the extra space available, which is 100 - (5 + 10 + 7) = 78 pixels. Therefore, columns 1 and 2 each get 39 pixels added to their widths, which means column 1 is 39 + 5 = 44 pixels, while column 2 is 39 + 10 = 49 pixels. The display area size for components of equal weighting will only be the same if the preferred sizes of the components in question are identical.

AWT TIP ...

Equal Weighting Does Not Necessarily Equate to Equal Display Area Sizes

If two components in the same row or column have equal weighting, that does not necessarily mean that their display areas will be the same size. Only if the preferred sizes of the two components are identical will their display areas wind up being the same size.

Weighting works the same in both the horizontal and vertical directions. Figure 10-23 takes us one step further, by specifying weights in the y direction for buttons 4, 7, and 10 as 0.25, 0.50, and 0.25, respectively.

Figure 10-23 Weighting Works the Same in Both Directions Buttons 4, 7, and 10 have `weighty` constraints of 0.25, 0.50, 0.25, respectively. All other image buttons have `weighty` constraints of 0.0.

GridBagConstraints.insets

Just as insets can be specified for a container, they can also be specified for a component's display area with an `Insets` object. Figure 10-24 shows our GridBagLab application, where button #5 has an insets value of (10,5,10,0). All of the other buttons have the default insets of (0,0,0,0).

Figure 10-24 `GridBagConstraints.insets` Constraint
Button #5 has an insets of (10,5,10,0).

The display area for button #5 is reduced as a result of setting the insets constraints, in much the same manner as setting the insets for a container reduces the available real estate for laying out components—see "Layout Managers and Container Insets" on page 332.

Insets can also be specified as negative, resulting in a component overstepping the bounds of its display area. Figure 10-25 shows button #5 fitted with an insets of (-10,-10,-10,-10).

Figure 10-25 A Negative Insets Value
Image button #5 has an insets constraint of (-10,-10,-10,-10). A negative insets constraint causes a component to overstep the boundaries of its display area.

As you can see, button #5 does indeed overstep the boundaries of its display area.

GridBagConstraints.ipadx and GridBagConstraints.ipady

While the `insets` constraint specifies an *external* padding between the edges of a component and its display area, `ipadx` and `ipady` specify an *internal* padding applied to the component (not the display area).

The rarely used `ipadx` and `ipady` constraints result in a component's preferred and minimum sizes increasing (for positive values) and decreasing (for negative values).

We're not sure exactly where you would want to use the padding constraints, but being the kitchen sink of layout managers, `GridBagLayout` supports this rarely used feature.

In Figure 10-25, the GridBagLab application has `ipadx` and `ipady` values of (50,50) for button #5 and (-50,-50) for button #10.

Figure 10-26 `ipadx` and `ipady` Constraints
Image button #5 has `ipadx` and `ipady` constraints of (50,50), and
image button #10 has `ipadx` and `ipady` constraints of (-50,-50).
Positive padding increases the size of the component; negative
padding decreases the component's size.

GridBagLab

Although our coverage of `GridBagLayout` should be sufficient to communicate
basic principles, we have found it most beneficial to run the GridBagLab
application in order to achieve a deeper understanding of how `GridBagLayout`
works. On the CD, under the `layout/gridbaglab` directory, you will find the
GridBagLab application.

Note: GridBagLab uses Swing components, so you must have either the 1.2
version (or later) of the JDK, or the Swing components and a 1.1.X version of the
JDK.

Figure 10-27 shows GridBagLab in action.

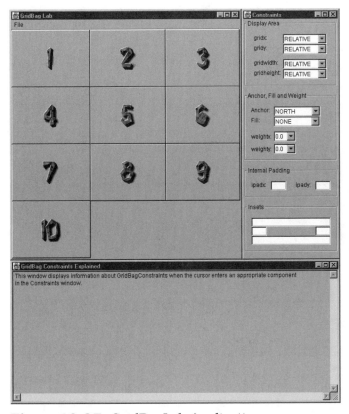

Figure 10-27 GridBagLab Application
The GridBagLab application provided on the CD allows grid bag
constraints to be set for the 10 image buttons displayed in the
applet's window.

GridBagLab is provided as a convenience for you to explore setting constraints on
components laid out by GridBagLayout. We hope that GridBagLab, combined
with the extensive coverage of GridBagLayout in *Graphic Java*, will empower
you to use this complicated, but extremely useful, layout manager with
confidence.

Our discussion of GridBagLayout will conclude with a look at a specialty of
GridBagLayout: laying out input forms.

GridBagLayout and Input Forms

One of the most common uses of GridBagLayout is to lay out input forms such as the one depicted in Figure 10-28. So, we'll take a short detour to discuss creating input forms with GridBagLayout.

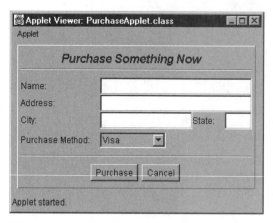

Figure 10-28 Using GridBagLayout to Lay Out an Input Form

GridBagLayout is often used to lay out input forms like the one pictured above.

The PurchaseApplet shown in Figure 10-28 is used to discuss keyboard traversal in "Standard AWT Components and Keyboard Traversal" on page 630; however, we do not discuss the applet's use of GridBagLayout there, so we will cover that ground here.

The applet contains an instance of ThreeDPanel, which in turn contains an instance of ButtonPurchaseForm:

```
public class PurchaseApplet extends Applet {
    public void init() {
        ThreeDPanel p = new ThreeDPanel();
        p.add(new ButtonPurchaseForm());
        add(p);
    }
}
class ThreeDPanel extends Panel {
    public void paint(Graphics g) {
        g.setColor(Color.lightGray);
        g.draw3DRect(0,0,getSize().width-1,
                          getSize().height-1,true);
    }
}
```

`ThreeDPanel` draws a 3D rectangle in order to give the input form a little panache. The interesting code, from the standpoint of `GridBagLayout`, resides in `ButtonPurchaseForm`, which extends `Panel` and instantiates all of the components used in the input form:

```
class ButtonPurchaseForm extends Panel {
    Separator sep = new Separator();
    Label title   = new Label("Purchase Something Now");
    Label name     = new Label("Name:");
    Label address = new Label("Address:");
    Label payment = new Label("Purchase Method:");
    Label phone    = new Label("Phone:");
    Label city     = new Label("City:");
    Label state    = new Label("State:");
    TextField nameField    = new TextField(25);
    TextField addressField = new TextField(25);
    TextField cityField    = new TextField(15);
    TextField stateField   = new TextField(2);
    Choice    paymentChoice = new Choice();
    Button    paymentButton = new Button("Purchase");
    Button    cancelButton  = new Button("Cancel");
    ...
```

A simple `separator` separates the title from the rest of the components in the panel. The `ButtonPurchaseForm` constructor contains all of the code that sets constraints for the components and adds them to the panel. The first order of business is to create instances of `GridBagLayout` and `GridBagConstraints` and then set the container's layout manager to the instance of `GridBagLayout`. In addition, the three payment options are added to the `paymentChoice` and the font of the `title` is set.

```
public ButtonPurchaseForm() {
    GridBagLayout       gbl = new GridBagLayout();
    GridBagConstraints gbc = new GridBagConstraints();

    setLayout(gbl);

    paymentChoice.add("Visa");
    paymentChoice.add("MasterCard");
    paymentChoice.add("COD");

    title.setFont(new Font("Times-Roman",
                     Font.BOLD + Font.ITALIC, 16));
    ...
```

Next, constraints for the components are set. First, constraints are set for the `title` (a `Label`), which is added to the container.

```
gbc.anchor    = GridBagConstraints.NORTH;
gbc.gridwidth = GridBagConstraints.REMAINDER;
add(title, gbc);
```

The anchor point for the title is specified as NORTH, so the title is centered at the top of the form. The gridwidth is set to REMAINDER, so the title is the last (and only) component in its row. Next, constraints are set for the separator.

```
gbc.fill      = GridBagConstraints.HORIZONTAL;
gbc.insets    = new Insets(0,0,10,0);
add(sep, gbc);
```

The same instance of GridBagConstraints is used to specify constraints for all of the components in the form. As stated earlier, constraints are copied, and therefore the same instance of GridBagConstraints can be used for multiple components with different constraints.

The fill constraint for the separator is set to HORIZONTAL, so that the separator spans the width of its grid cells. Insets are also specified for the separator as (0,0,10,0). The integer values passed to an Insets constructor specify, in order, top, left, bottom, and right margins. As a result, a bottom margin of ten pixels is specified for the separator, which provides some breathing room between the bottom of the separator and the top of the components in the panel.

Next, the name label and textfield are added to the panel.

```
gbc.anchor    = GridBagConstraints.WEST;
gbc.gridwidth = 1;
gbc.insets    = new Insets(0,0,0,0);
add(name, gbc);

gbc.gridwidth = GridBagConstraints.REMAINDER;
add(nameField, gbc);
```

The anchor constraint for the name label is set to WEST, and the gridwidth is set to 1. Even though the default value for gridwidth is 1, it must be explicitly set here because previously it had been set to REMAINDER.

For nameField, all the constraints are left as they were for the name label, except that the gridwidth is set to REMAINDER, which causes the textfield to be the last component in its row. Remember that previously the fill constraint was set to HORIZONTAL, and therefore the textfield, like the label, will fill its display area in the horizontal direction. Additionally, the anchor constraint was previously set to WEST, so both the label and textfield are left-justified in their respective display areas.

The constraints for the address label and textfield are set in a similar manner to the constraints for the name label and textfield.

```
gbc.gridwidth = 1;
add(address, gbc);

gbc.gridwidth = GridBagConstraints.REMAINDER;
add(addressField, gbc);
```

Next, the constraints are set for the city label and textfield.

```
gbc.gridwidth = 1;
add(city, gbc);
add(cityField, gbc);
```

Notice that the `gridwidth` for the textfield is not set to `REMAINDER`, because the textfield is not the last component in its row—the state label and field still need to be added to the row.

```
add(state, gbc);

gbc.gridwidth = GridBagConstraints.REMAINDER;
add(stateField, gbc);
```

The `stateField`, however, is the last component in the row, so its `gridwidth` constraint is set to `REMAINDER`.

Next, the payment label and choice have their constraints set and are added to the container.

```
gbc.gridwidth = 1;
add(payment, gbc);

gbc.insets = new Insets(5,0,5,0);

gbc.gridwidth = GridBagConstraints.REMAINDER;
gbc.fill      = GridBagConstraints.NONE;
add(paymentChoice, gbc);
```

The `insets` constraint for both the payment label and choice is set to five pixels top and bottom to provide a little separation for the payment components.

Finally, an instance of `ButtonPanel` (a panel containing a separator and buttons) is added to the panel. Two buttons are added to the button panel, which in turn has its constraints set and is added to the panel.

```
ButtonPanel buttonPanel = new ButtonPanel();
buttonPanel.add(paymentButton);
buttonPanel.add(cancelButton);

gbc.anchor    = GridBagConstraints.SOUTH;
gbc.insets    = new Insets(5,0,0,0);
gbc.fill      = GridBagConstraints.HORIZONTAL;
gbc.gridwidth = 4;
add(buttonPanel, gbc);
```

The `gridwidth` constraint for the button panel is set to 4. Since the row containing the city and state labels and fields consists of 4 grid cells, the button panel must have a `gridwidth` of 4 if its display area is to span the entire width of the form, as you can see from Figure 10-29. Similarly, of course, the `gridwidth` could have been set to `GridBagConstraints.REMAINDER`.[11]

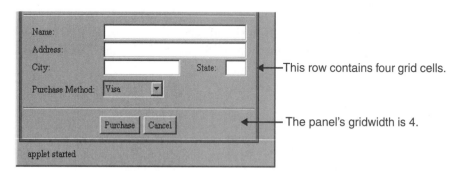

Figure 10-29 Specifying `GridBagConstraints.gridwidth`
The panel containing the separator and the buttons has its gridwidth set to 4 so that it spans the width of the container.

Additionally, the `fill` constraint for the `buttonPanel` is set to `HORIZONTAL` to ensure that the button panel itself, in addition to its display area, spans the entire width of the form.

Finally, an `insets` constraint is specified for the button panel, which gives the panel a top inset of 5 pixels. Notice that the pixel distance between the bottom of the purchase components and the top of the separator contained in the button panel is actually 10 pixels because the purchase components also have a bottom inset of 5 pixels.

11. See "GridBagConstraints.gridwidth and GridBagConstraints.gridheight" on page 369.

Laying Out Components in Nested Panels

A `Container` can contain components, and, fortunately for all involved, the AWT designers chose to make `Container` an extension of `Component`. What that means, of course, is that containers can contain not only components, but also other containers, since a `Container` is a `Component`. (This is an implementation of a design pattern known as *composite*.)[12]

This crucial ability—to nest containers inside of one another—is a necessity if we are to design screens of much complexity for use in applets. Attempting to lay out a complicated screenful of containers with a single layout manager can turn out to be an exercise in futility, no matter which layout manager you choose for the job.

Although we can give you some guidelines to follow, designing nested panels is something that is best learned by experimenting with different layout managers and layout situations. In *Advanced Topics* on page 667, we will explore designing nested panels in nearly every chapter; for now we'll take a look at a single contrived example—an applet that allows you to vary the settings of a `GridLayout`.

`GridLabApplet` employs an instance of `GridLayout` to display a grid of buttons. The applet includes controls for setting the number of rows and columns and for setting the horizontal and vertical gaps between the buttons. Figure 10-30 shows a picture of `GridLabApplet` in action.

This applet contains a number of nested panels, so we'll refer both to the diagram in Figure 10-31 and to appropriate sections of the `GridLabApplet` code to describe how the applet is assembled.

`GridLabApplet` sets its layout manager to an instance of `BorderLayout`. The north component is an instance of `Box`. A box is a simple extension of panel that draws an etched rectangle and title in its insets region. The north component is set like this:

```
add("North",  new Box(picker, "Grid Layout Settings"));
```

The box component contains a `Panel` named `Picker`. The constructor for the `Picker` class creates two more instances of `Panel`, one for the Row/Column and one for the Horizontal/Vertical gaps.

---

12. See Gamma, Helm, Johnson, Vlissides. *Design Patterns*, p. 163. Addison-Wesley, 1995.

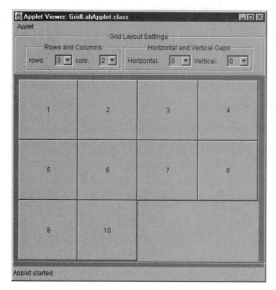

Figure 10-30 Nested Panels in an Applet
The GridLabApplet includes several layers of panels.

```
public Picker(ButtonPanel buttonPanel) {
    Panel rowCols = new Panel();
    Panel gaps    = new Panel();
    ...
    add(new Box(rowCols, "Rows and Columns"));
    add(new Box(gaps,    "Horizontal and Vertical Gaps"));
    ...
```

The rowCols and gaps panels are added to the Picker panel, but first they're
wrapped in boxes.

All of this results in the components in the "Grid Layout Settings" box being laid
out like so:

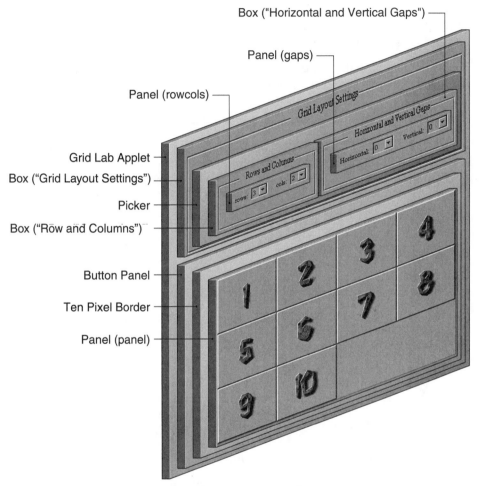

Figure 10-31 Nested Panel Layout Diagram

Now, in the center of the `GridLabApplet`, an instance of `Button Panel` is added:

```
add("Center", buttonPanel);
```

The `ButtonPanel` class creates an instance of `Panel` and an instance of `TenPixelBorder`:

```
private Panel           panel  = new Panel();
private TenPixelBorder border = new TenPixelBorder(panel);
```

As discussed previously, `TenPixelBorder` employs a `BorderLayout` to center the component it is passed and draws a gray border ten pixels thick around the component—see "TenPixelBorder" on page 336.

The `panel` passed to the `border` is the one that holds the buttons that will be positioned in a grid. First, several `Buttons` are declared:

```
private Button one, two, three, four, five,
                six, seven, eight, nine, ten;
```

The `ButtonPanel` constructor then creates instances of `Button`, adds them to the `panel`, and sets the layout manager for the `panel` to an instance of `GridLayout`:

```
public ButtonPanel(Applet applet) {
    URL cb = applet.getCodeBase();

    one   = new ImageButton(" 1 ");
    two   = new ImageButton(" 2 ");
    three = new ImageButton(" 3 ");
    ...
    panel.setLayout(new GridLayout(3,2));
    panel.add(one);    panel.add(two);    panel.add(three);
    panel.add(four);   panel.add(five);   panel.add(six);
    panel.add(seven);  panel.add(eight);  panel.add(nine);
    panel.add(ten);

    setLayout(new BorderLayout());
    add       (border, "Center");
}
```

Notice that at the end of the constructor, the `border`, which is the `TenPixelBorder` instance, is added to the center of the `ButtonPanel`. The `ButtonPanel` is centered beneath the north component and looks like this:

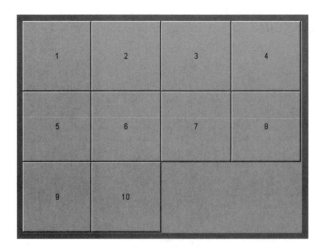

Communication Among Nested Panels

In applets with multiple nested panels, actions that occur in one panel may require a layout manager to reposition and resize components in other panels. That's certainly true in the `GridLabApplet`. When a user selects from the "Rows and Columns" or "Gaps" `Choice` components, the `ButtonPanel` needs to update accordingly. For example, look at the buttons in Figure 10-32.

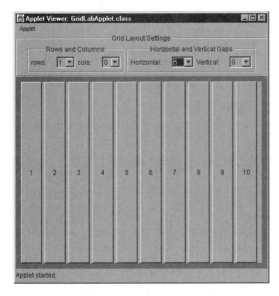

Figure 10-32 Nested Panel Updates
The `ButtonPanel` updates when selections are made in the `Picker` panel. The the `ButtonPanel` is shown above with one row specified and a horizontal gap of 5. (Note that when the number of rows has been set, the columns button value does not update because `GridLayout.getColumns()` returns the value last assigned via `setColumns()`, not the actual number of columns displayed.)

To force `ButtonPanel` to lay out its components after a selection has been made in a choice, we have to do a few things. First of all, we have to make sure that if a choice is selected, the `Picker` panel has access to the `ButtonPanel`. To accomplish that, we pass in an instance of `ButtonPanel` in the `Picker` constructor:

```
public Picker(ButtonPanel buttonPanel) {
```

Second, the `Picker` panel is added as an item listener for each `Choice`.

```
hchoice.addItemListener(this);
vchoice.addItemListener(this);
rowChoice.addItemListener(this);
colChoice.addItemListener(this);
```

`Picker.itemStateChanged()` makes sense of the selection made:

```
public boolean itemStateChanged(ItemEvent event) {
    int rows, cols, hgap, vgap;

    rows = Integer.parseInt(rowChoice.getSelectedItem());
    cols = Integer.parseInt(colChoice.getSelectedItem());
    hgap = Integer.parseInt(hchoice.getSelectedItem());
    vgap = Integer.parseInt(vchoice.getSelectedItem());

    buttonPanel.updateLayout(rows, cols, hgap, vgap);
}
```

The `itemStateChanged()` method extracts `integer` values from the four `Choice` objects it contains, like so:

```
numRows = Integer.parseInt(rowChoice.getSelectedItem());
```

`Integer.parseInt()` is a `static` method that parses a `String` and returns a `integer` value.

Once the integer values have been extracted from the choices, we pass the values to the `ButtonPanel` `updateLayout()` method:

```
public void updateLayout(int rows, int cols,
                             int hgap, int vgap) {
    try {
        gridLayout.setRows(rows);
        gridLayout.setCols(cols);
        gridLayout.setHgap(hgap);
        gridLayout.setVgap(vgap);

        panel.invalidate();
        border.validate();
    }
    catch(IllegalArgumentException e) {
        e.printStackTrace();
    }
}
```

The appropriate values for row, column and gaps are set for the `gridLayout`. Recall that invoking `setLayout()` invalidates the panel;[13] after invalidating the panel, the border—which is the parent container of the button panel—is validated.

---

13. See "`java.awt.Component` Methods That Depend Upon Peers" on page 440.

GridLabApplet Implementation

Now, let's look through the entire code for the GridLabApplet in Example 10-9. As you look through the code, refer to Figure 10-30 on page 386 and the two primary panels. One is called Picker; it is the north component of the applet and contains Box, Panel, Label, and Choice components. The other is called ButtonPanel; it is centered beneath Picker and contains a TenPixelBorder which (ultimately) contains the buttons displayed in a grid. Note that the Box class is not listed in Example 10-9; if you are interested in the implementation, the class is included on the CD. It is not listed here because its implementation is not germane to nested panels.

Example 10-9 GridLabApplet Class Listing

```
import java.applet.Applet;
import java.awt.*;
import java.awt.event.*;

public class GridLabApplet extends Applet {
    public void init() {
        ButtonPanel buttonPanel = new ButtonPanel(this);
        Picker      picker      = new Picker(buttonPanel);

        setLayout(new BorderLayout());
        add(new Box(picker, "Grid Layout Settings"), "North");
        add(buttonPanel, "Center");
    }
}

class ButtonPanel extends Panel {
    private Button      one, two, three, four, five,
                        six, seven, eight, nine, ten;

    private Panel          panel  = new Panel();
    private TenPixelBorder border = new TenPixelBorder(panel);
    private GridLayout     gridLayout;

    public ButtonPanel(Applet applet) {
        one   = new Button("  1  ");
        two   = new Button("  2  ");
        three = new Button("  3  ");
        four  = new Button("  4  ");
        five  = new Button("  5  ");
        six   = new Button("  6  ");
        seven = new Button("  7  ");
        eight = new Button("  8  ");
        nine  = new Button("  9  ");
        ten   = new Button("  10  ");

        panel.setLayout(gridLayout = new GridLayout(3,2));
```

```
        panel.add(one);    panel.add(two);    panel.add(three);
        panel.add(four);   panel.add(five);   panel.add(six);
        panel.add(seven);  panel.add(eight);  panel.add(nine);
        panel.add(ten);

        setLayout(new BorderLayout());
        add       ("Center", border);
    }
    public void updateLayout(int rows, int cols,
                             int hgap, int vgap) {
        try {
            gridLayout.setRows(rows);
            gridLayout.setColumns(cols);
            gridLayout.setHgap(hgap);
            gridLayout.setVgap(vgap);

            panel.invalidate();
            border.validate();
        }
        catch(IllegalArgumentException e) {
            e.printStackTrace();
        }
    }
}

class Picker extends Panel implements ItemListener {
    private Label   hgapLabel = new Label("Horizontal:");
    private Label   vgapLabel = new Label("Vertical:");
    private Label   rowLabel  = new Label("rows:");
    private Label   colLabel  = new Label("cols:");

    private Choice hchoice    = new Choice();
    private Choice vchoice    = new Choice();
    private Choice rowChoice  = new Choice();
    private Choice colChoice  = new Choice();

    private ButtonPanel buttonPanel;

    public Picker(ButtonPanel buttonPanel) {
        Panel rowCols = new Panel();
        Panel gaps    = new Panel();

        this.buttonPanel = buttonPanel;
        hchoice.addItem("0");
        hchoice.addItem("5");
        hchoice.addItem("10");
        hchoice.addItem("15");
        hchoice.addItem("20");

        vchoice.addItem("0");
        vchoice.addItem("5");
        vchoice.addItem("10");
```

```
        vchoice.addItem("15");
        vchoice.addItem("20");

        rowChoice.addItem("0");
        rowChoice.addItem("1");
        rowChoice.addItem("2");
        rowChoice.addItem("3");
        rowChoice.addItem("4");
        rowChoice.addItem("5");
        rowChoice.select (3);

        colChoice.addItem("0");
        colChoice.addItem("1");
        colChoice.addItem("2");
        colChoice.addItem("3");
        colChoice.addItem("4");
        colChoice.addItem("5");
        colChoice.select (2);

        rowCols.add(rowLabel);
        rowCols.add(rowChoice);
        rowCols.add(colLabel);
        rowCols.add(colChoice);

        gaps.add(hgapLabel);
        gaps.add(hchoice);
        gaps.add(vgapLabel);
        gaps.add(vchoice);

        hchoice.addItemListener(this);
        vchoice.addItemListener(this);
        rowChoice.addItemListener(this);
        colChoice.addItemListener(this);

        add(new Box(rowCols, "Rows and Columns"));
        add(new Box(gaps,    "Horizontal and Vertical Gaps"));
    }
    public void itemStateChanged(ItemEvent event) {
        int rows, cols, hgap, vgap;

        rows = Integer.parseInt(rowChoice.getSelectedItem());
        cols = Integer.parseInt(colChoice.getSelectedItem());
        hgap = Integer.parseInt(hchoice.getSelectedItem());
        vgap = Integer.parseInt(vchoice.getSelectedItem());

        buttonPanel.updateLayout(rows, cols, hgap, vgap);
    }
}
```

Null Layout Managers

Upon hearing of layout managers, newcomers to the AWT often have an overwhelming compulsion to simply set their container's layout manager to `null` and explicitly position and size the components displayed in their container.

Almost without exception, such a strategy is ill-fated. A container with a `null` layout manager will not be able to cope with resize events. As soon as this discovery is made, the next step is to override `paint()` to reposition and reshape the components laid out in the container. Once things have degenerated to this point, all of the benefits of the strategy pattern[14] go down the tubes. The algorithm for laying out components becomes hardcoded in the container, and therefore the container cannot easily change its layout strategy. Furthermore, once the layout strategy is hardcoded in the container, it is not available for others to reuse.

Sometimes, though, it is fitting to set a container's layout manager to `null`. For instance, in a drawing program where objects are created at random locations and dragged about, a `null` layout strategy may be the best choice. However, there are some pitfalls with using a `null` layout manager that you should be aware of. This section points out those pitfalls by discussing an applet with a `null` layout manager. The first two incarnations of the applet do not lay out their components properly. As a result, we will only list the working applet in its entirety, but we will show the pertinent code from the nonworking versions. All versions of the applet are on the CD, if you wish to run them for yourself.

The applet starts out by creating a handful of components and setting their locations.

```
public class TestApplet extends Applet {
    public void init() {
        setLayout(new BorderLayout());
        add(new NullLayoutTestPanel(), "Center");
    }
}
class NullLayoutTestPanel extends Panel {
    private Button      button;
    private Choice      choice;
    private TextField   textfield;
    private Checkbox    checkbox;
    private List        list;
    private Label       label;
    private Scrollbar   scrollbar;
```

14. See the "Layout Management and the Strategy Pattern" on page 330 for more discussion of the strategy pattern.

```
public NullLayoutTestPanel() {
    createComponents();
    setLayout(null);

    add(button); add(choice);
    add(textfield); add(checkbox);
    add(scrollbar); add(list);
    add(label);

    choice.setLocation(10,35);
    label.setLocation(230,120);
    checkbox.setLocation(120,120);
    textfield.setLocation(120,10);
    scrollbar.setLocation(120,160);
    button.setLocation(375,10);
    list.setLocation(230,10);
}
...
}
```

The `createComponents` method instantiates the components and sets properties for some of them. For instance, `createComponents` adds items to the choice and list.

When the applet runs, none of the components are visible. If the applet's `paint` method is modified to print out the bounds of each component and invoke `super.paint()`, the output looks like this:

```
java.awt.Rectangle[x=10,y=35,width=0,height=0]
java.awt.Rectangle[x=230,y=120,width=0,height=0]
java.awt.Rectangle[x=120,y=120,width=0,height=0]
java.awt.Rectangle[x=120,y=10,width=0,height=0]
java.awt.Rectangle[x=120,y=160,width=0,height=0]
java.awt.Rectangle[x=375,y=10,width=0,height=0]
java.awt.Rectangle[x=230,y=10,width=0,height=0]
```

Since the components are never explicitly sized, their sizes by default are (0,0), which makes them very difficult to see. Since components are usually sized by the layout manager that lays them out, it can be easy to forget to explicitly size them by hand when using a `null` layout manager.

Instead of invoking `setLocation()`, the `NullLayoutTestPanel` constructor is modified to invoke `setBounds()` for each component.

```
public NullLayoutTestPanel() {
    createComponents();
    setLayout(null);

    add(button); add(choice);
    add(textfield); add(checkbox);
```

```
        add(scrollbar); add(list);
        add(label);

        choice.setBounds(10,35,100,50);
        label.setBounds(230, 120,100,50);
        checkbox.setBounds(120, 120,100,50);
        textfield.setBounds(120,10,100,50);
        scrollbar.setBounds(120, 160,100,50);
        button.setBounds(375, 10,100,50);
        list.setBounds(230, 10,100,50);
    }
```

This version of the applet is much better except that the size of the checkbox is too large, which causes it to obliterate a portion of the scrollbar, as shown in Figure 10-33.

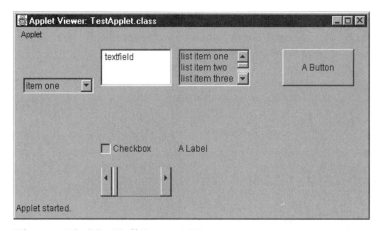

Figure 10-33 Null Layout Managers
The checkbox is sized too large and obliterates a portion of the scrollbar.

Perhaps it would be better to size the components according to their preferred sizes; that way, each component will be no larger than it needs to be. However, getPreferredSize() returns a dimension of (0,0) until a component's peer is created—see "Components and Peers" on page 439. As a result, the panel's addNotify method is overridden, and the components are sized according to their preferred sizes. At this point, all the components are visible and none of the components impinges upon the real estate of the others, as shown in Figure 10-34.

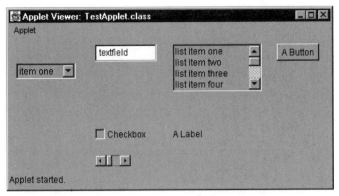

Figure 10-34 Null Layout Managers—Take II
All components are sized according to their preferred sizes.

The working version of the applet is listed in its entirety in Example 10-10.

Example 10-10 An Applet with a Panel That Employs a null Layout
Manager

```
import java.applet.Applet;
import java.awt.*;

public class TestApplet extends Applet {
    public void init() {
        setLayout(new BorderLayout());
        add(new NullLayoutTestPanel(), "Center");
    }
}
class NullLayoutTestPanel extends Panel {
    private Button          button;
    private Choice          choice;
    private TextField       textfield;
    private Checkbox        checkbox;
    private List            list;
    private Label           label;
    private Scrollbar       scrollbar;

    public NullLayoutTestPanel() {
        createComponents();
        setLayout(null);

        add(button);        add(choice);
        add(textfield); add(checkbox);
        add(scrollbar); add(list);
```

```
        add(label);
    }
    public void addNotify() {
        super.addNotify();

        Dimension ps;

        ps = choice.getPreferredSize();
        choice.setBounds(10,35,ps.width,ps.height);

        ps = label.getPreferredSize();
        label.setBounds(230,120,ps.width,ps.height);

        ps = checkbox.getPreferredSize();
        checkbox.setBounds(120,120,ps.width,ps.height);

        ps = textfield.getPreferredSize();
        textfield.setBounds(120,10,ps.width,ps.height);

        ps = scrollbar.getPreferredSize();
        scrollbar.setBounds(120,160,ps.width,ps.height);

        ps = button.getPreferredSize();
        button.setBounds(375,10,ps.width,ps.height);

        ps = list.getPreferredSize();
        list.setBounds(230,10,ps.width,ps.height);
    }
    public Insets getInsets() {
        return new Insets(10,10,10,10);
    }
    public void paint(Graphics g) {
        System.out.println(choice.getBounds());
        System.out.println(label.getBounds());
        System.out.println(checkbox.getBounds());
        System.out.println(textfield.getBounds());
        System.out.println(scrollbar.getBounds());
        System.out.println(button.getBounds());
        System.out.println(list.getBounds());
    }
    private void createComponents() {
        button      = new Button("A Button");
        choice      = new Choice();
        textfield   = new TextField("textfield");
        checkbox    = new Checkbox("Checkbox");
        list        = new List();
        label       = new Label("A Label");
        scrollbar   = new Scrollbar(Scrollbar.HORIZONTAL);
```

```
        choice.add("item one");
        choice.add("item two");
        choice.add("item three");
        choice.add("item four");

        list.add("list item one");
        list.add("list item two");
        list.add("list item three");
        list.add("list item four");
        list.add("list item five");
        list.add("list item six");
        list.add("list item seven");
        list.add("list item eight");
        list.add("list item nine");

        scrollbar.setValues(0,100,0,1000);
    }
}
```

AWT TIP ...

Setting Layout Managers to Null

Although it is almost always preferable to use a layout manager to position and size components, sometimes it is necessary to set a container's layout manager to null and to explicitly size and position components by hand.

When a container has a null layout manager, components must be positioned and sized—they will not be sized according to their preferred sizes. Also, if components are to be explicitly sized according to their preferred sizes, their sizes must be set after the component's peers have been created.

Custom Layout Managers

Although the AWT's standard layout managers are well equipped to handle most layout situations, there comes a time when they just won't do. You will also find that for certain types of layouts, it is simpler to use a custom layout manager that deals with an exact type of layout than it is to use one of the AWT's layout managers, even though one of them may suffice.

A custom layout manager involves implementing the LayoutManager or LayoutManager2 interfaces.

We've discussed each of these methods in detail earlier in this chapter, so instead of rehashing the responsibilities of each method, let's take a look at some custom layout managers that implement them.

BulletinLayout

This section describes a layout manager—BulletinLayout—which lays out components as though they were on a bulletin board. Components are positioned according to their location and shaped according to either their size or, if the component has not been explicitly sized, their preferred size.

BulletinLayout will serve as our first foray into implementing custom layout managers. Example 10-11 lists its implementation. Notice that BulletinLayout implements addLayoutComponent() and removeLayoutComponent() as no-ops, which indicates that it does not keep track of a finite set of components to lay out. Instead, it lays out all the components it finds in the container it is currently laying out.

Also note that BulletinLayout implements preferredLayoutSize() and minimumLayoutSize() to simply return the union of all the preferred and minimum sizes for all the visible components. These two methods invoke a number of container methods, such as getInsets(), countComponents(), and getComponent(), that are routinely used by layout managers.

BulletinLayout implements the required layoutContainer(), which operates on all visible components and reshapes them so that they reside at their specified location and are resized according to their (explicit or preferred) sizes.

Example 10-11 BulletinLayout Class Listing

```java
import java.awt.*;
import java.util.Hashtable;

public class BulletinLayout implements LayoutManager {
    private Hashtable hash = new Hashtable();

    public void addLayoutComponent(String s, Component comp) {
    }
    public void removeLayoutComponent(Component comp) {
    }
    public Dimension preferredLayoutSize(Container target) {
        Insets     insets     = target.getInsets();
        Dimension dim         = new Dimension(0,0);
        int        ncomponents = target.getComponentCount();
        Component comp;
        Dimension d;
        Rectangle size = new Rectangle(0,0);
        Rectangle compSize;

        for (int i = 0 ; i < ncomponents ; i++) {
            comp = target.getComponent(i);

            if(comp.isVisible()) {
```

```
            d = comp.getSize();
            compSize = new Rectangle(comp.getLocation());
            compSize.width  = d.width;
            compSize.height = d.height;

            size = size.union(compSize);
        }
    }
    dim.width  += size.width + insets.right;
    dim.height += size.height + insets.bottom;

    return dim;
}
public Dimension minimumLayoutSize(Container target) {
    Insets     insets      = target.getInsets();
    Dimension dim          = new Dimension(0,0);
    int        ncomponents = target.getComponentCount();
    Component comp;
    Dimension d;
    Rectangle minBounds = new Rectangle(0,0);
    Rectangle compMinBounds;

    for (int i = 0 ; i < ncomponents ; i++) {
        comp = target.getComponent(i);

        if(comp.isVisible()) {
            d = comp.getMinimumSize();
            compMinBounds =
              new Rectangle(comp.getLocation());
          compMinBounds.setSize(d.width, d.height);

            minBounds = minBounds.union(compMinBounds);
        }
    }
    dim.width  += minBounds.width  + insets.right;
    dim.height += minBounds.height + insets.bottom;

    return dim;
}
public void layoutContainer(Container target) {
    Insets     insets      = target.getInsets();
    int        ncomponents = target.getComponentCount();
    Component comp;
    Dimension sz, ps;
    Point loc;

    for (int i = 0 ; i < ncomponents ; i++) {
        comp = target.getComponent(i);

        if(comp.isVisible()) {
            sz   = comp.getSize();
          ps   = comp.getPreferredSize();
```

```
                loc   = getComponentLocation(comp);

            if(sz.width < ps.width || sz.height < ps.height)
                sz = ps;

            comp.setBounds(loc.x, loc.y, sz.width, sz.height);
          }
       }
    }
    private Point getComponentLocation(Component comp) {
        Insets insets = comp.getParent().getInsets();
        Point  loc    = comp.getLocation();

        if( ! hash.containsKey(comp)) {
           addComponentToHashtable(comp);
        }
        else {
           Point oldLocation = (Point)hash.get(comp);

           if(oldLocation.x != loc.x ||
              oldLocation.y != loc.y) {
              addComponentToHashtable(comp);
           }
        }
        return comp.getLocation();
    }
    private void addComponentToHashtable(Component comp) {
        Insets insets = comp.getParent().getInsets();
        Point  loc    = comp.getLocation();

        comp.setLocation(loc.x + insets.left,
                         loc.y + insets.top);
        hash.put(comp, comp.getLocation());
    }
  }
}
```

Notice that `BulletinLayout` maintains a hashtable of components and their locations.This was done to ensure that the top and left insets are added to the position of a component the first time it is laid out or if its location changes after it is laid out the first time.

Exercising the BulletinLayout Custom Layout Manager

`BulletinLayout` comes with a test applet that lays out a few random components at specific locations, as you can see from Figure 10-35.

The status line of the applet displays the minimum and preferred sizes of the container.

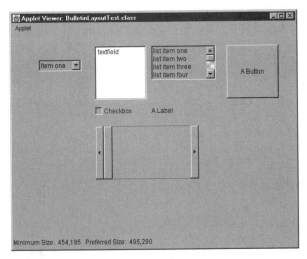

Figure 10-35 `BulletinLayout`
`BulletinLayout` positions components at their location and shapes them according to either their explicit or preferred size.

The test applet for `BulletinLayout` is rather lengthy, but much of the code is taken up with creating and setting parameters for the components displayed in the applet.

Locations for all of the components are explicitly set, whereas only four of the components have their sizes explicitly set; the rest will be sized to their preferred sizes.

```
choice.setLocation(10,35);
label.setLocation(230, 120);
checkbox.setLocation(120, 120);

textfield.setLocation(120,10);
textfield.setSize(100,100);

scrollbar.setLocation(120, 160);
scrollbar.setSize(200,100);

button.setLocation(375, 10);
button.setSize(100,100);

list.setLocation(230, 10);
list.setSize(100,100);
```

The choice, label, and checkbox are sized according to their preferred sizes since their size was not explicitly set. The `BulletinLayoutTest` applet is listed in Example 10-12.

Example 10-12 `BulletinLayoutTest` Class Listing

```java
import java.applet.Applet;
import java.awt.*;

public class BulletinLayoutTest extends Applet {
    public void init() {
        add(new BulletinLayoutTestPanel(this), "Center");
    }
}
class BulletinLayoutTestPanel extends Panel {
    private Applet      applet;
    private Button      button;
    private Choice      choice;
    private TextField   textfield;
    private Checkbox    checkbox;
    private List        list;
    private Label       label;
    private Scrollbar   scrollbar;

    public BulletinLayoutTestPanel(Applet applet) {
        this.applet = applet;

        createComponents();
        setLayout(new BulletinLayout());

        add(button);       add(choice);
        add(textfield); add(checkbox);
        add(scrollbar); add(list);
        add(label);

        choice.setLocation(10,35);
        label.setLocation(230, 120);
        checkbox.setLocation(120, 120);

        textfield.setLocation(120,10);
        textfield.setSize(100,100);

        scrollbar.setLocation(120, 160);
        scrollbar.setSize(200,100);

        button.setLocation(375, 10);
        button.setSize(100,100);

        list.setLocation(230, 10);
        list.setSize(100,100);
    }
    public Insets getInsets() {
```

```
            return new Insets(10,10,10,10);
    }
    public void paint(Graphics g) {
        Dimension ps = getPreferredSize();
        Dimension ms = getMinimumSize();

        super.paint(g);
        applet.showStatus("Minimum Size:  " + ms.width + ","
                        + ms.height + "    " +
                        "Preferred Size:  " + ps.width + ","
                        + ps.height);
    }
    private void createComponents() {
        button      = new Button("A Button");
        choice      = new Choice();
        textfield   = new TextField("textfield");
        checkbox    = new Checkbox("Checkbox");
        list        = new List();
        label       = new Label("A Label");
        scrollbar   = new Scrollbar(Scrollbar.HORIZONTAL);

        choice.add("item one");
        choice.add("item two");
        choice.add("item three");
        choice.add("item four");

        list.add("list item one");
        list.add("list item two");
        list.add("list item three");
        list.add("list item four");
        list.add("list item five");
        list.add("list item six");
        list.add("list item seven");
        list.add("list item eight");
        list.add("list item nine");

        scrollbar.setValues(0,100,0,1000);
    }
}
```

RowLayout

You might wonder why we need custom layout managers at all. After all, we've shown that the standard AWT layout managers are fairly comprehensive in what they can do and that the GridBagLayout layout manager is powerful enough to lay out almost anything. However, there are occasions when it's simpler and more straightforward to encapsulate some layout functionality in a custom layout manager than it is to commit to memory the constraints necessary to manipulate GridBagLayout. In fact, the GridLabApplet offers a case in point. Look at Figure 10-36 and notice what happens to the Picker panel when the applet is resized horizontally to smaller in the horizontal direction.

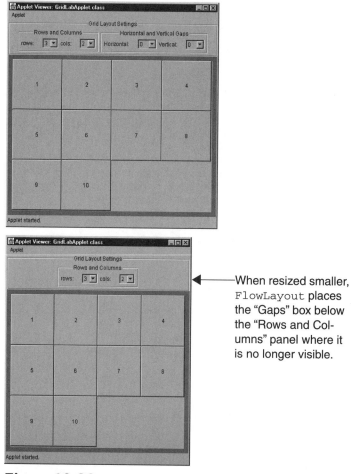

Figure 10-36 FlowLayout Resize Behavior
FlowLayout moves components to the next row if they don't fit in
the current row.

The Picker panel does not have a layout manager explicitly set, so it is using
the default layout manager for Panel, which is FlowLayout. From Figure 10-
36, it appears that FlowLayout is unable to position the "Gaps" box
appropriately. Actually, FlowLayout has positioned it, but you can't see it.
When the applet is resized small enough that there's no longer enough room to
place another component to the right of the previous one, FlowLayout places
the next component in the next row. In GridLabApplet, this behavior is

causing the "Gaps" box to be hidden—FlowLayout doesn't care if the Picker panel is tall enough to display the "Gaps" box it has placed below the "Rows and Columns" box.

We want the buttons in the boxes centered, even if both boxes don't entirely fit in the panel, so here's a case where the default layout manager is insufficient for the behavior we want. And although we could probably use GridBagLayout to accomplish the desired behavior, we want a more general-purpose solution that won't require us to deal with a variety of constraints each and every time we want to employ it.

Additionally, there are times when you just want to lay out components in a row or column and be guaranteed that the components will stay aligned in their row or column, no matter what kind of resizing adversity comes their way. To this end, we'll implement two custom layout managers: RowLayout and ColumnLayout.

The RowLayout layout manager is useful for components, such as toolbars, that might contain image buttons displayed in a row. As its name suggests, RowLayout lays out components in a row. At construction time, horizontal and vertical orientations and the gaps between components can be specified.

To start with, take a look at Table 10-14, which shows the responsibilities of the RowLayout class. You'll notice that these are the standard five methods that must be defined by any class that implements LayoutManager.

Table 10-14 RowLayout **Responsibilities**

Methods	Description
void addLayoutComponent(String name, Component comp)	Is a *no-op* implementation
void removeLayoutComponent(Component comp)	Is a *no-op* implementation
Dimension preferredLayoutSize(Container targert)	Returns the preferred container height and width for the layout manager
Dimension minimumLayoutSize(Container targert)	Returns the minimum container height and width for the layout manager
void layoutContainer(Container target)	Positions components in a container

RowLayout implements addLayoutComponent() and removeLayoutComponent() as no-ops—RowLayout does not keep track of individual components but instead lays out all of the components in containers it is called upon to lay out.

RowLayout is a fairly involved layout manager, so before looking at the entire listing for it, we'll highlight some details about its implementation. As described in Table 10-14, RowLayout addLayoutComponent() and removeLayoutComponent() are no-op methods, so the implementations of the other methods from the LayoutManager interface reveal exactly how RowLayout works. We'll start with preferredLayoutSize():

```
public Dimension preferredLayoutSize(Container target) {
    Insets      insets      = target.getInsets();
    Dimension dim           = new Dimension(0,0);
    int         ncomponents = target.countComponents();
    Component comp;
    Dimension d;
    ...
```

preferredLayoutSize() calculates the preferred width and height for the container it is passed. The insets for the container that RowLayout is going to lay out are obtained, and the preferredLayoutSize() return value is initialized to 0,0. The Component comp is a reference to the next component to be positioned and sized in the container. The Dimension d is used to hold the preferred size of each component in the container.

Next, preferredLayoutSize() loops through the components in the container and calculates the preferred size of the container.

```
    ...
    for (int i = 0; i < ncomponents; i++) {
        comp = target.getComponent(i);

        if(comp.isVisible()) {
            d = comp.getPreferredSize();

            dim.width  += d.width;
            dim.height = Math.max(d.height, dim.height);

            if(i > 0) dim.width += gap;
        }
    }
    dim.width  += insets.left + insets.right;
    dim.height += insets.top + insets.bottom;

    return dim;
}
```

The `for` loop cycles through every component in the container. If the `component` is visible, then the component's `getPreferredSize()` is assigned to d. As the method loops through each component in the container, the component's preferred width is added to `dim.width`. The preferred width of the container will be equal to the sum of the widths of all visible components plus the gaps between them.

The preferred height of the container winds up being the height of the tallest component in the row.

The gap between components is factored in n-1 times, where n is the number of components contained in the container.

The left and right insets of the container are also added to the preferred width, and the top and bottom insets of the container are added to the preferred height.

The `minimumLayoutSize()` implementation is calculated exactly like the `preferredLayoutSize()` except that `Dimension d` holds the minimum size of each component in the container instead of the preferred size.

Note that this method of looping through the container's components is typically the way `preferredLayoutSize()` and `minimumLayoutSize()` are implemented. The algorithms for each method are often mirror images of each other, with the exception of gathering either the preferred or minimum size of the component, respectively.

Note: Rather than duplicate the algorithm for `preferredLayoutSize()` and `minimumLayoutSize()`, we could have coded the algorithm in a third method and passed a `boolean` value to determine whether we were calculating the preferred or minimum size. However, for the sake of illustration and because custom layout managers are often implemented with two distinct but very similar methods, we've chosen to be somewhat redundant.

The `layoutContainer()` implementation defines exactly how components in a container are positioned and sized:

```
public void layoutContainer(Container target) {
    Insets    insets      = target.getInsets();
    int       ncomponents = target.countComponents();
    int       top         = 0;
    int       left        = insets.left;
    Dimension tps         = target.getPreferredSize();
    Dimension targetSize  = target.getSize();
    Component comp;
    Dimension ps;

    if(horizontalOrientation == Orientation.CENTER)
```

```
      left = left + (targetSize.width/2) - (tps.width/2);
   if(horizontalOrientation == Orientation.RIGHT)
      left = left + targetSize.width - tps.width;

   for (int i = 0; i < ncomponents; i++) {
      comp = target.getComponent(i);

   if(comp.isVisible()) {
      ps  = comp.getPreferredSize();

   if(verticalOrientation == Orientation.CENTER)
      top = (targetSize.height/2) - (ps.height/2);
   else if(verticalOrientation == Orientation.TOP)
      top = insets.top;
   else if(verticalOrientation == Orientation.BOTTOM)
      top = targetSize.height - ps.height - insets.bottom;

      comp.setSize(left,top,ps.width,ps.height);
      left += ps.width + gap;
   }
}
```

The left edge is set according to the horizontal orientation.[15] If the orientation is CENTER, the left edge is set to half of the container's width minus half of the container's preferred size. If the horizontal orientation is RIGHT, then the left edge is set to the width of the container minus the preferred width of the container.

Then, layoutContainer() cycles through all of the components in the container and assesses their vertical orientations.

Note that the setSize() call uses the left and top we've just calculated and also uses the component's preferred height and width. As a result, RowLayout will not stretch or shrink any component to any size other than the component's preferred height and width.

Now, let's take a look at the RowLayout code in Example 10-13. Notice that a RowLayout has four constructors that take a variety of orientation and gap settings. As is our practice, the first three constructors call the fourth one, which does the work:

---

15. The Orientation class is not part of the AWT. It is included on the CD.

Example 10-13 RowLayout Class Listing

```java
import java.awt.*;

public class RowLayout implements LayoutManager {
    static private int _defaultGap = 5;

    private int gap;
    private Orientation verticalOrientation;
    private Orientation horizontalOrientation;

    public RowLayout() {
        this(Orientation.CENTER,
            Orientation.CENTER, _defaultGap);
    }
    public RowLayout(int gap) {
        this(Orientation.CENTER, Orientation.CENTER, gap);
    }
    public RowLayout(Orientation horizontalOrient,
                Orientation verticalOrient) {
        this(horizontalOrient, verticalOrient, _defaultGap);
    }
    public RowLayout(Orientation horizontalOrient,
                Orientation verticalOrient, int gap) {
        if(gap < 0 ||
            (horizontalOrient != Orientation.LEFT    &&
            horizontalOrient != Orientation.CENTER &&
            horizontalOrient != Orientation.RIGHT) ||

            (verticalOrient    != Orientation.TOP    &&
            verticalOrient    != Orientation.CENTER &&
            verticalOrient    != Orientation.BOTTOM)) {
          throw new IllegalArgumentException(
                    "bad gap or orientation");
        }
        this.gap                 = gap;
        this.verticalOrientation = verticalOrient;
        this.horizontalOrientation = horizontalOrient;
    }

    public void addLayoutComponent(String name, Component comp) {
    }
    public void removeLayoutComponent(Component comp) {
    }

    public Dimension preferredLayoutSize(Container target) {
        Insets     insets      = target.getInsets();
        Dimension dim          = new Dimension(0,0);
        int       ncomponents = target.getComponentCount();
        Component comp;
        Dimension d;
```

```
      for (int i = 0 ; i < ncomponents ; i++) {
          comp = target.getComponent(i);

          if(comp.isVisible()) {
              d = comp.getPreferredSize();

              dim.width  += d.width;
              dim.height = Math.max(d.height, dim.height);

              if(i > 0) dim.width += gap;
          }
      }
      dim.width  += insets.left + insets.right;
      dim.height += insets.top + insets.bottom;

      return dim;
  }
  public Dimension minimumLayoutSize(Container target) {
      Insets     insets      = target.getInsets();
      Dimension dim          = new Dimension(0,0);
      int        ncomponents = target.getComponentCount();
      Component comp;
      Dimension d;

      for (int i = 0 ; i < ncomponents ; i++) {
          comp = target.getComponent(i);

          if(comp.isVisible()) {
              d = comp.getMinimumSize();

              dim.width  += d.width;
              dim.height = Math.max(d.height, dim.height);

              if(i > 0) dim.width += gap;
          }
      }
      dim.width  += insets.left + insets.right;
      dim.height += insets.top + insets.bottom;

      return dim;
  }
  public void layoutContainer(Container target) {
      Insets     insets      = target.getInsets();
      int        ncomponents = target.getComponentCount();
      int        top         = 0;
      int        left        = insets.left;
      Dimension tps          = target.getPreferredSize();
      Dimension targetSize   = target.getSize();
      Component comp;
      Dimension ps;

      if(horizontalOrientation == Orientation.CENTER)
          left = left + (targetSize.width/2) - (tps.width/2);
      if(horizontalOrientation == Orientation.RIGHT)
```

```
        left = left + targetSize.width - tps.width;

    for (int i = 0 ; i < ncomponents ; i++) {
        comp = target.getComponent(i);

        if(comp.isVisible()) {
            ps  = comp.getPreferredSize();

            if(verticalOrientation == Orientation.CENTER)
                top = (targetSize.height/2) - (ps.height/2);
            else if(verticalOrientation == Orientation.TOP)
                top = insets.top;
            else if(
                verticalOrientation == Orientation.BOTTOM)
                top = targetSize.height -
                        ps.height - insets.bottom;

            comp.setBounds(left,top,ps.width,ps.height);
            left += ps.width + gap;
        }
    }
    }
}
```

Exercising the RowLayout Custom Layout Manager

Now that we've seen the implementation of the RowLayout, let's see it in action. For an idea of how RowLayout works, take a look at Figure 10-37, which shows a RowLayoutApplet.

You may have noticed that there are several parallels between RowLayoutApplet and GridLabApplet, which we explored earlier in this chapter. If you followed that discussion, then you'll quickly see what's going on in RowLayoutApplet. Table 10-15 summarizes the similarities between the two applets.

Table 10-15 GridLabApplet and RowLayoutApplet Comparison

GridLabApplet **Panels**	RowLayoutApplet **Panels**	**Position**
ButtonPanel	RowButtonPanel	North
Picker	RowPicker	Center

Besides the panel construction and layout, also notice that just as GridLabApplet implements itemStateChanged() and updateLayout() to communicate among panels, RowLayout has itemStateChanged() and updateOrientations() to communicate among panels. Also, just as GridLabApplet has a ButtonPanel and Picker Panel, RowLayoutApplet has RowButtonPanel and RowPicker.

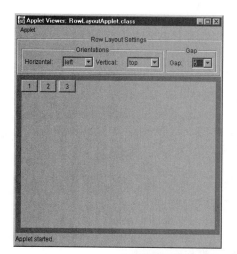

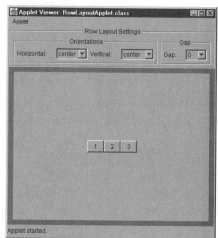

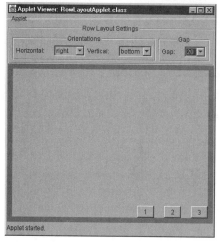

Figure 10-37 RowLayout at Work
This sequence of pictures shows RowLayout positioning image
buttons in a row, with various orientation and gap settings.

To illustrate how panels are layered in the RowLayoutApplet, take a look at
Figure 10-38 before we go through the code.

Now, let's take a look at some of the unique characteristics of
RowLayoutApplet, starting with its init method, where two panels are
positioned with an instance of BorderLayout. One panel is in the north and one
is in the center:

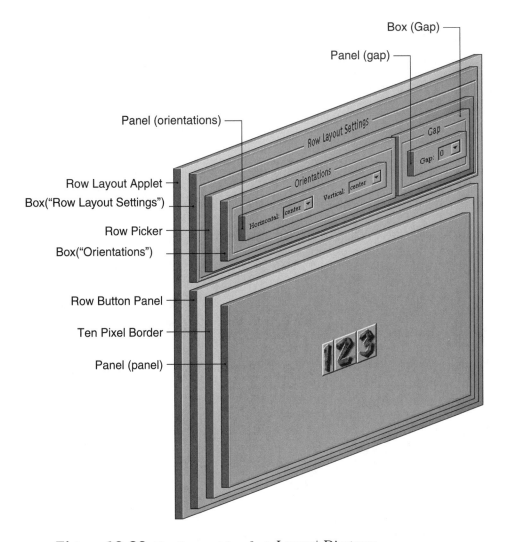

Figure 10-38 RowLayoutApplet Layout Diagram

```java
public void init() {
    setLayout(new BorderLayout());
    add(buttonPanel = new RowButtonPanel(), "Center");
    add(new Box(new RowPicker(buttonPanel),
                        "Row Layout Settings"), "North");
}
```

The `RowPicker` is a bit more complex than the `RowButtonPanel`, so we'll look at it first.

```
class RowPicker extends Panel implements ItemListener {
    private Label  horientLabel = new Label("Horizontal:");
    private Label  vorientLabel = new Label("Vertical:");
    private Label  gapLabel     = new Label("Gap:");
    private Choice hchoice   = new Choice();
    private Choice vchoice   = new Choice();
    private Choice gapChoice = new Choice();
    private RowButtonPanel buttonPanel;

    public RowPicker(RowButtonPanel buttonPanel) {
        Panel orientations = new Panel();
        Panel gap          = new Panel();

        this.buttonPanel = buttonPanel;

        hchoice.addItemListener(this);
        hchoice.addItem("left");
        hchoice.addItem("center");
        hchoice.addItem("right");
        hchoice.select(1);

        vchoice.addItemListener(this);
        vchoice.addItem("top");
        vchoice.addItem("center");
        vchoice.addItem("bottom");
        vchoice.select(1);

        gapChoice.addItemListener(this);
        gapChoice.addItem("0");
        gapChoice.addItem("5");
        gapChoice.addItem("10");
        gapChoice.addItem("15");
        gapChoice.addItem("20");

        orientations.add(horientLabel);
        orientations.add(hchoice);
        orientations.add(vorientLabel);
        orientations.add(vchoice);

        gap.add(gapLabel);
        gap.add(gapChoice);

        add(new Box(orientations, "Orientations"));
        add(new Box(gap,          "Gap"));
    }
    ...
}
```

The first order of business is to create the `Label` and `Choice` components. The `RowPicker` constructor is passed a `buttonPanel`. `RowPicker` maintains a reference to the `RowButtonPanel` in order to update it when the choice values are modified.

Two panels are created to hold the `Label` and `Choice` components. These panels will each be enclosed in a `Box` component.

Next, let's look at `RowButtonPanel`. The `RowButtonPanel` is the center component in Figure 10-38.

```
class RowButtonPanel extends Panel {
    private Button      one, two, three;
    private Panel            panel  = new Panel();
    private TenPixelBorder border = new TenPixelBorder(panel);

    public RowButtonPanel() {
        one   = new Button(" 1  ");
        two   = new Button(" 2  ");
        three = new Button(" 3  ");

        panel.setLayout(new RowLayout(0));
        panel.add(one);
        panel.add(two);
        panel.add(three);

        setLayout(new BorderLayout());
        add       (border, "Center");
    }
    public void updateOrientations(Orientation horient,
                                   Orientation vorient,
                                   int gap) {
        panel.setLayout(new RowLayout(horient, vorient, gap));
        border.validate();
    }
}
```

Note that `panel` is passed to the `TenPixelBorder` constructor. The layout manager of the `panel` is set to an instance of `RowLayout`. The `setLayout()` call sets the layout manager for the `RowButtonPanel` to be an instance of `BorderLayout`, which will center the border. So, what we have here is three instances of `Button` being laid out by `RowLayout` inside a panel inside a border being laid out by `BorderLayout`. Clear as mud? Refer back to Figure 10-38 on page 415 and that should help.

We haven't mentioned it yet, but `RowLayoutApplet` allows the specification of both the horizontal and vertical orientations in the `Choice` components. `RowPicker.itemStateChanged()` method is invoked whenever a selection is made in one of the choices.

```
public void itemStateChanged(ItemEvent event) {
    String horient, vorient;
    int     gap;

    horient = hchoice.getSelectedItem();
    vorient = vchoice.getSelectedItem();
    gap     = Integer.parseInt(gapChoice.getSelectedItem());

    buttonPanel.updateOrientations(
                Orientation.fromString(horient),
                  Orientation.fromString(vorient), gap);
}
```

The selected string in the gap choice is converted into an integer value. Then, fromString() from the Orientation class is invoked to convert the string selected in the choice to an Orientation constant.

Orientation.fromString() returns an appropriate Orientation constant, given a string representing the constant. The orientation constants are then passed along to updateOrientations().

The updateOrientations method uses the orientation values to create and set a new instance of RowLayout:

```
public void updateOrientations(Orientation horient,
                               Orientation vorient,
                               int gap) {
    panel.setLayout(new RowLayout(horient, vorient, gap));
    border.validate();
}
```

Recall that setLayout() invalidates the panel and its container (border), and therefore the call to border.validate() results in the panel being laid out.

RowLayoutApplet Implementation

Now, let's look through the RowLayoutApplet class in Example 10-14. As you look through the code, particularly note the use of RowButtonPanel and RowPicker. You may also want to refer to the 3D layout diagram in Figure 10-38 on page 415.

Example 10-14 RowLayoutApplet Class Listing

```
import java.applet.Applet;
import java.awt.*;
import java.awt.event.*;

public class RowLayoutApplet extends Applet {
    private RowButtonPanel buttonPanel;

    public void init() {
        setLayout(new BorderLayout());
```

```java
        add(buttonPanel = new RowButtonPanel(), "Center");
        add(new Box(new RowPicker(buttonPanel),
                           "Row Layout Settings"), "North");
    }
}
class RowButtonPanel extends Panel {
    private Button      one, two, three;
    private Panel          panel  = new Panel();
    private TenPixelBorder border = new TenPixelBorder(panel);

    public RowButtonPanel() {
        one   = new Button("  1  ");
        two   = new Button("  2  ");
        three = new Button("  3  ");

        panel.setLayout(new RowLayout(0));
        panel.add(one);
        panel.add(two);
        panel.add(three);

        setLayout(new BorderLayout());
        add        (border, "Center");
    }
    public void updateOrientations(Orientation horient,
                                   Orientation vorient,
                                   int gap) {
        panel.setLayout(new RowLayout(horient, vorient, gap));
        border.validate();
    }
}
class RowPicker extends Panel implements ItemListener {
    private Label   horientLabel = new Label("Horizontal:");
    private Label   vorientLabel = new Label("Vertical:");
    private Label   gapLabel     = new Label("Gap:");

    private Choice hchoice   = new Choice();
    private Choice vchoice   = new Choice();
    private Choice gapChoice = new Choice();

    private RowButtonPanel buttonPanel;

    public RowPicker(RowButtonPanel buttonPanel) {
        Panel orientations = new Panel();
        Panel gap          = new Panel();

        this.buttonPanel = buttonPanel;

        hchoice.addItemListener(this);
        hchoice.addItem("left");
        hchoice.addItem("center");
        hchoice.addItem("right");
        hchoice.select(1);
```

```
            vchoice.addItemListener(this);
            vchoice.addItem("top");
            vchoice.addItem("center");
            vchoice.addItem("bottom");
            vchoice.select(1);

            gapChoice.addItemListener(this);
            gapChoice.addItem("0");
            gapChoice.addItem("5");
            gapChoice.addItem("10");
            gapChoice.addItem("15");
            gapChoice.addItem("20");

            orientations.add(horientLabel);
            orientations.add(hchoice);
            orientations.add(vorientLabel);
            orientations.add(vchoice);

            gap.add(gapLabel);
            gap.add(gapChoice);

            add(new Box(orientations, "Orientations"));
            add(new Box(gap,          "Gap"));
        }
        public void itemStateChanged(ItemEvent event) {
            String horient, vorient;
            int    gap;

            horient = hchoice.getSelectedItem();
            vorient = vchoice.getSelectedItem();
            gap     = Integer.parseInt(gapChoice.getSelectedItem());

            buttonPanel.updateOrientations(
                    Orientation.fromString(horient),
                      Orientation.fromString(vorient), gap);
        }
    }
```

ColumnLayout

The ColumnLayout layout manager is very similar in design and capability to the RowLayout layout manager, except that it positions components in columns instead of rows. You'll notice in Table 10-16 that, like all custom layout managers, ColumnLayout implements the standard LayoutManager methods.

Since the ColumnLayout implementation is so similar to the RowLayout custom layout manager, we won't bother to discuss it. Example 10-15 lists the ColumnLayout code for completeness.

Table 10-16 ColumnLayout **Responsibilities**

Methods	Description
void addLayoutComponent(String name, Component comp)	Is a no-op implementation
void removedLayoutComponent(Component comp)	Is a no-op implementation
Dimension preferredLayoutSize(Container targert)	Returns the preferred container height and width for the layout manager
Dimension minimumLayoutSize(Container targert)	Returns the minimum container height and width for the layout manager
void layoutContainer(Container target)	Positions components in a container

Example 10-15 ColumnLayout Class Listing

```
import java.awt.*;

public class ColumnLayout implements LayoutManager {
    static private int _defaultGap = 5;

    private int        gap;
    private Orientation horizontalOrientation;
    private Orientation verticalOrientation;

    public ColumnLayout() {
        this(Orientation.CENTER,
            Orientation.CENTER, _defaultGap);
    }
    public ColumnLayout(int gap) {
        this(Orientation.CENTER, Orientation.CENTER, gap);
    }
    public ColumnLayout(Orientation horizontalOrient,
                        Orientation verticalOrient) {
        this(horizontalOrient, verticalOrient, _defaultGap);
    }
    public ColumnLayout(Orientation horizontalOrient,
                        Orientation verticalOrient, int gap) {
        if(gap < 0 ||
            (horizontalOrient != Orientation.LEFT   &&
            horizontalOrient != Orientation.CENTER &&
            horizontalOrient != Orientation.RIGHT)  ||

            (verticalOrient   != Orientation.TOP    &&
            verticalOrient    != Orientation.CENTER &&
            verticalOrient    != Orientation.BOTTOM)) {
            throw new IllegalArgumentException(
                "bad gap or orientation");
```

```
    }
    this.gap                = gap;
    this.verticalOrientation   = verticalOrient;
    this.horizontalOrientation = horizontalOrient;
}

public void addLayoutComponent(String name,
                               Component comp) {
}
public void removeLayoutComponent(Component comp) {
}

public Dimension preferredLayoutSize(Container target) {
    Insets     insets      = target.getInsets();
    Dimension dim          = new Dimension(0,0);
    int        ncomponents = target.getComponentCount();
    Component comp;
    Dimension d;

    for (int i = 0 ; i < ncomponents ; i++) {
        comp = target.getComponent(i);

        if(comp.isVisible()) {
            d = comp.getPreferredSize();
            if(i > 0)
                dim.height += gap;

            dim.height += d.height;
            dim.width   = Math.max(d.width, dim.width);
        }
    }
    dim.width  += insets.left + insets.right;
    dim.height += insets.top  + insets.bottom;
    return dim;
}
public Dimension minimumLayoutSize(Container target) {
    Insets     insets      = target.getInsets();
    Dimension dim          = new Dimension(0,0);
    int        ncomponents = target.getComponentCount();
    Component comp;
    Dimension d;

    for (int i = 0 ; i < ncomponents ; i++) {
        comp = target.getComponent(i);

        if(comp.isVisible()) {
            d = comp.getMinimumSize();

            dim.width  = Math.max(d.width, dim.width);
            dim.height += d.height;

            if(i > 0) dim.height += gap;
```

```
            }
        }
        dim.width  += insets.left + insets.right;
        dim.height += insets.top  + insets.bottom;

        return dim;
    }
    public void layoutContainer(Container target) {
        Insets    insets        = target.getInsets();
        int       top           = insets.top;
        int       left          = 0;
        int       ncomponents   = target.getComponentCount();
        Dimension preferredSize = target.getPreferredSize();
        Dimension targetSize    = target.getSize();
        Component comp;
        Dimension ps;

        if(verticalOrientation == Orientation.CENTER)
            top += (targetSize.height/2) -
                   (preferredSize.height/2);
        else if(verticalOrientation == Orientation.BOTTOM)
            top = targetSize.height - preferredSize.height +
                  insets.top;

        for (int i = 0 ; i < ncomponents ; i++) {
            comp = target.getComponent(i);
            left = insets.left;

            if(comp.isVisible()) {
                ps = comp.getPreferredSize();

                if(horizontalOrientation == Orientation.CENTER)
                    left = (targetSize.width/2) - (ps.width/2);
                else if(
                   horizontalOrientation == Orientation.RIGHT) {
                    left = targetSize.width - ps.width -
                           insets.right;
                }
                comp.setBounds(left,top,ps.width,ps.height);
                top += ps.height + gap;
            }
        }
    }
}
```

Exercising the ColumnLayout Custom Layout Manager

Figure 10-39 shows the ColumnLayoutApplet. As you can see, the
ColumnLayout layout manager positions components in column format
according to the orientations specified in the Choice selections in the top panel of
the applet.

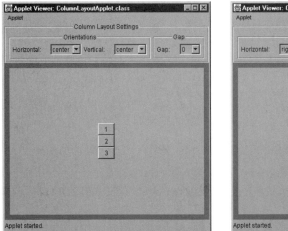

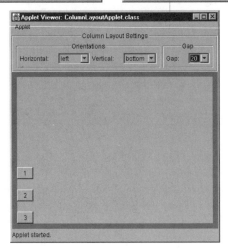

Figure 10-39 `ColumnLayout` at Work
This sequence of pictures shows `ColumnLayout` positioning
image buttons in their container.

Example 10-16 lists the `ColumnLayoutApplet` code so you can see how it
employs the `ColumnLayout` layout manager. Again, since
`ColumnLayoutApplet` is very similar to `RowLayoutApplet`, we won't discuss
the code.

425

Example 10-16 ColumnLayoutApplet Class Listing

```java
import java.applet.Applet;
import java.awt.*;
import java.awt.event.*;

public class ColumnLayoutApplet extends Applet {
    private ColumnButtonPanel buttonPanel;

    public void init() {
        setLayout(new BorderLayout());
        add(buttonPanel = new ColumnButtonPanel(), "Center");
        add(new Box(new ColumnPicker(buttonPanel),
                           "Column Layout Settings"), "North");
    }
}
class ColumnButtonPanel extends Panel {
    private Button    one, two, three;
    private Panel         panel = new Panel();
    private TenPixelBorder border = new TenPixelBorder(panel);

    public ColumnButtonPanel() {
        one   = new Button("  1  ");
        two   = new Button("  2  ");
        three = new Button("  3  ");

        panel.setLayout(new ColumnLayout(0));
        panel.add(one);
        panel.add(two);
        panel.add(three);

        setLayout(new BorderLayout());
        add       (border, "Center");
    }
    public void updateOrientations(Orientation horient,
                                   Orientation vorient,
                                   int gap) {
        panel.setLayout(new ColumnLayout(horient, vorient, gap));
        border.validate();
    }
}
class ColumnPicker extends Panel implements ItemListener {
    private Label   horientLabel = new Label("Horizontal:");
    private Label   vorientLabel = new Label("Vertical:");
    private Label   gapLabel     = new Label("Gap:");

    private Choice hchoice   = new Choice();
    private Choice vchoice   = new Choice();
    private Choice gapChoice = new Choice();

    private ColumnButtonPanel buttonPanel;
```

```java
public ColumnPicker(ColumnButtonPanel buttonPanel) {
    Panel orientations = new Panel();
    Panel gap          = new Panel();

    this.buttonPanel = buttonPanel;

    hchoice.addItemListener(this);
    hchoice.addItem("left");
    hchoice.addItem("center");
    hchoice.addItem("right");
    hchoice.select(1);

    vchoice.addItemListener(this);
    vchoice.addItem("top");
    vchoice.addItem("center");
    vchoice.addItem("bottom");
    vchoice.select(1);

    gapChoice.addItemListener(this);
    gapChoice.addItem("0");
    gapChoice.addItem("5");
    gapChoice.addItem("10");
    gapChoice.addItem("15");
    gapChoice.addItem("20");

    orientations.add(horientLabel);
    orientations.add(hchoice);
    orientations.add(vorientLabel);
    orientations.add(vchoice);

    gap.add(gapLabel);
    gap.add(gapChoice);

    add(new Box(orientations, "Orientations"));
    add(new Box(gap,          "Gap"));
}
public void itemStateChanged(ItemEvent event) {
    String horient, vorient;
    int    gap;

    horient = hchoice.getSelectedItem();
    vorient = vchoice.getSelectedItem();
    gap     = Integer.parseInt(gapChoice.getSelectedItem());

    buttonPanel.updateOrientations(
        Orientation.fromString(horient),
        Orientation.fromString(vorient), gap);
}
}
```

Summary

Containers in the AWT delegate positioning and shaping the components they contain to a layout manager. The AWT provides a set of five layout managers that are sufficient for most layout needs.

The tricky part about using the standard AWT layout managers is knowing when to use which one, but there are a few tips that can help until you've gained enough practice and experience that the decision is second nature.

The standard layout managers are fairly comprehensive in terms of the number of ways they can arrange components in a display. However, for those occasions when they just don't provide the desired behavior, you can implement your own implementation of the `LayoutManager` (or `LayoutManager2`) interface and create your own custom layout manager. This process is as simple as defining the five methods in the `LayoutManager` interface, as we've shown in the `BulletinLayout`, `RowLayout`, and `ColumnLayout` custom layout managers.

PART FOUR

AWT Components

CHAPTER
11

The AWT Component Class

Nearly half of all the classes in the AWT are components that are derived from the `java.awt.Component` class. In this chapter, we introduce the `Component` class and the services it provides for its extensions. In subsequent chapters, we'll discuss specific AWT components, such as buttons, labels, scrollbars, lists, dialogs, etc.

Components

All of the standard AWT components in the 1.1 release of the AWT are heavyweight components, which means that each component is rendered in a native, opaque window. While the 1.1 version of the AWT provides a framework for developing lightweight custom components,[1] it does not provide any specific lightweight components. Lightweight versions of all existing heavyweight components will be provided in a subsequent release of the AWT.

All of the standard AWT components have native, platform-dependent peers that do much of the work behind the scenes. Implementing a peer-based design enabled the original designers of the AWT to rapidly develop a user interface toolkit that retained native look-and-feel across platforms. However, even though most developers do not have to deal directly with peers, the peer approach results in a number of drawbacks when the AWT is used to develop user interfaces.[2] The

---

1. See *Lightweight Components* on page 651 for a discussion of lightweights.

Swing set of components provides peerless counterparts of the heavyweight AWT components to give developers the option of circumventing the peer-based approach. Table 11-1 repeats the standard AWT components listed in Table 1-2 on page 9.

Table 11-1 AWT Heavyweight Components

Component	Superclass	Description
Button	Component	A textual button for triggering an action
Canvas	Component	A canvas for painting graphics
Checkbox	Component	A checkable boolean component
Choice	Component	Popdown menu of textual entries
Dialog	Window	A window that can be modal
FileDialog	Dialog	A platform-dependent dialog for selecting files
Frame	Window	Top-level window with titlebar and optional menubar
Label	Component	Component that displays a string
List	Component	A scrollable list of textual entries
Panel	Container	A generic container of components
Scrollbar	Component	An Adjustable component for scrolling items
ScrollPane	Container	A scrollable container
TextArea	TextComponent	A multiline, scrollable textfield
TextComponent	Component	Base functionality for TextArea and TextField
TextField	TextComponent	A single-line component for entering text
Window	Container	A borderless window with no title

Note that some components, namely, Dialog, FileDialog, Frame, Panel, Window, and ScrollPane, are containers that can contain other components.

java.awt.Component

Every AWT component is ultimately an extension of the java.awt.Component class. java.awt.Component is an abstract class that encapsulates the common functionality among AWT components. In fact, so much functionality is

---

2.   See "Peers and Platform Independence" on page 5 and "Components and Peers" on page 439 for discussions of the advantages and disadvantages of peers.

embedded in the Component class that it provides a whopping 120 public methods. Instead of discussing each and every method, we'll focus on the basic aspects of components that you are likely to deal with on a regular basis. Note that some aspects of components are discussed in other places in *Graphic Java*, for instance, attaching a popup menu to a component is discussed in "Popup Menus" on page 619, and containers are discussed at length in "Components, Containers, and Layout Managers" on page 327—we will not repeat such discussions in this chapter.

Component Properties

All components share a common set of properties that can be obtained and set after construction; the properties are listed in Table 11-2.

Table 11-2 java.awt.Component Properties Modifiable at Runtime

Property	Set/Get Methods
Background Color	`void setBackground(Color)` `Color getBackground()`

Bounds	`void setBounds(Rectangle)`
	`void setBounds(int,int,int,int)`
	`Rectangle getBounds()`

Cursor	`void setCursor(Cursor)` `Cursor getCursor()`
Drop Target	`void setDropTarget(DropTarget)` `DropTarget getDropTarget()`
Enabled	`void setEnabled(boolean)` `boolean isEnabled()`
Font	`void setFont(Font)` `Font getFont()`
Foreground Color	`void setForeground(Color)` `Color getForeground()`
Locale	`void setLocale(Locale)` `Locale getLocale()`

Location	`void setLocation(Point)`
	`void setLocation(int,int)`
	`Point getLocation()`
	`Point getLocationOnScreen()`

Table 11-2 java.awt.Component Properties Modifiable at Runtime (Continued)

Property	Set/Get Methods
Name	void setName() String getName()
Size	void setSize(Dimension) Dimension getSize()
Visible	void setVisible(boolean) boolean isVisible()

All of the methods listed in Table 11-2 are `java.awt.Component` methods and therefore can be invoked on any extension of the `Component` class. Foreground and background colors, location, visibility, etc., can all be set for all AWT components.

Deprecated Methods

Table 11-2 purposely leaves out deprecated methods from the original AWT. Many component methods in the original version of the AWT were named inconsistently. For example, to get the font associated with a component, you would invoke `getFont()`; however, to get the bounds of a component, you would invoke `bounds()`. As a result, it was difficult to remember which methods were preceded with get/set and which were not. Fortunately, the 1.1 release of the AWT remedied the inconsistent naming, and as a result many of the old methods are now deprecated, meaning they will no longer be supported in subsequent releases of the AWT. In fact, `javac` comes with a *-deprecation* option, which issues warnings when a deprecated method is used.

Deprecated Methods and Compatibility

The 1.1 AWT methods that replace their deprecated counterparts simply call the deprecated method. For instance, `enable()` is deprecated—the new method to use is `setEnabled()`. The implementation of `Component.setEnabled()` looks like so:

```
public void setEnabled(boolean b) {
    enable(b);
}
```

Invoking `setEnabled()` or the deprecated `enable()` will result in the same code being executed. However, if you override either `setEnabled()` or `enable()`, things aren't quite so simple.

If you override `setEnabled()` in a custom component without overriding `enable()`, then existing client code that calls the deprecated `enable()` will get the wrong enabling behavior. If you override `enable()` without overriding `setEnabled()`, then you will get deprecation warnings when you compile your code. However, if you override *both* methods in the same manner as the Component class, the compiler will not issue a warning, and invoking either method will result in the same code being called:

```
/**
 * @deprecated as of JDK1.1
 */
public void setEnabled() {
    enable();
}
public void enable() {
    // new behavior ...
}
```

Therefore, if you need to override either a deprecated method or the method that replaces the deprecated version, you should override both methods and add a comment that includes the `@deprecated` tag for the deprecated version. This technique ensures that invoking either method will result in the same code being called, and the code will compile without compiler warnings.

AWT TIP ...

Override Deprecated Methods and Their Replacement Methods

If you need to override a method that replaces a deprecated method, you should override the deprecated version of the method in addition to the new version. The new version should simply invoke the deprecated method, like so:

```
/**
 * @deprecated - deprecated tag will suppress compiler warnings
 */
public Point location() {
    // new behavior ...
}
public Point getLocation() {
    return location();
}
```

This will ensure that the same code is invoked no matter which method is called and will also avoid compiler warnings about implementing deprecated methods.

Note: In the interest of both brevity and clarity, the listings that appear in *Graphic Java* do not adhere to the technique presented in the AWT Tip titled "Override Deprecated Methods and Their Replacement Methods."

Finally, to assist you in renaming deprecated AWT methods, Table 11-3 lists the AWT deprecated methods and their replacement methods (or alternative technique).

Table 11-3 AWT Deprecated Methods

Class/Interface	Deprecated Method	Replacement Method/Alternative
CheckboxGroup	getCurrent()	getSelectedCheckbox()
	setCurrent()	setSelectedCheckbox()
Choice	countItems()	getItemCount()
Component	action()	use ActionListener
	bounds()	getBounds()
	disable()	setEnabled(false)
	deliverEvent()	dispatchEvent()
	enable()	setEnabled(true)
	getPeer()	NO REPLACEMENT
	gotFocus()	processFocusEvent()
	handleEvent()	processEvent()
	hide()	setVisible(false)
	inside()	contains()
	keyDown()	processKeyEvent()
	keyUp	processKeyEvent()
	layout()	doLayout()
	locate()	getComponentAt()
	location()	getLocation()
	lostFocus()	processFocusEvent()
	minimumSize()	getMinimumSize()
	mouseDown()	processMouseEvent()
	mouseEnter()	processMouseEvent()
	mouseExit()	processMouseEvent()
	mouseMove()	processMouseEvent()
	mouseUp()	processMouseEvent()
	move()	setLocation()

Table 11-3 AWT Deprecated Methods (Continued)

Class/Interface	Deprecated Method	Replacement Method/Alternative
	nextFocus()	transferFocus()
	postEvent()	dispatchEvent()
	preferredSize()	getPreferredSize()
	reshape()	setBounds()
	resize()	setSize()
	size()	getSize()
	show()	setVisible()
Container	countComponents()	getComponentCount()
	deliverEvent()	dispatchEvent()
	insets	getInsets()
	layout()	doLayout()
	locate()	getComponentAt()
	minimumSize()	getMinimumSize()
	nextFocus()	transferFocus()
	preferredSize()	getPreferredSize()
FontMetrics	getMaxDecent()	getMaxDescent()
Frame	getCursorType()	getCursor()
	setCursor(int)	setCursor(Cursor)
Graphics	getClipRect()	getClipBounds()
LayoutManager	addLayoutComponent(String, Component)	addLayoutComponent(Component, Object)
List	allowsMultipleSelection()	isMultipleMode()
	clear()	removeAll()
	countItems()	getItemCount()
	delItems()	NO REPLACEMENT
	isSelected()	isIndexSelected()
	minimumSize()	getMinimumSize()
	preferredSize()	getPreferredSize()
	setMultipleSelections()	setMultipleMode()
Menu	countItems()	getItemCount()
	countMenus()	getMenuCount()
	disable()	setEnabled(false)

Table 11-3 AWT Deprecated Methods (Continued)

Class/Interface	Deprecated Method	Replacement Method/Alternative
	enable()	setEnabled(true)
	getPeer()	NO REPLACEMENT
Polygon	getBoundingBox()	getBounds()
Rectangle	inside()	inside()
	move()	setLocation()
	reshape()	setBounds()
	resize()	setSize()
ScrollPane	layout()	doLayout()
Scrollbar	getLineIncrement()	getUnitIncrement()
	getPageIncrement()	getBlockIncrement()
	getVisible()	getVisibleAmount()
	setLineIncrement()	setUnitIncrement()
	setPageIncrement()	setBlockIncrement()
	setVisible()	setVisibleAmount()
TextArea	appendText()	append()
	insertText()	insert()
	minimumSize()	getMinimumSize()
	preferredSize()	getPreferredSize()
	replaceText()	replaceRange()
TextField	minimumSize()	getMinimumSize()
	preferredSize()	getPreferredSize()
	setEchoCharacter()	setEchoChar()
Window	nextFocus()	transferFocus()
	postEvent()	dispatchEvent()

Component Location, Bounds, and Coordinates

A component's location is relative to the container in which it resides, whereas its bounds represent the actual pixel width and height of the component. If you'd like to find out the actual screen coordinates of a component, use the new method introduced in the 1.1 version of the AWT:

```
Point java.awt.Component.getLocationOnScreen()
```

Coordinates used in component methods are relative to the upper left-hand corner of the component in question. If you wish to draw a rectangle in a canvas, for example, and you specify the location of the rectangle as (10,10), the upper left-hand corner of the rectangle will be located 10 pixels below and to the right of the upper left-hand corner of the canvas.

Component Preferred, Minimum, and Maximum Sizes

Components can specify their preferred, minimum, and maximum sizes by overriding getPreferredSize(), getMinimumSize() and getMaximumSize(), respectively.

It is important to emphasize, however, that overriding the methods listed above does not guarantee anything about a component's size. The methods are merely guidelines that may well be ignored by the objects that size components—layout managers. Layout managers and component preferred sizes are discussed in "Components, Containers, and Layout Managers" on page 327.

Component Visibility and Responsiveness

All components, other than frames, windows, and dialogs,[3] are visible by default. You can use the setVisible method from java.awt.Component to set the visibility of individual components. If you need to toggle the visibility of a set of components, you should consider using the CardLayout layout manager—see "The CardLayout Layout Manager" on page 348—instead of individually managing the visibility of each component.

You can also toggle a component's responsiveness to user input by invoking the setEnabled method, passing either true or false to enable or disable, respectively, a component's responsiveness to user input. Components provide platform-dependent visual feedback when they are not enabled.

Components and Peers

Most developers do not have to deal directly with peers. However, a handful of Component methods will behave differently if they are invoked before a component's peer has been created—those methods are listed in Table 11-4.

Peers are created in a component's addNotify method. If it is necessary to invoke one of the methods listed in Table 11-4 before a component's peer has been created, you essentially have two choices. You can either invoke addNotify()

---

3. Invoking setVisible(true) on frames, windows, and dialogs makes them visible.

Table 11-4 `java.awt.Component` **Methods That Depend Upon Peers**

Method	Behavior Exhibited Before Peer Creation
`Image createImage(int,int)`	Returns `null`
`ColorModel getColorModel()`	Returns the toolkit's color model—not the component's
`Font getFont()`	Returns `null`
`FontMetrics getFontMetrics()`	Returns the toolkit's font metrics—not the component's
`Graphics getGraphics()`	Returns `null`
`Insets getInsets()`[1]	Returns an insets of (0,0,0,0)
`Dimension getPreferredSize()`	Returns minimum size—not preferred size
`Dimension getMinimumSize()`	Returns value of `getSize()`
`Dimension getSize()`	Returns a `Dimension` of zero width and height unless the component has been explicitly sized, in which case it returns the explicit size
`Toolkit getToolkit()`	Returns the default toolkit—not the component's
`boolean isFocusTraversable()`	Returns `false`
`boolean isValid()`	Returns `false`
`boolean isShowing()`	Returns `false`
`Point getLocationOnScreen()`	throws `IllegalComponentStateException`
`void requestFocus()`	Does nothing

1. `getInsets()` is a `java.awt.Container` method.

directly, which *may* cause the component's peer to be created, or you can override `addNotify()` and, after invoking `super.addNotify()`, call the methods that depend upon the peer's existence. For example, consider the applet listed in Example 11-1, which invokes some of the methods listed in Table 11-4 before and after the applet's peer has been created.

Example 11-1 Overriding addNotify()

```
import java.applet.Applet;
import java.awt.*;

public class OverrideAddNotify extends Applet {
    public OverrideAddNotify() {
        // peer is not created yet
        System.out.println("Before Peer is Created:");
        showPeerDependentProperties();
        System.out.println();
    }
    public void addNotify() {
        super.addNotify();

        // now peer exists
        System.out.println("After Peer is Created:");
        showPeerDependentProperties();
    }
    private void showPeerDependentProperties() {
        System.out.println("font:   " + getFont());
        System.out.println("graphics:  " + getGraphics());
        System.out.println("offscreen image:  " +
                           createImage(50,50));
    }
}
```

The output generated by the applet in Example 11-1 looks like so:

```
Before Peer is Created:
font:  null
graphics:  null
offscreen image:  null

After Peer is Created:
font:  java.awt.Font[family=Dialog,name=Dia-
log,style=plain,size=12]
graphics:  sun.awt.windows.WGraphics
offscreen image:  BufferedImage@20b7d5e3: type = 1 DirectColor-
Model: rmask=ff0000 gmask=ff00 bmask=ff amask=0 IntegerComponen-
tRaster: width = 50 height = 50 #Bands = 3 #DataElements 1 xOff =
0 yOff = 0 dataOffset[0] 0
```

Before the applet's peer is created, values for font, graphics, and the offscreen image are all null. When the same values are accessed in the overridden addNotify()—after super.addNotify() has been invoked—the values are all non-null.

In contrast, the applet listed in Example 11-2 invokes addNotify() directly.

Example 11-2 Invoking addNotify()

```
import java.applet.Applet;
import java.awt.*;

public class InvokeAddNotify extends Applet {
    public InvokeAddNotify() {
        addNotify();
        showPeerDependentProperties();
    }
    private void showPeerDependentProperties() {
        System.out.println("font:   " + getFont());
        System.out.println("graphics:  " + getGraphics());
        System.out.println("offscreen image:  " +
                        createImage(50,50));
    }
}
```

The output associated with the applet listed in Example 11-2 looks like so:

```
Before Peer is Created:
java.lang.NullPointerException: peer
        at sun.awt.windows.WCanvasPeer.create(Native Method)
        at sun.awt.windows.WComponentPeer.<init>(WComponent-
Peer.java:194)
        at sun.awt.windows.WCanvasPeer.<init>(WCan-
vasPeer.java:30)
        at sun.awt.windows.WPanelPeer.<init>(WPanelPeer.java:41)
        at sun.awt.windows.WToolkit.createPanel(WTool-
kit.java:208)
        at java.awt.Panel.addNotify(Panel.java:70)
        at InvokeAddNotify.<init>(InvokeAddNotify.java:10)
        at java.lang.Class.newInstance(Native Method)
        at sun.applet.AppletPanel.createApplet(Applet-
Panel.java:458)
        at sun.applet.AppletPanel.runLoader(AppletPanel.java:394)
        at sun.applet.AppletPanel.run(AppletPanel.java:233)
        at java.lang.Thread.run(Thread.java:484)
```

Invoking addNotify() directly, in this situation, throws a
NullPointerException, because the peer cannot be created at the time of the
call to addNotify().

In general, overriding addNotify() is the recommended approach. Invoking
addNotify() directly can be risky business because the AWT may not yet be
prepared to create the component's peer; if that is the case, invoking
addNotify() will result in a NullPointerException being thrown.

Overriding addNotify()

Component.addNotify() creates the component's peer. Therefore, if you need to ensure that the peer is created before performing some function, you can override addNotify() and take care of business. However, you must *always* call super.addNotify() when overriding addNotify() or else the platform-specific peers will not be created. Only after invoking super.addNotify() can you be assured that the component's peer has been created.

The Future of Peers

The Swing set of components provides peerless replacements for the AWT heavyweight components. Although the peer approach results in the retention of native look-and-feel, peers in general can cause more problems than they solve.

Rendering Components

Components are rendered in the `paint(Graphics)` method, which is typically invoked under one of the following circumstances:

1. A system paint or update event is generated

2. An explicit call to `repaint()` is made

System paint and update events are generated whenever the component needs to be repainted as a result of manipulation of the window in which it resides. For example, if an applet window is covered by another window and subsequently brought to the front, a `PaintEvent` is generated and sent to the components within the applet that need to be repainted.

`repaint()` is often invoked explicitly, sometimes by the component itself, when the component's graphical representation changes. `Component.repaint()` is overloaded as listed in Table 11-5.

All overloaded versions of `repaint()` invoke the `paint` method for the component's peer. If the component to be repainted is a lightweight component, the call is passed up the component's container hierarchy until a heavyweight container is found,[4] and the `paint` method of the container's peer is invoked.

---

4. All lightweight components must have a heavyweight container in their container ancestry. See the "Lightweight Components" chapter beginning on page 651

Table 11-5 Component **Repaint Methods**

Method	Implementation
void repaint()	Invokes update() as soon as possible
void repaint(int x, int y, int width, int height)	Invokes update() as soon as possible, with clipping set to specified rectangle
void repaint(long tm)	Invokes update() within tm milliseconds
void repaint(long tm, int x, int y, int width, int height)	Invokes update() within tm milliseconds, with clipping set to specified rectangle

Invoking a peer's repaint method ultimately results in a call to the component's update method. A call to repaint() then, results in the following sequence of calls:

repaint() —> peer.repaint() —> update() —> paint()

Component.update() clears the background for heavyweight components and subsequently invokes the component's paint method. As a result, if a heavyweight component needs to be updated continuously—for instance, a scrolling window or animation canvas—update() should be overridden to simply invoke paint(). Eliminating the erasing of the component can reduce flicker considerably.

One caveat should be mentioned concerning overriding update() to invoke paint(). If update() is invoked as a result of a paint event from the native windowing system, it is possible that the windowing system will clear the background of the component regardless of how update() is implemented. For example, if a component has its update method overridden to avoid clearing the background, then invoking repaint() explicitly (and thus ultimately update()) will repaint the component without clearing the background. However, if the window in which the component resides is covered and then brought to the front, the native windowing system may clear the background of the window before update() is invoked.

AWT TIP ...

Override update() to Avoid Flicker

Component.update() first clears the background of the component (if it is a heavyweight) and subsequently invokes paint(). As a result, heavyweight components may flicker if they are updated by repaint(), which ultimately results in a call to update(). To reduce the flicker associated with clearing the background, override update() to invoke paint() without clearing the background of the component.

Components and Zorder

Initial versions of the AWT made no guarantees about the depth, or *zorder*,[5] of components. With the advent of the 1.1 release of the AWT, zorder is defined to be the same as the order in which components are added to their containers, from front to back. The first component added to a container is the frontmost component, and the last component added will be displayed behind all other components in the component's container.

The applet shown in Figure 11-1 contains six buttons added to the applet in numerical order, starting with Button 1 and ending with Button 6. Although there is currently no support for setting the zorder of a component once it has been added to a container, the AWT does allow components to be added to and removed from a container at a specified position.

Whenever a button in the applet shown in Figure 11-1 is activated, it is removed from the applet, along with the component at position zero (the frontmost component). The buttons are then added back to the container with their zorders switched, so the button clicked on becomes the frontmost component, while the previously frontmost component assumes the zorder of the button selected. The picture on the right shows the applet after button 6 has been activated—Button 6 goes to the front, and Button 1 goes to the back, while the other buttons maintain their initial zorder.

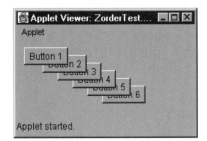 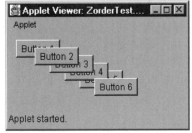

Figure 11-1 An Applet That Changes the Zorder of Its Buttons
Clicking on a button brings it to the top and sends the button that was previously on top to the back. The picture on the left is the applet in its initial state; the picture on the right is the applet after Button 6 is activated.

---

5. The term zorder comes from three-dimensional coordinate systems, where the z axis represents the third dimension.

Each button in the applet shares a single action listener that performs the aforementioned shenanigans, like so:

```
class Listener implements ActionListener {
    public void actionPerformed(ActionEvent event) {
        Button  button = (Button)event.getSource();
        int     zorder = getZorder(button);
        Button  top    = (Button)getComponent(0);

        remove(button);
        remove(top);

        add(button, 0);
        add(top, zorder);
        validate();
    }
    private int getZorder(Button button) {
        for(int i=0; i < getComponentCount(); ++i) {
            Component c = getComponent(i);
            if(c == button)
                return i;
        }
        return -1;
    }
}
```

The java.awt.Container class does not provide a method to obtain the zorder of a component, so we've implemented one ourselves. The action listener obtains the zorder of the button that fired the action event and then obtains the top component (whose zorder is zero). After both buttons are removed, the buttons are added back to the container with their zorders switched. Finally, validate() is invoked on the applet, which causes it to lay out all of its components. The applet is listed in its entirety in Example 11-3.

Example 11-3 ZorderTest Applet

```
import java.applet.Applet;
import java.awt.*;
import java.awt.event.*;

public class ZorderTest extends Applet {
    Button buttonOne   = new Button("Button 1");
    Button buttonTwo   = new Button("Button 2");
    Button buttonThree = new Button("Button 3");
    Button buttonFour  = new Button("Button 4");
    Button buttonFive  = new Button("Button 5");
    Button buttonSix   = new Button("Button 6");

    public void init() {
        Listener listener = new Listener();
```

```
        setLayout(new BulletinLayout());

        buttonOne.setLocation   (10,10);
        buttonTwo.setLocation   (35,20);
        buttonThree.setLocation(55,30);
        buttonFour.setLocation  (75,40);
        buttonFive.setLocation  (95,50);
        buttonSix.setLocation   (115,60);

        add(buttonOne);
        add(buttonTwo);
        add(buttonThree);
        add(buttonFour);
        add(buttonFive);
        add(buttonSix);

        buttonOne.addActionListener   (listener);
        buttonTwo.addActionListener   (listener);
        buttonThree.addActionListener(listener);
        buttonFour.addActionListener  (listener);
        buttonFive.addActionListener  (listener);
        buttonSix.addActionListener   (listener);
    }
    class Listener implements ActionListener {
        public void actionPerformed(ActionEvent event) {
            Button    button = (Button)event.getSource();
            int       zorder = getZorder(button);
            Button    top = (Button)getComponent(0);

            remove(button);
            remove(top);

            add(button, 0);
            add(top, zorder);
            validate();
        }
        private int getZorder(Button button) {
            for(int i=0; i < getComponentCount(); ++i) {
                Component c = getComponent(i);
                if(c == button)
                    return i;
            }
            return -1;
        }
    }
}
```

One thing to note about the applet is that the layout manager is set to an instance of BulletinLayout, which lays out components as though they were pinned to a bulletin board, at whatever their location has been set to. If a component has been explicitly resized, then bulletin layout lays them out at their current size;

otherwise, it lays them out according to their preferred size. Using `BulletinLayout` is preferable to setting a container's layout manager to null—see "BulletinLayout" on page 400.

Components and Cursors

The AWT supports the ability to set a component's cursor; to set the cursor for a component, you pass the component's `setCursor` method an instance of a `Cursor`. The `Cursor` class comes with a set of predefined cursors, which can be accessed by invoking `Cursor.getPredefinedCursor()`, which expects to be passed one of the integer constants listed in Table 11-6.

Table 11-6 `Cursor` **Constants for Predefined Cursors**

Cursor
DEFAULT_CURSOR
CROSSHAIR_CURSOR
TEXT_CURSOR
WAIT_CURSOR
SW_RESIZE_CURSOR
SE_RESIZE_CURSOR
NW_RESIZE_CURSOR
NE_RESIZE_CURSOR
N_RESIZE_CURSOR
S_RESIZE_CURSOR
W_RESIZE_CURSOR
E_RESIZE_CURSOR
HAND_CURSOR
MOVE_CURSOR

Figure 11-2 shows an applet equipped with a choice whose items represent predefined cursors. When a cursor is selected, the applet's cursor is changed to reflect the selection. Changing the cursor for a container, such as our applet, *may* also change the cursor for all of the container's components—therefore, changing the cursor in the applet shown in Figure 11-2, for example, also changes the cursor for the choice as well. Whether or not a container changes the cursor for all of its contained components is platform dependent.

 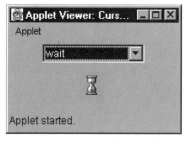

Figure 11-2 An Applet That Changes Its Cursor
When cursors are selected from the choice, the applet's cursor is
changed to the selected cursor. Changing the cursor for a
container changes the cursor for all of the container's
components.

Most of the action takes place in the `CursorChoice` custom component, which
extends `java.awt.Choice`, listed in Example 11-4. `CursorChoice` maintains
two arrays—an array of strings displayed in the choice and a corresponding array
of cursors obtained from calls to `Cursor.getPredefinedCursor()`.

Example 11-4 `CursorChoice` Custom Component

```java
import java.awt.*;

public class CursorChoice extends Choice {
    private String cursorNames[] = {
                    "default",          "cross hair",
                    "text",             "wait",
                    "southwest resize", "southeast resize",
                    "northwest resize", "northeast resize",
                    "north resize",     "south resize",
                    "west resize",      "east resize",
                    "hand",             "move" };

    private Cursor cursors[] = {
        Cursor.getPredefinedCursor(Cursor.DEFAULT_CURSOR),
        Cursor.getPredefinedCursor(Cursor.CROSSHAIR_CURSOR),
        Cursor.getPredefinedCursor(Cursor.TEXT_CURSOR),
        Cursor.getPredefinedCursor(Cursor.WAIT_CURSOR),
        Cursor.getPredefinedCursor(Cursor.SW_RESIZE_CURSOR),
        Cursor.getPredefinedCursor(Cursor.SE_RESIZE_CURSOR),
        Cursor.getPredefinedCursor(Cursor.NW_RESIZE_CURSOR),
        Cursor.getPredefinedCursor(Cursor.NE_RESIZE_CURSOR),
        Cursor.getPredefinedCursor(Cursor.N_RESIZE_CURSOR),
        Cursor.getPredefinedCursor(Cursor.S_RESIZE_CURSOR),
        Cursor.getPredefinedCursor(Cursor.W_RESIZE_CURSOR),
```

```
            Cursor.getPredefinedCursor(Cursor.E_RESIZE_CURSOR),
            Cursor.getPredefinedCursor(Cursor.HAND_CURSOR),
            Cursor.getPredefinedCursor(Cursor.MOVE_CURSOR) };

    public CursorChoice() {
        for(int i=0; i < cursors.length; ++i) {
            add(cursorNames[i]);
        }
    }
    public Cursor getSelectedCursor() {
        return Cursor.getPredefinedCursor(getSelectedIndex());
    }
    public void setSelectedCursor(Cursor cursor) {
        for(int i=0; i < cursors.length; ++i) {
            if(cursors[i].equals(cursor)) {
                select(i);
                break;
            }
        }
    }
}
```

Two methods are provided for getting and setting the currently selected cursor: `getSelectedCursor()` and `setSelectedCursor()`, respectively. The former method returns the cursor currently selected in the choice, and the latter allows the cursor selected in the choice to be set programmatically.

As an aside, note that we purposely did not name the methods `getCursor()` and `setCursor()`, because we would have overridden `Component.getCursor()` and `Component.setCursor()`, respectively. To allow the cursor for the choice to be set, we would have had to invoke the `Component` methods in each overridden method, but that would mean the cursor for the choice could not vary from the cursor displayed in the choice, so we chose to give the methods different names.

The applet displayed in Figure 11-2 is listed in Example 11-5.

Example 11-5 CursorChoiceTest Applet

```
import java.applet.Applet;
import java.awt.*;
import java.awt.event.*;

public class CursorChoiceTest extends Applet {
    private CursorChoice cursorChoice = new CursorChoice();

    public void init() {
        add(cursorChoice);
```

```
        cursorChoice.addItemListener(new ItemListener() {
            public void itemStateChanged(ItemEvent event) {
                setCursor(cursorChoice.getSelectedCursor());
            }
        });
    }
}
```

The applet contains a lone component—the `CursorChoice`. Whenever an item in the choice is selected, the applet's `setCursor` method is invoked with the currently selected cursor in the choice.

Custom Cursors

In addition to setting a component's cursor to the predefined cursors listed in Table 11-6 on page 448, custom cursors can also be set for AWT components. The `java.awt.Toolkit` class provides three methods pertaining to custom cursors, which are listed in Table 11-7.

Table 11-7 `java.awt.Toolkit` **Methods Pertaining to Custom Cursors**

Method	Implementation
`int getMaximumCursorColors()`	Returns the maximum number of colors that can be used for a custom cursor
`Dimension getBestCursorSize()`	Returns the best size for a custom cursor
`void setCustomCursor(Image, Point, String)`	Sets the cursor to the image with the specified hotspot. The string is used for accessibility purposes.

Not all windowing systems support custom cursors; if custom cursors are not supported, `Toolkit.getMaximumCursorColors()` will return 0 and `Toolkit.getBestCursorSize()` will return a `Dimension` of (0,0).

If an image passed to `Toolkit.setCustomCursor()` has colors whose number is greater than the maximum cursor colors, then the color palette used for the image will be flattened to the maximum cursor colors. Likewise, if the size of the image differs from the best cursor size, the image will be resized to fit the best cursor size. In either case, results may be less than desirable since converting low-resolution images can be a difficult proposition.

Figure 11-3 shows an applet with a custom cursor.

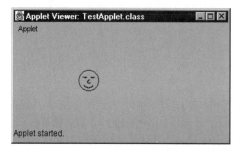

Figure 11-3 An Applet with a Custom Cursor

The applet is listed in Example 11-6.

Example 11-6 An Applet with a Custom Cursor

```
import java.applet.Applet;
import java.awt.*;

public class TestApplet extends Applet {
    public void start() {
        Toolkit tk = Toolkit.getDefaultToolkit();
        Image  cursorImage;
        Cursor cursor;
        Dimension bestSize = tk.getBestCursorSize(32,32);
        int    maxColors = tk.getMaximumCursorColors();

        System.out.println("Cursor size:  " + bestSize);
        System.out.println("Max cursor colors:  " + maxColors);

        if(maxColors == 0)
           System.out.println("custom cursors not supported");
        else {
           cursorImage = tk.getImage("smileCursor.gif");
           cursor = tk.createCustomCursor(cursorImage,
                                     new Point(1,1),
                                     "smile cursor");
           setCursor(cursor);
        }
    }
}
```

If the maximum cursor colors is 0, then the native windowing system does not support custom cursors, and therefore the cursor is not set. Otherwise, the image is loaded and passed to `Toolkit.createCustomCursor()`. The hotspot for the image is specified as (1,1), which means one pixel below and to the right of the upper left-hand corner of the image. The string passed to `createCustomCursor()` is meant to be used for accessibility purposes.

The applet also prints out the best cursor size and the maximum number of cursor colors allowed for custom cursors:

```
Cursor size:  java.awt.Dimension[width=32,height=32]
Max cursor colors:  2
```

The values printed above are for Windows NT; your mileage may vary.

Components and Serialization

AWT components provide built-in support for serialization. Actually, a more accurate statement is that the Java language provides support for serialization, and AWT components take advantage of that support. The AWT adds additional support for serializing event listeners associated with its components.

We won't discuss Java's support for serialization—that is beyond the scope of this book—however, we will discuss serializing AWT components because the AWT affords you the option of serializing a component's listeners along with the component itself.

Figure 11-4 shows an application initially containing a lone button. When the button is activated, the button's listener serializes the button and writes it to a file. Then, the listener turns around and reads the serialized button from the file, creating a new button that is added to the frame.

Figure 11-4 Serializing a Button
Activating the "Serialize Me" button serializes the button, writes it out to a file, and then creates a new button by reading the serialized button from the file. The new button is then added to the frame.

As you can probably guess, the application shown in Figure 11-4 writes out only the button itself, and not the button's listener. If the "No Listener" button is activated, no action will be performed. After the serialized button is read in, the button's label is modified to reflect the fact that the button has no action listener associated with it.

An `ObjectOutputStream` is wrapped in a `FileOutputStream`, and the stream's `writeObject` method is invoked and passed a reference to the button, which ultimately causes `java.awt.Button.writeObject()` to be invoked.

```
FileOutputStream fo = new FileOutputStream("button");
ObjectOutputStream so = new ObjectOutputStream(fo);
so.writeObject(button);
so.flush();
```

Then, the button is read from the file.

```
FileInputStream fi = new FileInputStream("button");
ObjectInputStream si = new ObjectInputStream(fi);
Button b = (Button)si.readObject();
b.setLabel("No Listener");
```

After the button is read in, its label is changed; otherwise, the label would be the same as the label of the button that was serialized to the file.

Finally, the button is added to the frame, which is subsequently packed.[6] The frame's visibility is toggled, which causes it to be redisplayed.

```
Frame f = SerializeTest.getFrame();
f.add(b);
f.pack();
f.setVisible(false);
f.setVisible(true);
```

Notice that we have not invoked any AWT methods whatsoever in order to serialize (and deserialize) the button—all of the serialization support is supplied by the Java language itself.

The entire application is listed in Example 11-7.

Example 11-7 `SerializeTest` Application

```
import java.awt.*;
import java.awt.event.*;
import java.io.*;

public class SerializeTest extends Frame {
    static Frame f;
    Button button;

    static public void main(String args[]) {
        f = new SerializeTest();
        f.pack();
        f.setVisible(true);
    }
    static public Frame getFrame() {
```

6. Packing a window reshapes it so that it is just large enough to display its contents.

```
        return f;
    }
    public SerializeTest() {
        super("Serialize Test");
        setLayout(new FlowLayout());

        add(button = new Button("Serialize Me"));
        button.addActionListener(new ButtonListener());

        addWindowListener(new WindowAdapter() {
            public void windowClosing(WindowEvent event) {
                dispose();
                System.exit(0);
            }
        });
    }
}
class ButtonListener implements ActionListener {
    public void actionPerformed(ActionEvent event) {
        try {
            doSerialize((Button)event.getSource());
        }
        catch(Exception e) {
            e.printStackTrace();
        }
    }
    private void doSerialize(Button button) throws
                                    IOException ,
                                    ClassNotFoundException {
        FileOutputStream fo = new FileOutputStream("button");
        ObjectOutputStream so = new ObjectOutputStream(fo);
        so.writeObject(button);
        so.flush();

        FileInputStream fi = new FileInputStream("button");
        ObjectInputStream si = new ObjectInputStream(fi);
        Button b = (Button)si.readObject();
        b.setLabel("No Listener");

        Frame f = SerializeTest.getFrame();
        f.add(b);

        f.pack();
        f.setVisible(false);
        f.setVisible(true);
    }
}
```

As we alluded to previously, the AWT adds the ability to serialize a component's listeners in addition to the component itself. In fact, if our listener had implemented the java.io.Serializable interface, it would have been serialized along with the button and read back in, thanks to the fact that `java.awt.Button` has overridden both `readObject()` and `writeObject()` to serialize and deserialize its action listeners. As a result, activating a reconstituted button would cause it to be serialized and deserialized also. Figure 11-5 shows our application after modifying ButtonListener to implement the `Serializable` interface.

Figure 11-5 Serializing a Button and Its `ActionListener`
The Serialize Me button *and* its action listener are serialized and deserialized. Clicking on any of the buttons in the application will cause it to be serialized to a file, read back in, and added to the frame.

Modifying the `ButtonListener` class to implement the `Serializable` interface and removing the line that modified the newly created button's label were the only changes that were made to the original application. As a result, the button's listener is serialized along with the button—therefore, activating the newly created button will result in it, too, being serialized and reconstituted.

AWT TIP ...

Have Listeners Implement java.io.Serializable If They Are to Be Serialized with Their Components

If you want listeners associated with your components to be serialized, you must make sure that the listeners implement java.io.Serializable. All of the AWT components themselves implement the Serializable interface, so custom components that extend AWT components do not need to explicitly implement the Serializable interface. However, since listeners do not implement Serializable by default, you must take matters into your own hands if you want a component's listeners to be serialized along with the component.

Components and Internationalization

The JDK includes support for internationalization; however, complete coverage of internationalization is beyond the scope of *Graphic Java*—none of the internationalization support resides in the `java.awt` package or its subpackages.

On the other hand, all AWT components have a `Locale` associated with them, so we'll take the time to briefly discuss the implications of that, and at the same time provide you with an applet that internationalizes an extremely simple graphical user interface (GUI). We will give you enough of an overview of internationalization so that you will be able to effectively internationalize a more complex user interface.

Locales

As you can see from "java.awt.Component Properties Modifiable at Runtime" on page 433, the `Component` class provides `getLocale` and `setLocale` methods, so obviously a component may have a `Locale` associated with it.

A locale is an *identifier* that represents a specific geographical, political, or cultural region. The `java.util.Locale` class provides a number of public `Locale` instances that save you the trouble of instantiating a `Locale` when the need arises.

The important thing to remember about locales is that they are simply an identifier—nothing more and nothing less. For instance, we can set a textfield's locale to `Locale.French`.

```
TextField field = new TextField();
field.setLocale(Locale.FRENCH);
```

However, doing so does not mean that the textfield will somehow magically display its text in French. All it means is that we've *identified* the textfield as an AWT component that should render its text in French. It is not the responsibility of the textfield to ensure that its text is in French—that responsibility is left for someone else, namely, you, to take care of. The rest of our discussion on internationalization will center on that responsibility.

Resource Bundles

A resource bundle contains locale-specific data that can be loaded at runtime. For instance, here's a resource bundle containing a single key/value pair.

```
import java.util.*;

public class LabelsBundle_en extends ListResourceBundle {
    static final Object[][] contents = {
                                   {"Identifier", "English GUI"}
    };
    public Object[][] getContents() {
        return contents;
    }
}
```

All bundles (classes ultimately derived from `java.util.ResourceBundle`) contain key/value pairs, where the key identifies a locale-specific object in the bundle.

The `LabelsBundle_en` class extends `ListResourceBundle`, (from the `java.util` package) and implements the lone abstract method defined by `ListResourceBundle.getContents()`. The `getContents` method returns an array—each item in the array is a key/value pair. Each key must be a string, while the value associated with the key may be any object. In our case, of course, the value is also a string. Additionally, we have only one key/value pair in our bundle, namely, the string "English GUI" that is identified by the key "Identifier."

Here's another bundle that we'll put to use, along with `LabelsBundle_en` in just a moment.

```
import java.util.*;

public class LabelsBundle_fr extends ListResourceBundle {
    static final Object[][] contents = {
                                   {"Identifier", "GUI en Francais"}
    };
    public Object[][] getContents() {
        return contents;
    }
}
```

`LabelsBundle_fr` is a resource bundle that also contains a string resource: "GUI en Francais" that is also identified by the key "Identifier."

The SimpleI18NTest Applet

The internationalized applet shown in Figure 11-6 contains a choice and a label. When an item is selected from the choice, the locale of the label is changed to reflect the currently selected item in the choice. The applet then modifies the text of the label in response to the change in locale.

Figure 11-6 SimpleI18NTest Applet
Selecting an item in the choice causes the label's locale to be modified.

The first order of business for the applet is to create its complex GUI.

```
public class SimpleI18NTest extends Applet
                               implements ItemListener {
    private Label  guiLabel = new Label();
    private Choice choice   = new Choice();

    public void init() {
        choice.add(Locale.ENGLISH.getDisplayName());
        choice.add(Locale.FRENCH.getDisplayName());
        choice.addItemListener(this);

        add(choice);
        add(guiLabel);

        guiLabel.setLocale(Locale.ENGLISH);
        internationalize();
    }
    ...
}
```

The strings added to the choice are obtained from two of the public Locale objects available from the Locale class: Locale.ENGLISH and Locale.FRENCH. The Locale.getDisplayName method returns the name of the locale in the language of the default locale, which for us is English.

The choice and the label are then added to the applet, and the label's locale is initially set to Locale.ENGLISH. Finally, one of the applet's private methods, internationalize(), which we'll discuss shortly, is invoked.

The applet is specified as an item listener for the choice. Whenever an item is selected in the choice, the applet's itemStateChanged method is invoked.

```
public void itemStateChanged(ItemEvent event) {
    int index = choice.getSelectedIndex();

    if(index == 0) guiLabel.setLocale(Locale.ENGLISH);
    else            guiLabel.setLocale(Locale.FRENCH);

    internationalize();
    validate();
}
```

Whenever an item is selected in the choice, the locale of the `guiLabel` is set appropriately, and then `internationalize()` is invoked once again, followed by a call to `validate()`, which results in the applet's components being laid out.

```
private void internationalize() {
    String s = getIdentifierString(guiLabel.getLocale());

    if(s != null) {
        guiLabel.setText(s);
        guiLabel.invalidate();
    }
}
```

The `internationalize` method obtains the string for the text of the label by invoking another `private` method, `getIdentifierString()`, which is passed the locale of the `guiLabel`. If the string returned is non-`null`, the text of the `guiLabel` is set and the `guiLabel` is invalidated; thus, the call to `validate()` in `itemStateChanged()` results in the applet's components being laid out—see "Forcing a Container to Lay Out Its Components" on page 338.

Finally, we come to the interesting part of the applet, as far as internationalization is concerned: obtaining the value of the "Identifier" key from the appropriate resource bundle depending upon the locale of the `guiLabel`.

```
private String getIdentifierString(Locale l) {
    ResourceBundle bundle = null;
    try {
        bundle = ResourceBundle.getBundle("LabelsBundle", l);
    }
    catch(MissingResourceException e) {
        e.printStackTrace();
    }
    if(bundle == null)
        return null;
    else
        return (String)bundle.getObject("Identifier");
}
```

ResourceBundle.getBundle() is a `static` method that returns a ResourceBundle. The `getBundle` method is passed a string and a locale, which are used to identify the *class* of the appropriate bundle; a class loader is used to create an instance of the appropriate resource bundle, which is returned.

If the locale passed to `getBundle()` is `Locale.ENGLISH`, then `ResourceBundle.getBundle()` looks for a `LabelsBundle_en.class` file in the current CLASSPATH. If the locale is `Locale.FRENCH`, then a `LabelsBundle_fr.class` file is searched for. If the `.class` file is found, a class loader instantiates an instance of the class and returns the bundle. If the `.class` file is not found, a `MissingResourceException` is thrown. We should note that we have oversimplified the search mechanism used by `getBundle()`—see the JDK documentation for a complete description of the search algorithm used.

At any rate, if `getBundle()` was able to locate the appropriate `.class` file and instantiate an instance of the resource bundle, we invoke the bundle's `getObject` method, which is passed the appropriate key and returns the value associated with the key.

To recap: if `getBundle()` is passed the locale `Locale.ENGLISH`, for example, it appends "_en.class" to the string it is passed and searches for a file of that name in the current CLASSPATH. If the `.class` file is found, a class loader instantiates an instance of `LabelBundles_en` and returns it. The `getObject` method of `LabelBundles_en` is passed the "Identifier" string and returns "English GUI." If the locale is `Locale.FRENCH`, then `LabelBundles_fr.class` is searched for, and the `getObject` method of `LabelBundles_fr` returns "GUI en Francais" when passed the key "Identifier."

The `SimpleI18NTest` applet is shown in Example 11-8 for completeness.

Example 11-8 SimpleI18NTest Applet

```java
import java.applet.Applet;
import java.util.*;
import java.awt.*;
import java.awt.event.*;

public class SimpleI18NTest extends Applet
                       implements ItemListener {
    private Label  guiLabel = new Label();
    private Choice choice   = new Choice();

    public void init() {
        choice.add(Locale.ENGLISH.getDisplayName());
        choice.add(Locale.FRENCH.getDisplayName());
        choice.addItemListener(this);
```

```
            add(choice);
            add(guiLabel);

            guiLabel.setLocale(Locale.ENGLISH);
            internationalize();
        }
        public void itemStateChanged(ItemEvent event) {
            int index = choice.getSelectedIndex();

            if(index == 0) guiLabel.setLocale(Locale.ENGLISH);
            else           guiLabel.setLocale(Locale.FRENCH);

            internationalize();
            validate();
        }
        private void internationalize() {
            String s = getIdentifierString(guiLabel.getLocale());

            if(s != null) {
                guiLabel.setText(s);
                guiLabel.invalidate();
            }
        }
        private String getIdentifierString(Locale l) {
            ResourceBundle bundle = null;

            try {
                bundle = ResourceBundle.getBundle("LabelsBundle", l);
            }
            catch(MissingResourceException e) {
                e.printStackTrace();
            }
            if(bundle == null)
                return null;
            else
                return (String)bundle.getObject("Identifier");
        }
    }
```

Property Resource Bundles

As an alternative to implementing resource bundle classes, resources can be
specified in a properties file. Properties files have a .properties extension and
contain key/value pairs. For example, the following properties file—
LabelsBundle_en.properties—can be substituted for the
LabelsBundle_en class:

```
# SimpleI8N English Property Bundle

Identifier=English GUI
```

Lines in a properties file that begin with # are regarded as comments and are ignored. Likewise, a LabelsBundle_fr.properties file can be substituted for the LabelsBundle_fr class:

```
# SimpleI8N French Property Bundle

Identifier=GUI en Francais
```

When a resource bundle is searched for, if a .class file is not found in the CLASSPATH as previously described, a properties file of the same name, with a .properties extension, is searched for. If the properties file is found, a PropertyResourceBundle is instantiated and returned from the call to ResourceBundle.getBundle(). PropertyResourceBundle is an extension of ResourceBundle, which means that we can invoke its getObject method to get the object associated with an identifier.

Therefore, instead of implementing resource bundle classes, you can use properties files to specify locale-dependent strings. As a result, the applet listed in Example 11-8 will work unmodified with the properties files shown above instead of implementing resource bundle classes.

In general, properties files are easier to use than implementing resource bundle classes. The only drawback associated with properties files has to do with performance—the properties file must be parsed, which could be a performance consideration with large properties files. In reality, however, the performance penalty is usually small enough to be inconsequential.

Separating the GUI from Internationalization Code

One final note about internationalization is the fact that, by use of a class loader to instantiate the appropriate type of resource bundle, the internationalization data is totally separated from the GUI code. This fact allows Java applets and applications to be written once and internationalized externally. In other words, if we wanted to provide an Italian version of our GUI, we would need only to implement a LabelsBundle_it class that returned the appropriate Italian version of the identifier string and make sure that the .class file for LabelsBundle_it is in our CLASSPATH.[7]

---

7. Of course, we would also have to add an option to our choice, but that is an implementation detail of how the GUI switches from one language to another that could be generalized in a better fashion.

Available Locales and Two-Letter Codes

Before we move on, we will leave you with a table, Table 11-8, of the `Locale` constants provided by the `Locale` class, and the two-letter codes for both countries and languages. The codes in the table can be found at the following websites:

- Countries: *http://www.chemie.fu-berlin.de/diverse/doc/ISO_3166.html*
- Languages: *http://www.ics.uci.edu/pub/ietf/http/related/iso639.txt*

Table 11-8 Locales and Codes for Countries and Languages

Country/Language	Code
Locale.CANADA	CA
Locale.CANADA_FRENCH	--
Locale.CHINA	CN
Locale.CHINESE	zh
Locale.ENGLISH	en
Locale.FRANCE	FR
Locale.FRENCH	fr
Locale.GERMAN	de
Locale.GERMANY	DE
Locale.ITALIAN	it
Locale.ITALY	IT
Locale.JAPAN	JP
Locale.JAPANESE	ja
Locale.KOREA	KP
Locale.KOREAN	ko
Locale.PRC	--
Locale.SIMPLIFIED_CHINESE	--
Locale.TAIWAN	TW
Locale.TRADITIONAL_CHINESE	--
Locale.UK	UK
Locale.US	US

Components and JavaBeans

All AWT components qualify as java beans by virtue of the fact that they adhere to JavaBeans design patterns for method signatures. The term design pattern does not equate to the popular object-oriented term[8] but instead simply refers to a method naming convention. By adhering to JavaBeans design patterns for property accessors and event handling methods, any AWT component can be manipulated in a JavaBeans builder tool.

In addition to using JavaBeans design patterns for method signatures, AWT components also come with (the ability to implement) bound properties.

Bound Properties

Bound properties are properties that result in a notification when their value changes. The notification takes the form of a `PropertyChangeEvent`, which is sent to a list of `PropertyChangeListeners` that have registered interest in changes to the property in question. The term bound property is used because changes to a bound property are *bound* to a set of `PropertyChangeListeners` that are notified of changes to the property.

`java.awt.Component` provides the methods listed in Table 11-9 for implementing bound properties.

`java.beans.PropertyChangeListener` is a simple interface that defines a lone method:

```
propertyChange(PropertyChangeEvent e)
```

`PropertyChangeListeners` can be registered with a component as a whole; when any of the component's bound properties changes value, the listener's `propertyChange` method is invoked.

Additionally, `PropertyChangeListeners` can be registered for a specific property and will be notified only when the property with the appropriate name is modified.

In addition to providing the infrastructure for implementing bound properties, the following properties associated with a `java.awt.Component` are bound:

- Font
- Foreground color
- Background color

---

8. See Gamma, Helm, Johnson, Vlissides. *Design Patterns*, Addison-Wesley, 1994.

Table 11-9 Component **Methods for Implementing Bound Properties**

Method	Implementation
```public void addPropertyChangeListener(PropertyChangeListener)```	Registers the specified `PropertyChangeListener` with the list of listeners maintained by the component
```public void removePropertyChangeListener(PropertyChangeListener)```	Removes the specified `PropertyChangeListener` from the list of listeners maintained by the component
```public void addPropertyChangeListener(String, PropertyChangeListener)```	Registers the specified `PropertyChangeListener` for the named property
```public void removePropertyChangeListener(String, PropertyChangeListener)```	Removes the specified `PropertyChangeListener` from the list of listeners associated with the named property
```protected void firePropertyChange(String, Object oldValue, Object newValue)```	Fires a property change for the named property with specified old and new values to the appropriate `PropertyChangeListeners`

For example, the applet shown in Figure 11-7 contains a `ColorChoice` and a canvas. When the color in the `ColorChoice` is modified, the background color of the canvas is updated to reflect the color selected.

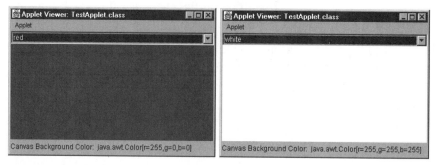

Figure 11-7 AWT Components and the Bound Background Property

The applet implements the `PropertyChangeListener` interface and registers itself as being interested in the background color of the canvas.

```
public class TestApplet extends Applet
                        implements PropertyChangeListener {
    ...
    public void init() {
        ...
        canvas.addPropertyChangeListener("background", this);
        ...
    }
}
```

The applet registers interest only in the "background" property of the canvas. Alternatively, the applet could register itself as interested in *any* of the properties associated with the canvas by invoking an overloaded version of `Component.addPropertyChangeListener`.

```
canvas.addPropertyChangeListener(this);
```

When the background color of the canvas is changed, the applet's `propertyChange` method is invoked, and the applet updates its status bar.

```
public void propertyChange(PropertyChangeEvent e) {
    Color color = (Color)e.getNewValue();
    showStatus("Canvas Background Color:  " + color);
}
```

The new color value is obtained from the `PropertyChangeEvent`, which comes complete with methods that return the name of the property, the property's old and new values and the property's propagation ID. The `public` methods of the `java.beans.PropertyChangeEvent` class are listed in Table 11-10.

Table 11-10 `java.beans.PropertyChangeEvent` **Public Methods**

Method	Implementation
Object getNewValue()	Returns the new value associated with the property
Object getOldValue()	Returns the old value associated with the property
String getPropertyName()	Returns the name of the property
Object getPropagationId()	Returns the propagation ID—which is reserved for future use
void setPropagationId(Object)	Sets the propagation ID

The applet shown in Figure 11-7 is listed in its entirety in Example 11-9.

Note: the `ColorChoice` listing is omitted in Example 11-9—see "Exercising the Rubberband Classes" on page 782 for a listing of the `ColorChoice` class.

Example 11-9 An Example of a Component's Bound Background Property

```
import java.applet.Applet;
import java.awt.*;
import java.awt.event.*;
import java.beans.*;

public class TestApplet extends Applet
                        implements PropertyChangeListener {
    public void init() {
        final Canvas canvas = new Canvas();
        final ColorChoice colorChoice = new ColorChoice();

        setLayout(new BorderLayout());
        add(colorChoice, "North");
        add(canvas, "Center");

        canvas.addPropertyChangeListener("background", this);

        colorChoice.setColor(Color.lightGray);

        colorChoice.addItemListener(new ItemListener() {
            public void itemStateChanged(ItemEvent e) {
                canvas.setBackground(colorChoice.getColor());
            }
        });
    }
    public void propertyChange(PropertyChangeEvent e) {
        Color color = (Color)e.getNewValue();
        showStatus("Canvas Background Color:  " + color);
    }
}
```

Implementing Bound Properties in Custom Components

The applet in the preceding section relies upon the fact that a component's background color is a bound property. This section discusses implementing a bound property in a custom component.

Figure 11-8 shows two custom components in the BeanBox.[9] The component selected in the top picture is an instance of `ColorPatch`—a simple extension of `java.awt.Canvas` with a black border and a fill color. The component selected in the bottom picture is an `EmptyCanvas`—an equally simple extension of `java.awt.Canvas` that implements the `PropertyChangeListener` interface.

---

9. The BeanBox is JavaSoft's freely available reference bean container.

In the top picture, the propertyChange event of the `ColorPatch` is selected and is hooked up to the `EmptyCanvas.propertyChange` method in the bottom picture. The BeanBox generates code that registers the `EmptyCanvas` as a `PropertyChangeListener` of the `ColorPatch`; whenever a bound property of the `ColorPatch` is modified, `EmptyCanvas.propertyChange()` is invoked.

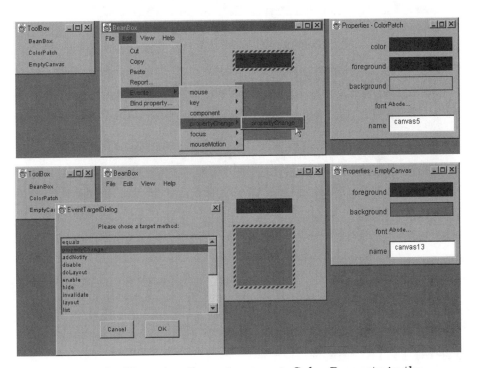

Figure 11-8 Changing the `ColorPatch` Color Property in the BeanBox.

As it turns out, the only bound property associated with the `ColorPatch`—other than inherited bound properties—is the color used to fill the interior of the `ColorPatch`. As a result, whenever the fill color of the `ColorPatch` is modified, `EmptyCanvas.propertyChange()` is invoked. The `EmptyCanvas` reacts to the color change by changing its own background color to match the new fill color, as illustrated in Figure 11-9.

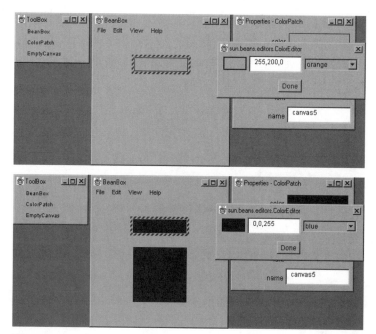

Figure 11-9 Hooking Up a Bound Property in the BeanBox.

Implementing the fill color of the `ColorPatch` as a bound property is a simple matter, thanks to the support methods listed in "`Component` Methods for Implementing Bound Properties" on page 466. The `ColorPatch` class is listed in Example 11-10.

Example 11-10 ColorPatch Class Listing

```
import java.awt.*;

public class ColorPatch extends Canvas {
    private Color color = Color.blue;

    public void paint(Graphics g) {
        Dimension size = getSize();
        g.setColor(Color.black);
        g.drawRect(0,0,size.width-1,size.height-1);
        g.setColor(color);
        g.fillRect(1,1,size.width-2,size.height-2);
```

```
    }
    public synchronized void setColor(Color c) {
        Color old = color;
        this.color = c;
        firePropertyChange("color", old, color);
    }
    public synchronized Color getColor() {
        return color;
    }
    public Dimension getMinimumSize() {
        return new Dimension(100,25);
    }
}
```

When the "color" property is set, ColorPatch.setColor() fires a property change event by invoking firePropertyChange(), which is passed the name of the property and the old and new values. The call to firePropertyChange() results in a call to propertyChange() for all PropertyChangeListeners that have expressed interest in the color property.

The EmptyCanvas class is listed in Example 11-11.

Example 11-11 EmptyCanvas Class Listing

```
import java.awt.*;
import java.beans.PropertyChangeEvent;
import java.beans.PropertyChangeListener;

public class EmptyCanvas extends Canvas
                    implements PropertyChangeListener {
    public EmptyCanvas() {
        setBackground(Color.gray);
    }
    public Dimension getMinimumSize() {
        return new Dimension(100,100);
    }
    public void propertyChange(PropertyChangeEvent e) {
        Color newColor = (Color)e.getNewValue();

        if(newColor != null && ! newColor.equals(getBackground()))
            setBackground(newColor);
    }
}
```

Like the applet listed in Example 11-9 on page 468, EmptyCanvas implements the PropertyChangeListener interface. The new color value is obtained from the PropertyChangeEvent and the background color of the EmptyCanvas is set accordingly.

Components and Tree Locking

The `Component` class instantiates a `static final Object`, referred to as the tree lock, that is used to synchronize access to a component's container hierarchy and layout methods. The idea is to prevent two threads from simultaneously accessing a component's hierarchy of containers (and layout methods), which could result in an inconsistent state without synchronizing access. For instance, the `Container` class uses the tree lock when removing a component, as listed in Example 11-12.

Example 11-12 `java.awt.Container.remove()` Uses the Component Tree Lock

```
// from java.awt.Container class ...

public void remove(int index) {
    synchronized (Component.LOCK) {
        ...
    }
}
```

`Container.remove()` synchronizes on the `Component` tree lock. Containers that remove components also synchronize on the tree lock to ensure that removing a component from a container is an atomic operation. For instance, the `ScrollPane` class has only one contained component at any given time. If a component is added to a scrollpane that already contains a component, the contained component is removed before the new component is added to the scrollpane. When a component is removed from a scrollpane, the operation is synchronized on the tree lock, as can be seen from Example 11-13.

Example 11-13 `java.awt.ScrollPane.addImpl()` Uses the Component Tree Lock

```
// from java.awt.ScrollPane class ...

protected final void addImpl(Component comp,
                         Object constraints, int index) {
    synchronized (Component.LOCK) {
        if (getComponentCount() > 0) {
            remove(0);
        }
        if (index > 0) {
            throw new IllegalArgumentException(
                        "position greater than 0");
        }
        super.addImpl(comp, constraints, index);
    }
}
```

Whenever an operation is performed on a component's container hierarchy, the operation should be synchronized on the component tree lock. The tree lock has package scope, so it cannot be accessed directly from outside the java.awt package. However, the Component class provides a public getTreeLock method that returns a reference to the lock for use outside of the java.awt package.

Example 11-14 lists a rather psychotic applet containing a panel that initially has five buttons. Two threads are created (and started) in the applet's init method. One thread—AddRemoveThread—alternately adds and then removes the last button from a panel. The other thread—ThrowThread—repeatedly tries to access all of the buttons contained in the panel.

Example 11-14 Psychotic Applet

```
import java.applet.Applet;
import java.awt.*;

public class TestApplet extends Applet {
    Panel panel = new Panel();

    public void init() {
        panel.add(new Button("button 1"));
        panel.add(new Button("button 2"));
        panel.add(new Button("button 3"));
        panel.add(new Button("button 4"));
        panel.add(new Button("button 5"));

        setLayout(new BorderLayout());
        add(panel, "Center");

        AddRemoveThread addRemoveThread = new AddRemoveThread();
        ThrowThread throwThread = new ThrowThread();

        addRemoveThread.start();
        throwThread.start();
    }
    class ThrowThread extends Thread {
        public void run() {
            while(true) {
                int cnt = panel.getComponentCount();

                System.out.println("throw Thread cnt:   " +
                                panel.getComponentCount());
                try {
                    Thread.currentThread().sleep(1500);
                }
                catch(InterruptedException e) {
                    e.printStackTrace();
                }
```

```
                       for(int i=0; i < cnt; ++i) {
                           try {
                               Button b = (Button)
                                           (panel.getComponent(i));
                           }
                           catch(NullPointerException e) {
                               e.printStackTrace();
                           }
                       }
                   }
               }
           }
       class AddRemoveThread extends Thread {
           public void run() {
               while(true) {
                   int cnt = panel.getComponentCount();

                   if(cnt == 5) {
                       System.out.println("removing");
                       panel.remove(panel.getComponent(cnt-1));
                   }
                   else {
                       System.out.println("adding");
                       panel.add(new Button("button 5"), cnt);
                   }
                   System.out.println("add/remove Thread cnt:   " +
                                   panel.getComponentCount());
                   panel.validate();

                   try {
                       Thread.currentThread().sleep(1000);
                   }
                   catch(InterruptedException e) {
                       e.printStackTrace();
                   }
               }
           }
       }
   }
```

Without synchronizing on the tree lock, the applet is bound to get into trouble, which is where ThrowThread gets its name. When the applet is run, the output is as follows:

```
removing
throw Thread cnt:   5
add/remove Thread cnt:   4
adding
add/remove Thread cnt:   5
throw Thread cnt:   5
removing
```

```
add/remove Thread cnt:   4
java.lang.ArrayIndexOutOfBoundsException: No such child: 4
adding
        at java.awt.Container.getComponent(Container.java:126)
        at TestApplet$ThrowThread.run(TestApplet.java:41)
```

ThrowThread invokes `Container.getComponentCount()` and then sleeps
for 1500 milliseconds. While ThrowThread is sleeping, AddRemoveThread
removes the fifth button from the panel. When ThrowThread wakes up and tries
to access the fifth button, an exception is thrown.

To remedy the situation, ThrowThread synchronizes on the component tree lock,
like so:

```
class ThrowThread extends Thread {
    public void run() {
        while(true) {
            synchronized(panel.getTreeLock()) {
                int cnt = panel.getComponentCount();

                System.out.println("throw Thread cnt:   " +
                                   panel.getComponentCount());
                try {
                    Thread.currentThread().sleep(1500);
                }
                catch(InterruptedException e) {
                    e.printStackTrace();
                }
                for(int i=0; i < cnt; ++i) {
                    try {
                        Button b = (Button)
                                    (panel.getComponent(i));
                    }
                    catch(NullPointerException e) {
                        e.printStackTrace();
                    }
                }
            }
        }
    }
}
```

Since `Container.remove()` also synchronizes on the component tree lock, the
remove method will not remove the button while ThrowThread is sleeping.
Instead, the panel will wait until ThrowThread releases the lock—meaning
ThrowThread exits the synchronized block—before removing the button.

Summary

AWT components extend `java.awt.Component`—a collection of basic, useful components for implementing user interfaces. All of the components are heavyweight components that have peers and render themselves in their own native, opaque windows. The AWT provides support for implementing lightweight components, but does not provide any specific lightweight components.[10]

`java.awt.Component` provides a great deal of functionality for its extensions, from setting/getting background/foreground colors to tracking location and size, to attaching cursors, to zordering components; the `Component` class covers a fair bit of ground.

Now that we've covered the `Component` class, we will explore the extensions of `Component` provided by the AWT.

10. The Swing set of components is a collection of mostly lightweight components.

CHAPTER
12

Basic Components: Labels, Buttons, Canvases, and Panels

This chapter covers the most basic of the AWT components: labels, buttons, canvases, and panels. Labels and buttons are simple components that display a label. Canvases provide a surface upon which to paint graphics; panels are the most basic container provided by the AWT.

Labels and Buttons

Label and Button are the simplest AWT components. Labels and buttons both display text—the difference is that buttons typically have a 3D border, and you can activate a button, which should initiate an action of some sort.

java.awt.Label

A Label is a simple textual label that doesn't do much; in fact a label doesn't do anything other than display text. You can set the component properties of a label, its foreground and background colors, font, cursor, etc.[1]

Since a label can be resized to be bigger than the text it displays, it comes with the ability to set its alignment—you can display the label's text justified left, right, or centered by specifying an alignment at construction time or after the label is

---

1. This is true, of course, for all extensions of java.awt.Component, so we will not mention the fact for any subsequent components we discuss.

constructed by invoking `Label.setAlignment()`. `java.awt.Label` defines three `public static` integer values for its alignment:

- `Label.LEFT`
- `Label.CENTER`
- `Label.RIGHT`

Because `Label` extends `Component`, labels fire component, mouse, and mouse motion events.[2] As a result, you can find out when a label is moved, resized, shown or hidden. Additionally, you can monitor mouse events that occur in a label if you wish. Since labels are not interested in accepting keyboard focus, they do not, by default, fire focus or key events.

We'll implement a simple extension of `Label` that prints out events and toggles between being selected and deselected when a mouse press occurs in the label, along with an applet that tests it out. You can see the applet in action in Figure 12-1.

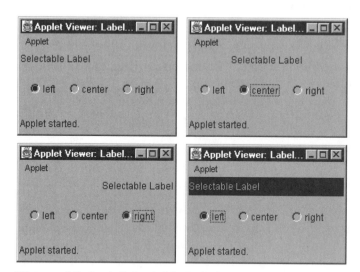

Figure 12-1 A Selectable Label
The `LabelTest` applet allows the alignment of a selectable label to be modified. The lower right picture shows the label selected.

---

2. Again, this is true of all extensions of `Component`, so we will not mention it for any components subsequently discussed in this chapter.

Before listing the entire applet, let's discuss the code that's pertinent to labels.

First of all, our applet implements `ItemListener` because checkboxes fire item events—see "Item Events" on page 276. When a checkbox is checked, we set the alignment of the label accordingly:

```
public void itemStateChanged(ItemEvent event) {
    Checkbox cbox = (Checkbox)event.getSource();
    if(cbox == left)   label.setAlignment(Label.LEFT);
    if(cbox == right)  label.setAlignment(Label.RIGHT);
    if(cbox == center) label.setAlignment(Label.CENTER);
}
```

The default alignment for labels is `Label.LEFT`, which you can see for yourself if you run the applet—we don't specify the alignment until a checkbox is checked, and the label is initially shown aligned to the left.

We also extend `Label` and add instances of debug listeners to listen for component, mouse, and mouse motion events. An anonymous inner class implementation[3] of `MouseListener` is added to the label that switches the foreground and background colors when a mouse press occurs, thereby toggling selection of the label:

```
class SelectableLabel extends Label {
    public SelectableLabel(String label) {
        super(label);

        addComponentListener(new DbgComponentListener());
        addMouseListener(new DbgMouseListener());
        addMouseMotionListener(new DbgMouseMotionListener());

        addMouseListener(new MouseAdapter() {
            public void mousePressed(MouseEvent event) {
                Color foreground = getForeground();
                setForeground(getBackground());
                setBackground(foreground);
            }
        });
    }
}
```

The applet, along with the implementation of `SelectableLabel`, is shown in its entirety in Example 12-1.

---

3.   See "Anonymous Inner Classes" on page 295.

Example 12-1 LabelTest Applet

```java
import java.applet.Applet;
import java.awt.*;
import java.awt.event.*;

public class LabelTest extends Applet implements ItemListener {
    CheckboxGroup group  = new CheckboxGroup();
    Checkbox left   = new Checkbox("left",   true,  group);
    Checkbox right  = new Checkbox("right",  false, group);
    Checkbox center = new Checkbox("center", false, group);
    Label    label  = new SelectableLabel("Selectable Label");

    public void init() {
        Panel checkboxPanel = new Panel();

        left.addItemListener(this);
        right.addItemListener(this);
        center.addItemListener(this);

        checkboxPanel.add(left);
        checkboxPanel.add(center);
        checkboxPanel.add(right);

        setLayout(new BorderLayout(10,10));
        add(label, "North");
        add(checkboxPanel, "Center");
    }
    public void itemStateChanged(ItemEvent event) {
        Checkbox cbox = (Checkbox)event.getSource();
        if(cbox == left)   label.setAlignment(Label.LEFT);
        if(cbox == right)  label.setAlignment(Label.RIGHT);
        if(cbox == center) label.setAlignment(Label.CENTER);
    }
}
class SelectableLabel extends Label {
    public SelectableLabel(String label) {
        super(label);

        addComponentListener(new DbgComponentListener());
        addMouseListener(new DbgMouseListener());
        addMouseMotionListener(new DbgMouseMotionListener());

        addMouseListener(new MouseAdapter() {
            public void mousePressed(MouseEvent event) {
                Color foreground = getForeground();
                setForeground(getBackground());
                setBackground(foreground);
            }
        });
    }
}
```

Remember that the debug listeners print out events as they occur. If we start the applet, wheel the mouse into the label, click the mouse button, and wheel the mouse back out of the label, we see the following output being printed (we've compressed some of the mouse move events):

```
java.awt.event.MouseEvent[MOUSE_ENTERED,(0,10),mods=0,click-
Count=0] on label1
java.awt.event.MouseEvent[MOUSE_MOVED,(0,10),mods=0,click-
Count=0] on label1
java.awt.event.MouseEvent[MOUSE_PRESSED,(3,10),mods=0,click-
Count=1] on label1
java.awt.event.MouseEvent[MOUSE_RELEASED,(3,10),mods=0,click-
Count=1] on label1
java.awt.event.MouseEvent[MOUSE_CLICKED,(3,10),mods=0,click-
Count=1] on label1
java.awt.event.MouseEvent[MOUSE_MOVED,(0,9),mods=0,click-
Count=0] on label1
java.awt.event.MouseEvent[MOUSE_EXITED,(379,219),mods=0,click-
Count=0] on label1
```

java.awt.Button

Buttons, like labels, display text. Buttons, however, typically have a 3D appearance and trigger some action when they are activated—buttons fire action events when they are activated.

The applet shown in Figure 12-2 contains two panels, each of which contains exactly one button. The North panel uses its default layout—a `FlowLayout`, so the button is sized to its preferred size,[4] which is just big enough to hold the text it displays plus a little elbow room. The center panel employs a `BorderLayout` and adds its button as the center component; therefore, the button is stretched to the width and height of the panel. The top button, when activated, toggles the enabled state of the bottom button, and vice versa.

Our `ButtonTest` applet is listed in Example 12-2. Notice that the top button implements an inner class representation of its action listener, and, simply for illustration, the bottom button opts to add an action listener that is a separate, top-level class. Whether a button's listener is an inner class representation or a separate class does not have any behavioral effect—either way, the `performAction` method of the listener associated with the button is invoked when the button is activated.

4. See "The FlowLayout Layout Manager" on page 351.

Figure 12-2 ButtonTest Applet
Two buttons reside in separate panels with different layout
managers—thus, the buttons are shaped differently. The top
button toggles the enabled state of the bottom button, and vice
versa.

Buttons, unlike labels, are interested in accepting focus. When the mouse is
pressed in an enabled button, it is given focus (whether or not the mouse is
released inside the button). Since buttons are willing to accept focus, they also fire
key events. When a button has focus, it will fire key events, regardless of the
location of the mouse.[5]

Example 12-2 ButtonTest Applet

```java
import java.applet.Applet;
import java.awt.*;
import java.awt.event.*;

public class ButtonTest extends Applet {
    Button top    = new Button("Toggle bottom button");
    Button bottom = new Button("Toggle top button");

    public void init() {
        Panel bottomPanel = new Panel();
        Panel topPanel    = new Panel();

        bottomPanel.setLayout(new BorderLayout());
        bottomPanel.add(bottom, "Center");

        topPanel.add(top);

        setLayout(new BorderLayout());
        add("North",  topPanel);
        add("Center", bottomPanel);
```

5.   This is true for all components that accept keyboard focus.

```
         top.addActionListener(new ActionListener() {
             public void actionPerformed(ActionEvent event) {
                 if(bottom.isEnabled()) bottom.setEnabled(false);
                 else                   bottom.setEnabled(true);
             }
         });
         bottom.addActionListener(new BottomActionListener(top));
     }
 }
 class BottomActionListener implements ActionListener {
     private Button otherButton;

     public BottomActionListener(Button otherButton) {
         this.otherButton = otherButton;
     }
     public void actionPerformed(ActionEvent event) {
         if(otherButton.isEnabled())
             otherButton.setEnabled(false);
         else
             otherButton.setEnabled(true);
     }
 }
```

Canvases and Panels

The aptly named canvas provides a surface upon which you can perform graphical operations. A panel is essentially the same as a canvas, except that a panel, unlike a canvas, is also a container that can contain other components. Neither Canvas nor Panel, by default, is interested in accepting keyboard focus, and therefore do not fire key or focus events.

Until the advent of lightweight components in the 1.1 release of the AWT, Canvas and Panel were the components of choice to extend when developing custom components.[6] For custom components that did not contain other components, such as an image button, Canvas was the logical choice for the component's superclass. On the other hand, a custom component that needed to contain other components, such as a border, would be a likely candidate for extending Panel. Now, of course, one must decide whether to implement a lightweight component by extending Component instead of Canvas, or to implement a lightweight container by extending Container instead of Panel.

---

6.   The lightweight component framework provides the ability to extend Component and Container directly. See "Lightweight Components" on page 651.

java.awt.Canvas

Canvas is a simple component that you can draw into. Although you can create an instance of Canvas and draw into it, it is much more common to extend Canvas and override its paint method. That way, whenever a canvas is repainted, it redraws its contents correctly.

As you can see in Figure 12-3 and the subsequent listing in Example 12-3, our applet for exercising the Canvas class implements an extension of Canvas that draws two borders around the canvas: a 3D border inside of a black border, so that we can see the bounds of the canvas. Additionally, we employ the graphics object associated with the canvas to paint some text and graphics inside the canvas.

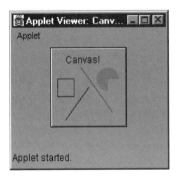

Figure 12-3 CanvasTest Applet
A Canvas is a component that provides a surface upon which to perform graphical operations, such as drawing text and graphics.

Example 12-3 CanvasTest Applet

```
import java.applet.Applet;
import java.awt.*;
import java.awt.event.*;

public class CanvasTest extends Applet {
    public void init() {
        Canvas canvas = new ExampleCanvas();
        canvas.addComponentListener(new DbgComponentListener());
        add(canvas);
    }
}
```

```
class ExampleCanvas extends Canvas {
    public void paint(Graphics g) {
        Dimension size = getSize();
        g.drawRect(0,0,size.width-1,size.height-1);
        g.setColor(Color.lightGray);
        g.draw3DRect(1,1,size.width-3,size.height-3,true);

        g.setColor(Color.blue);
        g.drawString("Canvas!",20,20);

        g.setColor(Color.orange);
        g.fillRect(10,40,20,20);
        g.setColor(Color.red);
        g.drawRect(9,39,22,22);

        g.setColor(Color.gray);
        g.drawLine(40,25,80,80);
        g.setColor(Color.black);
        g.drawLine(50,50,20,90);

        g.setColor(Color.cyan);
        g.fillArc(60,25,30,30,0,270);
    }
    public Dimension getPreferredSize() {
        return new Dimension(100,100);
    }
}
```

Notice that getPreferredSize() is overridden to return a dimension 100 pixels wide and 100 pixels tall. If the call to getPreferredSize() is commented out, the applet will look like the one pictured in Figure 12-4.

The reason for the invisible canvas becomes apparent after looking at the output generated by the debug component event listener attached to our canvas:

```
java.awt.event.ComponentEvent[COMPONENT_MOVED (100,5 0x0)] on
canvas0
```

While the canvas has been moved to (100,5), its size is (0,0). The Applet class has a FlowLayout layout manager by default, and FlowLayout lays out components according to their preferred size. As a result, one of the most common mistakes made by developers starting out with the AWT is to create a canvas, paint into it, and add it to an applet, only to have the canvas be a no-show. The solution, of course, is to override getPreferredSize() for the canvas in question.

Figure 12-4 A `Canvas` Extension With (0,0) Size
If an extension of `Canvas` does not override
`getPreferredSize()`, the canvas may not show up at all,
depending upon the layout manager that lays it out and whether
it has been explicitly sized.

java.awt.Panel

You can think of a panel as a canvas that can contain other components. As a matter of fact, if you take the `CanvasTest` applet and replace every occurrence of `Canvas` with `Panel`, you'll wind up with an applet that looks like the one in Figure 12-5.

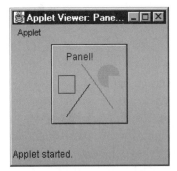

Figure 12-5 `PanelTest` Applet
A panel can be drawn into in exactly the same manner as for a canvas.

Panels, then, are a generic container that you can also paint into. Panels, like other AWT containers, use a layout manager to lay out the components they contain—a panel's default layout manager is a FlowLayout.[7]

While the Panel class is commonly extended to implement custom components, you are much more likely to simply instantiate a panel for the purpose of adding components. For instance, that is exactly what we did for our ButtonTest applet, listed in Example 12-2 on page 484; we created two panels—topPanel and bottomPanel, each of which contained a single button.

Since panels are containers and containers can contain other containers, panels are often nested in order to lay out user interface screens. Our PanelTest2 applet, shown in Figure 12-6, contains an instance of WorkPanel, which in turn contains two other panels—one that contains the label and textfield and another that contains the Ok and Cancel buttons.

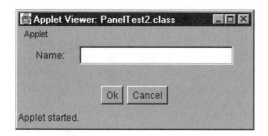

Figure 12-6 PanelTest2 Applet
The applet contains an instance of WorkPanel, which contains two panels—one for the label and textfield and another that contains the buttons.

The PanelTest2 applet is listed in Example 12-4. The WorkPanel class is an extension of Panel that might come in handy when implementing custom dialogs, for example. WorkPanel sets its layout to a BorderLayout and adds a center panel and a south panel. The center panel must be provided at construction time—the contents of the center panel would vary depending upon the user input

---

7.   See "Container Default Layout Managers" on page 345.

required. The south panel contains the buttons that would typically be activated when the user was done entering input into the components residing in the center panel.

Example 12-4 PanelTest2 Applet

```java
import java.applet.Applet;
import java.awt.*;

public class PanelTest2 extends Applet {
    public void init() {
        Panel     center    = new Panel();
        WorkPanel workPanel = new WorkPanel(center);

        workPanel.addButton("Ok");
        workPanel.addButton("Cancel");

        center.add(new Label("Name:"));
        center.add(new TextField(25));

        setLayout(new BorderLayout());
        add(workPanel);
    }
}
class WorkPanel extends Panel {
    Panel centerPanel;
    Panel buttonPanel = new Panel();

    public WorkPanel(Panel centerPanel) {
        this.centerPanel = centerPanel;

        setLayout(new BorderLayout());
        add(centerPanel, "Center");
        add(buttonPanel, "South");
    }
    public void addButton(String label) {
        buttonPanel.add(new Button(label));
    }
}
```

Summary

Labels, buttons, canvases, and panels are the most basic components provided by the AWT. Labels and buttons both display a label; canvases and panels both provide a surface upon which to perform graphical operations. Out of the four components, panels are the only component which also doubles as a container that can contain other components.

CHAPTER
13

Item Selectables: Checkboxes, Choices, and Lists

We've grouped checkboxes, choices, and lists together because they are the only AWT components that implement the ItemSelectable interface.[1] Before we discuss each of the three components in detail, we'll briefly discuss the ItemSelectable interface.

The java.awt.ItemSelectable Interface

Classes that implement the ItemSelectable interface have zero or more items that can be selected, or in the case of checkboxes, checked. We've listed the methods defined in the ItemSelectable interface in Table 13-1. As you can probably gather, classes that implement the ItemSelectable interface fire *item* events, thus, the item listener registration methods. The ItemListener interface defines one method: void itemStateChanged(ItemEvent). Whenever an item in an ItemSelectable changes state, an item event is fired to all currently registered item listeners.[2]

---

1. CheckboxMenuItem also implements the ItemSelectable interface but is not a component. See "Checkbox Menu Items" on page 610.
2. See "Item Events" on page 276.

Table 13-1 `java.awt.ItemSelectable` Interface

Method	Intent
`Object[] getSelectedObjects()`	Returns an array of the currently selected items
`void addItemListener(ItemListener)`	Adds an item listener, which will be notified whenever an item changes state
`void removeItemListener(ItemListener)`	Removes an item listener

java.awt.Checkbox

A checkbox is a component that represents a boolean state. We've already seen checkboxes in action in our `LabelTest` applet shown in "`LabelTest` Applet" on page 482.

Checkboxes fire item events whenever they are checked or unchecked. In order to react to a checkbox being checked or unchecked, an item listener is added to the checkbox. When the checkbox fires an item event, the item listener's `itemStateChanged` method is invoked and passed an instance of `ItemEvent`.

Since checkboxes often exist in mutually exclusive groups, they can be added to a `java.awt.CheckboxGroup`, which ensures that only one checkbox in the group is checked at any given time. Note that a `CheckboxGroup` is not a component and therefore cannot be added to a container. As a result, regardless of whether or not you add checkboxes to a checkbox group, you must individually add the checkboxes to the container in which they reside.

Typically, checkboxes are used under one of two circumstances: a group of checkboxes that are not mutually exclusive or a group that are mutually exclusive. Our first applet deals with the former, and our next applet deals with the latter.

Non-Mutually Exclusive Groups of Checkboxes

You can use checkboxes to represent a set of boolean options that are not mutually exclusive. For example, in a print dialog, you might want to let the user select a number of printing options, as shown in Figure 13-1.

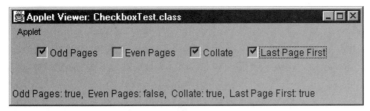

Figure 13-1 CheckboxTest Applet
A set of non-mutually exclusive checkboxes for printing options.

Checking or unchecking any of the four checkboxes in the applet updates the applet's status bar to reflect which items are checked and which are not. The applet is listed in Example 13-1.

Example 13-1 CheckboxTest Applet

```java
import java.applet.Applet;
import java.awt.*;
import java.awt.event.*;

public class CheckboxTest extends Applet {
    public void init() {
        setLayout(new BorderLayout());
        add(new PrintOptionsPanel(this), "Center");
    }
}
class PrintOptionsPanel extends Panel {
    Checkbox  oddPages, evenPages, collate, lastFirst;
    Listener  listener = new Listener();
    Applet    applet;

    public PrintOptionsPanel(Applet anApplet) {
        applet    = anApplet;
        oddPages  = new Checkbox("Odd Pages");
        evenPages = new Checkbox("Even Pages");
        collate   = new Checkbox("Collate");
        lastFirst = new Checkbox("Last Page First");

        oddPages.addItemListener (listener);
        evenPages.addItemListener(listener);
        collate.addItemListener  (listener);
        lastFirst.addItemListener(listener);

        add(oddPages);
        add(evenPages);
        add(collate);
        add(lastFirst);
```

```
        }
        class Listener implements ItemListener {
            public void itemStateChanged(ItemEvent event) {
                applet.showStatus(
                    "Odd Pages: "         + oddPages.getState()  + ",   " +
                    "Even Pages: "        + evenPages.getState() + ",   " +
                    "Collate: "           + collate.getState()   + ",   " +
                    "Last Page First: " + lastFirst.getState());
            }
        }
    }
```

Notice that the PrintOptionsPanel contains a named inner class[3] that implements ItemListener. One instance of the Listener class is instantiated and specified as the listener for each of the checkboxes. As a result, whenever a checkbox is checked or unchecked, the itemStateChanged method in the Listener class is invoked. PrintOptionsPanel.itemStateChanged() calls the applet's showStatus method, invoking getState() for each checkbox. Checkbox.getState() returns a boolean value indicating whether the checkbox in question is checked.

Mutually Exclusive Groups of Checkboxes

It is often the case that a group of checkboxes is used to represent a set of mutually exclusive options. Our next applet adds a pair of checkboxes to a checkbox group to facilitate choosing whether to print all the pages of a hypothetical document or whether to print only a specified range of pages. When the Print All checkbox is checked, the labels and textfields associated with range printing are disabled. Likewise, checking the Print Range checkbox enables the labels and textfields, in addition to requesting focus for the starting page textfield.

Figure 13-2 shows two snapshots of the applet, one with the Print All checkbox checked, and another with the Print Range checkbox checked.

Notice that checkboxes under Windows 95 change their appearance when they are part of a checkbox group. Example 13-2 lists the applet in its entirety.

---

3.   See "Named Inner Classes" on page 294.

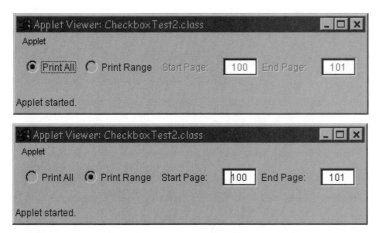

Figure 13-2 `CheckboxTest2` Applet
A pair of mutually exclusive checkboxes for specifying which
pages to print. Checking the Print All checkbox disables the
labels and textfields for printing a range of pages. Checking the
Print Range checkbox enables them.

Example 13-2 `CheckboxTest2` Applet

```
import java.applet.Applet;
import java.awt.*;
import java.awt.event.*;

public class CheckboxTest2 extends Applet {
    public void init() {
        add(new PrintRangePanel(100, 101));
    }
}
class PrintRangePanel extends Panel {
    Checkbox   printAll, printRange;
    Label      startPage, endPage;
    TextField     startField, endField;

    public PrintRangePanel(int start, int end) {
        CheckboxGroup group= new CheckboxGroup();
```

```
printAll   = new Checkbox("Print All", false, group);
printRange = new Checkbox("Print Range", true, group);

startPage = new Label("Start Page:");
endPage   = new Label("End Page:");

startField = new TextField(Integer.toString(start));
endField   = new TextField(Integer.toString(end));

add(printAll);   add(printRange);
add(startPage);  add(startField);
add(endPage);    add(endField);

printRange.addItemListener(new ItemListener() {
    public void itemStateChanged(ItemEvent event) {  ·
        if(printRange.getState()) {
            startField.setEnabled(true);
            endField.setEnabled  (true);
            startPage.setEnabled (true);
            endPage.setEnabled   (true);  ·

            startPage.repaint();
            endPage.repaint();

            startField.requestFocus();
        }
    }
});
printAll.addItemListener(new ItemListener() {
    public void itemStateChanged(ItemEvent event) {
        if(printAll.getState()) {
            startField.setEnabled(false);
            endField.setEnabled  (false);
            startPage.setEnabled (false);
            endPage.setEnabled   (false);

            startPage.repaint();
            endPage.repaint();
        }
    }
});
    }
}
```

The first thing to note is that we've invoked a different Checkbox constructor—one that takes a CheckboxGroup argument. The constructor adds the checkbox to the specified checkbox group. Additionally, note that the constructor also takes a boolean variable signifying whether the checkbox is initially checked.

The item listeners for the two checkboxes take care of setting the enabled state of the labels and fields associated with range printing. Also, when the Print Range checkbox is checked, it requests focus for the starting page field. After the starting page field is filled in, a TAB will move the focus to the ending page field—because the ending page field is added to the panel after the starting page field.[4]

Choices and Lists

Choices and lists both display a list of strings that can be selected. Whereas a list supports multiple selection, a choice allows only single selection of its items. Lists typically display one or more of their items at all times, while choices display only the selected item until they are activated, at which time a popup list of their items becomes available for making a selection.

Making a Choice: List or Choice?

It is often the case that choices and lists may be used interchangeably. The choice, if you will, whether to use a list or a choice in a given situation often depends upon the following:

- The amount of screen real estate available
- Whether it is desirable to display more than one item at all times
- Whether multiple selection is required

If more than one item needs to be displayed at all times or multiple selection is required, a list is the way to go. If screen real estate is tight and only single selection is required, then choices often get the nod.

Another consideration when deciding whether to use a choice or a list is the number of items in the component. Under Windows 95, the popup list for a choice may (automatically) be equipped with a scrollbar, depending upon the number of items in the choice. However, under Motif, the popup list does not provide a scrollbar no matter how many items need to be displayed. Since very long popup lists are unwieldy to manipulate, it often makes sense to use a list instead of a choice when there are a large number of items to choose from.

Figure 13-3 shows two applets, one that employs choices and another that employs lists for selecting a font.

---

4. Actually, the ending page label is between the two textfields, but labels do not accept focus.

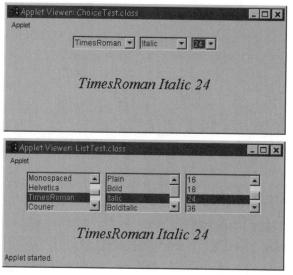

Figure 13-3 Two Applets for Selecting a Font
Both of the applets shown above contain a panel for selecting a
font. The top applet uses choices for font family, style, and size
selection; the bottom applet uses lists for the same purpose.

java.awt.Choice

We'll start our discussion of choices by taking a look at the implementation of the
applet that employs choices shown in Figure 13-3. Since our applet is rather
lengthy, we'll start out by showing you the code pertinent to choices, and then
we'll list the applet in its entirety.

The choices reside in an extension of Panel—FontPanel:

```
class FontPanel extends Panel {
    private ChoiceTest choiceTest;
    private Choice familyChoice = new Choice(),
                   styleChoice  = new Choice(),
                   sizeChoice   = new Choice();

    public FontPanel(ChoiceTest applet) {
        Listener listener = new Listener();

        choiceTest = applet;

        populateFonts();
        populateStyles();
```

```
        populateSizes();

        add(familyChoice);
        add(styleChoice);
        add(sizeChoice);

        familyChoice.addItemListener(listener);
        styleChoice.addItemListener (listener);
        sizeChoice.addItemListener  (listener);
    }
    ...
}
```

After populating the three choices in the populateFonts(), populateStyles, and populateSizes methods, the FontPanel constructor adds an instance of Listener to each choice; Listener is a named inner class that implements ItemListener. We'll take a look at Listener.itemStateChanged(), which is invoked when any of the items in the three choices changes state, but first we look at the methods that populate the choices.

```
private void populateFonts() {
    String fontNames[] = getToolkit().getFontList();

    for(int i=0; i < fontNames.length; ++i)
        familyChoice.add(fontNames[i]);
}
private void populateStyles() {
    styleChoice.add("Plain");
    styleChoice.add("Bold");
    styleChoice.add("Italic");
    styleChoice.add("BoldItalic");
}
private void populateSizes() {
    String sizes[] = {"12", "14", "16", "18", "24", "36"};

    for(int i=0; i < sizes.length; ++i)
        sizeChoice.add(sizes[i]);
    }
}
```

java.awt.Choice provides an add method that takes a string for adding items, which we make liberal use of for adding items to the family, style, and sizes choices.

The only other method of interest, as far as choices are concerned, is the itemStateChanged method of the Listener class:

```
public class Listener implements ItemListener {
    public void itemStateChanged(ItemEvent event) {
        choiceTest.updateLabel(getSelectedFont());
    }
}
```

The `choiceTest` variable is a member of the `FontPanel` class and is a reference to the applet itself. Whenever an item in any of the three choices changes state, the listener attached to each of the choices invokes the applet's `updateLabel` method and passes the currently selected font. You can see the `ChoiceTest.updateLabel` method in our complete listing of the applet in Example 13-3.

Example 13-3 `ChoiceTest` Applet

```
import java.applet.Applet;
import java.awt.*;
import java.awt.event.*;

public class ChoiceTest extends Applet {
    private FontPanel fontPanel = new FontPanel(this);
    private Label     label     = new Label(" ", Label.CENTER);

    public void init() {
        setLayout(new BorderLayout());
        add(fontPanel, "North");
        add(label, "Center");
    }
    public void start() {
        updateLabel(fontPanel.getSelectedFont());
    }
    public void updateLabel(Font font) {
        label.setText(fullNameOfFont(font));
        label.setFont(font);
    }
    private String fullNameOfFont(Font font) {
        String family = font.getFamily();
        String style  = new String();

        switch(font.getStyle()) {
            case Font.PLAIN:  style = " Plain ";  break;
            case Font.BOLD:   style = " Bold ";   break;
            case Font.ITALIC: style = " Italic "; break;

            case Font.BOLD + Font.ITALIC:
                style = " Bold Italic ";
                break;
        }
        return family + style + Integer.toString(font.getSize());
    }
}
class FontPanel extends Panel {
    private ChoiceTest choiceTest;
    private Choice familyChoice = new Choice(),
                   styleChoice  = new Choice(),
                   sizeChoice   = new Choice();
```

```
public FontPanel(ChoiceTest applet) {
    Listener listener = new Listener();

    choiceTest = applet;

    populateFonts();
    populateStyles();
    populateSizes();

    add(familyChoice);
    add(styleChoice);
    add(sizeChoice);

    familyChoice.addItemListener(listener);
    styleChoice.addItemListener (listener);
    sizeChoice.addItemListener  (listener);
}
public class Listener implements ItemListener {
    public void itemStateChanged(ItemEvent event) {
        choiceTest.updateLabel(getSelectedFont());
    }
}
public Font getSelectedFont() {
    return new Font(familyChoice.getSelectedItem(),
                    styleChoice.getSelectedIndex(),
                Integer.parseInt(
                    sizeChoice.getSelectedItem()));
}
private void populateFonts() {
    String fontNames[] = getToolkit().getFontList();

    for(int i=0; i < fontNames.length; ++i)
        familyChoice.add(fontNames[i]);
}
private void populateStyles() {
    styleChoice.add("Plain");
    styleChoice.add("Bold");
    styleChoice.add("Italic");
    styleChoice.add("BoldItalic");
}
private void populateSizes() {
    String sizes[] = {"12", "14", "16", "18", "24", "36"};

    for(int i=0; i < sizes.length; ++i)
        sizeChoice.add(sizes[i]);
}
}
```

A major complaint about the java.awt.Choice class in the original release of
the AWT was the fact that there was no way to delete an item from a choice.
Choices that had to represent a dynamic, as opposed to a static, list of strings
often had to resort to replacing the original choice with a brand new choice that

contained the pertinent items of the moment. Fortunately, the 1.1 release of the AWT fixed that oversight, by providing a number of methods that are variations on deleting items from a choice.

Our next applet provides a mechanism for adding items to, and deleting items from, a choice. As you can see from Figure 13-4, our applet provides a textfield that always contains a string representing the currently selected item in the choice with a remove item button alongside it. Activating the Remove Item button deletes the currently selected item. The applet also provides a second textfield/button combination for adding items to the choice. The Add Item button adds the string currently displayed in the corresponding textfield to the choice.

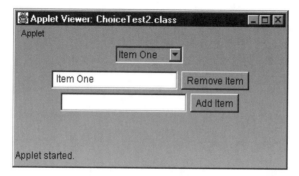

Figure 13-4 An Applet That Programmatically Manipulates a `Choice`
Items can be deleted from, and added to, the choice.

All of the action worth discussing takes place in the event handlers for the choice and the two buttons. When an item in the choice is selected, we must set the text in the Remove Item textfield to reflect the currently selected item in the choice, which is a simple task:

```
choice.addItemListener(new ItemListener() {
    public void itemStateChanged(ItemEvent event) {
        removeField.setText(choice.getSelectedItem());
    }
});
```

When an item in the choice is selected, we invoke
`Choice.getSelectedItem()`, which returns the string for the currently
selected item in the choice, which we pass along to the textfield's `setText`
method. Note that `getSelectedItem()` may return `null` only if the choice
contains no items; if a choice has one or more items, one of the items is always
selected.

When the Remove Item button is activated, we delete the item from the choice
with the same string contained in the textfield:

```
removeButton.addActionListener(new ActionListener() {
    public void actionPerformed(ActionEvent event) {
        String fieldStr = removeField.getText();

        if( ! isValidItem(fieldStr)) {
            ChoiceTest2.this.showStatus(
                                    "That's cheating!");
            removeField.setEnabled(false);
        }
        else if(choice.getItemCount() > 1) {
            choice.remove(removeField.getText());

            Object[] objs = choice.getSelectedObjects();
            removeField.setText((String)objs[0]);
        }
    }
});
```

First, we need to check that the text contained in the textfield is a valid item in the
choice, and unfortunately, the `Choice` class does not provide such a method, so
we must take matters into our own hands. The `isValidItem` method iterates
over the items in the choice until it finds a match for the string it was passed, at
which time it returns `true` to signify that the string passed in is a valid item in the
choice. If no match was found, the method returns `false`. If the string in the
textfield is not a valid item, then we've run across a malicious user, so we disable
the textfield by invoking its `setEnabled` method with a `false` value.

```
boolean isValidItem(String string) {
    int numItems = choice.getItemCount();

    for(int i=0; i < numItems; ++i) {
        if(choice.getItem(i).equals(string))
            return true;
    }
    return false;
}
```

If the string in the textfield represents a valid item in the choice and if there is more than one item in the choice,[5] we invoke `remove()` on the choice, passing it the string that represents the item to be removed. Once the item has been removed, the remove textfield is now out of synch, so we invoke `Choice.getSelectedObjects()`, which returns an array of, well, of selected objects.

You may find it curious that `Choice` implements a method that returns an array of selected objects, when it can only have strings as its items, and furthermore, only supports single selection. The Choice class implements `getSelectedObjects()` because it implements the `ItemSelectable` interface, which is a more general representation of components that can contain one or more selectable items. For a choice, `getSelectedObjects()` will always return either `null` if there are no selected items (meaning there are no items at all), or it will return an array of strings with the selected item as the first string in the array. Then, we set the remove textfields text to the first string in the selected objects array.

Finally, when the Add Item button is selected, we pass the text in the corresponding textfield to the choice's add method:

```
addButton.addActionListener(new ActionListener() {
    public void actionPerformed(ActionEvent event) {
        choice.add(addField.getText());
    }
});
```

The applet shown in Figure 13-4 is listed in its entirety in Example 13-4.

Example 13-4 Programmatically Manipulating a Choice

```
import java.applet.Applet;
import java.awt.*;
import java.awt.event.*;

public class ChoiceTest2 extends Applet {
    private TextField addField     = new TextField(20);
    private TextField removeField  = new TextField(20);
    private Choice    choice       = new Choice();
    private Button    addButton    = new Button("Add Item");
    private Button    removeButton = new Button("Remove Item");
```

5. We could have let the number of items in the choice go to zero, but doing so would have complicated matters.

```java
public void init() {
    Panel north  = new Panel();
    Panel center = new Panel();

    north.add(choice);

    center.add(removeField);
    center.add(removeButton);
    center.add(addField);
    center.add(addButton);

    setLayout(new BorderLayout());
    add(north, "North");
    add(center, "Center");

    choice.add("Item One");
    choice.add("Item Two");
    choice.add("Item Three");

    removeField.setText(choice.getItem(0));

    choice.addItemListener(new ItemListener() {
        public void itemStateChanged(ItemEvent event) {
            removeField.setText(choice.getSelectedItem());
        }
    });
    addButton.addActionListener(new ActionListener() {
        public void actionPerformed(ActionEvent event) {
            choice.add(addField.getText());
        }
    });
    removeButton.addActionListener(new ActionListener() {
        public void actionPerformed(ActionEvent event) {
            String fieldStr = removeField.getText();

            if( ! isValidItem(fieldStr)) {
                ChoiceTest2.this.showStatus(
                              "That's cheating!");
                removeField.setEnabled(false);
            }
            else if(choice.getItemCount() > 1) {
                choice.remove(removeField.getText());

                Object[] objs = choice.getSelectedObjects();
                removeField.setText((String)objs[0]);
            }
        }
    });
}
```

```
      boolean isValidItem(String string) {
          int numItems = choice.getItemCount();
          for(int i=0; i < numItems; ++i) {
              if(choice.getItem(i).equals(string))
                  return true;
          }
          return false;
      }
  }
```

java.awt.List

As we mentioned previously, the `List` and `Choice` components have a great deal in common. As a matter of fact, if you take the applet listed in "ChoiceTest Applet" on page 502 and do a global search and replace on every occurrence of *Choice* with `List`, you very nearly wind up with the applet that employs lists shown in "Two Applets for Selecting a Font" on page 500. The only difference to account for is the fact that choices always have (only) one item selected if they have one or more items, while lists do not have any items initially selected.

Recall that in the "ChoiceTest Applet" on page 502, we overrode the applet's start method to determine the font that was initially selected:

```
public void start() {
    updateLabel(fontPanel.getSelectedFont());
}
```

The pitfall associated with using this approach with lists, of course, is that lists don't have items initially selected, so in the `FontPanel.getSelectedFont` method, after our global search and replace mentioned above, we have:

```
public Font getSelectedFont() {
    return new Font(familyList.getSelectedItem(),
                    styleList.getSelectedIndex(),
                    Integer.parseInt(
                        sizeList.getSelectedItem()));
}
```

Since no item is currently selected in any of the lists, the call to `familyList.getSelectedItem()` returns a null reference, and the `Font` constructor does not take kindly to being passed a `null` reference for the name of the font. As a result, an exception is thrown.

The simple fix, then, is to select an item each of the lists after they are created, which we accomplish by invoking `List.select(0)` for each list, which selects the first item in the list:

```
public FontPanel(ListTest applet) {
        Listener listener = new Listener();
```

```
        listTest = applet;

        populateFonts();
        populateStyles();
        populateSizes();

        add(familyList);
        add(styleList);
        add(sizeList);

        familyList.addItemListener(listener);
        styleList.addItemListener (listener);
        sizeList.addItemListener  (listener);

        familyList.select(0);
        styleList.select(0);
        sizeList.select(0);
    }
```

After globally replacing `Choice` with `List` in the `ChoiceTest` applet and
applying the simple fixes shown above, we now have a working applet that
allows selection of a font with lists instead of choices. For completeness, we'll list
the entire applet in Example 13-5.

Example 13-5 `ListTest` Applet

```
import java.applet.Applet;
import java.awt.*;
import java.awt.event.*;

public class ListTest extends Applet {
    private FontPanel fontPanel = new FontPanel(this);
    private Label     label     = new Label(" ", Label.CENTER);

    public void init() {
        setLayout(new BorderLayout());
        add(fontPanel, "North");
        add(label, "Center");
    }
    public void start() {
        updateLabel(fontPanel.getSelectedFont());
    }
    public void updateLabel(Font font) {
        label.setText(fullNameOfFont(font));
        label.setFont(font);
    }
    private String fullNameOfFont(Font font) {
        String family = font.getFamily();
        String style  = new String();

        switch(font.getStyle()) {
            case Font.PLAIN: style = " Plain ";  break;
            case Font.BOLD:  style = " Bold ";   break;
```

```
            case Font.ITALIC: style = " Italic "; break;

            case Font.BOLD + Font.ITALIC:
                style = " Bold Italic ";
                break;
        }
        return family + style + Integer.toString(font.getSize());
    }
}
class FontPanel extends Panel {
    private ListTest listTest;
    private List familyList = new List(),
                 styleList  = new List(),
                 sizeList   = new List();

    public FontPanel(ListTest applet) {
        Listener listener = new Listener();

        listTest = applet;

        populateFonts();
        populateStyles();
        populateSizes();

        add(familyList);
        add(styleList);
        add(sizeList);

        familyList.addItemListener(listener);
        styleList.addItemListener (listener);
        sizeList.addItemListener  (listener);

        familyList.select(0);
        styleList.select(0);
        sizeList.select(0);
    }
    public class Listener implements ItemListener {
        public void itemStateChanged(ItemEvent event) {
            listTest.updateLabel(getSelectedFont());
        }
    }
    public Font getSelectedFont() {
        return new Font(familyList.getSelectedItem(),
                        styleList.getSelectedIndex(),
                    Integer.parseInt(
                        sizeList.getSelectedItem()));
    }
    private void populateFonts() {
        String fontNames[] = getToolkit().getFontList();

        for(int i=0; i < fontNames.length; ++i)
            familyList.add(fontNames[i]);
```

```
    }
    private void populateStyles() {
        styleList.add("Plain");
      styleList.add("Bold");
        styleList.add("Italic");
      styleList.add("BoldItalic");
    }
    private void populateSizes() {
        String sizes[] = {"12", "14", "16", "18", "24", "36"};

        for(int i=0; i < sizes.length; ++i)
            sizeList.add(sizes[i]);
    }
}
```

A Double-List Component

Our next applet implements a common user interface component that contains two lists; items can be moved back and forth between the two lists. We'll name our component DoubleList and give it an applet to test it out. You can see our applet in action in Figure 13-5. DoubleList exercises a good percentage of the public methods provided by the List class.

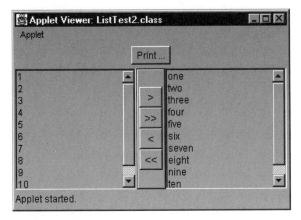

Figure 13-5 A DoubleList Component
Items can be moved back and forth from one list to the other by activating the buttons in the center panel.

The buttons in the center of the component work like so:

- > moves selected items from the left list to the right list
- >> moves all items from the left list to the right list
- < moves selected items from the right list to the left list
- << moves all items from the right list to the left list

Additionally, items moved from one side to the other must appear at the top of the list they are moved to so that they can be seen without scrolling. Also, selection of items must be preserved when they are moved from one list to another. Finally, the DoubleList component provides the following accessor methods:

- String[] getRightSideItems()
- String[] getRightSideSelectedItems()
- String[] getLeftSideItems()
- String[] getLeftSideSelectedItems()

The applet contains, in addition to the DoubleList component, a Print button to print out the items and selected items in each list, using the aforementioned methods. The applet is quite lengthy, so we'll digest it in small pieces and restrict our discussion to the code that is pertinent to lists.

First, let's take a look at the DoubleList implementation. DoubleList maintains references to the two lists it contains and a reference to the panel containing the buttons, referred to as the controlPanel:

```
class DoubleList extends Panel {
    private List left = new List(), right = new List();
    private Panel controlPanel = new ControlPanel(this);

    public DoubleList(String[] leftStrs, String[] rightStrs) {
        ...
        left.setMultipleMode(true);
        right.setMultipleMode(true);
        ...
        for(int i=0; i < leftStrs.length; ++i)
            left.add(leftStrs[i]);

        for(int i=0; i < rightStrs.length; ++i)
            right.add(rightStrs[i]);
    }
    ...
}
```

The omitted code sets the layout manager to an instance of `GridBagLayout`,[6] sets constraints for the two lists and control panel, and adds them to the double list (note that `DoubleList` extends `Panel`). `List.setMultipleMode()` is invoked for each list and is passed `true`, which as you might guess, enables multiple selection mode for the lists. Then, we add strings to the appropriate list by invoking `List.add(String)`, which adds an item to the end of a list.

`DoubleList.moveLeftToRight()` is invoked when the > button is activated, and moves all selected items in the left list to the right list.

```
public class ListTest2 extends Applet {
    private DoubleList list;
    private Button   printButton = new Button("Print ...");

    private String[] leftStrs = { "1", "2", "3", "4", "5",
                                  "6", "7", "8", "9", "10"};
    private String[] rightStrs = { "one", "two", "three", "four",
                                   "five", "six", "seven",
                                   "eight", "nine", "ten"};
    public void moveLeftToRight() {
        String[] leftSelected = left.getSelectedItems();
        int[]    leftSelectedIndexes = left.getSelectedIndexes();

        for(int i=0; i < leftSelectedIndexes.length; ++i) {
            left.remove(leftSelectedIndexes[i]-i);
        }
        for(int i=0; i < leftSelected.length; ++i) {
            right.add(leftSelected[i], i);
            right.select(i);
        }
    }
}
```

First, all of the selected items and selected indexes in the left list are obtained by invoking `List.getSelectedItems()` and `List.getSelectedIndexes()`, respectively.

Then, each of the selected items is removed from the left list.

At this point, you probably have two questions. First, why are we using indices to remove items when the `List` class provides a `remove(String)` method? Second, why is the rather curious argument of `(leftSelectedIndexes[i]-i)` passed to `remove(int)`?

The answer to the first question is that `List.remove(String)` removes the *first* item in the list that matches the string passed in. If we had duplicate items in the list and we removed by string, we could potentially remove the wrong item.

---

6. For an in-depth look at `GridBagLayout`, see "The GridBagLayout Layout Manager" on page 356.

The answer to the second question stems from the fact that we are modifying the list each time through the loop by removing one item, so we must decrement each index by the number of items that we've deleted.

Finally, the items are added to the right list.

Each item is added by invoking `List.add(String, int)`, where the `integer` argument specifies the position in the list where the item will be added. The positions, of course, start at zero, and increase by one each time through the loop, which means the items are added at the top of the list. Finally, we select each item by invoking `List.select(int)`, because we are retaining selection when moving items and all of the items that we are moving were originally selected.

`DoubleList.moveRightToLeft()` is implemented in exactly the same manner as `moveLeftToRight()` except that the lists are swapped, so we won't bother to discuss it.

Next, we have the straightforward `moveAllRightToLeft()`, which moves all the items in the right list (selected or not) to the left list and retains selection.

```
public void moveAllRightToLeft() {
    int rightCnt = right.getItemCount();

    for(int i=0; i < rightCnt; ++i) {
        left.add(right.getItem(i), i);

        if(right.isIndexSelected(i))
            left.select(i);
    }
    right.removeAll();
}
```

All of the items in the right list are cycled through, and each item is added to the left list, once again employing `List.add(String, int)` to ensure that the added items show up at the top of the left list. In addition, if the item was selected in the right list, we select it in the left list. When all the items have been moved, we invoke `List.removeAll()`, which removes all of the items in the right list. Once again, `moveAllLeftToRight()` is implemented in exactly the same manner as `moveAllRightToLeft()`, so we won't bother to discuss it.

Finally, we have the accessor methods that return all of the items and all of the selected items for each list.

```
public String[] getRightSideItems() {
    return right.getItems();
}
public String[] getRightSideSelectedItems() {
    return right.getSelectedItems();
}
public String[] getLeftSideItems() {
    return left.getItems();
}
public String[] getLeftSideSelectedItems() {
    return left.getSelectedItems();
}
```

The methods listed above simply delegate to the appropriate list, invoking either
List.getItems() or List.getSelectedItems(), both of which return an
array of strings.

One final note about DoubleList. Even though its name implies that it contains
lists, DoubleList does not provide accessors to its lists, even though it would
have been easier to implement List getLeftList() and List
getRightList methods and let the caller dig out the items and selected items
directly from the lists themselves.

In general, it is preferable to implement delegation methods that return pertinent
information, rather than expose the implementation of a class by returning
references to enclosed objects. Hiding the implementation of a class by not
providing accessors to enclosed objects affords a class more leeway in changing
its implementation in the future.

In the case of DoubleList, you might argue that it really doesn't matter whether
the implementation is hidden or not, since it is highly unlikely that DoubleList
would ever swap out its lists for a different type of object. Consider, however, that
the AWT in the future will provide lightweight versions of all its (heavyweight)
components, and therefore DoubleList might like to swap out its heavyweight
lists for a lightweight version, in which case hiding the implementation was good
foresight.

Typically, deciding whether to provide accessors to enclosed objects is a trade-off
between hiding the implementation of the class and providing clients with the
information they need. Another alternative to returning direct references to
enclosed objects is to return a reference to an interface that the enclosed object
implements, as discussed in the OO Tip "Hide Implementations of Enclosed
Objects by Returning References to Interfaces" on page 274.

Now, without further ado, we present the applet shown in Figure 13-5 on
page 511 in its entirety.

Example 13-6 ListTest2 Applet

```java
import java.applet.Applet;
import java.awt.*;
import java.awt.event.*;

public class ListTest2 extends Applet {
    private DoubleList list;
    private Button    printButton = new Button("Print ...");
    private String[] leftStrs = { "1", "2", "3", "4", "5",
                                  "6", "7", "8", "9", "10"};
    private String[] rightStrs = { "one", "two", "three", "four",
                                   "five", "six", "seven",
                                   "eight", "nine", "ten"};
    public void init() {
        Panel controlPanel = new Panel();
        controlPanel.add(printButton);

        setLayout(new BorderLayout());
        add(controlPanel, "North");
        add(list = new DoubleList(leftStrs, rightStrs), "Center");

        printButton.addActionListener(new ActionListener() {
            public void actionPerformed(ActionEvent event) {
                String[] left  = list.getLeftSideItems();
                String[] right = list.getRightSideItems();
                String[] sleft  = list.getLeftSideSelectedItems();
                String[] sright = list.getRightSideSelectedItems();

                System.out.println("Left Side Items:");
                for(int i=0; i < left.length; ++i)
                    System.out.println(left[i]);
                System.out.println();

                System.out.println("Right Side Items:");
                for(int i=0; i < right.length; ++i)
                    System.out.println(right[i]);
                System.out.println();

                System.out.println("Left Side Selected Items:");
                for(int i=0; i < sleft.length; ++i)
                    System.out.println(sleft[i]);
                System.out.println();

                System.out.println("Right Side Selected Items:");
                for(int i=0; i < sright.length; ++i)
                    System.out.println(sright[i]);
                System.out.println();
            }
        });
    }
}
```

```
class DoubleList extends Panel {
    private List left = new List(), right = new List();
    private Panel controlPanel = new ControlPanel(this);

    public DoubleList(String[] leftStrs, String[] rightStrs) {
        GridBagLayout      gbl = new GridBagLayout();
        GridBagConstraints gbc = new GridBagConstraints();

        left.setMultipleMode (true);
        right.setMultipleMode(true);

        setLayout(gbl);

        gbc.fill    = GridBagConstraints.BOTH;
        gbc.weightx = 1.0;
        gbc.weighty = 1.0;
        gbl.setConstraints(left, gbc);

        gbc.fill    = GridBagConstraints.VERTICAL;
        gbc.weightx = 0;
        gbc.weighty = 1.0;
        gbl.setConstraints(controlPanel, gbc);

        gbc.fill    = GridBagConstraints.BOTH;
        gbc.weightx = 1.0;
        gbc.weighty = 1.0;
        gbl.setConstraints(right, gbc);

        add(left);
        add(controlPanel);
        add(right);

        for(int i=0; i < leftStrs.length; ++i)
            left.add(leftStrs[i]);

        for(int i=0; i < rightStrs.length; ++i)
            right.add(rightStrs[i]);
    }
    public void moveLeftToRight() {
        String[] leftSelected = left.getSelectedItems();
        int[]    leftSelectedIndexes = left.getSelectedIndexes();

        for(int i=0; i < leftSelectedIndexes.length; ++i) {
            left.remove(leftSelectedIndexes[i]-i);
        }
        for(int i=0; i < leftSelected.length; ++i) {
            right.add(leftSelected[i], i);
            right.select(i);
        }
    }
    public void moveRightToLeft() {
        String[] rightSelected = right.getSelectedItems();
```

```
            int[]   rightSelectedIndexes =
                              right.getSelectedIndexes();

            for(int i=0; i < rightSelectedIndexes.length; ++i) {
               right.remove(rightSelectedIndexes[i]-i);
            }
            for(int i=0; i < rightSelected.length; ++i) {
               left.add(rightSelected[i], i);
               left.select(i);
            }
        }
        public void moveAllRightToLeft() {
            int rightCnt = right.getItemCount();

            for(int i=0; i < rightCnt; ++i) {
               left.add(right.getItem(i), i);
               if(right.isIndexSelected(i))
                  left.select(i);
            }
            right.removeAll();
        }
        public void moveAllLeftToRight() {
            int leftCnt = left.getItemCount();

            for(int i=0; i < leftCnt; ++i) {
               right.add(left.getItem(i), i);
               if(left.isIndexSelected(i))
                  right.select(i);
            }
            left.removeAll();
        }
        public String[] getRightSideItems() {
            return right.getItems();
        }
        public String[] getRightSideSelectedItems() {
            return right.getSelectedItems();
        }
        public String[] getLeftSideItems() {
            return left.getItems();
        }
        public String[] getLeftSideSelectedItems() {
            return left.getSelectedItems();
        }
    }
    class ControlPanel extends Panel {
        private DoubleList  doubleList;
        private Button leftToRight     = new Button(">");
        private Button allLeftToRight  = new Button(">>");
        private Button rightToLeft     = new Button("<");
        private Button allRightToLeft  = new Button("<<");
        private Font   buttonFont      = new Font("TimesRoman",
                                            Font.BOLD, 14);
```

```java
public ControlPanel(DoubleList dblList) {
    this.doubleList = dblList;

    GridBagLayout       gbl = new GridBagLayout();
    GridBagConstraints gbc = new GridBagConstraints();

    setLayout(gbl);

    gbc.gridwidth = GridBagConstraints.REMAINDER;
    gbc.fill      = GridBagConstraints.HORIZONTAL;
    gbl.setConstraints(leftToRight,     gbc);
    gbl.setConstraints(allLeftToRight,  gbc);
    gbl.setConstraints(rightToLeft,     gbc);
    gbl.setConstraints(allRightToLeft,  gbc);

    add(leftToRight);
    add(allLeftToRight);
    add(rightToLeft);
    add(allRightToLeft);

    leftToRight.setFont     (buttonFont);
    allLeftToRight.setFont(buttonFont);
    rightToLeft.setFont     (buttonFont);
    allRightToLeft.setFont(buttonFont);

    leftToRight.addActionListener(new ActionListener() {
        public void actionPerformed(ActionEvent event) {
            doubleList.moveLeftToRight();
        }
    });
    allLeftToRight.addActionListener(new ActionListener() {
        public void actionPerformed(ActionEvent event) {
            doubleList.moveAllLeftToRight();
        }
    });
    rightToLeft.addActionListener(new ActionListener() {
        public void actionPerformed(ActionEvent event) {
            doubleList.moveRightToLeft();
        }
    });
    allRightToLeft.addActionListener(new ActionListener() {
        public void actionPerformed(ActionEvent event) {
            doubleList.moveAllRightToLeft();
        }
    });
}
public Insets getInsets() {
    return new Insets(4,4,4,4);
}
public void paint(Graphics g) {
    Dimension size = getSize();
```

```
            g.setColor(Color.black);
            g.drawRect(0,0,size.width-1,size.height-1);
            g.setColor(Color.lightGray);
            g.fill3DRect(1,1,size.width-2,size.height-2,true);
        }
    }
```

OO·TIP

Hide Enclosed Objects

When a class contains other objects, it is often tempting to provide accessors to the enclosed objects so that clients can obtain information directly from the enclosed objects. However, providing such accessors reveals the implementation of a class, and thus restricts implementation changes that the class can make in the future. It is often a better design to implement delegation methods that return information pertaining to enclosed objects. In reality, deciding whether to provide accessor methods to enclosed objects is often a trade-off between the likelihood of implementation changes that swap out the enclosed objects with different types of objects versus the amount of information clients of the class need to access.

Summary

The AWT offers three components that implement the `ItemSelectable` interface: choices, checkboxes, and lists. Item selectables, of course, are components that contain zero or more selectable items. Item selectables are also capable of firing item events whenever an item is selected or deselected.

Choices and lists serve similar purposes; which one to employ in a given situation depends upon the needs of the moment. We have provided some guidelines for deciding whether to use a choice or list depending upon the requirements of the user interface in which they reside.

We've also provided some examples of common user interface components, such as a double list and a font panel for selecting a font.

CHAPTER 14

Text Components

The AWT provides two components for displaying editable text: TextArea and TextField. The TextField component provides a single line of editable text, and the TextArea component provides a multiline textarea that can be thought of as a miniature text editor.

Before we launch into our discussion concerning these two components, we should point out that although the components are useful in their own right, they can be difficult to extend in a meaningful manner because they are peer-based components. While this is true for all of the AWT's heavyweight components, we wish to emphasize the point here; it is not uncommon for newcomers to the AWT to attempt to extend or modify the functionality provided by the textarea to implement a custom text editor. For instance, if you wanted to change the textarea to underline text when selected, instead of displaying the text in reverse video, you'd be out of luck because that functionality is buried in the textarea's peer and cannot be modified.[1]

---

1. Future versions of the AWT will provide peerless versions of existing components.

java.awt.TextComponent

`TextField` and `TextArea` both extend the `TextComponent` class.
`TextComponent`, as a matter of fact, exists solely to provide fundamental text
editing capabilities for `TextArea` and `TextField`.

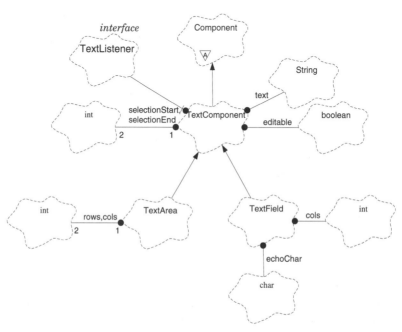

Figure 14-1 `TextComponent` Class Diagram
`TextComponent` maintains text, selection range, and editability
of the component. `TextComponent` cannot be instantiated by
classes outside the java.awt package.

As evidenced by the class diagram in Figure 14-1, `TextComponent` provides the
following functionality:

* Get and set text
* Get and set selected text

- Get and set editable mode
- Position the insertion caret[2]

Table 14-1 lists the public methods provided by the `TextComponent` class.

Table 14-1 `java.awt.TextComponent` **Public Methods**

Method	Description
`String getText()`	Returns the text currently in the component
`void setText(String)`	Sets the text
`String getSelectedText()`	Returns the selected text
`void select(int, int)`	Sets the selected text. The first `int` is the selection start; the second is the selection end.
`void selectAll()`	Selects all of the text in the component
`int getSelectionStart()`	Returns the staring position of the selection range
`void setSelectionStart(int)`	Sets the start of selection range
`int getSelectionEnd()`	Returns the end position of the selection range
`void setSelectionEnd(int)`	Sets the end of the selection range
`int getCaretPosition()`	Returns the caret (insert) position
`void setCaretPosition(int)`	Sets the caret (insert) position
`boolean isEditable()`	Returns whether the textarea is editable
`void setEditable(boolean)`	Sets the ability to edit text in the component
`void addTextListener(TextListener)`	Adds a text listener
`void removeTextListener(TextListener)`	Removes a text listener

`TextComponent` is not available for you to instantiate directly. Even though `TextComponent` is a concrete (meaning not abstract) class, it does not provide any public constructors, and therefore classes outside of the `java.awt` package cannot instantiate a `TextComponent`.

As you can see, all of the necessary get and set methods are provided to either inquire about, or set the value of, the textarea's text, selected text, caret position, and editable mode. In addition, `TextComponent` enables the addition of text listeners that will be notified whenever its text changes.

2. Since caret manipulation is handled by the peer, there is no evidence of caret responsibility in Figure 14-1.

Text Selection

As you can see from Table 14-1, a `TextComponent` maintains the range of the currently selected text. Figure 14-2 shows an applet with a lone textfield, whose selection range has been set. Although we used a `TextField`, we could have used a `TextArea` and gotten the same result because `TextField` and `TextArea` both inherit their text selection functionality from `TextComponent`.

Figure 14-2 Selection Range for Text Components
Selection range begins at zero. The range includes the low end but stops just short of the top end (the 3 is selected, but the 7 is not).

When figuring selection range, begin counting at zero. The selection range includes the lower end of the range, but not the upper. Notice in Figure 14-2 that the low end of the range (3) is selected, but the top end (7) is not. For the last character in the text to be selected, an index equal to the length of the string must be specified as the end of the selection range. If you're accustomed to C or C++, having the range start at zero makes you feel right at home, but using an index equal to the length of a string might make you think twice. Finally, if there is no selection, `getSelectionStart()` and `getSelectionEnd()` both return the caret position.

TextComponent Listeners

Text components, by default, accept focus and, as a result, fire key and focus events in addition to the events fired by all components (see "Components and Internationalization" on page 457). Text components also fire text events and therefore support adding and removing text listeners. The `TextListener`[3] interface defines one abstract method: `void` `textChangedValue(TextEvent)`. Text listeners are notified whenever the text they are interested in has been changed. As a result, a text listener can be attached to any extension of `TextComponent`, for keeping a watchful eye over each and every key entered or deleted.

Here's a small dose of pseudocode for hooking up a text listener to a textfield:

```
public class ATextListener implements TextListener {
    public void textChangedValue(TextEvent event) {
        System.out.println("TextField's text changed value");
    }
}
...

TextField field = new TextField(20);
ATextListener listener = new TextListener();

field.addTextListener(listener);

...
```

java.awt.TextField

Ok, so we know that `TextField` inherits all of the functionality provided by its superclass, `TextComponent`. A `TextField`, as a result, can manage selection, editable mode, and caret positioning. You can also add text listeners to a textfield and watch the text change in the field. So, let's take a look at the additional functionality `TextField` provides for editing its one line of text. First, take a look at the four constructors provided by the `TextField` class.

1. `TextField()`

2. `TextField(String text)`

3. `TextField(int columns)`

4. `TextField(String text, int columns)`

If someone were to put a gun to your head and shout "quick! what's the columns argument for, and you'd better be right!" we're pretty confident that you could calmly reel off the fact that the columns, of course, indicate how many characters fit in the textfield.

3.   See "java.awt.event Listener Interfaces and Methods" on page 249.

If the guy with the gun were really sharp, he might ask if specifying a column width of 9 means that there will always be 9 characters displayed, regardless of font family, style, and point size. The answer, of course, is probably not, because most fonts are not monospaced, so the width of different characters can vary, making one-size-fits-all-for-X-columns an ill-fated pursuit.

AWT TIP ...

Use Monospaced Font for Precise Column Width

Since most fonts are variable width, the sizes of individual characters in the font set can have varying widths, making a field with a certain number of columns an approximation. If a textfield must reflect an exact column width, setting the font for the textfield to monospaced will do. Here's how to change a fields font to a monospaced font:

```
field.setFont(new Font("Monospaced", Font.PLAIN, 12))
```

Table 14-2 lists the interesting `public` methods provided by `TextField`.

Table 14-2 `java.awt.TextField` **Public Methods**

Method	Description
`int getColumns()`	Gets the current number of columns displayed
`void setColumns(int)`	Sets the number of columns displayed
`char getEchoChar()`	Gets echo character
`void setEchoChar(char)`	Sets the echo character
`boolean echoCharIsSet()`	Is the echo character set?
`void addActionListener(ActionListener listener)`	Registers action listeners to listen for action events generated by typing enter in the textfield
`void removeActionListener(ActionListener listener)`	Removes an action listener

`TextField` also provides methods for calculating the preferred, minimum, and maximum sizes for itself for a given number of columns.

`TextField` turns out to be a pretty bland, but quite useful, tool in the AWT toolchest. It doesn't bring much to the party though, above and beyond what it gets from `TextComponent`, other than firing action events and providing manipulation for the *echo* character.

The echo character, of course, is what is echoed back into the field when characters are typed into the field. If you have a supersecret textfield with sensitive data, you can make the echo character be something like '*', or some other equally deceptive character.

A `TextField` fires action events when you activate the enter key—see "Semantic Events" on page 269.

We've got two applets concerning textfields coming up for you. Both deal with input validation, which is useful to have at your disposal, and will also help us illustrate some of the finer points of dealing with textfields.

Input Validation

The ugly task of input validation raises its head with amazing regularity, so we'll spend a bit of time talking about two kinds of input validation:

- Exit validation
- On-the-fly validation

The exit mechanism waits until an attempt has been made to exit the textfield, at which time parties guilty of entering invalid data into the textfield are punished accordingly.

The on-the-fly mechanism watches the textfield like a hawk, noting each and every keystroke and quickly assessing whether or not the new addition (or deletion) to the textfield is, in fact, legal. Once again retribution is swift.

Figure 14-3 Exit Validation
You can never leave the field on the left if you've typed in something that's not an `integer`.

Exit Validation

Our first applet dealing with input validation contains two textfields. When an attempt is made to leave the left textfield, whether by pressing the TAB key, pressing the enter key, or trying to mouse out, a check is made to make sure that the data entered in the left textfield is a valid integer. If not, focus is politely requested for the left textfield (and always granted), and then all of the text in the field is deservedly selected to admonish the integer challenged. The applet is listed in Example 14-1.

Example 14-1 ExitValidatorTest Applet

```java
import java.applet.Applet;
import java.awt.*;
import java.awt.event.*;

public class ExitValidatorTest extends Applet {
    TextField      fieldOne  = new TextField(3),
                   fieldTwo  = new TextField(3);
    ExitValidator validator = new ExitValidator();

    public void init() {
        fieldOne.addActionListener(validator);
        fieldOne.addFocusListener (validator);
        add(fieldOne);
        add(fieldTwo);
    }
}
class ExitValidator extends     FocusAdapter
                       implements ActionListener {
    public void actionPerformed(ActionEvent event) {
        validate((TextField)event.getSource());
    }
    public void focusLost(FocusEvent event) {
        validate((TextField)event.getSource());
    }
    private void validate(TextField field) {
        try {
            Integer.parseInt(field.getText());
        }
        catch(NumberFormatException e) {
            field.requestFocus();
            field.selectAll();
        }
    }
}
```

First, we should confess that the textfield on the right exists solely to provide another component to point the focus at—only the left hand textfield has the necessary listeners attached for validation.

ExitValidator deals with focus and action events. Focus lost events are generated when you try and leave the textfield. Typing enter in a textfield fires an action event, which is deftly handled by ExitValidator.

Our validation is pretty simple-minded. We ask the Integer class to parse the string in the left textfield. If the string does not represent a valid integer, Integer.toString() throws a NumberFormatException, which we catch. Once we've caught the exception, we request focus for the field and select all of the text within the field.

That was exciting enough, we're sure, but wait, there's more! Let's take a quick look at the fascinating world of on-the-fly field validation.

Validating on the Fly

This scenario involves watching keystrokes and not letting illegal characters see the light of day. It's interesting that this approach was not possible under previous releases of the AWT, because try as you might, you couldn't stop an event from being passed on to a component's peer. Input events can be consumed by invoking InputEvent.consume(),[4] which is exactly what we do in our next applet, shown in Figure 14-4. The applet itself is listed immediately following, in Example 14-2.

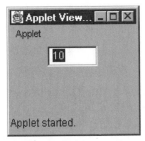

Figure 14-4 On-the-fly Validation
Offending characters are caught and their associated event is consumed before they can get to the textfield's peer, so the characters never show up in the field.

---

4. See "Consuming Input Events" on page 267.

Example 14-2 FlyValidatorTest Applet

```java
import java.applet.Applet;
import java.awt.*;
import java.awt.event.*;

public class FlyValidatorTest extends Applet {
    TextField    field = new TextField(5);
    FlyValidator validator = new FlyValidator();

    public void init() {
        field.addKeyListener(validator);
        add(field);
    }
}
class FlyValidator extends KeyAdapter {
    public void keyPressed(KeyEvent event) {
        TextField field     = (TextField)event.getSource();
        String    oldstring = field.getText();
        String    newstring = new String();
        int       value     = 0, newValue;

        try {
            if(!oldstring.equals(""))
                value = Integer.parseInt(oldstring);

            newstring += event.getKeyChar();
            newValue   = Integer.parseInt(newstring);
        }
        catch(NumberFormatException e) {
            event.consume();
            field.selectAll();
        }
    }
}
```

This time, we attach a key listener to the textfield and watch for key pressed events. The cool thing about intercepting key presses is that the key press hasn't been delivered to the textfield's peer yet,[5] so if we don't like the key pressed, we can consume the event and the keystroke never reaches the peer. This, of course, is exactly what we do if our exception-provoking tomfoolery catches the integer challenged in command of the keyboard.

Notice that we don't have to be concerned with focus events when validating on the fly. Since we're validating every keystroke as it comes in and consuming events associated with illegal characters, the textfield always displays a valid integer (or an empty string).

5. Event listeners get a crack at input events before their peers.

As an aside, note that we check the string in the textfield against the empty string: `""`. That's because both `TextField` and `TextArea` initialize their text to an empty string if you don't specify what the initial text should be.

TextArea.getText() May Return an Empty String

Textfields and textareas devoid of text return an empty string: `""`. To see whether a textfield or textarea currently has no text, check the string against `""`, like so:

```
if(field.getText().equals("")) // field is empty
```

java.awt.TextArea

`TextArea` and `TextField` are nearly identical except for one rather obvious difference: A textarea provides more than one row of text, while a textfield provides only a single line of text. `TextArea`, like `TextField`, is quite generous about providing ample constructors to choose from.

- `TextArea()`
- `TextArea(String)`
- `TextArea(int rows, int cols)`
- `TextArea(String s, int rows, int cols)`
- `TextArea(String s, int rows, int cols, int scrollbarPolicy)`

Of course, if you really want the textarea to be sized precisely, you should set the textarea's font to monospaced, as we advised for textareas.

The scrollbar policy passed to the last constructor listed must be one of the following:

- `TextArea.SCROLLBARS_NONE`
- `TextArea.SCROLLBARS_BOTH`
- `TextArea.SCROLLBARS_HORIZONTAL_ONLY`
- `TextArea.SCROLLBARS_VERICAL_ONLY`

We'll leave the interpretation of the constants listed above as an exercise for the reader.

Table 14-3 lists the interesting public methods implemented by `java.awt.TextArea`. As you can see, `TextArea` provides minimal functionality for text replacement and setting the number of rows and columns. `TextArea`, like `TextField`, inherits most of its functionality from `TextComponent`.

Table 14-3 `java.awt.TextArea` **Public Methods**

Method	Description
`int getColumns()`	Returns the number of columns
`void setColumns(int)`	Sets the number of columns (characters)
`int getRows()`	Returns the number of text rows
`void setRows(int)`	Sets the number of text rows
`void insert(String,int)`	Inserts text at specified location
`void append(String)`	Adds text to the end of the component
`void replaceRange(String s, int start,int end)`	Replaces range starting at `start` and ending at end with the string s
`int getScrollbarVisibility()`	Returns scrollbar visibility policy

A `TextArea` can contain more than one row of text, whereas a `TextField` is restricted to one row. Nonetheless, each class implements the same method for returning the text it contains: `String getText()`. The difference is that the `TextArea` implementation of `getText()` embeds newline characters in its string whenever a new row of text begins (excluding the first row).

Search and Replace

Perhaps you noticed that the `TextArea` class provides few methods for text manipulation: `insert()`, `append()`, and `replaceRange()`. That may not strike you as odd until you realize that `TextField` has no such methods; `TextField` and its superclass, `TextComponent`, have no text editing capabilities whatsoever. It would be better for all involved if `TextComponent` could wrest the text editing mantle from `TextArea`, and then `TextField` could reap the benefits.

Since `TextArea` is the only text component with editing capabilities, our next applet, shown in Figure 14-5, is a simple text editor that implements find, change, and change & find capabilities.

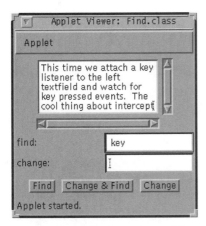

Figure 14-5 Search and Replace in a `TextArea`
The text editing capabilities of a `TextArea` are used to implement
search and replace functionality.

We'll take a look at the areas of the applet pertaining to text editing in a textarea,
and then we'll list the applet in its entirety. The applet maintains references to all
of the AWT components shown in the applet:

```
TextArea editor = new TextArea(5,20);
..
TextField findField = new TextField(5),
          changeField = new TextField(5);
```

When the Change button is selected, the currently selected text in the textarea, if
any, is replaced with the text contained in the "change:" textfield, by invocation of
the applet's `replace` method.

```
void replace(String change) {
    int start = editor.getSelectionStart(),
        end   = editor.getSelectionEnd();

    if(start != end)
        editor.replaceRange(change,start,end);
}
```

`TextArea` does not provide a method to determine if text is selected, so we check
to see if the starting position of the selection range differs from the end position. If
the start and end positions differ, then the text is selected, and we invoke the
textarea's `replaceRange` method to replace the text.

Our only other task is to find text in the textarea.

```
void findNext(String find) {
    String edit  = editor.getText();
    int start  = editor.getSelectionStart(),
        end    = editor.getSelectionEnd(),
        index  = -1;

    index = edit.indexOf(find, start+1);

    if(index == -1 && start != 0) {
        index = edit.indexOf(find);
    }
    if(index != -1) {
        editor.setSelectionStart(index);
        editor.setSelectionEnd(index + find.length());
    }
}
```

Once again, we get the start and end positions of the selection range, along with the text in the textfield. If there is selected text (meaning start != end), we invoke `String.indexOf()` to search for the index of the next occurrence of the find string, starting at the character after the start of the selection range. If `String.indexOf()` returns -1, then no substring was found.

If no substring was found and start is not at the beginning of the string, we call a version of `String.indexOf()` that starts the search at the beginning of the string. This call ensures that once we get to the end and there are no further matches, the search starts over at the beginning.

If we've got an index that's something other than -1, we reset the selection range.

The entire applet is listed in Example 14-3.

Example 14-3 Find Applet

```
import java.applet.Applet;
import java.awt.*;
import java.awt.event.*;

public class Find extends Applet {
    TextArea    editor          = new TextArea(5,20);
    Label       findLabel       = new Label("find:"),
                changeLabel     = new Label("change:");

    TextField   findField       = new TextField(5),
                changeField     = new TextField(5);

    Button      findButton      = new Button("Find"),
                changeFindButton = new Button("Change & Find"),
                changeButton    = new Button("Change");
```

```
public void init() {
    Panel north  = new Panel(),
          center = new Panel(),
          south  = new Panel();

    north.add(editor);

    center.setLayout(new GridLayout(2,2));
    center.add(findLabel);
    center.add(findField);
    center.add(changeLabel);
    center.add(changeField);

    south.add(findButton);
    south.add(changeFindButton);
    south.add(changeButton);

    setLayout(new BorderLayout());
    add(north, "North");
    add(center, "Center");
    add(south, "South");

    findButton.addActionListener(new ActionListener() {
        public void actionPerformed(ActionEvent event) {
            findNext(findField.getText());
        }
    });
    changeButton.addActionListener(new ActionListener() {
        public void actionPerformed(ActionEvent event) {
            replace(changeField.getText());
        }
    });
    changeFindButton.addActionListener(new ActionListener() {
        public void actionPerformed(ActionEvent event) {
            int start = editor.getSelectionStart(),
                end   = editor.getSelectionEnd();

            if(start != end)
                replace(changeField.getText());

            findNext(findField.getText());
        }
    });
}
void replace(String change) {
    int start = editor.getSelectionStart(),
        end   = editor.getSelectionEnd();

    if(start != end)
        editor.replaceRange(change,start,end);
}
```

```
void findNext(String find) {
    String edit   = editor.getText();
    int    start  = editor.getSelectionStart(),
           end    = editor.getSelectionEnd(),
           index  = -1;

    index = edit.indexOf(find, start+1);

    if(index == -1 && start != 0) {
        index = edit.indexOf(find);
    }
    if(index != -1) {
        editor.setSelectionStart(index);
        editor.setSelectionEnd(index + find.length());
    }
}
}
```

Summary

This chapter covered the text components provided by the AWT: textfields and textareas. We've discussed not only textfields and textareas but also taken a look at their superclass: TextComponent, which provides a number of services shared by textfields and text areas. Additionally, we've taken a short detour to discuss input validation for textfields, both exit validation and on-the-fly validation.

CHAPTER

15

Scrolling: Scrollbars and Scrollpanes

When you are developing applets, or any graphical user interface, for that matter, it usually doesn't take long before the need arises to scroll something. In the world of the AWT, that *something* is nearly always a component—usually a container—or an image.

Before the 1.1 version of the AWT, implementing scrolling required you to manually attach scrollbars to a container and then subsequently monitor scrollbar events in order to scroll the contents of the container accordingly, which was a fairly complicated and error-prone process.

Releases of the AWT from 1.1 on still provide a basic scrollbar component, but it also comes with a ScrollPane container. ScrollPane greatly simplifies the process of scrolling a component—a component is simply added to the scrollpane, and all of the scrolling details are handled without programmer intervention.

java.awt.Scrollbar

Although the advent of ScrollPane takes away much of Scrollbar's thunder, scrollbars are still useful in their own right; for instance, a scrollbar could be used to implement a quick and dirty slider component—a component, in fact, that we'll use to illustrate the properties and events associated with scrollbars. Our slider contains a scrollbar and a label that displays the scrollbar's current value. For visual effect, we'll wrap the scrollbar and label in a 3D rectangle outlined with a black border. Figure 15-1 shows our slider component in action.

Figure 15-1 A Slider Component
A slider consists of a scrollbar and a label that displays the scrollbar's current value. The scrollbar and label are contained in a panel with an outlined 3D border.

Instead of embedding the functionality that paints the 3D border and black outline in the Slider class itself, we'll create a separate class, BorderedPanel. By encapsulating the bordering functionality in a separate class, we make it available for others to use. The BorderedPanel class is a simple panel, listed in Example 15-1, which overrides paint() in order to paint its borders.

Example 15-1 BorderedPanel Class Listing

```java
import java.awt.*;

public class BorderedPanel extends Panel {
    public Insets getInsets() {
        return new Insets(2,2,2,2);
    }
    public void paint(Graphics g) {
        Dimension size = getSize();

        g.setColor(Color.black);
        g.drawRect(0,0,size.width-1,size.height-1);

        g.setColor(Color.lightGray);
        g.draw3DRect(1,1,size.width-3,size.height-3,true);
    }
}
```

BorderedPanel also overrides getInsets() so that the components contained in the panel do not encroach upon the area in which the 3D border and outline are drawn. If BorderedPanel did not override getInsets(), the borders would be drawn underneath the panel's components and therefore would not be visible. See "Painting a Container's Components" on page 335 for more information on painting graphics in a container.

The Slider class extends BorderedPanel and implements the Adjustable interface. It sets its layout to an instance of BorderLayout and adds a label as the north component and a scrollbar as the south component. An anonymous inner class implementing AdjustmentListener is added to the scrollbar so that whenever the scrollbar's value changes, the label's text is set to reflect the current value of the scrollbar.

```
public class Slider extends BorderedPanel implements Adjustable {
    Scrollbar scrollbar;
    Label     valueLabel;

    public Slider(int initialValue, int visible,
                  int min, int max) {
        String initialValueStr = Integer.toString(initialValue);

        valueLabel = new Label(initialValueStr, Label.CENTER);
        scrollbar  = new Scrollbar(Scrollbar.HORIZONTAL,
                                   initialValue,
                                   visible, min, max);

        setLayout(new BorderLayout());
        add(valueLabel, "North");
        add(scrollbar, "Center");

        scrollbar.addAdjustmentListener(new AdjustmentListener() {
            public void adjustmentValueChanged(AdjustmentEvent e) {
                valueLabel.setText(
                    Integer.toString(scrollbar.getValue()));
            }
        });
    }
    ...
}
```

The rest of the implementation for the Slider class implements the methods defined in the Adjustable interface by delegating to the enclosed scrollbar—see "Adjustable Interface" on page 273.

Note that it would have been much easier to forgo implementing the Adjustable interface by providing an accessor to the scrollbar instead, so that clients could directly manipulate the scrollbar itself, but that approach would have exposed the implementation of the Slider class. In this case, the slider's scrollbar is a likely candidate to be replaced with something that more closely resembles a real slider component in the future, and therefore the effort required to keep the slider's implementation hidden is justifiable.

Example 15-2 lists the Slider class in its entirety.

 Example 15-2 Slider Class Listing

```java
import java.awt.*;
import java.awt.event.*;

public class Slider extends BorderedPanel implements Adjustable {
    Scrollbar scrollbar;
    Label     valueLabel;

    public Slider(int initialValue, int visible,
                  int min, int max) {
        String initialValueStr = Integer.toString(initialValue);

        valueLabel = new Label(initialValueStr, Label.CENTER);
        scrollbar  = new Scrollbar(Scrollbar.HORIZONTAL,
                                   initialValue,
                                   visible, min, max);

        setLayout(new BorderLayout());
        add(valueLabel, "North");
        add(scrollbar, "Center");

        scrollbar.addAdjustmentListener(new AdjustmentListener() {
            public void adjustmentValueChanged(AdjustmentEvent e) {
                valueLabel.setText(
                    Integer.toString(scrollbar.getValue()));
            }
        });
    }
    public void addAdjustmentListener(AdjustmentListener l) {
        scrollbar.addAdjustmentListener(l);
    }
    public void removeAdjustmentListener(AdjustmentListener l) {
        scrollbar.removeAdjustmentListener(l);
    }
    public int getOrientation() {
        return scrollbar.getOrientation();
    }
    public void setOrientation(int orient) {
        scrollbar.setOrientation(orient);
    }
    public int getValue() {
        return scrollbar.getValue();
    }
    public int getVisibleAmount() {
        return scrollbar.getVisibleAmount();
    }
    public int getMinimum() {
        return scrollbar.getMinimum();
    }
    public int getMaximum() {
```

```
        return scrollbar.getMaximum();
    }
    public int getUnitIncrement() {
        return scrollbar.getUnitIncrement();
    }
    public int getBlockIncrement() {
        return scrollbar.getBlockIncrement();
    }
    public void setValue(int value) {
        scrollbar.setValue(value);
        valueLabel.setText(Integer.toString(value));
    }
    public void setVisibleAmount(int value) {
        scrollbar.setVisibleAmount(value);
    }
    public void setMinimum(int min) {
        scrollbar.setMinimum(min);
    }
    public void setMaximum(int max) {
        scrollbar.setMaximum(max);
    }
    public void setUnitIncrement(int inc) {
        scrollbar.setUnitIncrement(inc);
    }
    public void setBlockIncrement(int inc) {
        scrollbar.setBlockIncrement(inc);
    }
}
```

The Adjustable Interface

The java.awt.Adjustable interface defines methods for setting and getting
the properties associated with an adjustable object—value, minimum, maximum,
etc. The applet shown in Figure 15-2 implements a control panel for dynamically
changing the properties of a slider and exercises all of the methods in the
Adjustable interface.

The SliderTest applet creates an instance of ControlPanel and an instance
of Slider, specifying the former as the north component and the latter as the
center component of the applet itself.

```
public class SliderTest extends Applet {
    private Slider       slider       = new Slider(35,10,0,100);
    private ControlPanel controlPanel = new ControlPanel(slider);

    public void init() {
        setLayout(new BorderLayout(10,10));
        add(controlPanel, "North");
        add(slider, "Center");
    }
}
```

`ControlPanel` employs an instance of `GridBagLayout` to lay out two columns, where the left column consists of labels and the right column consists of controls (mostly textfields). We'll show you the applet in its entirety, but we won't discuss the use of `GridBagLayout` for the `ControlPanel`. "The GridBagLayout Layout Manager" on page 356 provides an in-depth discussion of `GridBagLayout`.

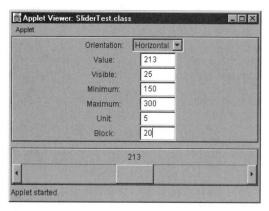

Figure 15-2 `SliderTest` Applet
The applet allows the properties of a slider (scrollbar) to be modified and tracked.

`ControlPanel` first instantiates its components.

```
class ControlPanel extends    BorderedPanel
                   implements AdjustmentListener {
   private Slider slider;

   private Label orientLabel  = new Label("Orientation:"),
                 valueLabel   = new Label("Value:"),
                 minLabel     = new Label("Minimum:"),
                 maxLabel     = new Label("Maximum:"),
                 visibleLabel = new Label("Visible:"),
                 unitLabel    = new Label("Unit:"),
                 blockLabel   = new Label("Block:");

   private Choice orientChoice = new Choice();
```

```
private TextField valueField   = new TextField(5),
                  minField     = new TextField(5),
                  maxField     = new TextField(5),
                  visibleField = new TextField(5),
                  unitField    = new TextField(5),
                  blockField   = new TextField(5);
```

The `ControlPanel` constructor takes a reference to the slider it manipulates and adds itself as an *adjustment listener* of the slider. Remember that the slider implements the `Adjustable` interface and delegates `Adjustable` methods to the enclosed scrollbar, so adjustment listeners can be added to the slider, which in turn adds them to the scrollbar itself.

```
public ControlPanel(Slider aSlider) {
    slider = aSlider;
    slider.addAdjustmentListener(this);
    readSliderValues();
...
}
```

Whenever the slider's value changes, the control panel's `adjustmentValueChanged()` is invoked to obtain the current value for the slider and to set the value of the `valueField` textfield appropriately.

```
public void adjustmentValueChanged(AdjustmentEvent e) {
    valueField.setText(Integer.toString(slider.getValue()));
}
```

After adding itself as an adjustment listener for the slider, the control panel reads in the initial values of the slider by invoking `Adjustable` methods implemented by the slider.

```
void readSliderValues() {
    String value = Integer.toString(slider.getValue()),
        min    = Integer.toString(slider.getMinimum()),
        max    = Integer.toString(slider.getMaximum()),
        vis    = Integer.toString(slider.getVisibleAmount()),
        unit   = Integer.toString(slider.getUnitIncrement()),
        blck   = Integer.toString(slider.getBlockIncrement());

    valueField.setText   (value);
    minField.setText     (min);
    maxField.setText     (max);
    visibleField.setText (vis);
    unitField.setText    (unit);
    blockField.setText   (blck);
}
```

In addition to updating the text displayed in the `valueField` textfield whenever the slider's value changes, we also want the properties of the slider to be updated whenever a value is specified in the control panel. This goal is accomplished by adding action listeners to all of the textfields in the control panel.[1]

```
valueField.addActionListener(new ActionListener() {
     public void actionPerformed(ActionEvent event) {
        slider.setValue(
           Integer.parseInt(valueField.getText()));
     }
});
visibleField.addActionListener(new ActionListener() {
     public void actionPerformed(ActionEvent event) {
        slider.setVisibleAmount(
           Integer.parseInt(visibleField.getText()));
     }
});
minField.addActionListener(new ActionListener() {
     public void actionPerformed(ActionEvent event) {
        slider.setMinimum(
           Integer.parseInt(minField.getText()));
     }
});
maxField.addActionListener(new ActionListener() {
     public void actionPerformed(ActionEvent event) {
        slider.setMaximum(
           Integer.parseInt(maxField.getText()));
     }
});
unitField.addActionListener(new ActionListener() {
     public void actionPerformed(ActionEvent event) {
        slider.setUnitIncrement(
           Integer.parseInt(unitField.getText()));
     }
});
blockField.addActionListener(new ActionListener() {
     public void actionPerformed(ActionEvent event) {
        slider.setBlockIncrement(
           Integer.parseInt(blockField.getText()));
     }
});
```

The action listeners for the textfields all invoke `TextField.getText()` to obtain the string currently displayed in the textfield, which is then passed to `Integer.parseInt()`, which returns an integer value.[2] Once we have the

---

1. A textfield fires an action event whenever enter is typed in the textfield. See "Action Events" on page 270.
2. Of course, the value typed into the textfield must be a valid integer value, or an exception will be thrown, which we do not bother to catch.

integer value in hand, it is passed to the appropriate `Adjustable` method implemented by the slider (which is in turn passed to the scrollbar contained in the slider).

An item listener that controls the orientation of the slider is added to the choice.

```
orientChoice.addItemListener(new ItemListener() {
    public void itemStateChanged(ItemEvent event) {
        int index = orientChoice.getSelectedIndex();

        if(index == 0)
            slider.setOrientation(Scrollbar.HORIZONTAL);
        else
            slider.setOrientation(Scrollbar.VERTICAL);

        readSliderValues();
    }
});
```

There are a couple of points of interest here. First, note that we could take a peek in the `java.awt.Scrollbar` class and discover the following:

```
public class Scrollbar extends Component implements Adjustable {
    public static final intHORIZONTAL = 0;
    public static final intVERTICAL   = 1;
    . . .
}
```

Having knowledge of the explicit values for `Scrollbar.HORIZONTAL` and `Scrollbar.VERTICAL`, coupled with the fact that indices for a choice start at zero, we could simplify the implementation of the item listener associated with the `orientChoice`, like so:

```
orientChoice.addItemListener(new ItemListener() {
    public void itemStateChanged(ItemEvent event) {
        slider.setOrientation(orientChoice.getSelectedIndex());
        readSliderValues();
    }
});
```

How_ver, we would be committing one of the cardinal object-oriented sins: relying upon the implementation of a class. If, in the future, the `Scrollbar` class changed the values of the `HORIZONTAL` and `VERTICAL` constants, our not-so-clever shortcut would break. As a result, we opt for a few more lines of code to ensure that our code will continue to work even if the implementation of `Scrollbar` changes.[3]

---

3. Of course, the values for the constants must still be integers, but we can only do so much.

Second, we invoke `readSliderValues()` after changing the orientation because we found that some of the scrollbar's values are reset when the orientation of the scrollbar is modified, resulting in our fields being out of synch.

The `SliderTest` applet is shown in Example 15-3.

Example 15-3 `SliderTest` Applet

```
import java.applet.Applet;
import java.awt.*;
import java.awt.event.*;

public class SliderTest extends Applet {
    private Slider        slider      = new Slider(35,10,0,100);
    private ControlPanel controlPanel = new ControlPanel(slider);

    public void init() {
        setLayout(new BorderLayout(10,10));
        add(controlPanel, "North");
        add(slider, "Center");
    }
}
class ControlPanel extends      BorderedPanel
                   implements AdjustmentListener {
    private Slider slider;

    private Label orientLabel  = new Label("Orientation:"),
                  valueLabel   = new Label("Value:"),
                  minLabel     = new Label("Minimum:"),
                  maxLabel     = new Label("Maximum:"),
                  visibleLabel = new Label("Visible:"),
                  unitLabel    = new Label("Unit:"),
                  blockLabel   = new Label("Block:");

    private Choice orientChoice = new Choice();

    private TextField valueField   = new TextField(5),
                      minField     = new TextField(5),
                      maxField     = new TextField(5),
                    visibleField = new TextField(5),
                      unitField    = new TextField(5),
                      blockField   = new TextField(5);

    public void adjustmentValueChanged(AdjustmentEvent e) {
        valueField.setText(Integer.toString(slider.getValue()));
    }
    public ControlPanel(Slider aSlider) {
        slider = aSlider;
        slider.addAdjustmentListener(this);
        readSliderValues();

        GridBagLayout        gbl = new GridBagLayout();
```

```
GridBagConstraints gbc = new GridBagConstraints();

orientChoice.add("Horizontal");
orientChoice.add("Vertical");

setLayout(gbl);

gbc.gridwidth = 1;
gbl.setConstraints(orientLabel, gbc);
add(orientLabel);

gbc.gridwidth = GridBagConstraints.REMAINDER;
gbl.setConstraints(orientChoice, gbc);
add(orientChoice);

gbc.gridwidth = 1;
gbl.setConstraints(valueLabel, gbc);
add(valueLabel);

gbc.gridwidth = GridBagConstraints.REMAINDER;
gbl.setConstraints(valueField, gbc);
add(valueField);

gbc.gridwidth = 1;
gbl.setConstraints(visibleLabel, gbc);
add(visibleLabel);

gbc.gridwidth = GridBagConstraints.REMAINDER;
gbl.setConstraints(visibleField, gbc);
add(visibleField);

gbc.gridwidth = 1;
gbl.setConstraints(minLabel, gbc);
add(minLabel);

gbc.gridwidth = GridBagConstraints.REMAINDER;
gbl.setConstraints(minField, gbc);
add(minField);

gbc.gridwidth = 1;
gbl.setConstraints(maxLabel, gbc);
add(maxLabel);

gbc.gridwidth = GridBagConstraints.REMAINDER;
gbl.setConstraints(maxField, gbc);
add(maxField);

gbc.gridwidth = 1;
gbl.setConstraints(unitLabel, gbc);
add(unitLabel);

gbc.gridwidth = GridBagConstraints.REMAINDER;
```

```
    gbl.setConstraints(unitField, gbc);
    add(unitField);

    gbc.gridwidth = 1;
    gbl.setConstraints(blockLabel, gbc);
    add(blockLabel);

    gbc.gridwidth = GridBagConstraints.REMAINDER;
    gbl.setConstraints(blockField, gbc);
    add(blockField);

    orientChoice.addItemListener(new ItemListener() {
        public void itemStateChanged(ItemEvent event) {
            int index = orientChoice.getSelectedIndex();

            if(index == 0)
                slider.setOrientation(Scrollbar.HORIZONTAL);
            else
                slider.setOrientation(Scrollbar.VERTICAL);

            readSliderValues();
        }
    });
    valueField.addActionListener(new ActionListener() {
        public void actionPerformed(ActionEvent event) {
            slider.setValue(
                Integer.parseInt(valueField.getText()));
        }
    });
    visibleField.addActionListener(new ActionListener() {
        public void actionPerformed(ActionEvent event) {
            slider.setVisibleAmount(
                Integer.parseInt(visibleField.getText()));
        }
    });
    minField.addActionListener(new ActionListener() {
        public void actionPerformed(ActionEvent event) {
            slider.setMinimum(
                Integer.parseInt(minField.getText()));
        }
    });
    maxField.addActionListener(new ActionListener() {
        public void actionPerformed(ActionEvent event) {
            slider.setMaximum(
                Integer.parseInt(maxField.getText()));
        }
    });
    unitField.addActionListener(new ActionListener() {
        public void actionPerformed(ActionEvent event) {
            slider.setUnitIncrement(
                Integer.parseInt(unitField.getText()));
        }
```

```
        });
        blockField.addActionListener(new ActionListener() {
            public void actionPerformed(ActionEvent event) {
                slider.setBlockIncrement(
                    Integer.parseInt(blockField.getText()));
            }
        });
    }
    void readSliderValues() {
        String value = Integer.toString(slider.getValue()),
               min   = Integer.toString(slider.getMinimum()),
               max   = Integer.toString(slider.getMaximum()),
               vis   = Integer.toString(slider.getVisibleAmount()),
               unit  = Integer.toString(slider.getUnitIncrement()),
               blck  = Integer.toString(
                                  slider.getBlockIncrement());

        valueField.setText   (value);
        minField.setText     (min);
        maxField.setText     (max);
        visibleField.setText (vis);
        unitField.setText    (unit);
        blockField.setText   (blck);
    }
}
```

java.awt.ScrollPane

If you've had to manually implement scrolling with the previous versions of the AWT, you'll surely appreciate the `java.awt.ScrollPane` class, which made its debut in the 1.1 release of the AWT.

`java.awt.ScrollPane` is a container, although it differs from other AWT containers in two ways:

- Its layout manager is `null` and cannot be set.
- It can contain only one component at a time.

`ScrollPane` has a `null` layout manager;[4] its peer controls the placement of the scrollbars and the viewport. As a result, `ScrollPane` does not allow its layout manager to be set. `ScrollPane.setLayout()`, which is implemented as `final` so that it cannot be overridden in extensions, throws an exception if invoked.

---

4.   `Containers` have `null` layout managers by default.

ScrollPane overrides Container.addImpl()[5] to ensure that the scrollpane always contains exactly one component. Therefore, if you invoke any of the add methods provided by the Container class on a scrollpane, the existing component contained in the scrollpane will be removed and the component added will be the only component contained in the scrollpane. Of course, the component contained in a scrollpane may be a container, so a scrollpane can scroll more than one component at a time.

ScrollPane also allows a scrollbar display policy to be set at construction time only. The valid constants for the scrollbar display policy are:

- ScrollPane.SCROLLBARS_AS_NEEDED (Default)
- ScrollPane.SCROLLBARS_ALWAYS
- ScrollPane.SCROLLBARS_NEVER

As you can probably guess, setting the display policy to SCROLLBARS_AS_NEEDED results in scrollbars being displayed only if the component being scrolled is larger than the scrollpane itself, whereas setting the display policy SCROLLBARS_ALWAYS or SCROLLBARS_NEVER results in scrollbars being displayed all the time or never, respectively. SCROLLBARS_AS_NEEDED is the default display policy if you construct an instance of ScrollPane without specifying a policy. You may wonder why the third option is provided at all—what good is a scrollpane if the contents cannot be scrolled? The answer is that a scrollpane can still be scrolled programmatically even if no scrollbars are displayed. We'll discuss programmatic scrolling a little later on.

Scrolling Components

Our first applet concerning the Scrollpane class is shown in Figure 15-3. The applet scrolls components and provides a button that toggles the component currently contained in the scrollpane. The components that are scrolled are both extensions of Panel. One of the panels contains 50 buttons, and the other contains 100 labels. The buttons and labels are laid out in a simplistic fashion with instances of GridBagLayout.

As you can see from Figure 15-3, the scrollbars in the scrollpane adjust to accommodate the size of the component being scrolled.

---

5. Container.addImpl is a protected method that is invoked by the overloaded add methods in the Container class.

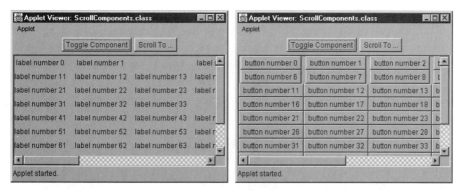

Figure 15-3 A `ScrollPane` That Toggles the Containers It Scrolls

A scrollpane is quite simple to use. For instance, the applet shown in Figure 15-3 initially creates the two panels that will be displayed in the scrollpane, the scrollpane itself. Subsequently, the `ManyLabelsPanel` instance is added to the scrollbar.

```
public class ScrollComponents extends Applet {
    private ScrollPane scroller;
    private ManyLabelsPanel labels;
    private ManyButtonsPanel buttons;

    public void init() {
        setCursor(
            Cursor.getPredefinedCursor(Cursor.WAIT_CURSOR));

        labels = new ManyLabelsPanel();
        buttons= new ManyButtonsPanel();
        scroller = new ScrollPane();

        scroller.add(labels);

        setLayout(new BorderLayout());
        add(new TogglePanel(scroller, labels, buttons), "North");
        add(scroller, "Center");
    }
    public void start() {
        setCursor(
            Cursor.getPredefinedCursor(Cursor.DEFAULT_CURSOR));
    }
}
```

In fact, since scrolling is handled automatically by the scrollpane, the rest of the applet consists only of the implementation of the toggle panel that contains a button for toggling the component being scrolled and another button for programmatically scrolling the component. Since we'll discuss programmatic scrolling later, we won't repeat that discussion here; instead, we'll show you the code pertinent to toggling the component currently displayed in the scrollpane.

```
toggleButton.addActionListener(new ActionListener() {
    public void actionPerformed(ActionEvent event) {
        if(scroller.getComponent(0) == labels)
            scroller.add(buttons);
        else
            scroller.add(labels);

        scroller.getParent().validate();
    }
});
```

A reference is obtained to the first component contained in the scrollpane by invoking `Container.getComponent()` and passing an index of zero, which returns the first—and only—component in the scrollpane. If the component currently being scrolled is the panel with labels, then the panel with buttons is added to the scrollpane, and vice versa.

After the component is added to the scrollpane, `validate()` is invoked on the scrollpane's container in order to force the scrollpane to be laid out, which updates the scrollbars associated with the scrollpane. It is not necessary to remove the current component before adding a component because, as we mentioned previously, that is taken care of automatically.

The entire applet is listed in Example 15-4.

Example 15-4 ScrollComponents Applet

```
import java.applet.Applet;
import java.awt.*;
import java.awt.event.*;

public class ScrollComponents extends Applet {
    private ScrollPane scroller;
    private ManyLabelsPanel labels;
    private ManyButtonsPanel buttons;

    public void init() {
        setCursor(
            Cursor.getPredefinedCursor(Cursor.WAIT_CURSOR));

        labels = new ManyLabelsPanel();
        buttons= new ManyButtonsPanel();
```

```
        scroller = new ScrollPane();

        scroller.add(labels);

        setLayout(new BorderLayout());
        add(new TogglePanel(scroller, labels, buttons), "North");
        add(scroller, "Center");
    }
    public void start() {
        setCursor(
            Cursor.getPredefinedCursor(Cursor.DEFAULT_CURSOR));
    }
}
class TogglePanel extends Panel {
    Button   toggleButton = new Button("Toggle Component");
    Button   scrollButton = new Button("Scroll To ...");
    ScrollDialog dialog;
    ScrollPane scroller;
    ManyButtonsPanel buttons;
    ManyLabelsPanel      labels;

    public TogglePanel(ScrollPane scrollpane,
                       ManyLabelsPanel store,
                   ManyButtonsPanel panel) {
        this.labels = store;
        this.buttons    = panel;
        this.scroller   = scrollpane;

        add(toggleButton);
        add(scrollButton);

        scrollButton.addActionListener(new ActionListener() {
            public void actionPerformed(ActionEvent event) {
                Point loc = TogglePanel.this.getLocationOnScreen();

                if(dialog ==null) {
                    dialog = new ScrollDialog(scroller);
                }
                dialog.setLocation(loc.x, loc.y);
                dialog.show();
            }
        });

        toggleButton.addActionListener(new ActionListener() {
            public void actionPerformed(ActionEvent event) {
                if(scroller.getComponent(0) == labels)
                    scroller.add(buttons);
                else
                    scroller.add(labels);

                scroller.getParent().validate();
            }
```

```
            });
      }
}
class ManyButtonsPanel extends Panel {
   GridBagLayout gbl = new GridBagLayout();
   GridBagConstraints gbc = new GridBagConstraints();

   public ManyButtonsPanel() {
      setLayout(gbl);

      for(int i=0; i < 50; ++i) {
         if(i != 0 && i % 5 == 0)
            gbc.gridwidth = GridBagConstraints.REMAINDER;
         else
            gbc.gridwidth = 1;

         add(new Button("button number " + i), gbc);
      }
   }
}
class ManyLabelsPanel extends Panel {
   GridBagLayout gbl = new GridBagLayout();
   GridBagConstraints gbc = new GridBagConstraints();

   public ManyLabelsPanel() {
      setLayout(gbl);

      for(int i=0; i < 100; ++i) {
         if(i != 0 && i % 10 == 0)
            gbc.gridwidth = GridBagConstraints.REMAINDER;
         else
            gbc.gridwidth = 1;

         add(new Label("label number " + i), gbc);
      }
   }
}
```

Scrolling Images

So far, we've seen how to scroll a component, but what if you need to scroll an image? Images are not components, and therefore an image cannot be added to a scrollpane. The answer, of course, is to stick the image in a container and then add the container to the scrollpane, which is just what our next applet does, shown in Figure 15-4.

The first order of business, therefore, is to implement a container that contains an image.

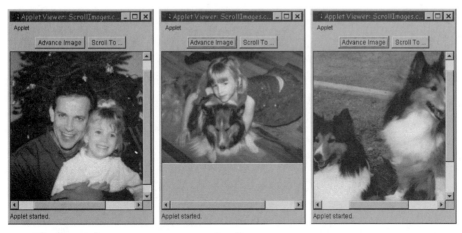

Figure 15-4 ScrollImage Applet
A scrollpane that cycles through an array of pictures. The
Advance Image button advances the image to the next one in the
array.

```
class ImageCanvas extends Canvas {
    private Image image;

    public ImageCanvas(Image image) {
        MediaTracker mt = new MediaTracker(this);
        mt.addImage(image, 0);

        try                 { mt.waitForID(0);       }
        catch(Exception e) { e.printStackTrace(); }

        this.image = image;
    }
    public void paint(Graphics g) {
        g.drawImage(image, 0, 0, this);
    }
    public void update(Graphics g) {
        paint(g);
    }
    public Dimension getPreferredSize() {
        return new Dimension(image.getWidth(this),
                             image.getHeight(this));
    }
}
```

The `ImageCanvas` constructor waits for the image it was passed to load; the image is drawn in the `ImageCanvas.paint` method. Notice that we've also overridden `update()` to invoke `paint()` directly; otherwise, the canvas will be cleared each time `update()` is called. Also, we've overridden `getPreferredSize()` to return the width and height of the image.

The applet itself creates a scrollpane and loads up an array of images, in addition to creating a control panel that will contain the advance image and scroll buttons. The control panel is added to the applet as the north component, and the scrollpane is added as the center component.

```
public class ScrollImages extends Applet {
    private ScrollPane   scroller = new ScrollPane();
    private Image[]      images   = new Image[4];

    public void init() {
        loadImages(getCodeBase());

        scroller = new ScrollPane();
        scroller.add(new ImageCanvas(images[0]));

        setLayout(new BorderLayout());
        add(new ControlPanel(scroller, images), "North");
        add(scroller, "Center");
    }
    private void loadImages(URL base) {
        images[0] = getImage(base, "gifs/ashleyAndRoy.gif");
        images[1] = getImage(base, "gifs/ashleyAndSabre.gif");
        images[2] = getImage(base, "gifs/anjinAndMariko.gif");
        images[3] = getImage(base, "gifs/ashleyAndAnjin.gif");
    }
}
```

As with our previous applet, the only point of interest left to discuss is the advancing of the images, which is done by the Advance button in the control panel.

```
advanceButton.addActionListener(new ActionListener() {
    public void actionPerformed(ActionEvent event) {
        Container container = scroller.getParent();

        container.setCursor(Cursor.getPredefinedCursor(
                            Cursor.WAIT_CURSOR));

        curImage = (curImage == images.length - 1) ?
                    0 : curImage + 1;

        scroller.add(new ImageCanvas(images[curImage]));
        container.validate();
```

```
container.setCursor(Cursor.getPredefinedCursor(
                           Cursor.DEFAULT_CURSOR));
    }
});
```

Since the image may take a perceptible amount of time to load, we set the scrollpane container's cursor to the wait cursor before creating a new instance of image canvas, and then reset to the default cursor after we're done creating and adding the new image canvas to the scrollpane. Note that as before, we invoke `validate()` on the scrollpane's container to force the scrollpane to be laid out.

The entire applet is listed in Figure 15-4.

Example 15-5 ScrollImages Applet

```
import java.applet.Applet;
import java.net.URL;
import java.awt.*;
import java.awt.event.*;

public class ScrollImages extends Applet {
    private ScrollPane  scroller = new ScrollPane();
    private Image[]      images   = new Image[4];

    public void init() {
        loadImages(getCodeBase());

        scroller = new ScrollPane();
        scroller.add(new ImageCanvas(images[0]));

        setLayout(new BorderLayout());
        add(new ControlPanel(scroller, images), "North");
        add(scroller, "Center");
    }
    private void loadImages(URL base) {
        images[0] = getImage(base, "gifs/ashleyAndRoy.gif");
        images[1] = getImage(base, "gifs/ashleyAndSabre.gif");
        images[2] = getImage(base, "gifs/anjinAndMariko.gif");
        images[3] = getImage(base, "gifs/ashleyAndAnjin.gif");
    }
}
class ControlPanel extends Panel {
    ScrollPane    scroller;
    ScrollDialog  dialog;
    Button        advanceButton = new Button("Advance Image");
    Button        scrollButton  = new Button("Scroll To ...");
    Image[]       images;
    int           curImage = 0;

    public ControlPanel(ScrollPane scrollpane, Image[] pics) {
        scroller = scrollpane;
        images   = pics;
```

```
            advanceButton.addActionListener(new ActionListener() {
                public void actionPerformed(ActionEvent event) {
                    Container container = scroller.getParent();

                    container.setCursor(Cursor.getPredefinedCursor(
                                     Cursor.WAIT_CURSOR));

                    curImage = (curImage == images.length - 1) ?
                             0 : curImage + 1;

                    scroller.add(new ImageCanvas(images[curImage]));
                    container.validate();

                    container.setCursor(Cursor.getPredefinedCursor(
                                     Cursor.DEFAULT_CURSOR));
                }
            });
            scrollButton.addActionListener(new ActionListener() {
                public void actionPerformed(ActionEvent event) {
                    Point loc =
                            ControlPanel.this.getLocationOnScreen();

                    if(dialog ==null) {
                        dialog = new ScrollDialog(scroller);
                    }
                    dialog.setLocation(loc.x, loc.y);
                    dialog.setVisible(true);
                }
            });
            add(advanceButton);
            add(scrollButton);
        }
    }
    class ImageCanvas extends Canvas {
        private Image image;

        public ImageCanvas(Image image) {
            MediaTracker mt = new MediaTracker(this);
            mt.addImage(image, 0);

            try                { mt.waitForID(0);     }
            catch(Exception e) { e.printStackTrace(); }

            this.image = image;
        }
        public void paint(Graphics g) {
            g.drawImage(image, 0, 0, this);
        }
        public void update(Graphics g) {
            paint(g);
        }
```

```
    public Dimension getPreferredSize() {
        return new Dimension(image.getWidth(this),
                             image.getHeight(this));
    }
}
```

Programmatic Scrolling

Scrollpanes also support programmatic scrolling by providing an overloaded
`setScrollPosition` method; one version of the method takes two integer
values, and the other takes a point. For the `setScrollPosition` methods to
work, the scrollpane must contain a component and the point specified must be
valid. A valid point lies within the following boundary:

- X: 0
- Y: 0
- Width: Width of component — width of viewport
- Height: Height of component — height of viewport

The size of the component, of course, can be obtained by invoking
`Component.getSize()`, and the size of the viewport can be obtained by
invoking `ScrollPane.getViewportSize()`. The size of the viewport is the
size of the scrollpane minus the scrollpane's insets. The insets account for the
width or height of the vertical or horizontal scrollbars, respectively, and any
borders drawn by the scrollpane's peer.

The applets discussed previously for scrolling components and images both
contain a provision for programmatic scrolling. Each applet contains a Scroll To
button that brings up a dialog for setting the x and y values to scroll to. The applet
and dialog are shown in Figure 15-5.

The Scroll To buttons have an action listener that shows the dialog—the dialog is
created if necessary, and its position is set to the upper left-hand corner of the
panel containing the Scroll To button. The code below is from the `ScrollImages`
applet:

```
scrollButton.addActionListener(new ActionListener() {
    public void actionPerformed(ActionEvent event) {
        Point loc = ControlPanel.this.getLocationOnScreen();

        if(dialog ==null) {
            dialog = new ScrollDialog(scroller);
        }
        dialog.setLocation(loc.x, loc.y);
        dialog.setVisible(true);
    }
});
```

Figure 15-5 Programmatically Scrolling a `ScrollPane`
A dialog allows the scrollpane in the applet to be scrolled
programmatically.

`Component.getLocationOnScreen()` is used to get the position of the
control panel, which is then used to set the dialog's location. Notice that the
dialog is passed the scrollpane when it is constructed.

The dialog contains two buttons—a Scroll button and a Done button. The action
listener for the scroll button invokes the dialog's `scroll` method, which extracts
the values from the textfields and invokes `setScrollPosition()` on the
scrollpane passed to the dialog's constructor.

```
scrollButton.addActionListener(new ActionListener() {
    public void actionPerformed(ActionEvent event) {
        scroll ();
    }
});
...
void scroll() {
    scroller.setScrollPosition(
        Integer.parseInt(xField.getText()),
        Integer.parseInt(yField.getText()));
}
```

The Done button's action listener checks to see if the current scroll position of the
scrollpane is different from the values in the textfields, and if so, it also invokes
`scroll()` before disposing of the dialog.[6]

```
doneButton.addActionListener(new ActionListener() {
    public void actionPerformed(ActionEvent event) {
        Point pos = scroller.getScrollPosition();
        int   x   = Integer.parseInt(xField.getText());
        int   y   = Integer.parseInt(yField.getText());

        if(pos.x != x || pos.y != y)
            scroll ();

        dispose();
    }
});
```

Finally, we've also added an instance of `FieldListener`, a named inner class of `ScrollDialog`, to the two textfields so that an `enter` typed into the textfield will also invoke the `scroll` method.

```
...
xField.addActionListener(listener);
yField.addActionListener(listener);
...

class FieldListener implements ActionListener {
    public void actionPerformed(ActionEvent event) {
        scroll();
    }
}
```

We should point out that our simple example performs no error checking, so, for instance, typing a value into the `xField` textfield and subsequently typing `enter` without typing a value into the `yField` textfield will result in an exception being thrown.

`ScrollPane` is a welcome addition to the AWT and is really an essential component for an industrial-strength user interface toolkit. The code for the `ScrollDialog` class is listed in Example 15-6.

Example 15-6 `ScrollDialog` Class Listing

```
import java.awt.*;
import java.awt.event.*;

public class ScrollDialog extends Dialog {
    private ScrollPane scroller;
    private Panel      buttonPanel  = new Panel();
    private Panel      controlPanel = new Panel();
```

---

6. See "Window.dispose() Disposes of the Window's Resources, Not the AWT Component" on page 579.

```java
private Button doneButton   = new Button("Done");
private Button scrollButton = new Button("Scroll");

private Label xLabel = new Label("X:"),
              yLabel = new Label("Y:");

private TextField xField = new TextField(3),
                  yField = new TextField(3);

public ScrollDialog(ScrollPane scrollpane) {
    super(getFrame(scrollpane), "Scroll To");
    FieldListener listener = new FieldListener();
    this.scroller = scrollpane;

    GridBagLayout      gbl = new GridBagLayout();
    GridBagConstraints gbc = new GridBagConstraints();

    controlPanel.setLayout(gbl);

    gbl.setConstraints(xLabel, gbc);
    controlPanel.add(xLabel);

    gbc.gridwidth = GridBagConstraints.REMAINDER;
    gbl.setConstraints(xField, gbc);
    controlPanel.add(xField);

    gbc.gridwidth = 1;
    gbl.setConstraints(yLabel, gbc);
    controlPanel.add(yLabel);

    gbc.gridwidth = GridBagConstraints.REMAINDER;
    gbl.setConstraints(yField, gbc);
    controlPanel.add(yField);

    buttonPanel.add(doneButton);
    buttonPanel.add(scrollButton);

    setLayout(new BorderLayout());
    add(controlPanel, "Center");
    add(buttonPanel, "South");

    xField.addActionListener(listener);
    yField.addActionListener(listener);

    scrollButton.addActionListener(new ActionListener() {
        public void actionPerformed(ActionEvent event) {
            scroll ();
        }
    });
    doneButton.addActionListener(new ActionListener() {
        public void actionPerformed(ActionEvent event) {
            Point pos = scroller.getScrollPosition();
```

```
            int    x    = Integer.parseInt(xField.getText());
            int    y    = Integer.parseInt(yField.getText());

            if(pos.x != x || pos.y != y)
                scroll ();

            dispose();
        }
    });
}
class FieldListener implements ActionListener {
    public void actionPerformed(ActionEvent event) {
        scroll();
    }
}
public void show() {
    pack();
    xField.requestFocus();
    super.show();
}
void scroll() {
    scroller.setScrollPosition(
        Integer.parseInt(xField.getText()).
        Integer.parseInt(yField.getText()));
}
static Frame getFrame(Component c) {
    Frame      frame = null;

    while((c = c.getParent()) != null) {
        if(c instanceof Frame)
            frame = (Frame)c;
    }
    return frame;
}
}
```

Summary

The 1.1 version of the AWT introduced the ScrollPane class, which makes scrolling a component a snap. Additionally, the AWT also provides a scrollbar class, in the event that you wish to take scrolling into your own hands.

In this chapter we've discussed scrollbars and scrollpanes at length and provided applets that scroll both components and images.

CHAPTER 16

Windows, Frames, and Dialogs

The AWT provides three components that display a window on screen: Window, Frame, and Dialog.[1] While all three components are windows, the differences between the three are not always readily apparent, and therefore it can sometimes be difficult to decide which component to use in a given situation. To clarify, we have summarized the properties of the three components in Table 16-1.

Table 16-1 Window, Frame, and Dialog Properties [1,2]

Property	Window	Frame	Dialog
Modal	No	No	No/CSG
Resizable	No	Yes/SG	Yes/SG
TitleBar	No	Yes	Yes
Border	No	Yes	Yes
Title	No	Yes/CSG	Yes/CSG
Menubar	No	Yes/SG	No
Focus Manager	Yes	Yes	Yes

1. There's also FileDialog, which we will discuss later on.

Table 16-1 Window, Frame, and Dialog Properties (Continued)[1,2]

Property	Window	Frame	Dialog
Warning String	Yes/G	Yes/G	Yes/G
Icon Image[3]	No	Yes/SG	No
Anchored To A Frame	Yes	No	Yes

1. Yes/No refers to default status of the property.
2. C = settable at construction time, S = setter method available,
   G = getter method available (either get...() or is...()).
3. Not all platforms support iconizing windows.

java.awt.Window is the most basic component of the three and, in fact, is the superclass of both Frame and Dialog. Windows have no border, titlebar, or menubar and cannot be resized. Windows are best suited for displaying something in a borderless rectangular region that needs to float on top of other components, such as a splash screen for displaying product information, or bubble help for a component, both of which we will take the time to explore shortly.

java.awt.Frame is an extension of Window that comes with a border and a titlebar and is resizable. Additionally, you can attach a menubar to a frame, as we have discussed at length in "Menus" on page 597. Frames are the component of choice when an application window that is required needs to be iconized or fitted with a menubar.

java.awt.Dialog is also an extension of Window that, like a frame, comes with a border and a titlebar and is resizable. Unlike a frame, a dialog cannot support a menubar, and dialogs can be modal, whereas frames and windows cannot. Dialogs are the window of choice when a temporary window is required to capture user input. The AWT also provides a lone extension of java.awt.Dialog—FileDialog, for selecting a file name to load or save.

Another thing to note is that windows and dialogs must be anchored to a frame, meaning that a frame must be passed to the Window and Dialog constructors. While this may seem somewhat limiting, it should be noted that the frame does not have to be visible, an important loophole that we'll take advantage of when discussing splash screens, for instance.

java.awt.Window

`java.awt.Window` is the superclass for both `Frame` and `Dialog` and provides a good deal of functionality for both of its extensions. Table 16-2 lists the public methods provided by `java.awt.Window` (we've omitted some overridden `Component` methods, such as `addNotify()`).

Table 16-2 `java.awt.Window` **Public Methods**

Method	Description
`void pack()`	Sets the size of the window to the minimum size that will display all contained components
`void show()`	Makes the window visible. If the window is already visible, it is brought to the front of all other windows.
`boolean isShowing()`	Returns `true` if the window is showing; `false` otherwise
`void dispose()`	Hides the window and disposes of the platform-dependent resources used by the window
`void toFront()`	Places the window in front of all other windows
`void toBack()`	Places the window behind all other windows
`String getWarningString()`	Returns the warning string
`void addWindowListener( WindowListener)`	Adds a `WindowListener` to the window
`void removeWindowListener( WindowListener)`	Removes a `WindowListener` from the window
`Component getFocusOwner()`	Returns the component that currently has keyboard focus
`InputContext getInputContext()`	Returns the window's input context
`Locale getLocale()`	Returns the locale associated with the window
`Window[] getOwnedWindows()`	Returns an array of windows owned by this window
`Window getOwner()`	Returns the window's parent window
`Toolkit getToolkit()`	Returns the window's toolkit

As indicated in Table 16-2, windows fire window events by virtue of the fact that window listeners can be added and removed to and from a window. See Table 9-3 on page 249 for a list of the methods defined by the `WindowListener` interface, and see Table 9-3 on page 249 for a list of the methods defined by the `WindowEvent` class.

Windows can also provide a reference to the component they contain that currently has keyboard focus. Each `Window` keeps a `FocusMgr` around to track the focus among the window's components. `Window.getFocusOwner()` asks the focus manager for a reference to the currently selected component and then passes it back. See "Standard AWT Components and Keyboard Traversal" on page 630 for more information on keyboard traversal.

Splash Screen

In addition to providing basic windowing functionality for frames and dialogs, the `java.awt.Window` class is useful in its own right. We'll start off with a Java application that displays a splash screen—a window that typically displays product information while an application loads. Our splash screen will display an image for ten seconds and then exit. The splash screen is shown in Figure 16-1.

The application creates a window that contains an image canvas that in turn displays the image. After the window and the image canvas are created, the location of the splash screen is calculated, using `Toolkit.getScreenSize()`, which returns the size in pixels of the desktop. Subsequently the window is shown and placed in front of all other windows.

```java
public class SplashTest extends Frame {
    Toolkit toolkit = Toolkit.getDefaultToolkit();
    Window  window;
    Image   image;

    static public void main(String[] args) {
        Frame frame = new SplashTest();
    }
    public SplashTest() {
        ImageCanvas canvas;

        window  = new Window(this);
        image   = toolkit.getImage("gifs/saint.gif");
        canvas  = new ImageCanvas(image);

        window.add(canvas, "Center");
```

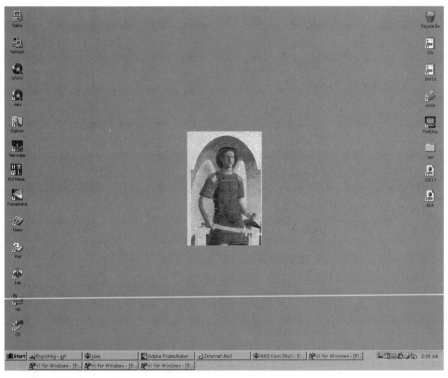

Figure 16-1 Splash Screen

A Java application displays a splash screen centered on the
desktop when it starts up. The splash screen is implemented with
a java.awt.Window.

```
Dimension   scrnSize  = toolkit.getScreenSize();
int         imgWidth  = image.getWidth(this),
            imgHeight = image.getHeight(this);

window.setLocation(scrnSize.width/2  - (imgWidth/2),
                   scrnSize.height/2 - (imgHeight/2));
window.setSize(imgWidth,imgHeight);
window.show();
window.toFront();

try { Thread.currentThread().sleep(10000); }
catch(Exception e) { e.printStackTrace(); }

window.dispose();
System.exit(0);
   }
}
```

There are a few points to note about the `SplashTest` class. First, note that we've explicitly resized the window instead of invoking `pack()` because `pack()` was not up to the task under Solaris. `Window.pack()` resizes (and lays out) the window so that it is just big enough to hold all of the components it contains. Under Windows 95, `pack()` worked just fine.

Second, we have invoked `toFront()` immediately after the call to `show()`. While you might expect `show()` to bring the window being shown to the front, that is not necessarily the case on all platforms, so if you want the window to come to the front when it is shown, you should call `toFront()` after invoking `show()`. Note that `show()` is guaranteed to bring the window to the front if the window is already visible, but the window will not necessarily be brought to the front if it is not already visible.

Third, before we exit the application, we invoke `Window.dispose()`, which hides the window and frees the resources associated with the *native* window.

The entire application is listed in Example 16-1.

AWT TIP ...

Invoke toFront() After show() for Windows That Are Not Visible

Window.show() is guaranteed to bring the window being shown to the front only if the window is currently visible. If the window is not visible, show() makes no such guarantee. Therefore, to ensure that a window being shown will wind up in front of all other windows, invoke toFront() after calling show().

Example 16-1 SplashTest Application

```
import java.awt.*;
import java.awt.event.*;

public class SplashTest extends Frame {
    Toolkit toolkit = Toolkit.getDefaultToolkit();
    Window  window;
    Image   image;

    static public void main(String[] args) {
        Frame frame = new SplashTest();
    }
    public SplashTest() {
        ImageCanvas canvas;
```

```java
        window  = new Window(this);
        image   = toolkit.getImage("gifs/saint.gif");
        canvas  = new ImageCanvas(image);

        window.add(canvas, "Center");

        Dimension    scrnSize  = toolkit.getScreenSize();
        int          imgWidth  = image.getWidth(this),
                     imgHeight = image.getHeight(this);

        window.setLocation(scrnSize.width/2  - (imgWidth/2),
                           scrnSize.height/2 - (imgHeight/2));
        window.setSize(imgWidth,imgHeight);
        window.show();
        window.toFront();

        try { Thread.currentThread().sleep(10000); }
        catch(Exception e) { e.printStackTrace(); }

        window.dispose();
        System.exit(0);
    }
}
class ImageCanvas extends Canvas {
    private Image image;

    public ImageCanvas(Image image) {
        MediaTracker mt = new MediaTracker(this);
        mt.addImage(image, 0);

        try                  { mt.waitForID(0);       }
        catch(Exception e) { e.printStackTrace(); }

        this.image = image;
    }
    public void paint(Graphics g) {
        g.drawImage(image, 0, 0, this);
    }
    public void update(Graphics g) {
        paint(g);
    }
    public Dimension getPreferredSize() {
        return new Dimension(image.getWidth(this),
                             image.getHeight(this));
    }
}
```

Bubble Help

One popular windowing system feature not supported by the AWT is bubble help (aka tool tips).[2] Bubble help consists of a small textual window that is typically displayed when the cursor rests over a component, such as an image button in a toolbar. Although the AWT does not explicitly support bubble help, it is nonetheless quite simple to implement, graphically speaking.

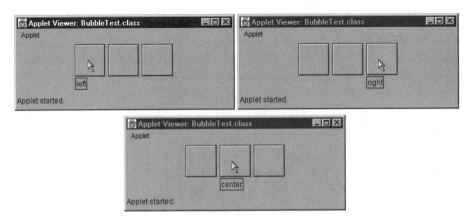

Figure 16-2 BubbleTest Applet
Three panels are equipped with a bubble—a popup window that displays a string.

Figure 16-2 shows an applet that displays three makeshift canvases whose `paint` method paints a 3D border. Each panel is equipped with a `Bubble`—an extension of `Window` that paints a rectangle with an enclosed string.

Example 16-2 Bubble Class Listing

```java
import java.awt.*;
import java.awt.event.*;

public class Bubble extends Window {
    private String text;

    public Bubble(Component comp, String text) {
        super(getFrame(comp));
```

2. The Swing components support tool tips.

```
            this.text = text;
            setForeground(SystemColor.textText);
        }
        public Dimension getPreferredSize() {
            Graphics    g  = getGraphics();
            FontMetrics fm = g.getFontMetrics();

            return new Dimension(fm.stringWidth(text)+4,
                                 fm.getHeight()+4);
        }
        public void paint(Graphics g) {
            Dimension   size = getSize();
            FontMetrics fm   = g.getFontMetrics();

            g.drawRect(0,0,size.width-1,size.height-1);
            g.drawString(text,2,fm.getAscent()+2);
        }
        public void show() {
            pack();
            super.show();
        }
        static Frame getFrame(Component c) {
            Frame frame = null;

            while((c = c.getParent()) != null)
                if(c instanceof Frame)
                    frame = (Frame)c;

            return frame;
        }
    }
```

Bubble has a lone constructor that takes a component (any component will do) and a string. The component to obtains a reference to a frame, which is then passed to the Window constructor. Additionally, the constructor sets its foreground color to SystemColor.textText, which simply represents text color—see "Mouseless Operation" on page 629. Bubble overrides paint() to paint a border around the window, and the string is passed to the constructor centered in the window. show() is overridden to invoke pack() and then call super.show(), which is a common technique when extending java.awt.Window.

The BubbleTest applet shown in Figure 16-2 is listed in Example 16-3.

Example 16-3 BubbleTest Applet

```java
import java.applet.Applet;
import java.awt.*;
import java.awt.event.*;

public class BubbleTest extends Applet {
    public void init() {
        BubblePanel left   = new BubblePanel("left");
        BubblePanel center = new BubblePanel("center");
        BubblePanel right  = new BubblePanel("right");

        add(left);
        add(center);
        add(right);
    }
}
class BubblePanel extends BorderedPanel {
    Bubble bubble;
    String bubbleText;

    public BubblePanel(String string) {
        bubbleText = string;

        addMouseListener(new MouseAdapter() {
            public void mouseEntered(MouseEvent event) {
                BubblePanel canvas  = BubblePanel.this;
                Point       scrnLoc = canvas.getLocationOnScreen();
                Dimension   size    = getSize();

                if(bubble == null)
                    bubble = new Bubble(canvas, bubbleText);

                bubble.setLocation(scrnLoc.x,
                                   scrnLoc.y + size.height + 2);
                bubble.show();
            }
            public void mouseExited(MouseEvent event) {
                if(bubble != null && bubble.isShowing())
                    bubble.dispose();
            }
        });
    }
    public Dimension getPreferredSize() {
        return new Dimension(50,50);
    }
}
```

BubblePanel is an extension of BorderedPanel (see "BorderedPanel Class Listing" on page 542) that has a bubble. When the mouse enters the bubble panel, the bubble associated with the bubble panel is constructed if it has not already been created and, after its location is set, is shown. When the mouse exits the bubble canvas, the bubble is disposed of.

Notice that a bubble panel may potentially call `dispose()` on its bubble many times, whereas the bubble itself is only created once. It is important to realize that `dispose()` does not dispose of the bubble object but merely releases the system resources associated with the window that the bubble represents. Therefore, we can dispose of and show a bubble repeatedly without having to construct a new bubble instance after every call to `dispose()`. Another important point to remember is that `dispose()` invokes `hide()` on the window, so not only does it release the system resources associated with the window, but it also hides the window.

AWT TIP

Window.dispose() Disposes of the Window's Resources, Not the AWT Component

Window.dispose() disposes of the native resources associated with a window. It does not dispose of the AWT component representing the window. As a result, a java.awt.Window object may be disposed of repeatedly without the AWT component requiring reconstruction. Additionally, Window.dispose() also hides the window, so when you need to hide a window, a single call to dispose() will do the job, and you can turn around and show() the window without having to reconstruct the AWT window component.

java.awt.Frame

If the `Window` class represents the base model of AWT window components, `Frame` is the fully loaded model. Features included with the `Frame` class are a border, titlebar, and an optional menubar. Frames can also be resized and fitted with an icon image, which will be displayed when the frame is iconified. The downside of frames is that they are tagged with a string warning potential users that your frame may be *untrustworthy*. Browsers are in charge of the warning string enforcement policy[3]—trusted applets that show a frame should not have the warning string displayed. And before you ask, the AWT provides no mechanism for modifying or removing the warning string, although a `getWarningString()` is provided by the `Frame` class in case the string is hard to read on screen.

---

3. Browsers typically have their own security manager and also decide the contents of the warning string.

One benefit of the Frame class is that you don't have to dig around for a frame to pass to the constructor, as you do when constructing a Window or a Dialog. Frames are standalone windows, whereas windows and dialogs must be anchored by a frame supplied at construction time.

"Menus" on page 597 has many examples of frames and menubars, so we won't bother to explore creating menubars and menus in this chapter. In addition, since frames are straightforward to use, we'll present a simple applet that creates and displays a frame with a lone button. The lone button is used to dispose of the frame. You can see our applet and its resultant frame in Figure 16-3.

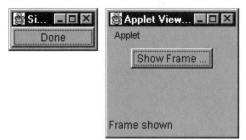

Figure 16-3 SimpleFrameTest Applet
An applet creates and shows a frame. The frame (on the left) has a full complement of system buttons in its titlebar: iconify, maximize, and close buttons, along with an image for when it is iconified. Contrast this to the dialog's titlebar in the similar-looking applet in Figure 16-4 on page 583.

The applet is fairly short-winded and easy to digest, so we'll list the entire applet in Example 16-4, and follow that by a short discussion.

Example 16-4 SimpleFrameTest Applet

```
import java.applet.Applet;
import java.awt.*;
import java.awt.event.*;

public class SimpleFrameTest extends Applet {
    Button launchButton = new Button("Show Frame ...");
    Frame  frame        = new Frame ("Simple Frame");

    public void init() {
        add(launchButton);
```

```
        launchButton.addActionListener(new ActionListener() {
            public void actionPerformed(ActionEvent event) {
                Frame myFrame = getFrame(SimpleFrameTest.this);
                Point scrnLoc = myFrame.getLocationOnScreen();
                Dimension frameSize = frame.getSize();

                frame.setLocation(scrnLoc.x - frameSize.width - 2,
                                  scrnLoc.y);
                showStatus(null);
                frame.show();
                showStatus("Frame shown");
            }
        });
    }
    public void start() {
        Button doneButton = new Button("Done");

        frame.add (doneButton);
        frame.pack();

        doneButton.addActionListener(new ActionListener() {
            public void actionPerformed(ActionEvent event) {
                frame.dispose();
                showStatus(null);
            }
        });
        frame.addWindowListener(new WindowAdapter() {
            public void windowClosing(WindowEvent event) {
                System.out.println("Window Closing");
                frame.dispose();
            }
            public void windowClosed(WindowEvent event) {
                showStatus("Window Closed");
            }
        });
    }
    static Frame getFrame(Component c) {
        Frame frame = null;

        while((c = c.getParent()) != null) {
            if(c instanceof Frame)
                frame = (Frame)c;
        }
        return frame;
    }
}
```

The applet's `init` method creates the complex user interface employed by the
applet and then adds an action listener to the launch button. When activated, the
location of the applet's frame is obtained in order to locate the frame created by
the applet.

The `start` method adds a button to the frame and then packs the frame. When the Done button is activated, the frame is disposed of. Our frame also listens for window closing and window closed events. `WindowListener.windowClosing()` is called when the window is closed through a system mechanism—using the close box or the window's system menu to close the window. If you don't call `dispose()` in the `windowClosing` method of one of the frame's window listeners,[4] then the window will not be closed.

Notice that we call the applet's `showStatus` method immediately after showing the frame. You can see the status line doing its thing in Figure 16-3 on page 580. The reason for updating the status line is to convince you that frames are not modal—they do not block thread execution while the frame is showing, nor do they block input to other windows. In other words, when the frame is shown, the status line of the applet is immediately updated. We'll experiment with modality in our next section on dialogs, but modality is one of the few options not available with the `Frame` class.

Frames Don't Close by Default

Frames, by default, will not close when their close box is activated or *Quit* is selected from the system menu (or whatever equivalent mechanisms the operating system provides). If you want the user to be able to close the frame through system means, you must listen for the window closing event to be fired by the frame. windowClosing() should invoke dispose() on the frame in order to go through with the closing of the window. Once the window is closed, a window closed event is generated and sent to all of the window's window listeners.

java.awt.Dialog

From an evolutionary perspective, dialogs lie between windows and frames. Dialogs share many of the amenities found in frames, but they lack the frame's status as being a fully operational application window. Dialogs cannot support menubars or be iconified, two essentials of application window functionality.

However, dialogs do have something that windows and frames do not—modality. Dialogs can be either modal or nonmodal, and before we go any further, let's define what that means. Being modal means blocking two things:

---

4.   It is highly advisable to call `dispose()` for a frame only once between calls to `show()`. A frame can have more than one window listener. Beware.

- Thread execution
- Input to other windows

When a modal dialog is shown, input is blocked to all other windows in the dialog's ancestry.[5] Also, execution of the thread that showed the dialog is blocked until the dialog is closed. Notice from Table 16-1 on page 569 that dialogs are not modal by default, and that modality can be set at construction time or at your leisure. The `Dialog` class also provides an accessor that will tell you the dialog's current modality setting in case you lose track.

Another noteworthy item concerning dialogs is that the AWT, compared to most user interface toolkits, is currently quite thin in the dialog department, with only one offering as far as `Dialog` extensions go: the `FileDialog`. In "Custom Dialogs" on page 735, we examine extending the `Dialog` class to provide a number of useful `Dialog` extensions, such as message, question, yes/no, and progress dialogs. If you want to explore dialogs in more detail, *page 735* is the place to go. For now, we'll look at an applet, `SimpleDialogTest`, which is similar to our `SimpleFrameTest`. Figure 16-4 shows a dialog; Example 16-5 lists the applet.

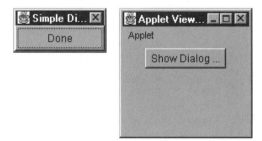

Figure 16-4 `SimpleDialogTest` Applet
An applet creates and shows a dialog. Notice the stripped-down titlebar for the dialog—no iconified image, iconify, or maximize buttons. Contrast the dialog's titlebar with that of the frame displayed in Figure 16-3 on page 580.

5. You didn't think we were passing frames to dialog constructors for nothing, did you?

Example 16-5 SimpleDialogTest Applet

```java
import java.applet.Applet;
import java.awt.*;
import java.awt.event.*;

public class SimpleDialogTest extends Applet {
    Button launchButton = new Button("Show Dialog ...");
    Dialog dialog;
    Frame myFrame;

    public void init() {
        add(launchButton);

        launchButton.addActionListener(new ActionListener() {
            public void actionPerformed(ActionEvent event) {
                Point scrnLoc = myFrame.getLocationOnScreen();
                Dimension dialogSize = dialog.getSize();

                dialog.setLocation(
                    scrnLoc.x - dialogSize.width - 2,
                    scrnLoc.y);

                showStatus(null);
                dialog.show();
                showStatus("Dialog shown");
            }
        });
    }
    public void start() {
        Button doneButton = new Button("Done");

        myFrame = getFrame(SimpleDialogTest.this);
        dialog  = new Dialog(myFrame, "Simple Dialog", true);

        dialog.add(doneButton);
        dialog.pack();
        dialog.setResizable(false);

        doneButton.addActionListener(new ActionListener() {
            public void actionPerformed(ActionEvent event) {
                dialog.dispose();
                showStatus(null);
            }
        });
```

```
        dialog.addWindowListener(new WindowAdapter() {
            public void windowClosing(WindowEvent event) {
                System.out.println("Window Closing");
                dialog.dispose();
            }
            public void windowClosed(WindowEvent event) {
                System.out.println("Window Closed");
            }
        });
    }
    static Frame getFrame(Component c) {
        Frame frame = null;

        while((c = c.getParent()) != null) {
            if(c instanceof Frame)
                frame = (Frame)c;
        }
        return frame;
    }
}
```

Like the "SimpleFrameTest Applet" on page 580, we have the paraphernalia associated with listening for action and window events, with the same results.

Notice that the applet's status bar does not show "Dialog Shown" until the dialog is closed. That's because our dialog is modal and, therefore, when it is shown, suspends execution of the thread that showed the dialog, so that the call below to showStatus() does not occur until the dialog is closed.

```
public void actionPerformed(ActionEvent event) {
    Point scrnLoc = myFrame.getLocationOnScreen();
    Dimension dialogSize = dialog.getSize();

    dialog.setLocation(
        scrnLoc.x - dialogSize.width - 2,
        scrnLoc.y);

    showStatus(null);
    dialog.show();
    showStatus("Dialog shown");
}
```

The applet's start method packs the dialog and sets its resizable property to false. Repeated attempts to size the dialog were consistently thwarted.

AWT TIP ...

The AWT's Meaning of Modality

Modal dialogs block input to all other windows in the dialog's ancestry. Modal dialogs also block execution of the thread that was responsible for showing the dialog. As a result, a line of code immediately following a call to setVisible(true) will not be invoked until a modal dialog has been dismissed:

```
Dialog d = new Dialog(frame, true); // true signifies modal
...
d.setVisible(true);
// This line of code is not executed until dialog is dismissed.
```

Modal Dialogs and Multithreading

Because modal dialogs block the thread that makes them visible, there is always the possibility that showing a modal dialog may result in thread deadlock. Consider the applet listed in Example 16-6, which shows a modal dialog when a mouse pressed event occurs in the applet.

Example 16-6 An Applet That Results in Deadlock

```
import java.applet.Applet;
import java.awt.*;
import java.awt.event.*;

public class TestApplet extends Applet {
    Dialog d = new DeadlockDialog();

    public void init() {
        addMouseListener(new MouseAdapter() {
            public synchronized void mousePressed(MouseEvent e) {
                try {
                    Thread.currentThread().sleep(2000);
                }
                catch(InterruptedException ex) {
                    ex.printStackTrace();
                }
                d.setVisible(true);
            }
        });
    }
    public void paint(Graphics g) {
        g.drawString("click in here twice in a row " +
                "within a span of 2 seconds", 20, 20);
    }
}
class DeadlockDialog extends Dialog {
```

```
    Button doneButton = new Button("doneButton");

public DeadlockDialog() {
    super(new Frame(), "Deadlock", true);
    add(doneButton);
    pack();

    doneButton.addActionListener(new ActionListener() {
        public void actionPerformed(ActionEvent e) {
            dispose();
        }
    });
    }
}
```

The DeadlockDialog class itself is quite unremarkable; we will focus our attention on the applet's mousePressed method.

If the instructions displayed in the applet are followed, namely, clicking twice in the applet within a span of two seconds, thread deadlock will occur. Here's why:

When the first mouse press occurs, the applet's mousePressed method is invoked, and a lock is acquired on the applet because the mousePressed method is synchronized. After acquiring the lock, the applet thread sleeps for two seconds.

If a second mouse pressed event occurs while the applet thread is sleeping,[6] the AWT event dispatch thread dispatches another call to the mousePressed method. However, since mousePressed is synchronized, the event dispatch thread must wait for the first call to mousePressed to return.

Meanwhile, after the applet thread wakes up, it shows the modal dialog. When a modal dialog is shown, it starts its own event dispatch thread[7] that dispatches events from the AWT event queue. Additionally, the dialog's peer blocks the thread that showed the dialog, so the mousePressed method cannot return until the dialog is dismissed.

At this point, the dialog's event dispatch thread is waiting for the next event to become available on the AWT event queue so it can dispatch the event for the dialog. The applet's event dispatch thread is waiting for the first call to mousePressed to return so that it can make the next event available on the AWT

---

6. Actually, anytime after the applet thread starts sleeping and before the modal dia-
    log starts its event dispatch thread.
7. If the thread that showed the dialog is an instance of EventDispatchThread.

event queue. However, the first call to `mousePressed` won't return until the dialog is dismissed, and the only way for that dismissal to happen is for the dialog's event dispatch thread to handle a mouse press on the dialog's button.

Thus, we have thread deadlock: two threads waiting on conditions that will never materialize. As a result, both the applet and the dialog become unresponsive, and the only way out of this mess is to hit CTRL-C, or whatever keystroke combination terminates wayward applications on your operating system of choice.

How can we modify the applet so that deadlock will not occur? One apparent solution is to deprive the applet of its short nap. Even then, however, deadlock can still occur if a user with an extremely quick trigger finger commandeers the applet. If the second mouse press occurs between the first mouse press and the point in time where the dialog blocks the applet's event dispatch thread, we've got the whole deadlock scenario all over again.

One sure-fire way of avoiding deadlock is to make the `mousePressed` method unsynchronized. In reality though, this solution is less than optimal, for there are often other valid reasons to synchronize event handling methods.

The best solution is to show the dialog on another thread, which is the approach taken by the applet listed in Example 16-7.

Example 16-7 Showing a Modal Dialog on a Different Thread

```
import java.applet.Applet;
import java.awt.*;
import java.awt.event.*;

public class TestApplet extends Applet implements Runnable {
    Thread thread;
    Dialog d = new NoDeadlockDialog();

    public void init() {
        addMouseListener(new MouseAdapter() {
            public synchronized void mousePressed(MouseEvent e) {
                try {
                    Thread.currentThread().sleep(2000);
                }
                catch(InterruptedException ex) {
                    ex.printStackTrace();
                }
```

```
            if(thread == null) {
                Thread thread = new Thread(TestApplet.this);
                thread.start();
            }
        }
    });
    }
    public void run() {
        d.setVisible(true);
        thread = null;
    }
    public void paint(Graphics g) {
        g.drawString("click in here twice in a row " +
                    "within a span of 2 seconds", 20, 20);
    }
}
class NoDeadlockDialog extends Dialog {
    Button doneButton = new Button("doneButton");

    public NoDeadlockDialog() {
        super(new Frame(), "NoDeadlock", true);
        add(doneButton);
        pack();

        doneButton.addActionListener(new ActionListener() {
            public void actionPerformed(ActionEvent e) {
                dispose();
            }
        });
    }
}
```

Showing the dialog on a different thread blocks the run method of the applet, which frees up the mousePressed method to return immediately after showing the dialog. Once the mousePressed method returns, the second call to mousePressed waiting in the wings can go about its business, which undams the flow of events from the AWT event queue, so that the dialog event dispatch thread can dispatch events to the dialog.

Notice that the second call to mousePressed will effectively be a no-op because it will just sleep for two seconds and return. In fact, if you run the applet from the CD, click twice in the applet, and immediately click on the dialog's button, you will notice an approximate delay of two seconds between clicking the mouse and activating the button.

AWT TIP ...

Show Modal Dialogs on a Separate Thread to Avoid Thread Deadlock

It should be noted that the author of this book is fully aware that the applets listed in Example 16-6 on page 586 and Example 16-7 on page 588 are contrived examples. However, that does not mean that thread deadlock in the real world does not occasionally bite the uninformed AWT developer. If you run across a deadlock situation as a result of showing a modal dialog, remember that a good solution is to show the dialog on another thread.

java.awt.FileDialog

The AWT provides a peer-based file dialog that in reality is the native file dialog for whatever platform you are running on. The file dialog—no surprises here—provides a mechanism for selecting a file name. The file dialog also allows for entries in the dialog to be filtered by specifying a file name filter. You can see the file dialogs for Solaris and Windows 95 in Figure 16-5.

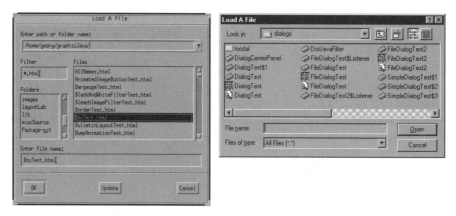

Figure 16-5   Solaris and Windows95 File Dialogs

It's a snap to put up a file dialog and decipher the file name selected, which is just what the applet shown in Figure 16-6 and listed in Example 16-8 does.

Figure 16-6 `FileDialogTest` Applet
The applet can open the file dialog in either load or save mode.
The file dialog displayed above is the loading version.

Example 16-8 `FileDialogTest` Applet

```
import java.applet.Applet;
import java.awt.*;
import java.awt.event.*;

public class FileDialogTest extends Applet {
    Button      loadButton = new Button("Load File ...");
    Button      saveButton = new Button("Save File ...");
    Listener    listener   = new Listener();
    FileDialog dialog;
    String      filename;

    public void init() {
        add(loadButton);
        add(saveButton);
        loadButton.addActionListener(listener);
        saveButton.addActionListener(listener);
    }
     class Listener implements ActionListener {
        public void actionPerformed(ActionEvent event) {
            Button button = ((Button)event.getSource());
            Frame myFrame = getFrame(button);

            showStatus(null);

            if(button == loadButton)
                dialog = new FileDialog(myFrame, "Load A File");
            else
                dialog = new FileDialog(myFrame, "Save A File",
                                        FileDialog.SAVE);
            dialog.show();
```

```
            if((filename = dialog.getFile()) != null) {
                showStatus(filename);
            }
            else {
                showStatus("FileDialog Cancelled");
            }
        }
    }
    static Frame getFrame(Component c) {
        Frame frame = null;

        while((c = c.getParent()) != null) {
            if(c instanceof Frame)
                frame = (Frame)c;
        }
        return frame;
    }
}
```

If the load button is activated, a file dialog is opened in its default mode, which is
`FileDialog.LOAD`. If the save button is activated, the file dialog is set to
`FileDialog.SAVE` mode. Whether you choose load or save, your motivation
doesn't change: you want to show the file dialog and subsequently obtain the file
name that was selected. Once you have the file name, it's up to you to do the
actual saving or loading—the file dialog doesn't save or load anything on its own.
You can see a file dialog in both LOAD and SAVE modes under Windows 95 in
Figure 16-7.

What it means to specify LOAD or SAVE mode is platform dependent—usually
it's a cosmetic change in the file dialog. The Windows 95 file dialog will confirm
file overwrites when in SAVE mode; the Solaris dialog allows selection of an
existing file name in SAVE mode, figuring that you'll handle the overwrite
dilemma yourself.

`FileDialog.getFile()` either returns a string representing the file name or
returns `null` if the dialog was cancelled.

Let's take a look at one more applet that specifies a file name filter for the file
dialog. Although the applet listed in Example 16-9 correctly specifies a file name
filter of *.java, the filter did not work correctly under the 1.2 version of the AWT.

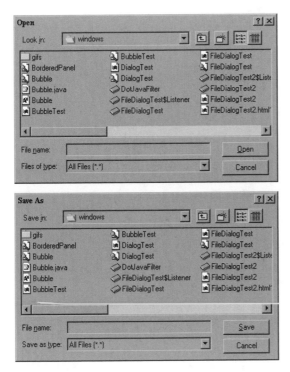

Figure 16-7 `FileDialog` in LOAD and SAVE Modes
The top picture shows a file dialog in LOAD mode, while the
bottom picture shows a file dialog in SAVE mode, both under
Windows 95.

Example 16-9 `FileDialogTest2` Applet

```java
import java.applet.Applet;
import java.awt.*;
import java.awt.event.*;
import java.io.*;

class DotJavaFilter implements FilenameFilter {
    public boolean accept(File dir, String name) {
        return name.endsWith(".java");
    }
}
```

```java
public class FileDialogTest2 extends Applet {
    Button    loadButton = new Button("Load File ...");
    Button    saveButton = new Button("Save File ...");
    Listener  listener   = new Listener();
    FileDialog dialog;
    String    filename;

    public void init() {
        add(loadButton);
        add(saveButton);
        loadButton.addActionListener(listener);
        saveButton.addActionListener(listener);
    }
    class Listener implements ActionListener {
        public void actionPerformed(ActionEvent event) {
            Button button = ((Button)event.getSource());
            Frame myFrame = getFrame(button);

            showStatus(null);

            if(button == loadButton)
                dialog = new FileDialog(myFrame, "Load A File");
            else
                dialog = new FileDialog(myFrame, "Save A File",
                                            FileDialog.SAVE);
            dialog.setFilenameFilter(new DotJavaFilter());
            dialog.setVisible(true);

            if((filename = dialog.getFile()) != null) {
                showStatus(filename);
            }
            else {
                showStatus("FileDialog Cancelled");
            }
        }
    }
    static Frame getFrame(Component c) {
        Frame frame = null;

        while((c = c.getParent()) != null) {
            if(c instanceof Frame)
                frame = (Frame)c;
        }
        return frame;
    }
}
```

Summary

The AWT provides three basic components that create a top-level window: `Window`, `Frame`, and `Dialog`.

Windows are the superclass of both frames and dialogs and are also the only component of the three that can be displayed without a border or titlebar. As a result, windows are used when a basic, borderless rectangular region is required, as is the case for either a splash screen or bubble help.

Frames are the component of choice when more than one application window is needed. Frames are the only AWT component that can be iconified or have a menubar attached—both of which are characteristics of a top-level application window.

Finally, dialogs are the only component that can be modal. Modal dialogs not only block input to other windows in their container ancestry but also block execution of the thread that makes the dialogs visible. The AWT provides a lone extension of the basic `java.awt.Dialog` class: `FileDialog`, for selecting a file name.

CHAPTER
17

Menus

The original release of the AWT supported only one type of menu: ones that reside in a menubar. Furthermore, AWT menus were not components, so it was not possible to draw into a menu (or menu item). As a result, menus could only contain textual information.

The current version of the AWT provides a `PopupMenu` class; however, menus are still not extensions of `java.awt.Component`, so it is still not possible to implement owner-drawn menus, which are a common feature under many windowing systems[1]. The current release of the AWT also provides support for a basic menu feature that was lacking in the original AWT—menu shortcuts, which are discussed in "Menu Shortcuts" on page 638.

Note that with the exception of the section covering popup menus, all of the examples in this chapter are applications and therefore must be run through the `java` interpreter directly instead of employing `appletviewer` or a browser to invoke the `java` interpreter for you. This behavior is required because a menubar may only be attached to a frame—AWT menubars cannot be attached to an applet. For instance, to run the `FileMenuTest` application, which we'll discuss shortly, you would execute the following command:

`java FileMenuTest`

---

1. The Swing set of components implements menus as components.

The Menu Classes

Figure 17-1 shows the relationships between the AWT's menu classes.

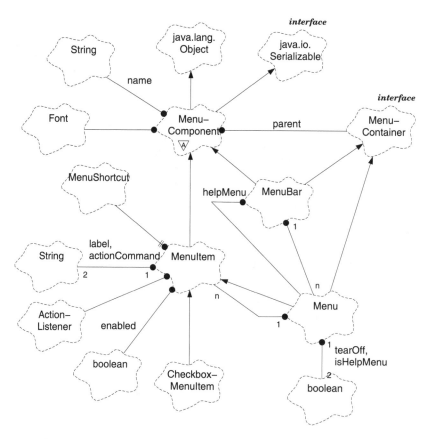

Figure 17-1 AWT Menu Classes Diagram

We will be concerned with four classes when dealing with menus: MenuBar, Menu, MenuItem, and PopupMenu. The first thing to note from the class diagram is that each of these classes extends MenuComponent; a MenuComponent is simply something that can be displayed in a menu. Second, notice that Menu and

Menubar both implement MenuContainer, meaning they may both contain instances of MenuComponent. Finally, note that Menu extends MenuItem; this enables the creation of cascading menus, as we shall soon discover.

It is worth repeating that none of the menu classes extend java.awt.Component. Although this may seem insignificant, consider that since menu items are not components, we may not paint or draw strings inside of a menu. This makes it impossible to render owner-drawn menus (a menu into which graphics may be drawn) in the current AWT.

A File Menu

Let's start off our discussion of menus residing in menubars with a simple example that creates the file menu in Figure 17-2.

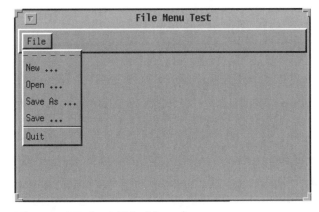

Figure 17-2 A File Menu

Most applications that provide a menubar have a file menu as the leftmost menu in their menubar, and most provide menu items similar to those we have added to our example. Implementing such a menu is straightforward, as illustrated in Example 17-1.

Example 17-1 `FileMenuTest Class Listing`

```java
import java.awt.*;
import java.awt.event.*;

public class FileMenuTest extends Frame {
    private MenuBar mbar;
    private MenuItem newItem, openItem,
                    saveAsItem, saveItem, quitItem;
    private MenuItemListener menuItemListener =
                            new MenuItemListener();

    public static void main(String args[]) {
        FileMenuTest test = new FileMenuTest("File Menu Test");
        test.setBounds(300,300,300,100);
        test.show();
    }
    public FileMenuTest(String s) {
        super(s);

        MenuBar mbar     = new MenuBar();
        Menu    fileMenu = new Menu("File", true);

        fileMenu.add(newItem = new MenuItem("New ..."));
        fileMenu.add(openItem = new MenuItem("Open ..."));
        fileMenu.add(saveAsItem = new MenuItem("Save As ..."));
        fileMenu.add(saveItem = new MenuItem("Save ..."));
        fileMenu.addSeparator();
        fileMenu.add(quitItem = new MenuItem("Quit"));

        mbar.add(fileMenu);
        setMenuBar (mbar);

        addWindowListener(new WindowAdapter() {
            public void windowClosing(WindowEvent event) {
                dispose();
                System.exit(0);
            }
        });
    }
}
```

This version of the `FileMenuTest` class extends `Frame` and provides a `main` method, signifying that it is an application, and not an applet. (See *Applets and Applications* on page 15 for a discussion of developing applets versus applications.) The `FileMenuTest` constructor takes a string, which is immediately passed to the superclass' (`Frame`) constructor. The string passed to the `Frame` constructor will be used as the title of the window.

The `FileMenuTest` constructor creates a `MenuBar` and a `Menu`. The string passed to the `Menu` constructor is the menu's title and will be displayed in the menubar.

Adding menu items to a menu is accomplished by invoking the `Menu.add` method and passing in a string that will be displayed in the menu item.

After creating the menubar and the menu, `FileMenuTest` adds the menu to the menubar and then calls `Frame.setMenuBar()` to set the frame's menubar.

The only event handling our application implements is detecting a window closing event, triggered when the window is closed via a system menu (or close box). See "java.awt.Frame" on page 579 for more information on handling window closing events.

Handling Menu Events

Menubars and menus take care of displaying themselves, but attaching behavior to menu items is something you must handle yourself. Example 17-2 expands `FileMenuTest` to print the label of the item selected and to quit the application when the "Quit" item is selected.

Since menu items fire action events when they are selected, an implementation of `ActionListener` obtains a reference to the menu item that generated the event and prints the label associated with the menu item. If the menu item is the Quit menu item, we exit the application, being careful to dispose of the frame before exiting. So that the `MenuItemListener` to do its thing, it is added as the action listener for every menu item created.

Example 17-2 Expanded FileMenuTest Class Listing

```
import java.awt.*;
import java.awt.event.*;

public class FileMenuTest extends Frame {
    private MenuBar mbar;
    private MenuItem newItem, openItem,
                saveAsItem, saveItem, quitItem;
    private MenuItemListener menuItemListener =
                        new MenuItemListener();

    public static void main(String args[]) {
        FileMenuTest test = new FileMenuTest("File Menu Test");
        test.setBounds(300,300,300,100);
        test.show();
    }
```

```java
    public FileMenuTest(String s) {
        super(s);

        MenuBar mbar     = new MenuBar();
        Menu    fileMenu = new Menu("File", true);

        fileMenu.add(newItem = new MenuItem("New ..."));
        fileMenu.add(openItem = new MenuItem("Open ..."));
        fileMenu.add(saveAsItem = new MenuItem("Save As ..."));
        fileMenu.add(saveItem = new MenuItem("Save ..."));
        fileMenu.addSeparator();
        fileMenu.add(quitItem = new MenuItem("Quit"));

        mbar.add(fileMenu);
        setMenuBar(mbar);

        newItem.addActionListener(menuItemListener);
        openItem.addActionListener(menuItemListener);
        saveAsItem.addActionListener(menuItemListener);
        saveItem.addActionListener(menuItemListener);
        quitItem.addActionListener(menuItemListener);

        addWindowListener(new WindowAdapter() {
            public void windowClosing(WindowEvent event) {
                dispose();
                System.exit(0);
            }
        });
    }
    class MenuItemListener implements ActionListener {
        public void actionPerformed(ActionEvent event) {
            MenuItem item = (MenuItem)event.getSource();
            System.out.println(item.getLabel());

            if(item == quitItem) {
                dispose();
                System.exit(0);
            }
        }
    }
}
```

Since a reference is needed for each menu item in order to add a listener to the items, a different `Menu` constructor is invoked—one that takes a `MenuItem`.

Tear-off Menus

Tear-off menus are implemented under Motif and are menus that, as their name implies, can be torn off and placed aside for quick access. Tear-off menus have aperforated line at the top of the menu. Once torn off, they are placed in their own window, as illustrated in Figure 17-3.

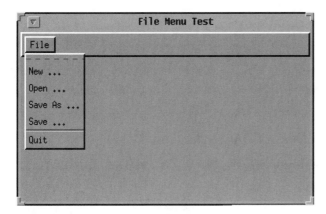 

Figure 17-3 Tear-off Menu
The left picture shows the perforated tear-off menu. The right picture shows the menu after it is torn off.

The Menu class provides a constructor that allows you to specify whether the menu is a tear-off menu. This constructor is invoked in Example 17-2 on page 601 and is passed true as the second argument. The true argument indicates that the menu should be of the tear-off variety.

Windows 95 does not support tear-off menus, so passing true as a second argument to the Menu constructor will have no effect under Windows 95.

A MenuBar Printer

To illustrate the relationships between menus, menubars, and menu items, we'll present a simple class in Example 17-3 that walks you through all the menus in a menubar and prints information about each item.

Example 17-3 MenuBarPrinter Class Listing

```java
import java.awt.Menu;
import java.awt.MenuItem;
import java.awt.MenuBar;

public class MenuBarPrinter {
    static public void print(MenuBar menubar) {
        int      numMenus = menubar.getMenuCount();
        Menu      nextMenu;
        MenuItem nextItem;

        System.out.println();
        System.out.println("MenuBar has "          +
                            menubar.getMenuCount() +
                            " menus");
        System.out.println();

        for(int i=0; i < numMenus; ++i) {
            nextMenu = menubar.getMenu(i);
            System.out.println(nextMenu);

            int numItems = nextMenu.getItemCount();

            for(int j=0; j < numItems; ++j) {
                nextItem = nextMenu.getItem(j);
                System.out.println(nextItem);
            }
            System.out.println();
        }
    }
}
```

The `MenuBarPrinter` class contains a lone `static` method, which is passed a `MenuBar` and prints information about each menu in the menubar. Notice that `MenuBar.countMenus()`, `MenuBar.getMenu()`, `Menu.countItems()`, and `Menu.getItem()` are used to traverse through all of the menu items contained in each menu in the menubar.

A `FrameWithMenuBar` **Class**

Applications containing a menubar typically do the following things:

1. Create a menubar

2. Add menus to the menubar

3. Set the frame's menubar

In good object-oriented fashion, we will encapsulate these tasks in a base class illustrated in Example 17-4. You can extend this class whenever you need a frame with a menubar.

Encapsulate Common Functionality in Base Classes

Encapsulating common functionality in a base class is one of the tenets of object-oriented development; it increases reuse and reduces reimplementation of similar functionality in more than one class. Often, such code is not identified until two or more classes have reimplemented the same functionality. In such cases, it is well worth your while to *refactor* the code in question and move the similar functionality into a base class.

Example 17-4 FrameWithMenuBar Class Listing

```java
import java.awt.*;
import java.awt.event.*;

public abstract class FrameWithMenuBar extends Frame {
    private MenuBar        mbar    = new MenuBar();
    private MenuBarPrinter printer;

    abstract protected void createMenus(MenuBar menuBar);

    public FrameWithMenuBar(String s) {
        super(s);

        createMenus(mbar);
        setMenuBar (mbar);

        addWindowListener(new WindowAdapter() {
           public void windowClosing(WindowEvent event) {
              quit();
           }
        });
    }
    protected void quit() {
     if(aboutToBeDestroyed())
         quitNoConfirm();
    }
    protected void quitNoConfirm() {
        System.exit(0);
    }
     public void printMenus() {
        if(printer == null)
            printer = new MenuBarPrinter();

        printer.print(mbar);
    }
    protected boolean aboutToBeDestroyed() {
       return true;
    }
}
```

Each `FrameWithMenuBar` comes complete with a `MenuBar` and `MenuBarPrinter` reference. `FrameWithMenuBar` leaves one abstract method for extensions to implement:

```
void createMenus(MenuBar)
```

Extensions of `FrameWithMenuBar` simply create the menus they wish to attach to the menubar and then add them to the menubar passed to `createMenus()`.

`FrameWithMenuBar` also takes care of the details of handling a window closing event. Before exiting the application, the `aboutToBeDestroyed` method is invoked. Classes that extend `FrameWithMenuBar` may override `aboutToBeDestroyed()` if they have unfinished business to take care of before the application is exited. Returning `false` from `aboutToBeDestroyed()` will abort the closing of the window.

Note that `aboutToBeDestroyed()` is a `protected` method. We chose to make `aboutToBeDestroyed()` `protected` instead of `public` to ensure that no hooligan developers run around directly invoking `aboutToBeDestroyed()`. Limiting the access of `aboutToBeDestroyed()` to extensions of `FrameWithMenuBar` ensures that the method will be invoked only when the frame is actually about to be destroyed.[2]

Finally, each `FrameWithMenuBar` comes with a `printMenus` method that prints information about all of the menus in the menubar. Notice that we use a technique known in object-oriented circles as *lazy instantiation* for creating the `MenuBarPrinter`. The `printMenus` method checks to see if the `MenuBarPrinter` instance is `null`. If so, it creates the `MenuBarPrinter`. This technique ensures that the `MenuBarPrinter` only gets created the first time it is needed.

OO TIP

Employ Lazy Instantiation for Rarely Used Class Members

FrameWithMenuBar can print out the label for each menu in its menubar. While this capability may at times be beneficial, in all honesty it will probably be used sparingly. As a result, it is a good idea to employ lazy instantiation to create the menubar printer. Lazy instantiation delays the creation of objects until they are needed for the first time.

---

2. Actually, the `aboutToBeDestroyed` method is accessible by extensions of `FrameWithMenuBar` *and* other classes in the same package.

FrameWithMenuBar in Action

To illustrate the use of FrameWithMenuBar, we present a FileEditMenuTest
application in Example 17-5. This extension of FrameWithMenuBar attaches
both a file and an edit menu to its menubar.

Example 17-5 FileEditMenuTest Class Listing

```
import java.awt.*;
import java.awt.event.*;

public class FileEditMenuTest extends FrameWithMenuBar {
    private MenuItem quitItem;

    public static void main(String args[]) {
        FileEditMenuTest test =
            new FileEditMenuTest("FileEdit Menu Test");

        test.setBounds(300,300,300,100);
        test.show();
    }
    public FileEditMenuTest(String s) {
        super(s);
    }
    public void createMenus(MenuBar mbar) {
        mbar.add(createFileMenu());
        mbar.add(createEditMenu());
    }
    private Menu createFileMenu() {
        Menu fileMenu = new Menu("File");

        fileMenu.add("New ...");
        fileMenu.add("Open ...");
        fileMenu.add("Save As ...");
        fileMenu.add("Save ...");
        fileMenu.addSeparator();
        fileMenu.add(quitItem = new MenuItem("Quit"));

        quitItem.addActionListener(new ActionListener() {
            public void actionPerformed(ActionEvent event) {
                MenuItem item = (MenuItem)event.getSource();

                if(item == quitItem) {
                    dispose();
                    System.exit(0);
                }
            }
        });

        return fileMenu;
    }
    private Menu createEditMenu() {
```

```
        Menu editMenu = new Menu("Edit");

        editMenu.add("Cut");
        editMenu.add("Copy");
        editMenu.add("Paste");

        return editMenu;
    }
}
```

The `createMenus` method is overridden in order to add a file menu and an edit menu to the menubar. Note that `FrameWithMenuBar` takes care of creating the menubar and attaching it to the frame, leaving us to take care of business specific to `FileEditMenuTest`, namely, creating the file and edit menus and adding them to the menubar.

In the remaining examples in this chapter, we will subclass `FrameWithMenuBar` when illustrating the use of AWT menus.

Help Menus

The AWT provides support for a help menu. A help menu is created and added to a menubar just like any other menu. Help menus, however, need to be identified by invocation of `MenuBar.setHelpMenu()`, which ensures that the help menu is the rightmost menu in the menubar, regardless of when it was added to the menubar.

Help menus under Motif are right-justified in the menubar itself, whereas help menus under Windows 95 are simply placed to the right of the other menus in the menubar, as illustrated in Figure 17-4.

Example 17-6 lists an implementation of a help menu.

Example 17-6 HelpTest Class Listing

```
import java.awt.*;
import java.awt.event.*;
import java.util.Vector;

public class HelpTest extends FrameWithMenuBar {
    private MenuItem quitItem;

    public static void main(String args[]) {
        HelpTest frame = new HelpTest("Help Menu Test");
        frame.setBounds(300,300,300,100);
        frame.show();
    }
    public HelpTest(String s) {
        super(s);
```

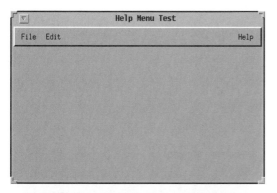

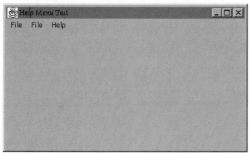

Figure 17-4 Motif and Windows 95 Help Menus
Motif help menus are right-justified in the menubar itself, as in
the top picture. Windows 95 help menus are placed to the right of
the other menus, as in the bottom picture.

```
    }
    public void createMenus(MenuBar mbar) {
        Menu helpMenu = createHelpMenu();

        mbar.add(createFileMenu());
        mbar.add(createEditMenu());
        mbar.add(helpMenu);

        mbar.setHelpMenu(helpMenu);
    }
    private Menu createFileMenu() {
        Menu fileMenu = new Menu("File");
        fileMenu.add(quitItem = new MenuItem("Quit"));

        quitItem.addActionListener(new ActionListener() {
            public void actionPerformed(ActionEvent event) {
                MenuItem item = (MenuItem)event.getSource();
                if(item == quitItem) {
```

```
                    dispose();
                    System.exit(0);
                }
            }
        });
        return fileMenu;
    }
    private Menu createEditMenu() {
        Menu editMenu = new Menu("Edit");

        editMenu.add("Cut");
        editMenu.add("Copy");
        editMenu.add("Paste");

        return editMenu;
    }
    private Menu createHelpMenu() {
        Menu helpMenu = new Menu("Help");

        helpMenu.add("Overview ...");
        helpMenu.add("Topics ...");
        helpMenu.add("About ...");

        return helpMenu;
    }
}
```

Once again, thanks to `FrameWithMenuBar`, we are only concerned with creating menus, adding them to the menubar, and reacting to menu events.

Checkbox Menu Items

The AWT provides a `CheckboxMenuItem` class. A `CheckboxMenuItem` is a menu item that toggles between checked and unchecked when activated. Figure 17-5 shows a `CheckboxMenuItem` at work.

A `CheckboxMenuItem` is often used in a menu that exhibits radio button behavior. That is, when one of the menu items is checked, the other items in the menu are all unchecked, so that only one checkbox menu item is checked at a time.

It is a simple matter to extend `Menu` and provide a `RadioMenu` class that adds `CheckboxMenuItem` items (only) and implements the mutually exclusive selection behavior. Example 17-7 lists the `RadioMenu` implementation.

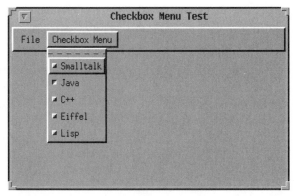

Figure 17-5 A Checkbox Menu Item
Activated menu items toggle between checked or unchecked.

Example 17-7 RadioMenu Class Listing

```java
import java.awt.Menu;
import java.awt.MenuItem;
import java.awt.CheckboxMenuItem;

public class RadioMenu extends Menu {
    public RadioMenu(String s, boolean tearOff) {
        super(s, tearOff);
    }
    public void add(String s) {
        add(new CheckboxMenuItem(s));
    }
    public MenuItem add(MenuItem item) {
        if(!item instanceof CheckboxMenuItem);
            throw new IllegalArgumentException("bad menuitem");

        return super.add(item);
    }
    public void selectItem(MenuItem item) {
        CheckboxMenuItem nextItem;
        int             numItems = getItemCount();

        for(int i=0; i < numItems; ++i) {
            if(item != getItem(i)) {
                nextItem = (CheckboxMenuItem)getItem(i);
                nextItem.setState(false);
            }
        }
    }
}
```

RadioMenu implements add(String) to ensure that the item being added to it is a CheckboxMenuItem. Additionally, RadioMenu overrides add(MenuItem) for the same purpose.

RadioMenu.selectItem() cycles through each of its menu items and sets its state to false (unchecked), except for the item that was activated. This behavior ensures that only one item at a time is checked.

RadioMenuTest in Example 17-8 illustrates the use of RadioMenu.

Example 17-8 RadioMenuTest Class Listing

```
import java.awt.*;
import java.awt.event.*;

public class RadioMenuTest extends FrameWithMenuBar {
    private RadioMenu        radioMenu;
    private MenuItem         quitItem;
    private CheckboxMenuItem stItem, javaItem, cppItem,
                             eiffelItem, lispItem;

    public static void main(String args[]) {
        RadioMenuTest test =
            new RadioMenuTest("FileEdit Menu Test");

        test.setBounds(300,300,300,100);
        test.show();
    }
    public RadioMenuTest(String s) {
        super(s);
    }
    public void createMenus(MenuBar mbar) {
        mbar.add(createFileMenu());
        mbar.add(createRadioMenu());
    }
    private Menu createFileMenu() {
        Menu fileMenu = new Menu("File");
        fileMenu.add(quitItem = new MenuItem("Quit"));

        quitItem.addActionListener(new ActionListener() {
            public void actionPerformed(ActionEvent event) {
                dispose();
                System.exit(0);
            }
        });
        return fileMenu;
    }
    private Menu createRadioMenu() {
        CheckboxItemListener checkboxItemListener =
                        new CheckboxItemListener();
        radioMenu = new RadioMenu("Radio Menu", true);
```

```
        stItem = new CheckboxMenuItem("Smalltalk");
        javaItem = new CheckboxMenuItem("Java");
        cppItem = new CheckboxMenuItem("C++");
        eiffelItem = new CheckboxMenuItem("Eiffel");
        lispItem = new CheckboxMenuItem("Lisp");

        radioMenu.add(stItem);
        radioMenu.add(javaItem);
        radioMenu.add(cppItem);
        radioMenu.add(eiffelItem);
        radioMenu.add(lispItem);

        stItem.addItemListener(checkboxItemListener);
        javaItem.addItemListener(checkboxItemListener);
        cppItem.addItemListener(checkboxItemListener);
        eiffelItem.addItemListener(checkboxItemListener);
        lispItem.addItemListener(checkboxItemListener);

        return radioMenu;
    }
    class CheckboxItemListener implements ItemListener {
        public void itemStateChanged(ItemEvent event) {
            CheckboxMenuItem item =
                (CheckboxMenuItem)event.getSource();

            radioMenu.selectItem(item);
        }
    }
}
```

Notice that `RadioMenuTest` calls `RadioMenu.selectItem()` to ensure the mutually exclusive behavior of the menu. Also, notice that checkbox menu items fire item events when activated, and menu items fire action events, as you can see from the manner in which events are handled for the `quitItem` and the checkbox menu items.

Cascading Menus

As previously alluded to, cascading menus are possible with the AWT by virtue of the fact that `Menu` extends `MenuItem`. As we have seen, `Menu.add(MenuItem)` adds a menu item to a menu. Since a `Menu` is a `MenuItem`, the `Menu.add(MenuItem)` method is perfectly happy to take a `Menu` as an argument, which it dutifully adds to itself.

Figure 17-6 shows the cascading menu created by Example 17-9.

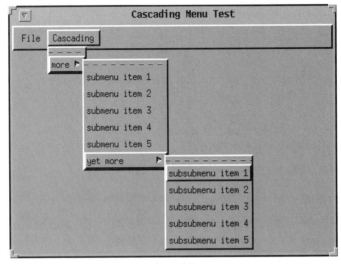

Figure 17-6 A Cascading Menu

Example 17-9 CascadingTest Class Listing

```java
import java.awt.*;
import java.awt.event.*;

public class CascadingTest extends FrameWithMenuBar {
    private MenuItem quitItem;

    public static void main(String args[]) {
        CascadingTest test =
            new CascadingTest("Cascading Menu Test");

        test.setBounds(300,300,300,100);
        test.show();
    }
    public CascadingTest(String s) {
        super(s);
    }
    public void createMenus(MenuBar mbar) {
        mbar.add(createFileMenu());
        mbar.add(createCascadingMenu());
    }
    private Menu createFileMenu() {
        Menu fileMenu = new Menu("File");
        fileMenu.add(quitItem = new MenuItem("Quit"));
```

```
        quitItem.addActionListener(new ActionListener() {
            public void actionPerformed(ActionEvent event) {
                dispose();
                System.exit(0);
            }
        });
        return fileMenu;
    }
    private Menu createCascadingMenu() {
        Menu cascading   = new Menu("Cascading", true);
        Menu submenu      = new Menu("more", true);
        Menu subsubmenu = new Menu("yet more", true);

        submenu.add("submenu item 1");
        submenu.add("submenu item 2");
        submenu.add("submenu item 3");
        submenu.add("submenu item 4");
        submenu.add("submenu item 5");

        subsubmenu.add("subsubmenu item 1");
        subsubmenu.add("subsubmenu item 2");
        subsubmenu.add("subsubmenu item 3");
        subsubmenu.add("subsubmenu item 4");
        subsubmenu.add("subsubmenu item 5");

        submenu.add(subsubmenu);
        cascading.add(submenu);

        return cascading;
    }
}
```

The `createCascadingMenu` method creates three menus:

- `cascading`
- `submenu`
- `subsubmenu`

`subsubmenu` is added to `submenu`, and `submenu` is added to `cascading`.
Notice that a `Menu` "knows" that we are adding a `Menu` instead of a `MenuItem`,
and it does the right thing, which in this case is to create a `MenuItem` with a pull-
right arrow on the far-right edge of the menu item that represents the added
menu.

Dynamically Modifying Menus

So far, we have modified menus before they are created, by adding items to them.
Sometimes it is necessary to modify a menu after it is created.

The `SelfModifyingMenu` illustrated in Figure 17-7 contains an item that is either enabled or disabled by the menu item above it. `SelfModifyingMenu` also contains two menu items for adding an item and removing the last item added to the menu.

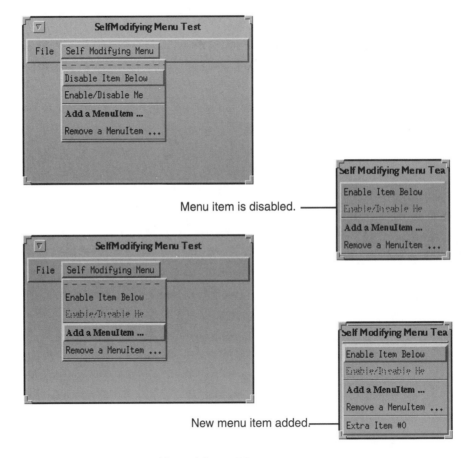

Figure 17-7 A Self-Modifying Menu
The top pair of pictures show the "Enable/Disable Me" item grayed out. The bottom pair of pictures show a menu item added to the menu. Tear-off menus are used to show the different states of the self-modifying menu.

Example 17-10 lists the `SelfModifyingMenu` class.

Example 17-10 SelfModifyingMenu Class Listing

```java
import java.awt.*;
import java.awt.event.*;
import java.util.Vector;

class SelfModifyingMenu extends Menu {
    private Vector    newItems = new Vector();
    private MenuItemListener menuItemListener =
                    new MenuItemListener();
    private MenuItem toggleItem, enablerItem,
                    addItem, removeItem;

    public SelfModifyingMenu() {
        super("Self Modifying Menu", true);

        add(enablerItem = new MenuItem("Disable Item Below"));
        add(toggleItem  = new MenuItem("Enable/Disable Me"));
        addSeparator();

        add(addItem     = new MenuItem("Add a MenuItem ..."));
        add(removeItem = new MenuItem("Remove a MenuItem ..."));
        addItem.setFont(new Font("TimesRoman", Font.BOLD, 12));
        addSeparator();

        enablerItem.addActionListener(menuItemListener);
        toggleItem.addActionListener(menuItemListener);
        addItem.addActionListener(menuItemListener);
        removeItem.addActionListener(menuItemListener);
    }
    public void addItem() {
        MenuItem newItem =
            new MenuItem("Extra Item #" + newItems.size());

        add(newItem);
        newItems.addElement(newItem);
    }
    public void removeLastItem() {
        if(newItems.size() == 0)
            System.out.println("Hey, nothing to remove!");
        else {
            MenuItem removeMe =
                (MenuItem)newItems.lastElement();

            remove(removeMe);
            newItems.removeElement(removeMe);
        }
    }
    public void toggleItem() {
        if(toggleItem.isEnabled()) toggleItem.setEnabled(false);
        else                        toggleItem.setEnabled(true);
    }
```

```
class MenuItemListener implements ActionListener {
public void actionPerformed(ActionEvent event) {
    MenuItem item = (MenuItem)event.getSource();

    if(item == enablerItem) {
        toggleItem();

        if(toggleItem.isEnabled())
            enablerItem.setLabel("Disable Item Below");
        else
            enablerItem.setLabel("Enable Item Below");
    }
    else if(item == addItem)     addItem();
    else if(item == removeItem) removeLastItem();
}
}
}
```

`MenuItemListener.actionPerformed()` is where all the interesting action takes place. If the menu item activated is the `enablerItem`, the `toggleItem` method is invoked; it toggles the enabled state of the `toggleItem`. After the state of `toggleItem` is toggled, the label for the `enablerItem` is modified to reflect the current enabled state of `toggleItem`.

If the menu item activated is the `addItem`, the `addItem` method is invoked; this method creates a new menu item and adds it to the `newItems` menu:

```
public void addItem() {
    MenuItem newItem =
        new MenuItem("Extra Item #" + newItems.size());

    add(newItem);
    newItems.addElement(newItem);
}
```

If the menu item activated is the `removeItem`, `removeLastItem()` is invoked; this method makes sure that a menu item is available for removal by invoking `MenuItem.size()`. After confirming that there is a menu item to remove, `Menu.lastElement()` is invoked to obtain a reference to the last menu item in the menu, and then `Menu.removeElement()` is subsequently invoked to remove the last menu item:

```
public void removeLastItem() {
    if(newItems.size() == 0)
        System.out.println("Hey, nothing to remove!");
    else {
        MenuItem removeMe = (MenuItem)newItems.lastElement();

        remove(removeMe);
        newItems.removeElement(removeMe);
    }
}
```

Example 17-11 lists an application that exercises the `SelfModifyingMenu` class.

Example 17-11 `SelfModifyingTest` Application

```java
import java.awt.*;
import java.awt.event.*;
import java.util.Vector;

public class SelfModifyingTest extends FrameWithMenuBar {
    private SelfModifyingMenu selfModifyingMenu;
    private MenuItem quitItem;

    public static void main(String args[]) {
        Frame frame =
            new SelfModifyingTest("SelfModifying Menu Test");

        frame.setBounds(100,100,300,100);
        frame.show();
    }
    public SelfModifyingTest(String s) {
        super(s);
    }
    public void createMenus(MenuBar mbar) {
        mbar.add(createFileMenu());
        mbar.add(selfModifyingMenu = new SelfModifyingMenu());
    }
    private Menu createFileMenu() {
        Menu fileMenu = new Menu("File");
        fileMenu.add(quitItem = new MenuItem("Quit"));

        quitItem.addActionListener(new ActionListener() {
            public void actionPerformed(ActionEvent event) {
                dispose();
                System.exit(0);
            }
        });
        return fileMenu;
    }
}
```

Popup Menus

Incredible as it may seem, popup menus were nowhere to be found in the original AWT. As a result, many developers implemented their own popups, but since such popups were drawn entirely in Java code and not implemented by a peer, the native look-and-feel was lost. Fortunately, this deficiency was remedied in the 1.1 version of the AWT with the introduction of a peer-based popup menu.

Popup menus are extremely easy to use. In this section, we'll discuss creating popups, displaying them, and handling the events they generate.

Popups and Components

Popup menus must be attached to an AWT component. In fact, `java.awt.Component` has two methods for attaching and removing popup menus:

- `add(PopupMenu popup)`
- `remove(MenuComponent popup)`

Creating a popup menu, attaching it to a component, and displaying it are trivial. The following applet creates a popup menu, adds it to an applet, and then adds four items to the popup menu. When the time is right—bear with us, we'll explain in a moment—the popup menu is shown at the location of the cursor:

Example 17-12 PopupTest Applet

```java
import java.applet.Applet;
import java.awt.*;
import java.awt.event.*;

public class PopupTest extends Applet {
    private PopupMenu popup = new PopupMenu();

    public void init() {
        add(popup);

        popup.add(new MenuItem("item one"));
        popup.add(new MenuItem("item two"));
        popup.add(new MenuItem("item three"));
        popup.add(new MenuItem("item four"));

        addMouseListener(new MouseAdapter() {
            public void mousePressed (MouseEvent e) {
                showPopup(e);
            }
            public void mouseClicked (MouseEvent e) {
                showPopup(e);
            }
            public void mouseReleased(MouseEvent e) {
                showPopup(e);
            }
        });
    }
    void showPopup(MouseEvent e) {
        if(e.isPopupTrigger())
            popup.show(this, e.getX(), e.getY());
    }
}
```

The popup menu is shown in action in Figure 17-8.

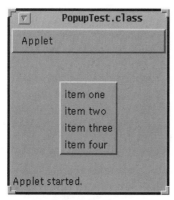

Figure 17-8 Popup Menu
Popup menus should be shown when
`MouseEvent.isPopupTrigger` method returns `true`.

There are a number of things to note concerning our simple applet.

First of all, we add the popup to the applet. Note that the `add` method invoked in the first line of `init()` is not the familiar `Container.add` method that adds a component to a container, but the `Component.add()`, which adds a popup menu to a component.

Second, note that menu items are added to a popup menu in exactly the same manner as items are added to a menu because the `PopupMenu` class extends `Menu`.

Third, we have added a mouse listener to the applet in the form of an inner class extending `MouseAdapter`, which overrides `mousePressed()`, `mouseClicked()`, and `mouseReleased()`, all of which invoke the `showPopup` method.

`showPopup()` checks the event it is passed to see whether the event is a popup trigger; if so, it shows the popup.

Two questions remain unanswered concerning our applet. First, why do we have to override the three mouse event handling methods, and second, why are we passing a reference to the applet to `PopupMenu.show()`?

The answer to the first question lies in the fact that popups are shown in response to a sequence of events, commonly known as the popup *trigger*. The popup trigger varies between platforms, for instance:

- **Motif Popup Trigger:** On a mouse button 3 DOWN, the popup is displayed and stays up if the button is held down or released within a short period of time. A subsequent mouse down, either outside of the popup or in one of the popup's items, brings the popup down.

- **Windows 95 Popup Trigger:** The popup is displayed on a mouse button 2 UP. A subsequent mouse button 1 or mouse button 2 down either over an item in the popup or outside of the popup menu brings the popup down.

Since the algorithm for popup triggers varies between platforms, the AWT must provide a unified mechanism for detecting when the popup trigger has been pulled, so to speak. Since the popup trigger is activated on all platforms as the result of a mouse event, the MouseEvent class comes equipped with an isPopupTrigger method that returns true if the trigger has been pulled, and false if it has not.

Out of all the mouse events that can occur in the AWT, mouse pressed, mouse clicked, and mouse released are the only ones that can cause the trigger to be pulled, so we must override them all to check for the trigger.

(This is a somewhat awkward way to have to detect the popup trigger. A better solution might have been to implement a popup trigger event that is fired by components equipped with popups. That way, we could register a popup trigger listener with components and not have to deal with generic mouse events. Not only would this be more convenient, but it would be much more in line with the delegation-based event model.)

The answer to the second question is that popups are shown at an offset to a component. You may be wondering why we have to pass the same component that the popup is attached to; the answer is that popups can come up relative to any component contained in the container hierarchy of the component to which the popup is attached. That way, a popup can be attached to, say, a frame, but can be shown relative to any component contained in the frame.

Handling Popup Events

As we saw in "Semantic Events" on page 269, menu items fire action events when they are selected. Example 17-13 lists an applet that handles the action events fired by a popup menu.

Example 17-13 PopupActionTest Applet

```
import java.applet.Applet;
import java.awt.*;
import java.awt.event.*;

public class PopupActionTest extends Applet {
    private PopupMenu popup = new PopupMenu();
    private MenuItem  itemOne, itemTwo, itemThree, itemFour;
    private PopupActionListener actionListener;

    public void init() {
        add(popup);

        popup.add(itemOne   = new MenuItem("item one"));
        popup.add(itemTwo   = new MenuItem("item two"));
        popup.add(itemThree = new MenuItem("item three"));
        popup.add(itemFour  = new MenuItem("item four"));

        actionListener = new PopupActionListener();

        itemOne.addActionListener  (actionListener);
        itemTwo.addActionListener  (actionListener);
        itemThree.addActionListener(actionListener);
        itemFour.addActionListener (actionListener);

        Menu m = new Menu("cascading");
        m.add("item one");
        m.add("item two");
        m.add("item three");
        m.add("item four");

        popup.add(m);

        addMouseListener(new MouseAdapter() {
            public void mousePressed (MouseEvent e) {
                showPopup(e);
            }
            public void mouseClicked (MouseEvent e) {
                showPopup(e);
            }
```

```
            public void mouseReleased(MouseEvent e) {
                showPopup(e);
            }
        });
    }
    void showPopup(MouseEvent e) {
        if(e.isPopupTrigger())
            popup.show(this, e.getX(), e.getY());
    }
    class PopupActionListener implements ActionListener {
        public void actionPerformed(ActionEvent event) {
            MenuItem mi = (MenuItem)event.getSource();
            showStatus(mi.getLabel());
        }
    }
}
```

The `PopupActionTest` applet is essentially the same as the previous applet, except that we've added event handling to detect when an item in the popup has been selected.[3] We maintain references to each item in the popup so that we can add a single instance of `ActionListener` to each menu item. When an item is selected from the popup, the action listener invokes the applet's `showStatus` method to display the label of the item selected in the status bar of the applet.

Showing Popups Relative to Components

As noted previously, `PopupMenu.show()` takes three arguments—a component and an x,y location. The location specifies an offset from the upper left-hand corner of the component. The component can be any component in the container hierarchy associated with the component to which the popup is attached. Our final popup applet, shown in Figure 17-9, illustrates showing a popup over different components in the applet's containment hierarchy.

The applet contains three `ColoredCanvas` instances, along with a `Choice` for selecting which colored canvas the popup will be shown relative to. When a selection is made from the choice, the popup is shown 5 pixels below and 5 pixels to the right of the colored canvas selected in the choice. Note that although the popup is attached to the applet, we don't detect the firing of the applet's popup trigger, and therefore the only mechanism provided for showing the popup is by making a selection from the choice. Once again, we'd like to point out that the call to `add(popup)` invokes `Component.add(PopupMenu)`, while the other calls to `add()` invoke `Container.add(Component)`, as we've indicated with comments in Example 17-14, which lists the source for the applet.

---

3.   Note that we're using inner classes here. See "Named Inner Classes" on page 294.

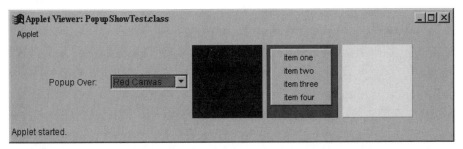

Figure 17-9 Popups Are Shown Relative to Specific Components
Popups can be shown relative to any component in the container
hierarchy of the component to which the popup is attached.

Example 17-14 `PopupShowTest` Applet

```java
import java.applet.Applet;
import java.awt.*;
import java.awt.event.*;

public class PopupShowTest extends Applet {
    Choice         choice = new Choice();
    PopupMenu      popup  = new PopupMenu();
    ColoredCanvas popupRelativeToMe;
    ColoredCanvas blueCanvas, redCanvas, yellowCanvas;

    public void init() {
        blueCanvas        = new ColoredCanvas(Color.blue);
        redCanvas         = new ColoredCanvas(Color.red);
        yellowCanvas      = new ColoredCanvas(Color.yellow);
        popupRelativeToMe = blueCanvas;

        popup.add(new MenuItem("item one"));
        popup.add(new MenuItem("item two"));
        popup.add(new MenuItem("item three"));
        popup.add(new MenuItem("item four"));

        add(popup);                      // Component.add(PopupMenu)

        Menu m = new Menu("Cascading");
        m.add("item one");
        m.add("item two");
        m.add("item three");
        m.add("item four");

        add(new Label("Popup Over:"));//Container.add(Component)
        add(choice);
```

```
        add(blueCanvas);               // Container.add(Component)
        add(redCanvas);                // Container.add(Component)
        add(yellowCanvas);             // Container.add(Component)

        choice.add("Blue Canvas");
        choice.add("Yellow Canvas");
        choice.add("Red Canvas");

        choice.addItemListener(new ItemListener() {
            public void itemStateChanged(ItemEvent event) {
                Choice c      = (Choice)event.getSource();
                String label = c.getSelectedItem();

                if(label.equals("Blue Canvas"))
                    popupRelativeToMe = blueCanvas;
                else if(label.equals("Red Canvas"))
                    popupRelativeToMe = redCanvas;
                else if(label.equals("Yellow Canvas"))
                    popupRelativeToMe = yellowCanvas;

                popup.show(popupRelativeToMe, 5, 5);
            }
        });
    }
}
class ColoredCanvas extends Canvas {
    private Color color;

    public ColoredCanvas(Color color) {
        this.color = color;
    }
    public void paint(Graphics g) {
        Dimension size = getSize();
        g.setColor  (color);
        g.fill3DRect(0,0,size.width-1,size.height-1,true);
    }
    public Dimension getPreferredSize() {
        return new Dimension(100,100);
    }
}
```

Summary

Menubars and menus are easy to create and display in the AWT; however, there is a certain amount of drudgery that every application with a menubar must implement. We have encapsulated that drudgery in a `FrameWithMenuBar` class that is extended by most of the example applications in this chapter. We have also presented a general-utility class, `MenuBarPrinter`, that prints each menu and menu item contained in a menubar.

Tear-off menus are supported by the AWT. A menu is designated as a tear-off menu at construction time by an additional boolean argument being passed to a `Menu` constructor; a `true` value indicates that the menu is to be a tear-off; a `false` value indicates that the menu is not a tear-off. Tear-off menus are not supported under Windows 95.

The AWT supports help menus, which are like ordinary menus in every respect except that they are always the rightmost menu in the menubar. Under Motif, the help menu is right-justified in the menubar itself. Under Windows 95, the menu is simply the rightmost menu in the menubar.

The AWT also supports checkbox menu items, and we have presented a general-purpose class—`RadioMenu`—which provides checkbox menu items that are mutually exclusive, ensuring that only one of its items is checked at any given time.

We have also explored implementing cascading menus and menus that can be modified dynamically. Since `Menu` extends `MenuItem`, a `Menu` can be added as an item to another menu. Menus can have their items enabled or disabled after their creation, and items can be added to or removed from a menu after construction.

Currently, setting a menu item's font does not work under Windows 95, and setting a menu item's label after construction does not work under either Motif or Windows 95.

CHAPTER
18

Mouseless Operation and Printing

This chapter explores both mouseless operation and printing.

The AWT supports mouseless operation on two fronts: tabbing between components and menu shortcuts. We'll explore both mechanisms in this chapter.

Printing support is seamlessly integrated into the existing AWT graphics model; as a result, it is intuitive and simple to use. The flip side of this, however, is that implementing platform-independent support for printing is notoriously tricky to nail down, so there were still some outstanding bugs concerning printing.

Mouseless Operation

Support for mouseless operation encompasses two mechanisms: keyboard traversal and menu shortcuts, both of which are quite simple to implement. We'll start off with keyboard traversal and then move on to menu shortcuts.

Keyboard Traversal

GUI users today expect to be able to navigate user interface components either by using the mouse or the keyboard. Although all components could be activated with the mouse in the original AWT, explicit support for keyboard traversal was only available if it was supported by the native windowing system. As a result, the mechanism for keyboard traversal was inconsistent between platforms and was not supported in the underlying AWT code.

The AWT provides a unified mechanism across platforms for moving the focus from one component to another:

- TAB moves focus forward to the next component.
- SHIFT-TAB moves focus backward to the previous component.

The order of traversal, i.e., which component is in front of or behind another component, is defined by the order in which components are added to their containers.[1] If the first component added to a container has focus, a TAB will move the focus to the second component added to the container, whereas a subsequent SHIFT-TAB moves the focus back to the first component. There is one catch, however: not all components are willing to accept focus on every platform. For instance, buttons are willing to accept focus under Windows 95 and Motif, but not on the Macintosh. The `java.awt.Component` class, as a result, comes equipped with an `isFocusTraversable` method, which returns `true` if the component supports accepting focus and `false` if it does not.

Standard AWT Components and Keyboard Traversal

`java.awt.Window` maintains an association with an instance of `java.awt.FocusManager`. The `FocusManager` class keeps track of which component currently has focus and manages moving the focus forward and backward in response to a TAB or SHIFT-TAB, respectively. If you are only dealing with standard AWT components, you don't have to give keyboard traversal a second thought, apart from ensuring that you add components to a container in the order desired for keyboard traversal. Our first applet illustrates keyboard traversal in a container that might be used to make a purchase of some sort, shown in Figure 18-1.

Keyboard traversal for the standard AWT components in our applet is handled by the window's focus manager—our rather long-winded applet is shown in Example 18-1. Note that we use two custom components: `Separator` and `ButtonPanel`, but they have little bearing on the concepts we are stressing here. The separator serves to visually spruce up the applet to a small degree, and the button panel simplifies the layout of the Purchase and Cancel buttons.

One thing worth noting about the custom components used in the applet, however, is that neither of them is interested in accepting focus. Custom components, unlike the standard AWT components, must provide explicit support for keyboard traversal, as we shall see in our next applet. Also, our applet employs an instance of `GridBagLayout` to lay out the components in an

---

1. This paradigm also defines the zorder of components—See "Components and Zorder" on page 445.

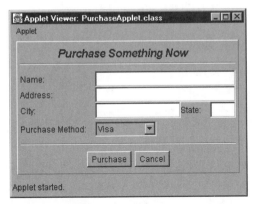

Figure 18-1 Keyboard Traversal with Standard AWT Components
Keyboard traversal is handled automatically for standard AWT
components. Order of traversal is defined by the order in which
components are added to their containers.

aesthetically pleasing manner; however, that is more the purview of
"GridBagLayout and Input Forms" on page 380. The intention of the
PurchaseApplet is to illustrate that keyboard traversal is handled
automatically for standard AWT components and that the order of traversal is
defined by the order in which components are added to their containers.

Example 18-1 PurchaseApplet Listing

```
import java.applet.Applet;
import java.awt.*;

public class PurchaseApplet extends Applet {
    public void init() {
        ThreeDPanel p = new ThreeDPanel();
        p.add(new ButtonPurchaseForm());
        add(p);
    }
}
class ThreeDPanel extends Panel {
    public void paint(Graphics g) {
        Dimension sz = getSize();
        g.setColor(Color.lightGray);
        g.draw3DRect(0, 0, sz.width-1, sz.height-1, true);
    }
}
class ButtonPurchaseForm extends Panel {
    Separator sep = new Separator();
```

```
Label title   = new Label("Purchase Something Now");
Label name    = new Label("Name:");
Label address = new Label("Address:");
Label payment = new Label("Purchase Method:");
Label phone   = new Label("Phone:");
Label city    = new Label("City:");
Label state   = new Label("State:");

TextField nameField    = new TextField(25);
TextField addressField = new TextField(25);
TextField cityField    = new TextField(15);
TextField stateField   = new TextField(2);

Choice    paymentChoice = new Choice();

Button    paymentButton = new Button("Purchase");
Button    cancelButton  = new Button("Cancel");

public ButtonPurchaseForm() {
    GridBagLayout      gbl = new GridBagLayout();
    GridBagConstraints gbc = new GridBagConstraints();

    setLayout(gbl);

    paymentChoice.add("Visa");
    paymentChoice.add("MasterCard");
    paymentChoice.add("COD");

    title.setFont(new Font("Times-Roman",
                        Font.BOLD + Font.ITALIC,
                        16));
    gbc.anchor    = GridBagConstraints.NORTH;
    gbc.gridwidth = GridBagConstraints.REMAINDER;
    add(title, gbc);

    gbc.fill      = GridBagConstraints.HORIZONTAL;
    gbc.insets    = new Insets(0,0,10,0);
    add(sep, gbc);

    gbc.anchor    = GridBagConstraints.WEST;
    gbc.gridwidth = 1;
    gbc.insets    = new Insets(0,0,0,0);
    add(name, gbc);

    gbc.gridwidth = GridBagConstraints.REMAINDER;
    add(nameField, gbc);

    gbc.gridwidth = 1;
    add(address, gbc);

    gbc.gridwidth = GridBagConstraints.REMAINDER;
    add(addressField, gbc);
```

```
        gbc.gridwidth = 1;
        add(city, gbc);

        add(cityField, gbc);

        add(state, gbc);

        gbc.gridwidth = GridBagConstraints.REMAINDER;
        add(stateField, gbc);

        gbc.gridwidth = 1;
        add(payment, gbc);

        gbc.insets = new Insets(5,0,5,0);

        gbc.gridwidth = GridBagConstraints.REMAINDER;
        gbc.fill      = GridBagConstraints.NONE;
        add(paymentChoice, gbc);

        ButtonPanel buttonPanel = new ButtonPanel();

        buttonPanel.add(paymentButton);
        buttonPanel.add(cancelButton);

        gbc.anchor    = GridBagConstraints.SOUTH;
        gbc.insets    = new Insets(5,0,0,0);
        gbc.fill      = GridBagConstraints.HORIZONTAL;
        gbc.gridwidth = 4;
        add(buttonPanel, gbc);
    }
}
```

Once again, the order in which we've added the components to their container defines the order in which keyboard focus is traversed. Obviously, our representation of the applet in Figure 18-1 cannot convey keyboard traversal, so you may wish to run the applet from the CD in order to verify that we have indeed been telling the truth.

Custom Components and Keyboard Traversal

While keyboard traversal is handled automatically for the standard AWT components, you are pretty much on your own if you are developing a custom component. Fortunately, implementing keyboard traversal support for custom components is very straightforward. We will start out by enumerating the steps involved, followed by an example; these should serve to set you well on your way to implementing support for keyboard traversal in your own custom components.

The first order of business when considering keyboard traversal is to decide whether or not your particular custom component is interested in accepting keyboard focus. For instance, in the previous applet, we used an instance of `Separator`, which has no interest whatsoever in accepting focus. If your component is interested in accepting focus, then you should adhere to the following:

1. Override `isFocusTraversable()` to return `true`.[2]

2. Implement a `FocusListener` that responds appropriately to gaining/losing focus. Typically, this involves some type of visual feedback.

3. Implement a `MouseListener` that invokes `requestFocus()` in the appropriate mouse handler method.

4. Add the focus listener and mouse listener implemented in steps 2 and 3 to the component.

That's all there is to supporting keyboard traversal in custom components. Let's take a look at a simple custom component whose only purpose is to illustrate implementing keyboard traversal.

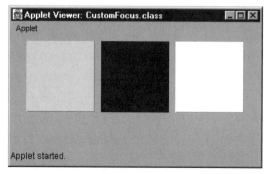

Figure 18-2 Keyboard Traversal with Custom Components
It is up to the developer to provide keyboard traversal support for custom components. The component on the left currently has focus.

---

2. By default, it is up to a component's peer to provide the return value from `isFocusTraversable()`.

Our custom component is simply a blotch of color that is interested in receiving keyboard focus. Since the implementation of `ColoredCanvas` is relatively short, we'll show you the code for the entire component in Example 18-2 and then discuss the code pertinent to supporting keyboard traversal.

Example 18-2 ColoredCanvas Tracking Focus

```java
import java.awt.*;
import java.awt.event.*;

public class ColoredCanvas extends Canvas {
    Color color;
    boolean hasFocus = false;

    public ColoredCanvas(Color color) {
        this.color = color;

        addMouseListener(new MouseAdapter() {
            public void mousePressed(MouseEvent event) {
                requestFocus();
            }
        });
        addFocusListener(new FocusListener() {
            public void focusGained(FocusEvent e) {
                hasFocus = true;
                repaint();
            }
            public void focusLost(FocusEvent event) {
                hasFocus = false;
                repaint();
            }
        });
        addKeyListener(new KeyAdapter() {
            public void keyPressed(KeyEvent event) {
                System.out.println("Key Pressed");
            }
        });
    }
    public boolean isFocusTraversable() {
        return true;
    }
    public void paint(Graphics g) {
        Dimension size = getSize();
        g.setColor   (color);
        g.fill3DRect(2,2,size.width-4,size.height-4,true);

        if(hasFocus == true) {
            g.setColor(Color.black);
            g.drawRect(0,0,size.width-1,size.height-1);
        }
    }
    public Dimension getPreferredSize() {
```

```
         return new Dimension(100,100);
      }
      public Frame getFrame() {
         Component c = this;

         while((c = c.getParent()) != null) {
            if(c instanceof Frame)
               return (Frame)c;
         }
         return null;
      }
   }
```

As required, `ColoredCanvas` implements `isFocusTraversable()` to return `true`. We have also implemented a `FocusListener` that responds appropriately to gaining/losing focus and added it to the component in one fell swoop, through the magic of inner classes.[3] In addition, we've implemented a `MouseListener` that requests focus whenever a mouse press occurs and added it to the component.

We've also implemented one additional step not listed above—we've tracked whether or not the component has focus. If the component has focus, then its `paint` method draws a black border around the component; if the component does not have focus, no border is drawn. This provides visual feedback when the component has focus and ensures that any subsequent repainting of the component will provide the correct visual feedback.

However, we have done a little more work than we need to in order to track whether or not the component currently has focus, for there is another object that is already doing that for us—the focus manager associated with the window in which the component resides. Example 18-3 lists a new and improved version of `ColoredCanvas` that asks the frame in which it resides whether or not it is the focus owner.

 Example 18-3 `ColoredCanvas Class—FocusManager Tracking Focus`

```
import java.awt.*;
import java.awt.event.*;

public class ColoredCanvas extends Canvas {
   Color color;

   public ColoredCanvas(Color color) {
      this.color = color;
```

---

3. See "Anonymous Inner Classes" on page 295 for a discussion of inner classes and event handling.

```java
            addMouseListener(new MouseAdapter() {
                public void mousePressed(MouseEvent event) {
                    requestFocus();
                }
            });
            addFocusListener(new FocusListener() {
                public void focusGained(FocusEvent e) {
                    repaint();
                }
                public void focusLost(FocusEvent event) {
                    repaint();
                }
            });
            addKeyListener(new KeyAdapter() {
                public void keyPressed(KeyEvent event) {
                    System.out.println("Key Pressed");
                }
            });
        }
        public boolean isFocusTraversable() {
            return true;
        }
        public void paint(Graphics g) {
            Dimension size = getSize();
            g.setColor  (color);
            g.fill3DRect(2,2,size.width-4,size.height-4,true);

            if(getFrame().getFocusOwner() == this) {
                g.setColor(Color.black);
                g.drawRect(0,0,size.width-1,size.height-1);
            }
        }
        public Dimension getPreferredSize() {
            return new Dimension(100,100);
        }
        public Frame getFrame() {
            Component c = this;

            while((c = c.getParent()) != null) {
                if(c instanceof Frame)
                    return (Frame)c;
            }
            return null;
        }
    }
```

Notice that this version of `ColoredCanvas` no longer explicitly keeps track of whether it currently has the keyboard focus. `Frame.getFocusOwner()` is invoked to determine if the component currently has the keyboard focus.

You may take issue with the fact that our new version of `ColoredCanvas` has traded tracking whether it has focus with having to implement a method that returns the frame in which the canvas resides. However, such functionality is better placed in a utility class that all classes have access to. Regardless of whether the component itself keeps track of whether it currently has the keyboard focus— we recommend that you let the focus manager handle that responsibility— `ColoredCanvas` is now able to accept keyboard focus, either by tabbing or pressing the mouse, and provides visual feedback indicating whether or not it currently has focus.

Finally, the `CustomFocus` applet is listed in Example 18-4.

Example 18-4   CustomFocus Applet

```
import java.applet.Applet;
import java.awt.*;
import java.awt.event.*;

public class CustomFocus extends Applet {
    ColoredCanvas yellowCanvas = new ColoredCanvas(Color.yellow);
    ColoredCanvas blueCanvas   = new ColoredCanvas(Color.blue);
    ColoredCanvas whiteCanvas  = new ColoredCanvas(Color.white);

    public void init() {
        add(yellowCanvas);
        add(blueCanvas);
        add(whiteCanvas);

        yellowCanvas.requestFocus();
    }
}
```

> **AWT TIP**
>
> *Let the Window's Focus Manager Track Focus For Custom Components*
>
> Every AWT window comes with an instance of FocusManager that is responsible for tracking which component in the window currently has keyboard focus. Windows also come with a method getFocusOwner(), that returns a reference to the component that currently has focus. Custom components should use the Window.getFocusOwner method to determine if they currently have keyboard focus.

Menu Shortcuts

Menu shortcuts provide the ability to activate a menu item by using the keyboard. Menu shortcuts are also known as menu accelerators or keyboard equivalents. Shortcuts have a key modifier that varies among platforms:

- Macintosh: \<Command\>
- Windows 95:   \<Control\>
- Motif: \<Control\>

The `java.awt.Toolkit` class provides a method that returns the appropriate modifier—`Toolkit.getMenuShortcutKeyMask()`—should you ever have the need to programmatically determine the modifier key on a particular platform.

Menu items must provide some kind of visual indication that a shortcut may be used to activate the menu item, when applicable. Such visual indication varies among platforms and is handled in a platform-dependent manner by the AWT.

Menu Classes and Shortcuts

Menu shortcuts are attached to menu items by instantiating an instance of `MenuShortcut`, which is passed either to a menu item's constructor or to a menu item's `setShortcut` method. Table 18-1 shows the public methods of the `java.awt.MenuShortcut` class.

Table 18-1 `java.awt.MenuShortcut` **Public Methods**

Method	Description
`int getKey()`	Returns raw key code, e.g., 'c', 't', etc.
`boolean usesShiftModifier()`	Returns `true` if SHIFT modifier is used
`boolean equals(MenuShortcut)`	If keycode and shift modifiers are the same, two shortcuts are equal
`String toString()`	Describes the shortcut

Table 18-2 shows the methods that have been added to the `java.awt.MenuItem` class to accommodate menu shortcuts.

Table 18-2 `java.awt.MenuItem` **Methods Dealing with Menu Shortcuts**

Method	Description
`MenuItem(String, MenuShortcut)`	Constructs with menu shortcut
`MenuShortcut getShortcut()`	Returns shortcut for item
`void setShortcut(MenuShortcut)`	Sets shortcut for item
`void deleteShortcut()`	Deletes an item's shortcut

Note that the first method in Table 18-2 is a `MenuItem` constructor; menu items can have their shortcut specified either at construction time or after construction. Additionally, `java.awt.MenuItem` provides methods for obtaining an item's shortcut and removing a shortcut from a menu item.

Finally, `java.awt.MenuBar` has some additional methods to deal with menu shortcuts, as you can see from Table 18-3.

Table 18-3 `java.awt.MenuBar` **Methods Dealing with Menu Shortcuts**

Method	Description
`MenuItem getShorcutMenuItem( MenuShortcut)`	Returns menu item with specified shortcut
`Enumeration shortcuts()`	Returns an enumeration of all shortcuts in the menu items contained in the menubar's menus
`boolean handleShortcut(KeyEvent)`	Process shortcut key event
`void deleteShortcut( MenuShortcut)`	Deletes shortcut from appropriate menu item

A Menu Shortcuts Example

Figure 18-3 shows a Java application that has a menubar with an Edit menu that has shortcuts for the cut, copy, and paste menu items.

Figure 18-3 Menu Shortcuts Displayed in a `MenuItem`
Menu shortcuts are attached to the cut, copy, and paste menu items in a Motif window. Visual indication of shortcuts in menu items varies between platforms.

Our application simply creates a menu shortcut for the cut, copy, and paste menu items and then constructs the menu items by passing in the appropriate shortcut. The applet is listed in its entirety in Example 18-5.

Example 18-5 `ShorcutTest` Application

```java
import java.awt.*;
import java.awt.event.*;

public class ShortcutTest extends Frame {
    private MenuItem quitItem;

    public static void main(String args[]) {
        ShortcutTest test =
            new ShortcutTest("FileEdit Menu Test");

        test.setBounds(300,300,300,300);
        test.show();
    }
    public ShortcutTest(String s) {
        super(s);

      MenuBar mbar = new MenuBar();

        mbar.add(createFileMenu());
        mbar.add(createEditMenu());
      setMenuBar(mbar);

      quitItem.addActionListener(new ActionListener() {
          public void actionPerformed(ActionEvent event) {
              dispose();
              System.exit(0);
          }
      });
    }
    private Menu createFileMenu() {
        Menu fileMenu = new Menu("File");
        fileMenu.add(quitItem = new MenuItem("Quit"));
        return fileMenu;
    }
    private Menu createEditMenu() {
        Menu editMenu = new Menu("Edit");

      MenuShortcut copyShortcut  = new MenuShortcut('c');
      MenuShortcut cutShortcut   = new MenuShortcut('x');
      MenuShortcut pasteShortcut = new MenuShortcut('p');

      MenuItemListener itemListener = new MenuItemListener();
      MenuItem cutItem  = new MenuItem("Cut",   cutShortcut),
               copyItem = new MenuItem("Copy",  copyShortcut),
               pasteItem= new MenuItem("paste", pasteShortcut);

      cutItem.addActionListener  (itemListener);
      copyItem.addActionListener (itemListener);
      pasteItem.addActionListener(itemListener);
```

```
            editMenu.add(cutItem);
            editMenu.add(copyItem);
            editMenu.add(pasteItem);

            return editMenu;
        }
    }
    class MenuItemListener implements ActionListener {
        public void actionPerformed(ActionEvent event) {
            MenuItem item = (MenuItem)event.getSource();
            System.out.println(item.getLabel());
        }
    }
```

It is in the `createEditMenu` method that all of the action takes place as far as menu shortcuts are concerned. Three shortcuts are created, each of which is passed to the appropriate `MenuItem` constructor. That's all there is to attaching shortcuts to menu items—from here on out the AWT will process the appropriate keystrokes to activate the menu item associated with a shortcut.

Printing

You can print a `Graphics` object—but not just any `Graphics` object; you can only print a `PrintGraphics` object. You can either manually draw into the graphics or have a component draw into it; either way, after you are done painting into the graphics, you can turn around and print it. If a component prints into the graphics object and the component is a container, you can choose to print all of the components contained within the container's containment hierarchy.

Obtaining a Reference to a PrintGraphics

Whether you want to paint a (hierarchy of) component(s) or you just want to paint into a graphics object and then print it, you must first obtain a reference to a special extension of the `Graphics` class—a `PrintGraphics`. This is a four-step process, outlined below:

1. Obtain a reference to a frame.
2. Obtain a reference to the default toolkit.
3. Invoke the toolkit's `getPrintJob` method, passing in the frame obtained in step 2, which returns a reference to a `PrintJob`.
4. Invoke the print job's `getGraphics` method, which returns a reference to a `PrintGraphics`.

Once you have a reference to a `PrintGraphics` object, you can either pass it to a component's `print` or `printAll` methods or you can paint into it as you would any graphics object. Printing the graphics merely requires you to invoke the graphics's `dispose` method, which flushes the graphics object to the printer. When you are done printing, you should invoke `end()` on the print job obtained in step 3 above.

An Applet That Prints Itself

Let's start out with a simple applet that prints itself, shown in Figure 18-4.

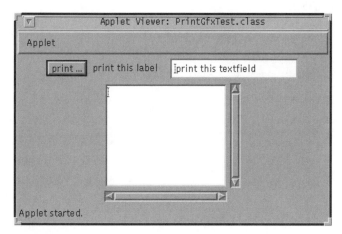

Figure 18-4 An Applet That Prints Itself
The print button prints out all of the components contained in the applet.

The listing for our applet is shown in Example 18-6.

Example 18-6 PrintApplet Listing

```
import java.applet.Applet;
import java.awt.*;
import java.awt.event.*;
import java.util.Properties;

public class PrintApplet extends Applet {
    Button printButton = new Button("print ...");

    static Frame getFrame(Component c) {
        while((c = c.getParent()) != null) {
            if(c instanceof Frame)
```

```
                return (Frame)c;
        }
        return null;
    }
    static void printComponents(Component c) {
        Toolkit    tk    = Toolkit.getDefaultToolkit();
        Frame      frame = getFrame(c);
        Properties props = new Properties();

        props.put("awt.print.printer",   "durango");
        props.put("awt.print.numCopies", "2");

        if(tk != null) {
            String    name = c.getName() + " print job";
            PrintJob pj    = tk.getPrintJob(frame, name, props);

            if(pj != null) {
                Graphics pg = pj.getGraphics();

                if(pg != null) {
                    try {
                        c.printAll(pg);
                    }
                    finally {
                        pg.dispose();
                    }
                }
                pj.end();
            }
            System.out.println(props);
        }
    }
    public void init() {
        add(printButton);
        add(new Label("print this label"));
        add(new TextField("print this textfield"));
        add(new TextArea(10,20));

        printButton.addActionListener(new ActionListener() {
            public void actionPerformed(ActionEvent event) {
                printComponents(PrintApplet.this);
            }
        });
    }
}
```

The most interesting method in our applet, of course, is the static
printComponents method. By the way, If printComponents() were placed
in a utility class, it would be available to print any component. After obtaining the
reference to the print graphics, we pass it to the component's (the component is
the applet in this case) printAll method and then invoke the graphics'

`dispose` method, which flushes it to the printer. Optionally, once we had the reference to the print graphics, we could have drawn directly into it and then printed it out:

```
if(pg != null) {
    try {
      pg.drawLine(10,10,50,50);
    }
    finally {
        pg.dispose();
    }
}
```

The Print Dialog and Its Properties

One thing that we've glossed over is the fact that `Toolkit.getPrintJob()` shows a platform-dependent print dialog. The Motif version of the print dialog is shown in Figure 18-5.

If the print button in the dialog is activated, `Toolkit.getPrintJob()` returns a non-null reference to a `PrintJob`. If the cancel button is activated, then a null reference is returned. So, you should always check the return value of `Toolkit.getPrintJob()` to find out whether the job was cancelled.

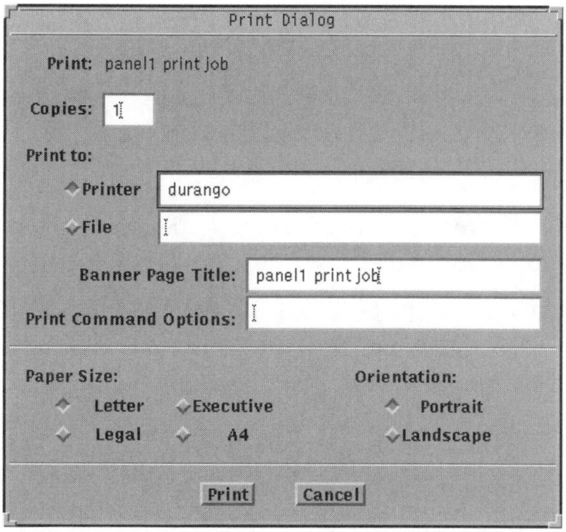

![Motif Print Dialog window titled "Print Dialog" with Print: panel1 print job, Copies: 1, Print to: Printer durango / File, Banner Page Title: panel1 print job, Print Command Options, Paper Size options (Letter, Executive, Legal, A4), Orientation options (Portrait, Landscape), and Print / Cancel buttons]

Figure 18-5 Motif Print Dialog
`Toolkit.getPrintJob()` shows a platform-dependent print dialog.

Another point we need to expand upon is that `Toolkit.getPrintJob()` takes two arguments in addition to a frame: the name of the print job and a `Properties` object. The properties passed in specify any platform-dependent printing properties; for instance, you could specify that "awt.print.printer" is "durango", and "awt.print.numCopies" is "2":

```
static void printComponents(Component c) {
    Toolkit    tk    = Toolkit.getDefaultToolkit();
    Frame      frame = getFrame(c);
    Properties props = new Properties();

    props.put("awt.print.printer",   "durango");
    props.put("awt.print.numCopies", "2");

    if(tk != null) {
        String    name = c.getName() + " print job";
        PrintJob pj    = tk.getPrintJob(frame, name, props);

        if(pj != null) {
            Graphics pg = pj.getGraphics();

            if(pg != null) {
                try {
                 c.printAll(pg);
                }
                finally {
                    pg.dispose();
                }
            }
            pj.end();
        }
        System.out.println(props);
    }
}
```

Specifying the two properties above results in those properties being set in the print dialog, as you can see in Figure 18-6.

Another nifty feature of `Toolkit.getPrintJob()` is that it modifies the properties it is passed so that the values match whatever the user entered in the print dialog. In the code snippet above, we print out the properties object after the call to `getPrintJob()` returns. In the print dialog, we changed the number of copies to 1 and changed the printer to sabre. As you can see from the output, those changes were stored in the properties object we passed in:

```
                          Print Dialog
      Print:  panel1 print job

    Copies:  2

    Print to:
          Printer   durango

          File     I

          Banner Page Title:   panel1 print job
    Print Command Options:  I


    Paper Size:                      Orientation:
        Letter    Executive             Portrait
        Legal     A4                    Landscape


                    Print    Cancel
```

Figure 18-6 Motif Print Dialog with Preset Properties
The number of copies and printer name were specified with the
properties object passed to `Toolkit.getPrintJob()`

```
{awt.print.numCopies=1, awt.print.printer=sabre,
awt.print.paperSize=letter, awt.print.destination=printer,
awt.print.orientation=portrait}
```

Pagination

You're on your own as far as pagination is concerned. Each print graphics will
print out a single page, so it's up to you to organize your print graphics when
printing multiple pages. However, the `PrintJob` class will lend a hand by
providing two methods concerning pagination:

- `Dimension getPageDimension()`
- `int getPageResolution()`

The former method returns the page dimension in pixels; the latter returns the
page resolution in pixels per inch. It's up to you to do the math.

Summary

The AWT provides three features that are essential to developing anything but the most trivial of applications: mouseless operation, and printing. For the most part, each feature is straightforward to use and fits well with the existing AWT infrastructure.

Mouseless operation is an expected feature for graphical user interfaces that was conspicuous in its absence in the original AWT. The AWT has laid the foundation for mouseless operation by providing two basic features: keyboard traversal and menu shortcuts. More support for mouseless operation will be added in future versions of the AWT.

Finally, the AWT has provided access to platform-dependent printing. The model used for printing is in line with the AWT's graphics model and is intuitive and easy to use. A major chunk of functionality is wrapped up in the toolkit's getPrintJob method, which posts a platform-dependent print dialog and provides a mechanism for getting and setting the properties in the dialog.

CHAPTER
19

Lightweight
Components

AWT components are heavyweight, meaning they have a native peer and are rendered in an opaque window of their own. Since a heavyweight component is rendered in its own opaque window, it must always be rectangular in shape; if you want a see-through component, a heavyweight won't cut the mustard. Also, as you might suspect, a 1:1 ratio of native window per AWT component is not exactly ideal from a performance perspective.

Lightweight components do not require a native window because they are rendered in their container's graphics. As a result, lightweight components require fewer resources than heavyweight components, and their backgrounds are transparent. Having transparent backgrounds means that lightweight components can appear to be nonrectangular, even though the bounding box of a lightweight component (obtained by invoking `Component.getBounds()`) is rectangular.

In addition, lightweights must have a heavyweight container in their container ancestry, or they will not have a window in which to draw. In practice, this requirement is not a problem because components reside in either an `Applet` or a `Frame`, both of which are heavyweight containers.

Introducing Lightweight Components

Developing custom components versions of the AWT prior to 1.1 typically involved extending either `java.awt.Canvas` or `java.awt.Panel`—the latter was extended when a custom component had to function as a container.

Lightweight custom components are implemented simply by extending either `java.awt.Component` or `java.awt.Container`. With previous versions of the AWT, `Component` and `Container` could be extended only by classes residing in the `java.awt package`, because their constructors had package scope. This restriction has been removed as of the 1.1 AWT—classes outside of the `java.awt` package may now extend either `Component` or `Container`.

The AWT: A Heavyweight World

In principle, creating a lightweight component (or container) is a simple matter: extend either `Component` or `Container`, and you have a lightweight component or container, respectively.

In the guts of the AWT code, however, things are not so simple. For quite some time, AWT code has been accustomed to being passed components that have their own native windows and that come complete with a native peer. Suddenly, the same code is being asked to deal with a different breed of component. As a result, there are some nuances pertaining to lightweight components; these subtleties are not obvious, and we will explore them in the pages ahead.

Lightweights vs. Heavyweights

Lightweights are lightweight by virtue of the fact that they do not require their own native window in which to be rendered. Instead, they are painted into their container's window. This fact has serious repercussions in the AWT code because code that used to rely on components having their own window—and, therefore, their own coordinate system—now has to watch for lightweights and translate them into the parent container's coordinate system.

Another distinction to enumerate is that lightweight components do not have a peer, as their heavyweight counterparts do.[1]

Our point here is that heavyweight components are peer-based components that are rendered in their own native window, whereas lightweights are peerless and are drawn into the windows of their container.

---

1.   Actually, the AWT provides a lightweight peer, but it is merely a placeholder that will be deprecated in subsequent releases of the AWT.

A Simple Lightweight Component

Lightweight components are extremely simple to implement—a lightweight component is lightweight because it extends either Component or Container. Since lightweights are components, lightweights can be manipulated in exactly the same manner as their heavyweight counterparts; that is, their locations can be set, they can be painted and added to containers, and so on.

A Simple Heavyweight Component

Let's start out by implementing a simple *heavyweight* component that extends Panel and paints an image. Then, to illustrate the ease of implementing lightweight components (and to point out a potential pitfall), we'll turn our heavyweight component into a lightweight—you can see the implementation of our simple heavyweight component in Example 19-1.

Example 19-1 A Simple Heavyweight Component That Paints an Image

```java
import java.applet.Applet;
import java.awt.*;

public class SimpleHeavyweight extends Applet {
    private Image dining, paper;

    public void init() {
        dining = getImage(getCodeBase(),"../gifs/Dining.gif");
        paper  = getImage(getCodeBase(),"../gifs/paper.gif");
        add(new Heavyweight(dining));
    }
    public void paint(Graphics g) {
        Util.wallPaper(this, g, paper);
    }
}
class Heavyweight extends Panel {
    private Image    image;

    public Heavyweight(Image image) {
        this.image = image;
        Util.waitForImage(this, image);
    }
    public void paint(Graphics g) {
        g.drawImage(image, 0, 0, this);
    }
    public Dimension getPreferredSize() {
        return new Dimension(image.getWidth(this),
                             image.getHeight(this));
    }
}
```

There are a couple of things to note about our simple heavyweight component and the applet that exercises it. First, note that we use two methods from the $Util^2$ class—one to wait for an image to load and another to wallpaper the background of the applet with an image. Second, as you can see from Figure 19-1, our heavyweight component is indeed drawn in its own opaque window.

Figure 19-1 A Simple *Heavyweight* Component
Note the opaque background of the component, which signifies that the component is painted within its own opaque window.

From Heavyweight to Lightweight

To turn our heavyweight component into a lightweight, we simply change its superclass to Component instead of Panel, as we've done in Example 19-2.

Example 19-2 A Simple Lightweight Component That Paints an Image

```
import java.applet.Applet;
import java.awt.*;

public class SimpleLightweight extends Applet {
    private Image dining, paper;

    public void init() {
        dining = getImage(getCodeBase(),"../gifs/Dining.gif");
        paper  = getImage(getCodeBase(),"../gifs/paper.gif");
        add(new Lightweight(dining));
    }
    public void paint(Graphics g) {
        Util.wallPaper(this, g, paper);
```

2.   The Util class is discussed in Util on page 794.

```
            super.paint(g);
        }
    }
class Lightweight extends Container {
    private Image    image;

    public Lightweight(Image image) {
        this.image = image;
        Util.waitForImage(this, image);
    }
    public void paint(Graphics g) {
        g.drawImage(image, 0, 0, this);
    }
    public Dimension getPreferredSize() {
        return new Dimension(image.getWidth(this),
                             image.getHeight(this));
    }
}
```

However, if you compile and run the SimpleLightweight applet, you may be surprised to find that the applet displays no components whatsoever! Although we have indeed turned our heavyweight component into a lightweight simply by changing its superclass to Component, the lightweight component is a no-show because we have overridden Container.paint()[3] in our applet class. Taking a look at the implementation of Container.paint() in Example 19-3 will shed some light on why our lightweight component is not showing up in our applet.

Example 19-3 java.awt.Container.paint() Implementation

```
public void paint(Graphics g) {
    if (isShowing()) {
        int ncomponents = this.ncomponents;
        Component component[] = this.component;
        Rectangle clip = g.getClipRect();

        for (int i = ncomponents - 1 ; i >= 0 ; i--) {
            Component comp = component[i];

            if (comp != null &&
             comp.peer instanceof java.awt.peer.LightweightPeer &&
             comp.visible == true) {
                Rectangle cr = comp.getBounds();

                if ((clip == null) || cr.intersects(clip)) {
                    Graphics cg = g.create(cr.x, cr.y,
                                            cr.width, cr.height);
                    try {
```

3. Container.paint() was added in 1.1 for the express purpose of painting lightweights—there was no Container.paint method in the 1.02 version of the AWT.

```
            comp.paint(cg);
        } finally {
            cg.dispose();
        }
    }
}
```

`java.awt.Container.paint()` is responsible for painting all of the lightweight components contained in the container, as long as they intersect the bounds of the clip rectangle associated with the container's graphics. Since our container—the applet—has overridden `Container.paint()`, none of the lightweight components are painted. The fix for our broken applet, then, is to invoke `super.paint()` to ensure that the lightweight component gets painted, as shown below.

```
public void paint(Graphics g) {
    Util.wallPaper(this, g, paper);
    super.paint(g);
}
```

Now our lightweight component is painted in the applet, as you can see in Figure 19-2. The order of invocation is significant in the `paint` method above. If we had invoked `super.paint()` before wallpapering the background, then the background would obliterate the lightweight components. Heavyweight components, on the other hand, would be unaffected.

Notice that there is no opaque border around the image—our lightweight component is painted in its container's graphics, not in an opaque window of its own.

Figure 19-2 A Simple Lightweight Component
Note that the lightweight is painted in its container's graphics, not in its own opaque window.

> **AWT TIP ...**
>
> *Remember to Invoke super.paint() When Overriding Container.paint()*
>
> In order to ensure that a container paints the lightweight components it contains, you must invoke super.paint() in overridden paint methods for your containers. Even if your container contains only heavyweight components, it is still a good idea to call super.paint(). Invoking super.paint() for a container with no lightweight components will resolve to a no-op, and you may very well decide to add lightweight components to the container in the future.

Lightweight Containers

Lightweight *components* extend `java.awt.Component`, and lightweight *containers* extend `java.awt.Container`. In Example 19-4, we've added a lightweight container to the previous applet. Just as with any other container, we can add components to a lightweight container, which we've done by adding an instance of `Lightweight` to our lightweight container.

Example 19-4 A `Lightweight Container`

```
import java.applet.Applet;
import java.awt.*;

public class SimpleLightweightContainer extends Applet {
    private Image dining, paper;

    public void init() {
        dining = getImage(getCodeBase(),"../gifs/Dining.gif");
        paper  = getImage(getCodeBase(),"../gifs/paper.gif");

        Container container = new LightweightContainer(paper);
        container.add(new Lightweight(dining));
        setLayout(new BorderLayout());
        add(container, "Center");
    }
}
class LightweightContainer extends Container {
    private Image wallpaperImage;

    public LightweightContainer(Image wallpaperImage) {
        this.wallpaperImage = wallpaperImage;
    }
    public void paint(Graphics g) {
        Util.wallPaper(this, g, wallpaperImage);
        super.paint(g);
    }
}
class Lightweight extends Component {
```

```
    private Image   image;

    public Lightweight(Image image) {
        this.image = image;
        Util.waitForImage(this, image);
    }
    public void paint(Graphics g) {
        g.drawImage(image, 0, 0, this);
    }
    public Dimension getPreferredSize() {
        return new Dimension(image.getWidth(this),
                                image.getHeight(this));
    }
}
```

Note that we've followed our own advice and invoked `super.paint()` in the lightweight container's overridden `paint` method to ensure that the lightweight components get painted. However, once again, much to our chagrin, our lightweight component is nowhere to be found. This time the catch is this: `Container`, unlike all other AWT containers, has no default layout manager, and therefore our lightweight component never gets laid out. The solution, of course, is to fit our lightweight container with a layout manager:

```
    public LightweightContainer(Image wallpaperImage) {
        this.wallpaperImage = wallpaperImage;
        setLayout(new FlowLayout());
    }
```

Once we've fitted our lightweight container with a layout manager, the container's components get laid out, and our applet once again looks like the applet in Figure 19-2 on page 656.

AWT TIP

Lightweight Containers Must Be Fitted with a Layout Manager

Lightweight containers, by default, have a null layout manager. If you want a lightweight container's components (regardless of whether they are lightweight or heavyweight components) to be painted, you must fit the lightweight container with a layout manager of some sort. Alternatively, you can manually set the locations of each component in the container, but the preferred approach is to fit the container with a layout manager.

Lightweight Components and Zorder

Zorder for lightweight components is determined in the same manner as zorder for heavyweight components.[4] Zorder is determined by the order in which lightweight components are added to their container. If more than one lightweight component is added to a container, the one that is added to the container first is displayed in front of all the other lightweights.

Figure 19-3 shows an applet containing three lightweight components and a single heavyweight component—a button. The zorder of the lightweights is determined by the order in which they are added to the applet. For example, the filmstrip lightweight is displayed in front of the frog lightweight because it is added to the applet first. The applet shown in Figure 19-3 is listed in Example 19-5.

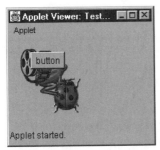

Figure 19-3 Lightweight Zorder
Heavyweight components are always placed in front of lightweight components.

Example 19-5 Zorder When Mixing Heavyweight and Lightweight Components

```
import java.applet.Applet;
import java.awt.*;
import java.net.URL;

public class TestApplet extends Applet {
    private Lightweight filmstrip, frog, ladybug;
    private Button button;
```

---

4. For details, see "Components and Zorder" on page 445.

```
public void init() {
    URL cb = getCodeBase();

    setLayout(new BulletinLayout());

    add(filmstrip = new Lightweight(
                getImage(cb, "../gifs/filmstrip.gif")));

    add(frog = new Lightweight(
                getImage(cb, "../gifs/frog.gif")));

    add(ladybug = new Lightweight(
                getImage(cb, "../gifs/ladybug.gif")));

    add(button = new Button("button"));

    filmstrip.setLocation(15, 15);
    frog.setLocation(35, 35);
    ladybug.setLocation(55, 55);
    button.setLocation(30, 20);
    }
}
```

Note: the applet listed in Example 19-5 employs an instance of `BulletinLayout` to position components at specific locations. `BulletinLayout` is discussed in "BulletinLayout" on page 400. Also, the `Lightweight` class is the lightweight component from Example 19-4 on page 657.

Although zorder is determined in the same manner for lightweight and heavyweight components, heavyweight components are always placed in front of lightweight components. For example, in Example 19-5 the button is added to the container after the lightweight components; however, the button (a heavyweight) is displayed in front of all the lightweights. This protocol can have significant repercussions when heavyweight and lightweight components are mixed together. For instance, the application shown in Example 19-4 contains a lightweight Swing component—a `JScrollPane`—that contains a heavyweight component—an extension of `java.awt.Canvas`.

Notice that even though the (lightweight) scrollpane contains the (heavyweight) canvas, the canvas is drawn in front of the scrollpane, and therefore the scrollpane is partially obliterated by the canvas.

Although this volume of *Graphic Java* does not deal with Swing components, the application is listed in Example 19-6 for completeness.

Figure 19-4 Zorder When Mixing Lightweights and Heavyweights

Example 19-6 Zorder When Mixing Lightweights and Heavyweights

```
import com.sun.java.swing.*;
import java.awt.*;
import java.awt.event.*;

public class Test extends JFrame {
    public Test() {
        super("Lightweight Zorder");

        JScrollPane sp = new JScrollPane();
        PaintCanvas pc = new PaintCanvas();

        sp.setViewportView(pc);

        getContentPane().setLayout(new BorderLayout());
        getContentPane().add(sp, "Center");
    }
    public static void main(String args[]) {
        final JFrame f = new Test();
        f.setBounds(100,100,150,150);
        f.setVisible(true);

        f.addWindowListener(new WindowAdapter() {
           public void windowClosing(WindowEvent e) {
              f.dispose();
              System.exit(0);
           }
```

```
            });
        }
    }
    class PaintCanvas extends Canvas {
        public void paint(Graphics g) {
            Dimension sz = getSize();
            g.setColor(Color.black);
            g.drawRect(0,0,sz.width-1,sz.height-1);
        }
        public Dimension getPreferredSize() {
            return new Dimension(500,500);
        }
    }
```

Lightweights and Their Graphics

Invoking getGraphics() on a lightweight component returns a copy of the Graphics for the lightweight's heavyweight container. Since lightweights are rendered in their (heavyweight) container's window, they have no Graphics of their own.

Figure 19-5 shows an applet with a simple heavyweight component.

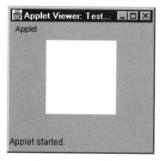

Figure 19-5 A Simple Heavyweight Component

The applet is listed in Example 19-7.

Example 19-7 A Heavyweight Component

```
import java.applet.Applet;
import java.awt.*;

public class TestApplet extends Applet {
    public void init() {
        Heavyweight hw = new Heavyweight();
        hw.setForeground(Color.white);
        add(hw);
    }
}
class Heavyweight extends Canvas {
    public void paint(Graphics g) {
        Dimension sz = getSize();
        g.fillRect(0,0,sz.width,sz.height);
    }
    public Dimension getPreferredSize() {
        return new Dimension(100,100);
    }
}
```

The heavyweight component extends `Canvas` and defines a preferred size of 100x100 pixels. In addition, the applet's `init` method sets the heavyweight's foreground color to white.

Setting the foreground color of the heavyweight modifies the current color of its `Graphics`, and therefore the call to `g.fillRect()` fills the rectangle with white.

Now consider the same applet, with the heavyweight component implemented as a lightweight, as in Example 19-8.

Example 19-8 A Lightweight Component

```
import java.applet.Applet;
import java.awt.*;

public class TestApplet extends Applet {
    public void init() {
        Lightweight lw = new Lightweight();
        lw.setForeground(Color.white);
        add(lw);
    }
}
class Lightweight extends Component {
    public void paint(Graphics g) {
        Dimension sz = getSize();
        g.fillRect(0,0,sz.width,sz.height);
    }
    public Dimension getPreferredSize() {
        return new Dimension(100,100);
    }
}
```

Graphic Java Mastering the JFC Volume I: AWT

The heavyweight is transformed into a lightweight because it now extends `Component` instead of `Canvas`. Other than a clever name change for the reference to the component, the applet is the same: the component's foreground color is set to white and the component is added to the applet.

The lightweight component, however, does not look like its heavyweight counterpart, as you can see in Figure 19-6.

Figure 19-6 A Simple Lightweight Component

Although the lightweight's foreground color is set to white, the `Graphics` passed to its paint method is the `Graphics` for the lightweight's container—the applet. Setting the foreground color for the lightweight does not affect the color of its `Graphics` because lightweights have no `Graphics` of their own. When the lightweight's paint method is invoked, it is passed the `Graphics` of the applet, which is unaffected by the call to `setForeground()` for the lightweight. As a result, the lightweight is filled with the default foreground color for the applet, which under Windows NT, is black.[5]

The moral of the story is this: Lightweight `paint` methods must be sure to initialize the (copy of the) `Graphics` they are passed.

Lightweights and Preferred Sizes

Preferred sizes for heavyweight components are calculated by the component's peer, whereas the preferred size for heavyweight containers are calculated by the container's layout manager.

5. Default colors are platform dependent.

On the other hand, by default, a one-pixel square is the value for preferred sizes for lightweight components. As a result, lightweight components should override `getPreferredSize()` to ensure that they are sized according to their preference. Of course, overriding `preferredSize()` does not guarantee that the lightweight will be sized according to the dimension returned from `preferredSize()` because the shape of both heavyweight and lightweight components depends upon the layout manager that lays them out—see "Layout Managers and Preferred Sizes" on page 335.

Summary

Lightweight components, unlike their heavyweight counterparts, do not require a native, opaque window in which to render themselves and, therefore, have transparent backgrounds. As a result, lightweight components can appear to be nonrectangular, although their bounding boxes are in fact rectangular.

Lightweight components are extremely simple to implement; they merely need to extend `java.awt.Component` (for lightweight components) or `java.awt.Container` (for lightweight containers).

There are a couple of pitfalls to be aware of when developing lightweight components and lightweight containers. First, custom containers that contain lightweight components and override `paint()` must be sure to invoke `super.paint()`, or the lightweight components will not be painted. Second, `java.awt.Container` is equipped with a `null` layout manager, so if you expect components residing in a lightweight container to be laid out, you must manually set the container's layout manager.

Lightweight components, unlike heavyweight components, are rendered entirely in Java—whereas heavyweights are rendered by a native peer—and therefore are best rendered in a double buffered container in order to reduce flicker.

Lightweight components (and containers) are a welcome and necessary addition to the AWT. Although the peer approach taken by the original designers of the AWT had a certain number of benefits, it also suffers from a number of drawbacks, not the least of which stems from the fact that AWT components are heavyweight; that is, they require native, opaque windows. The lightweight component framework provides an alternative to the peer approach and at the same time enables developers to develop components with transparent backgrounds that are not nearly as resource intensive as their heavyweight counterparts.

Advanced Topics

CHAPTER
20

Clipboard and Data Transfer

Nearly every modern windowing system includes support for a clipboard—a rendezvous point for data of various kinds; data can be transferred to and retrieved from the clipboard.

Although initial versions of the AWT did not explicitly support clipboard and data transfer, the current AWT comes complete with data transfer and clipboard support. In fact, the AWT provides access to two kinds of clipboards: the *system* clipboard, and *local* clipboards. As you might suspect, manipulation of the system clipboard actually manipulates the native windowing system clipboard. We mention this because copying data onto the system clipboard in a Java applet or application makes it available to other programs, not just to other AWT components. Alternatively, applets can also create, for their own internal use, local clipboards that do not involve the native windowing clipboard.

In this chapter, we'll take a look at the fundamental concepts behind data transfer and the clipboard, followed by examples that place data on both the system clipboard and local clipboards and retrieve data from the clipboards in some fashion. As of this writing, the `java.awt.datatransfer` package only provides explicit support for placing Java strings onto the clipboard, but we'll take a look at the steps involved in placing other kinds of data, such as images and custom AWT components, on the clipboard.

The java.awt.datatransfer Package

The clipboard and data transfer mechanism are implemented with a handful of classes and interfaces, all of which reside in the `java.awt.datatransfer` package. The classes and interfaces from `java.awt.datatransfer` are listed in Table 20-1.

Table 20-1 java.awt.datatransfer Classes and Interfaces

Class/Interface	Class or Interface	Purpose
Clipboard	Class	Transferables can be copied to and retrieved from the clipboard
ClipboardOwner	Interface	An interface for classes that copy data to the clipboard
DataFlavor	Class	Data flavors (formats) supported by a transferable
StringSelection	Class	A transferable that encapsulates textual data
Transferable	Interface	Interface for items that can be placed on the clipboard
UnsupportedFlavorException	Class	Thrown by a transferable when a requested data flavor is not supported

The concepts behind the clipboard and the data transfer mechanism are quite simple. First of all, only a `ClipboardOwner` can copy data onto the clipboard. By copying data onto the clipboard, the clipboard owner becomes the current owner of the data on the clipboard. Furthermore, only one type of object can be copied to or retrieved from the clipboard—a *transferable* object. Transferables encapsulate data of some sort and are able to provide their data in one or more different *data flavors*. For instance, a transferable that contains an image may choose to provide the image in two different flavors—either as a reference to an instance of `java.awt.Image` or as an array of pixels.

The Clipboard Class

`java.awt.datatransfer.Clipboard` is an extremely simple class. There are only three things you can do to a clipboard, other than construct one, as you can see from Table 20-2: get the name of the clipboard, set the contents of the clipboard, and retrieve the current contents of the clipboard. Notice that there is no `setName` method—setting the name of the clipboard is done at construction time. Furthermore, you can either create a local clipboard via the `Clipboard` constructor or you can obtain a reference to the system clipboard by invoking `Toolkit.getSystemClipboard()`.

Table 20-2 `java.awt.datatransfer.Clipboard` **Public Methods**

Method	Description
`String getName()`	Returns the name of the clipboard
`void setContents(Transferable, ClipboardOwner)`	Sets the contents of the clipboard to the transferable passed in; also sets the owner of the clipboard
`Transferable getContents(Object)`	Returns the contents of the clipboard; the `Object` parameter is the requestor of the clipboard contents

Copying Data to and Retrieving Data from a Clipboard

Before we launch into our first example, let's enumerate the steps involved in copying data to a clipboard and subsequently retrieving it.

To Copy Data to a Clipboard:

- Either instantiate a clipboard or obtain a reference to an existing clipboard.
- Wrap the data in a transferable object (which could involve implementing an extension of `Transferable`).
- Copy the transferable to the clipboard, specifying both the transferable and the owner of the clipboard.

To Retrieve Data from the Clipboard:

- Obtain a reference to the clipboard that contains the data you are interested in.
- (Optional.) Determine if the clipboard contents (a transferable) provides its data in a palatable flavor.
- If the transferable currently on the clipboard provides its data in a flavor acceptable to you, ask the transferable to produce its data in the flavor in question.

The ClipboardOwner Class

Depending upon the native facilities available for data transfer, the contents of the clipboard may not actually be copied to the clipboard until the data is requested from the clipboard. Such a scenario is known as a *lazy data mode* and is the reason for the `ClipboardOwner` interface. The clipboard owner is the object that puts the data on the clipboard, and it must make sure that the data placed on the clipboard is accessible up until the time its `lostOwnership` method is invoked. `lostOwnership()` is the only method defined by the `ClipboardOwner` interface and is invoked when another object places data on the clipboard. If, for some reason, a clipboard owner needs to release the resources associated with an item it placed on the clipboard, it is only safe to do so after the `lostOwnership` method is invoked. In practice, the `lostOwnership` method is almost always implemented as a no-op.

Ok, enough discussion about data transfer concepts and the steps involved in using the clipboard. Let's get on with some examples.

The System Clipboard

As you can see in Figure 20-1, our first applet contains a textfield, a textarea, and two buttons. After text is typed into the textfield, activating the Copy To System Clipboard button places the textfield's text onto the system clipboard. Subsequently, activating the "Paste From System Clipboard" button retrieves the text currently on the clipboard and places it in the textarea.

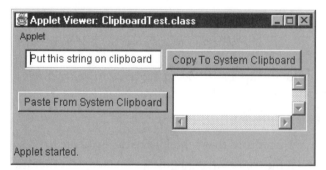

Figure 20-1 Copying a String to the System Clipboard
Activating the Copy To System Clipboard button copies the text from the textfield and places it on the system clipboard.

Before listing the applet in its entirety, let's take a look at the code that implements the steps outlined previously for placing data on and retrieving data from a clipboard.

First, we obtain a reference to the system clipboard:

```
public class ClipboardTest extends    Applet
                           implements ClipboardOwner {
private Clipboard clipboard;
private TextField copyFrom;
private TextArea  copyTo;
private Button    copy, paste;

public void init() {
    // Obtain a reference to the system clipboard
    clipboard = getToolkit().getSystemClipboard();
        ...
    }
}
```

As we noted earlier, a reference to the system clipboard is obtained by invoking the getSystemClipboard()[1] static method supplied by the Toolkit class. Next, we wrap the text contained in the textfield in a transferable and place the transferable on the system clipboard:

```
class CopyListener implements ActionListener {
    public void actionPerformed(ActionEvent event) {

        // Wrap the data in a transferable object
        StringSelection contents =
                    new StringSelection(copyFrom.getText());

        // Place the transferable onto the clipboard
        clipboard.setContents(contents, ClipboardTest.this);
    }
}
```

CopyListener is the action listener for the "Copy To System Clipboard" button. Note that the transferable is an instance of StringSelection, which is provided by the AWT for wrapping textual data.

Finally, we retrieve the text from the system clipboard when the Paste From System Clipboard button is activated:

```
class PasteListener implements ActionListener {
    public void actionPerformed(ActionEvent event) {
        Transferable contents = clipboard.getContents(this);

        // Determine if data is available in string flavor
        if(contents != null &&
              contents.isDataFlavorSupported(
                        DataFlavor.stringFlavor)) {
            try {
```

1. Note that Toolkit.getSystemClipboard() is subject to security restrictions.

```
                String string;
                // Have contents cough up string
                string = (String) contents.getTransferData(
                                  DataFlavor.stringFlavor);
                copyTo.append(string);
            }
            catch(Exception e) {
                e.printStackTrace();
            }
        }
    }
}
```

`PasteListener` is the action listener for the Paste From System Clipboard button, and the first thing its `actionPerformed` method does is to obtain the contents of the clipboard via the clipboard's `getContents` method.

`Clipboard.getContents()` requires us to pass a reference to the object that is requesting the data (the `PasteListener`). Once we have a reference to the transferable currently on the clipboard, we ask the transferable if the data it contains is available in the particular data flavor we are interested in. If there was indeed a transferable on the clipboard and it supports `DataFlavor.stringFlavor`, then we invoke the clipboard's `getTransferData()`, telling the transferable the type of data flavor we'd like returned. Finally, we append the string obtained from the transferable to the text area.

The fruits of our labor are shown in Figure 20-2, and the entire applet is listed in Example 20-1.

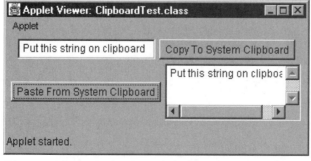

Figure 20-2 Retrieving a String from the System Clipboard Activating the Paste From System Clipboard button retrieves the text from the system clipboard and appends it to the textarea.

Example 20-1 ClipboardTest Applet

```java
import java.applet.Applet;
import java.awt.*;
import java.awt.event.*;
import java.awt.datatransfer.*;

public class ClipboardTest extends    Applet
                            implements ClipboardOwner {
    private Clipboard clipboard;
    private TextField copyFrom;
    private TextArea  copyTo;
    private Button    copy, paste;

    public void init() {
        // Obtain a reference to the system clipboard
        clipboard = getToolkit().getSystemClipboard();

        copyFrom = new TextField(20);
        copyTo   = new TextArea(3, 20);
        copy     = new Button("Copy To System Clipboard");
        paste    = new Button("Paste From System Clipboard");

        add(copyFrom);
        add(copy);
        add(paste);
        add(copyTo);

        copy.addActionListener (new CopyListener());
        paste.addActionListener(new PasteListener());
    }
    class CopyListener implements ActionListener {
        public void actionPerformed(ActionEvent event) {
            // Wrap the data in a transferable object
            StringSelection contents =
                    new StringSelection(copyFrom.getText());

            // Place the transferable onto the clipboard
            clipboard.setContents(contents, ClipboardTest.this);
        }
    }
    class PasteListener implements ActionListener {
        public void actionPerformed(ActionEvent event) {
            Transferable contents = clipboard.getContents(this);

            // Determine if data is available in string flavor
            if(contents != null &&
               contents.isDataFlavorSupported(
                       DataFlavor.stringFlavor)) {
                try {
                    String string;
```

```
                // Have contents cough up string
                string = (String) contents.getTransferData(
                                DataFlavor.stringFlavor);
                copyTo.append(string);
            }
            catch(Exception e) {
                e.printStackTrace();
            }
        }
    }
}
    public void lostOwnership(Clipboard    clip,
                            Transferable transferable) {
        System.out.println("Lost ownership");
    }
}
```

Pasting from the System Clipboard to Other Applications

As we alluded to earlier, copying data to the system clipboard makes it available to other programs in addition to other AWT components. After we copied the text onto the system clipboard, we opened a document in FrameMaker® and did a paste operation. The result is shown in Figure 20-3.

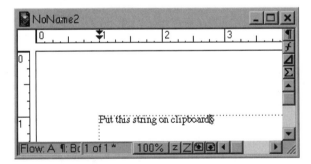

Figure 20-3 Pasting Clipboard Contents into Another Application Text placed on the clipboard from an applet is pasted into a FrameMaker document.

Local Clipboards

In Example 20-1 on page 675, we manipulated the system clipboard. You can also create local clipboards by invoking the lone Clipboard constructor that takes a string as an argument. The string specifies the name of the clipboard, so you can keep track of several clipboards if need be. As we saw in Table 20-2 on page 671, the Clipboard class comes with a getName method so that you can determine which clipboard you currently have in hand.

Data Transfer Mechanism

Now that we've introduced the basics of data transfer and manipulating a clipboard and provided a simple example of cutting and pasting text to/from the system clipboard, let's take a closer look at the data transfer mechanism.

Data Flavors

No, you cannot taste data; flavor, in this case, can be thought of as a synonym for format. One data flavor for an image, for instance, might be a java.awt.Image; another flavor for an image might be an array of pixels representing the image in question.

Data flavors fall into two general categories:

*   A Java class
*   MIME (Multipurpose Internet Mail Extensions) Type Representation[2]

All this means is that you can either construct a DataFlavor by specifying the particular Java class that the data flavor represents, or you can construct a data flavor by specifying a string that represents a data type. If you choose to construct a data flavor with a string representing the data type, the string should conform to a standard MIME type. If you construct a DataFlavor by specifying a Java class, it will be assigned the MIME type "application/x-javaserializedobject". For instance, if you look at the source for java.awt.datatransfer.DataFlavor, you will see that the DataFlavor class provides two constructors:

```
public DataFlavor(Class representationClass,
                  String humanPresentableName)

public DataFlavor(String mimeType, String humanPresentableName)
```

Regardless of which constructor you use, you must provide a human presentable name for your particular data flavor, but you probably figured that out on your own!

The DataFlavor class contains two static public instances of DataFlavor, each representing a different flavor of text. One flavor is represented by java.lang.String; the other is represented by a MIME type for plain text:

2.   If you want to read the gory details concerning MIME types, check out
     http://206.21.31.20/notes/rfcs1/30ee_1e2.htm.

```
static { // This is from the DataFlavor class
   try {
     stringFlavor =
         new DataFlavor(Class.forName("java.lang.String"),
                           "Unicode String");
     plainTextFlavor =
              new DataFlavor("text/plain; charset=unicode",
                           "Plain Text");
  ...
```

So, don't get hung up on MIME types. MIME types are simply a standard way to describe certain flavors of data, and since there is already a standard established, it makes perfect sense to use it instead of defining another standard. Table 20-3 lists the public methods provided by the `DataFlavor` class.

Table 20-3 `java.awt.datatransfer.DataFlavor` **Public Methods**

Method	Description
Object clone() throws CloneNotSupportedException	Returns a clone of the data flavor
String getParameter(String)	Returns the value of the named parameter
String getPrimaryType()	Returns the primary MIME type
String getSubType()	Returns the MIME subtype
String getMimeType()	Returns MIME type for data flavor
Class getRepresentationClass()	Returns the Java class the data flavor represents
String getHumanPresentableName()	Returns the human presentable name of the data flavor
void setHumanPresentableName(String)	Sets the human presentable name of the data flavor
boolean equals(DataFlavor)	Determines if another data flavor is equal to the data flavor on whose behalf the method is called
boolean equals(MimeType)	Determines if the data flavor is equal to the specified MIME type
boolean equals(Object)	Determines if the data flavor is equal to the specified object
boolean equals(String)	Determines if another data flavor is equal to the data flavor on whose behalf the method is called

Table 20-3 `java.awt.datatransfer.DataFlavor` **Public Methods (Continued)**

Method	Description
`boolean isMimeTypeEqual(DataFlavor)`	Determines if the data flavor has a MIME type equivalent to the MIME type of the data flavor passed in
`boolean isMimeTypeEqual(String)`	Determines if the data flavor has a MIME type equivalent to the `String` passed in
`boolean isMimeTypeEqual(DataFlavor)`	Convenience method implemented as: `return isMimeTypeEqual(flavor.getMimeType())`
`boolean isMimeTypeSerializedObject()`	Signifies whether the data flavor represents a serializable object
`boolean isRepresentationClassInput-Stream()`	Signifies whether the data flavor represents an input stream
`String normalizeMimeTypeParameter(String, String)`	Allows `DataFlavor` subclasses to modify how MIME types are normalized
`String normalizeMimeTypeParameter(String, String)`	Allows `DataFlavor` subclasses to handle special parameters
`void readObject(ObjectInputStream)`	Restores a serialized data flavor
`void writeObject(ObjectOutputStream)`	Serializes the data flavor

Transferables and Data Flavors

As we mentioned previously, there's only one type of object that can be placed on or retrieved from a clipboard—a `Transferable`, which is an interface that defines the three methods listed in Table 20-4.

A transferable then, is simply a wrapper around some piece of data. Since a given type of data can be packaged in different flavors, a transferable is a data wrapper that manages the flavors of the particular type of data it encapsulates.

Notice that `getTransferData()` can throw either an `UnsupportedFlavorException` if the requested data flavor is not supported or an `IOException` if an object representing the given data flavor cannot be created. Of course, you can avoid having an `UnsupportedFlavorException`

Table 20-4 `java.awt.datatransfer.Transferable` **Interface Public Methods**

Method	Intent
`DataFlavor[]` `getTransferDataFlavors()`	Provides an array of data flavors supported by the transferable
`boolean` `isDataFlavorSupported(DataFlavor)`	Determine if a particular data flavor is supported by the transferable

`Object`
`getTransferData(DataFlavor)`
`throws`
`UnsupportedFlavorException,`
`IOException;`
	Returns an `Object` representing the specified flavor

thrown by calling `isDataFlavorSupported()` to find out if a particular data flavor is supported before you invoke `getTransferData()`, as we did in Example 20-1 on page 675.

StringSelection

The `java.awt.datatransfer` package comes with one implementation of `Transferable` that encapsulates text: `StringSelection`. `StringSelection` can cough up its string in one of two different flavors: as a `java.lang.String` or as plain text. As you might guess, `StringSelection` uses the two (public) static instances of `DataFlavor` provided by the `DataFlavor` class for representing its string—see "Data Flavors" on page 677.

In Example 20-1 on page 675, we asked an instance of `StringSelection` obtained from the clipboard for its text in the form of a `java.lang.String`:

```
if(contents != null &&
      contents.isDataFlavorSupported(DataFlavor.stringFlavor))
{
    try {
        String string;

        // Have contents cough up string
        string = (String) contents.getTransferData(
                             DataFlavor.stringFlavor);
    ...
```

We could also have asked the `StringSelection` object for its text represented as plain text:

```
class PasteListener implements ActionListener {
    public void actionPerformed(ActionEvent event) {
        Transferable contents = clipboard.getContents(this);
        StringBuffer sb = new StringBuffer();
```

```
                // Determine if data is available in plain text flavor
                if(contents != null &&
                    contents.isDataFlavorSupported(
                               DataFlavor.plainTextFlavor)) {
                    try {
                        int i;
                        StringReader s = (StringReader)
                                     contents.getTransferData(
                                     DataFlavor.plainTextFlavor);

                        while( (i = s.read()) != -1) {
                            sb.append((char)i);
                        }
                    }
                    catch(Exception e) {
                        e.printStackTrace();
                    }
                    catch(java.util.mime.MimeTypeParseException e) {
                        e.printStackTrace();
                    }
                    copyTo.setText(sb.toString());
                }
            }
        }
```

`StringSelection.getTransferData()` returns a `StringReader` when asked for its data in plain text flavor.

Copying Images to a Clipboard

As we have seen, manipulating clipboards is relatively straightforward. Perhaps the most difficult aspect of the clipboard/data transfer mechanism is copying data other than text to a clipboard, and even that is not rocket science, especially once you get the hang of it.

ImageSelection—A Transferable for Encapsulating Images

The first order of business is to develop a class that implements `Transferable` and encapsulates an image. Our first version of such a class will offer a lone data flavor for representing the image—`java.awt.Image`. A little later on, we'll add another data flavor for good measure.

We'll follow the naming convention established by `StringSelection` and name our class `ImageSelection`. Additionally, as with `StringSelection`, we'll also implement the `ClipboardOwner` interface[3] as a convenience, so that the contents and the owner of the clipboard can be specified as the same object when the contents of the clipboard are set.

---

3.   See The ClipboardOwner Class on page 671. It is often the case that classes implementing `Transferable` also implement the `ClipboardOwner` interface.

```
public class ImageSelection implements Transferable,
                                       ClipboardOwner {
    static public DataFlavor ImageFlavor;

    private DataFlavor[] flavors = {ImageFlavor};
    private Image image;
    . . .
```

ImageSelection contains a `static public` instance of `DataFlavor` that clients can use to specify the data flavor in which they'd like the image to be produced. Since `ImageSelection` has only one data flavor for its image, it maintains an array of data flavors that has only one entry. The array, of course, will be returned from the `getTransferDataFlavors` method. Finally, `ImageSelection` maintains a reference to the image that it currently represents.

`ImageSelection` implements a static block that creates the `ImageFlavor` instance:

```
static {
    try {
        ImageFlavor = new DataFlavor(
                Class.forName("java.awt.Image"),"AWT Image");
    }
    catch(ClassNotFoundException e) {
        e.printStackTrace();
    }
}
```

Notice that the data flavor is constructed with a Java class instead of a MIME type, and with a human presentable name of "AWT Image".

`ImageSelection` provides a lone constructor that takes a reference to an image, and implements the three methods required by the `Transferable` interface:

```
public ImageSelection(Image image) {
    this.image = image;
}
public synchronized DataFlavor[] getTransferDataFlavors() {
    return flavors;
}
public boolean isDataFlavorSupported(DataFlavor flavor) {
    return flavor.equals(ImageFlavor);
}
public synchronized Object getTransferData(DataFlavor flavor)
                throws UnsupportedFlavorException, IOException {
    if(flavor.equals(ImageFlavor)) {
        return image;
    }
    else {
        throw new UnsupportedFlavorException(flavor);
    }
}
public void lostOwnership(Clipboard c, Transferable t) {
}
```

If the data flavor requested in getTransferData() is equal to the ImageFlavor instance, the image is returned; otherwise, an UnsupportedFlavorException is thrown. Also, as is typically the case, since ImageSelection never releases the resources associated with the image it encapsulates, its lostOwnership method is implemented as a no-op.

That's all there is to implementing a transferable that encapsulates an image. For completeness, ImageSelection is shown in its entirety in Example 20-2.

Example 20-2 ImageSelection Class Listing

```java
import java.awt.*;
import java.awt.datatransfer.*;
import java.io.*;

public class ImageSelection implements Transferable,
                                        ClipboardOwner {
    static public DataFlavor ImageFlavor;

    private DataFlavor[] flavors = {ImageFlavor};
    private Image image;

    static {
        try {
            ImageFlavor = new DataFlavor(
                Class.forName("java.awt.Image"), "AWT Image");
        }
        catch(ClassNotFoundException e) {
            e.printStackTrace();
        }
        catch(java.util.mime.MimeTypeParseException e) {
            e.printStackTrace();
        }
    }
    public ImageSelection(Image image) {
        this.image = image;
    }
    public synchronized DataFlavor[] getTransferDataFlavors() {
        return flavors;
    }
    public boolean isDataFlavorSupported(DataFlavor flavor) {
        return flavor.equals(ImageFlavor);
    }
    public synchronized Object getTransferData(DataFlavor flavor)
        throws UnsupportedFlavorException, IOException {
        if(flavor.equals(ImageFlavor)) {
            return image;
        }
        else {
            throw new UnsupportedFlavorException(flavor);
        }
    }
    public void lostOwnership(Clipboard c, Transferable t) {
    }
}
```

Now let's put our `ImageSelection` class to use by copying an image to a local clipboard and subsequently retrieving it.

Using the ImageSelection Class

As you can see from Figure 20-4, our applet contains two image canvases, one of which initially contains an image, along with a copy button and a paste button. The Copy button, of course, copies the image to a clipboard—this time, we'll copy the image to a local clipboard instead of the system clipboard. Activating the Paste button retrieves the image from the local clipboard and puts it into the right-hand image canvas.

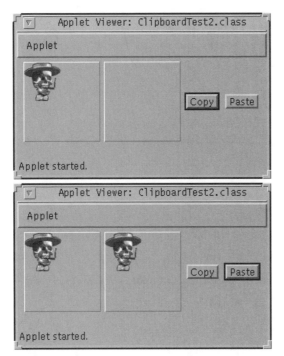

Figure 20-4 Copying and Retrieving an Image to/from a Clipboard
The top picture shows the applet in its initial state. After activating the copy and paste buttons, the applet looks like the bottom picture—the image has been copied to a clipboard and then pasted from the clipboard into the right-hand image canvas.

Our applet creates a local clipboard, with the name "image clipboard," along with the various AWT components used in the applet:

```
public class ClipboardTest2 extends      Applet
                              implements ClipboardOwner {
    private Clipboard   clipboard;
    private ImageCanvas copyFrom = new ImageCanvas();
    private ImageCanvas copyTo   = new ImageCanvas();
    private Button copy  = new Button("Copy" );
    private Button paste = new Button("Paste");

    public void init() {
        clipboard = new Clipboard("image clipboard");

        copyFrom.setImage(getImage(getCodeBase(),"skelly.gif"));
        add(copyFrom);
        add(copyTo);
        add(copy);
        add(paste);
        copy.addActionListener (new CopyListener());
        paste.addActionListener(new PasteListener());
    }
...
}
```

Next, event listeners are implemented for the two buttons:

```
class CopyListener implements ActionListener {
    public void actionPerformed(ActionEvent event) {
        ImageSelection contents =
                    new ImageSelection(copyFrom.getImage());

        clipboard.setContents(contents, ClipboardTest2.this);
    }
}
class PasteListener implements ActionListener {
    public void actionPerformed(ActionEvent event) {
        Transferable contents = clipboard.getContents(this);

        if(contents != null &&
           contents.isDataFlavorSupported(
                              ImageSelection.ImageFlavor)) {
            try {
                Image image;
                image = (Image) contents.getTransferData(
                              ImageSelection.ImageFlavor);
                copyTo.setImage(image);
            }
            catch(Exception e) {
                e.printStackTrace();
            }
            catch(java.util.mime.MimeTypeParseException e) {
                e.printStackTrace();
            }
        }
    }
}
```

`CopyListener.actionPerformed()` creates an instance of
`ImageSelection`, which it places on the clipboard. Notice that the clipboard
owner (the second argument to `setContents()`) is specified as
`ClipboardTest2.this` because `CopyListener` is an inner class of
`ClipboardTest2` and it is `ClipboardTest2`, not `CopyListener`, that
implements the `ClipboardOwner` interface.

`PasteListener.actionPerformed()`, after obtaining the contents of the
clipboard, checks to see if the transferable currently on the clipboard supports the
`ImageSelection.ImageFlavor` data flavor. Obviously, we are engaging in a
bit of paranoia here—we know who put the data on the clipboard, and so we
know that `ImageSelection.ImageFlavor` is supported, but such tight
coupling between the object that places data on the clipboard and objects that
retrieve the data is not always the case, so we make the check for the sake of
illustration. Finally, we retrieve the image from the transferable and place it in the
right-hand image canvas.

The entire applet is shown in Example 20-3. Note that the implementation of
`ImageCanvas` has no bearing on the concepts we are stressing but is included for
completeness.

Example 20-3 ClipboardTest2 Applet

```
import java.applet.Applet;
import java.awt.*;
import java.awt.event.*;
import java.awt.datatransfer.*;

public class ClipboardTest2 extends      Applet
                             implements ClipboardOwner {
    private Clipboard    clipboard;
    private ImageCanvas copyFrom = new ImageCanvas();
    private ImageCanvas copyTo   = new ImageCanvas();
    private Button copy  = new Button("Copy");
    private Button paste = new Button("Paste");

    public void init() {
        clipboard = new Clipboard("image clipboard");

        copyFrom.setImage(getImage(getCodeBase(),"skelly.gif"));
        add(copyFrom);
        add(copyTo);
        add(copy);
        add(paste);

        copy.addActionListener (new CopyListener());
        paste.addActionListener(new PasteListener());
    }
```

```java
    class CopyListener implements ActionListener {
       public void actionPerformed(ActionEvent event) {
          ImageSelection contents =
                  new ImageSelection(copyFrom.getImage());

          clipboard.setContents(contents, ClipboardTest2.this);
       }
    }
    class PasteListener implements ActionListener {
       public void actionPerformed(ActionEvent event) {
          Transferable contents = clipboard.getContents(this);

          if(contents != null &&
             contents.isDataFlavorSupported(
                ImageSelection.ImageFlavor)) {
             try {
                Image image;
                image = (Image) contents.getTransferData(
                        ImageSelection.ImageFlavor);
                copyTo.setImage(image);
             }
             catch(Exception e) {
                e.printStackTrace();
             }
          }
       }
    }
    public void lostOwnership(Clipboard    clip,
                              Transferable transferable) {
       System.out.println("Lost ownership");
    }
}
class ImageCanvas extends Panel {
    private Image image;

    public ImageCanvas() {
       this(null);
    }
    public ImageCanvas(Image image) {
       if(image != null)
          setImage(image);
    }
    public void paint(Graphics g) {
       g.setColor(Color.lightGray);

       g.draw3DRect(0,0,getSize().width-1,
                    getSize().height-1,true);

       if(image != null) {
        g.drawImage(image, 1, 1, this);
       }
    }
```

```
       public void update(Graphics g) {
          paint(g);
       }
       public void setImage(Image image) {
          this.image = image;
          try {
             MediaTracker tracker = new MediaTracker(this);
             tracker.addImage(image, 0);
            tracker.waitForID(0);
          }
          catch(Exception e) { e.printStackTrace(); }

          if(isShowing()) {
             repaint();
          }
       }
       public Image getImage() {
          return image;
       }
       public Dimension getPreferredSize() {
          return new Dimension(100,100);
       }
    }
```

Adding an Additional Flavor

Now we'll take our `ImageSelection` class and add support for another data
flavor.[4] Our additional flavor will take the form of an array of bits that represents
the image. The `ImageSelection2` class contains two `static public`
`DataFlavor` objects, which are placed in the `flavors` array. Additionally, the
static block now constructs both flavors:

```
    public class ImageSelection2 implements Transferable,
                                        ClipboardOwner {
       static public DataFlavor ImageFlavor;
       static public DataFlavor ImageArrayFlavor;
       private DataFlavor[] flavors = {ImageFlavor,
                                                ImageArrayFlavor};
       private Image image;
       private int   width, height;

       static {
          try {
             ImageFlavor = new DataFlavor(
                 Class.forName("java.awt.Image"), "AWT Image");

             ImageArrayFlavor = new DataFlavor("image/gif",
                                                "GIF Image");
          }
```

---

4.   Note that we have resisted bad jokes about Baskin-Robbins.

```
            catch(ClassNotFoundException e) {
                e.printStackTrace();
            }
            catch(java.util.mime.MimeTypeParseException e) {
                e.printStackTrace();
            }
        }
    ...
    }
```

The `ImageSelection2` constructor is passed the width and height of the image, which are needed to return an array of pixels representing the image. Once again, the methods defined in the `Transferable` interface are implemented.

```
    public ImageSelection2(Image image, int width, int height) {
        this.image  = image;
        this.width  = width;
        this.height = height;
    }
    public synchronized DataFlavor[] getTransferDataFlavors() {
        return flavors;
    }
    public boolean isDataFlavorSupported(DataFlavor flavor) {
        return flavor.equals(ImageFlavor) ||
                  flavor.equals(ImageArrayFlavor);
    }
    public synchronized Object getTransferData(
                                        DataFlavor flavor)
        throws UnsupportedFlavorException, IOException {
        if(flavor.equals(ImageFlavor)) {
            return image;
        }
        else if(flavor.equals(ImageArrayFlavor)) {
            return imageToArray();
        }
        else
            throw new UnsupportedFlavorException(flavor);
    }
```

By now, the methods listed above should need little commentary. Notice that `ImageSelection2.getTransferData()` returns the image as either a `java.awt.Image` or an array of pixels, depending upon the requested data flavor. Of course, the only mystery left to uncover involves the inner workings of the `imageToArray` method, which employs an instance of `PixelGrabber` for obtaining the pixels associated with the image:[5]

```
    private int[] imageToArray() {
        int[] pixels = new int[width*height];
```

5. See "Grabbing Pixels" on page 190 for more information on `PixelGrabber` and image manipulation.

```
        PixelGrabber pg = new PixelGrabber(image,0,0,
                            width,height,pixels,0,width);
        try { pg.grabPixels(); }
        catch(InterruptedException e) { e.printStackTrace(); }
        return pixels;
    }
```

`ImageSelection2` is listed in Example 20-4.

Example 20-4 `ImageSelection2 Class Listing`

```
import java.awt.*;
import java.awt.image.*;
import java.awt.datatransfer.*;
import java.io.*;

public class ImageSelection2 implements Transferable,
                                        ClipboardOwner {
    static public DataFlavor ImageFlavor;
    static public DataFlavor ImageArrayFlavor;

    private DataFlavor[] flavors = {ImageFlavor,
                                    ImageArrayFlavor};
    private Image image;
    private int   width, height;

    static {
        try {
            ImageFlavor = new DataFlavor(
                Class.forName("java.awt.Image"),
                "AWT Image");

            ImageArrayFlavor = new DataFlavor("image/gif",
                                              "GIF Image");
        }
        catch(ClassNotFoundException e) {
            e.printStackTrace();
        }
        catch(java.util.mime.MimeTypeParseException e) {
            e.printStackTrace();
        }
    }
    public ImageSelection2(Image image, int width, int height) {
        this.image  = image;
        this.width  = width;
        this.height = height;
    }
    public synchronized DataFlavor[] getTransferDataFlavors() {
        return flavors;
    }
    public boolean isDataFlavorSupported(DataFlavor flavor) {
        return flavor.equals(ImageFlavor) ||
                flavor.equals(ImageArrayFlavor);
```

```
    }
    public synchronized Object getTransferData(
                                    DataFlavor flavor)
        throws UnsupportedFlavorException, IOException {
        if(flavor.equals(ImageFlavor)) {
            return image;
        }
        else if(flavor.equals(ImageArrayFlavor)) {
            return imageToArray();
        }
        else
            throw new UnsupportedFlavorException(flavor);
    }
    public void lostOwnership(Clipboard c, Transferable t) {
    }
    private int[] imageToArray() {
        int[] pixels = new int[width*height];
        PixelGrabber pg = new PixelGrabber(image,0,0,
                            width,height,pixels,0,width);

        try { pg.grabPixels(); }
        catch(InterruptedException e) { e.printStackTrace(); }

        return pixels;
    }
}
```

All that's left is to modify our applet to ask for the new data flavor when retrieving the image from the clipboard:

```
class PasteListener implements ActionListener {
    public void actionPerformed(ActionEvent event) {
        Transferable contents = clipboard.getContents(this);

        if(contents != null) {
            try {
                int[] array = (int[])
                        contents.getTransferData(
                            ImageSelection2.ImageArrayFlavor);

                copyTo.setImage(waveThis(array,width,height));
            }
            catch(Exception e) {
                e.printStackTrace();
            }
        }
    }
}
```

We obtain the array of bits from the `ImageSelection2` instance by asking for the `ImageArrayFlavor`, and then we pass the array to the `waveThis` method, which, purely for entertainment purposes, runs the array through a sine wave filter and returns a new image, which we set as the image for the right-hand image canvas. You can see the results of our shenanigans in Figure 20-5. Since the `waveThis` method has no bearing on clipboard and data transfer, we won't bother to list it; the code, of course, is on the CD in the back of the book.[6]

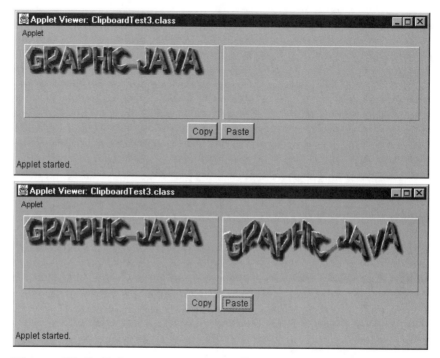

Figure 20-5 Retrieving an Image off the Clipboard as an Array of Bits
The picture on the left is copied to the clipboard and retrieved as an array of bits. The array of bits is run through a sine wave function, the result of which is displayed in the right-hand image canvas.

6.   A more extensive `WaveFilter` class is discussed in "Wave Filter" on page 160.

Transferring Custom AWT Components

Our final example, at the risk of beating data transfer to death, is to implement a transferable that encapsulates a custom component.

Note: A bug under the 1.2 release of the AWT causes the following applet to throw an exception under Windows NT (it works fine under Solaris).

A Transferable for Encapsulating a Custom Component

Our custom component will be a very simplistic image button, whose implementation we won't bother to discuss. Instead, we will simply show the implementation of `ImageButtonSelection` and the applet that exercises it. The complete implementation of `ImageButtonSelection` is listed in Example 20-5.

Example 20-5 ImageButtonSelection Class Listing

```java
import java.awt.*;
import java.awt.datatransfer.*;
import java.io.*;

public class ImageButtonSelection implements Transferable,
                                    ClipboardOwner {
    public static DataFlavor ImageButtonFlavor;
    private DataFlavor[] flavors = {ImageButtonFlavor};
    private ImageButton imageButton;

    static {
        try {
            ImageButtonFlavor = new DataFlavor(
                            Class.forName("ImageButton"),
                            "ImageButton");
        }
        catch(ClassNotFoundException e) {
            e.printStackTrace();
        }
        catch(java.util.mime.MimeTypeParseException e) {
            e.printStackTrace();
        }
    }
    public ImageButtonSelection(ImageButton imageButton) {
        this.imageButton = imageButton;
    }
    public synchronized DataFlavor[] getTransferDataFlavors() {
        return flavors;
    }
    public boolean isDataFlavorSupported(DataFlavor flavor) {
        return flavor.equals(ImageButtonFlavor);
    }
    public synchronized Object getTransferData(
```

```
                                   DataFlavor flavor)
        throws UnsupportedFlavorException, IOException {
        if(flavor.equals(ImageButtonFlavor)) {
            return imageButton;
        }
        else
            throw new UnsupportedFlavorException(flavor);
    }
    public void lostOwnership(Clipboard c, Transferable t) {
    }
}
```

We have but one lone data flavor—ImageButtonFlavor. By now, the implementation of ImageButtonSelection should require no explanation, so without further ado, we'll move on to an applet that copies image buttons to and from a clipboard.

ImageButton Transfer Applet

First, let's take a look at the applet, both in its initial state and after we've copied a single image button three times from the clipboard, in Figure 20-6.

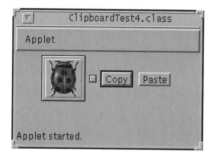 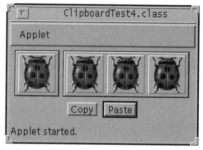

Figure 20-6 Copying and Retrieving an ImageButton to/from a Clipboard

The picture on the left shows the applet in its initial state. After we activate the Copy button once and the Paste button three times, the applet looks like the picture on the right.

Rather than bore you with the details of the inner workings of the applet, we'll have a brief discussion and show you the code. The applet is composed of four components: two instances of ImageButtonCanvas and two instances of java.awt.Button. An ImageButtonCanvas draws a 3D rectangle inside of a black rectangle and contains image buttons. ImageButtonCanvas, when it is laid out, expands to accommodate the image buttons it currently contains; thus, the original canvas on the left is just big enough to hold the single image button, while the image canvas on the right is initially at its minimum size.

Copying and retrieving image buttons to and from the clipboard is accomplished with the following (by now familiar) code:

```
class CopyListener implements ActionListener {
    public void actionPerformed(ActionEvent event) {
        ImageButton button = copyFrom.getImageButton();
        ImageButtonSelection contents =
                        new ImageButtonSelection(button);

        clipboard.setContents(contents, ClipboardTest4.this);
    }
}
class PasteListener implements ActionListener {
    public void actionPerformed(ActionEvent event) {
        Transferable contents = clipboard.getContents(this);

        if(contents != null) {
            try {
                ImageButton imageButton =
                    (ImageButton) contents.getTransferData(
                    ImageButtonSelection.ImageButtonFlavor);

                copyTo.setImageButton(imageButton);
                copyTo.invalidate();
                validate();
            }
            catch(Exception e) {
                e.printStackTrace();
            }
        }
    }
}
```

The copyTo ImageButtonCanvas is invalidated, and then validate() is invoked for its container—the applet—to force the image button canvas to be laid out whenever an image button is pasted to it. The entire applet is listed in Example 20-6.

Example 20-6 ClipboardTest4 Applet

```java
import java.applet.Applet;
import java.awt.*;
import java.awt.event.*;
import java.awt.datatransfer.*;

public class ClipboardTest4 extends     Applet
                            implements ClipboardOwner {
    private Clipboard    clipboard;
    private ImageButtonCanvas copyFrom = new ImageButtonCanvas();
    private ImageButtonCanvas copyTo   = new ImageButtonCanvas();
    private Button copy  = new Button("Copy");
    private Button paste = new Button("Paste");

    public void init() {
        clipboard = getToolkit().getSystemClipboard();

        copyFrom.setImageButton(
          new ImageButton(getImage(getCodeBase(),
                          "ladybug.gif")));

        add(copyFrom);
        add(copyTo);
        add(copy);
        add(paste);

        copy.addActionListener (new CopyListener());
        paste.addActionListener(new PasteListener());
    }
    class CopyListener implements ActionListener {
        public void actionPerformed(ActionEvent event) {
            ImageButton button = copyFrom.getImageButton();
            ImageButtonSelection contents =
                    new ImageButtonSelection(button);
            clipboard.setContents(contents, ClipboardTest4.this);
        }
    }
    class PasteListener implements ActionListener {
        public void actionPerformed(ActionEvent event) {
            Transferable contents = clipboard.getContents(this);

            if(contents != null) {
                try {
                    ImageButton imageButton =
                        (ImageButton) contents.getTransferData(
                          ImageButtonSelection.ImageButtonFlavor);
                    copyTo.setImageButton(imageButton);
                    copyTo.invalidate();
                    validate();
                }
                catch(Exception e) {
                    e.printStackTrace();
                }
            }
        }
    }
}
```

```
        }
    public void lostOwnership(Clipboard    clip,
                            Transferable transferable) {
        System.out.println("Lost ownership");
    }
}
class ImageButtonCanvas extends Panel {
    private ImageButton imageButton;

    public ImageButtonCanvas() {
        this(null);
    }
    public ImageButtonCanvas(ImageButton imageButton) {
        if(imageButton != null)
            setImageButton(imageButton);
    }
    public void paint(Graphics g) {
        g.setColor  (Color.black);
        g.drawRect  (0,0,getSize().width-1,getSize().height-1);

        g.setColor  (Color.lightGray);
        g.draw3DRect(1,1,getSize().width-3,
                    getSize().height-3,true);

    }
    public void setImageButton(ImageButton button) {
        imageButton = button;
        add(new ImageButton(imageButton.getImage()));

        if(isShowing()) {
            repaint();
        }
    }
    public ImageButton getImageButton() {
        return imageButton;
    }
}
```

Summary

The AWT includes support for clipboards, both local clipboards and access to the system clipboard. Copying data to the system clipboard makes the data available to other programs in addition to other AWT components.

The AWT's data transfer mechanism consists of transferables and data flavors. Transferables encapsulate data and can provide access to their data in one or more data flavors.

Transferring textual data is supported by the `java.awt.datatransfer` package; however, you are on your own when transferring data of other types. To illustrate transferring nontextual data types, we've demonstrated how to transfer both images and AWT custom components to and from clipboards.

CHAPTER

21

Drag and Drop

Drag and drop is an essential part of most modern software and, as of the 1.2 JDK, is available as part of the AWT. The `java.awt.dnd` package provides all of the essentials for implementing drag and drop among AWT components.

Regardless of what you may have heard in the past, drag and drop always starts with a drag, and a drag always starts with a gesture. The `java.awt.dnd` package provides the infrastructure for drag sources, drop targets, drag gesture recognizers, and assorted event and listener classes.

The java.awt.dnd Package

The classes and interfaces contained in the `java.awt.dnd` package are listed in Table 21-1.

Table 21-1 `java.awt.dnd` Classes and Interfaces

Class/Interface	Class or Interface	Purpose
Autoscroll	Interface	Can be implemented by scrollable drop targets
DnDConstants	Class	Enumeration of action constants
DragGestureEvent	Class	Passed to `gestureRecognized()`

Table 21-1 `java.awt.dnd` **Classes and Interfaces (Continued)**

Class/Interface	Class or Interface	Purpose
`DragGestureListener`	Interface	Implements `gestureRecognized()`
`DragGestureRecognizer`	Class	Invokes gestureRecognized()
`DragSource`	Class	Starts drag
`DragSourceContext`	Class	Maintains state with native peer
`DragSourceDragEvent`	Class	Notifies DragSourceListeners
`DragSourceDropEvent`	Class	Notifies DragSourceListeners
`DragSourceEvent`	Class	Base class for DragSourceDragEvent/ DragSourceDropEvent
`DragSourceListener`	Interface	Notified about drag source events
`DropTarget`	Class	Associated with component
`DropTargetContext`	Class	Maintains state with native peer
`DropTargetDragEvent`	Class	Notifies DropTargetListeners
`DropTargetDropEvent`	Class	Notifies DropTargetListeners
`DropTargetEvent`	Class	Base class for DropTargetDragEvent/ DropTargetDropEvent
`DropTargetListener`	Class	Notified about drop target events
`InvalidDndOperationException`	Classes	Native drag and drop is out of synch with AWT drag and drop
`MouseDragGestureRecognizer`	Class	Recognizes mouse drag and drop gestures

The `java.awt.dnd` classes fall naturally into three categories: recognizer, drag source, and drop target. Drag sources and drop targets both have a small hierarchy of event types and listeners. Drag sources and drop targets also have a context object that maintains state with the drag source for drop target peer.

Drag Sources and Drop Targets

Drag sources and drop targets are the fundamental building blocks upon which drag and drop is based. Drag sources, represented by the `DragSource` class, initiate a drag with the `DragSource.startDrag` method. Drop targets, represented by the `DropTarget` class, are targets for dropped data with the `DropTarget.drop` method.

As mentioned previously, drag and drop is initiated with a gesture. Typically, the gesture entails dragging the mouse outside of the bounds of a drag source; however, the gesture is window system dependent. The `java.awt.dnd` package provides a `DragGestureRecognizer` class for detecting a drag gesture. Instances of `DragGestureRecognizer` can be obtained from a drag source. The recognizer notifies a drag gesture listener that a drag gesture has occurred in the associated drag source, and the listener typically starts a drag with `DragSource.startDrag()`.

But we are getting ahead of ourselves, and an example of drag and drop will serve better than a textual description.

A Simple Drag and Drop Example

The application shown in Figure 22-1 contains two lists; the top list is a drag source and the bottom list is a drop target. Items from the top list (drag source) can be dragged into the bottom list (drop target).

The top left picture in Figure 22-1 shows the application after a selection has been made in the drop source list. The top right picture shows the applet after a drag gesture has been made in the drag source and the text associated with the selected item is being dragged. The bottom left picture shows the applet after the cursor has been moved over the drop target. At the bottom right, the drop target list has received the drop and has added the text that was dropped.

The application extends `java.awt.Frame` and implements the `DragGestureListener`, `DragSourceListener`, and `DropTargetListener` interfaces. The application creates two lists, one for the drag source and the other for the drop target.

```
public class Test extends Frame implements
                    DragGestureListener, DragSourceListener,
                                   DropTargetListener{

    // Create drag and drop components

    private List dragList = new List();
    private List dropList = new List();
    ...
```

Then the key ingredients for drag and drop are instantiated: a drag source, a drop target, and a drag gesture recognizer.

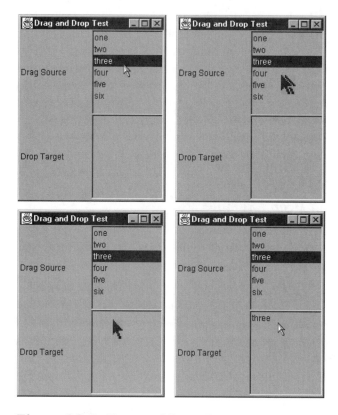

Figure 22-1 Drag and Drop Between Two Lists

```
// create drag source, drop target and drag gesture recognizer
...
private DragSource dragSource = new DragSource();

private DropTarget dropTarget =
      new DropTarget(
          dropList,  // Component
          DnDConstants.ACTION_COPY_OR_MOVE,  // actions
          this); // DragTargetListener

DragGestureRecognizer recognizer =
          dragSource.createDefaultDragGestureRecognizer(
            dragList,  // Component
            DnDConstants.ACTION_COPY_OR_MOVE,  // actions
            this); // DragGestureListener
...
```

The drop target and drag gesture recognizer are both constructed with the following three arguments: `Component`, `int`, `DragGestureListener/DragTargetListener`. The component represents the AWT component where either the drag gesture or drop will occur.

The `int` value represents the type of action and is one of the following values:

- `DndConstants.ACTION_COPY`
- `DndConstants.ACTION_COPY_OR_MOVE`
- `DndConstants.ACTION_LINK`
- `DndConstants.ACTION_MOVE`
- `DndConstants.ACTION_REFERENCE`

The application implements both the `DragTargetListener` and `DragGestureListener` interfaces and specifies itself as the listener for the drop target and drag gesture recognizer.

The application's constructor adds strings to the drag list, sets its layout manager to an instance of `GridLayout`, and adds the lists and labels that identify them.

```
public Test() {
    super("Drag and Drop Test");

    dragList.add("one");
    dragList.add("two");
    dragList.add("three");
    dragList.add("four");
    dragList.add("five");
    dragList.add("six");

    setLayout(new GridLayout(2,0)); // 2 rows, 0 columns

    add(new Label("Drag Source"));
    add(dragList);
    add(new Label("Drop Target"));
    add(dropList);
}
public static void main(String[] args) {
    ...
}
...
```

The application implements the `DragGestureListener` interface and specifies itself as the drag gesture listener for the drag source. As a result, when a drag gesture is detected in the drag source, `Test.dragGestureRecognized()` is invoked, which gets the drag underway by invoking `DragGestureEvent.startDrag()`.

DragGestureEvent.startDrag() is passed a cursor to use during the drop, a transferable, and a drag source listener that is the application.

```
// implement DragGestureListener interface ...

public void dragGestureRecognized(DragGestureEvent e) {
    String selectedItem = dragList.getSelectedItem();

    e.startDrag(
            DragSource.DefaultCopyDrop,  // cursor
            new StringSelection(selectedItem), // transferable
            this); // DragSourceListener
}
...
```

The application implements the DragSourceListener interface because a reference to a DragSourceListener must be passed to DragSource.startDrag(). However, the application is not interested in any events associated with the drag source, so the implementation of the methods leans towards simplistic.

```
// implement DragSourceListener interface ...

public void dragDropEnd(DragSourceDropEvent e) {}
public void dragEnter(DragSourceDragEvent e) {}
public void dragExit(DragSourceEvent e) {}
public void dragOver(DragSourceDragEvent e) {}
public void dropActionChanged(DragSourceDragEvent e) {}
```

The application's implementations for the methods defined by the DropTargetListener interface are listed below. The application is only interested in the drop itself, so the only meaningful implementations belong to the dragEnter and drop methods.

```
// implement DropTargetListener interface ...

public void dragEnter(DropTargetDragEvent e) {
    e.acceptDrag(DnDConstants.ACTION_COPY_OR_MOVE);
}
public void drop(DropTargetDropEvent e) {
    try {
        if(e.isDataFlavorSupported(DataFlavor.stringFlavor)){
            Transferable tr = e.getTransferable();

            e.acceptDrop (DnDConstants.ACTION_COPY_OR_MOVE);

            String s = (String)tr.getTransferData (
                                DataFlavor.stringFlavor);
```

```
                dropList.add(s);

                e.dropComplete(true);
            } else {
                e.rejectDrop();
            }
        }
        // catching exceptions omitted ...
    }
    public void dragExit(DropTargetEvent e) { }
    public void dragOver(DropTargetDragEvent e) { }
    public void dropActionChanged(DropTargetDragEvent e) { }
}
```

The dragEnter method accepts the drag if it is of the appropriate type.

The drop method obtains a reference to the transferable that was specified in the
call to DragSource.startDrag() above. If the transferable supports the string
data flavor, the string is extracted from the transferable and added to the drop
target list. See "Clipboard and Data Transfer" on page 669 for more information
concerning data transfer.

After the string is extracted and the list is updated, dropComplete() is invoked
to signal that the drop successfully completed. The boolean value passed to
dropComplete() indicates the success of the drop.

The application shown in Figure 22-1 is listed in its entirety in Example 21-1.

Example 21-1 Drag and Drop Between Two Lists

```
import java.applet.Applet;
import java.awt.*;
import java.awt.dnd.*;
import java.awt.datatransfer.*;
import java.awt.event.*;
import java.io.*;

public class Test extends Frame implements
                    DragGestureListener, DragSourceListener,
                                    DropTargetListener{

    private List dragList = new List();
    private List dropList = new List();

    private DragSource dragSource = new DragSource();

    private DropTarget dropTarget =
            new DropTarget(
                dropList,  // Component
                DnDConstants.ACTION_COPY_OR_MOVE,  // actions
                this); // DropTargetListener
```

```
DragGestureRecognizer recognizer =
        dragSource.createDefaultDragGestureRecognizer(
            dragList,  // Component
            DnDConstants.ACTION_COPY_OR_MOVE,  // actions
            this); // DragGestureListener

public Test() {
    super("Drag and Drop Test");

    dragList.add("one");
    dragList.add("two");
    dragList.add("three");
    dragList.add("four");
    dragList.add("five");
    dragList.add("six");

    setLayout(new GridLayout(2,0));
    add(new Label("Drag Source"));
    add(dragList);
    add(new Label("Drop Target"));
    add(dropList);
}
public static void main(String[] args) {
    Frame f = new Test();
    f.setBounds(300,300,200,175);
    f.setVisible(true);

    f.addWindowListener (new WindowAdapter() {
     public void windowClosing(WindowEvent e) {
     System.exit(0);
     }
     });
}

// DragGestureListener implementation follows ...

public void dragGestureRecognized(DragGestureEvent e) {
    String selectedItem = dragList.getSelectedItem();

    e.startDrag(
        DragSource.DefaultCopyDrop,  // cursor
        new StringSelection(selectedItem), // transferable
        this); // DragSourceListener
}

// DragSourceListener implementation follows ...

public void dragDropEnd(DragSourceDropEvent e) {}
public void dragEnter(DragSourceDragEvent e) {}
public void dragExit(DragSourceEvent e) {}
public void dragOver(DragSourceDragEvent e) {}
public void dropActionChanged(DragSourceDragEvent e) {}

// DropTargetListener implementation follows ...
```

```java
    public void dragEnter(DropTargetDragEvent e) {
        e.acceptDrag(DnDConstants.ACTION_COPY_OR_MOVE);
    }
    public void drop(DropTargetDropEvent e) {
        try {
            if(e.isDataFlavorSupported(DataFlavor.stringFlavor)){
                Transferable tr = e.getTransferable();

                e.acceptDrop (DnDConstants.ACTION_COPY_OR_MOVE);

                String s = (String)tr.getTransferData (
                                  DataFlavor.stringFlavor);
                dropList.add(s);
                e.dropComplete(true);
            } else {
                e.rejectDrop();
            }
        }
        catch (IOException io) {
            io.printStackTrace();
            e.rejectDrop();
        }
        catch (UnsupportedFlavorException ufe) {
            ufe.printStackTrace();
            e.rejectDrop();
        }
    }
    public void dragExit(DropTargetEvent e) {}
    public void dragOver(DropTargetDragEvent e) {}
    public void dropActionChanged(DropTargetDragEvent e) {}
}
```

AWT TIP ...

A Recipe for Drag and Drop

Drag and drop is easy to remember if you keep in mind the three major participants: drag source, drop target, and drag gesture recognizer:

1. Make instances of DragSource, DropTarget, and DragGestureRecognizer available for use.

2. Implement listeners for each of the objects listed above: DragSourceListener, DropTargetListener, and DragGestureListener, respectively.

DragGestureListener: Typically initiates drag with

DragSource.startDrag()

DragSourceListener: Monitors state of drop

DropTargetListener: Accept/reject drag and complete drop

Drag Gestures

Detecting a drag gesture in a drag source is a job for the aptly named `DragGestureRecognizer`. Drag gesture recognizers are unicast[1] event sources that are notified by a native peer when a drag gesture is made in an associated drag source. In turn, gesture recognizers notify a single listener that implements the `DragGestureListener` interface.

Instances of `DragGestureRecognizer` are rarely directly instantiated or manipulated because recognizers are a connection between native peers and drag gesture listeners. The connection can be seen from Figure 22-2, which shows the sequence of events leading up to a drag gesture listener notification.

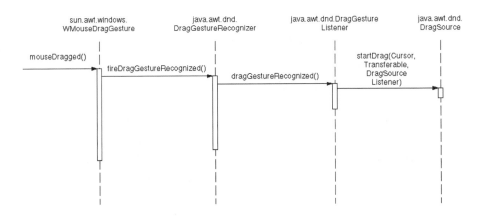

Figure 22-2 `DragGestureRecognizer` Sequence Diagram

In Figure 22-2, a mouse dragged event is sent to a peer—an instance of `sun.awt.windows.WMouseDragGesture`—which in turn invokes `fireDragGestureRecognized()` on a recognizer.

1.   Instances of unicast event sources have exactly one listener.

The `DragGestureRecognizer` notifies its drag gesture listener by invoking `DragGestureListener.dragGestureRecognized()`. The `DragGestureListener` in Figure 22-2 starts a drag by invoking `startDrag()` for a drag source, which is typical, but not mandatory, behavior.

As in the application listed in Example 21-1 on page 705, gesture recognizers are typically created through either `createDragGestureRecognizer()` or `createDefaultDragGestureRecognizer()` methods from the `DragSource` class:

```
// from application listed in Example 21-1 on page 705 ...

DragGestureRecognizer recognizer =
            dragSource.createDefaultDragGestureRecognizer(
            dragList,   // Component
            DnDConstants.ACTION_COPY_OR_MOVE,   // actions
            this); // DragGestureListener
  ...
```

When the gesture recognizer is created by the drag source, the `DragGestureListener` for the recognizer is specified. From there on out, a drag gesture in the drag source that created the recognizer will result in notification of the gesture listener (by way of the `dragGestureRecognized()` method).

Table 21-2 lists the `public` methods provided by the `DragGestureRecognizer` class.

Table 21-2 `java.awt.dnd.DragGestureRecognizer` **Methods**

Return Value	Method
void	addDragGestureListener(DragGestureListener)
Component	getComponent()
DragSource	getDragSource()
int	getSourceActions()
InputEvent	getTriggerEvent()
void	removeDragGestureListener(DragGestureListener)
void	resetRecognizer()
void	setSourceActions(int)

Drag Sources

Drag sources initiate drags and create drag gesture recognizers. Drag sources are typically used in the following manner:

- Create an instance of `DragSource` with the no-argument `DragSource` constructor.
- Obtain an instance of `DragGestureRecognizer` from the drag source.
- Invoke `DragSource.startDrag()` when a drag gesture is detected.

Drag sources are represented by the `DragSource` class, whose `public` methods are listed in Table 21-3.

Table 21-3 `java.awt.dnd.DragSource` **Methods**

Return Value	Method
DragGesture Recognizer	createDefaultDragGestureRecognizer(Component,int, DragGestureListener)
DragGesture Recognizer	createDefaultDragGestureRecognizer(Class, Component,int,DragGestureListener)
FlavorMap	getFlavorMap()
void	startDrag(DragGestureEvent,Cursor,Image,Point, Transferable,DragSourceListener)
void	startDrag(DragGestureEvent,Cursor,Image,Point, Transferable,DragSourceListener)
void	startDrag(DragGestureEvent,Cursor,Transferable, DragSourceListener,FlavorMap)
void	startDrag(DragGestureEvent,Cursor,Transferable, DragSourceListener)

Drag source listeners can be added to drag sources to monitor the state of a drag and drop operation. The methods defined by the `DragSourceListener` interface are listed in Table 21-4.

Table 21-4 `java.awt.dnd.DragSourceListener` **Methods**

Return Value	Method
void	dragDropEnd(DragSourceDropEvent)
void	dragEnter(DragSourceDragEvent)
void	dragExit(DragSourceEvent)
void	dragOver(DragSourceDragEvent)
void	dropActionChanged(DragSourceDragEvent)

Drop Targets

Drop targets, like drag sources, are the target of a gesture. The drop gesture typically consists of releasing the mouse button in the drop target's associated component; however, the drop gesture, like the drag gesture, is window system dependent.

Drop targets are actually more similar to drag gesture recognizers than are drag sources. Drop targets and recognizers are both unicast event sources; drop targets each have a single drop target listener of type DropTargetListener.

Also, creating a drop target associates the drop target, component, and drop target listener. After an instance of DropTarget is instantiated, everything is wired for action when a drop gesture is detected in the component. This is similar to instances of DragGestureRecognizer, and in fact both recognizers and drop targets are rarely used after they are instantiated.

The public methods implemented by the DropTarget class are listed in Table 21-5.

Table 21-5 java.awt.dnd.DropTarget **Methods**

Return Value	Method
void	addDropTargetListener(DropTargetListener)
void	dragEnter(DropTargetDragEvent)
void	dragExit(DropTargetEvent)
void	dragOver(DropTargetDragEvent)
void	drop(DropTargetDropEvent)
void	dropActionChanged(DropTargetDragEvent)
Component	getComponent()
int	getDefaultActions()
DropTarget Context	getDropTargetContext()
FlavorMap	getFlavorMap()
boolean	isActive()
void	removeDropTargetListener(DropTargetListener)
void	setActive(boolean)
void	setComponent(Component)
void	setDefaultActions(int)
void	setFlavorMap(FlavorMap)

Drop targets notify their drop target listener of a number of drop target events, as listed in Table 21-6.

Table 21-6 `java.awt.dnd.DropTargetListener` **Methods**

Return Value	Method
void	dragEnter(DropTargetDragEvent)
void	dragExit(DropTargetEvent)
void	dragOver(DropTargetDragEvent)
void	drag(DropTargetDropEvent)
void	dragDropEnd(DropTargetDropEvent)
void	dropActionChanged(DropTargetDragEvent)

Events

The `java.awt.dnd` package provides a number of event classes for events that are passed to `DragGestureListener`, `DragSourceListener`, and `DropTargetListener` methods. The tables that follow list the `public` methods defined by the event classes from the `java.awt.dnd` package.

Table 21-7 lists the `public` methods from the `DragGestureEvent` class.

Table 21-7 `java.awt.dnd.DragGestureEvent` **Methods**

Return Value	Method
Component	getComponent()
int	getDragAction()
Point	getDragOrigin()
DragSource	getDragSource()
DragGesture Recognizer	getSourceAsDragGestureRecognizer()
InputEvent	getTriggerEvent()
Iterator	iterator()
void	startDrag(Cursor,Transferable,DragSourceListener()
void	startDrag(Cursor,Image,Point, Transferable,DragSourceListener)
Object[]	toArray()
Object[]	toArray(Object[])

Drag gesture events are capable of initiating a drag, so you needn't be bothered with directly accessing the drag source yourself when a drag gesture occurs.

Instances of `DragGestureEvent` are passed to `DragSource.startDrag()` and `DragGestureListener.dragGestureRecognized()`.

DragSourceDragEvent and DragSourceDropEvent

Instances of `DragSourceDragEvent` and `DragSourceDropEvent` are passed to methods defined in the `DragSourceListener` interface. Both `DragSourceDragEvent` and `DragSourceDropEvent` are related to drag and drop events, respectively, that occur in a drop target.

Table 21-8 lists the `public` methods implemented by the `DragSourceDragEvent` class.

Table 21-8 `java.awt.dnd.DragSourceDragEvent` **Methods**

Return Value	Method
int	getDropAction()
int	getGestureModifiers()
int	getTargetActions()
int	getUserAction()
boolean	isLocalDropTarget()

Table 21-9 lists the `public` methods implemented by the `DragSourceDropEvent` class.

Table 21-9 `java.awt.dnd.DragSourceDropEvent` **Methods**

Return Value	Method
int	getDropAction()
boolean	getDropSuccess()

DropTargetDragEvent and DropTargetDropEvent

Instances of `DropTargetDragEvent` and `DropTargetDropEvent` are passed to methods defined in the `DropTargetListener` interface. Both `DropTargetDragEvent` and `DropTargetDropEvent` are related to drag and drop events, respectively, that occur in a drop target.

Table 21-10 lists the `public` methods implemented by the
`DropTargetDragEvent` class.

Table 21-10 `java.awt.dnd.DropTargetDragEvent` **Methods**

Return Value	Method
void	acceptDrag(int)
DataFlavor[]	getCurrentDataFlavors()
List	getCurrentDataFlavorsAsList()
int	getDropAction()
Point	getLocation()
int	getSourceActions()
boolean	isDataFlavorSupported(DataFlavor)
void	rejectDrag()

Table 21-11 lists the `public` methods implemented by the
`DropTargetDropEvent` class

Table 21-11 `java.awt.dnd.DropTargetDropEvent` **Methods**

Return Value	Method
void	acceptDrop(int)
void	dropComplete(boolean success)
DataFlavor[]	getCurrentDataFlavors()
List	getCurrentDataFlavorsAsList()
int	getDropAction()
Point	getLocation()
int	getSourceActions()
Transferable	getTransferable()
boolean	isDataFlavorSupported(DataFlavor)
boolean	isLocalTransfer()
void	rejectDrop()

Specialized Drag Sources and Drop Targets

The application shown in Figure 22-1 on page 702 and listed in Example 21-1 on
page 705 is implemented as a monolithic `Test` class that contains a drag source,
drag gesture recognizer, drop target, and two lists. The `Test` class also

implements the DragGestureListener, DragSourceListener, and DropTargetListener interfaces. In practice, such a design is useful for little more than illustration.

Using drag and drop involves more than the mechanics of starting drags and accepting drops. Typically, specialized drag sources and drop targets are implemented that are pertinent to the situation at hand. The next sections discuss designs for implementing specialized drag sources and drop targets.

Inheritance and Delegation

The application shown in Figure 22-1 on page 702 is rewritten below to use a specialized drag source and a specialized drop target. The drag source is represented by the ListDragSource class, that extends List. The drop target is represented by the ListDropTarget class, which delegates to an instance of List.

The constructor for the application creates an instance of ListDragSource, which is simply added to the application frame. A list is instantiated and used to construct an instance of ListDropTarget. The list is then added to the application frame.

```
public class Test extends Frame {
    public Test() {
        super("Drag and Drop Test");
        ListDragSource dragList = new ListDragSource();

        List dropList = new List();
        ListDropTarget dropTarget = new ListDropTarget(dropList);

        dragList.add("one");
        dragList.add("two");
        dragList.add("three");
        dragList.add("four");
        dragList.add("five");
        dragList.add("six");

        setLayout(new GridLayout(2,0));
        add(new Label("Drag Source"));
        add(dragList);
        add(new Label("Drop Target"));
        add(dropList);
    }
    public static void main(String[] args) {
        ...
    }
}
```

`ListDragSource` extends `List` and implements the `DragSourceListener` and `DragGestureListener` interfaces. When a drag gesture is detected in the drag source (the list), the selected item in the list is wrapped in a transferable that is designated as the data being dragged.

Because `ListDragSource` extends `List`, the `dragGestureRecognized` method calls `getSelectedItem()` to obtain a reference to the currently selected item.

```
class ListDragSource extends List
      implements DragSourceListener, DragGestureListener {
   ...
   public void dragGestureRecognized(DragGestureEvent e) {
      String item = getSelectedItem();
      e.startDrag(
            DragSource.DefaultCopyDrop,  // cursor
            new StringSelection(item), // transferable
            this); // DragSourceListener
   }
   ...
}
```

When a drop occurs in the `ListDropTarget` class, the dropped string is added to the list passed to the `ListDropTarget` constructor.

```
class ListDropTarget implements DropTargetListener {
   private List list;
   private DropTarget dropTarget;

   public ListDropTarget(List list) {
      this.list = list;
      ...
   }
   ...
   public void drop(DropTargetDropEvent e) {
      try {
         Transferable tr = e.getTransferable();

         if(tr.isDataFlavorSupported(DataFlavor.stringFlavor)){
            e.acceptDrop (DnDConstants.ACTION_COPY_OR_MOVE);
            String s = (String)tr.getTransferData (
                               DataFlavor.stringFlavor);
            list.add(s);
            e.dropComplete(true);
         } else {
            e.rejectDrop();
         }
      }
      ...
   }
   ...
}
```

ListDragSource extends an AWT component—List—and therefore can
simply invoke an inherited List method for obtaining the text associated with
the currently selected item in the list. ListDropTarget, on the other hand, does
not extend List but instead delegates to a List instance that is passed to its
constructor.

Delegation is generally preferable to inheritance because it is more flexible. For
example, a single instance of ListDropTarget could serve as a drop target for
multiple lists; however, a ListDragSource is bound by inheritance to a single
list.

The application shown in Figure 22-1 on page 702 is rewritten in Example 21-2,
using inheritance (for ListDragSource) and delegation (for
ListDropTarget) for implementing a custom drag source and drop target.

Example 21-2 Using Delegation and Inheritance

```
import java.applet.Applet;
import java.awt.*;
import java.awt.dnd.*;
import java.awt.datatransfer.*;
import java.awt.event.*;
import java.io.*;

public class Test extends Frame {
    public Test() {
        super("Drag and Drop Test");
        ListDragSource dragList = new ListDragSource();

        List dropList = new List();
        ListDropTarget dropTarget = new ListDropTarget(dropList);

        dragList.add("one");
        dragList.add("two");
        dragList.add("three");
        dragList.add("four");
        dragList.add("five");
        dragList.add("six");

        setLayout(new GridLayout(2,0));
        add(new Label("Drag Source"));
        add(dragList);
        add(new Label("Drop Target"));
        add(dropList);
    }
    public static void main(String[] args) {
        ...
    }
}
```

```
// ListDropTarget delegates to an instance of java.awt.List

class ListDropTarget implements DropTargetListener {
    private List list;
    private DropTarget dropTarget;

    public ListDropTarget(List list) {
        this.list = list;
        dropTarget = new DropTarget(
                    list, // component
                    DnDConstants.ACTION_COPY_OR_MOVE, // actions
                    this); // DropTargetListener
    }
    public void dragEnter(DropTargetDragEvent e) {
        e.acceptDrag(DnDConstants.ACTION_COPY_OR_MOVE);
    }
    public void drop(DropTargetDropEvent e) {
        try {
            Transferable tr = e.getTransferable();

            if(tr.isDataFlavorSupported(DataFlavor.stringFlavor)){
                e.acceptDrop (DnDConstants.ACTION_COPY_OR_MOVE);
                String s = (String)tr.getTransferData (
                                    DataFlavor.stringFlavor);
                list.add(s);
                e.dropComplete(true);
            } else {
                e.rejectDrop();
            }
        }
        catch (IOException io) {
            io.printStackTrace();
            e.rejectDrop();
        }
        catch (UnsupportedFlavorException ufe) {
            ufe.printStackTrace();
            e.rejectDrop();
        }
    }
    public void dragExit (DropTargetEvent e) { }
    public void dragOver (DropTargetDragEvent e) { }
    public void dropActionChanged (DropTargetDragEvent e) { }
}

// ListDragSource is a list that contains a drag source

class ListDragSource extends List
        implements DragSourceListener, DragGestureListener {
    DragSource dragSource;
    DragGestureRecognizer recognizer;

    public ListDragSource() {
        dragSource = new DragSource();
```

```
            recognizer =
                dragSource.createDefaultDragGestureRecognizer(
                        this,   // Component
                        DnDConstants.ACTION_COPY_OR_MOVE,   // actions
                        this);  // DragGestureListener
        }
    public void dragGestureRecognized(DragGestureEvent e) {
        String item = getSelectedItem();
        e.startDrag(
                DragSource.DefaultCopyDrop,   // cursor
                new StringSelection(item), // transferable
                this); // DragSourceListener
    }
    public void dragDropEnd(DragSourceDropEvent e) {}
    public void dragEnter(DragSourceDragEvent e) {}
    public void dragExit(DragSourceEvent e) {}
    public void dragOver(DragSourceDragEvent e) {}
    public void dropActionChanged(DragSourceDragEvent e) {}
}
```

Reflection

All other things being equal, delegation is more flexible than inheritance for relating AWT components to drag and drop classes. Delegation relationships can be specified (and modified) at runtime, whereas inheritance relationships are specified once and for all at compile time.

However, both delegation and inheritance are limited by the type of component that is delegated to or extended, respectively. For example, consider the dragGestureRecognized method from the ListDragSource class in the previous section and the drop method from the ListDropTarget.

```
// See previous section for full listings of ListDragSource
// and ListDropTarget

class ListDragSource extends List
        implements DragSourceListener, DragGestureListener {
    ...
    public void dragGestureRecognized(DragGestureEvent e) {
        String selectedItem = getSelectedItem();

        e.startDrag(
                DragSource.DefaultCopyDrop,   // cursor
                new StringSelection(selectedItem), // transferable
                this); // DragSourceListener
    }
    ...
}
```

```
class ListDropTarget implements DropTargetListener {
    // from DropTargetListener implementor
    ...
    public void drop(DropTargetDropEvent e) {
        try {
            if(e.isDataFlavorSupported(DataFlavor.stringFlavor)){
                ...
                dropList.add(s);
                ...
            } else {
                e.rejectDrop();
            }
        }
        ...
    }
    ...
}
```

Obviously, both `ListDragSource` and `ListDropTarget` will only work with instances of `java.awt.List` because of the manner in which the selected item is obtained and the dropped text is added to the list.

It would be much more useful if we could implement drag sources and drop targets that could be used with any type of object that could produce a string or have a string added to it, respectively. Java reflection gives us the opportunity to do just that.

The application listed below instantiates instances of `StringDragSource` and `StringDropTarget`, which use reflection to invoke an arbitrary method for an arbitrary object.

```
public class Test extends Frame {
    public Test() {
        super("Drag and Drop Test");

        List drag = new List(), drop = new List();

        StringDragSource source = new StringDragSource(
                drag, "getSelectedItem", new Class[]{});

        StringDropTarget target = new StringDropTarget(
                drop, "add", new Class[]{String.class});

        drag.add("one");
        drag.add("two");
        drag.add("three");
        drag.add("four");
        drag.add("five");
        drag.add("six");

        setLayout(new GridLayout(0,2));
```

```
        add(new Label("Drag Source"));
        add(drag);
        add(new Label("Drop Target"));
        add(drop);
    }
    public static void main(String[] args) {
        ...
    }
}
```

Both `StringDragSource` and `StringDropTarget` are constructed with three arguments:

- An `Object`
- A string representing a method name
- An array of `Class` objects

The string representing a method name is used to obtain a Method reference for the object passed to the constructor. The method is subsequently invoked with `java.lang.reflect.Method.invoke()`, which is passed the array of `Class` objects representing argument types for the method.

```
class StringDragSource
          implements DragSourceListener, DragGestureListener {

    Component component;
    DragSource dragSource;
    DragGestureRecognizer recognizer;
    Method dragMethod;
    String s;

    public StringDragSource(Component component,
                            String methodName,
                            Class[] args) {
        this.component = component;
        dragSource = new DragSource();

        recognizer =
            dragSource.createDefaultDragGestureRecognizer(
                component, // Component
                DnDConstants.ACTION_COPY_OR_MOVE, // actions
                this); // DragGestureListener
        try {
            dragMethod =
                component.getClass().getMethod(methodName, args);
        }
        catch(NoSuchMethodException ex) {
            ex.printStackTrace();
        }
    }
    ...
```

In the code fragment listed above, the method associated with the drag source component for obtaining a string to drag is obtained from the class of the component. Care is taken to ensure that the method name and arguments are valid for the class of the component by catching NoSuchMethodExceptions.

In the dragGestureRecognized method of the StringDragSource, the method obtained in the StringDragSource constructor is invoked to obtain a string to drag.

```
    ...
    public void dragGestureRecognized(DragGestureEvent e) {
       try {
          s = (String)dragMethod.invoke(
                              component, new Object[]{});
       }
       catch(InvocationTargetException ex) {
          ex.printStackTrace();
       }
       catch(IllegalAccessException iae) {
          iae.printStackTrace();
       }
       e.startDrag(DragSource.DefaultCopyDrop,  // cursor
               new StringSelection(s), // transferable
               this); // DragSourceListener
    }
    ...
}
```

Finally, the method associated with the drop target is obtained and invoked in the StringDropTarget constructor and drop method, respectively.

```
class StringDropTarget implements DropTargetListener {
      ...
    public StringDropTarget(Component component,
                            String methodName,
                            Class[] args) {
       this.component = component;

       dropTarget = new DropTarget(component,
                     DnDConstants.ACTION_COPY_OR_MOVE,
                     this);
       try {
          dropMethod =
             component.getClass().getMethod(methodName, args);
       }
       catch(NoSuchMethodException ex) {
          ex.printStackTrace();
       }
    }
    ...
```

```
public void drop(DropTargetDropEvent e) {
    try {
        Transferable tr = e.getTransferable();

        if(tr.isDataFlavorSupported(DataFlavor.stringFlavor)){
            e.acceptDrop(DnDConstants.ACTION_COPY_OR_MOVE);
            String s = (String)tr.getTransferData (
                                    DataFlavor.stringFlavor);

            dropMethod.invoke(component, new Object[]{s});
            e.dropComplete(true);
        }
    }
    ...
}
...
}
```

Using reflection to obtain a reference to a method for an arbitrary object and subsequently invoking the method enables us to implement very general drag sources and drop targets. The drag source and drop target discussed above will work with any type of object that can produce and subsume text.

Reflection enables us to specify methods at runtime instead of compile time, adding another degree of freedom that allows more generality. However, using reflection comes with a penalty, namely, that exceptions that would normally be caught by the compiler at compile time must be handled by the developer at runtime. Because of this penalty, reflection should be used sparingly.

The application is listed in its entirety in Example 21-3.

Example 21-3 Using Reflection for General Drag Sources and Drop Targets

```
import java.applet.Applet;
import java.awt.*;
import java.awt.datatransfer.*;
import java.awt.dnd.*;
import java.awt.event.*;
import java.io.*;
import java.lang.reflect.*;

public class Test extends Frame {
    public Test() {
        super("Drag and Drop Test");

        List drag = new List(), drop = new List();

        StringDragSource source = new StringDragSource(
                drag, "getSelectedItem", new Class[]{});
```

```
            StringDropTarget target = new StringDropTarget(
                    drop, "add", new Class[]{String.class});

            drag.add("one");
            drag.add("two");
            drag.add("three");
            drag.add("four");
            drag.add("five");
            drag.add("six");

            setLayout(new GridLayout(0,2));

            add(new Label("Drag Source"));
            add(drag);
            add(new Label("Drop Target"));
            add(drop);
        }
    public static void main(String[] args) {
        Frame f = new Test();
        f.setBounds(300,300,250,300);
        f.setVisible(true);

        f.addWindowListener (new WindowAdapter() {
         public void windowClosing(WindowEvent e) {
         System.exit(0);
         }
         });
    }
}
class StringDragSource
            implements DragSourceListener, DragGestureListener {
    Component component;
    DragSource dragSource;
    DragGestureRecognizer recognizer;
    Method dragMethod;
    String s;

    public StringDragSource(Component component,
                        String methodName,
                        Class[] args) {
        this.component = component;
        dragSource = new DragSource();

        recognizer =
            dragSource.createDefaultDragGestureRecognizer(
                component, // Component
                DnDConstants.ACTION_COPY_OR_MOVE, // actions
                this); // DragGestureListener
        try {
            dragMethod =
                component.getClass().getMethod(methodName, args);
        }
```

```
        catch(NoSuchMethodException ex) {
            ex.printStackTrace();
        }
    }
    public void dragGestureRecognized(DragGestureEvent e) {
        try {
            s = (String)dragMethod.invoke(
                            component, new Object[]{});
        }
        catch(InvocationTargetException ex) {
            ex.printStackTrace();
        }
        catch(IllegalAccessException iae) {
            iae.printStackTrace();
        }
        e.startDrag(DragSource.DefaultCopyDrop,  // cursor
                new StringSelection(s), // transferable
                this); // DragSourceListener
    }
    public void dragDropEnd(DragSourceDropEvent e) {}
    public void dragEnter(DragSourceDragEvent e) {}
    public void dragExit(DragSourceEvent e) {}
    public void dragOver(DragSourceDragEvent e) {}
    public void dropActionChanged(DragSourceDragEvent e) {}
}
class StringDropTarget implements DropTargetListener {
    Component component;
    DropTarget dropTarget;
    Method dropMethod;

    public StringDropTarget(Component component,
                        String methodName,
                        Class[] args) {
        this.component = component;

        dropTarget = new DropTarget(component,
                        DnDConstants.ACTION_COPY_OR_MOVE,
                        this);
        try {
            dropMethod =
                component.getClass().getMethod(methodName, args);
        }
        catch(NoSuchMethodException ex) {
            ex.printStackTrace();
        }
    }
    public void dragEnter(DropTargetDragEvent e) {
        e.acceptDrag(DnDConstants.ACTION_COPY_OR_MOVE);
    }
    public void drop(DropTargetDropEvent e) {
        try {
            Transferable tr = e.getTransferable();
```

```
          if(tr.isDataFlavorSupported(DataFlavor.stringFlavor)){
              e.acceptDrop(DnDConstants.ACTION_COPY_OR_MOVE);
              String s = (String)tr.getTransferData (
                                   DataFlavor.stringFlavor);

              dropMethod.invoke(component, new Object[]{s});
              e.dropComplete(true);
          }
      }
      catch(IOException io) {
          io.printStackTrace();
          e.rejectDrop();
      }
      catch(UnsupportedFlavorException ufe) {
          ufe.printStackTrace();
          e.rejectDrop();
      }
      catch(IllegalAccessException iae) {
          iae.printStackTrace();
          e.rejectDrop();
      }
      catch(InvocationTargetException ite) {
          ite.printStackTrace();
          e.rejectDrop();
      }
  }
  public void dragExit (DropTargetEvent e) { }
  public void dragOver (DropTargetDragEvent e) { }
  public void dropActionChanged (DropTargetDragEvent e) { }
}
```

AutoScrolling

Autoscrolling is the ability of a drop target to scroll its contents when the drag cursor is within specified insets. For example, the tree control on the left side of Windows Explorer is an autoscrolling drop target. If something is being dragged into the tree and the cursor is near the top or bottom, the tree will scroll toward the cursor.

Autoscrolling drop targets are implementations of the `java.awt.dnd.Autoscroll` interface, which defines two methods:

- `public Insets getAutoscrollInsets()`
- `public void autoscroll(Point)`

The `getAutoscrollInsets` method determines if the location of the drag cursor should cause an autoscroll to occur. If so, the `autoscroll()` method is invoked periodically as long as the cursor remains in the autoscroll insets area.

The application shown in Figure 22-3 contains a list and an image canvas. Items in the list correspond to different images; dragging an item from the list and dropping it on the image canvas will cause the appropriate image to be displayed.

If the drag cursor is kept within the autoscroll insets, the image currently displayed in the image canvas will autoscroll.

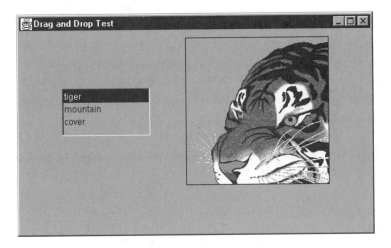

Figure 22-3 Autoscrolling in a Drop Target

The drop target component is an instance of the DragCanvas class, which extends ImageCanvas (a simple extension of java.awt.Canvas) and implements the Autoscroll interface.

DragCanvas.getAutoscrollInsets() returns an insets of ten pixels all the way around. DragCanvas.autoscroll() updates an offset depending upon the location of the cursor and invokes repaint(). DragCanvas.paint() translates its graphics by the offset calculated in the DragCanvas.autoscroll() method.

```
class DropCanvas extends ImageCanvas implements Autoscroll {
    private Insets insets = new Insets(10,10,10,10);
    private Point offset = new Point(0,0);

    . . .
```

```
public void paint(Graphics g) {
    Dimension size = getSize();
    g.drawRect(0,0,size.width-1,size.height-1);

    g.translate(-offset.x, -offset.y);
    super.paint(g);
}
...
public Insets getAutoscrollInsets() {
    return insets;
}
public void autoscroll(Point drag) {
    Dimension size = getSize();

    if(drag.x < insets.left) {
        if(offset.x + 10 < size.width -
                          insets.left - insets.right)
        offset.x += 10;
    }
    if(drag.x > size.width - insets.right) {
        if(offset.x - 10 >= 0)
            offset.x -= 10;
    }
    if(drag.y < insets.top) {
        if(offset.y + 10 < size.height -
                           insets.top - insets.bottom)
            offset.y += 10;
    }
    if(drag.y > size.height - insets.bottom) {
        if(offset.y - 10 >= 0)
            offset.y -= 10;
    }
    repaint();
}
}
```

The applet shown in Figure 22-3 is listed in its entirety in Example 21-4.

Example 21-4 Autoscrolling in a Drop Target

```
import java.applet.Applet;
import java.awt.*;
import java.awt.dnd.*;
import java.awt.datatransfer.*;
import java.awt.event.*;
import java.io.*;
import java.lang.reflect.*;

public class Test extends Frame {
    public Test() {
        super("Drag and Drop Test");

        List drag = new List();
```

```
        DropCanvas drop = new DropCanvas("cover");

        StringDragSource source = new StringDragSource(
                drag, "getSelectedItem", new Class[]{});

        StringDropTarget target = new StringDropTarget(
                drop, "loadImage", new Class[]{String.class});

        drag.add("tiger");
        drag.add("mountain");
        drag.add("cover");

        setLayout(new FlowLayout(FlowLayout.CENTER,50,10));
        add(drag);
        add(drop);
    }
    public static void main(String[] args) {
        Frame f = new Test();
        f.setBounds(300,300,500,400);
        f.setVisible(true);

        f.addWindowListener (new WindowAdapter() {
         public void windowClosing(WindowEvent e) {
         System.exit(0);
         }
         });
    }
}
class DropCanvas extends ImageCanvas implements Autoscroll {
    private Insets insets = new Insets(10,10,10,10);
    private Point offset = new Point(0,0);

    public DropCanvas() {
        this(null);
    }
    public DropCanvas(String imageName) {
        super(imageName);
    }
    public void paint(Graphics g) {
        Dimension size = getSize();
        g.drawRect(0,0,size.width-1,size.height-1);

        g.translate(-offset.x, -offset.y);
        super.paint(g);
    }
    public Dimension getPreferredSize() {
        return new Dimension(200,200);
    }
    public Insets getAutoscrollInsets() {
        return insets;
    }
    public void autoscroll(Point drag) {
```

```
        Dimension size = getSize();

        if(drag.x < insets.left) {
            if(offset.x + 10 < size.width -
                            insets.left - insets.right)
            offset.x += 10;
        }
        if(drag.x > size.width - insets.right) {
            if(offset.x - 10 >= 0)
                offset.x -= 10;
        }
        if(drag.y < insets.top) {
            if(offset.y + 10 < size.height -
                            insets.top - insets.bottom)
                offset.y += 10;
        }
        if(drag.y > size.height - insets.bottom) {
            if(offset.y - 10 >= 0)
                offset.y -= 10;
        }
        repaint();
    }
}
class ImageCanvas extends Canvas {
    Image image;

    public ImageCanvas(String imageName) {
        loadImage(imageName);
    }
    public void loadImage(String imageName) {
        image =
            Toolkit.getDefaultToolkit().getImage(
                                    imageName + ".gif");

        MediaTracker mt = new MediaTracker(this);
        try {
            mt.addImage(image, 0);
            mt.waitForID(0);
        }
        catch(InterruptedException ex) {
            ex.printStackTrace();
        }
        if(isShowing()) {
            repaint();
        }
    }
    public void paint(Graphics g) {
        g.drawImage(image, 0, 0, null);
    }
    public Dimension getPreferredSize() {
        return new Dimension(image.getWidth(null),
                        image.getHeight(null));
```

```
   }
}
class StringDragSource
       implements DragSourceListener, DragGestureListener {
    Component component;
    DragSource dragSource;
    DragGestureRecognizer recognizer;
    Method dragMethod;

    public StringDragSource(Component component,
                       String methodName,
                       Class[] args) {
        try {
            dragMethod =
                component.getClass().getMethod(methodName, args);
        }
        catch(NoSuchMethodException ex) {
            ex.printStackTrace();
        }
        this.component = component;
        dragSource = new DragSource();
        recognizer =
            dragSource.createDefaultDragGestureRecognizer(
                    component,  // Component
                    DnDConstants.ACTION_COPY_OR_MOVE,  // actions
                    this); // DragGestureListener
    }
    public void dragGestureRecognized(DragGestureEvent e) {
        String s = null;

        try {
            s = (String)dragMethod.invoke(
                             component, new Object[]{});
        }
        catch(InvocationTargetException ex) {
            ex.printStackTrace();
        }
        catch(IllegalAccessException iae) {
            iae.printStackTrace();
        }
        dragSource.startDrag(
                e,
                DragSource.DefaultCopyDrop,  // cursor
                new StringSelection(s), // transferable
                this); // DragSourceListener
    }
    public void dragDropEnd(DragSourceDropEvent e) {}
    public void dragEnter(DragSourceDragEvent e) {}
    public void dragExit(DragSourceEvent e) {}
    public void dragOver(DragSourceDragEvent e) {}
    public void dropActionChanged(DragSourceDragEvent e) {}
}
```

```java
class StringDropTarget implements DropTargetListener {
    Component component;
    DropTarget dropTarget;
    Method dropMethod;
    String string;

    public StringDropTarget(Component component,
                            String methodName,
                            Class[] args) {
        try {
            dropMethod =
                component.getClass().getMethod(methodName, args);
        }
        catch(NoSuchMethodException ex) {
            ex.printStackTrace();
        }
        this.component = component;
        dropTarget = new DropTarget(component,
                        DnDConstants.ACTION_COPY_OR_MOVE,
                        this);
    }
    public void dragEnter(DropTargetDragEvent e) {
        e.acceptDrag(DnDConstants.ACTION_COPY_OR_MOVE);
    }
    public void drop(DropTargetDropEvent e) {
        try {
            Transferable tr = e.getTransferable();

            if(tr.isDataFlavorSupported(DataFlavor.stringFlavor)){
                e.acceptDrop(DnDConstants.ACTION_COPY_OR_MOVE);

                string = (String)tr.getTransferData (
                                    DataFlavor.stringFlavor);
                System.out.println(string);

                dropMethod.invoke(component,
                                    new Object[]{string});

                e.getDropTargetContext().dropComplete(true);
            }
        }
        catch(IOException io) {
            io.printStackTrace();
            e.rejectDrop();
        }
        catch(UnsupportedFlavorException ufe) {
            ufe.printStackTrace();
            e.rejectDrop();
        }
        catch(IllegalAccessException iae) {
            iae.printStackTrace();
            e.rejectDrop();
```

```
            }
        catch(InvocationTargetException ite) {
            ite.printStackTrace();
            e.rejectDrop();
        }
    }
    public void dragExit(DropTargetEvent e) { }
    public void dragOver(DropTargetDragEvent e) { }
    public void dropActionChanged(DropTargetDragEvent e) { }
}
```

Summary

The AWT provides drag and drop that is intuitive and easy to use. This chapter has covered the fundamentals of the `java.awt.dnd` package and has explored customized drag sources and drop targets.

CHAPTER
22

Custom Dialogs

Dialogs were introduced in Part IV of *Graphic Java*—see "java.awt.Dialog" on page 582, where we mentioned that the AWT is pretty thin when it comes to dialogs. The AWT provides a basic `Dialog` class and only one `Dialog` extension: a `FileDialog` for selecting a file.

This chapter discusses the implementation of the following custom dialogs that are commonly found in user interface toolkits:

- `WorkDialog`
- `MessageDialog`
- `YesNoDialog`
- `QuestionDialog`

Discussing the dialogs listed above should considerably enhance your understanding of dialogs and their nuances. Additionally, we will introduce a couple of custom components used by the dialog classes that you may find useful in other contexts, namely, `ButtonPanel` and `Postcard`.

The `MessageDialog` displays a message and comes equipped with a lone button for dismissing the dialog.

Both `YesNoDialog` and `QuestionDialog` pose a question. The `YesNoDialog` provides two buttons (a *yes* button and a *no* button) for dismissing the dialog, while the `QuestionDialog` provides a textfield for typing in a response.

The WorkDialog class is the superclass of the YesNoDialog, MessageDialog, and QuestionDialog classes and provides a button panel and a work area in which to display a panel.

The Dialog Classes

Figure 22-1 illustrates the relationships between the dialog classes discussed in this chapter. Three fundamental abstractions are implemented in the dialog classes:

- GJTDialog takes care of low-level dialog gruntwork.
- ButtonPanel is a Panel extension that maintains a row of buttons centered at the bottom of the panel.
- WorkDialog contains a ButtonPanel and provides a dialog that has a work panel centered in the dialog and a row of buttons at the bottom of the dialog.

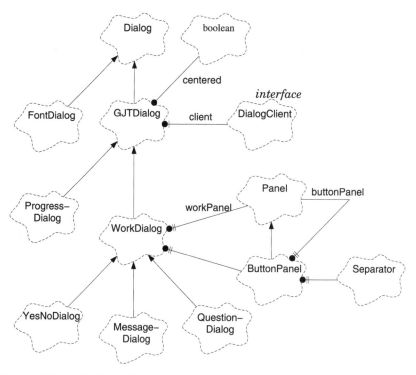

Figure 22-1 Dialog Classes Overview

GJTDialog

`GJTDialog` represents the most general abstraction embodied by the dialog classes. `GJTDialog` takes care of a pair of primitive dialog responsibilities—centering itself in its parent's frame and notifying a client when it has been dismissed or cancelled.

The responsibilities—`public` methods—of the `GJTDialog` class are listed in Table 22-1.

Table 22-1 `GJTDialog` **Responsibilities**

Methods	Description
`void setCentered(boolean b)`	Determines whether the dialog should be centered in its frame when shown
`void setClient(DialogClient c)`	Associates an instance of `DialogClient` with the dialog
`void dispose()`	Brings the dialog's frame to the front of other windows when the dialog is dismissed and notifies the dialog client of the dialog's dismissal.
`void setVisible(boolean b)`	Optionally centers the dialog in its frame and shows the dialog

Table 22-2 lists the associations—class members—for the `GJTDialog` class.

Table 22-2 `GJTDialog` **Associations**

Variable	Description
`DialogClient client`	An object that is notified when the dialog is dismissed or cancelled
`boolean centered`	If `true`, the dialog will be centered in its frame

We'll come back to `GJTDialog` shortly to discuss its implementation, but first we must take a short detour to discuss nonmodal dialogs and the `DialogClient` interface.

Nonmodal Dialogs and the DialogClient Interface

The `GJTDialog` class maintains an association with a `DialogClient`. `DialogClient` is a simple interface that defines two methods:

- `void dialogDismissed(Dialog)`
- `void dialogCancelled(Dialog)`

As was discussed previously in "java.awt.Dialog" on page 582, dialogs are distinguished from frames and windows in that a dialog can be modal. Being modal means that while the dialog is being shown, input to other windows within the dialog's ancestry is blocked. Additionally, and more importantly from our immediate perspective, a modal dialog also blocks execution of the thread that showed the dialog in the first place. For instance, consider the hypothetical someMethod() below:

```
public void someMethod() {
    Dialog dialog = new Dialog(Util.getFrame(this), false);
    dialog.setVisible(true);
    // do something interesting
}
```

If the dialog being shown is modal, then the "do something interesting" part of someMethod() is not executed until after the dialog is dismissed. However, if the dialog is nonmodal, the "do something interesting" part of someMethod() will be executed immediately after the dialog is shown.

This leaves somewhat of a dilemma for nonmodal dialogs, namely, how does the class that showed the nonmodal dialog get notified when the dialog is cancelled[1] or dismissed? One possibility is that the class responsible for showing the dialog implements the DialogClient interface, so that it can be notified of the dialog's impending dismissal or cancellation.

An instance of DialogClient may be associated with a GJTDialog. If a GJTDialog has a non-null instance of DialogClient, the dialog client will be notified when the dialog is dismissed or cancelled.

GJTDialog Revisited

Now that we have a basic understanding of modality, and thus the need for the DialogClient interface, let's take a look at the implementation of the GJTDialog class.

First of all, GJTDialog provides two constructors.

```
public GJTDialog(Frame         frame,
                 String        title,
                 DialogClient  aClient,
                 boolean       modal) {
    this(frame, title, aClient, true, modal);
}
```

---

1. By cancelled, we mean closed via the system menu or the close box of the dialog if the dialog is so equipped. See "java.awt.Frame" on page 579.

The first constructor merely invokes the second, passing a default value of true, signifying that the dialog will be centered in its frame when shown.

```
public GJTDialog(Frame        frame,
                 String       title,
                 DialogClient aClient,
                 boolean      centered,
                 boolean      modal) {
    super(frame, title, modal);

    setClient(aClient);
    setCentered(centered);

    addWindowListener(new WindowAdapter() {
        public void windowClosing(WindowEvent event) {
            dispose();

            if(client != null)
                client.dialogCancelled(GJTDialog.this);
        }
    });
}
```

The second constructor sets the client and the centered variables by invoking the setClient and setCentered methods, respectively. setClient() and setCentered() exist so that the dialog's client and centered status can be set after construction.

```
public void setCentered(boolean centered) {
    this.centered = centered;
}
public void setClient(DialogClient client) {
    this.client = client;
}
```

The second constructor also adds to the dialog a window listener that listens for window closing events. Recall from "java.awt.Frame" on page 579 that a window closing event is generated whenever a window is closed via the system menu or the window's close box (if the window is so equipped). Also, recall from the AWT Tip "Frames Don't Close by Default" on page 582 that for a window to actually close, the window must have dispose() invoked on it in response to a window closing event, which is exactly what the window listener does. Finally, notice that if the dialog has a non-null dialog client associated with it, the window listener invokes the dialog client's dialogCancelled method after the dialog is disposed of.

GJTDialog overrides Window.dispose() and Component.setVisible(). Both methods simply embellish their counterparts in Window and Component, respectively.

```
public void dispose() {
    Frame f = Util.getFrame(this);

    super.dispose();

    f.toFront();

    if(client != null)
        client.dialogDismissed(this);
}
public void setVisible(boolean visible) {
    pack();
    if(centered) {
        Dimension frameSize = getParent().getSize();
        Point     frameLoc  = getParent().getLocation();
        Dimension mySize     = getSize();
        int        x,y;

        x = frameLoc.x + (frameSize.width/2) -
                            (mySize.width/2);
        y = frameLoc.y + (frameSize.height/2) -
                            (mySize.height/2);

        setBounds(x,y,getSize().width,getSize().height);
    }
    super.setVisible(visible);
}
```

GJTDialog overrides dispose() in order to bring the dialog's frame to the front of all other windows and to invoke the dialog client's dialogDismissed method if the dialog client is non-null.

setVisible() is overridden in order to pack[2] the dialog before it is shown and to center the dialog in its frame if the centered variable is true.

As we said, GJTDialog is the ancestor of all the GJT custom dialogs. Before we discuss the extensions of GJTDialog, let's summarize the functionality encompassed by the GJTDialog class.

- It can be associated with an instance of DialogClient. The dialog client associated with a GJTDialog can be null, which is typically the case for modal dialogs. Nonmodal dialogs usually have a non-null dialog client.

- It notifies its dialog client when the dialog is dismissed or cancelled if the dialog client is non-null.

- It optionally centers the dialog in its frame when the dialog is shown.

2. pack() sizes the dialog so that it is just big enough to encompass the components it contains. See "Splash Screen" on page 572.

- It brings the dialog's frame to the front of all other windows when the dialog is dismissed or cancelled.

- It provides methods for setting the dialog client and the centering status after construction.

Example 22-1 lists the GJTDialog class in its entirety.

Example 22-1 GJTDialog Class Listing

```java
import java.awt.*;
import java.awt.event.*;

public class GJTDialog extends Dialog {
    protected DialogClient client;
    protected boolean      centered;

    public GJTDialog(Frame frame, String title,
                DialogClient aClient, boolean modal) {
        this(frame, title, aClient, true, modal);
    }
    public GJTDialog(Frame frame, String title,
                DialogClient aClient, boolean centered,
                boolean modal) {
        super(frame, title, modal);

        setClient(aClient);
        setCentered(centered);

        addWindowListener(new WindowAdapter() {
            public void windowClosing(WindowEvent event) {
                dispose();
                if(client != null)
                    client.dialogCancelled(GJTDialog.this);
            }
        });
    }
    public void setCentered(boolean centered) {
        this.centered = centered;
    }
    public void setClient(DialogClient client) {
        this.client = client;
    }
    public void dispose() {
        Frame f = Util.getFrame(this);

        super.dispose();

        f.toFront();

        if(client != null)
            client.dialogDismissed(this);
```

```
    }
    public void setVisible(boolean visible) {
        pack();

        if(centered) {
            Dimension frameSize = getParent().getSize();
            Point frameLoc  = getParent().getLocation();
            Dimension mySize    = getSize();
            int x,y;

            x = frameLoc.x + (frameSize.width/2) -
                        (mySize.width/2);
            y = frameLoc.y + (frameSize.height/2) -
                        (mySize.height/2);

            setBounds(x,y,getSize().width,getSize().height);
        }
        super.setVisible(visible);
    }
}
```

AWT TIP ...

Dialogs Are Nonmodal by Default

AWT dialogs allow their modality to be set either at construction time or after the dialog is constructed by invoking setModal(). The custom dialogs discussed in this chapter follow suit and are nonmodal by default. Of course, since the custom dialogs ultimately extend the java.awt.Dialog class, setModal() can be invoked on any of the dialogs to set modality after construction.

WorkDialog

Perhaps 90 percent of all dialogs contain a row of buttons along the bottom of the dialog and a work area above the buttons for user input—that is the rationale for the WorkDialog class.

WorkDialog is an extension of GJTDialog; it contains two panels—a work area into which a panel can be placed by extensions, and a button panel that can be populated with buttons.

The implementation of WorkDialog is straightforward, although it is somewhat lengthy because WorkDialog goes out of its way to implement a number of constructors in order to provide maximum flexibility for its extensions. We'll show you the entire implementation in one shot. WorkDialog employs an instance of ButtonPanel for managing its row of buttons; after taking a look at the WorkDialog implementation, we'll present the ButtonPanel class.

Example 22-2 WorkDialog Class Listing

```
import java.awt.*;
import java.awt.event.*;

public class WorkDialog extends GJTDialog {
    private ButtonPanel buttonPanel;
    private Panel        workPanel;

    public WorkDialog(Frame          frame,
                    DialogClient client,
                      String       title) {
        this(frame, client, title,
            null, Orientation.CENTER, false);
    }
    public WorkDialog(Frame          frame,
                    DialogClient client,
                      String       title,
                      boolean      modal) {
        this(frame, client, title,
            null, Orientation.CENTER, modal);
    }
    public WorkDialog(Frame          frame,
                    DialogClient client,
                      String       title,
                    Orientation  buttonOrientation,
                    boolean      modal) {
        this(frame, client, title,
            null, buttonOrientation, modal);
    }
    public WorkDialog(Frame          frame,
                    DialogClient client,
                      String       title,
                    Panel        workPanel,
                    Orientation  buttonOrientation,
                    boolean      modal) {
        super(frame, title, client, modal);
        this.workPanel = workPanel;

        setLayout(new BorderLayout(0,2));

        if(workPanel != null)
            add(workPanel, "Center");

        add("South", buttonPanel =
                    new ButtonPanel(buttonOrientation));
    }
    public void setWorkPanel(Panel workPanel) {
        if(workPanel != null)
            remove(workPanel);

        this.workPanel = workPanel;
```

```
          add(workPanel, "Center");

          if(isShowing())
              validate();
      }
      public Button addButton(String string) {
          return buttonPanel.add(string);
      }
      public void addButton(Button button) {
          buttonPanel.add(button);
      }
  }
```

We'll touch upon a couple of interesting points about WorkDialog, then move on to the implementation of ButtonPanel.

WorkPanel provides four constructors, so that extensions can construct a WorkPanel with a minimum of three arguments and a maximum of six. All of the constructors turn around and invoke the constructor with the most arguments (except for the one with the most arguments, of course). Notice from looking at the first constructor that a WorkDialog, like all custom dialogs presented in this chapter, is nonmodal by default.

The work panel (the panel above the button panel) can be set after construction. If a work panel is already in place, it is removed from the dialog and the new panel is subsequently added to the dialog. Then, if the dialog is showing, a call to validate() is made, which causes the dialog to be laid out—see "Forcing a Container to Lay Out Its Components" on page 338.

ButtonPanel

WorkDialog provides two methods for adding a button to the button panel— one that takes a string and another that takes a button. Notice that the WorkDialog add methods simply delegate to their enclosed instance of ButtonPanel, so without further ado, let's take a look at the implementation of ButtonPanel in Example 22-3.

Example 22-3 ButtonPanel Class Listing

```
import java.awt.*;

public class ButtonPanel extends Panel {
    Panel     buttonPanel = new Panel();
    Separator separator   = new Separator();

    public ButtonPanel() {
        this(Orientation.CENTER);
    }
```

```
public ButtonPanel(Orientation orientation) {
    int buttonPanelOrient = FlowLayout.CENTER;
     setLayout(new BorderLayout(0,5));

    if(orientation == Orientation.CENTER)
        buttonPanelOrient = FlowLayout.CENTER;
    else if(orientation == Orientation.RIGHT)
        buttonPanelOrient = FlowLayout.RIGHT;
    else if(orientation == Orientation.LEFT)
        buttonPanelOrient = FlowLayout.LEFT;

    buttonPanel.setLayout(new FlowLayout(buttonPanelOrient));
     add(separator, "North");
     add(buttonPanel, "Center");
}
public void add(Button button) {
    buttonPanel.add(button);
}
public Button add(String buttonLabel) {
    Button addMe = new Button(buttonLabel);
    buttonPanel.add(addMe);
    return addMe;
}
protected String paramString() {
    return super.paramString() + "buttons=" +
    getComponentCount();
}
}
```

`ButtonPanel` is a simple panel that contains a row of buttons. The orientation of the buttons can be specified at construction time by passing an instance of `Orientation` to the `ButtonPanel` constructor.[3] Additionally, `ButtonPanel` provides a default constructor that defaults the orientation of the buttons to center-justified. `ButtonPanel` sets its layout manager to an instance of `FlowLayout` with the appropriate orientation.

`ButtonPanel` provides two methods to add buttons to the panel—one that takes a `java.awt.Button` and another that takes a string. The method that takes a string creates a button and returns the button in case the caller has need of a reference to the button itself.

With the implementations of `ButtonPanel` and `WorkDialog` under our belts, we'll take one final detour—the `Postcard` class. Then, we'll look at the rest of the custom dialogs.

3. The `Orientation` class is not part of the AWT. It is included on the CD.

Postcard

`MessageDialog`, `QuestionDialog`, and `YesNoDialog` all extend
`WorkDialog`, and all provide the means to add not only text to the dialog, but an
image as well. Figure 22-2 shows instances of `MessageDialog`,
`QuestionDialog`, and `YesNoDialog` doing their thing.

Naturally, we don't want to reimplement the code for placing an image next to a
panel in each dialog class, so that functionality is embedded in the `Postcard`
class, which is listed in Example 22-4.

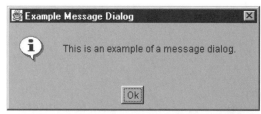

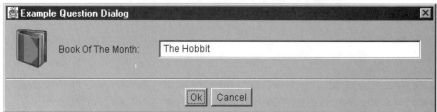

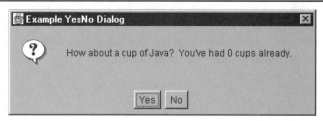

Figure 22-2 Message, Question, and Yes/No Dialogs
Message, question, and yes/no dialogs can be fitted with an
image and a panel.

Example 22-4 Postcard Class Listing

```java
import java.awt.*;

public class Postcard extends Panel {
    private Panel          panel, panelContainer = new Panel();
    private ImageCanvas canvas = new ImageCanvas();

    public Postcard(Image image, Panel panel) {
        if(image != null) setImage(image);
        if(panel != null) setPanel(panel);

        setLayout(new RowLayout());
        add(canvas);
        add(panelContainer);
    }
    public Panel getPanel() {
        if(panelContainer.getComponentCount() == 1)
            return (Panel)panelContainer.getComponent(0);
        else
            return null;
    }
    public void setImage(Image image) {
        Util.waitForImage(this, image);
        canvas.setImage(image);
    }
    public void setPanel(Panel panel) {
        if(panelContainer.getComponentCount() == 1) {
            panelContainer.remove(getComponent(0));
        }
        this.panel = panel;
        panelContainer.add(panel);
    }
    public Insets getInsets() {
        return new Insets(10,10,10,10);
    }
}
```

The Postcard class gets its name from the fact that postcards usually have an image on one side and text on the other. While the Postcard class name could be construed as somewhat of a misnomer because it cannot be turned over, it nevertheless was the best name that we could come up with.

At any rate, the Postcard class contains a panel and an image canvas.[4] Both the panel and the image displayed in the image canvas can be set at construction time or anytime afterward. The Postcard class also defines insets of ten pixels all the way around.

4. The ImageCanvas and Util classes are not part of the AWT but are provided on the CD.

MessageDialog

Object-oriented development typically results in classes that stand on the shoulders of a number of other classes—MessageDialog is a case in point. As you can see from Figure 22-3, MessageDialog extends WorkDialog, which in turn extends GJTDialog; all of the functionality wrapped up in the ancestry of MessageDialog is, of course, inherited. Additionally, MessageDialog employs an extension of Postcard which it places in its work panel. As a result, the implementation of MessageDialog is simple enough to show in one fell swoop. MessageDialog is listed in its entirety in Example 22-5.

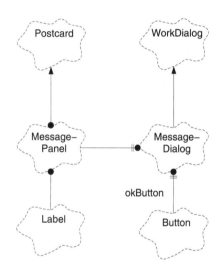

Figure 22-3 MessageDialog Class Diagram

 Example 22-5 MessageDialog Class Listing

```
import java.awt.*;
import java.awt.event.*;

public class MessageDialog extends WorkDialog
                           implements ActionListener {
    private Button       okButton;
    private MessagePanel messagePanel;
```

```
    public MessageDialog(Frame  frame, DialogClient client,
                  String title, String message,
                  Image  image) {
        this(frame, client, title, message, image, false);
    }
    public MessageDialog(Frame  frame, DialogClient client,
        String title, String      message,
        Image  image, boolean      modal) {

        super(frame, client, title, modal);

        messagePanel = new MessagePanel(image, message);
        okButton     = addButton("Ok");
        okButton.addActionListener(this);
        setWorkPanel(messagePanel);
    }
    /**
    * @deprecated as of JDK1.1
    */
    public void layout() {
        okButton.requestFocus();
        super.layout();
    }
    public void doLayout() {
        layout();
    }
    public void actionPerformed(ActionEvent event) {
        dispose();
    }
    private void setMessage(String message) {
        messagePanel.setMessage(message);
    }
    private void setImage(Image image) {
        messagePanel.setImage(image);
    }
}
class MessagePanel extends Postcard {
    private Label label;

    public MessagePanel(String message) {
        this(null, message);
    }
    public MessagePanel(Image image, String message) {
        super(image, new Panel());
        getPanel().add(label = new Label(message,Label.CENTER));
    }
    public void setMessage(String message) {
        label.setText(message);
    }
}
```

MessageDialog sets its work panel to an instance of MessagePanel, a simple extension of Postcard that adds a label representing the message to be displayed in the postcard's panel. The image displayed in the postcard is passed along to the Postcard constructor.

MessageDialog adds a lone button to the button panel contained in the work dialog. When the button is activated, dispose() is invoked on the dialog, which of course, invokes GJTDialog.dispose().

One point of interest is the overridden doLayout method.

```
public void doLayout() {
    okButton.requestFocus();
    super.doLayout();
}
```

The intent behind overriding doLayout() is to give the Ok button focus, so that the dialog can be dismissed without mousing around. doLayout() is invoked whenever the container is laid out—therefore, all of the components in the dialog have been created, and more importantly, the components have had their peers created.[5] As a result, the Ok button can receive focus. Note that super.doLayout() is invoked to ensure that the actual laying out of the components takes place.

Finally MessageDialog, like its counterparts that extend WorkDialog, allows both its image and text to be reset after construction.

MessageDialog Test Applet

Figure 22-4 shows a test applet for MessageDialog; Example 22-6 lists the applet.

---

5. See "java.awt.Component Methods That Depend Upon Peers" on page 440.

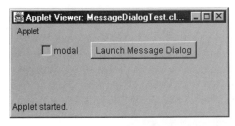

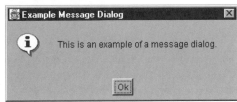

Figure 22-4 MessageDialogTest Applet

Example 22-6 MessageDialogTest Applet

```
import java.awt.*;
import java.awt.event.*;
import java.applet.Applet;

public class MessageDialogTest extends Applet {
    public void init() {
        setLayout(new BorderLayout());
        add(new MessageDialogLauncher(this), "Center");
    }
}
class MessageDialogLauncher extends Panel
                      implements DialogClient,
                                     ActionListener {
    private Applet applet;
    private Button messageDialogButton;
    private MessageDialog  messageDialog;
    private Image image = null;
    private Checkbox modal = new Checkbox("modal");

    public MessageDialogLauncher(Applet applet) {
        this.applet = applet;

        add(modal);

        add(messageDialogButton  =
               new Button("Launch Message Dialog"));
```

```
            messageDialogButton.addActionListener (this);
      }
      public void actionPerformed(ActionEvent event) {
         Image image = applet.getImage(applet.getCodeBase(),
                              "gifs/information.gif");
         if(messageDialog == null) {
            messageDialog = new MessageDialog(
                     Util.getFrame(this), this,
                     "Example Message Dialog",
                     "This is an example of a message dialog.",
                     image, modal.getState());
         }
         else {
            if(modal.getState()) messageDialog.setModal(true);
            else                 messageDialog.setModal(false);
         }
         messageDialog.setVisible(true);
      }
      public void dialogDismissed(Dialog d) {
         applet.showStatus("MessageDialog Dismissed");
      }
      public void dialogCancelled(Dialog d) {
         applet.showStatus("Message Dialog Cancelled");
      }
   }
```

`MessageDialogTest` contains a checkbox that controls the modality of the dialog, and `MessageDialogLauncher` implements the `DialogClient` interface to update the applet's status line when the dialog is dismissed or cancelled.

YesNoDialog

The `YesNoDialog` poses a question and provides two buttons for answering it—a yes button and a no button.

Like `MessageDialog`, `YesNoDialog` extends `WorkDialog` and employs an extension of `Postcard` that is displayed in its work panel. The class diagram for the YesNoDialog class is shown in Figure 22-5.

`YesNoDialog` is listed in Example 22-7.

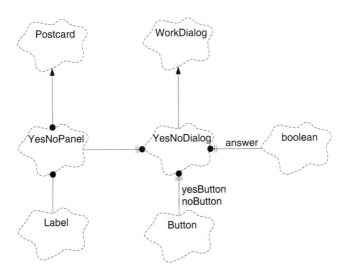

Figure 22-5 YesNoDialog Class Diagram

Example 22-7 YesNoDialog Class Listing

```
import java.awt.*;
import java.awt.event.*;

public class YesNoDialog extends WorkDialog {
    private Button      yesButton;
    private Button      noButton;
    private boolean     answer      = false;
    private ButtonPanel buttonPanel = new ButtonPanel();
    private YesNoPanel  yesNoPanel;

    public YesNoDialog(Frame  frame, DialogClient client,
                   String title, String question,
                   Image  image) {
        this(frame, client, title, question, image, false);
    }
    public YesNoDialog(Frame  frame, DialogClient client,
                   String title, String      question,
                   Image  image, boolean     modal) {
        super(frame, client, title, modal);

        ButtonListener buttonListener = new ButtonListener();

        yesButton = addButton("Yes");
        noButton  = addButton("No");
```

```
        yesButton.addActionListener(buttonListener);
        noButton.addActionListener(buttonListener);

        setWorkPanel(yesNoPanel = new YesNoPanel(image,question));

        if(image != null)
            setImage(image);
    }
    /**
     * @deprecated as of JDK1.1
     */
    public void layout() {
        yesButton.requestFocus();
        super.layout();
    }
    public void doLayout() {
        layout();
    }
    public void setYesButtonLabel(String label) {
        yesButton.setLabel(label);
    }
    public void setNoButtonLabel(String label) {
        noButton.setLabel(label);
    }
    public boolean answeredYes() {
        return answer;
    }
    public void setMessage(String question) {
        yesNoPanel.setMessage(question);
    }
    public void setImage(Image image) {
        yesNoPanel.setImage(image);
    }
    class ButtonListener implements ActionListener {
        public void actionPerformed(ActionEvent event) {
            if(event.getSource() == yesButton) answer = true;
            else                               answer = false;

            dispose();
        }
    }
}
class YesNoPanel extends Postcard {
    private Label label;
    public YesNoPanel(String question) {
        this(null, question);
    }
```

```
    public YesNoPanel(Image image, String question) {
        super(image, new Panel());
        getPanel().add(label = new Label(question,Label.CENTER));
    }
    public void setMessage(String question) {
        label.setText(question);
    }
}
```

Since `YesNoDialog` has two buttons, it implements an inner class implementation of `ActionListener` that deciphers which button was activated and records whether the answer to the question was yes or no. One instance of `ButtonListener` is instantiated, which serves as the action listener for both buttons.

`YesNoDialog.answeredYes()` returns `true` if the Yes button was activated and `false` if the No button was activated, thereby providing a means for discovering the answer to the question posed by the dialog.

YesNoDialog Test Applet

A test applet for the `YesNoDialog` is shown in Figure 22-6, and the listing for the applet is listed in Example 22-8.

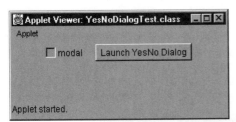

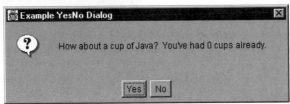

Figure 22-6 `YesNoDialog` Unit Test

Example 22-8 YesNoDialogTest Applet

```java
import java.awt.*;
import java.awt.event.*;
import java.applet.Applet;

public class YesNoDialogTest extends Applet {
    public void init() {
        setLayout(new BorderLayout());
        add(new YesNoDialogLauncher(this), "Center");
    }
}
class YesNoDialogLauncher extends Panel
                    implements DialogClient, ActionListener {
    private Applet        applet;
    private YesNoDialog   yesNoDialog;
    private int           cupCnt = 0, coffeeLimit = 3;
    private Image         image = null;
    private Checkbox      modal = new Checkbox("modal");

    private Button yesNoDialogButton;

    public YesNoDialogLauncher(Applet applet) {
        this.applet = applet;

        add(modal);
        add(yesNoDialogButton =
                new Button("Launch YesNo Dialog"));

        yesNoDialogButton.addActionListener(this);
    }
    public void actionPerformed(ActionEvent event) {
        String question = "How about a cup of Java?";
        Image image = applet.getImage(applet.getCodeBase(),
                              "gifs/question.gif");

        if(cupCnt >= 0 && cupCnt < coffeeLimit) {
            question += "  You've had " + cupCnt;

            if(cupCnt == 1) question += " cup already.";
            else            question += " cups already.";
        }
        else {
            question =
                "Are you sick and tired of coffee analogies?";
        }
        if(cupCnt >= 0 && cupCnt < coffeeLimit) {
            image = applet.getImage(applet.getCodeBase(),
                              "gifs/questionMark.gif");
        }
```

```
        else {
            image = applet.getImage(applet.getCodeBase(),
                            "gifs/punch.gif");
        }
        if(yesNoDialog == null) {
            yesNoDialog = new YesNoDialog(Util.getFrame(this),
                            this, "Example YesNo Dialog",
                            question, image, modal.getState());
        }
        else {
            if(modal.getState()) yesNoDialog.setModal(true);
            else            yesNoDialog.setModal(false);

            yesNoDialog.setImage(image);
            yesNoDialog.setMessage(question);
        }
        yesNoDialog.setVisible(true);
    }
    public void dialogDismissed(Dialog d) {
        if(yesNoDialog.answeredYes()) {
            ++cupCnt;

            if(cupCnt <= coffeeLimit)
                applet.showStatus("Cups Of Coffee:  " + cupCnt);
            else
                applet.showStatus("Me too");
        }
        else {
            if(cupCnt == 0)
                applet.showStatus("No coffee yet.");
            else if(cupCnt >= coffeeLimit)
                applet.showStatus("Me too");
        }
    }
    public void dialogCancelled(Dialog d) {
        applet.showStatus("Yes No Dialog Cancelled");
    }
}
```

Nearly all of the implementation of the unit test is wrapped up in
YesNoDialogLauncher.actionPerformed(), which concerns itself with
counting how many times the YesNoDialog has been shown. Once the
coffeeLimit is reached, both the image and the text displayed in the dialog are
modified.

QuestionDialog

A QuestionDialog, like the YesNoDialog, poses a question. Unlike the YesNoDialog, QuestionDialog provides a textfield instead of buttons for a response to the question. The class diagram for the QuestionDialog class is shown in Figure 22-7.

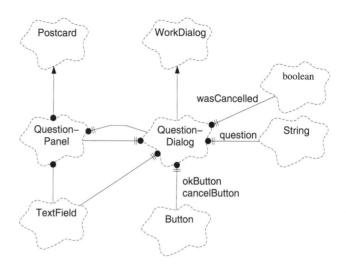

Figure 22-7 QuestionDialog Class Diagram

QuestionDialog is listed in Example 22-9.

 Example 22-9 QuestionDialog Class Listing

```
import java.awt.*;
import java.awt.event.*;

public class QuestionDialog extends WorkDialog
                            implements ActionListener{
    static private int   _defaultTextFieldSize = 20;
    private Button        okButton;
    private Button        cancelButton;
    private String        question;
    private TextField     textField;
    private boolean       wasCancelled;
    private ButtonPanel   buttonPanel = new ButtonPanel();
```

```java
public QuestionDialog(Frame   frame, DialogClient client,
                      String title, String question,
                      String initialResponse, Image image) {
   this(frame, client, title, question, initialResponse,
      _defaultTextFieldSize, image);
}
public QuestionDialog(Frame   frame, DialogClient client,
                      String title, String question,
                      Image image) {
   this(frame, client, title,
         question, null, _defaultTextFieldSize, image);
}
public QuestionDialog(Frame   frame, DialogClient client,
                      String title, String question,
                      int textFieldSize, Image image) {
   this(frame, client, title,
      question, null, textFieldSize, image);
}
public QuestionDialog(Frame   frame, DialogClient client,
                      String title, String question,
                      String initialResponse,
                      int textFieldSize, Image image) {
   this(frame, client, title, question, initialResponse,
      textFieldSize, image, false);
}
public QuestionDialog(Frame   frame, DialogClient client,
                      String title, String question,
                      String initialResponse,
                      int textFieldSize, Image image,
                      boolean modal) {
   super(frame, client, title, modal);

   QuestionPanel questionPanel;

   okButton     = addButton("Ok");
   cancelButton = addButton("Cancel");

   okButton.addActionListener(this);
   cancelButton.addActionListener(this);

   questionPanel = new QuestionPanel(this, question,
                                     initialResponse,
                                     textFieldSize,
                                     image);
   textField = questionPanel.getTextField();
   setWorkPanel(questionPanel);
}
public void actionPerformed(ActionEvent ae) {
   if(ae.getSource() == cancelButton)
      wasCancelled = true;
   else
```

```
                   wasCancelled = false;

              dispose();
         }
         public void setVisible(boolean b) {
              textField.requestFocus();
              super.setVisible(b);
         }
         public void returnInTextField() {
              okButton.requestFocus();
         }
         public TextField getTextField() {
              return textField;
         }
         public String getAnswer() {
              return textField.getText();
         }
         public boolean wasCancelled() {
              return wasCancelled;
         }
         private void setQuestion(String question) {
              this.question = question;
         }
    }
    class QuestionPanel extends Postcard {
         private TextField      field;
         private QuestionDialog dialog;

         public QuestionPanel(QuestionDialog dialog,
                              String question, Image image) {
              this(dialog, question, null, 0, image);
         }
         public QuestionPanel(QuestionDialog dialog, String question,
                              int columns, Image image) {
              this(dialog, question, null, columns, image);
         }
         public QuestionPanel(QuestionDialog myDialog,
                              String question,
                              String initialResponse, int cols,
                              Image image) {
              super(image, new Panel());

              Panel panel = getPanel();
              this.dialog = myDialog;
```

```
            panel.setLayout(new RowLayout());
            panel.add(new Label(question));

            if(initialResponse != null) {
                if(cols != 0)
                    panel.add(field =
                                new TextField(initialResponse, cols));
                else
                    panel.add(field =
                                new TextField(initialResponse));
            }
            else {
                if(cols != 0) panel.add(field = new TextField(cols));
                else           panel.add(field = new TextField());
            }

            field.addActionListener(new ActionListener() {
                public void actionPerformed(ActionEvent event) {
                    dialog.returnInTextField();
                }
            });
        }
        public TextField getTextField() {
            return field;
        }
    }
}
```

Although the listing for QuestionDialog is long-winded, it is nonetheless quite straightforward.

QuestionDialog provides five constructors for flexibility in specifying the size of the textfield and the initial response—if any—to be displayed in the textfield. QuestionDialog also provides a number of accessors for obtaining a reference to the textfield, finding out the response typed in the textfield, determining whether the Ok or Cancel button was activated, and so on.

The work panel for the QuestionDialog is set to an instance of QuestionPanel, which is where most of the complexity of the implementation resides. QuestionPanel constructs the textfield according to the parameters passed to its constructor and listens for action events in the textfield. When the enter key is typed in the textfield, QuestionPanel invokes QuestionDialog.returnInTextField(), which gives the focus to the Ok button.

QuestionDialog Test Applet

Figure 22-8 shows a `QuestionDialog` test applet in action; Example 22-10 lists the applet.

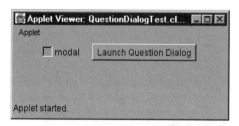

Figure 22-8 `QuestionDialog` Test Applet

 Example 22-10 QuestionDialogTest Applet

```java
import java.awt.*;
import java.awt.event.*;
import java.applet.Applet;

public class QuestionDialogTest extends Applet  {
    public void init() {
        setLayout(new BorderLayout());
        add(new QuestionDialogLauncher(this), "Center");
    }
}
class QuestionDialogLauncher extends Panel
                    implements DialogClient,
                    ActionListener {
    private Applet        applet;
    private QuestionDialog questionDialog;
    private Image          image = null;
    private Checkbox       modal = new Checkbox("modal");

    private Button questionDialogButton;
```

```
public QuestionDialogLauncher(Applet applet) {
    this.applet = applet;

    add(modal);
    add(questionDialogButton =
            new Button("Launch Question Dialog"));

    questionDialogButton.addActionListener(this);
}
public void actionPerformed(ActionEvent event) {
    Image image = applet.getImage(applet.getCodeBase(),
                                  "gifs/book.gif");
    if(questionDialog == null) {
        questionDialog =
                new QuestionDialog(Util.getFrame(this), this,
                        "Example Question Dialog",
                        "Book Of The Month:   ",
                        "The Hobbit",
                        45, image, modal.getState());
    }
    if(modal.getState()) questionDialog.setModal(true);
    else                 questionDialog.setModal(false);

    questionDialog.setVisible(true);
}
public void dialogDismissed(Dialog d) {
    if(questionDialog.wasCancelled())
        applet.showStatus("CANCELLED");
    else
        applet.showStatus("Book Of The Month:   " +

    questionDialog.getTextField().getText());
}
public void dialogCancelled(Dialog d) {
    applet.showStatus("Dialog Cancelled");
}
}
```

The dialogDismissed method obtains a reference to the textfield in the QuestionDialog to find out the text typed in the textfield.

Summary

In addition to introducing dialogs in "java.awt.Dialog" on page 582, we've now explored the intricacies of extending java.awt.Dialog by discussing the implementation of a number of custom dialogs.

We hope that you will find the custom dialogs useful in your own development, and that you will have gained some insights into AWT dialogs from our discussions in this chapter.

CHAPTER
23

Rubberbanding

Rubberbanding is an essential tool in the applet developer's toolkit. Rubberbands are useful in a number of different contexts; for instance, one method for selecting multiple items is to stretch a rubberband rectangle around the items to be selected. Drawing programs typically employ rubberbands that enable users to *rubberband* the shape they wish to draw before it is actually drawn on screen.

Rubberbanding involves dynamically updating a geometric shape whose boundary changes as the mouse is dragged. A rubberband must be careful not to disturb any existing graphics beneath it, which it accomplishes by painting in XOR mode.

This chapter presents a handful of classes for rubberbanding, including a `RubberbandPanel`, an extension of `Panel` that can be fitted with a rubberband. The chapter culminates with a simple drawing program that illustrates the use of rubberbands.

The Rubberband Classes

Figure 23-1 shows the class diagram for the rubberband classes discussed in this chapter.

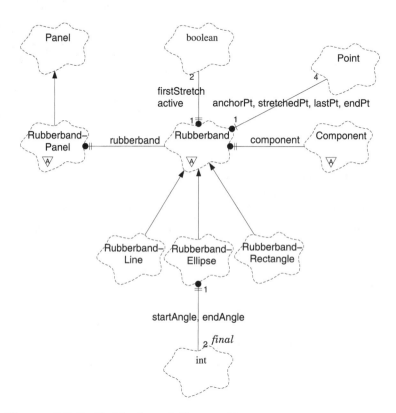

Figure 23-1 Rubberband Classes Diagram

The Rubberband Base Class

Before looking at the code for the Rubberband base class, let's briefly outline the steps involved in rubberbanding a shape on screen:

1. A mouse pressed event occurs in a Component equipped with a Rubberband.

2. The mouse is dragged inside the `Component` where the mouse pressed event occurred.

3. A mouse released event occurs in the same `Component`.

Step one defines the *anchor* point for the rubberband. The anchor point remains constant throughout the remaining steps.

Step two involves dynamically updating the *stretch* point for the rubberband; the stretch point is kept in synch with the last mouse drag location.

Step three defines the *end* point for the rubberband. After a rubberbanding operation is complete, a rubberband needs to be able to report the anchor point and the end point of the last rubberbanding operation that occurred, so that the rubberband client can determine the boundary of the rubberbanding operation and take whatever action is appropriate.

The `Rubberband` base class encapsulates the steps outlined above. Extensions of `Rubberband`, namely, `RubberbandLine`, `RubberbandRectangle`, and `RubberbandEllipse`, simply implement the actual drawing of the rubberband.

Rubberband Associations and Responsibilities

Table 23-1 and Table 23-2 summarize the responsibilities and associations of the `Rubberband` class. Note the two abstract methods in Table 23-1. Subclasses of `Rubberband` must implement `drawLast()` and `drawNext()` if they are to be concrete classes.

Table 23-1 `Rubberband` **Responsibilities**

Methods	Description
`void drawLast(Graphics g)`	**Abstract** method that draws the appropriate geometric shape at the *last* rubberband location
`void drawNext(Graphics g)`	**Abstract** method that draws the appropriate geometric shape at the *next* rubberband location
`void setComponent(Component c)`	Sets the component in which the rubberband is drawn
`void setActive(boolean b)`	Sets the state of the rubberband to either active or inactive
`boolean isActive()`	Indicates whether the rubberband is active or inactive
`Point getAnchor()`	Returns the point of origin of a rubberband operation

Table 23-1 Rubberband **Responsibilities (Continued)**

Methods	Description
Point getStretched()	Returns the current stretched location for a rubberband operation
Point getLast()	Returns the last point in a rubberband operation
Point getEnd()	Returns the final point in a rubberband operation
void anchor(Point p)	Sets the anchor point for a rubberband operation
void stretch(Point p)	Sets the stretched location for a rubberband operation
void end(Point p)	Sets the end point in a rubberband operation
Rectangle getBounds()	Returns the current boundary of the rubberband
Rectangle lastBounds()	Returns the last boundary of the rubberband

Table 23-2 Rubberband **Associations**

Variables	Description
Point anchorPt	The point of origin for a rubberband operation
Point stretchedPt	The current point in a rubberband operation
Point lastPt	The last point in a rubberband operation
Point endPt	The end point in a rubberband operation
boolean firstStretch	Indicates whether the rubberband has been stretched
Component component	The component where rubberbanding will take place

The Rubberband class provides two constructors—a default constructor and a constructor that takes a reference to a Component. A rubberband's component can be set after construction by invocation of setComponent().

Additionally, each rubberband registers itself as both a mouse listener and a mouse motion listener for the component in which it resides. Since a component can potentially have more than one rubberband associated with it, rubberbands can be designated as active or inactive. Only active rubberbands react to mouse events that occur in the rubberband's component.

```
public Rubberband(Component component) {
}
public Rubberband(Component component) {
    setComponent(component)
}
public void setComponent(Component c) {
    this.component = c;

    component.addMouseListener(new MouseAdapter() {
        public void mousePressed(MouseEvent event) {
            if(isActive())
                anchor(event.getPoint());
        }
        public void mouseClicked(MouseEvent event) {
            if(isActive())
                end(event.getPoint());
        }
        public void mouseReleased(MouseEvent event) {
            if(isActive())
                end(event.getPoint());
        }
    });
    component.addMouseMotionListener(new MouseMotionAdapter() {
        public void mouseDragged(MouseEvent event) {
            if(isActive())
                stretch(event.getPoint());
        }
    });
}
```

When a mouse pressed occurs in a component equipped with an active rubberband, the rubberband invokes its `anchor` method.

```
public void anchor(Point p) {
    firstStretch = true;
    anchorPt.x = p.x;
    anchorPt.y = p.y;

    stretchedPt.x = lastPt.x = anchorPt.x;
    stretchedPt.y = lastPt.y = anchorPt.y;
}
```

`Rubberband.anchor()` is passed the point where the mouse pressed event occurred. The `anchor` method sets the `anchor`, `stretched`, and `last` points to the point passed in, and `firstStretch` is set to `true`.

Subsequent mouse dragged events in a component equipped with an active rubberband result in the rubberband's `stretch` method being invoked. When a mouse released event occurs in the component, the active rubberband's `end` method is invoked.

Painting in XOR Mode

As we've pointed out, Rubberband is an abstract class that leaves two methods for extensions to implement:

```
abstract public void drawLast(Graphics g);
abstract public void drawNext(Graphics g);
```

Both of these methods are invoked from within Rubberband stretch and end methods. The stretch method is called when a mouse dragged event occurs.

```
public void stretch(Point p) {
    lastPt.x      = stretchedPt.x;
    lastPt.y      = stretchedPt.y;
    stretchedPt.x = p.x;
    stretchedPt.y = p.y;

    Graphics g = component.getGraphics();
    if(g != null) {
        try {
            g.setXORMode(component.getBackground());

            if(firstStretch == true) firstStretch = false;
            else                     drawLast(g);

            drawNext(g);
        }
        finally {
            g.dispose();
        }
    }
}
```

The first order of business for stretch() is to update both the stretched and last points. Next, the Graphics object associated with the component upon which rubberbanding is taking place is set to XOR mode. Setting XOR mode with the background color results in the following for all subsequent graphical operations using the Graphics object:

- Existing pixels with the current Graphics color are changed to the background color, and vice versa.

- Existing pixels that are not in the current color are changed unpredictably but reversibly—drawing the same color over the same pixel twice returns the pixel to its original color.

In essence, the call to setXORMode() effectively lets us paint on top of existing pixels without disturbing them.

If it is not the first time the rubberband has been stretched, `drawLast()` is invoked and draws the rubberband at its last location. Since XOR mode has been set, the call to `drawLast()` will effectively erase the rubberband at its last location. Note that the first time the rubberband is stretched, no erasing is necessary, thus the check against the `firstStretch` variable.

Finally, `drawNext()` is invoked to draw the rubberband at the next location, and the `Graphics` object is disposed of, as is required anytime we obtain a `Graphics` object via a call to `Component.getGraphics()`—see "Disposing of a Graphics" on page 40.

When a mouse released event occurs, an active rubberband invokes its `end` method.

```
public void end(Point p) {
    lastPt.x = endPt.x = p.x;
    lastPt.y = endPt.y = p.y;

    Graphics g = component.getGraphics();
    if(g != null) {
        try {
            g.setXORMode(component.getBackground());
            drawLast(g);
        }
        finally {
            g.dispose();
        }
    }
}
```

After the last and end points are updated, XOR mode is once again set for the `Graphics` object obtained from `Component.getGraphics()`, and `drawLast()` is invoked, which erases the rubberband one final time. Once again, we are careful to dispose of the `Graphics` object obtained from `Component.getGraphics()`.

The `Rubberband` class is listed in its entirety in Example 23-1.

Example 23-1 Rubberband Class Listing

```
import java.awt.*;
import java.awt.event.*;

abstract public class Rubberband {
    protected Point anchorPt    = new Point(0,0);
    protected Point stretchedPt = new Point(0,0);
    protected Point lastPt      = new Point(0,0);
    protected Point endPt       = new Point(0,0);

    private Component component;
```

```java
private boolean   firstStretch = true;
private boolean   active = false;

abstract public void drawLast(Graphics g);
abstract public void drawNext(Graphics g);

public Rubberband() {
}
public Rubberband(Component c) {
   setComponent(c);
}
public void setActive(boolean b) {
   active = b;
}
public void setComponent(Component c) {
   component = c;

   component.addMouseListener(new MouseAdapter() {
      public void mousePressed(MouseEvent event) {
         if(isActive()) {
            anchor(event.getPoint());
         }
      }
      public void mouseClicked(MouseEvent event) {
         if(isActive())
            end(event.getPoint());
      }
      public void mouseReleased(MouseEvent event) {
         if(isActive())
            end(event.getPoint());
      }
   });
   component.addMouseMotionListener(
                     new MouseMotionAdapter() {
      public void mouseDragged(MouseEvent event) {
         if(isActive())
            stretch(event.getPoint());
      }
   });
}
public boolean isActive    () { return active;      }
public Point   getAnchor   () { return anchorPt;    }
public Point   getStretched() { return stretchedPt; }
public Point   getLast     () { return lastPt;      }
public Point   getEnd      () { return endPt;       }

public void anchor(Point p) {
   firstStretch = true;
   anchorPt.x = p.x;
   anchorPt.y = p.y;

   stretchedPt.x = lastPt.x = anchorPt.x;
   stretchedPt.y = lastPt.y = anchorPt.y;
}
```

```java
public void stretch(Point p) {
    lastPt.x      = stretchedPt.x;
    lastPt.y      = stretchedPt.y;
    stretchedPt.x = p.x;
    stretchedPt.y = p.y;

    Graphics g = component.getGraphics();
    if(g != null) {
      try {
        g.setXORMode(component.getBackground());

        if(firstStretch == true) firstStretch = false;
        else                     drawLast(g);

        drawNext(g);
      }
      finally {
         g.dispose();
      }
    }
}
public void end(Point p) {
    lastPt.x = endPt.x = p.x;
    lastPt.y = endPt.y = p.y;

    Graphics g = component.getGraphics();
    if(g != null) {
      try {
        g.setXORMode(component.getBackground());
        drawLast(g);
      }
      finally {
         g.dispose();
      }
    }
}
public Rectangle getBounds() {
  return new Rectangle(stretchedPt.x < anchorPt.x ?
                       stretchedPt.x : anchorPt.x,
                       stretchedPt.y < anchorPt.y ?
                       stretchedPt.y : anchorPt.y,
                       Math.abs(stretchedPt.x - anchorPt.x),
                       Math.abs(stretchedPt.y - anchorPt.y));
}

public Rectangle lastBounds() {
  return new Rectangle(
              lastPt.x < anchorPt.x ? lastPt.x : anchorPt.x,
              lastPt.y < anchorPt.y ? lastPt.y : anchorPt.y,
              Math.abs(lastPt.x - anchorPt.x),
              Math.abs(lastPt.y - anchorPt.y));
}
}
```

Drawing Rubberband Lines

As the astute reader will probably figure out, the `RubberbandLine` class
rubberbands lines. Example 23-2 shows the `RubberbandLine` class source code.

Example 23-2 `RubberbandLine` Class Listing

```
import java.awt.*;

public class RubberbandLine extends Rubberband {
    public RubberbandLine() {
    }
    public RubberbandLine(Component component) {
        super(component);
    }
    public void drawLast(Graphics graphics) {
        graphics.drawLine(anchorPt.x, anchorPt.y,
                          lastPt.x,   lastPt.y);
    }
    public void drawNext(Graphics graphics) {
        graphics.drawLine(anchorPt.x,   anchorPt.y,
                          stretchedPt.x, stretchedPt.y);
    }
}
```

Like all extensions of `Rubberband`, `RubberbandLine` can either be constructed
with no arguments or with a component that it passes along to its superclass
constructor.

`RubberbandLine.drawLast()` draws a line from the anchor point to the last
point, and `drawNext()` draws a line from the anchor point to the stretch point.
`drawNext()` and `drawLast()` both use the `anchorPt`, `stretchedPt`, and
`lastPt` points from the `Rubberband` class.

`RubberbandLine` does not concern itself with drawing in XOR mode or tracking
the anchor, stretched, or end points of the rubberbanding operation; all of that
infrastructure is provided by its superclass, `Rubberband`.

Drawing Rubberband Rectangles and Ellipses

`RubberbandRectangle` and `RubberbandEllipse` work exactly the same as
`RubberbandLine` except that they draw rectangles and ellipses, as you can see
in Example 23-3 and Example 23-4, respectively.

Example 23-3 RubberbandRectangle Class Listing

```java
import java.awt.*;

public class RubberbandRectangle extends Rubberband {
    public RubberbandRectangle() {
    }
    public RubberbandRectangle(Component component) {
        super(component);
    }
    public void drawLast(Graphics graphics) {
        Rectangle rect = lastBounds();
        graphics.drawRect(rect.x, rect.y,
                          rect.width, rect.height);
    }
    public void drawNext(Graphics graphics) {
        Rectangle rect = getBounds();
        graphics.drawRect(rect.x, rect.y,
                          rect.width, rect.height);
    }
}
```

Example 23-4 RubberbandEllipse Class Listing

```java
import java.awt.*;

public class RubberbandEllipse extends Rubberband {
    private final int startAngle = 0;
    private final int endAngle   = 360;

    public RubberbandEllipse() {
    }
    public RubberbandEllipse(Component component) {
        super(component);
    }
    public void drawLast(Graphics graphics) {
        Rectangle r = lastBounds();
        graphics.drawArc(r.x, r.y,
            r.width, r.height, startAngle, endAngle);
    }
    public void drawNext(Graphics graphics) {
        Rectangle r = getBounds();
        graphics.drawArc(r.x, r.y,
            r.width, r.height, startAngle, endAngle);
    }
}
```

Both `RubberbandRectangle` and `RubberbandEllipse` invoke the
`Rubberband.lastBounds()` and `Rubberband.getBounds()` methods to
access the last and next boundaries of the rubberband, respectively.

`RubberbandRectangle` invokes the `Graphics.drawRect` method to draw its
rectangles; `RubberbandEllipse` invokes the `Graphics.drawEllipse`
method to draw its ellipses.

A Rubberband Panel

`RubberbandPanel` is an abstract extension of `Panel` that maintains an
association with an instance of `Rubberband`. `RubberbandPanel` implements no
constructors, so a default constructor (with no arguments) is generated for it.

`RubberbandPanel` provides a `setRubberband` method for associating a
rubberband with the panel. If a rubberband was previously associated with the
panel, it is made inactive. Next, if the rubberband passed to `setRubberband()`
is non-`null`, it is made active, and the rubberband's component is set to the
rubberband panel.

```
public void setRubberband(Rubberband rb) {
    if(rubberband != null) {
        rubberband.setActive(false);
    }
    rubberband = rb;

    if(rubberband != null) {
        rubberband.setActive(true);
        rubberband.setComponent(this);
    }
}
```

`RubberbandPanel` defines one abstract method.

```
abstract public void rubberbandEnded(Rubberband rb);
```

`rubberbandEnded()` is invoked by an overridden `processMouseEvent`
method if the event is a mouse released event and the rubberband associated with
the `RubberbandPanel` is non-`null`.

```
public void processMouseEvent(MouseEvent event) {
    super.processMouseEvent(event);  // fire to listeners

    if(rubberband != null &&
       event.getID() == MouseEvent.MOUSE_RELEASED)
        rubberbandEnded(rubberband);
}
```

If you recall, we previously recommended avoiding the inheritance-based mechanism provided by the delegation event model—see "Consuming Input Events" on page 267—and here we are, going against our own advice. RubberbandPanel uses the inheritance-based mechanism because there is no guarantee as to the order in which event listeners are notified of an event—see "Notification Order for Multiple Listeners Is Undefined" on page 247. Let us explain.

If RubberbandPanel were not an abstract class and did not override processMouseEvent(), how would a mouse release, and therefore the end of a rubberbanding operation, get handled? The answer, of course, would be to add a mouse listener to the RubberbandPanel and have the listener implement mouseReleased(). Realize that in such a scenario, there are at least two mouse listeners attached to the RubberbandPanel: one is listening for a mouse released event to determine when the rubberbanding operation is complete; the others are listening to any active rubberbands associated with the RubberbandPanel, which react to a mouse released event by erasing the last rubberbanding shape drawn.

Now consider that the delegation event model makes no guarantees as to the order in which multiple listeners attached to a component are notified of an event. Furthermore, consider a drawing program that draws the shape that was rubberbanded after the rubberbanding operation is complete—the rubberband erases the shape when a mouse released event occurs, whereas the drawing program draws the shape. If the rubberband is notified of the mouse released event first, everything is fine, but if the drawing program is notified first, the rubberband will wind up erasing the shape drawn by the drawing program.

The last piece to the puzzle is that Component.processMouseEvent() causes all listeners to be notified of the mouse event in question. To ensure that the rubberband erases the shape before extensions of RubberbandPanel are notified of the end of the rubberbanding operation, RubberbandPanel.processMouseEvent() invokes super.mouseEvent(event) before invoking the abstract rubberbandEnded method. Doing so ensures that mouse listeners are notified of the event before the RubberbandPanel derived class, which implements the rubberbandEnded method. As a result, our not-so-hypothetical drawing program works as expected.

The RubberbandPanel class is listed in its entirety in Example 23-5.

Example 23-5 RubberbandPanel Class Listing

```
import java.awt.*;
import java.awt.event.*;

abstract public class RubberbandPanel extends Container {
    private Rubberband rubberband;

    abstract public void rubberbandEnded(Rubberband rb);

    public void setRubberband(Rubberband rb) {
        if(rubberband != null) {
            rubberband.setActive(false);
        }
        rubberband = rb;

        if(rubberband != null) {
            rubberband.setActive(true);
            rubberband.setComponent(this);
        }
    }
    public Rubberband getRubberband() {
        return rubberband;
    }
    public void processMouseEvent(MouseEvent event) {
        super.processMouseEvent(event);  // fire to listeners

        if(rubberband != null &&
            event.getID() == MouseEvent.MOUSE_RELEASED)
            rubberbandEnded(rubberband);
    }
}
```

The DrawingPanel Class

This section presents a DrawingPanel class, which comes standard with three rubberbands: one each for rubberbanding lines, rectangles, and ellipses. When a rubberbanding operation is complete, DrawingPanel draws the shape that was rubberbanded. Optionally, the shape drawn may be filled.

DrawingPanel extends RubberbandPanel and creates rubberbands in its only constructor.

```
public class DrawingPanel extends RubberbandPanel {
    private Rubberband rbLine, rbRect, rbEllipse;
    private Color   color;
    private boolean fill;

    public DrawingPanel() {
        rbLine   = new RubberbandLine      ();
        rbRect   = new RubberbandRectangle();
        rbEllipse = new RubberbandEllipse  ();
        setRubberband(rbLine);
    }
    ...
```

Of course, DrawingPanel implements rubberbandEnded() in order to qualify as a concrete class. rubberbandEnded() invokes drawShape(), passing along the rubberband involved in the rubberbanding operation. DrawingPanel.drawShape() determines which of its rubberbands was responsible for the rubberbanding operation and draws the appropriate shape.

```
public void rubberbandEnded(Rubberband rubberband) {
    drawShape(rubberband);
}
protected void drawShape(Rubberband rb) {
    Graphics  g  = getGraphics();

    if(g != null) {
        try {
            g.setColor(color);

            if      (rb == rbLine)    drawLine      (rb, g);
            else if(rb == rbRect)     drawRectangle(rb, g);
            else if(rb == rbEllipse)  drawEllipse  (rb, g);
        }
        finally {
            g.dispose();
        }
    }
}
```

drawLine(), drawRectangle(), and drawEllipse() obtain the appropriate information from the rubberband they are passed, and do the actual drawing of the shape. Note that extensions of RubberbandPanel may override the protected drawShape() in the event that they have more rubberbands than the three provided by RubberbandPanel.

Finally, the drawLine, drawRectangle, and drawEllipse methods do the actual drawing of the appropriate shape.

```
protected void drawLine(Rubberband rb, Graphics g) {
    Point anchor = rb.getAnchor(), end = rb.getEnd();
    g.drawLine(anchor.x, anchor.y, end.x, end.y);
}
protected void drawRectangle(Rubberband rb, Graphics g) {
    Rectangle r = rb.getBounds();
    if(fill)
        g.fillRect(r.x+1, r.y+1, r.width-1, r.height-1);
    else
        g.drawRect(r.x, r.y, r.width, r.height);
}
protected void drawEllipse(Rubberband rb, Graphics g) {
    Rectangle r = rb.getBounds();
    if(fill)
        g.fillArc(r.x+1, r.y+1, r.width-1, r.height-1, 0, 360);
    else
        g.drawArc(r.x, r.y, r.width, r.height, 0, 360);
}
```

The DrawingPanel class is listed in its entirety in Example 23-6.

Example 23-6 DrawingPanel Class Listing

```
import java.awt.*;
import java.awt.event.*;

public class DrawingPanel extends RubberbandPanel {
    private Rubberband rbLine, rbRect, rbEllipse;
    private Color    color;
    private boolean fill;

    public DrawingPanel() {
        rbLine   = new RubberbandLine      ();
        rbRect   = new RubberbandRectangle();
        rbEllipse = new RubberbandEllipse  ();

        setRubberband(rbLine);
    }
    public void rubberbandEnded(Rubberband rubberband) {
        drawShape(rubberband);
    }
    public void drawLines      () { setRubberband(rbLine);    }
    public void drawRectangles() { setRubberband(rbRect);    }
    public void drawEllipses   () { setRubberband(rbEllipse); }
```

```java
    public void  setColor(Color color) { this.color = color; }
    public Color getColor()            { return color;       }

    public void    setFill(boolean b) { fill = b;    }
    public boolean getFill()          { return fill; }

    protected void drawShape(Rubberband rb) {
        Graphics   g = getGraphics();

        if(g != null) {
            try {
                g.setColor(color);

                if     (rb == rbLine)    drawLine      (rb, g);
                else if(rb == rbRect)    drawRectangle(rb, g);
                else if(rb == rbEllipse) drawEllipse  (rb, g);
            }
            finally {
                g.dispose();
            }
        }
    }
    protected void drawLine(Rubberband rb, Graphics g) {
        Point anchor = rb.getAnchor(), end = rb.getEnd();
        g.drawLine(anchor.x, anchor.y, end.x, end.y);
    }
    protected void drawRectangle(Rubberband rb, Graphics g) {
        Rectangle r = rb.getBounds();

        if(fill)
            g.fillRect(r.x+1, r.y+1, r.width-1, r.height-1);
        else
            g.drawRect(r.x, r.y, r.width, r.height);
    }
    protected void drawEllipse(Rubberband rb, Graphics g) {
        Rectangle r = rb.getBounds();

        if(fill)
            g.fillArc(r.x+1, r.y+1,
                        r.width-1, r.height-1, 0, 360);
        else
        g.drawArc(r.x, r.y, r.width, r.height, 0, 360);
    }
}
```

Exercising the Rubberband Classes

Figure 23-2 shows the DrawingPanel class in action. As usual, feel free to run the test application by invoking appletviewer on the RubberbandTest.html file provided on the CD. Doing so should help you to better understand the discussion of the application.

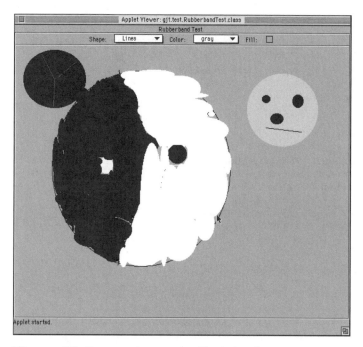

Figure 23-2 DrawingPanel Test Application

To see exactly how RubberbandTest is laid out in three dimensions, look at Figure 23-3.

RubberbandTest is listed in Example 23-7.

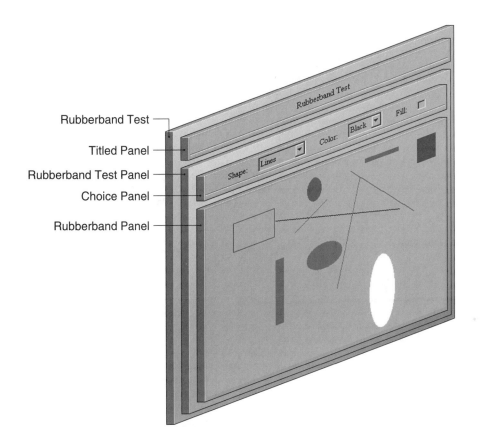

Rubberband Test

Titled Panel

Rubberband Test Panel

Choice Panel

Rubberband Panel

Figure 23-3 RubberbandTest Layout Diagram

Example 23-7 RubberbandTest Application

```java
import java.awt.*;
import java.awt.event.*;

public class RubberbandTest extends Frame {
    public RubberbandTest() {
        super("Rubberband Test");
        setLayout(new BorderLayout());
         add(new RubberbandTestPanel(), "Center");
    }
```

```
        public static void main(String args[]) {
            final Frame dbt = new RubberbandTest();
            dbt.setBounds(100,100,600,600);
            dbt.setVisible(true);

            dbt.addWindowListener(new WindowAdapter() {
                public void windowClosing(WindowEvent event) {
                    dbt.dispose();
                    System.exit(0);
                }
            });
        }
    }
    class RubberbandTestPanel extends RubberbandPanel {
        ColorChoice colorChoice= new ColorChoice();
        Choice rbChoice= new Choice();
        Rubberband linerb = new RubberbandLine(),
                   ellipserb = new RubberbandEllipse(),
                   rectanglerb= new RubberbandRectangle();

        public RubberbandTestPanel() {
            setRubberband(linerb);
            setForeground(Color.black);

            rbChoice.add("line");
            rbChoice.add("ellipse");
            rbChoice.add("rectangle");

            setLayout(new FlowLayout());
            add(rbChoice);
            add(colorChoice);

            rbChoice.addItemListener(new ItemListener() {
                public void itemStateChanged(ItemEvent event) {
                    int index = rbChoice.getSelectedIndex();
                    switch(index) {
                        case 0:setRubberband(linerb); break;
                        case 1: setRubberband(ellipserb); break;
                        case 2: setRubberband(rectanglerb); break;
                    }
                }
            });
            colorChoice.addItemListener(new ItemListener() {
                public void itemStateChanged(ItemEvent event) {
                    setForeground(colorChoice.getColor());
                }
            });
        }
        public void rubberbandEnded(Rubberband rb) {
            Graphics g = getGraphics();

            if(g != null) {
                try {
                    Point anchor = rb.getAnchor(), end = rb.getEnd();
```

```java
                int w = Math.abs(anchor.x - end.x);
                int h = Math.abs(anchor.y - end.y);

                g.setColor(getForeground());

                if(rb == linerb)
                    g.drawLine(anchor.x, anchor.y, end.x, end.y);
                else if(rb == ellipserb)
                    g.drawOval(anchor.x, anchor.y, w, h);
                else
                    g.drawRect(anchor.x, anchor.y, w, h);
            }
            finally {
                g.dispose();
            }
        }
    }
    public void update(Graphics g) {
        paint(g);
    }
}
class ColorChoice extends Choice {
    private String colorNames[] = {
                    "black", "blue", "cyan", "darkGray",
                    "gray", "green", "lightgray", "magenta",
                    "orange", "pink", "red", "white",
                    "yellow" };

    private Color colors[] = {Color.black,      Color.blue,
                        Color.cyan,       Color.darkGray,
                        Color.gray,       Color.green,
                        Color.lightGray, Color.magenta,
                        Color.orange,     Color.pink,
                        Color.red,        Color.white,
                        Color.yellow };
    public ColorChoice() {
        for(int i=0; i < colors.length; ++i) {
            add(colorNames[i]);
        }
    }
    public Color getColor() {
        return colors[getSelectedIndex()];
    }
    public void setColor(Color color) {
        for(int i=0; i < colors.length; ++i) {
            if(colors[i].equals(color)) {
                select(i);
                break;
            }
        }
    }
}
```

Refactoring the Unit Test

As an aside, we should mention that the `DrawingPanel` class was born out of a first attempt at a `RubberbandTest` applet, in the manner described below.

The object-oriented design process is an iterative one.[1] Classes are written, and as other classes are added to a system, insights are gained which often result in existing classes being *refactored*, meaning their implementations are modified to some degree according to a number of criteria. One of the mainstays of refactoring is to identify basic abstractions that can be shared among a number of different classes in the midst of specialized pieces of functionality. When such code is identified, it is separated from the specialized code and packaged into its own class or classes. The specialized code is then refactored to use the newly created class or classes.

For instance, the original test application for rubberbanding contained an extension of `RubberbandPanel` that was very similar to `DrawingPanel`. After the test application (a specialized piece of functionality) was implemented, it was observed that the unit test contained a basic abstraction that was much better placed in a class that could be made available for all to take advantage of. That abstraction, of course, was a drawing panel—a panel equipped with a set of rubberbands that could be used to draw geometric shapes. As a result, the unit test was refactored, meaning that `DrawingPanel` was implemented, and the unit test was reworked to use an instance of `DrawingPanel`. Not only did the refactoring produce a general-purpose class for drawing shapes, but it also considerably simplified the implementation of the unit tests—a win all the way around.

1. See Booch, Grady. *Object-Oriented Analysis And Design*, section 6.1. Benjamin/Cummings, 1991.

> **OO-TIP**
>
> *Refactor Classes to Extract Basic Abstractions*
>
> Object-oriented development involves refactoring of classes when it is determined that specialized pieces of functionality contain basic abstractions that are better off placed in their own class or set of classes. In addition to refactoring specialized functionality, it is often the case that one or more classes may contain redundant code that implements similar functionality. In such a case, a base class that implements the redundant functionality is often created, and the classes in question are refactored to extend the newly created base class.
>
> Refactoring involves repeatedly iterating over the implementation of classes and is one of the mainstays of object-oriented development.

Summary

The rubberband test application serves as a good reminder that all graphical activities in the AWT occur in a `Component`. All the work is accomplished by the use of a component's `Graphics` object.

We have discussed one of the cornerstones of object-oriented software development—refactoring existing code. One of the principal activities of refactoring is to identify basic abstractions that have been implemented in specialized code. Once the basic abstractions have been identified, they are extracted from the specialized code and placed in a class (or classes) of their own, and the original specialized code is refactored to use the newly created classes.

CHAPTER
24

Double Buffering

Double buffering was introduced previously in the *Image Filtering* chapter on page 129—and see "An Introduction to Double Buffering" on page 177. This chapter provides a more in-depth look at double buffering by examining a handful of classes used to implement draggable lightweight components and a double buffered container.

Double Buffering and Animation

From draggable lightweights, it's not too far a leap to a sprite class that can animate itself, as shown in Figure 24-1.

Sprites animate through a sequence of images; their movement, speed, and rate of animation are all settable. In the *Sprite Animation* chapter on page 813, you'll find a discussion of the `Sprite` class, a playfield on which sprites are animated, in addition to collision detectors capable of detecting collisions between sprites and between sprites and the boundaries of their playfield.

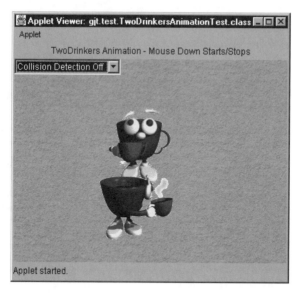

Figure 24-1 Sprites Animated on a Playfield

How Double Buffering Works

If the next frame of an animation is updated *onscreen*, you have single buffering—all the painting is done in a single buffer—not to mention potential flicker between frames. If the next frame is updated in an offscreen buffer and subsequently copied to the screen, you have double buffering and no flicker because the erasing takes place offscreen.

Flicker is a symptom of erasing part or all of the previous frame onscreen when rendering the next frame in an animation; the erasing can be impossible to avoid with animations of any complexity. Double buffering eliminates the flicker by preparing the next frame in an offscreen buffer, and then copying—or blitting—the completed frame to the screen, avoiding the onscreen erasing and flickering.

The documentation for lightweight components at the JavaSoft website[1] provides a simplistic example of double buffering—the `DoubleBufferPanel` listed in Example 24-1.

---

1. See http://www.javasoft.com/products/JDK/1.1/docs/guide/awt/
    designspec/lightweights.html

Example 24-1 DoubleBufferPanel—A Simplistic Double Buffering
Example

```
import java.awt.*;

public class DoubleBufferPanel extends Panel {
    Image offscreen;
    /**
     * null out the offscreen buffer as part of invalidation
     */
    public void invalidate() {
        super.invalidate();
        offscreen = null;
    }
    /**
     * override update to *not* erase the background before
     * painting
     */
    public void update(Graphics g) {
        paint(g);
    }
    /**
     * paint children into an offscreen buffer, then blast entire
     * image at once.
     */
    public void paint(Graphics g) {
        if(offscreen == null) {
            offscreen = createImage(getSize().width,
                                    getSize().height);
        }
        Graphics og = offscreen.getGraphics();
        og.setClip(0,0,getSize().width, getSize().height);
        super.paint(og);
        g.drawImage(offscreen, 0, 0, null);
        og.dispose();
    }
}
```

DoubleBufferPanel overrides update() to invoke paint() directly;
otherwise the inherited update() will erase the background of the component
before invoking paint(). DoubleBufferPanel.paint() paints the
component into an offscreen buffer and then copies the offscreen buffer into the
component's onscreen representation.

While DoubleBufferPanel does a good job of illustrating the basic technique
of double buffering, it is impractical for real-world usage for the following
reasons:

- Painting, erasing or moving a single component is not supported.

- Painting a background into the panel is not supported.

- The entire offscreen buffer is blitted to the screen even if only part of the
  buffer needs to be updated.

In the pages that follow, we'll implement a double buffered container that remedies all of the shortcomings listed above and provides some extra bells and whistles in the process. The double buffered container discussed in this chapter relies on two other classes:

- `Util`—Provides a couple of basic utility methods
- `BackingStore`—offscreen buffer associated with a component

Draggable Lightweights and a Double Buffered Container

Figure 24-2 shows an applet containing four draggable lightweight components that are displayed on a double buffered container.

Figure 24-2 `DoubleBufferedContainer` with Draggable Lightweights

The applet is listed in Example 24-2.

Example 24-2 DoubleBufferedContainerTest Applet

```
import java.applet.Applet;
import java.net.URL;
import java.awt.*;
import java.awt.event.*;

public class DoubleBufferedContainerTest extends Applet {
    private DoubleBufferedContainer container;

    public void init() {
        Toolkit tk = Toolkit.getDefaultToolkit();
        URL cb = getCodeBase();

        Image mandrill = getImage(cb, "gifs/mandrill.jpg");
        Image dining = getImage(cb, "gifs/Dining.gif");
        Image bg = getImage(cb, "gifs/rain.gif");
        Image skelly = getImage(cb, "gifs/skelly.gif");
        Image gj = getImage(cb, "gifs/gjMedium.gif");

        container = new DoubleBufferedContainer();
        container.setWallpaperImage(bg);

        container.add(new Lightweight(skelly));
        container.add(new Lightweight(dining));
        container.add(new Lightweight(gj));
        container.add(new Lightweight(mandrill, false));

        setLayout(new BorderLayout());
        add(container, "Center");
    }
    public void update(Graphics g) {
        paint(g);
    }
}
```

The applet contains an instance of DoubleBufferedContainer, which in turn contains four instances of Lightweight.

DoubleBufferedContainer sets its layout manager to a FlowLayout by default, so the applet is not concerned with setting the layout manager for the double buffered container.

Of course, in a static medium such as a book, we cannot show you the components being dragged about on our double buffered container—the best we can do is to show you an updated screen-shot of the applet after we've dragged the lightweights around. Of course, the applet is included on the CD that accompanies the book, so you can try it out for yourself. Figure 24-3 shows the applet after the lightweights have been dragged about. Lightweights can not only be dragged over the background of the container but can also be dragged over each other.

Figure 24-3   Lightweight Components After Being Dragged.
DoubleBufferedContainer is implemented so that lightweights
can be dragged over each other in addition to being dragged over
the background.

Now that we've illustrated the use of the DoubleBufferedContainer class,
let's take a look at how it's implemented. First, we'll discuss the Util and
BackingStore classes.

Util

The Util class provides two static methods: one method uses MediaTracker
to wait for an image to load and the other method wallpapers the background of a
component with a specified image.

The Util class is listed in Example 24-3.

Example 24-3 Util Class Listing

```
import java.awt.*;

public class Util {
    public static void waitForImage(Component component,
                                    Image image) {
        MediaTracker tracker = new MediaTracker(component);
        try {
            tracker.addImage(image, 0);
            tracker.waitForID(0);
        }
        catch(InterruptedException e) { e.printStackTrace(); }
    }
    public static void wallPaper(Component component,
                                 Graphics g,
                                 Image    image) {
        Dimension compsize = component.getSize();
        Util.waitForImage(component, image);

        int patchW = image.getWidth(component);
        int patchH = image.getHeight(component);

        for(int r=0; r < compsize.width; r += patchW) {
            for(int c=0; c < compsize.height; c += patchH) {
                g.drawImage(image, r, c, component);
            }
        }
    }
}
```

The Util methods should be self-explanatory; we have discussed the use of MediaTracker previously—see "MediaTracker" on page 117. Util.wallPaper() waits for the image it is passed to load and then repeatedly draws the image in the Graphics it is passed to wallpaper the image over the background of the component.

BackingStore

The BackingStore class maintains an offscreen buffer, which is simply an Image associated with a component. The BackingStore constructor is passed a reference to a Component, with which the backing store registers itself as a component listener. Whenever the component is resized, the backing store reallocates the offscreen buffer, if necessary, to accommodate the component's new size.

```
public class BackingStore extends ComponentAdapter {
    Image offscreen;
    Component component;
    Dimension size;

    public BackingStore(Component component) {
        setComponent(component);
    }
    public void setComponent(Component c) {
        if(component != null) {
            component.removeComponentListener(this);
        }
        component = c;
        component.addComponentListener(this);
    }
    public Component getComponent() {
        return component;
    }
    ...
    public void componentResized(ComponentEvent event) {
        if(needNewOffscreenBuffer())
            createBuffers();
    }
    ...
    private void createBuffers() {
        size = component.getSize();
        offscreen = component.createImage(size.width,
                                          size.height);
    }
    ...
}
```

In addition to maintaining the offscreen buffer, BackingStore also supplies a set of methods for blitting the offscreen buffer to various destinations.

```
    ...
    public void blitTo(Image im) {
        blitTo(im, null);
    }
    public void blitTo(Graphics graphics) {
        blitTo(graphics, null);
    }
    public void blitTo(Image im, Rectangle clip) {
        Graphics g = im.getGraphics();
        if(g != null) {
            try {
                if(clip != null)
                    g.setClip(clip);

                g.drawImage(offscreen, 0, 0, component);
            }
            finally {
```

```
            g.dispose();
        }
    }
}
public void blitTo(Graphics g, Rectangle clip) {
    if(g != null) {
        if(clip != null)
            g.setClip(clip);

        g.drawImage(offscreen, 0, 0, component);
    }
}
...
```

The offscreen image can be blitted to a graphics or another image, and clipping rectangles can be set for both blits. Notice the care taken to ensure that the Graphics obtained by a call to getGraphics() is disposed of—see "Disposing of a Graphics" on page 40.

The BackingStore class is listed in its entirety in Example 24-4.

Example 24-4 BackingStore Class Listing

```
import java.awt.*;
import java.awt.event.*;

public class BackingStore extends ComponentAdapter {
    Image offscreen;
    Component component;
    Dimension size;

    public BackingStore(Component component) {
        setComponent(component);
    }
    public void setComponent(Component c) {
        if(component != null) {
            component.removeComponentListener(this);
        }
        component = c;
        component.addComponentListener(this);
    }
    public Component getComponent() {
        return component;
    }
    public Image getImage() {
        if(offscreen == null)
            createBuffers();

        return offscreen;
    }
    public Graphics getGraphics() {
        if(offscreen == null)
```

```java
            createBuffers();

        return offscreen.getGraphics();
    }
    public void componentResized(ComponentEvent event) {
        if(needNewOffscreenBuffer())
            createBuffers();
    }
    public void blitTo(Image im) {
        blitTo(im, null);
    }
    public void blitTo(Graphics graphics) {
        blitTo(graphics, null);
    }
    public void blitTo(Image im, Rectangle clip) {
        Graphics g = im.getGraphics();
        if(g != null) {
            try {
                if(clip != null)
                    g.setClip(clip);

                g.drawImage(offscreen, 0, 0, component);
            }
            finally {
                g.dispose();
            }
        }
    }
    public void blitTo(Graphics g, Rectangle clip) {
        if(g != null) {
            if(clip != null)
                g.setClip(clip);

            g.drawImage(offscreen, 0, 0, component);
        }
    }
    private boolean needNewOffscreenBuffer() {
        Dimension newSize = component.getSize();

        return (offscreen == null ||
                newSize.width  > size.width ||
                newSize.height > size.height);
    }
    private void createBuffers() {
        size     = component.getSize();
        offscreen = component.createImage(size.width,
                                          size.height);
    }
}
```

DoubleBufferedContainer

DoubleBufferedContainer extends `java.awt.Container` directly and
therefore is a lightweight container. It maintains two backing stores: one
maintains only the background; another, called the workplace buffer, is used as
the offscreen buffer for the component. Since `java.awt.Container` has a `null`
layout manager by default, `DoubleBufferedContainer` fits itself with an
instance of `FlowLayout`.

```
public class DoubleBufferedContainer extends Container {
    private   Image wallPaperImage;
    protected BackingStore workplace, background;

    public DoubleBufferedContainer() {
        this(null);
    }
    public DoubleBufferedContainer(Image wallPaperImage) {
        if(wallPaperImage != null)
            setWallpaperImage(wallPaperImage);

        setLayout(new FlowLayout());

        workplace = new BackingStore(this);
        background = new BackingStore(this);
    }
    public void setWallpaperImage(Image wallPaperImage) {
        this.wallPaperImage = wallPaperImage;
        Util.waitForImage(this, wallPaperImage);
    }
```

`DoubleBufferedContainer.paint()` first checks to see if the window in
which the container resides has been damaged;[2] if so, it blits the workplace buffer
to the screen, clipped to the damaged area of the window, thus repainting only
the damaged area. `DoubleBufferedContainer.update()` is overridden to
invoke `paint()` directly, so the background of the container is not cleared before
it is repainted.

```
    ...
public void update(Graphics g) {
    paint(g);
}
public void paint(Graphics g) {
    if(windowDamaged(g)) {
        blitWorkplaceToScreen(g.getClipBounds());
    }
    else {
```

2. If the clipping rectangle associated with the `Graphics` passed to `paint()` is not
   equal to the size of the container, then the window in which the container resides
   has been damaged.

```
            Graphics wpg = getWorkplaceGraphics();

            if(wpg != null) {
                try {
                    Dimension size = getSize();
                    paintBackground();
                    wpg.setClip(0,0,size.width,size.height);
                    super.paint(wpg);
                    blitWorkplaceToScreen();
                }
                finally {
                    wpg.dispose();
                }
            }
        }
    }
    ...
    protected void paintBackground() {
        paintBackground((Rectangle)null);
    }
    protected void paintBackground(Rectangle clip) {
        Graphics g = getBackgroundGraphics();
        if(g != null) {
            try {
                if(clip != null)
                    g.setClip(clip);

                paintBackground(g);
                blitBackgroundToWorkplace();
            }
            finally {
                g.dispose();
            }
        }
    }
    protected void paintBackground(Graphics g) {
        if(wallPaperImage != null) {
            Util.wallPaper(this, g, wallPaperImage);
        }
    }
```

If the window has not been damaged, the entire container is painted. First,
paintBackground() is called, which in turn calls
paintBackground(Rectangle) with a null value for the clipping rectangle,
indicating that the entire background needs to be repainted.

paintBackground(Graphics) uses the Util.wallPaper method to
wallpaper the background of the workplace buffer if the wallpaper image is non-
null. Extensions of DoubleBufferedContainer can override
paintBackground(Graphics) if they wish to provide an alternate method of

painting the background. Regardless, the point is that, by default, `paintBackground(Graphics)` paints the background into the workplace buffer and not to the screen.

After the background is painted into the workplace buffer, `paint()` sets the clipping rectangle of the workplace buffer's graphics to the size of the container and invokes `super.paint(wpg)`. `Container.paint()` iterates over any lightweight components it contains and paints each lightweight component that intersects the clipping rectangle of the `Graphics` object it is passed.

Notice that up until now, all of the action has taken place in either the background buffer or the workplace buffer—nothing has been painted onscreen. Finally, the `paint` method blits the entire workplace to the screen, providing flicker-free painting of the lightweight components in the container.

`DoubleBufferedContainer` also provides methods for painting, erasing, and moving a single lightweight component. All three methods are overloaded; one version of the methods is passed an extra argument that indicates whether the onscreen representation of the component should be updated. `moveComponent()` calls `eraseComponent()` and `paintComponent()`, passing a `false` value to indicate that the onscreen representation of the component should not be updated. After the component has been erased, moved, and repainted in the workplace buffer, `moveComponent()` blits the workplace buffer to the screen, clipped by the union of the component's original and new bounds.

```
public void paintComponent(Component comp) {
    paintComponent(comp, true);
}
public void eraseComponent(Component comp) {
    eraseComponent(comp, true);
}
public void moveComponent(Component comp, Point location) {
    moveComponent(comp, location, true);
}
public void paintComponent(Component comp, boolean update) {
    Graphics  wpg     = getWorkplaceGraphics();
    Rectangle bounds = comp.getBounds();
    Graphics  compGraphics;

    if(wpg != null) {
        try {
            compGraphics = wpg.create(bounds.x,      bounds.y,
                                    bounds.width, bounds.height);
            comp.paint(compGraphics);
            if(update)
                blitWorkplaceToScreen(bounds);
        }
```

```
            finally {
                wpg.dispose();
            }
        }
    }
    public void eraseComponent(Component comp, boolean update) {
        Rectangle bounds = comp.getBounds();

        blitBackgroundToWorkplace(bounds);
        paintOverlappingComponents(comp);

        if(update)
            blitWorkplaceToScreen(bounds);
    }
    public void moveComponent(Component comp, Point newLoc,
                              boolean update) {
        Rectangle oldBounds = comp.getBounds();

        eraseComponent(comp, false);   // erase - no screen update
        comp.setLocation(newLoc);      // move component
        paintComponent(comp, false);   // paint comp - no update

        if(update)
            blitWorkplaceToScreen(
                            oldBounds.union(comp.getBounds())));
    }
```

DoubleBufferedContainer also provides a method that paints all of the components that overlap a given component.

paintOverlappingComponents() sets the clipping rectangle for the workplace buffer to the bounds of the component in question and sets the visibility of the component to false, so that the component itself is not drawn. Then Container.paint() is invoked, which paints each component that intersects the clipping rectangle of the component. Finally, the visibility of the component is set to true so that it will subsequently be drawn when calls to Container.paint() are made.

```
    protected void paintOverlappingComponents(Component comp) {
        Graphics  wpg     = getWorkplaceGraphics();
        Rectangle bounds  = comp.getBounds();

        if(wpg != null) {
            try {
                wpg.setClip     (bounds);
                comp.setVisible(false);
                super.paint     (wpg);
                comp.setVisible(true);
            }
```

```
        finally {
            wpg.dispose();
        }
    }
}
```

DoubleBufferedContainer is listed in its entirety in Example 24-5.

Example 24-5 DoubleBufferedContainer Class Listing

```
import java.awt.*;
import java.awt.event.*;

public class DoubleBufferedContainer extends Container {
    private    Image wallPaperImage;
    protected BackingStore workplace, background;

    public DoubleBufferedContainer() {
        this(null);
    }
    public DoubleBufferedContainer(Image wallPaperImage) {
        if(wallPaperImage != null)
            setWallpaperImage(wallPaperImage);

        setLayout(new FlowLayout());

        workplace = new BackingStore(this);
        background = new BackingStore(this);
    }
    public void setWallpaperImage(Image wallPaperImage) {
        this.wallPaperImage = wallPaperImage;
        Util.waitForImage(this, wallPaperImage);
    }
    public void update(Graphics g) {
        paint(g);
    }
    public void paint(Graphics g) {
        if(windowDamaged(g)) {
          blitWorkplaceToScreen(g.getClipBounds());
        }
        else {
           Graphics  wpg  = getWorkplaceGraphics();

           if(wpg != null) {
               try {
```

```
              Dimension size = getSize();
                  paintBackground();
                  wpg.setClip(0,0,size.width,size.height);
                  super.paint(wpg);
                  blitWorkplaceToScreen();
              }
              finally {
                  wpg.dispose();
              }
          }
      }
  }
  public void paintComponents(Rectangle clip, boolean update) {
      Graphics wpg = getWorkplaceGraphics();

      if(wpg != null) {
          try {
              wpg.setClip(clip);
              super.paint(wpg);

              if(update)
                  blitWorkplaceToScreen(clip);
          }
          finally {
              wpg.dispose();
          }
      }
  }
  public void paintComponent(Component comp) {
      paintComponent(comp, true);
  }
  public void eraseComponent(Component comp) {
      eraseComponent(comp, true);
  }
  public void moveComponent(Component comp, Point location) {
      moveComponent(comp, location, true);
  }
  public void paintComponent(Component comp, boolean update) {
      Graphics   wpg    = getWorkplaceGraphics();
      Rectangle bounds = comp.getBounds();
      Graphics  compGraphics;

      if(wpg != null) {
          try {
              compGraphics = wpg.create(bounds.x,     bounds.y,
                                 bounds.width, bounds.height);
              comp.paint(compGraphics);
```

```
            if(update)
                blitWorkplaceToScreen(bounds);
        }
        finally {
            wpg.dispose();
        }
    }
}
public void eraseComponent(Component comp, boolean update) {
    Rectangle bounds = comp.getBounds();

    blitBackgroundToWorkplace(bounds);
    paintOverlappingComponents(comp);

    if(update)
        blitWorkplaceToScreen(bounds);
}
public void moveComponent(Component comp, Point newLoc,
                          boolean update) {
    Rectangle oldBounds = comp.getBounds();

    eraseComponent(comp, false);  // erase - no screen update
    comp.setLocation(newLoc);     // move component
    paintComponent(comp, false);  // paint comp - no update

    if(update)
        blitWorkplaceToScreen(
                    oldBounds.union(comp.getBounds()));
}
public Graphics getWorkplaceGraphics() {
    return workplace.getGraphics();
}
public Graphics getBackgroundGraphics() {
    return background.getGraphics();
}
public void blitBackgroundToWorkplace() {
    blitBackgroundToWorkplace(null);
}
public void blitWorkplaceToScreen() {
    blitWorkplaceToScreen(null);
}
public void blitBackgroundToScreen() {
    blitBackgroundToScreen(null);
}
public void blitBackgroundToWorkplace(Rectangle r) {
    background.blitTo(workplace.getImage(), r);
}
```

```java
public void blitWorkplaceToScreen(Rectangle r) {
    Graphics g = getGraphics();

    if(g != null) {
        try {
            workplace.blitTo(g, r);
        }
        finally {
            g.dispose();
        }
    }
}
public void blitBackgroundToScreen(Rectangle r) {
    Graphics g = getGraphics();

    if(g != null) {
        try {
            background.blitTo(g, r);
        }
        finally {
            g.dispose();
        }
    }
}
public Image getWorkplaceBuffer () {
    return workplace.getImage();
}
public Image getBackgroundBuffer() {
    return background.getImage();
}
protected boolean windowDamaged(Graphics g) {
    Rectangle clip = g.getClipBounds();
    Dimension size = getSize();

    return ((clip.x != 0 || clip.y != 0) ||
            (clip.width  < size.width    ||
             clip.height < size.height));
}
protected void paintOverlappingComponents(Component comp) {
    Graphics  wpg    = getWorkplaceGraphics();
    Rectangle bounds = comp.getBounds();

    if(wpg != null) {
        try {
            wpg.setClip     (bounds);
            comp.setVisible(false);
            super.paint     (wpg);
            comp.setVisible(true);
        }
```

```
            finally {
                wpg.dispose();
            }
        }
    }
    protected void paintBackground() {
        paintBackground((Rectangle)null);
    }
    protected void paintBackground(Rectangle clip) {
        Graphics g = getBackgroundGraphics();

        if(g != null) {
            try {
                if(clip != null)
                    g.setClip(clip);

                paintBackground(g);
                blitBackgroundToWorkplace();
            }
            finally {
                g.dispose();
            }
        }
    }
    protected void paintBackground(Graphics g) {
        if(wallPaperImage != null) {
            Util.wallPaper(this, g, wallPaperImage);
        }
    }
}
```

Lightweight

Now that we've got an industrial-strength double buffered container, all that's left is to implement a lightweight component that can be displayed and dragged about on a double buffered container.

Each Lightweight maintains an instance of ImageIcon and Dragger. ImageIcon is a simple class that draws an image into a Graphics at a specified location.

```
class ImageIcon extends Object {
    Image image;
    Component component = new Component() { };

    public ImageIcon(Image image) {
        this.image = image;
        Util.waitForImage(component, image);
    }
```

```
     public void paintIcon(Component c, Graphics g, int x, int y) {
         g.drawImage(image,x,y,component);
     }
     public int getIconWidth() {
         return image.getWidth(null);
     }
     public int getIconHeight() {
         return image.getHeight(null);
     }
}
```

Dragger is a Lightweight inner class that monitors mouse events in the lightweight component and drags the lightweight around as appropriate.

```
class Dragger extends MouseAdapter
                           implements MouseMotionListener {
    Point press = new Point();
    boolean dragging = false;

    public void mousePressed(MouseEvent event) {
        press.x = event.getX();
        press.y = event.getY();
        dragging = true;
    }
    public boolean isDragging() {
        return dragging;
    }
    public void mouseReleased(MouseEvent event) {
        dragging = false;
    }
    public void mouseClicked(MouseEvent event) {
        dragging = false;
    }
    public void mouseMoved(MouseEvent event) {
        // don't care
    }
    public void mouseDragged(MouseEvent event) {
        if(dragging) {
            DoubleBufferedContainer c;
            Point loc = getLocation();
            Point pt  = new Point();

            pt.x = event.getX() + loc.x - press.x;
            pt.y = event.getY() + loc.y - press.y;

            c = (DoubleBufferedContainer)getParent();
            c.moveComponent(Lightweight.this, pt);
        }
    }
}
```

Notice that `Lightweight.Dragger` knows that the lightweight is contained in a `DoubleBufferedContainer`, and it takes advantage of this knowledge to smoothly drag the lightweight by invoking `DoubleBufferedContainer.moveComponent()`.

Lightweights can be specified as being mobile or immobile; the `Lightweight` class provides a constructor that allows the mobility parameter to be set at construction. In the applet shown in Figure 24-2 on page 792 and listed in Example 24-2 on page 793, the mandrill lightweight is specified as immobile; all of the other lightweights in the applet are mobile.

The `Lightweight` class is listed in its entirety in Example 24-6.

Example 24-6 `Lightweight Class Listing`

```java
import java.awt.*;
import java.awt.event.*;

public class Lightweight extends Component {
    private ImageIcon   icon;
    private Dragger dragger = new Dragger();
    private boolean isMobile = false;

    public Lightweight() {
        this(null, true);
    }
    public Lightweight(Image image) {
        this(image, true);
    }
    public Lightweight(Image image, boolean isMobile) {
        if(image != null)
            icon = new ImageIcon(image);

        this.isMobile = isMobile;

        if(isMobile) {
            addMouseListener       (dragger);
            addMouseMotionListener(dragger);
        }
    }
    public void paint(Graphics g) {
        if(isVisible() && icon != null)
            icon.paintIcon(this, g, 0, 0);
    }
```

```java
        public Dimension getPreferredSize() {
            Dimension rv = null;
            if(icon != null)
                rv = new Dimension(icon.getIconWidth(),
                                  icon.getIconHeight());
            else
                rv = super.getPreferredSize();
            return rv;
        }
    public boolean isBeingDragged() {
        return dragger.isDragging();
    }
    class Dragger extends MouseAdapter
                            implements MouseMotionListener {
        Point press = new Point();
        boolean dragging = false;

        public void mousePressed(MouseEvent event) {
            press.x = event.getX();
            press.y = event.getY();
            dragging = true;
        }
        public boolean isDragging() {
            return dragging;
        }
        public void mouseReleased(MouseEvent event) {
            dragging = false;
        }
        public void mouseClicked(MouseEvent event) {
            dragging = false;
        }
        public void mouseMoved(MouseEvent event) {
            // don't care
        }
        public void mouseDragged(MouseEvent event) {
            if(dragging) {
                DoubleBufferedContainer c;
                Point loc = getLocation();
                Point pt  = new Point();

                pt.x = event.getX() + loc.x - press.x;
                pt.y = event.getY() + loc.y - press.y;

                c = (DoubleBufferedContainer)getParent();
                c.moveComponent(Lightweight.this, pt);
            }
        }
    }
}
```

```
class ImageIcon extends Object {
    Image image;
    Component component = new Component() { };

    public ImageIcon(Image image) {
        this.image = image;
        Util.waitForImage(component, image);
    }
    public void paintIcon(Component c, Graphics g, int x, int y) {
        g.drawImage(image,x,y,component);
    }
    public int getIconWidth() {
        return image.getWidth(null);
    }
    public int getIconHeight() {
        return image.getHeight(null);
    }
}
```

Summary

Double buffering is an essential technique for dragging lightweight components and for implementing flicker-free animations. Double buffering is implemented by drawing the next frame in an animation into an offscreen buffer; once the offscreen buffer represents the next frame in the animation, it is copied to the screen. This chapter has presented a handful of reusable classes that you can use for implementing double buffering.

In the next chapter, we will build on the DoubleBufferedContainer class presented in this chapter by implementing a Playfield class that can contain animated sprites.

CHAPTER
25

Sprite
Animation

The AWT does not provide direct support for animation—there is no animation package, for example. However, the AWT does provide all of the underlying infrastructure necessary for implementing animations. This chapter presents an animation package that builds on double buffering techniques presented in the *Double Buffering* chapter on page 789.

The Participants

There are four major participants in the `animation` package presented in this chapter:

- `Playfield` — Is an extension of the `DoubleBufferedContainer` class upon which sprite animation takes place.
- `Sprite` — Is a lightweight component that is animated on a `Playfield`.
- `Sequence` — Maintains a sequence of images.
- `CollisionDetector` — Detects collisions between two sprites and collisions between sprites and the boundaries of a `Playfield`.

The premise behind the `animation` package is simple: sprites are animated on a playfield and can collide with other sprites and with the boundaries of their playfield. The rate at which sprites cycle through their images and the speed at which they move can both be set.

We'll begin our discussion with sprites and sequences and then describe playfields and collision detection.

Sequences and Sprites

Sprites must be able to perform two major functions:

- Cycle through a sequence of images
- Move about on a double buffered container

As previously mentioned, the rate at which each of these functions occurs can be set. A `Sprite` is responsible for moving itself about and timing its movement; however, it delegates the responsibility for cycling through a sequence of images to another object: a `Sequence`.

Sequence

Figure 25-1 shows the `Sequence` class diagram.

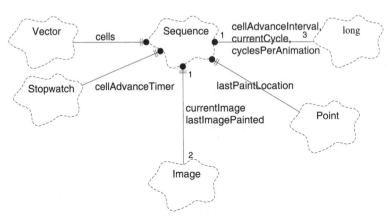

Figure 25-1 `Sequence` Class Diagram

As you can see, a `Sequence` maintains a vector of images that it cycles through. It also uses a stopwatch to control the rate at which it cycles through its images. The `cellAdvanceInterval` member of the `Sequence` class defines the elapsed time (in milliseconds) between the display of one image and the next.

If all Sequence objects simply cycled through their images only once, they wouldn't be of much use. Therefore, the number of cycles (defined as one complete pass through all the images) that a Sequence runs through can be set and is maintained in the cyclesPerAnimation member of the Sequence class. Additionally, an instance of Sequence keeps track of its current cycle and is able to report whether its animation is over. The responsibilities of the Sequence class are listed in Table 25-1.

Table 25-1 Sequence **Responsibilities**

Methods	Description
void start()	Starts the sequence
Image getLastImage()	Returns last image painted
Point getLastLocation()	Returns location of last image painted
int getNumImages()	Returns the number of images in the sequence
long getCurrentCycle()	Returns the number of the current cycle
void setCurrentCycle(long)	Sets the current cycle
long getCyclesPerAnimation()	Returns the number of cycles for one complete animation
void setCyclesPerAnimation(long)	Sets the number of cycles per animation
Image getFirstImage()	Returns the first image in the sequence
Image getCurrentImage()	Returns the current image
int getCurrentImagePosition()	Returns the position of the current image
Image getNextImage()	Returns the next image in the sequence
void setAdvanceInterval(long)	Sets the interval between image updates in milliseconds
void addImage(Component, Image)	Adds an image to the sequence
void removeImage(Image)	Removes an image from the sequence
boolean needsRepainting(Point)	Whether the sequence needs to repaint at a particular location
boolean isAtLastImage()	Whether the sequence is on the last image
boolean timeToAdvanceCell()	Whether it is time to advance to the next image
boolean animationOver()	Whether the animation is over
void advance()	Advances to the next image

Table 25-2 lists the associations of a `Sequence`.

Table 25-2 `Sequence` **Associations**

Variables	Description
`private static long infiniteCycle`	Defines an infinite cycle
`private Vector cells`	The images used in the sequence
`private Point lastPaintLocation`	The location at which the last image was painted
`private Stopwatch cellAdvanceTimer`	A timer for timing interval between image advances
`private Image currentImage`	The current image
`private Image lastImagePainted`	The last image painted
`private long cellAdvanceInterval`	The delay between image updates, in milliseconds
`private long currentCycle`	The current cycle
`private long cyclesPerAnimation`	The number of cycles per animation

Now that we have a basic understanding of the responsibilities and associations of a `Sequence`, let's take a look at the implementation of the `Sequence` class in Example 25-1.

Example 25-1 `Sequence Class Listing`

```
import java.util.Vector;
import java.awt.*;
import java.awt.image.ImageObserver;

public class Sequence {
    private static long infiniteCycle = -1;

    private Vector    cells              = new Vector();
    private Point     lastPaintLocation  = new Point(0,0);
    private Stopwatch cellAdvanceTimer   = new Stopwatch();
    private Image     currentImage, lastImagePainted;
    private long      cellAdvanceInterval = 0,
                      currentCycle        = 0,
                      cyclesPerAnimation  = 0;

    public Sequence() { }

    public Sequence(Component component, Image[] images) {
        for(int i=0; i < images.length; ++i) {
            addImage(component, images[i]);
        }
        cyclesPerAnimation = infiniteCycle;
```

```
    }
    public void  start          () { cellAdvanceTimer.start(); }
    public Image getLastImage    () { return lastImagePainted;  }
    public Point getLastLocation() { return lastPaintLocation; }
    public int   getNumImages    () { return cells.size();      }

    public long getCurrentCycle()        { return currentCycle; }
    public void setCurrentCycle(long c) { currentCycle = c;    }

    public long getCyclesPerAnimation() {
        return currentCycle;
    }
    public void setCyclesPerAnimation(long cyclesPerAnimation) {
        this.cyclesPerAnimation = cyclesPerAnimation;
    }
    public Image getFirstImage() {
        return (Image)cells.firstElement();
    }
    public Image getCurrentImage() {
        return currentImage;
    }
    public int getCurrentImagePosition() {
        return cells.indexOf(currentImage);
    }
    public Image getNextImage() {
        int    index = cells.indexOf(currentImage);
        Image image;

        if(index == cells.size() - 1)
            image = (Image)cells.elementAt(0);
        else
            image = (Image)cells.elementAt(index + 1);

        return image;
    }
    public void setAdvanceInterval(long interval) {
        cellAdvanceInterval = interval;
    }
    public void addImage(Component component, Image image) {
        if(currentImage == null)
            currentImage = image;

        Util.waitForImage(component, image);
        cells.addElement(image);
    }
    public void removeImage(Image image) {
        cells.removeElement(image);
    }
    public boolean needsRepainting(Point point) {
        return (lastPaintLocation.x != point.x ||
                lastPaintLocation.y != point.y ||
                lastImagePainted    != currentImage);
```

```
        }
        public boolean isAtLastImage() {
            return getCurrentImagePosition() == (cells.size() - 1);
        }
        public boolean timeToAdvanceCell() {
            return
              cellAdvanceTimer.elapsedTime() > cellAdvanceInterval;
        }
        public boolean animationOver() {
            return (cyclesPerAnimation != infiniteCycle) &&
                   (currentCycle >= cyclesPerAnimation);
        }
        public void advance() {
            if(isAtLastImage())
                ++currentCycle;

            currentImage = getNextImage();
            cellAdvanceTimer.reset();
        }
    }
```

A Sequence can be constructed with a component and an array of images. The sequence waits for all the images in the array to be loaded before returning from its constructor. The component's only role is as an accomplice to image loading; it is passed to Util.waitForImage(Component, Image).

Additionally, a Sequence can be constructed with no arguments. Presumably, images will be added to such a sequence through its addImage method before a call is made to Sequence.start(), which starts the sequence.

A Sequence is also able to report whether it needs to be repainted at a given location. If the last paint location is different from the given location or if the last image painted is not equal to the current image, then the current image in the sequence needs to be repainted.

A Sequence also has methods that return information about the sequence:

- isAtLastImage()
- timeToAdvanceCell()
- animationOver()

Sprites

It is important to realize that a Sequence is something of a simpleton that will continuously cycle through its sequence of images, no matter what its cyclesPerAnimation has been set to. It is up to another object to monitor the sequence's progress and determine if it is time to end the sequence. That object is a Sprite, as diagrammed in Figure 25-2.

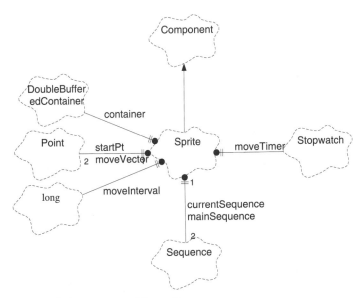

Figure 25-2 `Sprite` Class Diagram

Sprites are lightweight components[1] that can be animated on a
`DoubleBufferedContainer`.[2] Because `Sprite` extends `Component`, it inherits
all of the functionality provided by the `java.awt.Component` class.

The first thing that may strike you about the `Sprite` class is that it actually
maintains two sequences: one main sprite sequence and one temporary one. Our
sprites would be pretty boring if they endlessly cycled through only one
sequence; thus, it is imperative that we give sprites the ability to change their
sequence for a period of time. As a result, each sprite has a main sequence that it
cycles through endlessly and a temporary sequence that upstages the main
sequence for a specific number of cycles. Upstaging the main sequence is
accomplished by the `play(Sequence sequence, long cycles)` method.

As previously mentioned, a sprite is responsible for moving itself, so it is not
surprising to see that a sprite has both a stopwatch, which is used to time its
movement, and an interval, specified in milliseconds, which times the sprite's
movements from one location to the next.

1. See "Lightweight Components" on page 651.
2. See "DoubleBufferedContainer" on page 799.

Of course, in addition to timing its movements, a sprite must know the direction in which to move. The direction in which a sprite moves is stored in its moveVector, a point that defines how many pixels the sprite moves in the x and y directions each time it is told to move.

A sprite also keeps track of its width, height, and current location.

The responsibilities of the Sprite class are listed in Table 25-3.

Table 25-3 Sprite **Responsibilities (Public Methods)**

Methods	Description
void reverseX()	Reverses the sprite's horizontal direction
void reverseY	Reverses the sprite's vertical direction
void reverse()	Reverses both the horizontal and vertical directions of the sprite
void setMoveVector(Point p)	Sets the direction in which the sprite moves
Point getMoveVector()	Returns the move vector
void play(Sequence sequence, long cycles)	Plays a sequence other than the main sequence for a specified number of cycles
void animate()	Animates the sprite
void setMainSequence(Sequence sequence)	Sets the sprite's main sequence
Sequence getMainSequence()	Returns the sprite's main sequence
void setSequence(Sequence sequence)	Sets a temporary sequence
Sequence getSequence()	Gets the current sequence
boolean willIntersect(Sprite otherSprite)	Determines if the sprite will intersect with another sprite the next time they are moved
void setMoveInterval(long interval)	Sets the interval between movements
void setImageChangeInterval(long interval)	Sets the interval between image advancement
Point getNextLocation()	Returns the next location the sprite will be moved to
Rectangle getNextBounds()	Returns the bounds the sprite will occupy when it is moved to its next location
void paint(Graphics g)	Overridden Component method that paints the sprite

Table 25-3 `Sprite` **Responsibilities (Public Methods) (Continued)**

Methods	Description
`void update(Graphics g)`	Overridden `Component` method that invokes `paint()` directly to avoid erasing its background
`Dimension getPreferredSize()`	Overridden `Component` method that returns the width and height of the current image in the sprite's sequence
`void setLocation()`	Overridden `Component` method that resets move timer in addition to setting location

Table 25-4 lists the associations of a `Sprite`.

Table 25-4 `Sprite` **Associations**

Variables	Description
`private DoubleBufferedContainer container`	The double buffered container over which the sprite animates
`private Sequence currentSequence`	The sprite's current sequence
`private Sequence mainSequence`	The sprite's main sequence
`private Stopwatch moveTimer`	Timer used to time movements
`private Point startPoint`	The starting location for the sprite
`private Point moveVector`	The direction in which the sprite moves
`private long moveInterval`	Interval, in milliseconds, between movements

Example 25-2 lists the implementation of the `Sprite` class.

Example 25-2 `Sprite Class Listing`

```
import java.awt.*;
import java.util.Vector;

public class Sprite extends Component {
    private DoubleBufferedContainer container;
    private Sequence currentSequence, mainSequence;
    private Stopwatch moveTimer = new Stopwatch();

    private Point startPt     = new Point(0,0);
    private Point moveVector   = new Point(1,1);
    private long  moveInterval = 0;
```

```java
public Sprite(DoubleBufferedContainer container,
    Sequence                sequence,
    Point                   ulhc) {
    this.container = container;
    setSequence         (sequence);
    setMainSequence     (sequence);

    moveTimer.start        ();
    currentSequence.start();

    setLocation(ulhc);
}

public void   reverseX () { moveVector.x = 0-moveVector.x;   }
public void   reverseY () { moveVector.y = 0-moveVector.y;   }
public void   reverse  () { reverseX(); reverseY();          }

public void   setMoveVector (Point p) { moveVector = p;      }
public Point getMoveVector()          { return moveVector;   }

public void paint(Graphics g) {
    if(isVisible()) {
        Image image = currentSequence.getCurrentImage();
        g.drawImage(image, 0, 0, this);
    }
}
public void update(Graphics g) {
    paint(g);
}
/**
 * @deprecated as of JDK1.1
 */
public Dimension preferredSize() {
    Image image = currentSequence.getCurrentImage();
    return new Dimension(image.getWidth(this),
                         image.getHeight(this));
}
public Dimension getPreferredSize() {
    return preferredSize();
}
public void play(Sequence sequence, long cycles) {
    setSequence(sequence);
    sequence.setCyclesPerAnimation(cycles);
    sequence.setCurrentCycle(0);
}
public void animate() {
    if(currentSequence.animationOver())
        currentSequence = mainSequence;

    if(timeToChangeImage()) currentSequence.advance();

    if(timeToMove()) {
```

```
            advance();
      }
      else {
         if(needsRepainting()) {
            container.paintComponent(this);
         }
      }
   }
   public void setMainSequence(Sequence sequence) {
      mainSequence = sequence;
   }
   public Sequence getMainSequence() {
      return mainSequence;
   }
   public void setSequence(Sequence sequence) {
      currentSequence = sequence;
   }
   public Sequence getSequence() {
      return currentSequence;
   }
   public boolean willIntersect(Sprite otherSprite) {
      return getNextBounds().intersects(
            otherSprite.getNextBounds());
   }
   public void setLocation(int x, int y) {
      super.setLocation(x, y);
      moveTimer.reset();
   }
   public void setMoveInterval(long interval) {
      moveInterval = interval;
   }
   public void setImageChangeInterval(long interval) {
      currentSequence.setAdvanceInterval(interval);
   }
   public Point getNextLocation() {
      Rectangle bounds = getBounds();
      return new Point(bounds.x + moveVector.x,
                       bounds.y + moveVector.y);
   }
   public Rectangle getNextBounds() {
      Rectangle bounds = getBounds();
      Point nextLoc     = getNextLocation();
      return new Rectangle(nextLoc.x,    nextLoc.y,
                       bounds.width, bounds.height);
   }
   protected boolean timeToChangeImage() {
      return currentSequence.timeToAdvanceCell();
   }
   protected boolean timeToMove() {
      return moveTimer.elapsedTime() > moveInterval;
   }
   protected boolean needsRepainting() {
```

```
            Rectangle bounds = getBounds();
              return currentSequence.needsRepainting(
                        new Point(bounds.x, bounds.y));
        }
     protected void advance() {
        Rectangle bounds = getBounds();
        container.blitBackgroundToWorkplace(bounds);

        Image image = currentSequence.getCurrentImage();
        setBounds(bounds.x + moveVector.x,
                  bounds.y + moveVector.y,
                  image.getWidth(this), image.getHeight(this));

        container.paintComponents(bounds.union(getBounds()),
                                       true);
        }
     }
```

A `Sprite` must be constructed with a `DoubleBufferedContainer`, a main
Sequence, and a starting location:

```
   public Sprite(DoubleBufferedContainer container,
               Sequence sequence, Point ulhc) {
```

Sprites keep track of their `DoubleBufferedContainer`, main `Sequence`, and
location; by requiring that each of these is supplied at construction time, we leave
nothing to chance.

Notice that a sprite also implements a number of convenience methods. It is able
to reverse its x direction, y direction, or both, and it may have its move vector and
sequence set anytime after construction. Additionally, a sprite can tell whether it
will intersect with another sprite the next time it is moved.

One last thing to note about our implementation of the `Sprite` class is that it
requires that each image in its current sequence be the same size. While this may
seem restrictive, in practice it is usually not a problem; if a sprite is to grow or
shrink, it can always be fitted with a new sequence of images that are larger or
smaller. The only requirement is that each image in the sequence must have the
same size.

Playfield and DoubleBufferedContainer

Of course, a sprite is useless without a `DoubleBufferedContainer` upon
which to frolic, so let's turn our attention to the `Playfield` class and discuss the
animation functionality it provides.

Playfield

A `Playfield` is a double buffered container that adds animation capabilities to the double buffering functionality implemented by the `DoubleBufferedContainer` class. The class diagram for the `Playfield` class is shown in Figure 25-3.

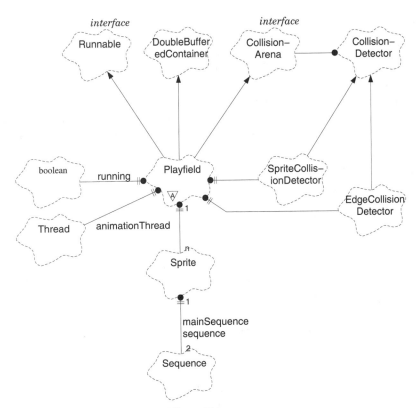

Figure 25-3 `Playfield` Class Diagram

`Playfield` extends `DoubleBufferedContainer`. We've already discussed the implementation of `DoubleBufferedContainer` in "Double Buffering" on page 789, so we won't bother to rehash that discussion here, other than to provide a brief recap of the `DoubleBufferedContainer` class.

DoubleBufferedContainer is a lightweight *container* upon which lightweight *components* can be rendered. DoubleBufferedContainer, as its name implies, employs double buffering to smoothly move lightweight components over its surface.

In any event, a playfield implements functionality specific to animation over and above the double buffering capabilities implemented by its superclass. The Playfield class implements two interfaces:

- Runnable
- CollisionArena

A playfield creates and maintains a thread that is used to animate the sprites that reside in the playfield; thus, it fulfills its obligations as a Runnable. Additionally, a playfield employs two collision detectors: a sprite collision detector and an edge collision detector. As their names suggest, the detectors detect collisions either between two sprites or between a sprite and the boundary of the playfield. The collision detectors merely *detect* collisions—they call back to the playfield to *handle* the collision. We will expound on this relationship more when we discuss collision detection.

Each playfield keeps track of the sprites that are currently animating on it. Because the double buffering functionality is implemented by its superclass, Playfield is a simple class. Table 25-5 lists the responsibilities of the Playfield class.

Table 25-5 Playfield **Responsibilities**

Methods	Description
void spriteCollision(Sprite, Sprite)	A no-op implementation of a CollisionArena method
void edgeCollision(Sprite, Orientation)	A no-op implementation of a CollisionArena method
void start()	Starts the animation
void stop()	Signifies that the animation is to stop
boolean running()	Returns whether the animation is currently running
Vector getSprites()	Returns the sprites in the playfield
void animateSprites()	Animates the sprites in the playfield
void run()	Animation loop

Table 25-6 lists the associations of a Playfield.

Table 25-6 Playfield Associations

Variables	Description
private boolean running	Whether the animation is running
private Thread animationThread	Thread controlling the animation
private CollisionDetector edgeCollisionDetector	Detects collisions between sprites and boundaries of the playfield
private CollisionDetector spriteCollisionDetector	Detects collisions between sprites

The Playfield constructor creates its collision detectors and sets its layout manager to an instance of BulletinLayout,[3] which simply positions components at their current location and shapes them to their preferred size.

```
public Playfield() {
    edgeDetector   = new EdgeCollisionDetector(this);
    spriteDetector = new SpriteCollisionDetector(this);
    setLayout(new BulletinLayout());
}
```

As we'll see when we discuss collision detectors, the CollisionArena interface that is implemented by the Playfield class defines two abstract methods, both of which Playfield implements as no-ops.

```
public void spriteCollision(Sprite sprite, Sprite other) { }
public void edgeCollision  (Sprite sprite, Orientation o){ }
```

By default then, the Playfield class takes no action when a collision occurs. Extensions of Playfield may override the methods in order to handle collisions if they so desire.

Playfield has both a start and a stop method, which start and stop the animation, respectively, along with a running method that can be used to determine if the animation is currently running. The start method creates a thread whose constructor is passed a reference to the Playfield so that Playfield. run() is invoked when the thread is started.[4]

```
public void start() {
    animationThread = new Thread(this);
    running = true;
    animationThread.start();
}
public void     stop   () { running = false;  }
public boolean running()  { return running;   }
```

---

3.   See "BulletinLayout" on page 400.
4.   A number of Java language books discuss threads in more detail.

The implementation of the `stop` method may seem odd, since it merely sets a `boolean` variable (`running`) to `false` and does nothing else. In reality, it does not stop anything. However, the `run` method runs as long as the `running` member is `true`; this state is checked at the top of the `run` method's `while` loop. If `running` has been set to `false`, `run()` returns after setting `animationThread` to `null`. This seemingly roundabout way of stopping the animation thread ensures that the thread is not stopped in the middle of painting one of the playfield's sprites.

Let's take a closer look at the `run` method to see exactly what it is that keeps a `Playfield` busy until someone calls the `stop` method:

```
public void run() {
    while(running == true) {
        edgeDetector.detectCollisions  ();
        spriteDetector.detectCollisions();

        animateSprites();

        try { Thread.currentThread().sleep(50); }
        catch(Exception e) { e.printStackTrace(); }
    }
    animationThread = null;
}
```

First, each of the `Playfield` collision detectors is told to detect collisions. If a collision is detected, the detectors invoke either `Playfield.spriteCollision()` or `Playfield.edgeCollision()`, depending upon the type of collision that was detected. Next, the playfield animates the sprites and then invokes `sleep(50)` on the current thread to give other processes some breathing room. (After all, when the boss walks by while you're playing the hottest new Internet game, a `Playfield` must be able to quickly allow someone else to take over the display.)

`Playfield.animateSprites()` runs through each `Component` contained in the playfield,[5] and, if the component is a sprite, invokes the sprite's `animate` method:

```
protected void animateSprites() {
    int           ncomps = getComponentCount();
    Component     comp;

    for(int i=0; i < ncomps; ++i)
        if((comp = getComponent(i)) instanceof Sprite)
            ((Sprite)comp).animate();
}
```

5. `Playfield` ultimately extends `java.awt.Container`.

That's about all there is to the Playfield class. The entire implementation of the Playfield class is listed in Example 25-3.

Example 25-3 Playfield Class Listing

```java
import java.awt.*;
import java.util.*;

public class Playfield extends DoubleBufferedContainer
                    implements Runnable,
                                CollisionArena {
    private    boolean running = false;
    private    Thread  animationThread;
    private    CollisionDetector spriteDetector, edgeDetector;

    public Playfield() {
        edgeDetector    = new EdgeCollisionDetector(this);
        spriteDetector = new SpriteCollisionDetector(this);
        setLayout(new BulletinLayout());
    }
    public void spriteCollision(Sprite sprite, Sprite other) { }
    public void edgeCollision  (Sprite sprite, Orientation o){ }

    public void    stop    ()  { running = false;  }
    public boolean running()   { return running;   }

    public void start() {
        animationThread = new Thread(this);
        running = true;
        animationThread.start();
    }
    public void run() {
        while(running == true) {
            edgeDetector.detectCollisions  ();
            spriteDetector.detectCollisions();

            animateSprites();
            try { Thread.currentThread().sleep(50); }
            catch(Exception e) { e.printStackTrace(); }
        }
        animationThread = null;
    }
    public Vector getSprites() {
        int         ncomps = getComponentCount();
        Component   comp;
        Vector      vector = new Vector();

        for(int i=0; i < ncomps; ++i) {
            if((comp = getComponent(i)) instanceof Sprite)
                vector.addElement(comp);
        }
        return vector;
```

```
        }
        protected void animateSprites() {
            int         ncomps = getComponentCount();
            Component   comp;

            for(int i=0; i < ncomps; ++i)
                if((comp = getComponent(i)) instanceof Sprite)
                    ((Sprite)comp).animate();
        }
    }
```

Collision Detection

Now that we've covered the `Sequence`, `Sprite`, and `Playfield` classes, the
only topic left to discuss is collision detection. Collision detection is defined by an
interface and an abstract class: `CollisionArena` and `CollisionDetector`,
respectively. As we discuss collision detection, don't forget that `Playfield`
implements `CollisionArena`, so everything discussed concerning
`CollisionArena` goes for `Playfield`.

CollisionArena

The `CollisionArena` interface defines the behavior of an arena in which
collisions take place, as you can see in Example 25-4.

Example 25-4 `CollisionArena` Interface Listing

```
    import java.awt.Dimension;
    import java.awt.Insets;
    import java.util.Vector;

    public interface CollisionArena {
        Vector      getSprites();
        Dimension getSize    ();
        Insets      getInsets();

        void        spriteCollision(Sprite sprite, Sprite other);
        void        edgeCollision(Sprite sprite, Orientation orient);
    }
```

A `CollisionArena` is responsible for producing a `Vector` of sprites that it
contains, reporting the size and insets of the collision arena, and handling
collisions between two `Sprite` objects and between a `Sprite` and a boundary.
Notice that the `CollisionArena` is not responsible for actually *detecting*
collisions but is responsible for handling the aftermath of a collision by
implementing `spriteCollision()` and `edgeCollision()`.

CollisionDetector

The abstract `CollisionDetector` class establishes the relationship between itself and a `CollisionArena` but leaves the actual collision detection to extensions, as illustrated in Example 25-5.

Example 25-5 CollisionDetector Class Listing

```
abstract public class CollisionDetector {
    protected CollisionArena arena;

    abstract public void detectCollisions();

    public CollisionDetector(CollisionArena arena) {
        this.arena = arena;
    }
}
```

A `CollisionDetector` must be constructed with a reference to a `CollisionArena`. Remember that a `CollisionArena` is responsible for handling the aftermath of a collision, whereas a `CollisionDetector` is only responsible for detecting collisions.

SpriteCollisionDetector

`CollisionDetector` has two subclasses that do the grunt work of actually detecting collisions: `SpriteCollisionDetector` and `EdgeCollisionDetector`. Let's first look at `SpriteCollisionDetector` in Example 25-6, which detects collisions between sprites.

Example 25-6 SpriteCollisionDetector Class Listing

```
import java.awt.*;
import java.util.Enumeration;
import java.util.Vector;

public class SpriteCollisionDetector extends CollisionDetector {
    public SpriteCollisionDetector(CollisionArena arena) {
        super(arena);
    }
    public void detectCollisions() {
        Enumeration sprites = arena.getSprites().elements();
        Sprite      sprite;

        while(sprites.hasMoreElements()) {
            sprite = (Sprite)sprites.nextElement();

            Enumeration otherSprites =
                        arena.getSprites().elements();
            Sprite otherSprite;
```

```
        while(otherSprites.hasMoreElements()) {
            otherSprite=(Sprite)otherSprites.nextElement();

            if(otherSprite != sprite)
                if(sprite.willIntersect(otherSprite))
                    arena.spriteCollision(sprite,otherSprite);
        }
    }
}
}
```

Simply put, SpriteCollisionDetector gets all of the sprites from its associated CollisionArena and cycles through each one to see if it will intersect with any of the other sprites the next time they are moved. If so, SpriteCollisionDetector invokes its collision arena's spriteCollision method, passing along the sprites involved in the collision.

EdgeCollision

EdgeCollisionDetector in Example 25-7 detects collisions between a sprite and the boundaries of its collision arena.

Example 25-7 EdgeCollisionDetector Class Listing

```java
import java.awt.*;
import java.util.Enumeration;
import java.util.Vector;

public class EdgeCollisionDetector extends CollisionDetector {
    public EdgeCollisionDetector(CollisionArena arena) {
        super(arena);
    }
    public void detectCollisions() {
        Enumeration sprites    = arena.getSprites().elements();
        Dimension   arenaSize   = arena.getSize();
        Insets      arenaInsets = arena.getInsets();
        Sprite      sprite;

        while(sprites.hasMoreElements()) {
            sprite = (Sprite)sprites.nextElement();

            Point nl      = sprite.getNextLocation ();
            Point mv      = sprite.getMoveVector();
            int   width   = sprite.getBounds().width;
            int   height  = sprite.getBounds().height;
            int   nextRightEdge   = nl.x + width;
            int   nextBottomEdge  = nl.y + height;
            int   arenaBottomEdge = arenaSize.height -
                                    arenaInsets.bottom;
            int   arenaRightEdge  = arenaSize.width -
                                    arenaInsets.right;
```

```
            if(nextRightEdge > arenaRightEdge)
                arena.edgeCollision(sprite, Orientation.LEFT);
            else if(nl.x < arenaInsets.left)
            arena.edgeCollision(sprite, Orientation.RIGHT);

            if(nextBottomEdge > arenaBottomEdge)
                arena.edgeCollision(sprite, Orientation.BOTTOM);
            else if(nl.y < arenaInsets.top)
                arena.edgeCollision(sprite, Orientation.TOP);
        }
    }
}
```

Note that when a sprite collides with the boundary of the collision arena, it is not enough to simply state that a particular sprite ran into a boundary. We must also tell the collision arena which edge of the sprite collided with the boundary. This is the reason for the orientation argument in the arena's edgeCollision method.

We've now covered the details of the Sprite, Playfield, and Sequence classes and collision detection and double buffering; it's time to have a little fun and take a look at the applet for the animation package.

Exercising the Animation Package

When animations are created with the animation package, Playfield is typically extended and spriteCollision() and edgeCollision() are overridden in order to handle sprite-on-sprite and sprite-boundary collisions, respectively. The only other coding necessary is to create the sprites and their associated sequences, define the sprites initial location and move vector, and add them to the playfield.

Simple Animation

To start off, we'll look at a simple animation applet that you can use as a starting point for your own animations. Our simple animation has one instance of Sprite that bounces off the walls of the Playfield. Figure 25-4 shows the applet, but of course, you can see the full animation by running the applet included on the CD yourself. Simply run appletviewer on the SimpleAnimationTest.html file.

As you look through the animation applet in Example 25-8, notice that SimpleAnimationTestPanel centers a SimplePlayfield instance; once that is done, all that is left is to implement SimplePlayfield.

SimplePlayfield.edgeCollisions() is implemented such that our sprite bounces off the walls of the Playfield. If the orientation of the collision is right or left, then we know the sprite has bumped into a vertical wall, and we reverse

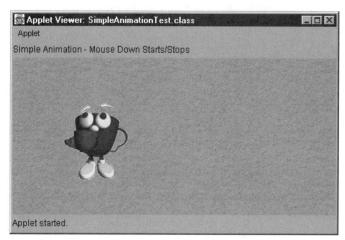

Figure 25-4 Simple Animation Applet
This sprite moves on the playfield and bumps off the walls.

its x direction. If the orientation is anything else (top or bottom), then we know the sprite has collided with the floor or ceiling of the `Playfield`, and we reverse its y direction.

`makeSequencesAndSprites()` first loads the 19 images used in the `Sprite` object's main sequence and then creates a sequence from the images loaded. Next, it creates the sprite itself (`javaDrinker`), passing a reference to the `Playfield`, the main sequence, and the starting location for `javaDrinker`. We set the move vector to (2,2), meaning the `Sprite` will move 2 pixels in the x direction and 2 pixels in the y direction every time it moves. Lastly, we add the `Sprite` to the `Playfield`. Figure 25-5 depicts the layout for all three of the sprite animation applets.

Now let's look at the applet, which is listed in Example 25-8.

 Example 25-8 SimpleAnimationTest Class Listing

```
import java.net.URL;
import java.applet.Applet;
import java.awt.*;
import java.awt.event.*;

public class SimpleAnimationTest extends Applet {
    public void init() {
        setLayout(new BorderLayout());
        add(
```

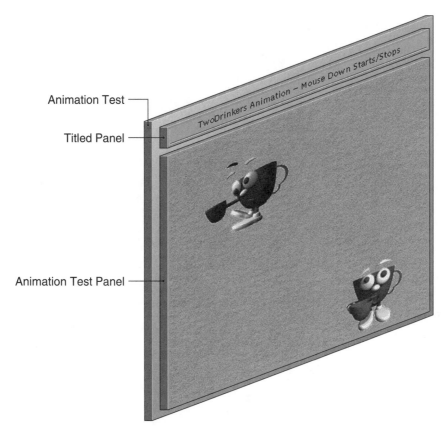

Animation Test

Titled Panel

Animation Test Panel

Figure 25-5 Sprite Animation Applets Layout.

```
        new Label("Simple Animation - Mouse Down Starts/Stops"),
        "North");
        add(new SimpleAnimationTestPanel(this), "Center");
    }
}
class SimpleAnimationTestPanel extends Panel {
    public SimpleAnimationTestPanel(Applet applet) {
        setLayout(new BorderLayout());
        add(new SimplePlayfield(applet), "Center");
    }
    public void update(Graphics g) {
        paint(g);
    }
}
class SimplePlayfield extends Playfield {
    private Applet    applet;
    private URL       cb;
```

```
        private Sprite   javaDrinker;
        private Sequence spinSequence;

        public SimplePlayfield(Applet applet) {
           this.applet = applet;
           cb = applet.getCodeBase();

           makeSequencesAndSprites();

           setWallpaperImage(
                 applet.getImage(cb, "gifs/background.gif"));

           addMouseListener(new MouseAdapter() {
              public void mousePressed(MouseEvent event) {
                 if(running() == true) stop ();
                 else                  start();
              }
           });
        }
     public void edgeCollision(Sprite sprite,
                        Orientation orientation) {
        if(orientation == Orientation.RIGHT ||
                     orientation == Orientation.LEFT)
           sprite.reverseX();
        else
           sprite.reverseY();
     }
     private void makeSequencesAndSprites() {
        String  file;
        Point   startLoc   = new Point(10, 10);
        Image[] spinImages = new Image[19];

        for(int i=0; i < spinImages.length; ++i) {
           file = "gifs/spin";

           if(i < 10) file += "0" + i + ".gif";
           else       file += i + ".gif";

           spinImages[i] = applet.getImage(cb, file);
        }
        spinSequence = new Sequence(this, spinImages);
        javaDrinker  = new Sprite(this, spinSequence, startLoc);

        javaDrinker.setMoveVector(new Point(1,1));
        add(javaDrinker);
        }
     }
```

Notice that SimplePlayfield implements an animation that can be stopped
and started with a mouse down, complete with collision detection, in a mere 50
lines of code. All that was necessary on our part was to:

1. Subclass `Playfield` in order to handle collisions.
2. Set the wallpaper image for painting the background.
3. Create the sprites and their associated sequences.
4. Add the sprites to the playfield.

Bump Animation

Now, let's add some more behavior to our `javaDrinker` when he bumps into the boundaries of the `Playfield`. We will create another sequence that `javaDrinker` will play when he bumps into a wall. Just to make things a little more interesting, we will have our `javaDrinker` cycle through the *bump* sequence once for collisions with the left wall and twice for collisions with the right wall. We will also slow down the rate at which `javaDrinker` cycles through its images. You can see a picture of the bump sequence in Figure 25-6.

Figure 25-6 Bump Animation Applet
This sprite goes through a bump sequence after bumping into a wall.

Our applet in Example 25-9 looks exactly the same as the one in Example 25-8 on page 834, except the names of the classes have changed. In `BumpPlayfield`, we create a second sequence, `bumpSequence`, and set the advance interval for the spin sequence to 100 milliseconds and the advance interval for the bump sequence to 200 milliseconds.

The edgeCollision method has also been modified so that a bump into the right or left walls causes javaDrinker to play the bump sequence the appropriate number of times. When the orientation is RIGHT, the right side of the sprite has collided with a playfield boundary, meaning our javaDrinker has run into the left wall.

Example 25-9 BumpAnimationTest Class Listing

```
import java.net.URL;
import java.applet.Applet;
import java.awt.*;
import java.awt.event.*;

public class BumpAnimationTest extends Applet {
    public void init() {
        setLayout(new BorderLayout());
        add(
        new Label("Bump Animation - Mouse Down Starts/Stops"),
        "North");

        add(new BumpAnimationTestPanel(this), "Center");
    }
}

class BumpAnimationTestPanel extends Panel {
    public BumpAnimationTestPanel(Applet applet) {
        setLayout(new BorderLayout());
        add(new BumpPlayfield(applet), "Center");
    }
    public void update(Graphics g) {
        paint(g);
    }
}

class BumpPlayfield extends Playfield {
    private Applet    applet;
    private URL       cb;
    private Sprite    javaDrinker;
    private Sequence  spinSequence, bumpSequence;

    public BumpPlayfield(Applet applet) {
        this.applet = applet;
        cb          = applet.getCodeBase();

        makeSequencesAndSprites();
        setWallpaperImage(
            applet.getImage(cb, "gifs/background.gif"));

        addMouseListener(new MouseAdapter() {
        public void mousePressed(MouseEvent event) {
          if(running() == true) stop ();
```

```
            else                 start();
        }
    });
}
public void edgeCollision(Sprite     sprite,
                          Orientation orientation) {
    if(orientation == Orientation.RIGHT ||
       orientation == Orientation.LEFT) {
        if(sprite.getSequence() != bumpSequence) {
            sprite.reverseX();

            if(orientation == Orientation.RIGHT)
                sprite.play(bumpSequence, 1);
            else
                sprite.play(bumpSequence, 2);
        }
    }
    else
        sprite.reverseY();
}
private void makeSequencesAndSprites() {
    String  file;
    Point   startLoc   = new Point(10, 10);
    Image[] spinImages = new Image[19];
    Image[] bumpImages = new Image[6];

    for(int i=0; i < spinImages.length; ++i) {
        file = "gifs/spin";

        if(i < 10) file += "0" + i + ".gif";
        else       file += i + ".gif";

        spinImages[i] = applet.getImage(cb, file);
    }
    for(int i=0; i < bumpImages.length; ++i) {
        file = "gifs/bump0" + i + ".gif";
        bumpImages[i] = applet.getImage(cb, file);
    }
    spinSequence = new Sequence(this, spinImages);
    bumpSequence = new Sequence(this, bumpImages);
    javaDrinker  = new Sprite(this, spinSequence, startLoc);

    spinSequence.setAdvanceInterval(100);
    bumpSequence.setAdvanceInterval(200);

    javaDrinker.setMoveVector(new Point(1,1));
    javaDrinker.setImageChangeInterval(50);
    add(javaDrinker);
    }
}
```

Now, let's look at one final applet that illustrates sprite-on-sprite collisions.

Two-Sprite Collision

The next applet adds another `javaDrinker` to the `Playfield`. We'll have one of the `javaDrinker` objects spin fast and move slow, while the other will spin slow and move fast. We will also create two bump sequences, one fast and the other slow. When the two `javaDrinker` objects collide, we'll have one of them play the slow bump sequence and the other the fast bump sequence. You can see the applet in action in Figure 25-7.

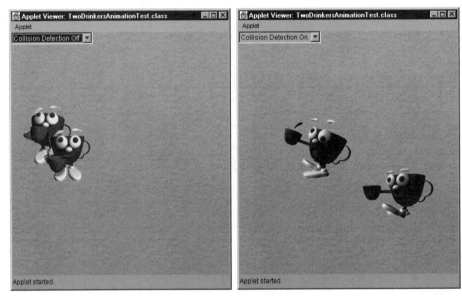

Figure 25-7 Two-Sprite Collision Animation Applet
The sprites each go through their individual bump sequences when they collide if collision detection is turned on, and pass over each other when it is turned off.

We've added one additional twist to our applet—we've added a choice that toggles collision detection on and off. Since `Playfield` extends `DoubleBufferedContainer`, and `DoubleBufferedContainer` extends `java.awt.Container`, we can add AWT components to a playfield, as well as sprites.

When collision detection is turned off, the sprites move over each other. Since sprites are components, the sprite that is on top is the sprite that has the highest zorder, or the sprite that was added to the container first. See "Components and Zorder" on page 445 for more on components and zorder.

Example 25-10 lists the applet. It is identical to the previous animation tests, except that this one creates a `TwoDrinkersPlayfield`. This time around, we will just show you the code without any accompanying commentary; it should be apparent what we're up to with the `TwoDrinkersPlayfield`.

Example 25-10 TwoDrinkersAnimationTest Class Listing

```java
import java.net.URL;
import java.applet.Applet;
import java.awt.*;
import java.awt.event.*;
import java.awt.Panel;

public class TwoDrinkersAnimationTest extends Applet {
    public void init() {
        setLayout(new BorderLayout());
        add(new Label(
        "TwoDrinkers Animation - Mouse Down Starts/Stops"));
        add(new TwoDrinkersAnimationTestPanel(this));
    }
}
class TwoDrinkersAnimationTestPanel extends Panel {
    public TwoDrinkersAnimationTestPanel(Applet applet) {
        setLayout(new BorderLayout());
        add(new TwoDrinkersPlayfield(applet), "Center");
    }
    public void update(Graphics g) {
        paint(g);
    }
}
class TwoDrinkersPlayfield extends Playfield
                            implements ItemListener {
    private Applet    applet;
    private Choice    collisionChoice;
    private boolean   collisionsEnabled = true;
    private URL       cb;
    private Sprite    moveFastSpinSlow, moveSlowSpinFast;
    private Sequence  fastSpinSequence,
                      slowSpinSequence,
                      fastBumpSequence,
                      slowBumpSequence;

    public TwoDrinkersPlayfield(Applet applet) {
        this.applet = applet;
        cb          = applet.getCodeBase();
        makeSequencesAndSprites();
        add(collisionChoice = new Choice());
        collisionChoice.add("Collision Detection On");
```

```java
        collisionChoice.add("Collision Detection Off");

        collisionChoice.addItemListener(this);

        addMouseListener(new MouseAdapter() {
            public void mousePressed (MouseEvent event) {
                if(running() == true) stop ();
                else                  start();
            }
        });
    }
    public void paintBackground(Graphics g) {
        Image bg = applet.getImage(cb, "gifs/background.gif");
        Util.wallPaper(this, g, bg);
    }
    public void itemStateChanged(ItemEvent event) {
        if(event.getSource() == collisionChoice) {
            if(collisionChoice.getSelectedIndex() == 0) {
                collisionsEnabled = true;
            }
            else {
                collisionsEnabled = false;
            }
        }
    }
    public void spriteCollision(Sprite sprite, Sprite sprite2) {
        if(collisionsEnabled) {
            if(moveSlowSpinFast.getSequence() !=
                    fastBumpSequence) {
                sprite.reverse();
                sprite2.reverse();

                moveSlowSpinFast.play(fastBumpSequence, 3);
                moveFastSpinSlow.play(slowBumpSequence, 3);
            }
        }
    }
    public void edgeCollision(Sprite      sprite,
                              Orientation orientation) {
        if(orientation == Orientation.RIGHT ||
           orientation == Orientation.LEFT)
            sprite.reverseX();
        else
            sprite.reverseY();
    }
    private void makeSequencesAndSprites() {
        String  file;
        Image[] spinImages = new Image[19];
        Image[] bumpImages = new Image[6];
        Image[] volleyball = new Image[4];

        for(int i=0; i < spinImages.length; ++i) {
```

```
        file = "gifs/spin";

        if(i < 10) file += "0" + i + ".gif";
        else       file += i + ".gif";

        spinImages[i] = applet.getImage(cb, file);
    }
    for(int i=0; i < bumpImages.length; ++i) {
        file = "gifs/bump0" + i + ".gif";
        bumpImages[i] = applet.getImage(cb, file);
    }
    fastSpinSequence = new Sequence(this, spinImages);
    slowSpinSequence = new Sequence(this, spinImages);

    fastBumpSequence = new Sequence(this, bumpImages);
    slowBumpSequence = new Sequence(this, bumpImages);

    moveFastSpinSlow =
        new Sprite(this,
            slowSpinSequence, new Point(25, 75));

    moveSlowSpinFast =
        new Sprite(this,
            fastSpinSequence, new Point(250,250));

    fastSpinSequence.setAdvanceInterval(50);
    slowSpinSequence.setAdvanceInterval(300);

    fastBumpSequence.setAdvanceInterval(25);
    slowBumpSequence.setAdvanceInterval(200);

    moveFastSpinSlow.setMoveVector(new Point(2,3));
    moveSlowSpinFast.setMoveVector(new Point(-1,-1));

    moveSlowSpinFast.setMoveInterval(100);

    add(moveFastSpinSlow);
    add(moveSlowSpinFast);
  }
}
```

Summary

By introducing the animation package, we have covered a number of animation-related topics, such as creating sprites, playfields, and animation sequences.

After exploring a number of animation applets in this chapter, it should be apparent how to go about creating your own animations. The first applet, "SimpleAnimationTest Class Listing" on page 834, is simple enough that it should be a good starting point for developing your own animations.

APPENDIX

A

AWT Class Diagrams

Imagine a world where architects write volumes of prose describing their buildings instead of drawing blueprints. While such a scenario would certainly be absurd, many software engineers are quick to eschew the software developer's equivalent of blueprints: the class diagram.

Class diagrams are to software development what blueprints are to the world of architecture. Class diagrams are essential for succinctly communicating one's design to others, and *Graphic Java* uses class diagrams extensively for documenting the classes from the Graphic Java Toolkit and the Abstract Window Toolkit.

The class diagrams throughout *Graphic Java* are of the *Booch* variety.[1] For those of you unfamiliar with Booch diagrams, we show a legend on the next page and then discuss a simple, yet fairly complete class diagram.

---

1.   See Booch, Grady. *Object-Oriented Analysis And Design.* Benjamin/Cummings.

Legend

The following is a legend of the elements used in our class diagrams.

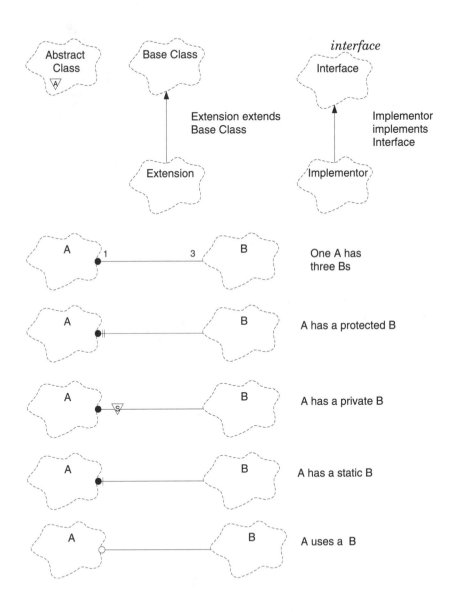

A Look at an Example Class Diagram

The class diagram below is for the `java.awt.Component` class.

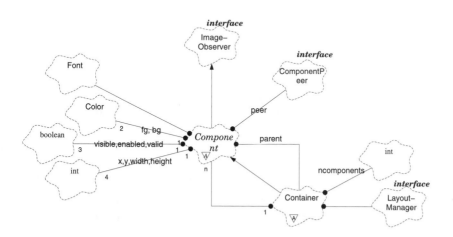

`Container` extends `Component`. Both `Container` and `Component` are abstract classes, meaning they have either declared or inherited abstract methods that they have not implemented. `Component`, on the other hand, implements the `ImageObserver` interface[2] and maintains an association with a `ComponentPeer`. Each `Component` has:

- Four `integer` values, named `x`, `y`, `width`, and `height`
- Three `boolean` values, named `visible`, `enabled`, and `valid`
- Two colors, `fg` and `bg`, and one `Font`

Note that the relationship between `Component` and `Font` is not labeled—we do not label relationships unless the name of the object adds some value. We chose to label the `int`, `boolean`, and `Color` relationships because the roles of those particular objects are not apparent without a label. Also note that `int` and `boolean` are not really objects; they are intrinsic types. We denote intrinsic types by changing the font of their "class" names.

One `Container` has potentially many `Components`. A `Container` also maintains a relationship with a `LayoutManager` and keeps track of the number of components it currently contains with an `integer` named `ncomponents`.

---

2. We denote interfaces by adorning them with an "interface" label. There is currently no notation in the Booch method for depicting interfaces.

APPENDIX
B

The Graphic Java CD-ROM

The *Graphic Java* CD was mastered to support a standard ISO 9660 file system with both RockRidge (for UNIX) and Joliet (for Windows 95) extensions. All of the files should be readable on any system with a CD-ROM drive that supports these specifications.

As we went to press, the JDK 1.2 was not yet available for the Macintosh. When the 1.2 version of the JDK is available for the Macintosh, the code examples on the CD should work without modification on the Macintosh.

There are two directories on the CD: Source Code and JDK. The Source Code directory contains the source code from the book. The code can be used without modification on UNIX and Windows systems that support JDK 1.1 or JDK 1.2. See Running the Code Examples below for more information. The JDK directory contains the most current version of the Java Development Kit (JDK) that was available at press time. The Solaris subdirectory contains a .sh file named jdk12-beta4-solaris2-sparc.sh (17,711,491 bytes) that you can copy onto any Sparc-based Solaris system following the instructions below. The Windows subdirectory contains a file named jdk12-beta4-win32.exe (16,630,031 bytes) that you can install on any Windows 95 or Windows NT system following the instructions below. You should check the JavaSoft website at http://java.sun.com for a more up-to-date version of the JDK or for more detailed installation instructions.

Installing the JDK on Windows 95 and Windows NT

The JDK installation file provided on the CD-ROM and the instructions below are based on what was available when this book went to press in August 1998. The JDK is subject to the License Agreement reprinted on page 879. Please read the License Agreement before proceeding.

The installation and configuration process can be broken down into the following steps:

- Run the JDK installer
- Update PATH and CLASSPATH variables
- Run the JDK tools

If you experience trouble along the way, check the Troubleshooting the Installation section below.

1. Run the JDK installer

The JDK software file (jdk12-beta4-win32.exe) and the JDK documentation file (available for download from the JDK download page) should be unpacked in the same directory. Unpacking them in the same directory ensures that HTML links in the JDK documentation and demo files will work properly.

You can install the software file and the documentation file in any order. If you've already installed the JDK documentation, however, you must unpack the JDK software file in the same directory.

To run the JDK installer, double-click on the icon of the file jdk12-beta4-win32.exe. This launches an install program that will guide you through the process of installing the JDK. Follow the onscreen instructions provided. When the installation is complete, you can delete the jdk12-beta4-win32.exe file to recover disk space.

2. Update PATH and CLASSPATH Variables

Note: **Windows NT only** — If you are using Windows NT, it is preferable to make the following environment variable changes in the Control Panel instead of in AUTOEXEC.BAT. Start the Control Panel, select System, then edit the environment variables.

Updating the PATH Variable

Set the PATH variable if you want to be able to run the executables (javac.exe, java.exe, javadoc.exe, etc.) from any directory. If you don't set the PATH variable, you need to specify the PATH to the executable when running it. The PATH variable is merely a convenience; setting it is not a requirement.

To find out the current value of your PATH, at the DOS prompt type:

C:\> **path**

To change the PATH permanently, open the AUTOEXEC.BAT file and make the change to the PATH statement. To edit the AUTOEXEC.BAT file in Windows 95:

1. Start a text editor by choosing "Start", "Programs", "Accessories", and choosing WordPad or NotePad.

2. Choose Open from the File menu and type **c:\autoexec.bat** for the filename. This will open the file for editing.

3. Look for the PATH statement. Notice that the PATH statement is a series of directories separated by semi-colons (;). Windows looks for programs in the PATH directories in order, from left to right. Look for other JDK versions in the PATH. There should only be one PATH to a classes.zip file. When in doubt, put the java directory at the end of the PATH statement. (Note: To make the PATH take effect, restart your system.)

Setting the CLASSPATH Environment Variable

Note: If you followed the default installation for the JDK, you do not need to set CLASSPATH, because the tools automatically look in the lib directory if it is next to the bin directory.

If CLASSPATH is set and you want to unset it, you typically need to change the current value (at the command line) and the startup value (in a startup file or script). For example, to see if it is currently set, type:

C:\> **set**

This lists all of the environment variables. CLASSPATH will not appear if it is not set. If it is set, you can unset the current value by setting it to no value:

C:\> **set CLASSPATH=**

Also open your startup file (AUTOEXEC.BAT) or script and remove the PATH to the JDK classes from the CLASSPATH environment variable, if you want the change to be permanent.

3. Run the JDK Tools

Your computer system should now be configured and ready to use the Java Development Kit. You start a tool by typing its name into the DOS window with a filename as an argument. None of the Java tools are Windows programs with GUI interfaces—they are all run from the DOS command line. You can't run a JDK tool by double-clicking its icon.

You can specify the PATH to a tool either by typing the PATH in front of the tool each time, or by adding the PATH to the startup file (AUTOEXEC.BAT). For example, if the JDK is installed at C:\jdk1.2beta4, to run the compiler on a file named myfile.java, go to a DOS shell and type the following:

```
C:\jdk1.2beta4\bin\javac myfile.java
```

If you added C:\jdk1.2beta4\bin to your PATH statement, at the command line you simply type:

```
javac myfile.java
```

Assuming you have already set your PATH (as described above), you can also, for example, run the AppletViewer with an html file containing an embedded applet by changing to the proper directory and executing the following command:

```
C:\JDK1.2BETA2\DEMO\APPLETS\TICTACTOE> appletviewer
example1.html
```

Troubleshooting the Installation

If you see the following error message:

```
net.socketException: errno = 10047
```

or

```
Unsupported version of Windows Socket API
```

check which TCP/IP drivers you have installed on your system. The AppletViewer supports only the Microsoft TCP/IP drivers included with Windows 95. If you are using third-party drivers (e.g., Trumpet Winsock), you'll need to change over to the native Microsoft TCP/IP drivers if you want to load applets over the network.

If the AppletViewer does not load applets then you might try the following:

1. set HOMEDRIVE=c:
set HOMEPATH=\
and restart the AppletViewer (in the same DOS window)

2. set HOME=c:\
and restart the AppletViewer (in the same DOS box)

If none of these work, try:

```
java -verbose sun.applet.AppletViewer
```

This lists the classes that are being loaded. From this output, you can determine which class the AppletViewer is trying to load and where it's trying to load it from. Check to make sure that the class exists and is not corrupted in some way.

Installing the JDK on Solaris

The installation and configuration process can be broken down into the following steps:

- Unpack the .sh file (jdk12-beta4-solaris2-sparc.sh)
- Update PATH and environment variables
- Start using the JDK!

1.   Unpack the .sh File

The JDK software file and the JDK documentation file (available for download from the JDK download page) should be unpacked in the same directory. Unpacking them in the same directory ensures that links between HTML files will work properly.

You can install the software file and the documentation file in any order. If you've already installed the JDK documentation, you must unpack the JDK software file in the same directory from which you unpacked the documentation. For example, if you installed the JDK software at /usr/local/, then you should place the downloaded JDK software file in /usr/local/ before proceeding.

In a shell window, execute the commands given below.

For SPARC (must be unpacked on a SPARC machine running Solaris 2.4 or greater):

```
% chmod a+x jdk12-beta4-solaris2-sparc.sh
% ./jdk12-beta4-solaris2-sparc.sh
```

2.   Update PATH and Environment Variables

PATH Variable

Set the PATH variable if you want to be able to run the executables (javac, java, javadoc, etc.) from any directory. If you don't set the PATH variable, you need to specify the PATH to the executable when running it. The PATH variable is merely a convenience to the developer and not necessary to set.

a.   To find out if the PATH is currently set for any java tools, execute:

```
% which java
```

This will print the PATH to the java tool, if it can find it.

b.   To set the PATH permanently, set the PATH in your startup file. For example, if you use the C shell (csh), you can set the PATH in your startup file (~/.cshrc) as follows:

```
set path=($path /usr/local/jdk1.2beta4/bin)
```

c.   Then load the startup file and verify that the PATH is set by repeating the "which" command above:

```
% source ~/.cshrc
% which java
```

CLASSPATH Environment Variable

If you follow the default installation, you do not need to set CLASSPATH, because the shell scripts automatically set it for you. If your CLASSPATH is currently not set, you can skip this step.

Testing and Unsetting CLASSPATH

If you have previously set the CLASSPATH variable and want to unset it, you normally need to change the current value (at the command line) and the startup value (in your startup file or script). To see if it is currently set, type:

```
% echo $CLASSPATH
```

If it is set, you can unset the current value by typing:

```
% unsetenv CLASSPATH
```

Also open your startup file (~/.cshrc) or script and remove the PATH to the JDK classes from the CLASSPATH environment variable if you want the change to be permanent.

3.   Start Using the JDK!

Your computer system should now be configured and ready to use the Java Development Kit. You start a tool by typing its name at a shell window command line, with a filename as an argument. If you didn't set the PATH variable to point to the tools in step 2, you must specify the PATH to a tool by typing the PATH in front of the tool.

Running the Code Examples

The directory structure for the source code is depicted in Figure B-1. The source code is contained in directories corresponding to the parts and chapters of the book. For example, image manipulation is discussed in Part II, and therefore the source code for the image manipulation chapter can be found in the partTwo/images directory.

The simplest way to run the source code examples from the book is to copy the contents of the CD to your hard disk and go to the directory that contains the code you are interested in. You should ensure that the current directory (typically specified with '.') is included in your CLASSPATH.

Figure B-1 *Graphic Java* CD Source Code Directory Structure

Index

Java™ Development Kit Version 1.1.6 Binary Code License

This binary code license ("License") contains rights and restrictions associated with use of the accompanying software and documentation ("Software"). Read the License carefully before installing the Software. By installing the Software you agree to the terms and conditions of this License.

1. Limited License Grant. Sun grants to you ("Licensee") a non-exclusive, nontransferable limited license to use the Software without fee for evaluation of the Software and for development of Java(tm) compatible applets and applications. Licensee may make one archival copy of the Software and may re-distribute complete, unmodified copies of the Software to software developers within Licensee's organization to avoid unnecessary download time, provided that this License conspicuously appear with all copies of the Software. Except for the foregoing, Licensee may not re-distribute the Software in whole or in part, either separately or included with a product. Refer to the Java Runtime Environment Version 1.1.6 binary code license (http://java.sun.com/products/JDK/1.1/index.html) for the availability of runtime code which may be distributed with Java compatible applets and applications.

2. Java Platform Interface. Licensee may not modify the Java Platform Interface ("JPI", identified as classes contained within the "java" package or any subpackages of the "java" package), by creating additional classes within the JPI or otherwise causing the addition to or modification of the classes in the JPI. In the event that Licensee creates any Java-related API and distributes such API to others for applet or application development, Licensee must promptly publish an accurate specification for such API for free use by all developers of Java-based software.

3. Restrictions. Software is confidential copyrighted information of Sun and title to all copies is retained by Sun and/or its licensors. Licensee shall not modify, decompile, disassemble, decrypt, extract, or otherwise reverse engineer Software. Software may not be leased, assigned, or sublicensed, in whole or in part. Software is not designed or intended for use in on-line control of aircraft, air traffic, aircraft navigation or aircraft communications; or in the design, construction, operation or maintenance of any nuclear facility. Licensee warrants that it will not use or redistribute the Software for such purposes.

4. Trademarks and Logos. This License does not authorize Licensee to use any Sun name, trademark or logo. Licensee acknowledges that Sun owns the Java trademark and all Java-related trademarks, logos and icons including the Coffee Cup and Duke ("Java Marks") and agrees to: (i) to comply with the Java Trademark Guidelines at http://java.sun.com/trademarks.html; (ii) not do anything harmful to or inconsistent with Sun's rights in the Java Marks; and (iii) assist Sun in protecting those rights, including assigning to Sun any rights acquired by Licensee in any Java Mark.

5. Disclaimer of Warranty. Software is provided "AS IS," without a warranty of any kind. ALL EXPRESS OR IMPLIED REPRESENTATIONS AND WARRANTIES, INCLUDING ANY IMPLIED WARRANTY OF MERCHANTABILITY, FITNESS FOR A PARTICULAR PURPOSE OR NON-INFRINGEMENT, ARE HEREBY EXCLUDED.

6. Limitation of Liability. SUN AND ITS LICENSORS SHALL NOT BE LIABLE FOR ANY DAMAGES SUFFERED BY LICENSEE OR ANY THIRD PARTY AS A RESULT OF USING

OR DISTRIBUTING SOFTWARE. IN NO EVENT WILL SUN OR ITS LICENSORS BE LIABLE FOR ANY LOST REVENUE, PROFIT OR DATA, OR FOR DIRECT, INDIRECT, SPECIAL, CONSEQUENTIAL, INCIDENTAL OR PUNITIVE DAMAGES, HOWEVER CAUSED AND REGARDLESS OF THE THEORY OF LIABILITY, ARISING OUT OF THE USE OF OR INABILITY TO USE SOFTWARE, EVEN IF SUN HAS BEEN ADVISED OF THE POSSIBILITY OF SUCH DAMAGES.

7. Termination. Licensee may terminate this License at any time by destroying all copies of Software. This License will terminate immediately without notice from Sun if Licensee fails to comply with any provision of this License. Upon such termination, Licensee must destroy all copies of Software.

8. Export Regulations. Software, including technical data, is subject to U.S. export control laws, including the U.S. Export Administration Act and its associated regulations, and may be subject to export or import regulations in other countries. Licensee agrees to comply strictly with all such regulations and acknowledges that it has the responsibility to obtain licenses to export, re-export, or import Software. Software may not be downloaded, or otherwise exported or re-exported (i) into, or to a national or resident of, Cuba, Iraq, Iran, North Korea, Libya, Sudan, Syria or any country to which the U.S. has embargoed goods; or (ii) to anyone on the U.S. Treasury Department's list of Specially Designated Nations or the U.S. Commerce Department's Table of Denial Orders.

9. Restricted Rights. Use, duplication or disclosure by the United States government is subject to the restrictions as set forth in the Rights in Technical Data and Computer Software Clauses in DFARS 252.227-7013(c) (1) (ii) and FAR 52.227-19(c) (2) as applicable.

10. Governing Law. Any action related to this License will be governed by California law and controlling U.S. federal law. No choice of law rules of any jurisdiction will apply.

11. Severability. If any of the above provisions are held to be in violation of applicable law, void, or unenforceable in any jurisdiction, then such provisions are herewith waived to the extent necessary for the License to be otherwise enforceable in such jurisdiction. However, if in Sun's opinion deletion of any provisions of the License by operation of this paragraph unreasonably compromises the rights or increase the liabilities of Sun or its licensors, Sun reserves the right to terminate the License and refund the fee paid by Licensee, if any, as Licensee's sole and exclusive remedy.

JDK Version 1.2 Beta 4 Binary Code Evaluation License

SUN MICROSYSTEMS, INC., THROUGH ITS JAVASOFT BUSINESS ("SUN") IS WILLING TO LICENSE THE JAVA DEVELOPMENT KIT VERSION 1.2 BETA 4 SOFTWARE AND THE ACCOMPANYING DOCUMENTATION INCLUDING AUTHORIZED COPIES OF EACH (THE "SOFTWARE") TO LICENSEE ONLY ON THE CONDITION THAT LICENSEE ACCEPTS ALL OF THE TERMS IN THIS AGREEMENT.

PLEASE READ THE TERMS CAREFULLY BEFORE INSTALLING THE SOFTWARE. BY INSTALLING THE SOFTWARE, LICENSEE ACKNOWLEDGES THAT LICENSEE HAS READ AND UNDERSTANDS THIS AGREEMENT AND AGREES TO BE BOUND BY ITS TERMS AND CONDITIONS.

IF LICENSEE DOES NOT ACCEPT THESE LICENSE TERMS, SUN DOES NOT GRANT ANY LICENSE TO THE SOFTWARE, AND LICENSEE SHOULD NOT INSTALL THE SOFTWARE.

1. EVALUATION LICENSE PERIOD

Licensee may use the binary Software for a period of ninety (90) days from the date Licensee installs the Software (the "Term"). At the end of the Term, Licensee must immediately cease use of and destroy the Software or, upon request from Sun, return the Software to Sun. The Software may contain a mechanism which (i) disables the Software at the end of the Term or (ii) advises the end user that the license has expired.

2. LICENSE GRANT

(A) License Rights

Licensee is granted a non-exclusive and non-transferable license to download, install and internally use the binary Software for beta testing and evaluation purposes only. Licensee may make one copy of the Software only for archival purposes in support of Licensee's use of the Software, provided that Licensee reproduce all copyright and other proprietary notices that are on the original copy of the Software.

(B) License Restrictions

The Software is licensed to Licensee only under the terms of this Agreement, and Sun reserves all rights not expressly granted to Licensee. Licensee may not use, copy, modify, or transfer the Software, or any copy thereof, except as expressly provided for in this Agreement. Except as otherwise provided by law for purposes of decompilation of the Software solely for inter-operability, Licensee may not reverse engineer, disassemble, decompile, or translate the Software, or otherwise attempt to derive the source code of the Software. Licensee may not rent, lease, loan, sell, or distribute the Software, or any part of the Software. No right, title, or interest in or to any trademarks, service marks, or trade names of Sun or Sun's licensors is granted hereunder.

(C) Acknowledgment that Software is Experimental

Licensee acknowledges that Software furnished hereunder is experimental and may have defects or deficiencies which cannot or will not be corrected by Sun and that Sun is under no obligation to release the Software as a product. Licensee will release and discharge Sun from any liability from any claims that any product released by Sun is incompatible with the Software. Further, Licensee will defend and indemnify Sun from any claims made by Licensee's customers that are based on incompatibility between the Software and any products released by Licensee. Licensee will have sole responsibility for the adequate protection and backup of Licensee's data and/or equipment used with the Software.

(D) Aircraft Product and Nuclear Applications Restriction
SOFTWARE IS NOT DESIGNED OR INTENDED FOR USE IN ON-LINE CONTROL OF AIRCRAFT, AIR TRAFFIC, AIRCRAFT NAVIGATION OR AIRCRAFT COMMUNICATIONS; OR IN THE DESIGN, CONSTRUCTION, OPERATION OR MAINTENANCE OF ANY NUCLEAR FACILITY. SUN DISCLAIMS ANY EXPRESS OR IMPLIED WARRANTY OF FITNESS FOR SUCH USES. LICENSEE REPRESENTS AND WARRANTS THAT IT WILL NOT USE THE SOFTWARE FOR SUCH PURPOSES.

3. CONFIDENTIALITY
The Software is the confidential and proprietary information of Sun and/or its licensors. The Software is protected by United States copyright law and international treaty. Unauthorized reproduction or distribution is subject to civil and criminal penalties. Licensee agrees to take adequate steps to protect the Software from unauthorized disclosure or use.

4. TERM, TERMINATION AND SURVIVAL
(A) The Agreement is effective until expiration of the Term, unless sooner terminated as provided for herein.

(B) Licensee may terminate this Agreement at any time by destroying all copies of the Software.

(C) This Agreement will immediately terminate without notice if Licensee fails to comply with any obligation of this Agreement.

(D) Upon termination, Licensee must immediately cease use of and destroy the Software or, upon request from Sun, return the Software to Sun.

(E) The provisions set forth in paragraphs 2(B), 3, 7, 8, 9, and 10 will survive termination or expiration of this Agreement.

5. NO WARRANTY
THE SOFTWARE IS PROVIDED TO LICENSEE "AS IS". ALL EXPRESS OR IMPLIED CONDITIONS, REPRESENTATIONS, AND WARRANTIES, INCLUDING ANY IMPLIED WARRANTY OF MERCHANTABILITY, SATISFACTORY QUALITY, FITNESS FOR A PARTICULAR PURPOSE, OR NON-INFRINGEMENT, ARE DISCLAIMED, EXCEPT TO THE EXTENT THAT SUCH DISCLAIMERS ARE HELD TO BE LEGALLY INVALID.

6. MAINTENANCE AND SUPPORT
Sun has no obligation to provide maintenance, support, updates or error corrections for the Software under this Agreement. In the event Sun, in its sole discretion, provides updates to Licensee, Licensee agrees to install and update the Software with such updates within fifteen (15) days from notification by Sun of the updates availability. Updates will be deemed Software hereunder and unless subject to terms of a specific update license, will be furnished to Licensee under the terms of this Agreement.

7. LIMITATION OF DAMAGES
TO THE EXTENT NOT PROHIBITED BY APPLICABLE LAW, SUN'S AGGREGATE LIABILITY TO LICENSEE OR TO ANY THIRD PARTY FOR CLAIMS RELATING TO THIS AGREEMENT, WHETHER FOR BREACH OR IN TORT, WILL BE LIMITED TO THE FEES PAID BY LICENSEE FOR SOFTWARE WHICH IS THE SUBJECT MATTER OF THE CLAIMS. IN NO EVENT WILL SUN BE LIABLE FOR ANY INDIRECT, PUNITIVE,

SPECIAL, INCIDENTAL OR CONSEQUENTIAL DAMAGE IN CONNECTION WITH OR ARISING OUT OF THIS AGREEMENT (INCLUDING LOSS OF BUSINESS, REVENUE, PROFITS, USE, DATA OR OTHER ECONOMIC ADVANTAGE), HOWEVER IT ARISES, WHETHER FOR BREACH OR IN TORT, EVEN IF SUN HAS BEEN PREVIOUSLY ADVISED OF THE POSSIBILITY OF SUCH DAMAGE. LIABILITY FOR DAMAGES WILL BE LIMITED AND EXCLUDED, EVEN IF ANY EXCLUSIVE REMEDY PROVIDED FOR IN THIS AGREEMENT FAILS OF ITS ESSENTIAL PURPOSE.

8. GOVERNMENT USER

Rights in Data: If procured by, or provided to, the U.S. Government, use, duplication, or disclosure of technical data is subject to restrictions as set forth in FAR 52.227-14(g)(2), Rights in Data-General (June 1987); and for computer software and computer software documentation, FAR 52-227-19, Commercial Computer Software-Restricted Rights (June 1987). However, if under DOD, use, duplication, or disclosure of technical data is subject to DFARS 252.227-7015(b), Technical Data-Commercial Items (June 1995); and for computer software and computer software documentation, as specified in the license under which the computer software was procured pursuant to DFARS 227.7202-3(a). Licensee shall not provide Software nor technical data to any third party, including the U.S. Government, unless such third party accepts the same restrictions. Licensee is responsible for ensuring that proper notice is given to all such third parties and that the Software and technical data are properly marked.

9. EXPORT LAW

Licensee acknowledges and agrees that this Software and/or technology is subject to the U.S. Export Administration Laws and Regulations. Diversion of such Software and/or technology contrary to U.S. law is prohibited. Licensee agrees that none of this Software and/or technology, nor any direct product therefrom, is being or will be acquired for, shipped, transferred, or reexported, directly or indirectly, to proscribed or embargoed countries or their nationals, nor be used for nuclear activities, chemical biological weapons, or missile projects unless authorized by the U.S. Government. Proscribed countries are set forth in the U.S. Export Administration Regulations. Countries subject to U.S. embargo are: Cuba, Iran, Iraq, Libya, North Korea, Syria, and the Sudan. This list is subject to change without further notice from Sun, and Licensee must comply with the list as it exists in fact. Licensee certifies that it is not on the U.S. Department of Commerce's Denied Persons List or affiliated lists or on the U.S. Department of Treasury's Specially Designated Nationals List. Licensee agrees to comply strictly with all U.S. export laws and assumes sole responsibility for obtaining licenses to export or reexport as may be required.

Licensee is responsible for complying with any applicable local laws and regulations, including but not limited to, the export and import laws and regulations of other countries.

10. GOVERNING LAW, JURISDICTION AND VENUE

Any action related to this Agreement shall be governed by California law and controlling U.S. federal law, and choice of law rules of any jurisdiction shall not apply. The parties agree that any action shall be brought in the United States District Court for the Northern District of California or the California superior Court for the County of Santa Clara, as applicable, and the parties hereby submit exclusively to the personal jurisdiction and venue of the United States District Court for the Northern District of California and the California Superior Court of the county of Santa Clara.

11. NO ASSIGNMENT

Neither party may assign or otherwise transfer any of its rights or obligations under this Agreement, without the prior written consent of the other party, except that Sun may assign its right to payment and may assign this Agreement to an affiliated company.

12. OFFICIAL LANGUAGE

The official text of this Agreement is in the English language and any interpretation or construction of this Agreement will be based thereon. In the event that this Agreement or any documents or notices related to it are translated into any other language, the English language version will control.

13. ENTIRE AGREEMENT

This Agreement is the parties' entire agreement relating to the Software. It supersedes all prior or contemporaneous oral or written communications, proposals, warranties, and representations with respect to its subject matter, and following Licensee's acceptance of this license by clicking on the "Accept" Button, will prevail over any conflicting or additional terms of any quote, order, acknowledgment, or any other communications by or between the parties. No modification to this Agreement will be binding, unless in writing and signed by an authorized representative of each party.

License Agreement and Limited Warranty

Agreement as to warranties, limitation of liability, remedies or damages, and our ownership rights shall survive termination.

7.   MISCELLANEOUS: This Agreement shall be construed in accordance with the laws of the United States of America and the State of New York and shall benefit the Company, its affiliates, and assignees.

8.   LIMITED WARRANTY AND DISCLAIMER OF WARRANTY: The Company warrants that the SOFTWARE, when properly used in accordance with the Documentation, will operate in substantial conformity with the description of the SOFTWARE set forth in the Documentation. The Company does not warrant that the SOFTWARE will meet your requirements or that the operation of the SOFTWARE will be uninterrupted or error-free. The Company warrants that the media on which the SOFTWARE is delivered shall be free from defects in materials and workmanship under normal use for a period of thirty (30) days from the date of your purchase. Your only remedy and the Company's only obligation under these limited warranties is, at the Company's option, return of the warranted item for a refund of any amounts paid by you or replacement of the item. Any replacement of SOFTWARE or media under the warranties shall not extend the original warranty period. The limited warranty set forth above shall not apply to any SOFTWARE which the Company determines in good faith has been subject to misuse, neglect, improper installation, repair, alteration, or damage by you. EXCEPT FOR THE EXPRESSED WARRANTIES SET FORTH ABOVE, THE COMPANY DISCLAIMS ALL WARRANTIES, EXPRESS OR IMPLIED, INCLUDING WITHOUT LIMITATION, THE IMPLIED WARRANTIES OF MERCHANTABILITY AND FITNESS FOR A PARTICULAR PURPOSE. EXCEPT FOR THE EXPRESS WARRANTY SET FORTH ABOVE, THE COMPANY DOES NOT WARRANT, GUARANTEE, OR MAKE ANY REPRESENTATION REGARDING THE USE OR THE RESULTS OF THE USE OF THE SOFTWARE IN TERMS OF ITS CORRECTNESS, ACCURACY, RELIABILITY, CURRENTNESS, OR OTHERWISE.

IN NO EVENT, SHALL THE COMPANY OR ITS EMPLOYEES, AGENTS, SUPPLIERS, OR CONTRACTORS BE LIABLE FOR ANY INCIDENTAL, INDIRECT, SPECIAL, OR CONSEQUENTIAL DAMAGES ARISING OUT OF OR IN CONNECTION WITH THE LICENSE GRANTED UNDER THIS AGREEMENT, OR FOR LOSS OF USE, LOSS OF DATA, LOSS OF INCOME OR PROFIT, OR OTHER LOSSES, SUSTAINED AS A RESULT OF INJURY TO ANY PERSON, OR LOSS OF OR DAMAGE TO PROPERTY, OR CLAIMS OF THIRD PARTIES, EVEN IF THE COMPANY OR AN AUTHORIZED REPRESENTATIVE OF THE COMPANY HAS BEEN ADVISED OF THE POSSIBILITY OF SUCH DAMAGES. IN NO EVENT SHALL LIABILITY OF THE COMPANY FOR DAMAGES WITH RESPECT TO THE SOFTWARE EXCEED THE AMOUNTS ACTUALLY PAID BY YOU, IF ANY, FOR THE SOFTWARE.

SOME JURISDICTIONS DO NOT ALLOW THE LIMITATION OF IMPLIED WARRANTIES OR LIABILITY FOR INCIDENTAL, INDIRECT, SPECIAL, OR CONSEQUENTIAL DAMAGES, SO THE ABOVE LIMITATIONS MAY NOT ALWAYS APPLY. THE WARRANTIES IN THIS AGREEMENT GIVE YOU SPECIFIC LEGAL RIGHTS AND YOU MAY ALSO HAVE OTHER RIGHTS WHICH VARY IN ACCORDANCE WITH LOCAL LAW.

ACKNOWLEDGMENT

YOU ACKNOWLEDGE THAT YOU HAVE READ THIS AGREEMENT, UNDERSTAND IT, AND AGREE TO BE BOUND BY ITS TERMS AND CONDITIONS. YOU ALSO AGREE THAT THIS AGREEMENT IS THE COMPLETE AND EXCLUSIVE STATEMENT OF THE AGREEMENT BETWEEN YOU AND THE COMPANY AND SUPERSEDES ALL PROPOSALS OR PRIOR AGREEMENTS, ORAL, OR WRITTEN, AND ANY OTHER COMMUNICATIONS BETWEEN YOU AND THE COMPANY OR ANY REPRESENTATIVE OF THE COMPANY RELATING TO THE SUBJECT MATTER OF THIS AGREEMENT.

Should you have any questions concerning this Agreement or if you wish to contact the Company for any reason, please contact the publisher, in writing at the address below.

Robin Short
Prentice Hall PTR
One Lake Street
Upper Saddle River, New Jersey 07458

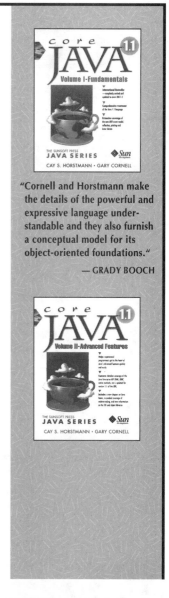

GRAPHIC JAVA 1.2
Volume I—Mastering the JFC, Third Edition

DAVID M. GEARY

850 pages; (includes CD-ROM)
ISBN: 0130796662

Written for experienced programmers looking for thorough and detailed explanations of the 1.2 AWT class libraries, Volume 1 covers all aspects of the AWT. It also includes coverage of advanced topics such as clipboard and data transfer, double buffering, custom dialogs, and sprite animation. Focuses heavily on bringing programmer's up to speed quickly on the new GUI services like:
- Drag and Drop
- the newest lightweight components
- the delegation event model

JUST JAVA 1.1,
Third Edition

PETER van der LINDEN

652 pages; (includes CD-ROM)
ISBN 0-13-784174-4

In JUST JAVA 1.1, the author of the classic EXPERT C PROGRAMMING: DEEP C SECRETS brings his trademark enthusiasm, straight talk, and expertise to the challenge of learning Java and object-oriented programming.

In this updated Third Edition, you'll find all the fundamentals of Java programming, including Java object-oriented techniques, types, statements, string processing, as well as more sophisticated techniques like networking, threads, and using the Abstract Window Toolkit. You'll also discover more examples than ever, along with updated coverage of future Java APIs—including the Java Database Connectivity (JDBC) API completely updated to include coverage of JDK 1.1.

TOPICS INCLUDE:
- The Story of O—object-oriented programming
- Applications versus applets
- Identifiers, comments, keywords, and operators
- Arrays, exceptions, and threads
- GIGO—Garbage In, Gospel Out
- On the Internet No One Knows You're a Dog

The CD-ROM includes all source code for examples presented in the book along with the latest JDK for Solaris, Windows 95, Windows NT, and Macintosh.

JAVA BY EXAMPLE,
Second Edition
JERRY R. JACKSON and
ALAN L. McCLELLAN

380 pages; (includes CD-ROM)
ISBN 0-13-272295-X

There's no better way to learn Java than by example. If you're an experienced programmer, JAVA BY EXAMPLE is the quickest way to learn Java. By reviewing example code written by experts, you'll learn the right way to develop Java applets and applications that are elegant, readable, and easy to maintain.

Step-by-step, working from examples, you'll learn valuable techniques for working with the Java language. The Second Edition provides even more extensive coverage.

TOPICS INCLUDE:

- Memory and constructors
- Input/output
- Multithreading
- Exception handling
- Animation
- Remote methods invocation (RMI)
- Networking
- Java Database Connectivity (JDBC) API

The CD-ROM includes all source code for examples presented in the book along with the JDK for Solaris, Windows 95, Windows NT, and Macintosh.

INSTANT JAVA, Second Edition
JOHN A. PEW

398 pages; (includes CD-ROM)
ISBN 0-13-272287-9

INSTANT JAVA™ applets—no programming necessary! Now anyone can use Java to add animation, sound, and interactivity to their Web pages! Instant Java is your guide to using more than 75 easy-to-customize Java applets. The Second Edition

contains even more applets and examples—plus updated, foolproof instructions for plugging them into your Web pages.

APPLETS INCLUDE:

- Text applets
- Image applets
- Animation applets
- Slide shows
- Tickers

You'll find all the applets on the cross-platform CD-ROM—along with sample HTML pages and the JDK for Solaris,™ Microsoft Windows 95, Microsoft Windows NT, and Macintosh. This is an invaluable tool for adding Java special effects to your HTML documents!

NOT JUST JAVA
PETER van der LINDEN

313 pages; ISBN 0-13-864638-4

NOT JUST JAVA is the book for everybody who needs to understand why Java and other Internet technologies are taking the software industry by storm. Peter van der Linden, author of the best-selling JUST JAVA, carefully explains each of the key technologies driving the Internet revolution and provides a much-needed perspective on critical topics including:

- Java and its libraries—present and future
- Security on intranets and the Internet
- Thin clients, network computers, and webtops
- Multi-tier client/server system
- Software components, objects and CORBA
- The evolution and role of intranets
- JavaBeans™ versus ActiveX

Also included are case studies of leading-edge companies that show how to avoid the pitfalls and how to leverage Java and related technologies for maximum payoff.

"...the most complete and effective treatment of a programming topic since Charles Petzold's classic Programming Windows."

— COMPUTER SHOPPER

"Fantastic book/CD package for HTML authors...practical, hands-on instructions get you off to a fast start."

— COMPUTER BOOK REVIEW

INSIDE JAVA WORKSHOP 2.0,
2nd Edition
LYNN WEAVER

380 pages; ISBN 0-13-899584-2
(includes CD-ROM)

A guide for new and experienced Java WorkShop users, INSIDE JAVA WORKSHOP 2.0 provides a task-based tour of every tool in the Java development environment from Sun and also highlights how to use the significant new features in version 2.0.

You will quickly learn the basics of the development model, including setting development preferences, building Java projects interactively, analyzing Java program performance, editing code with the enhanced Source Editor,and debugging applets across the Internet. You'll also learn how to use advanced debugging and GUI building features, and how to create, import and deploy JavaBeans projects.

The CD-ROM includes a 30-day, full-functioning version of Java WorkShop along with project examples and sample programs, complete with source code. It also features links to Java resources on the Web.

JUMPING JAVASCRIPT

JANICE WINSOR and BRIAN FREEMAN

1200 pages; (includes CD-ROM)
ISBN 0-13-841941-8

JUMPING JAVASCRIPT™ is a hands-on tutorial with loads of examples that will show both programmers and non-programmers how to use JavaScript to easily incorporate the interactivity of Java into their Web sites. It covers both basics such as scripting concepts, embedded Java applets, image maps, and buttons as well as advanced topics such as creating JavaScript objects and the cookies property. CD-ROM contains all the scripts discussed

in the book.

WEB PAGE DESIGN
A Different Multimedia
MARY E. S. MORRIS and
RANDY J. HINRICHS

200 pages; ISBN 0-13-239880-X

Everything you always wanted to know about practical Web page design! Anyone can design a web page, but it takes more than basic HTML skill to build a world-class Web site. Written for Web page authors, this hands-on guide covers the key aspects of designing a successful Web site and shows how to integrate traditional design techniques into Web sites. Contains sixteen full color examples of successful Web pages, and techniques for:
- Cognitive and content design
- Audience consideration
- Interactivity, organization, and navigational pathways
- Designing with VRML and Java
- Working with templates, style sheets, and Netscape™ Frames
- Evolving your design

HTML FOR FUN AND PROFIT,
3rd Edition
MARY E. S. MORRIS and
JOHN E. SIMPSON

400 pages; ISBN 0-13-079672-7

The international best seller has been completely revised and updated to feature in-depth coverage of the fundamentals and all the hottest new HTML innovations. You will quickly master using tags, adding hyperlinks, graphics and multimedia, and creating clickable imagemaps. You will also learn the benefits of tables and frames and how to generate pages "on the fly." You will also find information on Dynamic

EXPERT C PROGRAMMING:
Deep C Secrets
PETER van der LINDEN

352 pages; ISBN 0-13-177429-8

EXPERT C PROGRAMMING is a very different book on the C language! In an easy, conversational style, the author reveals coding techniques used by the best C programmers. EXPERT C PROGRAMMING explains the difficult areas of ANSI C, from arrays to runtime structures, and all the quirks in between. Covering both IBM PC and UNIX systems, this book is a must read for anyone who wants to learn more about the implementation, practical use, and folklore of C!

CHAPTER TITLES INCLUDE:
- It's not a bug, it's a language feature!
- Thinking of linking
- You know C, so C++ is easy!
- Secrets of programmer job interviews

CONFIGURATION AND CAPACITY PLANNING FOR SOLARIS SERVERS
BRIAN L. WONG

428 pages; ISBN 0-13-349952-9

No matter what application of SPARC architecture you're working with this book can help you maximize the performance of your Solaris-based server. This is the most comprehensive guide to configuring and sizing Solaris servers for virtually any task, including:
* World Wide Web, Internet email, ftp and Usenet news servers * NFS servers
* Database management
* Client/server computing
* Timesharing
* General purpose application servers Internet firewalls

PANIC!
UNIX System Crash Dump Analysis
CHRIS DRAKE and KIMBERLEY BROWN

480 pages; (includes CD-ROM)
ISBN 0-13-149386-8

UNIX systems crash—it's a fact of life. Until now, little information has been available regarding system crashes. PANIC! is the first book to concentrate solely on system crashes and hangs, explaining what triggers them and what to do when they occur. PANIC! guides you through system crash dump postmortem analysis towards problem resolution. PANIC! presents this highly technical and intricate subject in a friendly, easy style that even the novice UNIX system administrator will find readable, educational, and enjoyable.

TOPICS COVERED INCLUDE:
- What is a panic? What is a hang?
- Header files, symbols, and symbol tables
- A comprehensive tutorial on adb, the absolute debugger
- Introduction to assembly language
- Actual case studies of postmortem analysis

A CD-ROM containing several useful analysis tools—such as adb macros and C tags output from the source trees of two different UNIX systems—is included.

SUN PERFORMANCE AND TUNING
Java and the Internet, Second Edition
ADRIAN COCKCROFT and RICHARD PETTIT

500 pages; ISBN 0-13-095249-4

Hailed in its first edition as an indispensable reference for system administrators, SUN PERFORMANCE AND TUNING has been revised and expanded to cover Solaris 2.6, the newest generation of SPARC hardware and the latest Internet and Java server technologies.

Featuring "Quick Tips and Recipes," as well as extensive reference tables, this book is indispensable both for developers who need to design for performance and administrators who need to improve overall system performance.

KEY TOPICS COVERED INCLUDE:

- Web Server Sizing and Performance Management Tools
- Performance Management and Measurement
- Software Performance Engineering
- Kernel Algorithms and Tuning
- Java Application Servers

To get up to speed quickly on critical perfomance issues, this is the one book any Sun administrator, integrator, or developer needs.

WABI 2:
Opening Windows
SCOTT FORDIN and SUSAN NOLIN

383 pages; ISBN 0-13-461617-0

WABI 2: OPENING WINDOWS explains the ins and outs of using Wabi software from Sun Microsystems to install, run, and manage Microsoft Windows applications on UNIX systems. Easy step-by-step instructions, illustrations, and charts guide you through each phase of using Wabi—from getting started to managing printers, drives, and COM ports to getting the most from your specific Windows applications.

AUTOMATING SOLARIS INSTALLATIONS
A Custom Jumpstart Guide
PAUL ANTHONY KASPER and ALAN L. McCLELLAN

282 pages; (includes a diskette) ISBN 0-13-312505-X

AUTOMATING SOLARIS INSTALLATIONS describes how to set up "hands-off" Solaris installations for hundreds of SPARC™ and x86 systems. It explains in detail how to configure your site so that when you install Solaris, you simply boot a system and walk away—the software installs automatically! The book also includes a diskette with working shell scripts to automate pre- and post-installation tasks, such as:

- Updating systems with patch releases
- Installing third-party or unbundled software on users' systems
- Saving and restoring system data
- Setting up access to local and remote printers
- Transitioning a system from SunOS™ 4.x to Solaris 2

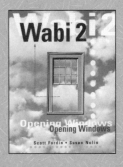

"This book is a must for all Solaris 2 system administrators."
— TOM JOLLANDS,
Sun Enterprise Network Systems

SOLARIS IMPLEMENTATION
A Guide for System Administrators
GEORGE BECKER,
MARY E. S. MORRIS, and
KATHY SLATTERY

345 pages; ISBN 0-13-353350-6

Written by expert Sun™ system administrators, this book discusses real world, day-to-day Solaris 2 system administration for both new installations and for migration from an installed Solaris 1 base. It presents tested procedures to help system administrators improve and customize their networks and includes advice on managing heterogeneous Solaris environments. Provides actual sample auto install scripts and disk partitioning schemes used at Sun.

TOPICS COVERED INCLUDE:

- Local and network methods for installing Solaris 2 systems
- Configuring with admintool versus command-line processes
- Building and managing the network, including setting up security
- Managing software packages and patches
- Handling disk utilities and archiving procedures

SOLARIS PORTING GUIDE,
Second Edition
SUNSOFT DEVELOPER ENGINEERING

695 pages; ISBN 0-13-443672-5

Ideal for application programmers and software developers, the SOLARIS PORTING GUIDE provides a comprehensive technical overview of the Solaris 2 operating environment and its related migration strategy.

The Second Edition is current through Solaris 2.4 (for both SPARC and x86 platforms) and provides all the information necessary to migrate from Solaris 1 (SunOS 4.x) to Solaris 2 (SunOS 5.x). Other additions include a discussion of

emerging technologies such as the Common Desktop Environment from Sun, hints for application performance tuning, and extensive pointers to further information, including Internet sources.

TOPICS COVERED INCLUDE:

- SPARC and x86 architectural differences
- Migrating from common C to ANSI C
- Building device drivers for SPARC and x86 using DDI/DKI
- Multithreading, real-time processing, and the Sun Common Desktop Environment

ALL ABOUT ADMINISTERING NIS+,
Second Edition
RICK RAMSEY

451 pages; ISBN 0-13-309576-2

Take full advantage of your Solaris distributed operating environment by learning how to effectively use the networking power of NIS+ technology. Updated and revised for Solaris 2.3, this book is ideal for network administrators who want to know more about NIS+: its capabilities, requirements, how it works, and how to get the most out of it.

INTERACTIVE UNIX OPERATING SYSTEM
A Guide for System Administrators
MARTY C. STEWART

275 pages; ISBN 0-13-161613-7

Written for first-time system administrators and end users, this practical guide goes step-by-step through the character-based menus for configuring, tailoring, and maintaining the INTERACTIVE™ UNIX® System V/386 Release 3.2, Version 3.0 through Version 4.1. It is also a great reference for any system based on UNIX SVR 3.2.

DEVELOPING VISUAL APPLICATIONS
XIL: An Imaging Foundation Library
WILLIAM K. PRATT

368 pages; ISBN 0-13-461948-X

A practical introduction to using imaging in new, innovative applications for desktop computing. DEVELOPING VISUAL APPLICATIONS breaks down the barriers that prevent developers from easily integrating imaging into their applications. It covers the basics of image processing, compression, and algorithm implementation and provides clear, real-world examples for developing applications using XIL™ a cross-platform imaging foundation library. More experienced imaging developers can also use this book as a reference to the architectural features and capabilities of XIL.

READ ME FIRST!
A Style Guide for the Computer Industry
SUN TECHNICAL PUBLICATIONS

256 pages; (includes CD-ROM)
ISBN 0-13-455347-0

User documentation should be an asset, not an afterthought. The READ ME FIRST! style guide can help technical publications groups outline, organize, and prepare high quality documentation for any type of computer product. Based on the award-winning Sun Microsystems documentation style guide, READ ME FIRST! includes complete guidelines—from style pointers to legal considerations, from writing for an international audience to forming a documentation department.

TOPICS INCLUDE:

• Grammar and punctuation guidelines
• Technical abbreviations, acronyms, and units of measurement
• How to set up your own documentation department

The CD-ROM includes ready-to-use FrameMaker templates for instant page design and the entire book in searchable FrameViewer and HTML format for easy reference.

INTRANET SECURITY:
Stories From the Trenches
LINDA McCARTHY

300 pages; ISBN 0-13-894759-7

Do you have response procedures for systems break-ins? Is your e-mail encrypted? Is your firewall protecting your company? Is your security staff properly trained? These are just a few of the security issues that are covered in INTRANET SECURITY: STORIES FROM THE TRENCHES. Author Linda McCarthy, who in her job as a worldwide security team leader at Sun broke into thousands of corporate intranets, presents detailed case studies of real-life break-ins that will help you make your systems safer. She explains how each breach occurred, describes what steps were taken to fix it, and then provides a practical and systematic solution for preventing similar problems from occurring on your network!

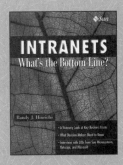

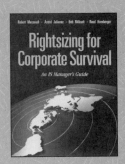

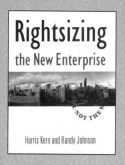

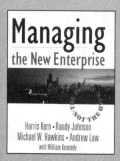

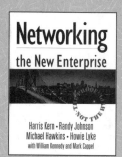

RIGHTSIZING THE NEW ENTERPRISE:
The Proof, Not the Hype
HARRIS KERN and RANDY JOHNSON

326 pages; ISBN 0-13-490384-6

The "how-to's" of rightsizing are defined in this detailed account based on the experiences of Sun Microsystems as it re-engineered its business to run on client/server systems. This book covers rightsizing strategies and benefits, management and system administration processes and tools, and the issues involved in transitioning personnel from mainframe to UNIX support. RIGHTSIZING THE NEW ENTERPRISE presents you with proof that rightsizing can be done...and has been done.

MANAGING THE NEW ENTERPRISE:
The Proof, Not the Hype
HARRIS KERN, RANDY JOHNSON, MICHAEL HAWKINS, and ANDREW LAW, with WILLIAM KENNEDY

212 pages; ISBN 0-13-231184-4

MANAGING THE NEW ENTERPRISE describes how to build a solid technology foundation for the advanced networking and systems of the enterprise. Learn to re-engineer your traditional information technology (IT) systems while reducing costs! As the follow-up to RIGHTSIZING THE NEW ENTERPRISE, this volume is about relevant, critical solutions to issues challenging corporate computing in the 1990s and beyond.

TOPICS INCLUDE:
- Creating reliable UNIX distributed systems
- Building a production-quality enterprise network
- Managing a decentralized system with centralized controls
- Selecting the right systems management tools and standards

NETWORKING THE NEW ENTERPRISE:
The Proof, Not the Hype
HARRIS KERN, RANDY JOHNSON, MICHAEL HAWKINS, and HOWIE LYKE, with WILLIAM KENNEDY and MARK CAPPEL

212 pages; ISBN 0-13-263427-9

NETWORKING THE NEW ENTERPRISE tackles the key information technology questions facing business professionals today—and provides real solutions. The book covers all aspects of network computing, including effective architecture, security, the Intranet, Web sites, and the resulting people issues culture shock.

OTHER NETWORKING TOPICS INCLUDE:
- Building a production quality network that supports distributed client/server computing
- Designing a reliable high-speed backbone network
- Centralizing and controlling TCP/IP administration
- Evaluating and selecting key network components

Like RIGHTSIZING THE NEW ENTERPRISE and MANAGING THE NEW ENTERPRISE, its best-selling companion volumes, NETWORKING THE NEW ENTERPRISE is based on the authors' real-life experiences. It's the expert guide to every strategic networking decision you face. AND THAT'S NO HYPE.

The Graphic Java 1.2 CD-ROM is a standard ISO-9660 disc.
Software on this CD-ROM requires Windows 95, Windows
NT, or Solaris 2.

Windows 3.1 IS NOT SUPPORTED